LAKE SUPERIOR

LAKE MICHIGAN

LAKE HURON

L. ONTARIO

LAKE ERIE

C E N T R A L

River

Ohio River

OZARK PLATEAU

Mississippi River

L O W L A N D

C O A S T A L   P L A I N

A P P A L A C H I A N

PIEDMONT PLATEAU

MOUNTAINS

ATLANTIC COASTAL PLAIN

GENERAL WASHINGTON AT THE BATTLE OF TRENTON.

By John Trumbull.

A SHORT HISTORY OF
THE AMERICAN PEOPLE

Volume I (1492-1865)

By

OLIVER PERRY CHITWOOD

and

FRANK LAWRENCE OWSLEY

SEVENTH PRINTING

D. VAN NOSTRAND COMPANY, INC.

TORONTO   NEW YORK   LONDON

NEW YORK

D. Van Nostrand Company, Inc., 250 Fourth Avenue, New York 3

TORONTO

D. Van Nostrand Company (Canada), Ltd., 228 Bloor Street, Toronto 8

LONDON

Macmillan & Company, Ltd., St. Martin's Street, London, W.C. 2

First Published May 1945

Reprinted January 1946, September 1946
February 1947, August 1947, September 1947
September 1948

To the Memory
of a sound scholar and inspiring teacher
JOHN LESLIE HALL
late professor and dean at
the College of William and Mary

Preface

IN preparing this text for college students we have endeavored to present such facts as are necessary to show the political, economic and social development of the United States to the end of the War for Southern Independence. We have not attempted to cover all the important events. If such an effort had been made, either the book would have been too voluminous or the account would have been unduly abbreviated. To avoid the second horn of this dilemma we have tried, as far as space limitations would permit, to clothe all statements with sufficient detail to cover the bare framework of the narrative.

Our discussions have in the main been based only on such data as are generally accepted by reliable historians. Wherever recent scholarship has challenged the accuracy or correctness of old established views, we have either accepted the later opinion or indicated in a footnote its divergence from the traditional interpretation.

One difficulty has been to maintain the proper perspective in the allocation of space to the various events and movements. In the endeavor to solve this problem we have been anxious to avoid giving such overemphasis to certain facts as would lend too great a prominence to some periods of history or to some sections of the country. In pursuit of this aim considerable space has been given to the colonial period; for we feel that the laying of the foundations of American society was an important stage in the development of the Republic. A greater difficulty has been to discuss without bias controversial questions bearing on international and sectional affairs. At this distance from the millennium no one should expect perfect objectivity in the handling of such questions. We have, however, made a strenuous effort to suspend our political and sectional prejudices and even our patriotism while discussing international disputes and the controversies that led to the Civil War. We have left it to the reader to evaluate the ethics of these conflicts and have made no effort to apportion praise or blame to the contestants. Indeed, we do not feel that in any of these controversies one side was altogether right and the other altogether wrong. Right and wrong cannot be charted along geographical lines; the sheep cannot be separated from the goats by parallels of latitude or meridians of longitude.

This attitude of neutrality left us somewhat in a quandary as to how to designate the war between the North and the South. Since it was, and still is, a disputed question whether secession was in violation of the Constitution, to be strictly correct we should have used only such names as the War for Southern Independence and the War of Secession, which are noncommittal on this point, rather than Civil War, which, if used in the ordinary sense, implies the acceptance of the Northern contention that secession was illegal. But, inasmuch as the term Civil War seems to have lost its original connotation and is now widely employed—by Southern historians as well as others, we have for the sake of convenience frequently substituted it for the somewhat awkward longer designations.

One feature of the book is the unusual amount of space devoted to thumbnail sketches of historical characters. The reason for inserting these sketches is the conviction that personality has played an important part in the development of the Republic. Individual leadership has not had as marked an influence on the trend of events as was formerly thought, but it has certainly colored—even though it has not determined—the stream of history. We feel therefore that college students should know something of the personality of the men and women who have played a part in the exciting drama of the history of the United States.

Acknowledgments

IN hammering this work into final shape we have had the benefit of helpful criticism, for which we express our grateful appreciation. We are especially indebted to Professor David Dale Johnson, head of the Department of English of West Virginia University; to Professors James M. Callahan and Charles H. Ambler, of the Department of History of West Virginia University; and to Professor Irby R. Hudson, of the Department of Political Science, and Professors Dan M. Robison and Henry Lee Swint, of the Department of History, of Vanderbilt University. Professor Johnson read all the manuscript except the last five chapters and offered numerous corrections as to style. Professors Callahan and Ambler carefully examined the greater part of the work and made many valuable suggestions regarding style and content. Professors Hudson, Robison, and Swint performed a like service for the chapters on the Civil War. Mrs. Harriet Chappell Owlsey and Mrs. Agnes Cady Chitwood also rendered valuable assistance, both in revising the manuscript and in reading the proof.

We also acknowledge our indebtedness to the following scholars and writers, each of whom read a part of the manuscript and proposed useful emendations: Dr. W. E. Brooks, Pastor of the First Presbyterian Church of Morgantown; Dr. C. H. Quenzel, Librarian of Mary Washington College; Professor Fred H. Harrington, of the University of Wisconsin; Dr. Dominic da le Salandra, Cultural Attaché of the State Department; Professor Harold Wentworth, of Temple University; and Professors Festus P. Summers, Fred M. Smith, and J. P. Brawner, of West Virginia University. Helpful comments regarding the school system of the Old South were made by Professor Edgar W. Knight, of the University of North Carolina.

We wish also to express our thanks to certain publishers who have given us permission to use quotations from their works. Of these our greatest indebtedness is to Harper and Brothers and to the American Historical Association. Through the courtesy of Harper and Brothers we have been able to lean heavily on O. P. Chitwood's *The History of Colonial America* in the preparation of the chapters on the Colonial and Revolutionary periods. Two whole paragraphs (indicated in a footnote, page 172) have been taken over and a number of sentences have been copied with little or no change in wording. The borrowings have been especially free in the following pages of the present work: 7–9, 11, 21–23, 173–174, 178, 237, and 602. In writing certain chapters on the Middle period we took similar liberties with another work by the same author, *John Tyler: Champion of the Old South*. This privilege was kindly extended to us by the American Historical Association, which sponsored the publication of the latter book. The numerous extracts from this work occur mainly on the following pages of the present work: 477–448, 464, 469–474, 477–479, 482–490, 492–493, 601, and 611–612. Acknowledgments for other quotations, usually short ones, are given in the footnotes.

OLIVER PERRY CHITWOOD
West Virginia University

FRANK LAWRENCE OWSLEY
Vanderbilt University

Contents

PART I: THE COLONIAL ERA TO 1763

ix

PART III: THE FEDERAL PERIOD, 1783–1860

List of Illustrations

List of Maps

PART I

The Colonial Era to 1763

CHAPTER I

Introduction: The Land and Its Original Inhabitants

PHYSICAL FEATURES OF THE UNITED STATES

THE history of the United States is to a great extent an account of the exploitation of the natural resources of this country by the European peoples and their descendants who have held the land for the past three centuries. A white race with centuries of civilization behind it came to a new world and thus had a virgin field on which to try out a new experiment in civilization. The political and social order of Europe was brought over by the settlers and subjected to the test of frontier conditions. Under this process the European heritage underwent slow and gradual but none the less important modifications. The United States of today is therefore the outcome of old world heredity and new world environment. Hence to understand American history we must know something about the geographical background against which the old world civilization was placed.

The area of the United States proper, exclusive of Alaska and the island possessions, is a little less than three million square miles, which is about three fourths that of Europe. This vast area, stretching across twenty-four degrees of latitude, has a great variety of soil and climate, which gives rise to a wide diversity in products and occupations. As a consequence, the country is insured against a complete failure of any crop over the entire area; but the great variety of occupations leads to a conflict of interests between different regions, which tends towards sectionalism in political beliefs and policies.

Area

The territory of the United States is divided into five geographical regions: (1) The Atlantic Slope; (2) The Appalachian Highland; (3) The Mississippi Valley; (4) The Cordilleran Highland; and (5) The Pacific Slope.

Geographical divisions

(1) The Atlantic Slope is the region between the Appalachian Mountains and the ocean, extending across the entire length of the country. It is divided into two parts, the Coastal Plain and the Piedmont Plateau.

The Atlantic Slope

3

*The Coastal
Plain*

T.Q.

   The former is an alluvial belt following the Atlantic coast from
New York to Florida, and the Gulf of Mexico from Florida into
Mexico. Beginning in the north as a narrow strip, the Coastal Plain
broadens out as it extends southward until in Georgia it attains a
width of about two hundred miles. Along the Gulf it is from fifty to
one hundred miles wide and in one place extends as far north as the
mouth of the Ohio. Everywhere the elevation above sea level is
slight, and the larger streams are navigable across the entire belt.
In some sections the tide runs up the navigable portions of these
streams, and for this reason the term Tidewater Belt is sometimes
used to designate the Coastal Plain. In that part of this alluvial region which borders on the Gulf, the land is fertile and well-watered.
In other sections the soil of the river bottoms is often rich, but with
this exception the land is not unusually fertile and in some places
is quite unproductive. In a good portion of the Coastal Plain, especially in the south, there are swamps which render the near-by localities unhealthful.

   Since the Atlantic Slope is the portion of the United States which
is nearest Europe, the first English settlements were naturally made
in this area. The physical features of this region are also favorable
to colonization. The land is easily accessible to seagoing traffic, for
there are a number of good harbors all along the coast from Virginia
to New England. Bays and navigable streams also afford good transportation facilities some distance into the interior. The climate,
except in the southern portion, is quite similar to that of England.
This was a great advantage to the English colonists for it enabled
them to grow the food crops in America which they were accustomed
to raise in the homeland.

*The Fall
Line*

   The outer edge of the Coastal Plain is marked by waterfalls or
rapids in the rivers. These falls separate the navigable from the un-
navigable portions of the streams. The imaginary line which con-
nects these rapids is known as the Fall Line. Between the Fall Line
and the first tier of the Appalachian Mountains lies the Piedmont

*The
Piedmont
Plateau*

Plateau. It extends from Canada to middle Alabama, with a varying
width which in the middle region broadens out to about one hundred and fifty miles. It is well drained, has few swamps, and is therefore comparatively free from those diseases which are caused by mosquitoes. Much of the soil is fertile, especially along the rivers.

*The Appa-
lachian
Highland*

   (2) The Appalachian Highland is a region of considerable elevation, comprising mountains, plateaus, and valleys. It extends from
northern New Brunswick to the interior of Alabama and Georgia.
The northeastern part of this highland is separated from the rest
by the trough through which the waters of Lake Champlain flow

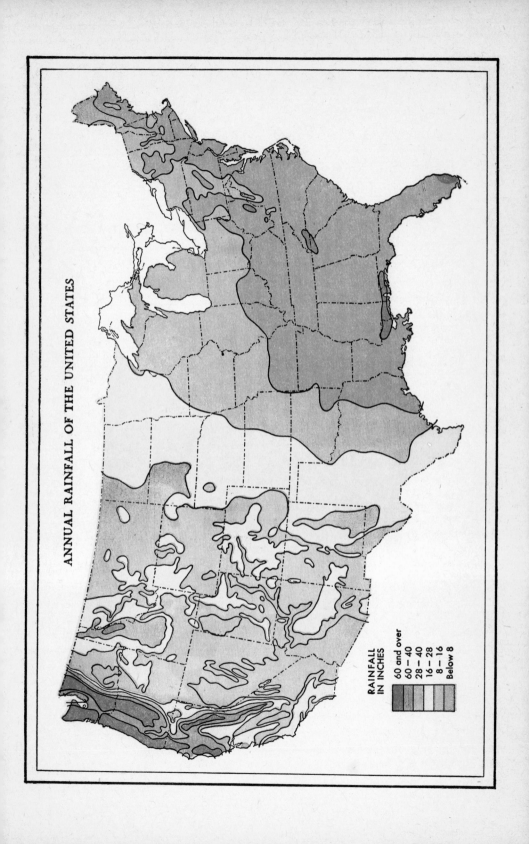

ANNUAL RAINFALL OF THE UNITED STATES

RAINFALL
IN INCHES

60 and over
60 — 40
28 — 40
16 — 28
8 — 16
Below 8

northward, and by the valleys of the Hudson and Mohawk Rivers. In this portion are located the White, Green, and Adirondack Mountains.

South of these two rivers is the Appalachian region proper. Its eastern border is a continuous range of mountains, the major portion of which is known as the Blue Ridge. Directly west of this eastern line of mountains is located the Appalachian Valley, which under different names extends from the Hudson to central Alabama. The soil has a limestone base and is for the most part quite fertile. Beyond the Great Valley lies an elevated region traversed by parallel ranges of mountains running northeast and southwest and separated from each other by narrow plateaus and valleys. Of these mountains, the most important are the Allegheny and Cumberland. The greater part of the land in the Appalachian region is too steep for profitable cultivation, and only in the valleys and plateaus can farming be successfully carried on. The chief value of this region lies in its valuable forests and rich deposits of coal, limestone, and sandstone.

(3) Between the Appalachian Highland and the Rocky Mountains lies the Mississippi Valley, a great plain extending from the Gulf of Mexico to Canada.[1] It is in reality only the southern part of a greater plain extending through the middle of the continent from the Arctic Ocean to the Gulf of Mexico. For the sake of convenience we may divide it into three parts—namely, the Great Plains, the Prairie Plains, and the Forest Plains. *The Mississippi Valley*

The Great Plains is a term usually applied to a semiarid region extending from the Rocky Mountains eastward to about the 100th meridian. Except along the rivers, the rainfall in this belt is not sufficient to support agriculture without irrigation. It is also generally too dry for trees. There is, however, enough moisture for grass and so in time stockraising became a profitable business on the Great Plains. *The Great Plains*

The Prairie Plains cover a large area of irregular dimensions extending from western Ohio through Indiana and Illinois across the Mississippi to the Great Plains, and from Mexico far into Canada. The width of this region at one point is about eight hundred miles, and the total area about a half million square miles. The land is level or rolling and the soil is exceedingly fertile. "It is the most productive agricultural area of comparable size in North America, if not in the world." The rainfall is sufficient for agriculture, but these rich meadows, originally covered everywhere with a fine sod of grass, *The Prairie Plains*

---

[1] Within this area there is an upland region, covering southern Missouri and portions of Arkansas and Oklahoma, which is known as the Ozark Plateau. There are some mountains in this region, the highest of which attain an elevation of twenty-five hundred feet. (See map on front cover.)

were treeless when they were first discovered. The reason for this is
not known. The most plausible theory is that the Indians destroyed
the trees by fires in order to have better pasturage for the buffaloes.
Owing to the absence of trees, the prairies were easily brought under
cultivation. This advantage, together with the remarkable fertility
of the soil, accounts for the fact that the West was so rapidly settled.

*The Forest
Plains*

The other sections of the Mississippi Valley were all originally
covered with forests and to them we may apply the name of Forest
Plains. As a rule these regions were fertile, well-watered, and well-
suited to agriculture.

The Mississippi Valley became a bone of contention between
England and France in the eighteenth century, and the resulting
rivalry culminated in the French and Indian War. Except for this,
however, this vast region did not play an important role in colonial
history. But in later years it became the breadbasket of the country
and figured prominently in the political and social life of the
United States.

*The Cor-
dilleran
Highland*

(4) West of the Great Plains there is a broad region of high elevation known as the Cordilleran Highland. This includes the Rocky
Mountains on the east, the Sierra Nevada and Cascade Mountains on
the west, and a central area of elevated plateaus interspersed with
mountains. The region is rich in mineral resources but poorly adapted
to agriculture. Only about one fifth of the surface is too steep and
rocky to be cultivated; but the coldness of the climate due to elevation, and the scantiness and uncertainty of the rainfall, render a still
larger portion sterile. The prevailing winds come from the west and
are robbed of most of their moisture by the mountains on the western border, leaving little for the central and eastern portions. A good
deal of the district is very dry, and fires have destroyed the original
forest covering of large areas which cannot now be reforested on
account of the lack of rainfall.

*The Pacific
Slope*

(5) Between the western wall of the Cordilleran Highland and
the Pacific Ocean is located the region known as the Pacific Slope.
It includes a small area of lowland in southern California, the Coast
Range Mountains, and the beautiful river valleys of California,
Oregon, and Washington. These valleys are remarkably fertile, and
are especially adapted to grain and fruit growing. But for some
crops they have to be irrigated, as the rainfall occurs mostly in
the winter.

The Cordilleran Plateau and the Pacific Slope had only a minor
place in the history of the United States until the last decades of the
period covered by this volume. In the colonial era these areas were
unoccupied, except by a few Spanish settlers and missionaries in the

southwest and the far west. It was not until the eighteen forties and fifties that this region became an important factor in the development of the country.

While our ancestors of the colonial era did not exploit, except to *Forests* a very limited extent, the great wealth of minerals which has given this country its industrial primacy in the machine age, they did appreciate and utilize the natural resources which were adapted to their stage of economy. These were a favorable climate, a fertile soil, sufficient rainfall, an abundance of timber, and the numerous waterfalls which furnished power for primitive manufactures. Nearly all the territory occupied by the English settlers in the colonial period was originally covered with valuable forests. Although the trees were in a sense an obstacle to settlement, owing to the difficulty of clearing them off the land, still the forest was of great benefit to both the whites and the red men. From it came wood for fuel, and lumber for building purposes and domestic manufactures as well as for export. Hogs fed on the acorns and nuts which fell from the trees in the autumn season. On the game procured in forest and stream the Indian depended mainly and the immigrant partially for his supply of food. The wild animals found in the forest were also a source of supply for the skins and furs which were used for clothing by both settlers and the natives, and which were one of the most valuable of the colonial exports.

INDIANS

At the beginning of the sixteenth century there were about half a *Primitive* million Indians living in North America, and the great majority of *conditions* these were located on the present territory of the United States. In *among the* Mexico and northern Central America the natives had made considerable advance in the arts of civilized life; and those in the southwestern area of the present United States had, under the influence of their southern neighbors, made some progress toward civilization. In nearly all the remaining portions of the continent, however, the Indians had not risen above a very primitive state of living. They had made only a slight beginning at cultivating the lands over which they roamed. The little rudimentary farming practiced by them barely scratched the surface of the great agricultural opportunities which the fertile soil afforded. Although they had lived for centuries in one of the finest regions in the world they had done almost nothing to advance civilization.

This lack of progress is not easy to understand. It cannot be explained on the theory of racial inferiority, for the part played in

American history by Indian leaders shows that they were not lacking
in mental vigor. The fact that they had no milch cattle, no beasts of
burden, and no domestic animals except the dog, accounts in part
for their economic backwardness. As a rule, civilization rests upon
agriculture as its foundation, and agriculture cannot be carried on

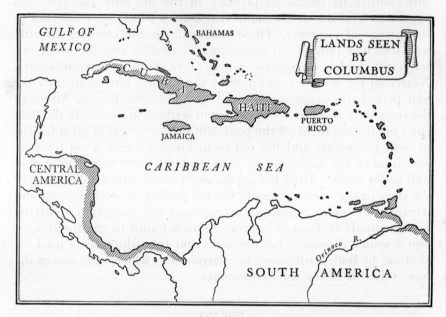

extensively by the unaided efforts of man, especially if he has the use
of only crude implements. Another reason for the lack of progress
on the part of the natives of middle North America was that they
had no contacts with the civilized Indians of South America and
southern North America, and were entirely shut off from the European and Asiatic centers of culture. There was therefore no way by
which they could learn from those peoples who had become the
disseminators of civilization.

*Part played
by the natives
in American
history*
Despite their backwardness, however, the Indians acted an important role in the early history of this country. They served as
guides to the whites in their journeys through the trackless forest
and gave them valuable lessons in woodcraft, hunting, and trapping.
From them the settlers learned how to make maple sugar and moc-
casins, and to construct the birch-bark canoe, which was a most valuable aid in traversing the wilderness. They also taught the newcomers how to clear the land and raise corn, tobacco, and other
native plants. Most of the furs which were exported from the colonies were collected by the natives. One permanent contribution

made by them was the transmission to us of many euphonious names for our mountains, streams, and lakes, which have given a tinge of poetry to American goegraphy. Aside from this contribution, American life has not been modified by Indian influence.

INDIAN FORTIFIED VILLAGE.

The Town of Pomeioc (present State of North Carolina) from DeBry, America, part I, Frankfurt-am-Main, 1590, engraved from John White's painting, which is in the British Museum. (From DeBry collection in W. L. Clements Library, Univ. of Michigan.)

CHAPTER II

The Discovery of America

EUROPE FINDS A NEW WORLD

The Norse discoveries

I T is quite probable that the Norsemen were the first Europeans to visit the continent of North America. Iceland had been occupied by them in 874, and a century later (about 985) a settlement had been made in Greenland by an Icelander, Eric the Red. According to a tradition recorded in the Icelandic sagas, the son of Eric the Red, Leif Ericsson, sailed from Norway in the year 1000 to join his father at the settlement in Greenland. On the voyage over he was driven out of his course and came to an unknown land where wheat and grapes were growing wild. So abundant were the grapes that he gave to the new country the name of Vinland. A settlement was planted and for a dozen years voyages were made between Vinland and Greenland; but it was very difficult to sustain a colony so far from the homeland and the attempt was finally abandoned. While modern scholarship is inclined to accept the fact of the Norse discoveries, it is still very uncertain as to the location of Vinland. It was probably somewhere between the northern coast of Labrador and the southern coast of New England.

The Renaissance

The unsuccessful effort at colonization made by the Norsemen showed that Europe was not yet ready to stake off a claim in America. Considerable progress in the science of navigation and the art of war would have to be made before civilization could extend itself to this far-off land and maintain its hold in opposition to native savagery. Europe had thus to make a great intellectual advance before it would be equal to the task of colonization; it had to pass from the mediaeval to the modern age. This transition was effected by the intellectual awakening known as the Renaissance.

This movement began in Italy in the fourteenth century, reached its height there in the fifteenth century, and later spread throughout western and central Europe. It started as a revival of interest in the Latin and Greek languages, literature, art, and philosophy. The scholars of that time showed a zeal that amounted to a religion in the study of the writings and architectural remains of the ancients. As a result of these efforts, the cultural and artistic ideals of the

10

Greeks and Romans were brought to light. The invention of print-ing (which occurred about the middle of the fifteenth century) made possible the dissemination of the newly-acquired information, thus putting the people in possession of the heritage of the past.

The Renaissance was not merely the revival of an old civilization, but was also the beginning of a new. The ideas and inspiration ac-quired from the study of Latin and Greek literature and art served as a tonic to the mind and stimulated originality in thought and creative activity in painting, sculpture, and architecture. The chief significance of the Renaissance for our purposes lies in the fact that it gave a new spirit to Europe. It inspired the people with optimism, self-reliance, and an adventurous faith in their own powers. They were relieved of many of the inhibitions that had trammeled the mediaeval mind. With this daring attitude of mind, Europe had the spiritual equipment necessary for launching out on exploring ventures. A scientific curiosity was also aroused and this led to a renewed interest in geography.

Land and sea routes to the East

In the late Middle Ages that part of the world which excited the greatest interest was the Far East—central, eastern, and southeastern Asia. Europeans had vague and incorrect notions of this distant land. The Crusades had aroused curiosity and had brought to Europe some information regarding the farther East. This interest was still further stimulated by the marvelous stories told by the missionaries and the few travelers who had made journeys into this wonderful region. From these dramatic but inaccurate accounts Europe re-ceived a glamorous idea of Cipangu (Japan), Cathay (China), and the Spice Islands. These faraway lands were pictured as a region of fabulous wealth—abounding in gold, precious stones, and spices.

These articles, along with silks, drugs, and ornamental woods, were finding their way to Europe, where there was a strong and growing demand for them. Native merchants would collect these products in China, Japan, and the East Indies, and bring them to Calcutta, Malacca, and other ports in the East. From these centers they were transported, partly by caravan and partly by ship, over long routes to the Mediterranean cities. Here they were bought by Italian, French, and Spanish merchants and by them carried to other leading European ports for distribution among the people.

Such a method of conveying goods was expensive and hazardous. In the costs of transportation had to be included the hardships en-dured in seasons of excessive heat and cold, and the dangers from robber bands incurred by the caravans in the ungoverned districts through which they passed. These drawbacks accentuated the desire of the people of Europe for a better means of procuring the goods of the East. It was this desire that prompted the efforts to find a sea route to the Indies. Furthermore, the major portion of the profit from this trade went to the Italian cities; and the other European states were eager to share in these gains. If a water route to the Indies could be found, the cities on the Atlantic coast would become the ports of entry for this sea-borne Eastern merchandise, and they would have a decided advantage in competing with their Italian rivals.

There were two possible ways by which India could be reached by sea. One was by sailing around the southern tip of Africa and eastward through the Indian Ocean; the other was by advancing into the unknown western waters and approach it from the other side of the world. Both of these daring feats were performed by seamen at the end of the fifteenth century, and the countries to which the world is indebted for these noted achievements are Portugal and Spain.

Portugal

By the end of the fifteenth century these powers had a rank in the family of nations out of proportion to their size and population. They had fallen heir to the possessions in the Spanish peninsula which the Mohammedan Moors had held since the early part of the eighth century (711). In the long struggle waged by the native Christians against their Moorish conquerors, the latter had gradually been driven southward until by the middle of the thirteenth century (1266) they had lost all their territory except the southern principality of Grenada. Out of this regained area there grew up a number of small Christian states. Prominent in this list was the kingdom of Portugal, which by 1263 had attained its present territorial limits.

Spain

There was a general trend toward consolidation among the other states and by the end of the thirteenth century the two largest, Castile and Aragon, were in possession of the greater part of the peninsula. These two states were combined by the marriage (1469) of Isabella of Castile and Ferdinand of Aragon. By the absorption of other principalities, including Grenada which was acquired (1492) by conquest, Castile and Aragon had by the end of the fifteenth century come into possession of all of present-day Spain. The joint kingdom now had a territorial basis which raised it to the rank of a first-class power, and its rulers were in a position to promote the discoveries and explorations which added to their possessions an extensive empire in the Western Hemisphere.

Prince Henry

By the middle of the fourteenth century European seamen had discovered the Canary, Madeira, and Azores Islands, and had explored the west coast of Africa as far south as Cape Bojador. Italian sailors had played the leading part in these early ventures, but in the voyages south of this headland the initiative was taken by Portuguese navigators. In these early explorations the Portuguese sea-men received aid and encouragement from Prince Henry, a younger son of King John I. At his astronomical observatory on the promon-tory of Sagres, Prince Henry was surrounded by scientists who de-voted their time to map making and the study of geography and navigation. The policy inaugurated by Prince Henry received ample financial support from the farseeing Portuguese rulers, who were also reaping profits from the slave trade growing out of the explo-rations. Under the stimulus of this patronage, the seamen trained in the school of Prince Henry the Navigator pushed farther and farther toward the south until, about a quarter of a century after his death, they reached the most southerly point of Africa.

In 1486 Bartholomew Diaz, a Portuguese explorer, while sailing *Diaz* along the western coast of Africa, was driven by a violent storm around the southern headland, which he called the Cape of Storms. King John II soon afterwards changed the name to the Cape of Good Hope, because the new discovery encouraged the hope that a waterway to the East Indies would soon be found.

This expectation was realized a dozen years later (1498) when *Vasco* another Portuguese explorer, Vasco da Gama, sailed to Calcutta *da Gama* and thus proved that there was an all-sea route to India. It was not long before the new water route had superseded the old land routes in the trade with the East. The elation felt by the King of Portugal because his country was the first to find a waterway to the real land of spices was tempered by the regret that it had failed to avail itself of a greater opportunity. For in the meantime Columbus had made his famous discovery, Spain having rendered him the aid which Por-tugal had previously denied (see p. 14).

By the end of the fifteenth century, Europe was ready for expan-sion into the Western Hemisphere. The compass and instruments for reckoning latitude were now in use among sailors and long voy-ages on the high seas could be made with a measure of safety. This progress in the science of navigation enabled the Europeans to find America, and a like advance in the arts of peace and war made it possible for them to appropriate the new land against the opposition of the natives. All that was now needed was a leader of courage and vision who would forge ahead and point out the way. Such a leader was Christopher Columbus.

He was born and reared in Genoa, one of the important city-states *Columbus:* of Italy. The Italian Renaissance was at its height during the time *The historic* of his childhood and youth, and he was doubtless influenced greatly *voyage* by the awakening spirit of the day. To it he probably owed his intense interest in geography and navigation. In pursuit of this interest he made a number of sea voyages and thus gained valuable experience as a navigator before he ventured upon his great undertaking. Believing that the earth was round, he was convinced that China and the East Indies could be reached by sailing to the west. Columbus' idea of the shape of the earth was not new. It had been advanced by Greek and Roman scholars and was held by all the leading geographers of his day; however, to others this belief was only an academic opinion, but to Columbus it was a conviction on which he was willing to stake his career.

As Columbus did not have the money to purchase and equip the ships needed for the voyage, he decided to ask for financial aid from a ruler of one of the European powers. His first application was made to King John II of Portugal, who after a long delay decided against risking money on such an uncertain venture. He then approached Ferdinand and Isabella with the hope of enlisting their support for his plan. These Spanish rulers kept him in suspense for five years and then gave a decision in his favor.

Since he hoped to find new lands, as well as a sea route to the Indies, Columbus was given authority by his commission to rule over all unclaimed lands which he might add to the Spanish realm. The title of Admiral was also conferred upon him by Queen Isabella. Seven eighths of the funds needed for the expedition were supplied by the city of Palos and the royal treasury. The other eighth was furnished by friends of the Admiral, who were to receive a proportionate share of the profits.

With this public and private support, Columbus was able to equip three small vessels with crews of ninety men in all. Leaving Palos (August 3, 1492), he sailed to the Canaries and from there steered westward hoping in due course to reach Japan. The incidents of the voyage are too well known to bear repetition. However, it might be pointed out that the persistence and courage exhibited by the Admiral in carrying out his great undertaking, his unwavering determination to sail on despite the fears and murmurings of his crew, and the calm assurance with which he pursued his course under the most discouraging circumstances, have won for him a deservedly high place among the heroes venerated by every schoolboy of modern times. It is true, however, that the only dangers encountered on the voyage were those created by the imagination of the men. For the weather was fine, and this late summer excursion might have been a delightful experience if the superstitious fears of the ignorant sailors had not conjured up one horror after another from the unknown Sea of Darkness.

Finally, when land was sighted, their apprehensions and deferred hopes gave way to transports of joy. The newly-found land was one of the Bahama Islands (probably the one now known as Watling Island), to which Columbus gave the name of San Salvador. A dramatic landing was made on Friday, October 12, 1492. When the Admiral stepped ashore his men crowded around him, the officers coming up to embrace him and the sailors to ask forgiveness for their complaints on the voyage. This demonstration took place in the presence of a group of naked savages, who looked on in silent wonder at the antics of these strange beings who had apparently dropped from the skies.

After touching at some of the other Bahama Islands, Columbus sailed along the coasts of Haiti and Cuba. Instead of finding people clad in silk and living in large cities adorned with fine palaces, as was supposed to be the case in the Indies, he saw only naked savages dwelling in villages of rude huts under conditions of primitive squalor. How anyone could identify these new lands with the magic East is almost beyond our comprehension. But the creative imagination of a romantic dreamer can weave a beautiful fabric out of commonplace materials, and so Columbus really thought that he had found a sea route to the Indies. Accordingly, he called the natives Indians, a term which has ever since been applied to the aborigines of the Western Hemisphere. When it later became known that these islands were not the East Indies, they were properly designated the West Indies.

As both Portugal and Spain were now engaged in the discovery of new lands, there was a danger that their rivalry would lead to a clash between these two Christian powers. In an effort to prevent this, Pope Alexander VI suggested a plan by which the unclaimed portion of the world could be divided between them. He issued four bulls, in which he drew an imaginary line one hundred leagues west of the Cape Verde Islands, allocating to Spain all lands not occupied by Christians which were west of the line, and to Portugal all those east of it. Portugal's dissatisfaction with this plan led to negotiations between the two powers which resulted in a treaty of division (1494). By this treaty the line was located at three hundred and seventy leagues west of the Cape Verde Islands. *The papal line of demarcation*

England and France did not recognize the right of Spain and Portugal to appropriate all the unoccupied area of the planet. Francis I of France is reported to have said derisively to the King of Spain: "Your Majesty and the King of Portugal have divided the world between you, offering no part of it to me. Show me, I pray you, the will of our father Adam, so that I may see if he has really made you his only universal heirs."

Columbus made three other voyages to the new world. On his third expedition (1498) he touched on the mainland of South America at the mouth of the Orinoco River. From the volume of water poured out by this stream he concluded that he had discovered a new continent and that the islands to the north were a part of the group lying east and south of the coast of Asia. To reach Asia it was therefore necessary to go farther west, beyond the northern limits of this newly-discovered continent. The hope of finding such a water route was the motive which prompted his fourth and last expedition (1502). On this voyage he sailed along the Caribbean coast of Central America, from Honduras to Panama, vainly searching for a channel which would lead into Asiatic waters.

Before starting on his historic voyage, Columbus sent his brother Bartholomew to England to solicit the support of Henry VII for the plan of the great Admiral. It is said that a promise of financial aid was given, but it came too late. Henry's interest in discovery caused him a few years later (1496) to issue a patent to John Cabot, a Venetian navigator, granting him governmental authority over any lands which he might discover in the east, north, and west. With the hope of finding a sea route to Cathay and the Spice Islands, Cabot left Bristol, England, in May, 1497, and sailed northward and westward until he reached the mainland of North America. Turning southward, he went along the coast for three hundred leagues and then returned to England. While the exact place at which he first saw land cannot be definitely located, it was somewhere in the neighborhood of Cape Breton Island. The following year he made a second voyage and this time sailed along the coast, probably as far as South Carolina.[1]

The significance of the Cabot voyages lies in the fact that they were the basis of England's claim to North America. They also revealed to Europe the value of the Newfoundland fisheries, which were profitably exploited by English, French, Spanish, and Portuguese seamen all during the sixteenth century.

One would naturally expect that the new world would have been named for Columbus. This honor, however, went to another navigator, who owed the undeserved distinction to the fact that his deeds were more successfully publicized than were those of the great Admiral. This over-advertised seaman was the Florentine, Amerigo Vespucci, who is generally known by his Latinized name, Americus Vespucius. He had accompanied an expedition along the coast of South America (1501), led by a Portuguese captain. In two letters

---

[1] John Cabot may have been accompanied by his son Sebastian on these voyages, though there is some doubt as to the correctness of this supposition.

written to friends, Vespucius gave vivid descriptions of the lands seen by him on this voyage and three others. These interesting letters had been translated into Latin before any report of Columbus' expedition to South America had been published in that language. As Latin was the literary language of the time, Vespucius ran ahead of Columbus in reaching the reading public with his observations about the southern mainland. In this way he received the honor, to which Columbus was entitled, of having first seen South America, or "Mundus Novus"—the "New World"—as he termed it.

In 1507 Martin Waldseemüller published a short treatise on geography, and with it one of the letters of Vespucius. In this little book, Americus Vespucius was represented as the discoverer of "Mundus Novus," and the suggestion was made that the newly-found continent be called "Amerigo" or "America" in his honor. The proposal was readily adopted and in this way the southern continent received the name of America. For a time the lands north of the Isthmus of Panama were still designated as the Indies, but later the northern mainland was given the name of North America. Then the term "America" was applied to the entire Western Hemisphere, and the region originally known as "Mundus Novus" now became South America.

SPANISH EXPLORATIONS IN THE WESTERN HEMISPHERE

Spain began at once to reinforce, by exploration and colonization, her rights in America which had been gained by the Columbian voyages and the papal grant. By the end of the first quarter of the sixteenth century Spanish navigators had explored the Atlantic coast of the Americas from Nova Scotia to the Strait of Magellan. One bold adventurer, Vasco Nuñez de Balboa, had penetrated the jungles *Balboa* of the Isthmus of Panama and reached the Pacific Ocean (1513). Ferdinand Magellan, a Portuguese seaman in the service of Spain, *Magellan* had led an expedition which had circumnavigated the globe (1519-1522). Settlement had gone hand in hand with exploration. Colonies had been planted in the West Indies and on the mainland of both North and South America. Spain had staked off for herself all South America except Brazil and had made considerable headway in the occupation and exploration of Central America and Mexico.

The natives of Mexico, Central America, and Peru were more *Pizarro* advanced in civilization than were the Indians in other parts of the *and Cortez* new world and had accumulated valuable stores of gold and silver. They did not, however, have iron tools and weapons, and with their copper weapons they were not a match for the Spanish invaders.

Accordingly, the Incas of Peru were conquered (1531-1534) by a
band of Spaniards led by Francisco Pizarro, an unscrupulous adventurer, and from them were taken large amounts of gold and silver.
In like manner the Aztecs of Mexico were conquered by Hernando
Cortez (1519-1522) and robbed of a rich store of the precious metals.

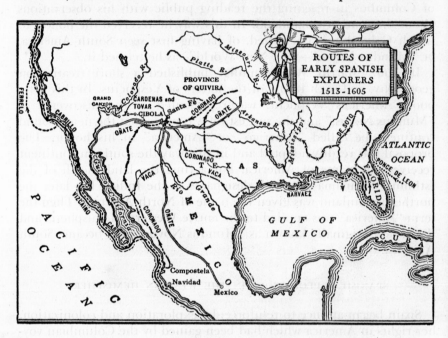

*Spanish ex-
plorations
within the
present
United
States:*

De Soto

Coronado

The most noted of the Spanish conquistadors who took part in
exploring the region now belonging to the United States were Hernando de Soto and Francisco Vásquez Coronado. Before the middle
of the sixteenth century these two adventurers, led on by the hope
of finding gold, had made extensive explorations respectively in the
southeastern and southwestern portions of the present United States.
Landing at Tampa Bay (1539), De Soto with more than six hundred
men entered upon a long march which carried him northward as
far as North Carolina and westward to the Arkansas region. In the
course of his wanderings he discovered the Mississippi River (1541),
beneath whose waters he was afterward buried. Coronado operated
from Mexico as a base and traversed a wide area in the southwest,
going as far east as central Kansas. Spanish seamen had also sailed
along the Pacific coast as far north as Oregon (1540-1541). By these
land and sea expeditions the geographical knowledge of middle
North America was greatly increased and Spain's claim was considerably strengthened.

The Spaniards did not confine their activities in the north to ex- *St. Augustine founded* ploration and gold hunting, but in the sixteenth century made a number of attempts at settlement within the territory now held by the United States. All of these were unsuccessful until 1565, when St. Augustine, the oldest town in this country, was founded. Near the end of the century (1598) the settlement of San Juan was established in New Mexico.

While Spain had not gone far by the end of the sixteenth century *Spanish achieve-ments in the Western Hemisphere* in occupying the territory now comprising the United States, she had built up a colonial empire in the Western Hemisphere which was the envy of her European rivals. Settlements had been made in the West Indies, and large areas in South America, Central America, and southern North America had been brought under her control. In 1574 there were in the new world approximately two hundred Spanish towns and cities with a white population of one hundred and sixty thousand or more. About five million Indians had been brought under Spanish authority. A number of fine churches had been erected and hundreds of monasteries had been built. Schools for the instruction of the Indians, and colleges for the training of priests, had also been established. The University of Mexico was a thriving institution and was turning out graduates in law and theology.

Portugal also carved out for herself a good slice of land in the *Cabral* Western Hemisphere. In 1500 one of her bold seamen, Pedro Alvarez Cabral, touched upon the coast of Brazil and took possession in the name of his sovereign. The eastern part of Brazil is west of the line agreed upon between the Spanish and Portuguese rulers and therefore Spain could not contest the claim of her rival. Cabral's discovery was followed by colonization, and so Brazil became a Portuguese possession.

FRANCE CONTESTS SPAIN'S CLAIM TO AMERICA

Before the end of the first quarter of the sixteenth century, France *Ver-razano* had also entered the contest for possessions in the new world. In 1524 Francis I, the ambitious King of France, dispatched the Florentine, Giovanni da Verrazano, on an exploring venture. He sailed along the eastern coast of North America from Cape Fear to Newfoundland, hunting in vain for a passage to the Pacific Ocean.

A decade later, Jacques Cartier was sent out by the French king *Cartier* in search of a sea route to the East. On this expedition he discovered (1534) the gulf to which he gave the name of St. Lawrence. Returning to the St. Lawrence region a year later, he ascended the river

hoping it might prove to be a waterway to China and India. This
hope was shattered when he reached the La Chine rapids. On these
voyages and others made later by Cartier, France based her claim to
the St. Lawrence valley, a right which she tried to strengthen by colonization. Two attempts at settlement on the St. Lawrence were
made at that time but both were costly failures.

EARLY FRENCH
EXPLORATIONS
1524-1535

Ribaut

   No further effort at colonization was made by the French for the
next two decades. In the meantime Admiral Coligny, a noted Protestant who was in high favor with King Charles IX, had become
interested in planting French settlements in America. Through his
influence, an expedition under the command of Jean Ribaut was
sent over to establish a Protestant colony in Florida (1562). A landing was effected at Port Royal, South Carolina, where Charles Fort
(named in honor of the king) was built and a band of forty volun-

teers left to hold the region for France. But it was not long before the settlers, after having become the victims of hunger, strife, and bloodshed, relinquished the post and returned to Europe.

The French had not, however, abandoned their purpose of occupying Florida, and in 1564 a large expedition was sent over under the command of Laudonnière, another Protestant. A settlement known as Fort Caroline was made on the St. John's River about five miles above its mouth. But Fort Caroline was on land which Philip II of Spain had staked off for his own country and he determined to destroy the French colony. He felt justified in breaking up this nest of heretics for several reasons. The post might easily be used—as it actually was—as the base for piratical incursions into the Spanish West Indies. Furthermore, by planting the settlement France had, as he considered, poached upon Spain's preserves. To wipe out the infant colony would therefore advance the interests of his country, by getting rid of foreign interlopers, and would help the Catholic Church by exterminating heretics. Seldom does a ruler have so plausible an excuse for performing such an evil deed. *Laudonnière*

The undertaking was carried out by Pedro Menendez de Aviles, whose cruelty and boldness well fitted him for the task. Menendez first landed about fifty miles south of Fort Caroline and laid the foundations of the settlement of St. Augustine (1565). From this point he marched through the tangled forests and made a surprise attack on the French settlement. The post was taken without resistance and most of the captured French were put to death. With this tragedy France's effort to challenge Spain's blanket claim to North America ended for the time. It was not until near the end of the century that France made another attempt at American colonization.

BRITISH AND SPANISH RIVALRY IN AMERICA

By destroying the French settlement in Florida, Spain had won an easy victory in the first clash between European powers in the new world. It was for only a short time, however, that she was left in undisturbed possession of North America. For it was not long before she had to cope with another rival, who was destined to wrest from her the supremacy of the seas and limit her expansion in North America. This second antagonist was England. To understand how this came about it is necessary to take a glance at the European background of the drama performed in America.

At the beginning of the sixteenth century the Roman Catholic Church held sway over all of Europe except Russia and the Balkan peninsula. The people in the latter regions, except for some Alba- *The Protestant Reformation*

nians and Turks in the Balkans, all adhered to the Greek Catholic
Church. The Roman Catholic Church, thanks to its efficient organization with the pope at its head, had been able to suppress the
various outbursts of heresy which had occasionally occurred. It had
maintained its unity until the second decade of the sixteenth century,
when a serious ecclesiastical revolt was begun under the leadership
of Martin Luther. Starting in Germany as a protest against certain
practices and doctrines of the church (1517), it soon developed into
an irreparable breach. This movement is known as the Protestant
Reformation, or Protestant Revolt. The final outcome of it was a
"rent in the seamless robe of Christ," that is, the permanent division
of the western church into two rival groups—Protestants and Catholics. The latter have held to the doctrines and traditions of the old
church while the former have accepted the tenets of Luther or other
reformers.

Protestantism soon spread throughout western Europe and became especially strong in the north German states, Switzerland, the
Dutch Netherlands, the Scandinavian peninsula, England, and
Scotland. It also made considerable headway in France. The clash
between the old and new faith in France led to a series of civil wars,
the final outcome of which was unfavorable to Protestantism. The
Huguenots, as the French Protestants were called, were thereafter
considerably in the minority, but they were an influential group in
the country.

John Calvin   While Martin Luther was the most outstanding of the Protestant
leaders, his influence on American life was not as great as that of
John Calvin. For a number of years (beginning in 1536) the little
state of Geneva was dominated, both politically and religiously, by
this noted theologian. He was the clearest thinker and the ablest
writer among the early reformers, and his great work, *The Institutes
of the Christian Religion,* was more widely read than any other theological treatise produced by the Protestant leaders.

Calvin was the great moral and religious teacher of our ancestors.
It is doubtful whether any man who has lived since the days of the
Apostle Paul has influenced American thinking along ecclesiastical
and ethical lines more than has the great Genevan theologian. In
colonial times his theological views were the basis of the doctrines
held by the Congregationalists, the Presbyterians, most of the Baptists, the adherents of the Dutch Reformed and German Reformed
Churches, and a good many of the Anglicans. It was with these denominations that the great majority of church members were affiliated in colonial days.

During the sixteenth century (from 1485 to 1603) England was

ruled by the powerful Tudors. The first of the line, Henry VII, came *England in the sixteenth century*
to the throne (1485) at the end of the Wars of the Roses and founded
the strong monarchy. His son and successor, Henry VIII, increased
the power of the kingship and was able to wield an authority greater
than that exercised by any of his predecessors. The strong monarchy
continued under Henry's successors, Edward VI, Mary, and Elizabeth, though the crown had lost much of its power by the end of the
Tudor period (1603).

Henry VIII was opposed to the new religion and wrote a book *Ecclesiastical changes under the Tudors*
against Lutheranism which won for him the title of "Defender of
the [Catholic] Faith." Later, as a result of a controversy between
him and the pope, Henry brought about the separation of the church
of England from that of Rome, with the king as the head of the
English church (1534). This change did not, however, involve a
departure from the Catholic doctrines, and it was not until the accession of Edward VI that the English church became Protestant.
Under Edward's successor, Mary, who was a sincere advocate of the
old faith, there was a return to the Catholic Church and England
again accepted the authority of the pope. After ruling for a short
period of five years, Mary was succeeded by Elizabeth, whose glorious
reign lasted for nearly half a century (1558-1603). When she came
to the throne, Protestantism was restored and the Anglican was made
the established church. Laws were passed compelling the recognition of the queen as the head of the church and requiring all ministers to accept the Thirty Nine Articles of Faith and the Prayer
Book, both of which were in accord with the Protestant doctrines.

In the meantime Scotland had come into the Protestant fold. The *John Knox*
leader in the reform movement there was John Knox, a zealous disciple of John Calvin. Knox had imbibed strong Presbyterian convictions from the writings of the Genevan theologian, and so most
of the Scotch became Presbyterians. Ireland remained loyal to the
Catholic faith.

At the end of the sixteenth century the British realm comprised *Union of England and Scotland*
England, Wales, and a district in the eastern part of Ireland. When
James I came to the throne he brought England and Scotland into
a personal union, for he was already ruler of the latter country. During the next century, however, the crown was the only bond of union
between the two countries. By the Act of Union of 1707, provision
was made for a joint Parliament for both kingdoms. Since the enactment of this measure the entire island of Britain has been united
under one government.

The reign of Queen Elizabeth was an important era in the history *The Elizabethan era*
of British expansion. The Renaissance was in full bloom in England

and was stimulating thought and action in every phase of effort. Industry and commerce were expanding, and population and wealth were rapidly increasing. Protestantism, which had been accepted by the people, was still young enough to inspire its adherents with its nascent zeal for religion, and thus impart to every great movement a tinge of idealism. A navy which had recently grown into strength and importance had given the government self-confidence in its relations with other powers. The time was thus ripe for England to challenge the exclusive claims of Spain and Portugal to the new world and to reassert her own rights in America.

John Hawkins

In arousing Britain's interest in America and her hostility to Spain, leading parts were played by John Hawkins and Francis Drake. Both of these bold seamen were firm in their Protestant convictions and therefore had no love for Catholic Spain. Hawkins violated the trade regulations of Spain by selling to her American colonies Negro slaves which he had transported from Africa. In this way he antagonized the Spanish American authorities and helped to keep alive the ill feeling between the two powers. His great service to his country was the introduction, by him and his associates, of reforms in the British navy which strengthened it for the great contest with the Spanish Armada.

Francis Drake

Of the English sea dogs who led semi-piratical expeditions in the Spanish Main, the most noted was Francis Drake. He robbed Spanish treasure ships and levied contributions on Spanish American towns, although Spain and Britain were technically at peace. Instead of punishing him for these acts, the queen gave him encouragement by accepting a portion of the booty and by conferring on him the honor of knighthood. The greatest of Drake's expeditions was the one on which he circumnavigated the globe. In 1578 he passed through the Strait of Magellan and sailed northward, seizing Spanish ships heavily loaded with gold and silver. Fearing that he would be intercepted by the Spaniards and forced to disgorge his loot if he should steer southward, he continued his course toward the north until he reached the coast of California. After vainly searching for a waterway across to the Atlantic, he turned boldly toward the west and came home by way of the Spice Islands and the Cape of Good Hope, thus completing the second voyage around the world.

Defeat of the Spanish Armada

Elizabeth and Philip II of Spain were the outstanding Protestant and Catholic rulers, respectively, and this difference in religious ideology lay behind much of the friction between their countries. There were other causes of strife, and finally the rivalry between the two powers became an irrepressible conflict. War was declared by Philip, who placed great reliance on his powerful fleet, known as the

Invincible Armada. The decisive event of the contest was a great naval battle in the English Channel (July, 1588) in which the Spanish fleet was badly defeated and then driven northward into the North Sea. A heavy additional toll of Philip's ships was taken by wind and storm and those that finally returned to Spain were only a remnant of the once proud Armada. By this great victory the prestige of England's fleet was greatly enhanced and that of Spain's correspondingly lowered. England's high rank as a sea power made it possible for her to occupy a good portion of North America, despite Spain's efforts to monopolize that continent. Spain now had a fear of the English navy which made her reluctant to risk another contest with it; and so America was made safe for British colonization.

Even before the Spanish Armada had been defeated, however, *Gilbert* England had gained a foothold in America. The first effort to establish an English colony in the new world was made by Sir Humphrey Gilbert, who was granted a patent by Queen Elizabeth (1578), authorizing him to explore and occupy "remote heathen and barbarous lands, countreys and territories not actually possessed by any Christian prince or people." Acting on this grant, Gilbert made an attempt to plant a settlement on Newfoundland. The venture was unsuccessful, and he lost his life at sea on the return voyage.

The rights under Gilbert's patent now descended to his half- *Raleigh* brother, Walter Raleigh, whose colorful personality had won the favor of the queen. Sharing his brother's ambition to extend British influence to America, Raleigh sent out an expedition to choose a place of settlement. An exploring party spent two months in the midsummer of 1584 on the coast of North Carolina and returned to give a glowing account of the region, which was described as "the most plentiful, sweet, fruitful, and wholesome of all the world." This report aroused great interest in the new country, which was given the name of Virginia, in honor of Elizabeth, the Virgin Queen.

Encouraged by the possibilities revealed by this expedition, Raleigh decided to establish a colony in Virginia. About one hundred emigrants were sent over in a fleet of seven ships under the command of Sir Richard Grenville, who left a group of settlers on Roanoke Island in charge of Ralph Lane (1585). Owing to the mismanagement of their leader, the settlers were within a year threatened with destruction by famine and the dangerous hostility of the savages. They were saved from this fate by Sir Francis Drake. Stopping at Roanoke Island on his return from a raid in the Spanish Main, he generously complied with their request and took them back to England.

Raleigh did not, however, abandon his purpose of planting a colony in Virginia. By enlisting the aid of some capitalists, he was able to procure funds for a second attempt. A large expedition was fitted out and in due time one hundred and fifty prospective settlers, including seventeen women, were on their way to Virginia (1587). A plan of government for the colony was drawn up, with John White as governor. On reaching the coast of Carolina the immigrants chose a site for their settlement on the ill-fated Roanoke Island.

Governor White remained in the colony for only a short time before going back to England with the returning ships to provide for the speedy sending over of more supplies. Through the influence of Raleigh, two small supply ships were made ready and in a few months White was on his way back to Roanoke. These vessels were attacked by Spanish men-of-war and were so seriously damaged that they had to return to a home port. A second attempt made by Raleigh to send relief to the colony was unsuccessful, and White was unable to go back to Virginia until 1591. When he arrived at Roanoke Island none of the settlers could be found. Just what had happened to the "Lost Colony" has never been satisfactorily determined. Whether the settlers were killed or absorbed by the Indians or were the victims of some other misfortune is one of the unsolved, if not unsolvable, problems of history.

Courtesy of the New-York Historical Society, New York City

CHRISTOPHER COLUMBUS.
After engraving, DeBry, 1595.

CHAPTER III

The Birth of a Nation

"THE CRADLE OF THE REPUBLIC"

*B*Y the end of the sixteenth century England had not obtained a permanent foothold in the new world, but a lively interest in colonization had been awakened. There were a number of reasons for this interest which made a strong appeal both to the government and public-spirited capitalists. Among them, the following were important:

(1) The expectation of procuring gold and silver in the new *Motives for* world.—The British promoters of colonization were hopeful of re- *English* peating the experience of the Spaniards, who had reaped such a rich *colonization* harvest of the precious metals in their American possessions.

(2) The hope of discovering a waterway across the mainland to the Pacific Ocean.—In the early part of the seventeenth century it was still generally believed that North America was only a narrow strip of land separating the Atlantic from the Pacific Ocean. The nation which should find and control a channel linking the two oceans would have a great advantage over its commercial rivals in the race for the Eastern trade. A colony planted in North America could serve as a base for the discovery and occupation of such a passage.

(3) The decision to contest Spain's claim to North America.— From her settlement at St. Augustine, Spain might push northward along the Atlantic as she afterwards did on the Pacific coast. By planting a colony in Virginia, England could check this expansion and stake out a large part of America for herself before the ground had been pre-empted by her rival.

(4) The expectation of using the colonies as a source of raw materials for British industry.—The list of raw materials imported by England included lumber, silks, iron, and also pitch, tar, rosin, and other naval stores. It was hoped that these products could be furnished by the colonials. If so, the money spent for them would be kept within the empire and the supply would not be subject to the trade restrictions which an outside power might impose.

(5) The belief that the colonies would serve as a market for English goods.—It was thought that the settlers, and probably the In-

27

dians, would buy large quantities of the coarse woolen goods then produced in England.

(6) The hope that colonization would promote the growth of the British merchant marine and strengthen the navy.—Trade between the possessions and the homeland would lead to the construction of additional merchant ships, which could be used in time of war as transports and carriers of food supplies.

(7) The desirability of finding a vent for the surplus population. —To the colonies could be sent criminals and other undesirables, as well as many worthy people who could not find employment at home. This latter class was large, owing to the inability of many laborers to make an adjustment to the economic changes which had recently taken place in England.

(8) The religious motive.—Colonization, it was said, would afford an opportunity to bring the Indians to a knowledge of Christianity. This worthy objective made an appeal to the softhearted religious leaders who were promoting the movement but had little, if any, influence on the hardheaded business men who were putting up the money. Later the desire to create in America a refuge for adherents of persecuted religious groups was an important factor in establishing colonies, notably those of New Plymouth, Massachusetts, Maryland, Rhode Island, and Pennsylvania.

At the accession of James I (1603) there were no English settlers on American soil. The British government had not, however, abandoned its purpose of gaining a foothold in the new world. About that time a fresh interest in colonization was aroused by several exploring and trading expeditions which had gone from England to the coast of North America. Raleigh's experience showed that the establishment of a colony was too great an undertaking for a private individual. The high costs and heavy risks involved made it desirable that the financial responsibility for such a venture be assumed by an organization of capitalists. But the government was also interested and wanted to have a hand in the project. Accordingly, the first successful attempt at colonization resulted from the co-operation of the government and private capital.

The London and Plymouth Companies: The First Charter

A joint-stock company was organized and granted a charter by the king (1606). It was composed of two groups of stockholders, one at London and the other at Plymouth. The two groups are often referred to as separate companies, the former being known as the London Company and the latter as the Plymouth Company. By this charter the London patentees were given the right to plant a colony anywhere on the continent of North America between the thirty-fourth and forty-first parallels of latitude; the Plymouth group, anywhere between the thirty-eighth and forty-fifth parallels; but no settlement was to be made by either company within a hundred miles of one already made by the other. To each company was granted a square of land extending along the coast fifty miles north and fifty miles south of the first settlement and going back one hundred miles into the interior.

The companies were to assume complete financial responsibility for the project and receive all the profits that might accrue from it. The king, however, was to have indirect control over the management of the colony. There was to be a general council, appointed by the king, which was to reside in England and have supervision over both colonies. In each colony there was to be a local council chosen by the general council. This local council was to be a self-perpetuating body, as it was authorized to fill vacancies in its own organization. It had power to manage the business of the colony and govern the settlers. The arrangement was thus a combination of private ownership and public control.

Each company made an attempt at colonization in the summer of 1607. An expedition sent out by the Plymouth Company landed in August at the mouth of the Kennebec River and built a fort which was named St. George. The settlers endured terrible sufferings during the following winter, and in the spring the survivors returned to England. The Plymouth Company thereafter devoted its efforts to fishing and fur trading, and it was not until a dozen years later (when the Pilgrims arrived) that a permanent settlement was made in New England. *The Plymouth Company makes an unsuccessful attempt at settlement*

The London Company was more persistent in its efforts and was able to make the first permanent English settlement in the new world. In December, 1606, this company sent out three small vessels with one hundred and twenty emigrants to occupy the land which had been granted to it. As the ships went the long route, by way of the Canaries and the West Indies, they did not reach the American coast until the spring of 1607. The expedition ascended a broad stream, called Powhatan by the Indians but now given the name of James in honor of the English king. The settlers landed on a peninsula about thirty miles above the mouth of the river (May 24, 1607) and at once began to erect huts for dwellings, a storehouse, a church, and a palisaded fort for protection. This was the beginning of Jamestown, the birthplace of a great nation. *The settlement at Jamestown*

The site chosen was in some respects a suitable one for settlement. The peninsula (now an island) was surrounded by water except for a narrow neck of land connecting it with the northern shore of the river. It was therefore accessible to ships and could be easily defended against outside attack; but the land was only a few feet above high tide and nearby was a malaria-breeding swamp. Besides, the peninsula was covered over with a dense forest, which furnished a good hiding place for prowling savages and added greatly to the difficulty of clearing the land.

Nature greeted the new venture with a smiling welcome. The spring weather was at its best and the clean atmosphere was sweet with the fragrance of young leaves, strawberries, and wild flowers, and vocal with the music of hundreds of birds. So charmed were the English with their new surroundings that one of them (Captain John Smith), in speaking of this favored land, said that "heaven and earth never agreed better to frame a place for man's habitation."

Sufferings of the early settlers

The first few years of the little settlement were a period of great suffering. This was occasioned by hunger and disease, mismanagement on the part of the leaders, and fear of the Indians. With the hot days of August there came famine and sickness, and death took a heavy toll. Adequate food supplies could not be obtained, although two expeditions bringing immigrants and provisions came to Jamestown in 1608. The forest was alive with game, and the rivers and Chesapeake Bay abounded in fish and oysters. But the Indians were hostile, and the settlers were afraid to venture out and garner what nature had provided. These Indians, who belonged to the Algonquian stock, were ruled by Powhatan, the emperor of thirty-four tribes occupying the region from Roanoke River to the head of Chesapeake Bay.

These troubles were aggravated by the overanxiety of the company for immediate gain. In its eagerness for profits, the company on two occasions had the colonists stop their work to get ready return cargoes, such as lumber, tar, pitch, iron, and other commodities. Time was also lost in hunting for gold and in digging for an ore falsely thought to be gold. So much energy was consumed with these activities that only four acres of corn were planted in the spring of 1608. The plan of the company required that all work should be done in common and the products of this labor put in a common storehouse. This took away the human incentive of gain, which is always a prod to effort. Because of the bitter strife among the members of the local council, the local government was paralyzed by inefficiency.

John Smith

The only man who showed any ability as a leader in these troublous times was Captain John Smith. He was one of the original members of the local council, and for a time was the only member of that body, the others having been removed by death and expulsion.

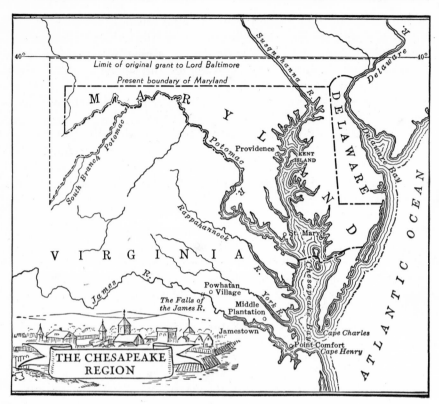

THE CHESAPEAKE REGION

While sole councillor, he acted as a benevolent despot. He had a blockhouse and twenty cabins built, a well dug, and thirty or forty acres of corn planted. He also procured corn from the Indians and treated them with a firmness which inspired them with a wholesome respect for the settlers.[1]

The terrible experiences of the first years called loudly for a *The Second Charter* change in the management of affairs. Such a change was made in 1609, when a second charter was obtained from the king. By this charter the company (which from this time on is known as the Virginia Company) had its land grant enlarged so as to include all the territory two hundred miles north and two hundred miles south of Point Comfort, extending west and northwest to the Pacific Ocean. A third charter was granted by the king in 1612 which added the *The Third Charter* Bermuda Islands to the territory of the company. By these two charters the company was given complete governmental authority over the colony.

---

[1] Smith wrote an account of the early events in the colony and gave a description of the country. He also made a map of the Chesapeake region, which is remarkabie for its accuracy.

In the meantime, an important change had been made in the local government of the colony. After receiving the second charter, the company appointed a governor for Virginia and conferred upon him almost absolute authority in local affairs. He was to be assisted by six councillors, but they did not limit his power, as they could act only in an advisory capacity. In this way the local administration was unified and the former dissensions ceased.

Lord Delaware was chosen as the first governor of the colony, but as he was not ready to leave at once, Sir Thomas Gates was sent over to act for a time as his deputy. The vessel on which Gates sailed was driven by a violent storm to the Bermuda Islands, where he was detained for nine months. In the spring of 1610 he and the survivors of his wrecked vessel sailed to Jamestown in two rough boats which had been constructed during their long sojourn in the Bermudas. When in May they pulled up to the Jamestown wharf they were greeted by a handful of half-starved and half-demented settlers who had tottered down to the landing to meet them. These were the survivors of a time of suffering during which famine and disease had renewed their ravages on the colony.

This horrible experience was due in large measure to the feeble policy of the local government. Smith had received a severe burn from an accidental explosion of gunpowder, and while he was helpless, his enemies were able to depose him from the presidency of the council. Furthermore, he could not get proper medical attention at Jamestown and consequently returned to England in the fall of 1609. There was now no one in the colony who was able to cope with the difficult situation. The settlers were intimidated by the Indians, who hemmed them in at Jamestown and at times came up and drove off their livestock. From these conditions there resulted a period of famine in the winter of 1609-10 which is known as the "Starving Time." To such straits were the settlers brought that their number was reduced by starvation from five hundred to about sixty. This was the most terrible instance of suffering experienced by any group of Englishmen who had a share in laying the foundations of the United States.

Since Gates had with him only a small amount of supplies he decided to abandon the colony. After a short stay he placed the survivors on his boats and started for the fishing stations in Newfoundland. They had not gone far before they met Lord Delaware, who was bringing supplies and more settlers for the sorely-beset colony. Gates now turned back, and he and Lord Delaware reestablished the settlement at Jamestown.

Returning to England a year later, Lord Delaware governed Virginia through deputy governors until 1618. Prominent in the list of these early representatives of the governor was Thomas Dale, who placed the colony under strict military rule and subjected the people to cruel and inhuman punishments without trial by jury. Many of the settlers needed a policy of strict discipline to bring them into habits of industry and obedience, but there was no adequate reason for the extreme severity practiced by the High Marshal, as Dale was called. *Thomas Dale*

Dale did, however, carry out some constructive measures which were very helpful to the colony. The plan of working in common was modified, and everyone was forced to depend upon his own labor for his support. Each settler was granted a small amount of land to be cultivated for his own benefit. He had to pay a high rent for this allotment, and still had to work for a month each year for the company. By this new arrangement an appeal was made to the self-interest of the laborer, who now had a stronger incentive for working than he had had under the earlier communal plan.

By a policy of craftiness and firmness, Dale was able to keep the natives quiet during his entire administration. Pocahontas, the daughter of Powhatan, was kidnapped by him and kept at Jamestown as a hostage. She had been a loyal friend of the English settlers, and (if we can accept Smith's account of the incident) had on one occasion saved his life at the risk of her own. While at Jamestown she was converted to Christianity and married to John Rolfe, one of the leading planters. This family tie bound the old chief to a policy of friendship with the English. It was also during Dale's administration that Rolfe discovered a process of curing tobacco which added greatly to its market value. Virginia tobacco was now able to compete in the British market with that from the Spanish West Indies and soon became a valuable export. This gave the colony a firm economic basis and caused it to take on new life. *Pocahontas*

A new process of curing tobacco

Under the charter of 1612, the Virginia Company had developed into an important legislative and administrative body. The stockholders were soon divided into two groups, the conservative, or "court" party, and the liberal, or "country" party. The former was at first the dominant faction and was responsible for the military regime inaugurated by Dale. When the liberals got control they put an end to military rule and allowed the settlers the rights of free Englishmen. Every planter who had resided in the colony for seven years was also granted a hundred acres of land for himself and each member of his family. *The beginning of representative government*

It was in line with this liberal policy that provision was made for a legislative assembly in Virginia. In obedience to instructions from the company, Governor George Yeardley called together the first representative assembly which was ever convened in the Western Hemisphere. It met at Jamestown in August, 1619, and was composed of the governor and his council and two representatives from each of the eleven plantations or boroughs. Out of this body there developed a bicameral assembly, the governor and his council constituting the upper house, and the representatives of the boroughs (burgesses), the lower house, known as the House of Burgesses. At first the functions of the assembly were administrative and judicial, as well as legislative, but later became mainly legislative. The organization of this body marks the beginning of representative government in the new world, and this assembly is the prototype of the Congress of the United States and of the legislature of every American state.[1]

Indian massacre

As long as Powhatan lived, the English settlers had little or nothing to fear from the Indians, for this able chief was held to a peace policy by family bonds. But his successor, Opechancanough, hated the whites because they were holding Indian lands, and he longed for an opportunity to exterminate them. In the early years, however, he concealed his resentment behind an appearance of friendship, and the settlers, lulled into a false security, failed to take proper precautions against sudden attack. Profiting by this inexcusable thoughtlessness, the Indians made simultaneous attacks on the scattered, defenseless settlements and killed about three hundred and fifty of the colonists (1622). So aroused were the whites over this massacre that they inflicted a terrible punishment on the redskins, and the latter remained peaceable for more than a score of years.

The charter of the company annulled

The troubles of the colony did not cease when the liberal party got control of the company. There was still great suffering from famine, disease, and death—more than can be accounted for from the normal hazards of pioneering in a new world. Much of this unnecessary suffering was justly blamed on the mismanagement of the company, among whose leaders there were dissensions and personal bickerings which made it difficult to carry out a wise and effective policy. The company was in dire financial straits and, by the summer of 1621, was on the verge of bankruptcy. Instead of devoting its meager resources to the furnishing of food supplies, livestock, and agricultural equipment for the settlers, it kept sending more and more emigrants to Virginia. In this way the colony was overrun with settlers for whom food supplies and adequate housing facilities had not been provided. The impatience of the stockholders for immediate

---

[1] Another important event of this year was the landing at Jamestown of a cargo of Negroes (see page 126).

returns caused the diversion of the energies of the colonists from the raising of food to making experiments in the manufacture of iron, the culture of silk, and other like projects.

Complaints against the company were made to King James, who had a committee appointed to investigate the charges. After making its investigation the commission brought an indictment against the company and its charter was annulled (June, 1624). Virginia was now a royal province, but no substantial change in the government was made, except that the appointment of the governor and the council was vested in the king instead of the company. After a brief suspension, the House of Burgesses was restored (by 1629) and it continued as the representative branch of the assembly from that time until the end of the colonial era.

VIRGINIA A ROYAL PROVINCE: THE INTERREGNUM

Governor Berkeley

Among the early governors sent to Virginia by the king, the most noted was Sir William Berkeley. As he was an intolerant Churchman, he bore down heavily upon the Puritans in Virginia and caused about one thousand of them to leave for Maryland. Fortunately, however, he had some good qualities to offset his intolerance. He had courage, ability, and decision of character, and advocated liberal reforms in the colony, such as increasing the powers of the assembly and abolishing the unfair poll tax.

Two years after Berkeley's arrival in Virginia, Opechancanough, now old and nearly blind, made another surprise attack upon the unsuspecting settlers and massacred hundreds of them (1644). Whereupon the young governor, at the head of the Virginia forces, conducted a series of campaigns against the Indians and administered such a severe defeat to them that their power in Tidewater Virginia was broken for all time.

The Puritan Revolution

On the death of James I (1625), Charles I came to the throne of England. His arbitrary policy in both church and state aroused the fierce antagonism of Parliament, and a war between Parliament and king was the result. The Puritans supported Parliament, and so this civil war is known as the Puritan Revolution. After seven years of strife (1642-1649), Parliament came out victorious and the king was executed. For more than a decade, the period of the Interregnum, England was governed without king or House of Lords. At first the government was in the hands of the House of Commons, but later Oliver Cromwell assumed control and ruled with the title of Lord Protector. The people grew tired of the Puritan regime and, shortly after Cromwell's death, called Charles II to the throne (1660).

Virginia loyal to the Stuarts

The planter aristocrats who dominated social and political life in Virginia were loyal to the Stuart cause and strongly opposed to the Puritan party. For this reason Berkeley had no difficulty in inducing the assembly to condemn the execution of Charles I and recognize the younger Charles as the rightful ruler of the English realm. This support of the exiled prince won for Virginia the designation of the Old Dominion. Thanks to this loyalty, Virginia became a haven for Cavaliers, as the adherents of the Stuart cause were called, and a considerable number of them migrated thither after the king had been defeated and executed.[1]

Virginia under the Commonwealth

The Puritan government in England did not overlook the defiant attitude of the Virginia colony and was determined to force it into an acceptance of the new regime. Accordingly, a commission supported by warships was sent to reduce the Chesapeake colonies to obedience. When the little squadron arrived at Jamestown, Berkeley wished to call out the militia and resist the demands of the commissioners. The belligerency of the governor was overruled, however, by the good sense of the councillors and burgesses, and the colony yielded without any attempt at resistance.

The terms of the surrender were very favorable to the colonists. The authority of Parliament was recognized and the Puritan party was put in control of the government of Virginia, but the Anglicans were allowed religious freedom. The governor and councillors were chosen by the House of Burgesses, the members of which were elected directly by the voters. No taxes could be levied without the consent of the popular branch of the assembly. The people were thus given a larger share in the government than they had ever had at any previous time. During the Interregnum, Virginia was a self-governing republic, managing its own affairs with little or no interference from the home authorities. This period of eight years was one of prosperity and rapid increase in population. It was a golden age for the yeoman farmers, who enjoyed an economic and political importance which had never before been accorded them.

---

1 According to the older historians, most of the Cavaliers who came to Virginia were of the gentry, some of them being younger sons of the nobility. These patrician immigrants gave to the social life of the province an aristocratic cast which was exceptional for the colonies. This view has, however, been challenged by Professor Thomas J. Wertenbaker, who contends that the number of Cavaliers who emigrated is not nearly so large as was formerly believed and the majority of those who did come were of the middle class and not of the gentry. See Wertenbaker's *Patrician and Plebeian in Virginia* (1910).

BACON'S REBELLION

Prosperity and the right of self-government did not wean the Old Dominion away from her loyalty to the lost cause, and the upper class was determined to seize the first opportunity to go back under Stuart authority. Accordingly, after Cromwell's death, Berkeley was chosen governor (March, 1660) and the Puritan regime came to an end in Virginia. *Berkeley recalled to the governorship*

This choice, which was afterwards confirmed by a commission from the king, was a most unfortunate one for the people of Virginia. In retirement and disappointment, for eight years Berkeley had been nursing his wrath and chafing his spiritual wounds. His natural bent toward intolerance had been accentuated by the humiliation which he felt as a result of Puritan supremacy in England and America. His increasing years were bringing on a premature senility which was hardening his faults and softening his virtues. His principles had degenerated into prejudices, and his covetousness had grown into rapacity. Always loyal to the king, he had now become a "royalist fanatic." His governmental policy was one of tyranny in both church and state. He was zealous in his efforts to enforce the laws against religious heresy and subjected the Quakers to persecution.

From such a governor only despotic rule could be expected, unless he were restrained by the council or assembly. Unfortunately, these checks were not now in operation. The views of the councillors were in entire agreement with those of the governor, and the assembly, which had been chosen in the first flush of royalist enthusiasm, was also disposed to do his bidding. Berkeley strengthened his grip on both houses of the assembly by a judicious use of patronage, for he gave most of the lucrative offices to councillors and burgesses. So well pleased was he with this assembly that he refused to call a new election for a period of fifteen years. *His tyrannical rule*

The right to vote, which was enjoyed by all freemen during the Commonwealth period, was now (1670) restricted to freeholders, and thus many of the people were disfranchised. Besides, the voters had no effective way to register their dissatisfaction with the government. Owing to the long continuance of the assembly, the people could not give any fresh mandates to the House of Burgesses. Nor did they have any voice in the local government. The administration of the counties and the parishes was in the hands of the justices of the peace and the vestrymen, respectively, and these officials were chosen from the aristocracy. All the openings for the escape of steam were thus closed and discontent could express itself only by an explosion.

Other grievances of the people

Furthermore, the people were conscious of many grievances. The Navigation Acts (see p. 179) worked a hardship on the planters. By them, freight rates on trans-Atlantic commerce were increased, and the sale of tobacco in continental Europe was greatly hampered. As a result of these drawbacks, the price of tobacco became so low that the Virginia farmers could earn no profit from raising it. The situation was aggravated by several crop failures in the early sixteen-seventies. Taxes were high and so apportioned as to impose a heavy burden on the common people, and a light one on the privileged class. The small landowners were unable to make ends meet and were forced more and more to cover their farms with mortgages.

Rebellion precipitated by Berkeley's Indian policy

The grievance which precipitated conflict was Berkeley's refusal to protect the outlying settlements against the danger of Indian attack. In 1675 unrest was stirring among the Indians, and the frontiersmen sent a petition to the governor, requesting the appointment of a military commander to lead them against the savages. Berkeley not only refused to heed this request but issued an order forbidding the submission of any more petitions. The settlers in the back country lost patience with this inaction and determined to take the defense of their homes into their own hands. At a large meeting, held in a frontier community, Nathaniel Bacon was chosen to lead the people against the Indians.

Nathaniel Bacon

Although Bacon had been in Virginia for only fourteen months, he had won the high esteem and confidence of his neighbors. He was a member of the governor's council and had influential family connections, both in the homeland and in the colony. Despite these associations with the privileged class, destiny had assigned him the role of champion of the people against the misrule of the governor and his aristocratic henchmen. And he was well-suited to the part. Ambitious, high-spirited, and energetic, he was not disposed to acquiesce tamely in the violation of his and the people's rights, either by the Indians or the provincial government. Moreover, he had the gift of eloquence and by stirring speeches could arouse his followers to a high pitch of enthusiasm for, and devotion to, his cause.

Part played by Bacon in the rebellion

Without the authorization of the governor, Bacon led his men in a series of successful campaigns against the Indians and reduced them to a condition of peace and quiet. For this service he won the gratitude of the masses, and became the idol of the frontiersmen and the plain people generally. Berkeley, however, considered that he had acted in defiance of the government and denounced him as a rebel and traitor. Bacon picked up the gauntlet hurled at him by the governor and a civil war was the result. Not only did Bacon fight against the forces of the governor but he also bound a number of his followers by oath (August, 1676) to support him against the troops of both Berkeley and the king, until the latter could be correctly informed as to the state of affairs in the province.

Berkeley was able to assemble a nondescript army with which he undertook to defend Jamestown against the attack of the rebels. When this undisciplined rabble was attacked by Bacon's troops, it was easily defeated and Berkeley was forced from the little capital. Bacon could not spare enough men to hold the town and, as he feared that Berkeley would return and use it as a base against him, he reluctantly decided to burn it. Every house in the village was destroyed by the conflagration, which was started when Lawrence, one of Bacon's chief lieutenants, set fire to his own house.

Shortly after his victory at Jamestown, Bacon was stricken with *Berkeley's* dysentery and fever, which brought on his death (October, 1676). *vengeance* The rebels did not now have a leader who was equal to the task of carrying on a successful fight, and so Berkeley was able to put an end to the revolt. With a vindictiveness worthy of an Assyrian despot, the aged governor signalized his success with a satanic cruelty toward the rebels. About twenty-three of them were hanged and the estates of a number of others were confiscated.

The king did not approve of the extreme cruelty which had been meted out to the insurgents and is said to have exclaimed: "That old fool has hanged more men in that naked country than I have for the death of my father." Sir William, having been summoned to England to explain his course, died soon after his arrival there. His end was probably hastened by grief and humiliation over the disapproval of his policy by his royal master.

Despite the brave fight put up by Bacon and his followers, the *Results and* immediate results of the outbreak were quite unsatisfactory, though *significance* in the final outcome some gains were made for the rights of the *of the* people. At the beginning of the uprising the governor called for the *rebellion* election of a new assembly, which passed a number of reform measures, among them one providing for the restoration of the right of suffrage to all freemen. All of these liberal acts, which were known as "Bacon's Laws," were rescinded by order of the king, but in later years some of the more important ones were re-enacted by the assembly.

The chief significance of Bacon's Rebellion lies in the fact that it is the first instance in American history of a revolt of the yeomanry, not only against the provincial government, but also against the dominance of the privileged class. Most of the large planters were aligned with the governor, while Bacon's adherents were recruited mainly from the common people, many of whom were from the outlying settlements. It was, therefore, largely a struggle between patrician and plebeian, and of the frontier against the older part of the colony. This conflict between east and west was the first of a series of sectional disputes which have from time to time disturbed the harmony or threatened the unity of this country.

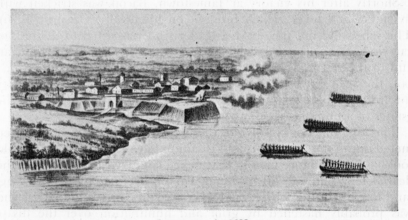

JAMESTOWN in 1622.

from a contemporary Dutch print.
From Lyon G. Tyler's "The Cradle of the Republic".

CHAPTER IV

The Establishment of Puritanism in New England

THE COLONY OF NEW PLYMOUTH

*A*FTER the tragic failure of its effort to plant a settlement on the Kennebec River (1607-08), the Plymouth Company lost its early zeal for establishing plantations in America. Some of the stockholders, however, were still interested in colonization, and a group of them reorganized the company under the name of the Council for New England. The new company received a charter from the king (1620), granting it all the land between the fortieth and forty-fourth parallels of north latitude, extending from the Atlantic to the Pacific Ocean. It also received authority to govern the colonies which it might establish on this large domain. *The Council for New England*

In the meantime, a number of trading and fishing expeditions had gone to the northeastern coast of the present United States and brought back to England information regarding this region. One of the most noted of these voyages was that made by Captain John Smith, of Virginia fame. He gave an account and made a map of the region explored by him, to which he gave the name of New England.

Instead of planting colonies on its grant, the Council for New England adopted the policy of bestowing large tracts of land on individuals and groups of settlers. In this way it had disposed of the greater part of its holdings and by 1635 was ready to surrender its charter. Of the groups to which large grants were made, the most important were those that founded the colonies of New Plymouth and Massachusetts Bay.

When the Anglican became the established church of England it was not accepted by all the Protestants of the realm. There was a radical wing of Protestants who felt that the Anglicans had retained too much of the doctrines and practices of the Catholic Church and were not living up to as high a moral standard as they should. These ultra-Protestants were known as Puritans. There was considerable disagreement among the Puritans as to church practices, and it is difficult to frame a definition which would apply to all the groups. Each of them held to the doctrines of Calvin and practiced a stern moral code. They insisted upon a strict observance of the Sabbath *The English Puritans*

41

and regarded as wicked some types of amusement which the Anglicans considered innocent. Of the various groups of Puritans, the two which took the leading part in the founding of New England were *Nonconformists* the Nonconformists and the Separatists. The Nonconformists objected to some of the doctrines and the ritual of the state church but did not carry their opposition to the point of withdrawing from it. They tried to bring about certain reforms in the establishment and thus make it conform to their views.

Separatists The Separatists, however, were so opposed to the beliefs and practices of the Anglicans that they refused to associate with them in a church relation. Accordingly, they separated from the established church and organized themselves into independent churches. For this reason they were known as Separatists, or Independents. They held that any group of worshippers, binding themselves together by a mutual covenant, could form a church or congregation. The members of this congregation could choose its minister and other officials and manage its affairs without any outside interference. This method of church government is known as the congregational.

The Pilgrims Early in the seventeenth century (1606), a Separatist church was organized at Scrooby in northern England. The membership of this congregation was recruited mainly from the humbler class, such as "had been used to a plaine countrie life, and the innocente trade of husbandry." But in this little group of earnest believers there were several men of outstanding ability and character. Prominent in this list was the minister, John Robinson, and two laymen, William Brewster and William Bradford.

The Pilgrims emigrate to the Netherlands The unconventional views held by these pious Separatists, and their refusal to have spiritual fellowship with the Anglicans, made them unpopular with their neighbors and "they were both scoffed and scorned by the prophane multitude."[1] Furthermore, their meetings were held in violation of an act of Parliament (1593), which made it unlawful for any one to be absent from the services of the Anglican Church or to participate in any other form of worship. The Scrooby Separatists fell under the censure of this law and were subjected to a persecution which, though not very severe, was humiliating to them and made them uneasy as to their safety in the future. To avoid this persecution and escape other unpleasant experiences, the members of the Scrooby church left the homeland (1607-08) and went to the Netherlands, where religious freedom was enjoyed by all Christians. After staying at Amsterdam for a year they moved to Leyden, and there reorganized themselves into a church, with John Robinson as pastor and William Brewster as elder.

---

[1] William Bradford, *History of Plymouth Plantation* (*Original Narratives of Early American History*, Macmillan Co.), 30, 33.

For twelve years the Pilgrims (as these English Separatists are *Why the Pilgrims left the Netherlands* usually called) lived at Leyden and enjoyed perfect freedom of worship. They won the respect and esteem of their Dutch associates by their honesty, industry, and general reliability. But life in a foreign land had many drawbacks, and Leyden was not a suitable place for their permanent home. They had been farmers in England and were therefore not skilled in the trades which afforded employment to their Dutch neighbors. Owing to this lack of training and their alien citizenship they were not admitted to the craft guilds which enjoyed a monopoly of the most profitable trades. They had therefore to work as unskilled laborers, and the children had to supplement the earnings of their parents by performing tasks which overtaxed their strength. Furthermore, it was difficult to maintain parental authority over the rising generation in the face of the temptations of city life, which was luring it into extravagance and immorality. The Pilgrims, who were strongly attached to the institutions and customs of the homeland, wanted their children brought up with English manners and speech, and this could not be done in a foreign country. A further incentive was the desire to establish their religious system without outside influence or interference. This purpose could be realized only in a new and unoccupied country. By settling in the new world they felt that they could lay the foundation for the propagating and advancing of the gospel of the Kingdom of Christ in those remote parts of the world.

Permission was obtained from the London Company to plant a settlement on its territory, and an oral promise was received from the king that he would connive at them and not molest them, provided they carried themselves peaceably. The capital for financing the undertaking was furnished by a joint-stock company composed of London merchants.

These arrangements having been made, thirty-five of the Pilgrims *The voyage of the Mayflower* left Leyden for Southampton, England. Here they were joined by fellow Separatists from London, and both groups embarked on the *Speedwell* and the *Mayflower* for the new world. Leaks in the *Speedwell* forced the expedition to return twice for repairs. Finally, this ill-fated ship was abandoned and all the emigrants were transferred to the *Mayflower*. This historic vessel left Plymouth (September 16, 1620) with one hundred and two passengers on board. Prominent in the list of emigrants were Captain Miles Standish, their military leader; John Carver, the governor; and William Bradford, who was to play the leading role in laying the foundations of the colony.

At the end of a long and stormy voyage the *Mayflower* sighted Cape Cod and shortly afterwards made a temporary landing at Provincetown. Exploring parties were sent out to find a suitable place for settlement. The site chosen was Plymouth, which had been so named by John Smith on his map of New England. The *Mayflower* anchored in Plymouth harbor (December 26, 1620), and here the Pilgrims made their first settlement. Since the winter was well-advanced when they landed, the Pilgrims were unable to provide

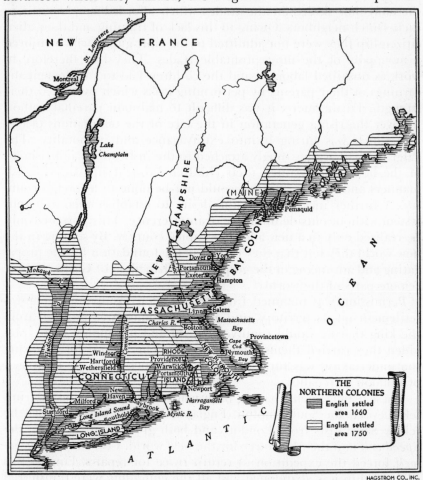

HAGSTROM CO., INC.

THE NORTHERN COLONIES
English settled area 1660
English settled area 1750

adequate housing facilities for all the settlers and there was great suffering during the winter months. Disease was brought on by exposure, and so severe was the epidemic (which apparently was contagious) that nearly half of the immigrants died during the first winter. At one time only about a half-dozen were well enough to care for the others. This little band of helpers performed their merciful task of caring for the sick with a kindly sympathy and self-forgetful devotion which won the lasting gratitude of their brethren.

Fortunately, the Pilgrims were not disturbed by the Indians in the *Relations with the Indians* time of their great distress. The natives had recently suffered from a plague which had destroyed most of those near Plymouth, and the survivors were so cowed that they were not inclined to venture an attack on the plantation. Not knowing this, the whites lived in constant fear of their redskin neighbors, who prowled around timidly, occasionally showing themselves at a distance. Finally in March, one of them, Samoset, walked boldly into the settlement and told them in broken English of the misfortune which had befallen his people. Some days later he returned to Plymouth bringing with him Massasoit, the sachem of his tribe. Massasoit showed a friendly disposition toward the English and made a treaty with them which was kept by both parties for more than fifty years.

In April, 1621, the first governor, John Carver, died and William *William Bradford* Bradford was chosen to succeed him. This was a fortunate selection, for Bradford was eminently qualified for leadership in an infant Puritan commonwealth struggling with pioneer conditions. In his well-poised character, deep religious convictions were combined with a sound common sense which served him in good stead in the handling of the many difficulties which confronted him. So wise was his management of affairs that he was kept in the governor's chair for more than thirty years. He also wrote an account of the Pilgrims, and his *History of Plymouth Plantation* is our best source of information for the early history of the colony.

As the Pilgrims had settled outside the limits of the Virginia Com- *Land patents* pany, the patent received from this corporation was of no value. In the beginning, therefore, the settlers had no legal title to their lands and no authority to establish a government. Later two patents were received from the Council for New England (1621, 1630) by which a valid title to its land was conferred upon the colony. But probably no governmental authority went with these grants, and as no royal charter was ever obtained by the colony, it is quite likely that the government of New Plymouth never rested on a strictly legal basis until it was united with Massachusetts.

The Pilgrim Fathers, however, were not disposed to deny them- *The May-flower Compact* selves the benefits of political organization out of deference to fine-spun political theories, but proceeded at once to organize a government in accordance with that fundamental natural right, the consent of the governed. When it was decided that the settlement would be made in New England, and therefore the patent of the Virginia Company would have no validity, some of the immigrants refused to recognize the authority of the leaders. To allay this rising discontent and ensure order, the men entered into an agreement that they would make just and equal laws and would yield obedience to such rules and regulations as should be made by a majority of the voters. This agreement was signed on board the *Mayflower* before they landed at Plymouth and is known as the Mayflower Compact.

The signers of this compact reaffirmed their allegiance to the king and had no thought of setting up an independent state. Their purpose was to organize themselves into a body politic and to create such governmental machinery as would be needed in preserving order. The Mayflower Compact was the first of a number of plantation covenants, signed by groups of New Englanders, on establishing civil governments for themselves. In entering into this agreement, the Pilgrim Fathers were extending to civil affairs the principle of the church covenant, which was a mutual pledge by which the members of every Congregational church bound themselves together in fraternal association.

Government

The most important place in the government of the colony was that of governor. In the performance of his numerous duties, the governor was assisted by a small group of advisers known as the board of assistants. At first there was only one assistant, but the number was later increased to seven. In the early years the voters, or "freemen," as they were called, had meetings from time to time, and out of this practice there soon developed a regular legislative assembly, known as the General Court. This was at first a primary assembly made up of the governor, the assistants, and all the freemen who would attend the meetings of the assembly. Later (by 1639) it had developed into a representative assembly consisting of the governor and the assistants, and deputies chosen by the towns. The assembly was never divided into two houses, as was done in all but one of the other colonies.

THE COLONY OF MASSACHUSETTS BAY

Beginning of the Massachusetts Bay Colony

The Massachusetts Bay Colony had its origin in a fishing station which had been established at Cape Ann in 1623. The promoters of this settlement were a group of business men in Dorchester, England, who felt that fishing and fur trading could be carried on successfully from this post; but the site chosen was not a favorable one for either fishing or farming and the experiment soon proved a failure. With bankruptcy facing them, the Dorchester promoters withdrew all financial support from the undertaking and most of the settlers returned to England (1626). The few planters (about thirty including women and children) who decided to remain, afterwards moved southward to a better location and settled at Naumkeag, later known as Salem.

Prominent among those who had taken an active interest in the Cape Ann venture was Reverend John White, of Dorchester, an Anglican minister with Puritan leanings. He felt that the little colony at Salem might serve as a base for religious instruction to the European fishermen who frequented that region, and as a center of missionary activity among the Indians. He therefore made an earnest effort to obtain funds for the support of the planters and a patent which would put the colony on a firm financial and legal basis. As a result of his exertions, a new company was formed, known as the New England Company. Through the influence of the Earl of Warwick this new organization received a patent from the Council for New England (1628), granting it all the land extending from three miles south of the Charles River to three miles north of the Merrimac River and westward to the Pacific Ocean. *The New England Company*

About forty emigrants were now sent over by the company as a reinforcement to the settlement at Naumkeag, and with them went John Endicott, who was to be governor of the plantation. The company, however, had no strictly legal authority for thus establishing a government for the colony, and its title to certain of its lands was contested by other claimants whose patents antedated that of the New England Company. All disputes as to land ownership and governmental authority could be settled by a charter of incorporation granted by the king. The company therefore applied for a royal charter, being able again to enlist the support of the Earl of Warwick. The petition was granted and a charter was received from the king (March 4, 1629) by which the New England Company was merged into a new corporation, which is generally known as the Massachusetts Bay Company. The new company was confirmed in all the landed possessions held by the old under the grant by the Council for New England, and was given authority to admit new members and to govern the settlers. *The Massachusetts Bay Company: Its charter*

The stockholders, or freemen, had authority to choose the officers of the corporation and to make all laws and regulations which were necessary for the management of the company and the government of the colony. The full membership was to meet four times a year, and at these sessions all important business was to be transacted. These quarterly meetings were known as General Courts. Matters of lesser significance were to be looked after by the governor, deputy governor, and a board of eighteen assistants. These officials were to be chosen at the Easter quarterly court, which was known as the Court of Election. There were clauses in the charter declaring that the authority of the king must be recognized and that the laws in Massachusetts must be in harmony with the laws of England. Except for these general restrictions, the authority of the company in the government of the colony was unlimited.

From the beginning, the Puritans were in the majority in the membership of the company, and the establishment of Puritanism in New England was one of the purposes of the organization. The hope of gain from trade was another incentive, for the colony in Massachusetts had been established as a commercial venture to promote fishing, farming, and fur trading rather than to serve as a haven for persecuted Puritans. The religious motive, however, gradually grew more important until finally it became the predominant purpose of the corporation.

The Cambridge Agreement

The charter of the Massachusetts Bay Company was different in one important respect from the type of charter usually obtained by colonizing corporations at that time. There was no provision requiring the stockholders to have their meetings in England and therefore they could hold their sessions in New England if they wished to do so. This possibility was noted by John Winthrop and eleven other prominent Nonconformists, who in a written agreement signed at Cambridge (August 29, 1629) promised to go to New England with their families if the management of the company should be turned over to them. This is known as the Cambridge Agreement.

The proposal was accepted by the company since the leaders who dominated it were anxious to promote the establishment of a Puritan commonwealth in the new world. All officers of the company who were unwilling to leave England resigned and their places were taken by the Puritan leaders who were going to New England. Winthrop was chosen governor of both the company and the colony, and the charter was turned over to him to be taken to Massachusetts. The future meetings of the company were to be in the colony and none were held in England after Winthrop was established in Massachusetts. The control of the corporation was henceforth in the hands of the Puritan members in New England, and the stockholders remaining in the homeland were reduced to the position of silent business partners.

The Great Migration

This was the proper time for a great Puritan exodus from England. There was strong dissatisfaction among Nonconformists because of unfavorable political, economic, and religious conditions in England. In the year of the Cambridge Agreement, Charles I dissolved Parliament and for the next decade ruled the country autocratically without the assistance of Parliament. In religious affairs the king followed the advice of William Laud, then Bishop of London but later to become head of the Anglican Church as Archbishop of Canterbury. Laud was determined to uphold the authority of the state church and to drive the Nonconformist ministers out of their pulpits. The policy of the king was therefore very objectionable to those who believed in the rights of Parliament and adhered to the doctrines of the Puritans.

Political and religious discontent were also reinforced by economic unrest. In the eastern and southeastern counties, where the Puritans were especially numerous, the people were suffering from business depression. Clothmaking, which was a leading industry in this section, had been undergoing a severe decline for several years, and this had caused widespread unemployment. There were thus in these counties a number of Puritans and persons of other beliefs who were anxious to go to a new country where land was cheap and the comforts and necessaries of life could be won by industry and thrift. Among the rank and file of the prospective settlers, the hope of bettering their economic condition was probably the main incentive to emigration, although with the leaders, dissatisfaction with the political and religious situation in the homeland was the impelling force.

These conditions made it easy for the Puritan leaders to enlist recruits for their New England colony. So many went over in 1630 that the exodus has been termed the Great Migration. The movement was led by John Winthrop, who left England (March 29, 1630) with a fleet of four ships carrying seven hundred passengers. Other vessels were sent over later, and during the year a total of more than a thousand immigrants were landed in Massachusetts. This was not only the largest number of settlers which had ever been sent from England to the colonies in any single year, but it also included a greater proportion of men of wealth, influence, and education than had any previous group of emigrants.

The selection of Winthrop to take charge of the venture was a *John* wise choice, for probably no other man in all England was better *Winthrop* suited to act "as the Moses of the great Puritan exodus."[1] Now at the age of forty-two, he was in his prime. With the seriousness and deep piety of the typical Puritan he combined the sound judgment, practical common sense, and the will power of a hardheaded man of the world. He had been a student at Cambridge and so had had good opportunities for education. His ability and self-control, which had won him a position of influence in England, gave promise of success in the administration of business affairs in the Bay Colony, while his earnestness in religion served him in good stead in the leadership of a Bible commonwealth.

---

[1] John Fiske, *New France and New England,* 102.

After the Massachusetts Bay Company received its charter, it assumed control of the settlement at Salem. A year later Endicott was superseded by Winthrop, who except for a few brief intervals was governor of the colony for two decades. The early history of the plantation therefore centers in him, and he more than anyone else was responsible for its establishment and early development. He also wrote a history of New England, which is the best contemporary narrative we have of the events in Massachusetts from 1630 to 1649.

New settle-
ments

The immigrants who came over in 1630 founded several new towns, one of which was Boston. During the first winter after the arrival of the newcomers there was considerable suffering from a shortage of food and two hundred had died by spring. Food was scarce at other times, but the Massachusetts settlers never experienced the horrors of famine to which the Jamestown pioneers were subjected. Since Charles continued his highhanded policy in church and state until he was curbed by the Long Parliament, a large stream of religious and political malcontents continued to pour into Massachusetts, numbering altogether more than twenty thousand by 1643. By that time, however, the Puritans had come to grips with the king, and the English Puritans were all needed at home. Furthermore, it looked as if their party would win the contest and thus secure control of the government. Owing to this favorable turn in the Puritan cause, the tide of emigration turned backward and for a few years flowed from Massachusetts to England.

Emigration
to Massa-
chusetts
discouraged
by the civil
war in
England

The Puritans who settled in Massachusetts in 1630 were not Separatists, but Nonconformists; that is, they were members of the Anglican Church but were dissatisfied with some of its beliefs and practices. Their allegiance to Anglicanism had, however, been subjected to a severe strain by the persecutions of Bishop Laud, and the slender bond which held them to the state church was in most cases snapped after they had crossed the Atlantic and established a self-governing commonwealth. Independence in religion was the logical corollary of the autonomy in government which had been granted them by their charter. The first step toward ecclesiastical independence had been taken before the Great Migration; for in the summer of 1629, Governor Endicott, acting under the influence of a deacon from Plymouth, had the church at Salem organized on a congregational basis. This was the first Congregational church in the colony of Massachusetts Bay. A church of the congregational type was also established at Charlestown by Winthrop on his arrival there. These examples were followed by the other communities, and in time there was a Congregational church in every town in the colony.

Congrega-
tionalism
established
in the Mas-
sachusetts
Bay Colony

There came over with Winthrop in the first part of the Great

Migration only about a dozen or slightly more of the stockholders of the company. These freemen had complete authority to govern the colony. As has already been seen, the population of Massachusetts had greatly increased by the end of the year 1630. To expect this large number of people to submit to the rule of a baker's dozen of their fellow citizens was to assume too much, even in that aristocratic age. Therefore, when the small group of stockholders met at Boston in the first General Court, a petition was received asking that one hundred and eighteen settlers be added to the list of freemen. Winthrop and the ruling clique feared that if the petitioners were denied the right of suffrage they and their supporters might weaken the colony by moving northward into what are now New Hampshire and Maine, or southward into the colony of New Plymouth. On the other hand, if they were admitted into the membership of the company with all the powers of the original grantees, they might get control of the government and manage the plantation in such a way as to defeat the religious purposes for which it had been founded.

A compromise arrangement was accepted by which the request of the petitioners was granted, but the power of all freemen was limited to that of electing the assistants. In this way all governmental power would be vested in the governor, deputy governor, and the assistants. As a further bulwark to the supremacy of the Puritan oligarchy, it was provided that in the future only church members would be made freemen and therefore receive the right to vote. Additional names were added to the list of freemen from time to time and so the number of voters gradually increased. As long as this first charter was in effect, however, no one could exercise the right of suffrage in a colonial election until he had been admitted to membership in the company.

The freemen were not satisfied with the limited rights which had been granted them but soon began to demand a stronger voice in the government. As a result of this pressure, representatives chosen by the voters were a few years later (1634) granted the right to sit with the governor and the assistants in the sessions of the General Court. The General Court had now become a representative assembly and by 1644 had developed into a bicameral legislature, with the governor and assistants constituting the upper house, and the representatives of the freemen, the lower.

In this way a corporation had grown into a commonwealth. Mas- sachusetts was an autonomous republic, regulating its own internal affairs with little or no restraints from the homeland. The government was decidedly aristocratic. The majority of the people had no voice in the control of provincial affairs, and the minority who enjoyed the right of suffrage accepted the leadership of the upper class. The ministers, being usually men of ability and intelligence, exerted a great influence in governmental affairs. Since the Puritan leaders were trying to shape the government in accordance with Biblical principles, the pastors of the Congregational churches, the expounders of Biblical doctrines, were looked up to as political as well as religious authorities. Accordingly, their advice was frequently asked by the magistrates when important questions had to be decided. Owing to the political influence of the clergy and the prominence given to the precepts of the Bible in the laws, the government of the Bay Colony is sometimes classed as a theocracy and the colony termed a Bible commonwealth.

Character of the government

The management of affairs in Massachusetts was thus in the hands of those who were best qualified to assume the responsibilities of government. The rulers were selected from the wealthy and educated class and were as a rule strongly imbued with the religious ideals of Puritanism. The administration was honest and efficient and comparatively free from that curse of oligarchies—the desire to exploit the masses for the benefit of the privileged class; but it was too narrow and conservative to make the proper adjustment to pioneer conditions. It was characterized by a spirit of intolerance, which put a curb on initiative and individuality. Forgetting their former nonconformity, the leaders tried to impose a uniformity of belief on the people. Many of the actual and prospective settlers were men of marked individuality, and such a narrow policy was unacceptable to them. Some emigrants of this type were discouraged from coming to the colony by the intolerance of the ruling class, while others who had already settled were expelled. In this way the normal growth in population was retarded and the colony lost some leaders of exceptional ability and originality.

The expulsion of Roger Williams

One of the first victims of this intolerant policy was Roger Williams, a brilliant young minister who had come to New England in 1631. He was a graduate of the University of Cambridge and had made some influential connections in England. Ablaze with the fine idealism which is inspired by deep piety and saintliness of character, and endowed with the courage to uphold his convictions, he was a born crusader. Unfortunately, however, Puritan New England was not a good field for crusading. Besides, he was not entirely free from the shortcomings which sometimes go with the prophetic temperament. He was morbidly conscientious and did not always display sound judgment and intellectual poise.

Shortly after his arrival in Massachusetts he began to proclaim, with earnestness and eloquence, opinions which were considered dangerous by the orthodox rulers. He advocated the complete separation of church and state, and absolute religious freedom. Not even such offenses as blasphemy, Sabbath breaking, and perjury should, he contended, be punished by the civil authorities. Nor did he confine his criticisms to church practices, but boldly declared that the company had no right to its land, since its title rested on a patent from the king and the king had no authority to grant away Indian lands. In the opinion of the Puritan oligarchy which ruled the Bay Colony these doctrines were striking at the foundations of both church and state. They would have been objectionable under ordinary circumstances, but at this time they were regarded as especially dangerous. The enemies of Massachusetts had been trying to have the charter recalled, and there was a feeling of uneasiness in the colony with reference to its relations with the royal authority. Such criticisms as Williams was leveling against the established order in Massachusetts tended to bring it into still further disfavor with the crown, and were considered disloyal propaganda by the rulers. They wished therefore to get rid of this troublemaker, and consequently secured a vote of the General Court expelling him from the commonwealth. Knowing that plans had been made to send him back to England, he escaped and took refuge with his friends, the Narragansett Indians. A few months later he and a handful of his followers made a settlement at the head of Narragansett Bay (1636), to which he gave the name of Providence.

Soon after Roger Williams was expelled there occurred another and more serious controversy over heresy—one which shook the established order to its foundations. The trouble arose when a strong-minded, earnest woman began to express convictions which did not agree with those of the orthodox leaders and were therefore regarded as dangerous heresies. This disturber of Puritan complacency was Anne Hutchinson, the wife of a man of means and high standing in Boston. By her kindly sympathy and efficient helpfulness in times of sickness and distress, she had won the esteem and affection of the other women of the community. Nor was her following confined to the women, but at one time it included nearly the entire membership of the Boston church. Her influence had now become so great that the old guard began to feel that orthodoxy was in peril. Among those who regarded her opinions as heresy, Winthrop was the most outstanding. *Mrs. Anne Hutchinson*

An adjustment of the quarrel could have been made if it had been kept out of politics. But as church and state were closely united, the contest developed into a bitter political fight which resulted in a defeat of the Hutchinsonians at the election. Winthrop was elected governor and the orthodox party was now in the saddle. It signalized its victory by the expulsion of Mrs. Hutchinson and Rev. John Wheelwright, her brother-in-law and most outstanding lieutenant. Wheelwright and a considerable group of followers went northward and founded a settlement in New Hampshire, while Mrs. Hutchinson, with her husband and a few of her supporters, moved southward and settled on the island of Aquidneck in Rhode Island.

Persecution of the Baptists and Quakers

The effort to stamp out error, as exemplified in the persecution of Roger Williams and Anne Hutchinson, did not prove a successful quarantine against heresy. In a few years orthodoxy had to combat the objectionable doctrines of the Baptists and Quakers. Soon after Mrs. Hutchinson's banishment, Baptists began to get a foothold in Rhode Island, the one area of religious freedom in New England. From this center these sectaries might spread their doctrine in Mas-

Courtesy of the Commonwealth of Massachusetts

PORTRAIT OF JOHN WINTHROP, SR.

First governor of Massachusetts Bay Colony. Painted in England, artist unknown.

sachusetts. To guard against this danger a law was passed by the General Court (1644) imposing the penalty of banishment upon all who should hold to Baptist beliefs. A few years later three prominent Baptists from Rhode Island came to Massachusetts to visit one of their brethren who was ill. While there, one of the visitors from Rhode Island preached to a small group at the home of his host. For this offense the minister and his two associates were arrested and fined. One of them refused to pay the fine and was brutally flogged with a three-corded whip.

Still severer treatment was meted out to the Quakers. A law was passed providing for the expulsion of all Quakers, and the infliction of the death penalty on those who returned. Under this measure four Quakers were executed, one of them being a woman.

All of these victims of persecution were persons of fine character, and the treatment accorded them was a severe indictment against the leadership of the Bible commonwealth. It was another instance of Jerusalem stoning her prophets.

CHAPTER V

Puritan Expansion in New England

CONNECTICUT

WITH the founding of the plantations of New Plymouth and Massachusetts Bay, Puritanism had gained two centers from which it soon began to expand into the unoccupied spaces toward the north, south, and west. The causes of this new movement were very much the same as those which had been behind the original migration of the Puritans from the old world to the new. In both cases the hope of economic betterment and the expectation of a happier religious adjustment figured as leading motives. Religious nonconformity was an important factor in the expansion southward into Rhode Island, and to a lesser extent a reason for the emigration northward into New Hampshire, while the economic motive was the main one in the movement westward into Connecticut and New Haven.

The founding of Connecticut

The Connecticut Valley offered an attractive field for settlement. The bottom lands along the Connecticut River were more productive and more easily cultivated than were the rocky hillsides of Massachusetts and New Plymouth. The river was navigable for a considerable distance into the interior and thus afforded an excellent means of communication for the planters. Both the Dutch and the English cast longing glances toward this fruitful land and both set up claims to it. The Dutch got the start on their competitors by establishing a military post, Fort Good Hope, at the present site of Hartford. The New Englanders were not discouraged, however, by this forward step of their opponents but went ahead with their settlements.

Four towns were soon established on the river. The first of these, Windsor, was founded (1633) by the Pilgrims from Plymouth. The other three, Wethersfield, Hartford, and Springfield, were settled by emigrants from the Bay Colony. The trek westward from Massachusetts to Connecticut was a series of migrations similar in character to those made later into the interior of the continent. Prominent in the list of pioneers in this early westward movement was Thomas

56

Hooker, a brilliant young minister who was somewhat dissatisfied with the religious and political situation in Massachusetts. The members of his church at Newtown (or Cambridge) felt the lure of the west and under the leadership of Hooker and another minister left in a body for the land of promise. These pioneers threaded their way one hundred miles through the wilderness, driving their hogs and cattle slowly along, and at the end of two weeks reached Hartford. Hooker was active in laying the foundations of the new colony and played a prominent part in its later development.

In the meantime, the Dutch were stubbornly holding on to Fort Good Hope, although the post was surrounded by New England farmers. Refusing to give up their claim to the land, the Dutch stood their ground until 1654, when they were forced out by the war between England and the Dutch Netherlands.

In 1637 the planters in the three river towns of Windsor, Hartford, and Wethersfield[1] organized a government for Connecticut, which was the name of the new colony. Two years later the legislature, or General Court, framed a number of laws, known as the "Fundamental Orders," which served as a sort of constitution for the commonwealth. A scheme of government similar to that of Massachusetts was outlined by this constitution. *The government organized*

NEW HAVEN

Soon after the settlements were made on the Connecticut River a second colony was established within the present limits of Connecticut. This was New Haven. The plantation was founded by a group of well-to-do English Puritans who came to New England under the leadership of John Davenport, a minister, and Theophilus Eaton, a wealthy merchant. The immigrants hoped to establish a Puritan colony which would soon become a profitable trading center. In pursuit of these aims, they selected as the site of their first settlement a place known by the Indians as Quinnipiack, which was located on a good harbor on Long Island Sound, about thirty miles west of the mouth of the Connecticut. Here on land bought from the Indians they laid out the town of New Haven (1638). *The settlement at New Haven*

No patent or charter for this colony was ever received from the king or any company, and therefore the settlers had no legal title to their lands and no authority to establish a government. They went

---

[1] It was soon discovered that Springfield was within the limits of Massachusetts and therefore this town took no part in the organization of the Connecticut government.

ahead, however, and organized their plantation into a Puritan commonwealth with a form of government like that of Massachusetts. For a while the settlement of New Haven was the only one in the little republic, but later, other towns were founded, and by 1644 these had united with the original settlement to form the colony of New Haven. In this little Bible commonwealth, Eaton played a part similar to that of William Bradford in New Plymouth and John Winthrop in Massachusetts. Eaton was the first governor, and for seventeen years—until the year of his death—he was annually re-elected.

The government established in Connecticut under the "Fundamental Orders" was not supported by the proper legal sanction, since it did not rest on any authority from the king. Nor had the Connecticut colony secured a clear title to the greater portion of its land. Such irregularities were condoned by the English authorities as long as the Puritans were in control in the homeland; but with the overthrow of the Puritan regime in England and the restoration of Charles II, the British government began to take a more critical attitude toward the New England colonies. Connecticut was, therefore, anxious to obtain a royal charter which would give her uncontested title to her land and authority to establish a government.

The governor of the colony, John Winthrop, Jr., was accordingly sent to England to get a charter from the king. Winthrop was a proper choice for such a mission. He was well educated and widely traveled, and the outer shell of his Puritanism had been smoothed down by contact with the world. Furthermore, he was well supplied with funds, which were an invaluable aid in dealing with the corrupt politicians who surrounded the king. He was successful in getting a charter that was quite to the liking of the people of Connecticut. By it boundaries were fixed for the colony, and the government which had grown up around the "Fundamental Orders" was given the stamp of legality. So pleased was Connecticut with this charter that, when she seceded from the British empire in the Revolutionary period, she kept it, and used it as her state constitution until 1818.

The boundaries of Connecticut were so defined in the charter as to include the towns of New Haven. This latter colony therefore, much to the disappointment of its settlers, lost its separate existence and henceforth was a part of Connecticut.

RHODE ISLAND

The colony of Rhode Island and Providence Plantations owed its origin to religious refugees from Massachusetts. These religious radicals were dissenting from the orthodoxy of New England, just as the early Massachusetts settlers had dissented from the orthodoxy of old England. The new nonconformists had been accorded a treatment by the Puritans of New England as severe as that received by the latter at the hands of the Anglicans in the homeland. *The founding of Providence*

As has already been shown, the first of these settlements was made at Providence (1636) by Roger Williams and a few of his followers. These planters, following the example of the Pilgrims, entered into a mutual covenant to obey the laws which should be made by a majority of the householders. The type of government thus established was very democratic in character. There was perfect freedom in religion, and liberty in general was stressed more than good order. The result was that Providence became a haven for the discontented and undesirable elements from the older and more staid Puritan commonwealths. The responsibility for controlling this unruly mob in the interest of law and order caused Williams much anxiety and worry.

Another group of heretics from Massachusetts founded the settlement of Portsmouth on the northern end of the island of Aquidneck. These settlers included Mrs. Hutchinson and some of her followers, who were under the leadership of William Coddington. Here another jurisdiction, based on Biblical principles, was organized by a plantation covenant. *Portsmouth*

The extreme individualism which had prevented the Hutchinsonians from making proper adjustments in the Bay Colony now caused dissensions in this their own miniature republic. The result was a secession from the plantation by a group of malcontents who moved to the southern part of the island and founded the town of Newport. *Newport*

A fourth settlement was made at Warwick, on the western shore of Narragansett Bay, twelve miles south of Providence. The founder of this town was Samuel Gorton, a religious radical who had aroused antagonism in Boston and Providence and had been expelled from Portsmouth and Plymouth. *Warwick*

These little states were regarded with disfavor by the orthodox Puritan colonies. The latter feared that their own people might be infected with political and religious heresy from these centers of contagion. The former in turn were alarmed lest their powerful neighbors might find some excuse for annexing or absorbing them. In the early years none of these small republics had a patent on which to base a claim to its land, or a legal sanction for its government. Union under a charter granted by the British authorities *The federation of the four colonies* would prevent them from being swallowed up by the adjoining colonies and would legalize their land tenure and political organization. The initial move toward such a union was the consolidation of the two island plantations under one jurisdiction (1640). As a further step toward federation, Roger Williams, acting as the agent of Providence and the island plantations, obtained a charter (1644) from the Parliamentary commissioners who had charge of colonial affairs. By this charter the Rhode Island communities were given titles to their land, and authority to unite and form a joint government. A few years later (1647) Providence, Portsmouth, and Newport were federated into a union, of which Warwick afterwards became a member. The government thus established for the united plantations was similar in form to that of Massachusetts and Connecticut.

The second charter

The united colonies of Rhode Island carried on under this patent until 1663, when a second charter was obtained from Charles II. In the new charter the old form of government was continued. The reason for applying for a new charter was that Charles could hardly be expected to recognize a grant made by the agents of a Parliament which had been responsible for the execution of his father. Rhode Island therefore sent Dr. John Clarke to England for a new patent. At that time John Winthrop, Jr., was in London working for the Connecticut charter and he used his influence at court in favor of the Rhode Island application.

Religious freedom

So well did the people of the little commonwealth like their charter that they not only held tenaciously to it to the end of the colonial period, but also used it as their state constitution after the Revolutionary War, and it was not until 1843 that a new constitution was adopted. One noted provision of the charter was that no one should be in "any wise molested, punished, disquieted, or called in question for any differences of opinion in matters of religion." This was the legal recognition of the practice of religious freedom which had already become a tradition in the colony. The people had been indoctrinated in this tradition by the teachings of Roger Williams, and to him more than anyone else is due the credit for this liberal principle.

NEW HAMPSHIRE AND MAINE

Early settlements

The occupation of the New Hampshire region was begun before the end of the first quarter of the seventeenth century. A temporary settlement was made in 1623 at the present site of Rye, and in the next two decades a few other towns were established in southeastern New Hampshire. One of these was Exeter, founded by the Rev. John Wheelwright and a group of his followers whom he had led northward after his expulsion from Massachusetts. Settlements were also made in Maine, though there were very few in this region prior to 1640.

In the meantime, a patent had been issued by the Council for New England granting about all the territory now included in Maine and New Hampshire to Sir Ferdinando Gorges and Captain John Mason and their associates. A few years later (1629) Mason and Gorges agreed upon a partition of their territory, the former receiving the land south and west of the Piscataqua River and the latter that between the Piscataqua and the Kennebec. Mason gave to his share the name of New Hampshire, after his native county in England, while the area east of the Piscataqua was known as Maine. Ten years later Gorges received a royal charter which confirmed his claim, enlarged his grant, and conferred on him authority to establish a government for his province. *Territory granted to Gorges and Mason*

The rights of the Mason and Gorges proprietors were contested by Massachusetts, who contended that the New Hampshire and Maine settlements were within her domain. This claim was disputed by the heirs of Gorges and Mason, but Massachusetts was able to maintain her authority over the Maine settlements for some time, and over those of New Hampshire for thirty-six years. Finally, however, the authorities in England gave a decision against Massachusetts in the case of both regions (1677), and two years later New Hampshire was made a royal province. Massachusetts bought out the Gorges heirs and thus became the proprietor of Maine. For more than a dozen years she exercised jurisdiction over Maine by virtue of her proprietary authority. Then by the charter of 1691, the district was united with Massachusetts and the northern boundary was pushed up to the St. Croix River. From that time until 1820 Maine remained a part of Massachusetts. *Later history of Maine and New Hampshire*

INDIAN TROUBLES

When the whites occupied Connecticut they came in hostile contact with the Pequot Indians settled in that region. Strife was precipitated by an act of unjust cruelty toward the natives, perpetrated by the Massachusetts authorities. In the struggle, Connecticut and Massachusetts joined forces against the Pequots, and the latter were thoroughly defeated and their nation was destroyed. The survivors *The Pequot War* numbered only about two hundred, and they were absorbed by the Mohegans and the Narragansetts. This terrible defeat removed the Indian menace from Connecticut for nearly forty years and opened up the New England frontier to colonization.

Basis of con-
flict between
the whites
and the
Indians

A lasting peace between the natives and the white intruders was, however, out of the question, for there was an irrepressible conflict between the economic systems of the two races. With the Indians, hunting was the chief occupation and this demanded the conservation of the forests. The English, on the other hand, were chiefly interested in agriculture and this required the clearing of the land. These two economic systems could not exist side by side—one had to yield to the other. The observant Indians noticed with alarm the rapid increase in the white population, with a corresponding destruction of their own means of living.

King
Philip's War

At the beginning of the last quarter of the seventeenth century, there were conflicts between the redskins and the whites in several of the colonies. The most bitter of these contests was the one which occurred in New England. It is known as King Philip's War, because the most noted of the Indian leaders in the struggle was a chieftain whom the New Englanders called King Philip.[1] The Indians had been unjustly deprived of their lands, and Philip's enmity had been aroused by unfair and untactful treatment. The natives also felt that they were being encircled by the whites, who were now outnumbering the Indians in New England four to one. The time was thus ripe for a general uprising on the part of the red men against their white rivals.

As a result of the negotiations carried on by Philip, the savages throughout New England were united in their war against the whites. The fighting started with an Indian attack on Swanzea (June, 1675), and soon spread throughout all New England. The long and bitter struggle made a heavy drain on the man power and material resources of the white settlements. It is estimated that one sixteenth of the New Englanders of military age were killed in action. "In Massachusetts sixteen towns were wholly destroyed, or abandoned, and four in Rhode Island."[2] Although the Puritan leaders mismanaged the war, their overwhelming numbers and resources gave them such an advantage that they won a decisive victory over their savage foes. The whites signalized their victory by executing some of the Indian

---

[1] Massasoit, the old friend of the Pilgrims, had two sons who were great fighters, and for that reason the whites called one Alexander and the other Philip. It was in this way that an Indian brave received the name and title of the noted Macedonian warrior.

[2] J. T. Adams, *The Founding of New England* (The Atlantic Monthly Press), 363.

leaders and by quartering Philip's body and hanging it up on trees. Some of the captives, including Philip's wife and nine-year-old son, were sold into slavery.

THE NEW ENGLAND CONFEDERATION

One of the earliest of a number of experiments in federation which preceded the formation of the American union was the New England Confederation. It was composed of the Puritan colonies of Massachusetts, New Plymouth, Connecticut, and New Haven. The Rhode Island communities, and those in the Maine-New Hampshire region, were not invited to become members. One reason for passing by these towns was the alleged political disorder in the northern, and the religious and political heresy in the southern, settlements. Furthermore, the admission of these plantations to the confederation would have been a recognition of their separateness as colonies. Massachusetts had designs on these areas and was unwilling to make any admissions which would weaken her claim to them.

Members of the Confederation

The confederation was formed in 1643, under the name of "The United Colonies of New England." Its purposes were to afford joint protection against the Indians, the Dutch, and the French; and to furnish mutual advice and succor upon all just occasions, both for preserving and propagating the truths and liberties of the Gospel, and for their own mutual safety and welfare.

Purposes

The governmental agency of the confederation was a board of eight commissioners, two from each colony. The commissioners, who were chosen by the general courts, were to hold regular sessions once a year and extra meetings whenever the occasion might demand it. The board of commissioners, by a vote of six, could declare war, make peace, and apportion among the member colonies the quotas of men and supplies to be raised; "take measures for the prevention of quarrels between the colonies; see that escaped servants, prisoners, and fugitives from justice, fleeing from one colony to another should be returned . . .; and that Indian affairs should be justly regulated."[1]

Powers

The New England Confederation lasted forty years—until 1684, when Massachusetts lost her charter. It was a loose union and had no real authority. Its recommendations were in the nature of advice, since it had no power to enforce them. It gave to the greater portion

Nature of the union

---

[1] For the text of the Articles of Confederation, see W. MacDonald, *Select Charters,* 94-101.

of settled New England the semblance of unity and proved of some service in promoting the co-operation of the whites in their fight with King Philip and his Indians.

THE "GLORIOUS REVOLUTION" IN ENGLAND AND AMERICA

The Revolu-
tion of 1688
in England

At the death of Charles II, his brother, James II, came to the throne of England (1685). The new ruler was a Catholic, and therefore entered upon his reign with a serious handicap. In his effort to favor his co-religionists, he disregarded certain laws and in general pursued an autocratic policy. His unwise acts aroused a growing opposition to his rule which culminated in a successful uprising. As a result of this revolt, James was deposed and William and Mary became joint sovereigns of the realm. As this change in the government was effected without bloodshed in England, it is known as the "Bloodless Revolution." It is also sometimes termed the "Glorious Revolution." That this movement in the homeland would be followed by important repercussions in the colonies goes without saying. It was also natural that the American counterpart of the British revolution should start in New England, for it was in this section that feeling against Stuart misrule had been strongest.

The charter
of Massa-
chusetts
annulled

As has already been seen, the New England commonwealths had become autonomous republics during the period immediately preceding the Puritan Revolution, and for some years they managed their own affairs with little or no regard for imperial authority. After the Restoration they still hoped to continue their position of quasi-independence. Massachusetts was especially bold in the assertion of her right of self-government and paid slight heed to the claims of the British government. Charles had never had any love for the Puritans of the Bay Colony and was not in the mood to brook this defiance of his authority. Complaints against the Massachusetts government were coming in to him from various quarters and this strengthened his hand in the contest with the obstreperous commonwealth. Circumstances thus being favorable, judicial proceedings were taken against the charter and it was annulled in October, 1684.

The Domin-
ion of New
England

The Privy Council now devised a new plan of government which provided for the union of all of the New England commonwealths, New York, and the Jerseys, under one jurisdiction, known as the Dominion of New England. Rhode Island and Connecticut were forced to accept the new arrangement, although their charters were not annulled. The administration of the Dominion of New England was entrusted to a governor and council, who could exercise legislative, executive, and judicial authority. The assemblies were all abolished and so the people were to have no voice in the government. James II was now king, and this autocratic scheme of administration was in keeping with his highhanded practices in England.

Courtesy of Yale University Art Gallery

JOHN DAVENPORT.

Edmund Andros, who had been acting as Governor of New York for some time, was made Governor of the Dominion of New England. He was honest and capable but did not have sufficient control over his hot temper, and at times was untactful. But however tactful he may have been, his position would have been an impossible one, for no royal governor could have been satisfactory to the privileged group who had hitherto ruled the Bay Colony. It was a foregone conclusion therefore that friction would develop between Andros and the Puritan aristocracy.

There were several reasons for dissatisfaction with the new regime on the part of both the leaders and the people of New England. Most of these objections stemmed from the autocratic system of government which Andros was instructed to carry out. Heretofore taxes (except for local purposes) had been levied and laws made by popular assemblies, and now the people were to have no voice in the levy-

The revolution of 1689 in New England

ing of provincial taxes or the enactment of laws. Such a curtailment of their rights naturally aroused a general feeling of resentment and Governor Andros received the blame for this objectionable policy. There was thus, throughout New England and especially in Massachusetts, abundant material for an explosion. This could be touched off at any time by an outside event which should promise hope of success to an uprising. Such encouragement came when news was received in Boston (March, 1689) that James had been driven from the throne and William and Mary had been installed as rulers of England. Emboldened by this revolution, a mob rose in Boston and deposed Andros. He was imprisoned for some months and then sent to England. With the downfall of Andros the old governments were for the time being restored, not only in Massachusetts but also in New Plymouth, Rhode Island, and Connecticut. This proved to be a temporary arrangement for New Plymouth and Massachusetts and two years later these two colonies were united to form a royal province.

CHAPTER VI

The Middle and Southern Colonies

NEW NETHERLAND AND NEW SWEDEN

SOON after the English landed at Jamestown, the Dutch began to *Henry Hudson* show an interest in America. The Dutch East India Company was trying to find a shorter route to the East than that by the Cape of Good Hope, especially since the Portuguese were attempting to monopolize the latter. To this end it sent Henry Hudson, an Englishman, on a voyage to America with the hope that he would find a strait across the continent connecting the Atlantic with the Pacific Ocean. Hudson sailed along the coast of North America (1609) and entered the harbor of New York. Thinking that the river emptying into this harbor might prove the desired channel to the Pacific, he sailed up the Hudson beyond the present site of Albany. The narrowness and swiftness of the stream at this point proved that it was a river and not an ocean strait. Although Hudson had failed to find a northwest passage, he had discovered the river that bears his name and had given the Netherlands a claim to a fine portion of the new world.

On the basis of this discovery, the Dutch laid claim to that part of *Settlements* North America included between the fortieth and forty-fifth parallels of north latitude. To this area they gave the name of New Netherland. Dutch seamen noted the fine opportunities for fur trading afforded by this region and at once began to engage in an active traffic with the Indians. In furtherance of this traffic, a trading post was established at the present site of Albany in 1614, and another on Manhattan Island about the same time.

Permanent settlement was begun in 1624 when the Dutch West India Company sent over thirty families of emigrants to occupy New Netherland. These were distributed among several places. A considerable group of them settled at the present site of Albany, where Fort Orange was built, while a few went over to the Connecticut River to establish Fort Good Hope at the place later known as Hartford. A temporary settlement was also made on the Delaware River opposite Philadelphia. The remaining immigrants were located on Manhattan, Staten, and Long Islands. Two years later Manhattan Island was bought from the Indians for about $24.00. A fort was built on the southern tip of the island, and the little village of New Amsterdam which had been growing up there became the seat of government of New Netherland.

Government

The general administration of New Netherland was in the hands of the Dutch West India Company, which appointed the officials and issued instructions for the government of the colony. The local government was entrusted to a director, or governor, and an advisory council. There was no assembly representing the people, and the governor's power was almost absolute, since the council did not prove an effective curb on his authority.

Friendship with the Iroquois

The Dutch were fortunate in forming a friendship with the Iroquois Indians, who occupied the regions north and south of the Mohawk River. The Iroquois were a confederation of five nations of Indians and were more strongly organized politically than any other group within the present limits of the United States. The significance of this friendship lay in the fact that it protected the Dutch from attack by the French and greatly promoted the fur trade. By the use of the Mohawk and Hudson Rivers, the furs procured directly by the Iroquois and obtained by them from the Indians farther toward the west could be easily sent down to Fort Orange or New Amsterdam, and goods given in exchange for these furs could in like manner be transported without difficulty to the Indian country.

Patroons

The Dutch West India Company was more interested in trade than in colonization. It was, therefore, willing to offer strong inducements to individuals who would make settlements. In line with this policy, the company granted to any of its stockholders who would settle fifty families a large area of land bordering on any of the navigable streams. The recipient of such a patent was given a tract of land fronting sixteen miles on one side or eight miles on both sides of a stream and extending indefinitely into the back country. The persons receiving such grants were called patroons, and the great estates so created were known as patroonships. The patroons were not only landlords but also had power to appoint magistrates and other officials and, within certain limits, to govern the settlers on their estates. This was an effort to transplant the manorial system to the new world. This old and decaying institution could not take root in the wilderness; for lands could easily be obtained in absolute ownership by settlers, and few of them were willing to submit to the terms of the patroonship. Consequently, most of the big grants failed to obtain the number of tenants needed, and the experiment did not prove a success.

Swedish settlements

In 1638 a group of Swedish emigrants was sent over to the Delaware region by a Swedish trading company. They landed and settled on the Delaware River at Fort Christina (now Wilmington). Other settlements were made along this navigable stream, and the territory on both sides of Delaware Bay and River from Cape May to points beyond the present site of Philadelphia was claimed by the Swedes. The area thus staked off, which was called New Sweden, was within the limits of New Netherland, and the authorities of New Amsterdam protested against the Swedish occupation. It was not, however, until 1655 that this protest was implemented with action. In that year *New Sweden* Governor Stuyvesant sent an expedition from New Amsterdam up *annexed to New Netherland* the Delaware River to demand the surrender of the Swedish posts. *erland*

Courtesy of the New-York Historical Society,
New York City

GOVERNOR PETER STUYVESANT
(1592–1672).
Director General of New Netherland,
1646–1664. By unidentified artist.

As the Swedes were few in number and were not prepared for defense, they yielded to the demand of the Dutch governor without making any resistance. The settlers were allowed to remain and retain possession of their lands, but thereafter the territory was recognized as being a part of New Netherland.

Of the various governors of New Netherland the most important *Peter* was Peter Stuyvesant. He was brave, capable, and intensely loyal to *Stuyvesant* the company and to the established church (the Dutch Reformed).

He was, however, narrow-minded and intolerant, ill-tempered, and autocratic in his notions of government. True to his prejudices and conservative views, he persecuted Baptists and Quakers and forbade Lutherans to worship in public. These measures were carried out in opposition to the wishes of the company, which pursued a policy of religious freedom for all. To the people in the little colony the blustering and at times almost laughable efforts of the testy governor to lord it over them must have made him appear more like the caricature of a tyrant than a real despot.

Stuyvesant, however, had some outstanding achievements to his credit. By an agreement with the New England Confederation he fixed for the time being the boundary between New York and New England, and by conquering the Swedes he added the Delaware region to New Netherland. He also instituted some needed reforms in New Netherland.

NEW YORK

New Netherland taken over by the British

New Netherland had all along been claimed by the British as a part of their American domain, and the Dutch planters were therefore regarded by them as interlopers. The British objected to the Dutch occupation for several reasons. First, it divided the northern English colonies from those of the Chesapeake region. Second, the possession of the harbor of New York by a rival commercial power like that of Holland made it difficult for England to enforce the navigation laws, for New Amsterdam afforded a fine base for Dutch smuggling. Third, the English wished to take over the fur trade which was so profitable to the Dutch.

For some years, however, nothing was done toward ousting the Dutch from New Netherland. The reason for this delay was that the Thirty Years' War was going on in Europe, and England and the Netherlands, both being Protestant powers, made common cause against the Catholic belligerents on the Continent. But after the war was brought to a close by the Treaties of Westphalia (1648), the *entente cordiale* between the Dutch and the British ceased to exist. It was not long, therefore, before friction developed between these two commercial rivals, and the British government felt free to press its claim to the Hudson River region. Accordingly, in 1664 New Netherland was taken over by the English.

The king's brother, the Duke of York and Albany, had been made proprietor of New Netherland and some islands and other territory in New England. To put him in possession of this new grant, several ships and an army were sent over to reduce the Dutch to submission.

When the expedition appeared before New Amsterdam, Governor Stuyvesant wanted to offer battle; but as he was in no position to put up an effective defense and as his people were unwilling to fight, he was forced to surrender and to acknowledge the authority of the

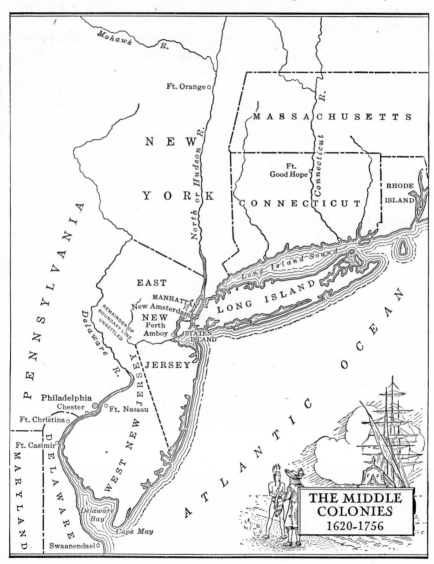

THE MIDDLE COLONIES 1620-1756

English. A few years later war broke out between England and the Netherlands, in the course of which New Amsterdam was recaptured by the Dutch; but by the terms of the treaty which ended the war (1674) New Netherland was returned to England.

British customs and laws were put into effect in the new acquisition, and English names of some places superseded those which had been used by the Dutch. For example, the name of the colony was changed from New Netherland to New York, and Fort Orange and New Amsterdam became, respectively, Albany and New York, after the Duke's titles.

The territory granted to the Duke of York was soon pared down by losses and voluntary grants to other colonies until only Long Island and the Hudson valley were left to him. Through the efforts of Thomas Dongan, the able governor of the province, the Iroquois Indians were induced to recognize the authority of the Duke, and in this way the limits of the colony were extended to the French territory on the west and northwest. The possessions of the proprietor were also extended southward to the forty-second parallel by the settlement of a boundary dispute with William Penn. In this way the original grant was expanded to the present extent of New York State.

When James became king (1685), New York was changed from a proprietary to a royal province, and shortly afterwards was joined to the Dominion of New England. The Dominion of New England was too large to be properly administered by one man, and so Andros was represented in New York by a deputy governor, Francis Nicholson, who was assisted by a local council. The deputy governor was in the trying position of having to administer an autocratic system of government, as the representative of a Catholic king, over a people practically all of whom were Protestants and many of whom believed in the right of self-government. This would have been a difficult task for the wisest of administrators, and Nicholson did not belong to this class. He was not lacking in ability, but at times he gave way to childish outbursts of temper which caused him to lose the respect of the people. He also aroused opposition by appointing Catholics to most of the important offices. There was a real, though unfounded, fear on the part of the masses that the deputy governor and the Catholic officials were plotting with the Catholics in Canada against the Protestants in New York.

When into this heavily-charged atmosphere there came the news of the downfall of James and Andros, Nicholson's doom was sealed. Taking advantage of an indiscreet remark made by him, the leading malcontents aroused the people into a revolt, and the deputy governor was forced to leave for England. The insurgents chose as their leader Jacob Leisler, an ardent Protestant of German birth, who took over the government in the name of William and Mary, despite the opposition of the aristocracy.

NEW JERSEY

Soon after receiving his patent, the Duke of York ceded to two of his friends, Sir George Carteret and Lord John Berkeley, a large area of land lying between the Delaware Bay and River and the Atlantic Ocean. To this region was given the name of New Jersey, to commemorate the brave defense of the island of Jersey which Carteret had made against the forces of Cromwell. Taking advantage of this grant, the proprietors proceeded at once to plant settlements and establish a government in New Jersey. There were already some Dutch settlers on the west side of the lower Hudson, and a few Dutch, Finns, and Swedes were located on the Delaware River. Soon after the seizure of New Netherland by England some Puritans from New England and Long Island came in and settled in the northeastern section of New Jersey. The first settlement established by the proprietors was at Elizabethtown (1665), which became the capital of the province. *New Jersey granted to Sir George Carteret and Lord Berkeley*

Early settlements

Immigration to New Jersey was encouraged by the liberal policy of the proprietors, who offered the settlers freedom of worship, a voice in the making of the laws, and grants of land on favorable terms. Thanks to these assurances, the province had a marked increase in population during the first decade. Some of the newcomers were from England, but most of them were from New England.

In 1674 Lord Berkeley sold his half of New Jersey to two English Quakers. This led to a division of the province between the Quaker proprietors, who took West New Jersey, and Sir George Carteret, who took East New Jersey. The Quakers proceeded to settle their territory, and in time West New Jersey became a stronghold of Quakerism. In 1682 the heirs of Sir George Carteret sold East New Jersey to William Penn and eleven other Quakers. These in turn shared their grant with twelve other proprietors, several of whom were Scotchmen. There were, therefore, twenty-four proprietors in East New Jersey. *The division of New Jersey*

The right of the proprietors to establish a government was questioned by the governor of New York, who represented the Duke of York. They also had a good deal of trouble in governing the settlers, especially those from New England, who objected to paying quitrents and in other ways showed their dissatisfaction. These complaints aided James II in his plan of taking over the government of the Jerseys, and for a short time (1688-1689) both East and West New Jersey were a part of the Dominion of New England. After the Dominion of New England collapsed, the Jerseys went back under the authority of the proprietors. Again troubles arose and the pro- *New Jersey becomes a royal province* prietors surrendered their governmental powers to the king, but retained their right to collect quitrents. The Jerseys were now united into one royal province (1702).

PENNSYLVANIA AND DELAWARE

The Quakers   The Quakers were a sect of radical dissenters that arose in England about the middle of the seventeenth century under the leadership of George Fox. Their beliefs and practices were at variance with those of both the Anglicans and the Puritans. They objected to the payment of tithes, refused to take oaths, and were opposed to war. The early Quakers at times allowed their zeal to lead them into emotional excesses, and frequently their preachers would be so overcome with feeling that they would tremble or quake. For this reason they were known as "Quakers," though they called themselves "Friends." Because of these views and their unconventional behavior, the Quakers were persecuted—both in England and in America—more than were most dissenters.

The policy of religious freedom in Rhode Island attracted a considerable number of Quakers to this little commonwealth, where they were able firmly to establish themselves. North Carolina and West New Jersey also became refuges for this harassed sect. The stronghold of the Quakers was, however, the province of Pennsylvania, and for the control of it they were indebted to William Penn, who while a student at Oxford had become a convert to their faith.

Pennsylvania and Delaware granted to William Penn   William Penn was the son of Admiral Sir William Penn, who had won the friendship of Charles II and his brother, James, the Duke of York. By the death of his father, William Penn inherited a claim of about $80,000 against the crown. To him had also descended the friendship of the king and his brother, the Duke of York. Owing to these favorable circumstances, Penn was able to obtain a grant from the king covering the present state of Pennsylvania in payment of his claims against the royal treasury. By the charter granted to him by the king (1681), he was made proprietor of Pennsylvania, having the right to dispose of the land and—within certain limitations—to govern the settlers. The region was so named by the king in honor of Penn's father. Next year Delaware was granted to Penn by the Duke of York.

The royal charter

Settlement of the province   Penn put forth every exertion to induce settlers to go to his province. Pamphlets advertising the advantages of Pennsylvania were circulated in Germany, Wales, and Ireland, as well as in England. As a result of this advertisement and the generous offers made as to land ownership and religious freedom, many immigrants were attracted to Pennsylvania. These included not only Quakers and others from England, but also quite a number of Germans who belonged to Protestant sects having views similar to those of the Quakers.

There were already in Pennsylvania in the region between Chester and Philadelphia a few Dutch, Swedish, and English settlers. Penn encouraged them to remain, and promised them freedom and the right to make their own laws. Other emigrants were sent over, and in 1682 Penn himself came to Pennsylvania. The town of Philadelphia (the city of brotherly love) had been laid out on a broad *The found-* plan with wide streets on which were erected large and comfortable *ing of* *Philadelphia* dwellings. The new colony prospered from the beginning. The climate was favorable, the soil good, and the transportation facilities excellent. The settlers were generally energetic and frugal and many of them were well-to-do. Philadelphia, therefore, never experienced the hardships which were characteristic of pioneering in other settlements.

One of Penn's motives in founding the colony was the desire to *Penn's ex-* perform a political and social experiment in America. He believed *periments in* that the ideals of Quakerism were practicable and that a political so- *government* ciety could be successfully organized on these principles. In the performance of this experiment he made trial at different times of three constitutions. The last one, put into effect in 1701, was the basis of the government in Pennsylvania from that time until the end of the colonial era. The government of Pennsylvania was similar to that of other proprietary provinces, except that after 1701 the council did not serve as the upper house of the assembly, the latter being a body of one house.

The laws in Pennsylvania were milder than they were in the other colonies. The death penalty was employed for fewer offenses and there was a saner attitude toward crime than elsewhere. From the *Religious* beginning, the law provided for freedom of worship for all persons *toleration* who believed in Almighty God. Only Christians, however, were allowed to vote, and later, as a result of pressure from the home government, the right to vote and hold office was denied Catholics as well as Jews.

After a sojourn of two years in his province, Penn returned to *The later* England. Later he came again to Pennsylvania and remained there *career of* for two years. He then went back and spent the rest of his life in *Penn* England. In these later years he was on very friendly terms with James, who had now become king. Owing to his association with this unpopular ruler, Penn lost the esteem of many of his admirers.

Delaware was at first governed as a part of Pennsylvania. The *Delaware* three counties into which it was divided sent representatives to the

Pennsylvania assembly, but in 1703 they were granted a separate assembly, which continued until the end of the colonial period. The governor of Pennsylvania, however, still had authority over Delaware.

MARYLAND

The charter granted to Lord Baltimore

In 1632 Cecilius Calvert, the second Lord Baltimore, received a charter from King Charles I granting him a large area of land north of Virginia, to which he gave the name of Maryland in honor of the Queen, Henrietta Maria. The charter conferred upon him the rights of a landlord and the authority to establish a government. He could sell, lease, or give away the land on such terms as he might wish to prescribe. In the exercise of his governmental powers he was restricted by the provisions that the laws of Maryland were to be in harmony with those of England and could not be made without the assent of a majority of the people or their representatives. Except for these two limitations, the proprietor had almost complete political authority. Maryland was thus to be a little constitutional monarchy with the proprietor as ruler.

The settlement at St. Mary's

Lord Baltimore sent over two or three hundred emigrants to Chesapeake Bay to plant a colony. They landed and established themselves at St. Mary's on St. George's River, a short distance above the mouth of the Potomac. The site chosen for the first settlement was a very desirable one inasmuch as it was high and well drained and therefore free from malarial swamps. The Indians in the vicinity were crossing over the Potomac into Virginia and were willing to sell their cleared lands to the settlers. The latter were also able to buy corn from the Indians and from the whites in the neighboring colonies. For these reasons St. Mary's did not go through a starving time as did the other early plantations.

The controversy between William Claiborne and Lord Baltimore

Virginia contended that Maryland was within the grant made to her by the charter of 1609 and therefore objected to Lord Baltimore's occupation of it. Before the settlement was made at St. Mary's, William Claiborne had established a flourishing trading post at Kent Island, in the central portion of Chesapeake Bay. Lord Baltimore demanded that Claiborne recognize his authority, for Kent Island was clearly within the limits of his grant. Claiborne, however, acting on the advice of the Jamestown government, refused to acknowledge the jurisdiction of the proprietor. Consequently, strife arose which led to bloodshed on both sides. The dispute was settled by a ruling, on the part of the English authorities, in Lord Baltimore's favor.

Since the charter provided that all laws should receive the assent of the citizens or their representatives, a primary assembly was or- *The government* ganized at St. Mary's soon after the arrival of the immigrants. For a while this mass meeting of all the citizens functioned as a legislative body. After other settlements were made, it was inconvenient for the settlers in distant towns to come to St. Mary's for these meetings, and this primary assembly gradually developed into a representative assembly. Maryland now had a government similar to that of Virginia, consisting of a governor and council appointed by the proprietor, and an assembly, the lower house of which was chosen by the voters. The governor and council constituted the upper house.

Lord Baltimore was a Catholic, and one of the reasons for found- *Religious toleration* ing his colony was the desire to provide a refuge for his fellow religionists who were persecuted in England. Therefore, many of the original settlers, including most of the influential and ruling class, were Catholics. These could not be protected in the exercise of their religion in Maryland unless the right of freedom of worship were granted to all the people. Furthermore, the promise of religious toleration would be an important inducement to prospective settlers. For these reasons Lord Baltimore allowed religious freedom from the beginning. This policy was embodied in law when the assembly passed the Toleration Act of 1649. By this act, freedom of worship was allowed to all persons who believed in Christ and the Holy Trinity.

Among those who were attracted to Maryland by its liberal reli- *Puritans emigrate from Virginia to Maryland* gious policy were a group of Puritans who were being persecuted in Virginia. A considerable number of them came over and made a settlement, to which they gave the name of Providence (now Annapolis). These Puritans later caused Lord Baltimore much trouble since they were strongly anti-Catholic.

When the civil war broke out in England, Maryland was wrong- *Maryland under the Commonwealth* fully accused of being opposed to the Parliamentary regime. For this reason this province, along with Virginia, was put under the ban of Parliament. The commissioners who had secured the surrender of Virginia appeared in Maryland to force a like recognition there of the authority of Parliament. Although the governor, who was the appointee of Lord Baltimore, was willing to accede to their demands, except for a few minor particulars, strife arose between him and the commissioners which ultimately led to bloodshed. William Claiborne, who was one of the commissioners, was largely responsible for this trouble. For a while Lord Baltimore was deprived of his authority in Maryland, and a government was established under the control of the Puritans. The latter signalized their victory by changing the Toleration Act and substituting for it a law by which Catholics were denied religious freedom. In a few years, however, Lord Baltimore regained his authority and the policy of toleration was restored.

The revolution of 1689

It was not long before there arose considerable dissatisfaction with the proprietary rule of Lord Baltimore, who had established a regime in his American province similar to that which had been inaugurated by James II in England. The suffrage was narrowed by a high property qualification, and laws were annulled by the proprietor after they had been accepted by the assembly and signed by him. Although a majority of the people were Protestants, the proprietor had appointed his relatives and other prominent Catholics to most of the important offices. Lord Baltimore had also antagonized some of the popular leaders, who were nursing their grievances and awaiting an opportunity to even scores with the absentee proprietor. Such an opportunity came when it was learned that James had been deposed. A revolt in the name of William and Mary broke out, and soon the Protestant insurgents were in control of almost the entire province. A convention was assembled which organized a provisional government to carry on until a governor chosen by the new rulers should arrive to take over the administration of the province.

No revolution in Virginia

When James II came to the throne there was still smoldering in Virginia some of the discontent which had been caused by the unjust policies of the governors sent over by Charles II, and which had found expression in Bacon's Rebellion. The accession of a Catholic king only made matters worse, and some excitement arose when it was known that William of Orange had landed in England. There was, however, no outbreak, and so Virginia was not seriously affected by the English revolution of 1688.

NORTH CAROLINA

Carolina granted to eight proprietors

At the accession of Charles II (1660) there was between Virginia and Florida a wide expanse of land suitable for colonization. Spain claimed this territory, but had not during the past three quarters of a century taken any steps to support her title by settlement. This left England free to appropriate this domain, to which she had already laid claim. Charles made use of this opportunity to reward some of his political supporters with a generous land gift. By two charters (1663, 1665), eight of his favorites were made joint proprietors of the territory lying between the parallels of 29° and 36° 30′ north latitude. To this region was given the name of Carolina, in honor of the king (*Carolus,* Latin for *Charles*). On this group of proprietors, which included some of the leading politicians and statesmen of England, were bestowed landed rights and governmental powers similar to those enjoyed by Lord Baltimore in Maryland.

THE CAROLINAS AND GEORGIA 1653-1760

Before these charters had been issued, a permanent settlement had been made in North Carolina. In 1653 a plantation was established on the Chowan River, near Albemarle Sound, by adventurers from Virginia, who had been attracted to this location by the lure of good land. The place selected was in some respects a suitable one for a settlement, as the soil was fertile and easily tillable and the site had access to navigable streams abounding in fish.

The first settlement in North Carolina

*Slow growth
of the colony*

Despite these favorable conditions, however, the growth of the colony was slow, mainly because of its isolation. It was separated from Virginia by a wide swamp and from other neighboring plantations by the barrier of great distance. The harbors that were within reach of the early settlers were too shallow for trans-Atlantic vessels and so there was little intercourse with England. The navigable streams, while furnishing transportation facilities to the interior, were too deep to be forded and were therefore difficult to cross. For this reason all roads running north and south were short and were very poor even according to colonial standards.

*Unsettled
conditions
in North
Carolina*

Owing to its isolation, North Carolina developed slowly, and in this province the frontier lingered longer in the coastal plain than it did in the other plantations. Therefore, during the seventeenth century pioneer conditions persisted, even in the older settlements. The North Carolinians had, along with the virtues, some of the faults of frontiersmen, among which was a lack of sufficient respect for law and order. Furthermore, they were neglected by the proprietors and did not always enjoy the salutary restraint of an effective government. They also had grievances against the proprietors, who were trying to collect from the people higher quitrents than they were willing to pay. The navigation acts, by imposing restrictions on the sale of tobacco, also worked a serious hardship upon them. Because of these grievances and the absence of adequate governmental authority, there were numerous insurrections in the northern province.

SOUTH CAROLINA

*The first
settlement
in South
Carolina*

The proprietors had had no part in the establishment of the colony on the Chowan River, but they soon took steps to promote the occupation of the southern part of their grant. They sent over a number of emigrants from England, and a few from Barbados, to plant a settlement in southern Carolina. The expedition sailed to the Ashley River and, a few miles above its mouth, established a plantation at a place which they called Albemarle Point (1670). The location was not a healthful one, and shortly afterwards some of the planters moved over to the land between the mouths of the Ashley

*The found-
ing of
Charleston*

and Cooper Rivers and began the settlement which later became Charleston. In 1680 Charleston was made the seat of government for the province and Albemarle Point was gradually abandoned.

In the decade of the sixteen-eighties, the population of South Carolina grew rapidly. Political and religious dissatisfaction in England caused a number of immigrants to come to this favored land. As a result, the population doubled during the two years from 1680 to 1682. Not all of the newcomers were from England. A very important group of foreign immigrants were the French Huguenots. Settling in Charleston and in other places in the colony, they proved a very valuable addition to the population. They were energetic, thrifty, and skilled in labor, and soon made a comfortable adjustment to their new situation. *French Huguenots in South Carolina*

Another group of non-English settlers were the Scotch, who came to Port Royal and founded the village of Stewart's Town (1683). The land occupied by them was within the territory claimed by Spain, and an expedition from Florida came up and attacked the settlement. Since the Scotch were unprepared for defense, Stewart's Town was completely destroyed by the enemy, and the survivors moved to Charleston. *The Scotch at Stewart's Town*

South Carolina, more than any of the other continental colonies, was influenced by the British West Indies. Some of the settlers and a few of their outstanding leaders came from Barbados and the Bahamas, and the Carolina proprietors also had authority over the Bahama Islands. This influence is especially noticeable in the slave legislation of South Carolina. In Barbados the number of slaves in proportion to whites was very great, and it was felt that stringent laws were necessary to keep the Negroes under control. Partly because of the influence of the Barbadian code and partly because of the large number of slaves in South Carolina, it too had very rigid slave restrictions. *South Carolina influenced by the British West Indies*

Since Spain contested England's claim to the Carolinas, she would have prevented the settlement at Albemarle Point if she had had the power. In 1676 a treaty was made between Spain and England whereby each country agreed to recognize the rights of the other to the territory already occupied. Spain construed this understanding to mean that England would claim no land south of Albemarle Point, and it was on the basis of this assumption that the Spaniards from Florida had attacked Stewart's Town. The agreement, however, did not put an end to controversy between the Spanish and English settlers. This controversy and the possibility of strife with the Indians, who might be incited against the South Carolinians by the Spaniards, gave the former a sense of insecurity which to some extent discouraged immigrants from coming to this region. When the wars between the Spanish and English governments broke out, South Carolina and Florida exchanged military blows. *Friction between the South Carolinians and the Spaniards in Florida*

In the Carolinas there seems to have been no marked reaction to the English revolution. There was, however, an uprising in North Carolina in 1689 which resulted in the removal of a disreputable governor. We cannot say positively, however, whether or to what extent this revolt was influenced by events in the homeland. About this time the North Carolinians seemed to have a flair for insurrection, and this uprising, like several others, may have resulted from local grievances.

Reproduced from THE PAGEANT OF AMERICA, *Copyright Yale University Press*

NEW AMSTERDAM, 1651.

CHAPTER VII

America between Two Revolutions

$\mathcal{T}$HE period between the English and American revolutions (1688-1775) is an important one in the political and social development of the British continental possessions. During this time there was a rapid growth in population and a noteworthy development in agriculture, industry, and commerce, which was attended by significant changes in the social life of the people. During this era too the English settlements were extended westward; the colony of Georgia was established, the Appalachian Valley and Carolina Piedmont were occupied by German and Scotch-Irish immigrants, and the supremacy of the continent was won by Britain as a result of a long contest with France. Aside from these great movements, there were other events of less dramatic appeal which deserve the attention of the student of this period.

The first problem which confronted William and Mary with reference to the overseas possessions was that of reconstructing the governments in those colonies which had revolted against their old rulers. These revolts had all been carried out in the name of the joint sovereigns and were imitations of the revolution in England to which William owed his crown. He therefore approved them and proceeded to form new governments to take the place of those which had been overthrown. *The problem of reconstruction*

The new regime was not free from disputes between local and imperial authority, for during this period important constitutional controversies were carried on in the royal provinces between the assembly and the royal governor. Since the governor felt duty-bound to uphold the interests of the empire, and the lower house of the assembly had a like responsibility to the people of the colony, there went on in some of the provinces a more or less constant dispute between the executive and the legislature during this entire period. The general principle beneath these controversies was a disagreement between the advocates of localism and the protagonists of imperialism. It was the clash between states' rights and nationalism. This controversy runs through the events of this period not like a *Constitutional controversies in the colonies*

silver thread, but rather like a knotted cord. It goes along from one administration to another with a sameness that is positively tiresome. Indeed, these perennial disputes between the executive and the legislature, if given in detail, would "bore the modern reader as much as they annoyed the provincial executive." Nor were these quarrels always kept on the high level of principle. On the contrary, they sometimes degenerated into undignified personal bickerings which were unworthy of a constitutional discussion. At times the governors showed a greater willingness to please their royal master than to serve the people of the province, and the representatives of the people were often disposed to sacrifice the interests of the empire to the selfish demands of their constituents.

In these contests the assemblies had the advantage of being in control of the purse strings. The governor could not get the appropriations needed for carrying out his measures without the consent of the representatives of the people, and in some provinces his salary was at their mercy. The power to withhold or reduce his salary was a weapon with which the assembly could cudgel the governor into conformity with its wishes. The assemblies were disposed to make full use of this power, and in some of them, notably Massachusetts and New York, they were able to impose hampering restrictions on the authority of the king's representative. In Massachusetts the assembly made an annual appropriation for the governor's maintenance instead of fixing a regular stipend, as the royal instructions prescribed. These grants were usually made at the end of the year, and the amount of the allowance might depend upon the behavior of the governor.

NEW ENGLAND

No attempt was made to restore the Dominion of New England, which had already broken up into its constituent elements. New Hampshire became a distinct royal province, and Rhode Island and Connecticut were allowed to continue under the governments which had been restored according to their old charters. The proceedings which had been instituted against these charters were dropped, and no further effort was ever made to annul them. Massachusetts also wished to have her charter restored, but this was not done. Instead, another charter, known as the Province Charter, was granted to her in 1691. Maine, New Plymouth, and for a short time New Brunswick,[1] were united with Massachusetts.

---

[1] Acadia, or New Brunswick as the English called it, had been wrested from the French the previous year; but as it was retaken by the latter in this same year (1691), Nova Scotia remained under the jurisdiction of Massachusetts for only a short period.

Under the charter of 1691 Massachusetts enjoyed a larger measure of self-government than did the other royal provinces. While the governor was appointed by the king, the council, which constituted the highest provincial court and the upper house of the assembly, after the first year was chosen by the two houses of the assembly meeting in joint session. The town meeting, whose powers had been curtailed by Andros, was restored to its old place as the chief agency in local government. With these exceptions the government of Massachusetts was like that of the other royal provinces. Suffrage was based on the ownership of property and not on church membership as it had been under the old regime. By this change the influence of the ministers in the government was lessened. They also lost prestige as the result of the witchcraft delusion which broke out at Salem soon afterward.

The Province Charter of Massachusetts

The last third of the seventeenth century was probably the darkest period intellectually that New England has ever known. The men and women of that era had been reared under a rigorous frontier environment and therefore had had few opportunities for formal education. In this respect they were more unfortunate than both their parents and their children. For the former had been brought up in England, and many of them had been trained in the schools of an old and established society; whereas the latter lived at a time when the agencies of education had been considerably improved as a result of the increase in wealth and population.

The Salem witchcraft delusion

The ignorance of the people at this time proved to be an expensive luxury, as it was purchased at the cost of a fierce outburst of superstition. This superstition took the form of a witchcraft frenzy which centered at Salem, Massachusetts, in the last decade of the century. The people might have been spared the evils of such a lapse into mediaevalism if they had been blest with an enlightened and progressive leadership. Most of the intellectual leaders of Massachusetts at that time were ministers, and they did not have the breadth of view necessary to steer the community safely through the dangers of a serious crisis. Puritanism and the discipline acquired in the wilderness school of hard knocks combined to stamp upon them a narrow and backward view of life. Even the most outstanding among them were upholding an outmoded obscurantism, which they were endeavoring to identify with religion. That with such blind guides the people would fall into the ditch of superstition was the only outcome that could be expected.

The delusion started in Boston (1688), but it was in Salem that it went to the greatest lengths and led to dire results. In 1692 some girls in Salem began to act as if they were bewitched. These young people were thought to be the victims of the black art, and certain persons in the town were accused of the crime. The craze, once started, spread rapidly, and it was not long before one hundred people were imprisoned and kept for trial.

The governor, Sir William Phips, appointed a special court to pass judgment upon the alleged offenders. The court was under the spell of the delusion, and a number of innocent people were adjudged guilty and put to death. "When a score of persons had been executed, when eight more were under sentence, when fifty others had confessed themselves to be witches, when one hundred and fifty were in prison and two hundred accused, things came to a sudden halt."[1] In the meantime the afflicted girls had overplayed their hand by accusing some persons of the highest standing, and the magistrates began to realize their terrible mistake. A reaction now set in, the special court was abolished, and the executions ceased.

Loss of prestige by the clergy

When normal sanity returned to the community it became conscious of the awful blunder which had been committed. One of the members of the special tribunal, Samuel Sewall, was so overcome with the consciousness of his mistake that he made public confession of his sin in church. Most of the ministers had used their influence in favor of the prosecution of the alleged witches, though some of them had objected to the unfair practices resorted to in the trials. There was considerable feeling, therefore, to the effect that the ministers had been largely responsible for the tragic mistake. Such an impression necessarily caused a lowering of the power and influence of the clergy.

NEW YORK

Party strife

It will be recalled that the revolution in New York which resulted in the expulsion of Governor Nicholson was led by Jacob Leisler, who was supported by the common people but opposed by the aristocracy. The feeling between the pro-Leislerians and the anti-Leislerians was very bitter, and for a half-generation was the main cause of party divisions. In appointing a governor for New York, William therefore properly decided to name an outsider, one who had had no part in the revolution; but in choosing Colonel Henry Sloughter for the position he made a bad selection, for Sloughter was a "profligate, needy, and narrow-minded adventurer."

The royal governors of New York

On Sloughter's arrival in New York, Leisler at first refused to surrender the fort to him but later yielded to the new governor's

---

[1] T. J. Wertenbaker, *The First Americans*, 161. (By permission of the Macmillan Company.)

authority. This hesitation on the part of Leisler was distorted into a charge of treason by his enemies, and he and his son-in-law were sentenced to death by the anti-Leislerian council. The death warrant was signed by the governor and these two victims of partisan hate were hanged. As the Leislerians considered this act of their opponents a judicial murder, the feeling between the two factions was made still more bitter.

Under Governor Sloughter a representative assembly was established (1691), and from that time until the end of the colonial period New York had a legislature of two houses. In other respects, too, the government of the colony was similar to that of the other royal provinces. In New York, as in Massachusetts, there were persistent disputes between the governor and the lower house of the assembly, and the causes of controversy in the former province were similar in character to those in the latter. Many, if not most, of the governors in New York were seriously handicapped in their contests with the assembly by their deserved unpopularity, for many of them were unworthy representatives of imperial authority. A very small number of them were honest, efficient, and tactful; a few were men of character and average ability, but were not fitted by temperament for the difficult task of colonial administration; while others were both dishonest and inefficient and proved to be downright grafters and rogues.

New York granted a representative assembly

One of the inefficient and unprincipled governors was William Cosby, who during his four-year term (1732-1736) aroused the antagonism of a group of prominent merchants and lawyers in and around the city of New York. These influential leaders were organized into a party of opposition and some of them wrote articles attacking the administration. These articles were published in a newspaper of which Peter Zenger was the editor. Governor Cosby resented these criticisms of his policy and had Zenger arrested on the charge of libel, for, as Zenger was publisher as well as editor of the newspaper, he was responsible for the articles. Zenger was defended in the trial by Andrew Hamilton, probably the ablest lawyer in America. The presiding judge, in accordance with the practice of the day, instructed the jury to pass upon the fact of publication only and leave it to the court to decide whether the statements were or were not libelous. Despite these instructions Hamilton made an eloquent plea to the jury to determine the truth or falsity of the statements and, if they were adjudged true, to declare in favor of the defendant. Acting under the spell of this stirring oratory, the jury brought in a verdict of not guilty.

The Zenger Case

The action of the jury in this case set a precedent in favor of hav-

ing juries instead of judges decide as to the truth or falsity of publications in libel cases. This precedent was followed in other trials
and finally became the regular practice throughout the colonies.
As juries were more inclined to be lenient with the critics of
British officials than were judges, who in many instances owed
their position to royal appointment, the new practice tended to promote a wider freedom in political discussion. For this reason the
Zenger case is an important milestone in the development of freedom of the press in America. Owing to this freedom, the newspapers
of the later colonial period became an important agency in molding
public opinion. Their columns were used for publishing the proceedings of town meetings and other public assemblies and for discussing American rights. In this way the newspaper became a means
of propaganda in fomenting the discontent against the mother country which ultimately led to the Revolution.

PENNSYLVANIA

*Penn loses
and regains
governmental
authority in
Pennsylvania*

When James was deposed and William and Mary placed on the
throne, Penn's political influence was gone and he was under suspicion by the new government. Furthermore, opposition in Pennsylvania was waged against him by some of his Anglican enemies.
The new rulers were desirous of bringing as many colonies as possible under the direct supervision of the crown, and so, taking advantage of this situation, deprived Penn of his political authority,
and made Pennsylvania a royal province (1692). Shortly thereafter
(1694) Penn regained his proprietary rights, and he and his family
remained proprietors of Pennsylvania and Delaware until the Revolution.

*Boundary
disputes*

Penn and his heirs had a series of disputes with neighboring
provinces as to the boundary of Pennsylvania. The dispute with New
York was settled at an early date, but there was a long controversy
with Maryland which was not settled until 1760. At that time Lord
Baltimore and the Penns agreed upon a boundary line which was
to be marked out by two surveyors, Charles Mason and Jeremiah
Dixon. In this way there was located the historic Mason and Dixon
Line. A good part of Pennsylvania was also claimed by Virginia and
Connecticut, and these disputes were not settled until after the
Revolution, when a decision was rendered in favor of Pennsylvania.

*Quaker paci-
fism and
imperial
military
policy*

The assembly in Pennsylvania was controlled by the Quakers
until the middle of the eighteenth century. These pacifistic legislators were placed in an awkward position while the French and
English colonies were at war. They found it difficult to practice the

doctrine of nonresistance without jeopardizing the safety of the empire. This conflict between pacifism and patriotism reached the danger point at the time of the French and Indian War. Pennsylvania occupied a strategic position of great importance, and the British authorities were unwilling for its government to remain in the hands of pacifists. A proposal was therefore made in Parliament requiring all members of the Pennsylvania legislature to swear allegiance to the crown. As the Quakers would not take oaths of any sort this measure, if passed, would automatically have excluded them from the assembly. To ward off such a drastic policy the Friends, except in a few instances, refused to run for the assembly, and so this body fell under the control of militant non-Quakers.

Although the Friends were opposed to war, they were as quick to resist any encroachment upon their rights as were other groups of Americans. This is shown in a contest which went on for some time between the Quaker legislature and the proprietors. One important bone of contention was the effort of the proprietors to have their lands and quitrents relieved of their just share of the tax burden. The controversy became so heated that the assembly sent Benjamin Franklin to England to uphold its claims before the king. This effort was successful and the proprietary lands were made taxable in the same way as were those of the people generally. The Penns, however, tried to evade this requirement by insisting that their good lands should be assessed at the rate of the worst lands of the colonials. This quibble was resented by the people, and again Franklin was sent to England as the agent of the assembly (1764). This time he was instructed to make an effort to have the government of the province taken away from the proprietors and turned over to the king. But as Parliament was at that time considering the Stamp Act, it looked as if going from proprietary to royal rule would be jumping from the frying pan into the fire, and so Franklin did not urge the change.

Controversy between the assembly and the proprietors

MARYLAND

The revolt against the authority of Lord Baltimore in Maryland gave King William the opportunity to take over the government of that province. According to an opinion given by the chief justice in England, the proprietor could be deprived of his governmental powers but must be allowed to retain his landed rights. Acting on this decision, the king took over the government, thus making Maryland a royal province (1691). Lord Baltimore still held the right to dispose of the unappropriated land, collect quitrents on individual holdings, and receive certain revenues.

Maryland becomes a royal province

A few years later (1702) the Anglican was made the established church and taxes for its support were levied on the people, including dissenters and Catholics. In keeping with the spirit of the Toleration Act of 1689, Protestant dissenters were granted the right of freedom of worship. They were not satisfied with the new arrangement, however, for they objected to paying taxes to maintain a religious denomination whose doctrines and practices they disliked. Catholics were deprived of the right to vote and hold office—and this in a colony which had been founded by a Catholic proprietor.

Maryland remained under royal control until 1715, when it again became a proprietary province under the fifth Lord Baltimore. The latter had transferred his allegiance from the Catholic to the Anglican Church and so the religious objection no longer obtained. From this time until the Revolution, Maryland remained a proprietary province under the authority of the Calvert family.

VIRGINIA

In Virginia the accession of William and Mary did not occasion any material change in the government. The incompetent and dishonest governor, Lord Howard of Effingham, had been a henchman of James II and should have been removed from office. Strange to say, however, he was permitted to retire to England with half pay as titular governor, while the duties of the office were performed by a deputy governor.

At the beginning of this period the Anglican Church in Virginia was sadly in need of reform. Many parishes were without ministers, and in many of those which had rectors the religious needs of the people were not properly cared for. The small salary received by the rector and the tenure of his position were under the control of the big planters who dominated the vestry. To expect a courageous and aggressive spiritual and moral leadership from such a dependent group was to look for figs on thorn bushes.

The Bishop of London, who had a sort of supervisory authority over the Anglican Church in the possessions, made an earnest effort to improve religious conditions in America. Dr. James Blair, a capable and persevering Scotchman, was made Commissary of Virginia, in which office he acted as the representative of the Bishop of London. Dr. Blair made a vigorous fight in favor of the much-needed reforms which he was instructed to put into effect. He tried to enforce a measure of discipline upon the clergy with the hope that they in their moral behavior would serve as better examples to their parishioners. A strenuous effort was made to increase the salaries of the rectors and give them a security of tenure which would not be at the mercy of the vestries. A college was also to be founded for the training of candidates for the ministry. In spite of a brave and persistent endeavor, Dr. Blair was not able to score a complete success for this program. One important aim, however, was realized when the College of William and Mary was established at Middle Plantation.

At the end of the century this village was also made the seat of government for the colony. Jamestown had recently been destroyed by fire, and it was decided to build the new state house at Middle Plantation. The latter, because of its better drainage and higher elevation, was comparatively free from mosquitoes and malaria and was therefore a more suitable location for a town than was Jamestown Island. The name Middle Plantation was changed, in honor of the king, to that of Williamsburg. As the capital of the province and the seat of the only college in the South, the village soon grew into a prosperous town and became an important intellectual, political, and social center. *Williamsburg made the capital of the province*

For more than sixty years (1705-1768) the governors of Virginia were absentee officials residing in England and drawing a large portion of the salary of the office without performing any of its duties. They were represented by a deputy, or lieutenant, governor who resided in the province and carried on the actual administration. *Absentee governors*

Of these deputy governors the most outstanding—and the ablest executive colonial Virginia ever had—was Alexander Spotswood. His administration of a dozen years (1710-1722) was signalized by a number of notable achievements. Education was encouraged and the growth of William and Mary College was promoted; iron furnaces were established which produced pig iron and some cast-iron utensils; the pirates that had been terrorizing the Virginia and Carolina coast were captured and hanged; and aid was sent to the South Carolinians in their struggle with the Yemassee Indians. In carrying out these wise policies Spotswood showed concern for the welfare of the people of the province as well as for the interests of the empire. He realized the danger of allowing the French to anticipate the English in the occupation of the trans-Allegheny region and recommended that the latter make settlements on the Great Lakes and occupy the mountain passes. It was in line with this interest that he led an exploring party across the Blue Ridge Mountains into the Valley of Virginia. *Alexander Spotswood*

NORTH CAROLINA

Quaker mis-
sionaries
in North
Carolina

Religion did not figure prominently as a motive in the settlement of North Carolina. The main incentive was land hunger, but the expectation of enjoying religious freedom may have been a favorable influence. Apparently the first settlers on the Chowan River were without religious instruction for a score of years. The first preachers in the colony were Quaker missionaries, prominent among whom was George Fox, the founder of the denomination. As a result of their activities the Quakers secured a firm foothold in North Carolina, and at one time one of their number held the place of governor.

The Anglican
Church
in North
Carolina

The Anglicans began their work in North Carolina at the beginning of the eighteenth century and soon a house of worship was constructed by them (1702). This was the first church building erected there, for the Quakers had been worshipping in private homes. Missionaries sent out by the Society for the Propagation of the Gospel in Foreign Parts were now active in the province, and in consequence the Anglican Church gradually grew in importance. Early in the eighteenth century an effort was made to make the Anglican the state church of North Carolina. Laws to this effect were passed, to which strong objection was raised by the dissenters, especially the Quakers. At one time this opposition went to the extreme of insurrection, and there was an outbreak known as Cary's Rebellion. Despite this opposition, however, an act was finally passed providing for the establishment of the Anglican Church. The measure was effective in the communities where there were enough Anglicans to make it practicable, but the church was not established in those sections where there were few or no Anglicans.

War with the
Tuscaroras

North Carolina had no serious trouble with the Indians until 1711, when the Tuscarora outbreak occurred. This was a long and bitter struggle, but the whites were aided by their neighbors from South Carolina and the result was a complete victory over the Tuscaroras. So badly were they defeated that the greater portion of them left North Carolina to join the Five Nations in New York.

Later
settlements

For some years the little colony on the Chowan River showed no sign of expanding southward, and it was not until 1690 that the permanent occupation of the region south of Albemarle Sound began. In that year a settlement was made on the Pamlico River, which was soon followed by others in that section. These new communities were established by adventurers from Albemarle, Virginia, and Europe. Prominent in the list of these later pioneers were the French Huguenots. One of the settlements founded by them (1704) was at Bath, which is noted as being the first incorporated town in

North Carolina. The Huguenots also established themselves in the region along the Neuse and Trent Rivers.

Another important contingent of non-English immigrants consisted of a group of Germans and Swiss who located on the Neuse River, forming a settlement (1710) which they called New Bern after the city of the same name in Switzerland. Hardly had they become established when the Tuscarora Indian War broke out. They suffered severely from the attack by the Indians, not only in the damage to their livestock, crops, and homes, but also in the loss of the lives of their people. So great was the destruction that the settlement was given up and the survivors were scattered among the other communities in North Carolina.

The German settlement at New Bern

In 1712 Carolina was permanently divided into two jurisdictions, and North Carolina thus became a separate proprietary province. The last of the rebellions had now been suppressed, and the people were more disposed than they had been at any previous time to settle down into obedience to law. There was still a great deal of dissatisfaction with the weak but meddlesome administration of the proprietors. The odium which attached to their rule was increased by their failure to aid the colonists in their life-and-death struggle with the Tuscarora Indians.

Carolina divided into two provinces

Despite this feeling, however, the North Carolinians did not join in the revolt (1719) which overthrew the proprietary regime in South Carolina (see pp. 94-95). The northern province had recently undergone the hardships of a rebellion and an Indian war, and was doubtless weary of strife and disorder. Furthermore, the assembly was not in session, and the people were, for the time being, without capable leadership. The governor and council were therefore able at this time to hold the province to its allegiance to the proprietors. A decade later the proprietors surrendered to the crown their political authority in North Carolina, and all but one of them sold to the crown their landed privileges in both provinces.[1] North Carolina now became a royal province (1729). The governor and council were thereafter appointed by the Privy Council, but no other material change was made in the government.

North Carolina becomes a royal province

Under royal rule North Carolina had a more efficient and stable government than it had had under the proprietary regime. As a result of this improvement in law and order, there was an increase in immigration to the colony. These new settlers, who came from

---

[1] Lord Carteret was the sole proprietor to retain his landed rights. Later he exchanged his one-eighth interest in the whole territory for an individual grant which comprised the northern half of North Carolina. In this vast area he had authority to dispose of the unoccupied lands and collect quitrents on individual holdings. Owing to this power the agents of the proprietor were able to defraud and exploit the settlers.

Expansion in the area of settlement

Europe and the other English plantations, occupied the central and southern portions of the province. Settlements were made on the lower reaches of the Cape Fear River, one of which developed into the town of Wilmington. As the harbor at the mouth of the Cape Fear could accommodate ocean-going vessels, North Carolina now had a window through which she could look out upon the outside world.

German and Scotch-Irish immigration

The settlements in North Carolina were confined to the coastal plain until the Scotch-Irish and Germans began to come in in large numbers. These immigrants, trekking southward from Pennsylvania through the Appalachian Valley, settled in the Carolina Piedmont in the middle decades of the eighteenth century. These newcomers made a large and important addition to the population of the province and a significant contribution to its rapid development in the later years of the colonial period (see p. 100).

SOUTH CAROLINA

The Anglican Church established

Early in the eighteenth century the Anglican was made the established church in South Carolina, and dissenters as well as Anglicans were taxed for its support. Missionaries sent out by the Society for the Propagation of the Gospel in Foreign Parts were active in southern as well as in northern Carolina, and the Anglican cause got a firmer hold on the people in the former than in the latter province.

The Yemassee War

Shortly after the Tuscaroras were overcome in North Carolina, South Carolina had to face a serious Indian danger. In 1715 the Yemassees, who lived on the southern border, made an attack on the South Carolinians and killed about two hundred of them. These Indians were encouraged by the Spaniards and were able to put up a strong fight against the whites; but the South Carolinians, with the aid of their neighbors, the Virginians and the North Carolinians, won a decisive victory in the struggle.

South Carolina becomes a royal province

Proprietary administration was unpopular in the southern as well as in the northern province. In the management of the colony the absentee proprietors seemed to be interested more in their private gains than in the welfare of the colonials. There was therefore considerable friction between the settlers and their overlords, and in the contests which arose between them the former were fortunate in having an able leadership. The home government was also dissatisfied with proprietary rule. The disorders in North Carolina and the activity of pirates and smugglers in both provinces were grounds for serious complaint. The proprietary regime could hardly be expected to hold out long against both external and internal opposition.

The crisis came when there arose a controversy over the method of electing representatives in the lower house of the assembly. Prior to 1716 the members of this body had been chosen by the voters assembling in Charleston. With the widening of the area of settlement this practice became unfair to distant planters who were seldom able to go to Charleston for the exercise of their right of suffrage. On the other hand, it gave the officials, merchants, and other citizens of Charleston an unfair advantage in the provincial elections. To remedy this inequality and inconvenience, the assembly passed an act in this year allowing elections for members of the Commons House (the lower house of the assembly) to be held in the rural precincts. This wise measure was, however, vetoed by the proprietors. Thereupon, the people in the province rose in revolt against proprietary rule and expressed the wish to be brought under the direct authority of the king. This request was granted and South Carolina was later made a royal province (1719).

As was the case in the northern province, the change from proprietary to royal rule made little or no change in internal administration in South Carolina. The governor and council, since they were now appointed by and responsible to the king, were disposed to champion the rights of the empire, while the Commons House was inclined to uphold the interests of the people of the province. The contest in South Carolina between localism and imperialism was thus very much the same as it was in other provinces. There were also sharp controversies between the upper and lower houses *Political* of the assembly. Two of the main causes of dispute between these *controversies* two bodies were: paper money and the right asserted by the council, or upper house, to amend money bills. So warm was this contest that twice there was a deadlock which held up legislation. The dispute as to paper money was settled by compromise, and the one over money bills was disposed of by a temporary acceptance on the part of the lower house of the contention of the upper.

GEORGIA

The contest which the English settlers in the south had carried *Reasons for* on with the Yemassee Indians and the Spaniards in Florida im- *the founding* pressed upon the South Carolinians the desirability of establishing *of Georgia* a buffer colony on their southern border. For the purpose of founding such a colony, a charter was issued by King George II to James Edward Oglethorpe and a group of philanthropists which granted them governmental authority over the territory between the Savannah and Altamaha Rivers. The new colony was to be named Georgia after its royal patron. Oglethorpe and his associates were to govern the colony as disinterested trustees, and none of them was allowed to own any land in Georgia.

Oglethorpe

Oglethorpe, who had been chosen governor, was the proper person to serve as the founder of the buffer state; for he had had successful experience as a soldier under Prince Eugene, and as a member of Parliament had always advocated an energetic policy toward Spain. He and his associates, however, had other reasons for establishing a new colony in America. They wanted to provide an asylum for some of the unfortunate Englishmen who had been imprisoned for debt. It was hoped that in the new world they would make a fresh start and get a new lease on life. These philanthropists also wanted to offer a refuge for German Protestants who were undergoing persecution in the homeland. Furthermore, it was expected that Georgia would serve as an important base in the fur trade with the Indians of the interior which would give the English traders the advantage in their competition with their Spansh rivals.

Early settlements

Oglethorpe brought over about one hundred and thirty emigrants and made a settlement near the mouth of the Savannah River. Here the city of Savannah was laid out with broad streets and numerous parks. For a while there was a continuous stream of new arrivals, of whom some were Germans and some Scotch Highlanders. The most important German settlement was the one made by the Lutheran Salzburgers on the Savannah River about twenty-five miles above its mouth (1734). These Protestant refugees had come originally from the principality of Salzburg, where they had suffered persecution at the hands of their Catholic ruler. They were given lands in Georgia, and their passage to America had been paid by an Anglican missionary society in London. In a spirit of thankfulness for the improvement in their fortunes, they called their settlement Ebenezer, meaning "Hitherto hath the Lord helped us."

Discontent among the settlers

The people had no voice in the government of the colony and in the early years Oglethorpe acted as a benevolent despot. He was legislator and judge, as well as chief executive and military leader. For some time there were a number of restrictions imposed upon the settlers. Their landholdings were small and they were not allowed the use of slaves. Furthermore, many of the immigrants, who had been unsuccessful in England, were not able to cope with frontier conditions in the new world. The small farmers of Georgia, with no Negroes to assist them, could not successfully compete with the big planters of South Carolina, who commanded the labor of numerous slaves. Many of the settlers therefore left the former province for the latter, and as late as 1760 the total population of Georgia was not more than five or six thousand.

So great was the discontent of the people that finally the proprietors abolished all these restrictions. The settlers continued to complain, however, and the trustees became so discouraged that they relinquished their authority in 1751. Georgia now became a royal province and remained so until the end of the colonial era.

Georgia becomes a royal province

THE OLD WEST

By the end of the seventeenth century the English had occupied a broken strip of territory on the Atlantic coast extending from Maine to South Carolina. Along the navigable streams this area of settlement had been pushed to a considerable distance into the interior (see map p. 98). At a number of places it had reached the line which separates the Coastal Plain from the Piedmont region. During the first half of the eighteenth century English colonization had extended westward into central and western New England, middle New York, the Piedmont section, and the great Appalachian Valley as well as southward into eastern Georgia. The territory occupied in this period of expansion is known as the Old West. Some of the settlers in the Old West had come from the eastern communities, but a large proportion of them were fresh immigrants from Europe. This latter class was made up almost entirely of Germans and Scotch-Irish.

Location of the Old West

At the end of the first decade of the eighteenth century there began the great immigration of Germans to America. These foreigners were mostly from the Rhine region, especially the Palatinate, Baden, and Württemberg, though some of them were from Switzerland. So many came from the Palatinate that all German immigrants were called Palatines. Württemberg and the Palatinate had not fully recovered from the terrible devastations of the Thirty Years' War (1618-1648) when they were again subjected to the ravages of the French invasion under Louis XIV. The poverty caused by these depredations was aggravated by the exploitation of the people by their greedy and incompetent rulers. There were also a number of Protestant sects that had been denied freedom of worship by their Catholic princes. In Switzerland conditions were not so bad, since this country had not suffered from invasion. But even in this more sheltered land the masses were exploited by their feudal lords and religious freedom was not allowed.

The great German migration

Reasons for the migration

In the spring of 1709, after an unusually severe winter which had

caused terrible suffering in the poverty-stricken sections of Württemberg and the Palatinate, about fifteen thousand Germans left the

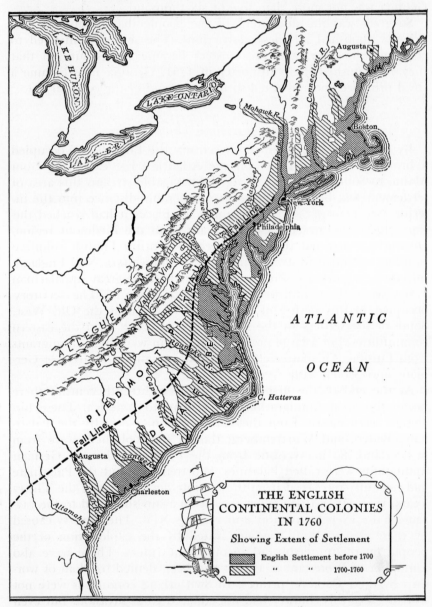

THE ENGLISH
CONTINENTAL COLONIES
IN 1760

Showing Extent of Settlement

English Settlement before 1700
"   "   1700-1760

homeland and sailed down the Rhine for England. After a brief
sojourn in England they began to move on to the British colonies.
The first immigrants went to the provinces of New York and North

Carolina. As has already been seen, the German colony in North Carolina was nearly destroyed by the Indians (see p. 93). The Palatines also had a series of unhappy experiences in New York, where they had been robbed by greedy landlords. Despite these drawbacks, however, a considerable number of the early German immigrants were permanently located in the Mohawk Valley.

The Palatines who came over later usually tried to avoid New York and North Carolina, and the greater part of them settled in Pennsylvania. The Germans who had been living there for a generation had become prosperous and their success offered a pleasing contrast to the unhappy experiences which their compatriots had had in North Carolina and New York. Cheap land and religious freedom were additional inducements offered by the Quaker province. Accordingly, Pennsylvania received more of the German immigrants than did any other colony. From about 1717 to the Revolution there was almost a continuous stream of these foreigners, and by the end of the colonial period the Germans constituted about one third of the population of this province. *Where the Germans settled*

Many of the Palatines were poor when they left the fatherland, and some were exploited and reduced to poverty by ship captains and others with whom they had relations on the voyage. Therefore, most of them were forced to bind themselves out for a period of service to pay for the transportation of themselves and their families. They thus became indentured servants and were known as "redemptioners." After finishing their terms of service they usually bought good limestone land in the Great Valley and by hard labor and Spartan thrift soon became prosperous. They held on to their own language and were thus not assimilated by their English neighbors. They were known as Pennsylvania Dutch (*Dutch* being a corruption of *Deutsch, German*). *"Redemptioners"*

Hardly had the German exodus got well under way when the great Scotch-Irish migration began to gather momentum. These new settlers came from northern Ireland (Ulster), which had been occupied by Scotchmen since the early years of the seventeenth century. Some of the Ulstermen settled in the English colonies in the seventeenth century, but it was not until 1718 that the stream of immigration had begun to assume large proportions. From that time until the Revolution emigrants from Ulster continued to come in a constant stream to America, and by the end of the colonial era the Scotch-Irish had become a large and important element in the population of the continental colonies. *The Scotch-Irish immigration to America*

An important reason for their leaving Ulster was economic and religious discontent. During the seventeenth century the manu- *Reasons for leaving Ulster* facture of woolen goods had become an important industry in Ireland. British producers were alarmed at the competition of their Irish rivals and had Parliament pass the Woolens Act (1699) for their own protection. By this law the Irish, as well as the Americans, were prohibited from sending woolen cloth to England or to any other country, a restriction which destroyed the woolen industry of Ireland. In 1717 a large number of land leases were expiring and the tenants on renewing them had to pay a much higher rental than before, sometimes double or triple the original figure. The interruptions in the commerce between England and the colonies caused by the pre-Revolutionary friction led to a great decline (after 1771) in the Irish linen industry. The famines of 1740 and 1741 also speeded up emigration. The religious policy of the government was another cause of complaint. As the Scotch-Irish of Ulster were Presbyterians, they objected to the payment of taxes for the support of the Anglican Church. Presbyterians, as well as other dissenters, were allowed freedom of worship but were debarred from holding office.

The German and Scotch-Irish trek southward

At the end of the colonial period there were some Scotch-Irish in all the colonies, but most of them had at first settled in Pennsylvania. After they had become well established in Pennsylvania, the Scotch-Irish and Germans in considerable numbers began to move southward settling in the Valley of Virginia and later passing through the water gaps into the Carolina Piedmont. Rich lands could be obtained in the Maryland and Virginia portions of the Valley on more favorable terms than those offered in Pennsylvania. The government of the Old Dominion encouraged these new settlements hoping that they would protect the frontier against Indian attack. In addition to cheap land the Carolinas presented the attraction of a mild winter climate.

In the trek southward the Germans and the Scotch-Irish were located in approximately the same areas, except that the latter were generally seated nearer the western frontier than were the former. There were also German settlements east of the Blue Ridge Mountains in the middle portion of Maryland and on the western border of the Virginia Piedmont.

Differences between East and West

As there were no rivers which could afford the new frontier settlements an outlet to the ocean, the Westerners had little communication with England and other European countries. This isolation prevented the inflow of the cultural influences of the homeland and gave the wilderness environment a free hand in molding the ideals of the settlers. Under the impact of frontier conditions the civilization of the old world often cast aside its European dress and donned the garb of the backwoods. In the meantime the older communities in the East were keeping in constant touch with Europe and were modelling their ideas and habits of living after the European pattern. It was inevitable, therefore, that the two sections would develop along widely divergent lines.

The economic and social differences between East and West were greatest in the Chesapeake and Southern provinces. In the western sections of these colonies there had grown up a New South which was more closely assimilated to the northern than to the southern colonies. The Valley of Virginia and the Carolina Piedmont were separated from the older portions of the South, in the one case by the Blue Ridge Mountains and in the other by the pine barrens, and the economic interests and social ideals of the one section were markedly different from those of the other. In the East there were large plantations on which were raised such staples as tobacco, rice, and indigo with the labor of slaves and indentured white servants. In the West the small landowners were engaged in diversified farming with free labor, and few slaves and indentured servants were used. In the East the people were generally of English stock and most of them were willing to accept the Anglican as the established church. In the West the greater part of the settlers were of non-English origin and as they belonged to dissenting sects were opposed to the union of church and state.

The New South

These social differences naturally gave rise to an antagonism between the older and newer communities, and this feeling was reflected in the political friction which developed between East and West. In every colony the clique of Eastern politicians which had control of local and provincial affairs refused to accord the Westerners their rightful share in the government. The frontiersmen felt that they were not fairly represented in the provincial assemblies and were forced to bear more than their share of the common burdens.

Friction between the old and new communities

It was in the Carolinas that the antagonism between lowland and upland went to the greatest lengths. In the later years of the colonial period there had grown up in the hill country of these provinces a bitter dissatisfaction with provincial and local administration. Among the causes of complaint were: high taxes, the corruption and inefficiency of the sheriffs, and the contraction of the currency. In South Carolina the Westerners organized themselves into associations (1764), whose members were known as "Regulators," and took up arms against the government. Frightened by this show of force,

The "Regulators"

the authorities made concessions and so insurrection was averted. In North Carolina the controversy led to a pitched battle at Alamance Creek (1771) between the "Regulators" and the governor's forces. The rebels were defeated and the insurrection collapsed, but many of the reforms demanded by them were embodied in the constitution of 1776.

Courtesy of the New-York Historical Society,
New York City

GENERAL OGLETHORPE.

After engraving by Ravenet.

CHAPTER VIII

British and French Rivalry in America

THE FRENCH IN CANADA AND THE MISSISSIPPI VALLEY

*I*T was some years after their tragic failure in the south (see pp. *Champlain* 20-21) before the French again launched upon a policy of colonization in North America. In the last years of the sixteenth century and the first decade of the seventeenth, explorations and attempts at settlement were made in the St. Lawrence region. The first of these colonizing ventures to succeed was the one directed by Samuel de Champlain at Quebec in 1608. Champlain was a man of exceptional courage, ability, and enthusiasm, and well deserves the honor of being known as the "Father of New France." By planting this colony he gave France a strong foothold on the continent. He also made a number of explorations, some of them extending far into the interior of Canada.

While on one of his exploring expeditions he aided his Indian *The French* allies in an attack on the Iroquois, or Five Nations. This skirmish *incur the enmity of the* occurred on the shores of the beautiful lake which had been dis- *Iroquois* covered by him and which now bears his name. It proved to be a very costly encounter, for by it the French incurred the lasting enmity of the Five Nations, the most powerful political organization among the Indians within the present limits of the United States. A few weeks later, Henry Hudson was feasting with the Iroquois and winning their friendship for the Dutch. The cordial understanding between the Five Nations and the Dutch was passed on to the English when they took New York. This alliance was cemented by a profitable fur trade between the Iroquois and the English and was continued until near the end of the colonial period. This friendship gave the English a great advantage over their French competitors in the race for furs. It also put a buffer state between New York and New France and protected the former from attack by the latter.

The site of Quebec was not a good one for a settlement; the soil *New France* was lacking in fertility and the winter climate was severe. It was, however, a suitable base for expansion into the interior as it commanded the waterway to the Great Lakes. Other settlements were made in the St. Lawrence basin, but the colony advanced slowly.

The cold and dreary land of Canada did not attract many Frenchmen from the comforts of the motherland. Consequently, at the end of a half-century the population of New France was only about twenty-five hundred, and was scattered over a very wide area. By this time, however, there had been established in the West Indies a number of thriving French colonies, which had attained a total population of fifteen thousand.

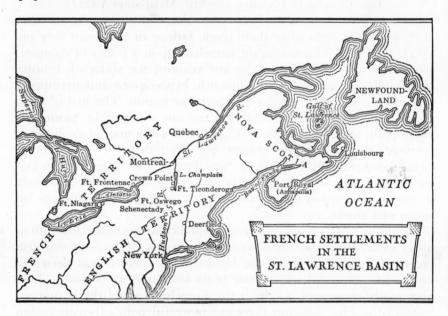

FRENCH SETTLEMENTS IN THE ST. LAWRENCE BASIN

Political organization   New France, as the French Canadian province was called, entered upon a more promising career when Louis XIV came of age and took over the reins of government in France (1658). Acting on the advice of his great minister, Colbert, he inaugurated a policy which put the colonial venture on a firm basis. The government was taken over by the crown and the colony was given a political organization like that of a French province. The chief officials in the provincial administration were: the governor, who had charge of civil and military affairs; the intendant, who was at the head of the judiciary and served as a check on the authority of the governor; and the bishop, who had political as well as ecclesiastical authority. The actual administration of the province was centered in this triumvirate, though there was also an advisory council made up of these three officials and other councillors appointed by the crown. The people had no voice in the administration of provincial affairs.

Despite the encouragement given New France by the home au-

thorities, the province never became prosperous. The rigorous cli- *Slow devel-*
mate may have been one cause of this, but the intolerant and pater- *opment of*
nalistic policy of the government was also partly responsible. Ini- *New France*
tiative on the part of the settlers was discouraged by excluding them
from all political activity and by denying them the right of freedom
of thought in religion, for Protestants were not allowed to settle in
the American province. But the main explanation is to be found in
the physical geography of the region. There were no high and
densely wooded mountains—as in the English colonies—to bar the
approach to the west, and the navigable streams led into the heart of
the continent. These conditions were a constant invitation to exploration and expansion. Consequently, the colonials devoted too
much energy to fur trading and exploration and not enough to the
pursuits of a settled life. Even the settlements which were made
were scattered over too wide an area for the co-operation needed in
taming a wilderness.

This tendency was also accentuated by the Jesuit missionaries, *Missionaries*
who traveled widely in their sacrificial efforts to spread their reli- *and fur*
gion among the natives, and founded numerous mission stations *traders*
throughout the interior. As a matter of convenience, a missionary
and a fur trader would often row together in the same canoe, although they were going on very different errands. The priest was
anxious to elevate the Indians to a higher moral and spiritual plane
and warn them against the evils of intemperance; whereas the fur
trader was too often bent on cheating them out of their furs and
tempting them into drunkenness with his firewater.

A good example of this kind of co-operation was the exploring *Father*
voyage of the Jesuit priest, Father Marquette, and Louis Joliet, the *Marquette*
fur trader. Leaving Lake Michigan, they went up the Fox River and *and Joliet*
carried their canoe over a two-mile portage to the Wisconsin. They
then followed this stream into the Mississippi, down which they
pursued their course to a point below the mouth of the Arkansas
River.

Some of the provincial authorities also felt that instead of con- *Count*
centrating their efforts on consolidating and strengthening the set- *Frontenac's*
tlements already made in Canada, the French colonials should stake *policy*
off a claim to the rich lands of the Mississippi Valley and thus pre-
empt the region before France's rival, England, could get possession
of it. Among those who advocated such a policy was Count Frontenac, the most capable of all the governors of New France. He was
ably supported in this policy by La Salle, the greatest of the French *La Salle*
explorers of the interior of the continent. His plan was for France to
strengthen her claim to the Mississippi Valley by establishing trad-

ing centers and military posts at strategic places throughout the entire region. In keeping with this purpose, he led a number of exploring expeditions in the west, the most noted of which was the voyage down the great river to its mouth (1682). To this lower Mississippi region he gave the name of Louisiana, in honor of Louis XIV of France.

The founding of Louisiana

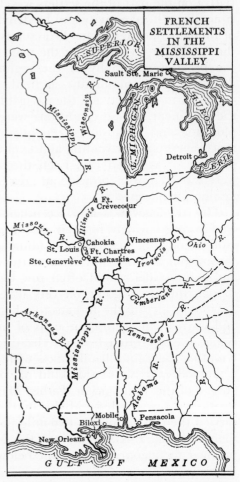

FRENCH SETTLEMENTS IN THE MISSISSIPPI VALLEY

Energetic efforts were made by the French authorities to realize the dreams of La Salle and Frontenac. In 1699 a colony was planted at Biloxi in southern Mississippi, which was the first attempt by the French to occupy Louisiana. Other settlements in this area were soon afterwards made and in 1718 New Orleans was founded. This town became the seat of government for the new province of Louisiana, which by 1731 had a population of five thousand whites and two thousand blacks.

French occupation of the Illinois region

The Illinois region was another center of French colonization. Before the end of the seventeenth century a military post and a mission station had been established at Fort St. Louis in north-central Illinois. In the Illinois country and adjacent areas, other missions and trading centers were founded which grew into permanent settlements. One of these, Vincennes (established in 1732), was located on the Wabash River, in Indiana. In the near-by Michigan area, Detroit (founded in 1701 by Lamothe Cadillac) was important as a fur-trading center and a military post commanding the waterway from Lake Erie to Lake Huron. The land on which the Illinois villages were located was fertile, and the farmers there were able to produce supplies which were sent east to Detroit and down the Mississippi to be sold in New Orleans and Mobile or reshipped to the West Indies.

By the middle of the eighteenth century the French had explored *Extent of* the Great West as far as the Rocky Mountains in both the northern *French expansion* and southern portions. Forts had been built at strategic locations both east and west of the Father of Waters, including a series of military posts extending from Louisiana to the Illinois and the lake regions, and another from Lake Superior almost to the Rocky Mountains. There were also a number of trading posts and mission stations, some of which had developed into permanent settlements.

THE FIRST THREE INTERCOLONIAL WARS

It is needless to say that England viewed with grave concern this westward expansion of her chief rival. Since the trading centers and settlements south of Canada were on territory claimed by England, a clash between the two powers was sooner or later inevitable. For a long time, however, the English and French plantations were so far from each other that the question as to the ownership of the trans-Allegheny region was only an academic dispute. There was some friction between the French and British colonials over the fur trade and the Newfoundland fisheries, but not enough to bring on war. Conflict in America therefore might have been postponed until the middle of the eighteenth century had not conditions in Europe changed for the worse.

After the Revolution of 1688 Britain became more anxious than *England's at-* ever over the balance of power in Europe and began to take a prom- *titude toward* inent part in continental affairs. As a result of this new foreign *of power in* policy, she was drawn into a series of wars with France which lasted, *Europe* with long and short intervals of peace, for more than a hundred years. In these struggles many of the other European powers played a secondary role as allies of one or the other of the main contestants. The American possessions of the European belligerents were involved in most of these wars, and between the French and English colonies in America there were four conflicts, in all but one of which the Spanish colonies were aligned with those of France.

The American part of the first of these wars between England *King* and France was known as King William's War (1689-1697). The *William's War* struggle in Europe made such demands on the resources of both England and France that neither was able to give much aid to her subjects in America. A few regular troops were furnished by the British, and merchant vessels were convoyed across seas by the British fleet. No troops were supplied by France, but Count Frontenac was sent over for the second time, now to act as governor and director of military affairs. The war was carried on therefore mainly by the colonials and their Indian allies.

Fighting was confined to New England, New York, and the St. Lawrence basin. Indian raids, directed by French leaders and accompanied by brutal atrocities on helpless villages, harried the frontiers of New York and New England. These barbarities brought terror to the outlying settlements, but did not materially affect the military situation. The plan of the British was to capture the enemy strongholds of Quebec, Montreal, and Port Royal. Efforts to take these places were all failures except that Port Royal was captured by the English, only to be retaken by the French shortly thereafter.

Treaty of Ryswick

The war in both Europe and America was brought to a close by the Treaty of Ryswick, by the terms of which England and France were each to retain the territory in America it had held before the conflict started.

Queen Anne's War

This treaty proved to be a truce of only short duration, for in a few years there broke out another long European conflict, the War of the Spanish Succession. The American part of this contest is known as Queen Anne's War (1701-1713).

Owing to the neutrality of the Iroquois, New York was free from attack and so took no part in the struggle for the first seven years. In the north most of the fighting was between the New Englanders and the French and their Indian allies, and in the south between the South Carolinians and the Spaniards. The French, pursuing very much the same tactics as they had in the previous war, resumed their raids on the New England frontier. Again efforts were made by the English to capture Montreal and Quebec but without success. Finally, however, after two failures Port Royal was captured (1710) by a joint force of British marines and New England militiamen in co-operation with the British fleet.

Peace of Utrecht

The war was brought to a close by the Peace of Utrecht (1713). By the terms of this treaty Britain received from France—Acadia, Newfoundland, and the Hudson Bay region, and her protectorate over the Iroquois was recognized by France. England also received for thirty years a monopoly of supplying the Spanish colonies with slaves.

There was a long interval between this war and the next one. During this time of peace France was strengthening her hold on the Mississippi Valley, and England was occupying the Old West and expanding southward into Georgia. Each party was therefore getting ready for the great contest which was looming ahead.

The renewal of the war came first as a conflict between England

and Spain. English merchants continued to violate the regulations
which Spain had imposed on the trade with her colonies, and many
of these English smugglers were severely punished by the Spanish
officials. These merchants complained loudly of this alleged mistreatment and succeeded in winning the ear of Parliament. Spain
also resented the occupation of Georgia as an infringement of her
rights. Accordingly, war broke out between England and Spain
(1739), which widened into a European conflict, the War of the
Austrian Succession, which was known in America as King George's
War (1744-1748).

Again there was fighting in the south, this time between the Spaniards in Florida and the English settlers in Georgia. In the north the
war assumed the same pattern followed in the two previous conflicts.
The most important event of the contest in America was the capture
of Louisbourg by the New Englanders. This stronghold, which had
been built by the French to compensate for the loss of Port Royal,
dominated the Gulf of St. Lawrence and could serve as a base for
French privateers and men-of-war in their attacks on British shipping. Its possession by the French gave them a great advantage over
the New Englanders in the competition for the fisheries. In making
the attack the British fleet effectively co-operated with the New England militiamen.

By the Treaty of Aix-la-Chapelle, which ended the conflict, Louisbourg was returned to the French, and in America the territorial
arrangement was restored to what it had been before the war. The
New Englanders were sorely disappointed over the loss of their prize,
but England had to yield Louisbourg in order to induce France to
relax her hold on the Netherlands.

THE FRENCH AND INDIAN WAR

After a six-year period of peace following the Treaty of Aix-la-
Chapelle, there broke out another great war, the American phase of
which is known as the French and Indian War, and the European,
the Seven Years' War. Unlike the first three intercolonial wars (all
of which were of European origin), this conflict began in America
and spread to the old world. The cause of this war was a dispute between England and France as to the ownership of the trans-Allegheny country and especially of the Ohio Valley.[1] The occupation

---

[1] The region between the Allegheny Mountains and the Mississippi River was
claimed by both nations although neither had done much to support this claim by
occupation. France, as has been seen, had established settlements and military posts
on the outer fringe while England had secured a number of trading posts in the interior. The rivalry between British and French fur traders in this region was generating
friction, but the real cause of conflict lay deeper.

of the Ohio region would greatly shorten the chain of water communication which held together the French possessions in Canada, the Illinois country, and Louisiana. If the French were thus entrenched they "could join hands behind the backs"[1] of the English and limit their expansion westward. The English colonies would also have hostile backdoor neighbors who would be in a position to arouse the western Indians against them and thus keep their frontier in a state of perpetual insecurity. With such an advantage the French might dispossess their rivals of the territory they held east of the mountains.

Relative strength of the contestants

As world powers Britain and France were about evenly matched. The latter had the larger army and the former the stronger navy. In America, however, England had a decided lead over her rival. On the mainland of North America the population of the English colonies was greatly in excess of that of the French provinces, and this disparity was accentuated by the fact that the French settlements were spread over a wide area and it was difficult for them to coordinate their military operations. Furthermore, in the British colonies there was an abundance of food products, whereas the French provinces did not produce enough food supplies for their soldiers and the civilian population. But this advantage was lessened to a considerable extent by the unpatriotic conduct of some British colonials, who persisted in selling supplies to the enemy in violation of the law.

One handicap under which Britain labored was the inability of her colonies to act in unison. There was no bond holding the possessions together except a common loyalty to the empire, and this feeling was not so strong as their concern for provincial rights. The tradition in favor of self-government also interfered with the sacrifices as to local interests which were demanded by the exigencies of war. It was impossible, therefore, to get the thirteen separate commonwealths to pull together effectively in the war harness.

The Albany Congress

A step toward remedying this situation was taken at the beginning of the war by the Albany Congress (June, 1754). This body, which was made up of representatives from seven colonies, had been called by the British authorities to arrange an agreement with the Iroquois Indians. An understanding with the Iroquois was reached and a plan of union was formulated. This plan, which had been drawn up by Benjamin Franklin, provided for a president-general chosen by the king and a federal council made up of representatives from all the colonies. To this general council was delegated the power to

---

[1] W. Wood, *The Fight for Canada.* 35.

supervise Indian affairs, enact measures of general interest, declare war, and raise armies and levy taxes for their support. This scheme of union was rejected by all the provincial assemblies on the ground that it would too greatly limit their powers. A plan offered by the Board of Trade met with a like refusal.

About the middle of the century, both England and France began aggressively to assert their claims to the Ohio region. The Virginia government made a large grant of land in that area to a group of land speculators (1749), on which they were expected to plant a colony. In that same year the Governor of Canada sent Céloron de Bienville on an expedition to reaffirm France's rights in the upper Ohio country. He made a circuit from Lake Erie *via* Lake Chautauqua and the Allegheny River to the Ohio and down that stream to the mouth of the Miami and thence up the Miami and down the Maumee back to Lake Erie. At various points along the journey, leaden plates were buried on which were inscriptions affirming France's title to the region. In this ceremonious manner France proclaimed her determination to contend for the disputed Ohio Valley. *Aggressive measures of the English and French*

It was not long before France began to assert her claim to the west in more aggressive fashion. Three forts were built in northwestern Pennsylvania, and one of them (Fort Venango) was on the site of a trading post from which English traders had been thrust out by the French. The colonial governors were instructed by the British authorities not to act on the offensive, but to oppose by force any effort on the part of the French to occupy lands which undoubtedly belonged to England. Acting on these instructions, Lieutenant-Governor Robert Dinwiddie of Virginia sent George Washington, a young man of twenty-one, to these new forts to bear a message of protest against this infringement of Britain's landed rights (1753). The commanders of these posts politely but firmly refused to give them up and reaffirmed France's right to the land occupied. *Washington's mission*

Diplomacy having failed, war was now left as the only alternative and both sides made ready for the fray. The present site of Pittsburgh, where the Allegheny and Monongahela Rivers unite to form the Ohio, was the gateway to the West and both sides were eager to get possession of it. Governor Dinwiddie sent forward a force of Virginia militia to hold this important strategic center. But before this expedition could reach the scene of action the French had seized the forks of the Ohio after having driven off a small band of Englishmen who had started to build a fort there. The French now erected a strongly-fortified post on the same location, to which they *Beginning of hostilities*

gave the name of Fort Duquesne, in honor of the able governor of
New France.

The advance guard of the Virginia troops, led by Washington,
had proceeded a few miles west of the Great Meadows, when it en-

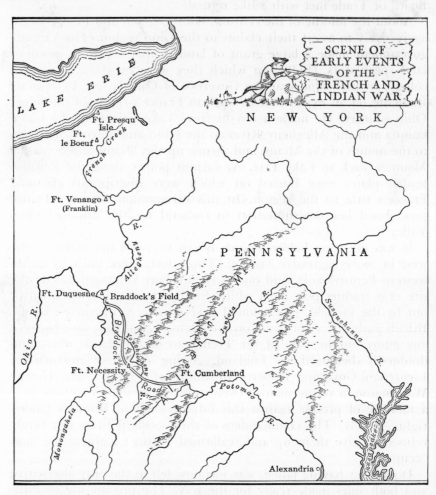

countered a band of Frenchmen from Fort Duquesne (May 28,
1754). Washington gave the order to fire, and a skirmish ensued in
which Jumonville, the French commander, and twenty of his men
were killed, and the rest were forced to surrender. Washington fell
back to Great Meadows, where he built Fort Necessity and five
weeks later took a stand against a superior French force from Fort
Duquesne. After holding out against attack during the entire day of
July 3, Washington capitulated and his men were allowed to with-

draw with the honors of war. In this way began a new war in America which was destined to widen into a European conflict.

The French held certain key positions which would have to be taken if the British were to win the war. Next to Fort Duquesne, those of chief importance were: Louisbourg, the strongest military post on the eastern coast of North America; Fort Crown Point, on Lake Champlain, which controlled the waterway to Canada by way of Lake Champlain and the Richelieu River; Fort Frontenac, on Lake Ontario, which guarded the French line of communication with the West; Fort Niagara, standing sentinel at the portage between Lake Ontario and Lake Erie; and Quebec, in the heart of the province, sitting apparently in impregnable security at the top of an inaccessible precipice. The capture of these places would not only deprive the enemy of bases of attack on the English colonies but would also open the gates to the French possessions. *Strategic positions of the French*

The plan of the British was to send regular troops across seas to co-operate with the colonials in an effort to wrest these strongholds from the French. The English navy was to prevent the landing of any enemy troops in Canada. Most of the French ships, however, were able to elude the vigilance of the British admiral and land their contingents of trained soldiers. The French were therefore in a position to put up a strong fight in defense of their fortified posts. Accordingly, in the early part of the war the British met with many severe reverses. *Early reverses of the British*

Of these early defeats the most humiliating was the one sustained by General Edward Braddock, who had been sent over from England with approximately one thousand regulars. With this force and about one thousand provincials, Braddock proceeded slowly from Fort Cumberland, as he had to cut a road for his army. When he had advanced to a point about eight miles from Fort Duquesne, he relaxed his usual caution and allowed himself to be outmaneuvered by the enemy. An attack was made upon him by a smaller force of Indians and French and he was badly defeated and mortally wounded.[1] His successor withdrew his forces although he was still strong enough to have captured the fort. *Braddock's defeat*

The Indian allies of the French were aroused into great activity by this victory. The frontier from Pennsylvania to North Carolina was now open to attack and the settlements west of the Allegheny Mountains had to be abandoned. Washington, with a force of one thousand (later fifteen hundred) militiamen, did what he could to protect the exposed line of three hundred and fifty miles. Stockaded *The frontier open to Indian attack*

---

[1] For a good discussion of the reasons for Braddock's defeat see an article by Stanley Pargellis in the *American Historical Review*, XLI, 253-269.

blockhouses manned by frontiersmen were erected in the mountain passes west of the main settlements, and a fierce struggle was carried on between the whites and the redskins for the duration of the war.

The American conflict becomes a world war

For about two years the struggle between England and France went on as an undeclared war and was confined to America. In the meantime there had been a new alignment of the European powers. When war was finally declared by England (May, 1756) she was in alliance with Prussia, and France with Austria. Later (1762) Spain came in as the ally of France. The American conflict had now widened into a world war (the Seven Years' War) and was carried on not only in America but also in Europe and in India.

French successes

The great victory over General Braddock was followed by a series of French successes, and the tide did not turn strongly in favor of the British until 1758. The French owed these later successes mainly to the able leadership of the Marquis of Montcalm, who came over early in 1756 to assume the chief command of the Canadian troops. British defeats in the early part of the war were in large measure due to poor management on the part of the imperial authorities. Too often were appointments in the army and navy made on the basis of birth, seniority, and political influence rather than on merit. As a result, there were in both branches of the service a number of officers who were not equal to the responsibilities of their positions. Many of them were untactful, as well as incompetent, and antagonized the colonials by their haughty bearing. Under such conditions hearty co-operation between the imperial and colonial groups was impossible.

War policy of Pitt

Fortunately, the British people became aware of the situation and began to clamor for a better leadership. The pressure was so strong that William Pitt was called to the ministry in the autumn of 1756, and the following year was put in entire control of the war. The "Great Commoner" discharged his grave responsibilities with energy, enthusiasm, and marked ability. Appointments in the army and navy were made with reference to merit and not to social position and political influence. Agreements were reached with the colonial governments whereby they were induced to give greater aid in the prosecution of the war. These changes raised the morale and efficiency of the army and navy, which were reflected in one success after another for the British cause. The strategic positions mentioned above were all wrested from the French, and in time complete victory perched on the British banner.

The most spectacular of all these successes was the capture of

Quebec by the English. At the head of the British troops was a *The capture* brilliant young officer, General James Wolfe, who was now arrayed *of Quebec* against the Marquis of Montcalm, the ablest of the French commanders. In the battle which preceded and led to the surrender of Quebec, Wolfe was killed and Montcalm was mortally wounded. The sacrifice of these fine young leaders accentuated the tragedy of this battle.

Next year Montreal was taken by General Amherst and all of Canada passed under English control. It was not until three years later, however, that the treaty of peace was signed. In the meantime Spain's belated entrance into the war (1762) had given Britain the opportunity to seize Cuba and the Philippine Islands.

The Seven Years' War came to an end with the treaty of peace *The Treaty* signed at Paris in 1763. The treaty provided for the surrender by *of Paris* France to England of all but two of her colonies in India and the return to France of some of her West Indian colonies which had been seized by England. France ceded Canada to England and yielded to England her claim to all territory east of the Mississippi except the island of Orleans. As the British government was not aware of the capture of the Philippines when the preliminary treaty was signed, these islands were returned to Spain. Britain received Florida from Spain and agreed to restore Cuba to her. As a compensation for the loss of Florida, France ceded to Spain the island of Orleans and Louisiana west of the Mississippi. France had thus lost all her possessions on the continent of North America except two small islands in the Gulf of St. Lawrence, which were useful as fishing stations.

At the end of this war England enjoyed supremacy in India and *Results of* North America and was the leading naval and colonial power of the *the war* world. The defeat of the French, and the victory over Pontiac which followed soon afterwards, relieved the English colonials to a considerable extent of the Indian danger in the Ohio region and thus removed the greatest barrier to westward expansion. But these gains were offset by some important economic and spiritual losses. During the four intercolonial wars the fur trade and foreign commerce had declined, and privateering and speculation, especially in land and commerce, had greatly increased. War profiteers and smugglers who carried on an illicit trade with the enemy were able to reap excessive profits. The large amount of metallic money sent over from England to purchase supplies for the soldiers changed the balance of trade between the plantations and the homeland so that it came to favor the former.

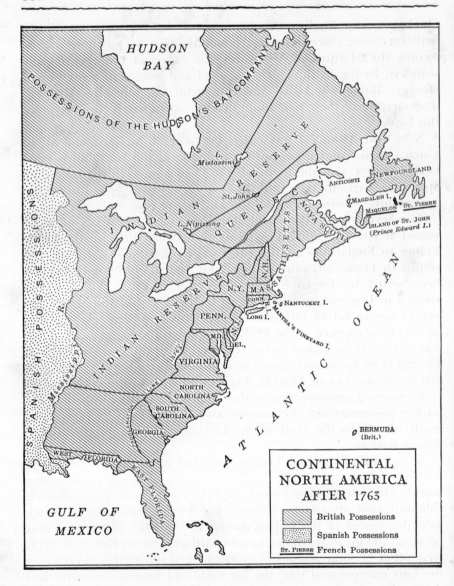

HUDSON BAY

POSSESSIONS OF THE HUDSON'S BAY COMPANY

L. Mistassini

L. St. John

ANTICOSTI

NEWFOUNDLAND

MAGDALEN I.

MIQUELON ST. PIERRE

ISLAND OF ST. JOHN
(Prince Edward I.)

L. Nipissing

Q U E B E C

N O V A S C O T I A

I N D I A N   R E S E R V E

N.Y.

N.H.

MASS.

CONN.

NANTUCKET I.

LONG I.

MARTHA'S VINEYARD I.

PENN.

S P A N I S H   P O S S E S S I O N S

MD.

DEL.

N.J.

VIRGINIA

NORTH CAROLINA

SOUTH CAROLINA

GEORGIA

Mississippi R.

BERMUDA
(Brit.)

WEST   FLORIDA

EAST FLORIDA

GULF OF MEXICO

A T L A N T I C   O C E A N

CONTINENTAL NORTH AMERICA AFTER 1763

British Possessions

Spanish Possessions

ST. PIERRE French Possessions

THE OCCUPATION OF THE TRANS-ALLEGHANY REGION

*The royal
proclamation
cf 1763*

The accession of territory which came to England as a result of
her victory over France had placed new responsibilities on the British government. A plan of administration had to be devised for the
new lands and a policy had to be formulated which would insure
peace between the whites and the western Indians. The royal proclamation of 1763, issued on the advice of the Board of Trade, was an

effort to solve these problems. It provided for the creation of the provinces of East and West Florida in the south, and the Province of Quebec in Canada.

By this same proclamation an important change was made in the *The Procla-* supervision of Indian affairs. Heretofore, relations between the *mation Line* whites and the red men had been under the management of the colonial governments. This arrangement made it impossible to carry out a uniform practice and permitted the exploitation of the Indians by fur traders and land speculators. Indian relations were now to be under the exclusive control of imperial agents, and in the future no lands could be purchased from the natives except by these agents. The land west of the crest of the Allegheny Mountains was set aside as an Indian reservation, and for the time being no white settlements could be made in that area, and those which had already been made there had to be abandoned. By this policy of segregation it was hoped that friction between the two races would be reduced to a minimum and that the fur trade would be promoted by protecting the trans-Allegheny forests against the destructive activities of the colonial farmers.

Although this was a temporary arrangement to remain in effect until Indian relations could be stabilized, there was strenuous objection to it by the land speculators who had hoped to secure large land grants in that region. Moreover, the backwoodsmen who wanted to settle in the west chafed under these restraints and often refused to recognize this imaginary barrier as the boundary of westward expansion. The colonial authorities also objected to the Proclamation Line because its location was a denial of the rights of the colonies to the trans-Allegheny country, which they claimed under the sea-to-sea grants of their charters.

Before this new policy had gone into effect there had occurred a *Pontiac's War* serious uprising among the Indians in the west. This was led by Pontiac, an Ottawa chief of unusual ability. He had succeeded in enlisting the support of most of the western tribes in this struggle, which has been improperly termed Pontiac's "Conspiracy." The main cause of this outbreak was the encroachment of the white settlers on the Indian lands. English pioneers were coming in and rapidly clearing the land for farming purposes. In this way they were destroying the forests which sheltered the wild life on which the Indians largely depended for a living. The French backwoodsmen, on the other hand, had generally been fur traders and not farmers, and their activities had promoted rather than hindered the Indian occupation of hunting. There was therefore a clash between the economy of the English frontiersmen and that of the natives which menaced the whole mode of life of the latter. For some time discontent had been smoldering among the Indians because of the sharp practices engaged in by the English traders. This ill feeling became more intense at the end of the French and Indian War when the British government began to withhold the presents which it had been giving to them. The redskins were also deceived by the French traders into believing that a large French force would assist them in their fight against the English.

The outbreak began in May, 1763, by a surprise attack on the western forts. The English were taken unawares and soon all but two of their forts (Detroit and Pitt) were in Indian hands. But the odds against the natives were too great for lasting success, and in the following year Pontiac was defeated and the uprising came to an end.

Treaties with the Indians

In 1768 the imperial agents negotiated two treaties with the Indians, one with the Iroquois at Fort Stanwix and the other with the Cherokees at Hard Labor. By these treaties the English received a narrow strip of land in New York and an immense area including southwestern Pennsylvania, most of West Virginia, and the region between the Ohio and Tennessee Rivers. The validity of the title received by the English to these lands was not above question, as some of it was claimed by tribes that were not signatory to the treaties; but the British authorities proceeded on the assumption that their rights were unassailable.

Vandalia

The purchase of these lands by the British agents opened up a large area in the west for settlement despite the barrier previously erected by the Proclamation Line of 1763. To take advantage of this opportunity a group of American and British capitalists organized a syndicate and petitioned the crown for a large land grant on which a new colony, to be known as Vandalia, was to be established. In the membership of this company were included such prominent Americans as Benjamin Franklin and Sir William Johnson (the imperial agent who had negotiated the Treaty of Fort Stanwix) and also some English politicians of influence. The petitioners were thus able to bring strong pressure to bear upon the English authorities, who yielded to their request for a patent granting them nearly all the land of present West Virginia and eastern Kentucky. This patent had gone through all the necessary legal stages except that of receiving the king's signature, when the outbreak of the Revolution put an end to the scheme.

Settlements on the upper Ohio

The collapse of the Vandalia project did not delay the occupation of the trans-Allegheny region. Soon after the French and Indian War and the war with Pontiac were over, the frontier again began to move across the mountains. Between 1766 and 1774 a number of

permanent settlements were made on the upper Ohio and its tributaries. Of these settlements the most promising were the villages of
Wheeling and Pittsburgh.

During the decade preceding the outbreak of the Revolution, *The Watauga*
other settlements were made in the trans-Appalachian region. In *settlements*
1769 a colony was established on the Watauga River in the present
state of Tennessee by frontiersmen who had come down from southwest Virginia. Two years later the infant colony was strengthened by
the arrival of seventeen additional families that had been led across
the mountains from western North Carolina by James Robertson.
Next year John Sevier, the son of a Huguenot immigrant, came from
Virginia to join his fortunes with those of the new colony. Both he
and Robertson were men of exceptional ability and well suited to
pioneer life. The community, therefore, was fortunate in having a
capable leadership.

Watauga was within the limits of North Carolina but was separated from the older section of the province by nearly one hundred
miles of wilderness. The arm of the North Carolina government did
not reach so far, and these pioneers had to look to themselves for the
preservation of law and order. Acting under the guidance of Sevier
and Robertson, the different settlements in the Watauga region
united in organizing a government for the community. A mass
meeting was held and a written constitution was adopted which
provided for a representative assembly to make laws and a board of
commissioners to interpret and administer them. This miniature
commonwealth carried on as an independent republic until 1778,
when it was incorporated into North Carolina as a part of the newly
created county of Washington.

Just on the verge of the Revolution another conflict broke out on *Lord*
the western frontier, this time in the upper and middle Ohio Valley. *Dunmore's*
The Shawnees had been nursing a grudge against the whites since *War*
Pontiac's defeat, and this feeling was stirred into active hostility
when they saw their hunting grounds south and east of the Ohio
rapidly giving way to the cleared spaces of the white farmer. In 1774
the Shawnees led an uprising in northwestern Virginia in which they
were aided by other tribes of that region.

Lord Dunmore, the Governor of Virginia, organized two expedi- *Battle of*
tions to be sent against the troublemakers, one to be led by himself *Point*
and the other by General Andrew Lewis. With an army composed *Pleasant*
of untrained but straight-shooting backwoodsmen, Lewis had
marched across the wilderness and reached the mouth of the Ka-
nawha River at the present site of Point Pleasant. Dunmore in the
meantime had advanced into the Ohio country to Pickaway Plains,

near the Indian town of Chillicothe. Lewis was on the point of breaking camp to join Dunmore when he discovered that he was confronted by Cornstalk, the Shawnee leader, who had crossed the Ohio with a strong force to attack him. The battle was joined at once (October, 1774), and after a bloody struggle in which both sides suffered heavy losses the Indians retired and the Virginians claimed a victory. Cornstalk now signed a treaty of peace by which the Shawnees surrendered their claim to the land south and east of the Ohio River.

DANIEL BOONE.

The founding of Kentucky

By this treaty Kentucky was opened up to settlement by the whites. This region offered fine opportunities to hunters, as herds of elk and buffalo were attracted to its salt licks. Its fertile bluegrass lands were also very inviting to farmers. These advantages had been made known to the settlers on the frontier by hunters who had journeyed into the "dark and bloody ground" (the meaning of the Indian word, *Kentucky*), and a settlement was made in 1774 at Harrodsburg by James Harrod of Pennsylvania. In this same year Judge Richard Henderson, of North Carolina, and some other land speculators formed a partnership, known as the Transylvania Company, for the purpose of promoting a colony in Kentucky. They hoped to establish a new province over which they would exercise the authority of proprietors. They bought from the Cherokee Indians all the land between the Kentucky and Cumberland Rivers and sent forward Daniel Boone with a squad of thirty men to make a trail from *Daniel Boone* the Holston River to the Kentucky River. The trail thus broken later developed into an important highway, known as the Wilderness Road.

On reaching the end of his journey, Boone proceeded to lay the *Transylvania* foundations of the village of Boonesborough on the Kentucky River (1775). Other settlements were soon made in the vicinity, and at once there was felt the need of some sort of political organization.

A VIEW OF THE FRONTIER CABIN.
From Woestemeyer & Gambrill's "The Westward Movement,"
D. Appleton-Century Company, Inc.

In response to this need Henderson took the lead in organizing a government for the new province, which was called Transylvania. A convention composed of delegates from four settlements met under a large elm tree at Boonesborough and devised a scheme of government for the little colony (May, 1775).

But the new commonwealth was not able to stand alone in this faraway wilderness. The Revolutionary War had begun, and Transylvania was in grave danger from attack by the Indians, who had been incited against the Kentuckians by Henry Hamilton, the British governor at Detroit. It was therefore necessary for Transylvania to link up with some outside jurisdiction which could afford adequate protection to the wilderness republic. The proprietors sent a delegate to the Continental Congress with the request that Transylvania be recognized by that body as one of the United Colonies. The people of Harrodsburg, on the other hand, sent a petition to the Virginia assembly asking that the mother state take the Kentucky colony under her wing. The request of the proprietors was denied by Congress, while that of the Harrodsburg settlers was granted by the legislature of the Old Dominion. The result was that Transylvania became a part of the new county of Kentucky and ceased to exist as an independent commonwealth (December, 1776).

CHAPTER IX

Economic Development in the Colonies

POPULATION AND LABOR

*I*N 1760 the total population of the thirteen colonies was slightly *Diversity in* above a million and a half. The majority of the colonials were of *population* English origin, though other stocks were also largely represented. There were Dutch in New York, Swedes in Delaware, and Germans and Scotch-Irish in the West. The non-English groups also included Welshmen, Scotchmen, Irishmen, and a considerable number of French Huguenots. As a rule the people of foreign descent were in accord with English political ideals, and many of them had adopted the English language. It has been estimated that at the end of the colonial period the English language was in daily use among four fifths of the entire population.

The first Jews to come to continental North America were those *Jews* who landed at New Amsterdam (New York) about the middle of the seventeenth century. Other Jewish immigrants came to this town later, and it became the chief center of the Jewish element. The Jews were also attracted to other cities and towns, notably Newport, Philadelphia, and Charleston. By the end of the colonial era many of them had become prosperous. When the Revolutionary War broke out, most of the Jews gave loyal support to the patriot cause.

Of the groups of foreigners who settled in the colonies one of the *French* most important was that of the Huguenots, or French Protestants. *Huguenots* They began to come over in large numbers in the latter part of the seventeenth century, having left France on account of the severe persecutions which had been inflicted upon them by their king, Louis XIV. The Huguenots were very desirable colonists, since a large proportion of them were skilled workmen, professional men, or prosperous merchants. While these choice immigrants were distributed among a number of the colonies, South Carolina received more than did any of the others. The Huguenots, with characteristic French adaptability, adjusted themselves easily to their new environment, and so were everywhere gladly welcomed as settlers.

There was a great demand for labor in all the colonies. Lands had to be cleared and cultivated, roads and bridges made, and barns and dwelling houses built. Moreover, there was a constant drain on the supply of labor because many workers soon left the ranks of the employees to join those of the employers. Land was cheap and any energetic hired man could, in a few years, earn and set aside enough money to begin farming for himself on land either rented or purchased on credit. Or if he wanted to become an independent artisan, it did not take long for him to acquire the necessary means for equipping a shop.

Labor was also more productive in America than in Europe; for in industry it was applied to easily obtained raw materials, and in farming, often to virgin soil. Owing to the restrictions usually imposed on the suffrage, the laboring class exerted little or no influence on the government, and so the laws were as a rule framed by and for the employers. Efforts were therefore made from time to time in some of the colonies to put a ceiling above wages. But these enactments usually had to give way to the stronger law of supply and demand, and so wages were generally higher in the colonies than in the homeland.

Among the small farmers, who everywhere were more numerous than the big planters, most, and often all, of the labor of cultivating the land was performed by members of the family. The father and his sons were frequently assisted in the farm work by a hired man or so, and in emergencies the wife and daughters would lend a helping hand in the fields. Generally, however, the latter were busy with household duties, which included spinning and weaving. The children, except the very youngest, were also assigned to light tasks and so became breadwinners at an early age.

The neighbors would be called in to help when houses had to be raised, logs rolled together for burning, the corn crop "shucked," or other tasks performed which required the co-operative efforts of several families. At these working bees, work and social diversion were combined in most pleasant fashion. At the noon hour the men, with appetites sharpened by the exertions of the long forenoon, would eagerly partake of the palatable food which had been prepared for them in such abundance by the hostess with the assistance of other housewives in the neighborhood. During the midday meal and the rest period following it, there was offered a fine opportunity for conversation as to crop prospects and for an interchange of opinions on topics of general and local interest. These working parties were thus a means of relieving the tedium of farm routine and keeping alive the spirit of co-operation.

The demand for labor was met in part by white servitude. In

all the colonies white men and women were bound out for service for a number of years. Persons under such bonds were known as indentured servants. There were two classes of indentured servants, voluntary and involuntary. The former were those who came to America of their own accord and agreed to work for a master for a certain length of time to pay their transportation charges. The latter consisted of paupers, criminals, and kidnapped persons who were sent over by the British authorities and sentenced to a period of labor in the colonies. In the case of criminals this service in America took the place of more serious punishments in England. *White servitude: Voluntary and involuntary servants*

The term of service required of convicts was usually from seven to fourteen years, while that of the voluntary servants was generally not so long. The bondsmen were deprived of many rights enjoyed by white freemen. They were subject to corporal punishment, and could not marry without the consent of their masters. A runaway was punished by a lengthening of his term by double the time lost while away. There was also an additional extension of his term to discharge jail fees, sheriff fees, and other expenses incurred in recovering him. The master was required to give his servants proper maintenance, medical attention, and opportunities for religious instruction. *Treatment of servants*

After serving his term, the indentured servant became a freeman with all the rights of other freemen. In some colonies he received a grant of fifty acres of land from the public domain, and in the others he could buy land at a low price. An energetic and thrifty ex-servant could therefore in a few years acquire a small farm and thus be admitted into the ranks of the yeomanry. Since the freed servants were thus absorbed into the community, they never constituted a separate class as they did in ancient Rome. Most of them became hired laborers, overseers, renters, and owners of small farms, but a few finally ascended to the high rank of the aristocracy. *Status of freed white servants*

The convicts sent to America were usually undesirable immigrants and from them the pauper and criminal classes in the colonies were largely recruited. Often, too, women convicts were unchaste and their behavior tended to lower the standard of morality among the freemen. *Evils of white servitude*

There were, however, some decided advantages of white servitude to offset the evils of the system. It made possible the immigration to America of many desirable settlers who otherwise could not have found the means of transportation; it met in part the demand for both skilled and unskilled labor; it increased the number of small farmers and so brought numerous recruits to the yeomanry; it relieved England of a portion of her socially unde- *Advantages of white servitude* sirable class and helped to solve her problem of unemployment; and it gave many worthy but unfortunate people of the old world the opportunity of a second chance in the new.

Slavery: Origin of Negro Slavery in the colonies

American slavery had its origin in the Spanish West Indies. After having taken root in these islands, it was easily transplanted to the English continental colonies. In 1619 the captain of a Dutch vessel stopped at Jamestown and sold twenty Negroes to the planters. For several decades thereafter blacks were brought to Virginia in small lots and later in greater number. Negroes were also sold in the other colonies and in time were distributed throughout the entire English American possessions. Scholars now maintain that the first Negroes brought to Jamestown did not become slaves but indentured servants. It was not many years, however, before black servitude had developed into slavery. Negro slavery had obtained legal recognition in Virginia by 1661 and at earlier dates in some of the other colonies.

More slaves in the South than in the North

While there were slaves in all the colonies, the number in the South was greater than in any other section. In New England the small-scale diversified farming did not lend itself to the profitable employment of a large number of slaves. In the South, on the other hand, both climatic conditions and the agricultural system were favorable to slavery. Here much of the farming was on a large scale, devoted to the raising of the great staples, tobacco, rice, and indigo. The Negro was well adapted to the cultivation of these crops. Rice was grown in hot, swampy areas, where mosquitoes were numerous and malaria widely prevalent. In these places the white laborer was an easier victim of disease and excessive heat than the Negro, whose long residence in tropical Africa had inured him to the heat and given him a partial immunity from malaria.

Attitude of the colonials toward slavery and the slave trade

There was little or no effective opposition to slavery on moral grounds during the entire colonial era, except that made by the Friends. In the beginning most of the leaders of this group raised no objection to it, but in a few years the Quaker conscience began to be troubled at human bondage. There was a gradual development of this feeling and, by the end of the colonial period, the Friends were definitely committed as a denomination to the principle of abolition. In several of the colonies, however, attempts were made to restrict the further importation of slaves. These efforts were especially persistent in Virginia and South Carolina, where the proportion of blacks to whites was greatest. Acts were passed by the provincial assemblies providing for a tax on imported slaves, and other measures to discourage the traffic. This policy was prompted by the fear that the security of the whites would be menaced by the presence of too large a number of blacks. These acts were all disallowed, either by the king or by the royal governors acting under instructions from the Privy Council.

As a labor system, slavery offered both advantages and disadvantages. It gave to the master a cheap and constant supply of labor, one which would enable him to make his plans for years ahead. There was, however, the drawback of inelasticity, for the owner could not adjust his labor supply to the demand for his output. It opened up for rice culture large areas in the South which, it is thought, could not have been exploited by white labor. It relieved the families of the well-to-do of the drudgery of routine tasks and afforded them leisure for intellectual and artistic pursuits. To this escape from drudgery the South was indebted for the charming social life of the big plantation. This leisure was in some instances wasted in frivolous amusement and even in dissipation, but in many cases it was devoted to statecraft and other public affairs. Slavery disciplined the Negro into habits of self-control and diligence, gave him a rudimentary skill in agriculture and primitive industry, and taught him Christianity and inspired him with the glowing hopes of that religion. *Advantages and disadvantages of slavery*

On the other hand, the evils inherent in slavery cropped out in the colonial period. The power of the master over his slave was not adequately restrained by legal responsibility. There was therefore always the possibility of the slave's becoming the victim of mistreatment. While many, and probably most, masters were kind to their servants, there were always some who would abuse their power. Furthermore, the desire to "keep the Negro in his place" and the necessity of guarding against insurrection and other trouble led to restrictions on what would otherwise have been the normal activities of the slaves. Slavery also tended to cultivate in the Negro the trait of servility rather than the virtue of self-respect. The right of the master (though probably seldom used) to separate husband and wife, and parents and children, was not promotive of morality and of the integrity of the home among the Negroes. As the activities of the Negro were closely supervised by the whites, the race was kept too long in leading strings and thus was not given proper opportunity for the development of individuality. But what in present-day opinion was the greatest of all the evils of slavery— the wrong of any person holding a fellow human being in bondage —did not, as we have seen, figure prominently as an objection to the institution except among a few who had enjoyed exceptional spiritual illumination.

TRANSPORTATION AND TRADE

Water trans-portation
During the seventeenth century nearly all the colonials lived on or near navigable streams, and transportation was mainly by water. Even during the eighteenth century the waterways continued to be the main channels of commercial intercourse for the older settlements. Boats, large and small, were used by the families living on the rivers, very much as are automobiles and busses on the highways of today. Owing to this reliance on water transportation, the need of good roads was not deeply felt and their development was not greatly encouraged in the colonial period.

Roads; methods of travel
Considerable use, however, was made of roads from the beginning to the end of the colonial era. None of these roads were hard-surfaced and very few were well constructed. Clouds of dust in the summer and fall, and deep mud in the winter and spring, made transportation and travel uncomfortable and at times impossible. In the seventeenth century the most common mode of travel on the roads was on foot or on horseback. Women sometimes rode on side-saddles, but often they were seated on cushions behind their husbands or near relatives. In the eighteenth century sleighs were much in use for winter travel in the Northern and Middle colonies. By the beginning of the middle third of the eighteenth century the stagecoach had come in as a means of public conveyance, and carriages were in wide use by the wealthy class. On the big plantations in Virginia these carriages were sometimes drawn by six horses and each carriage was attended by a black coachman, postilion, and footman.

At the outbreak of the Revolution all the leading towns and cities had been linked together by roads and there was a chain of highways extending from Boston to Savannah. Roads had also been built connecting the western with the eastern settlements; the most noted of these were the military roads to Pittsburgh, constructed during the French and Indian War by Generals Braddock and Forbes.

Taverns
In all the colonies there were located on the highways at the villages and the county-seat hamlets numerous taverns, which offered food and shelter to the traveler and his horse. At these public houses drinks were also served and often there were bowling alleys and pool tables for amusement and for gambling. In the lobby, heated in winter by a roaring fire, the village loafers would congregate for conversation and to hear the news brought in from the outside world by the transient guests. The taverns were also some-

times used for public meetings and social gatherings, such as balls and concerts.

The colonial postal system went through three stages of develop- *The postal* ment. During the first period, extending from the beginning to *system in* 1691, there was no general plan for distributing mail throughout *colonial days* the colonies. Letters were sent by private messengers and Indians were sometimes employed for this purpose. In Virginia public documents were transmitted from one plantation to another until they reached their final destination. In Massachusetts and Connecticut this service was performed by official riders, and in Pennsylvania, by constables, sheriffs, and justices of the peace. Massachusetts (1677) and Pennsylvania (1683) adopted plans for carrying and distributing private mail within their respective jurisdictions.

The second period (1691-1707) was one during which the American post office was under proprietary management. Thomas Neale was made postmaster general of all the British plantations in the new world and was granted a monopoly for twenty-one years of the right to distribute mail in the American possessions. He was to assume all financial risks involved in running the business and receive all the profits derived from it. A deputy postmaster general was selected by him, and with the co-operation of the assemblies, a postal system was established for all the colonies from New Hampshire to Pennsylvania. As there were no profits but a constant loss from the venture, Neale was glad to surrender his monopoly (1707) before the term of his patent had expired.

A few years later the British government provided for a unified postal system for the whole empire (effective 1711). The postmaster of London became imperial postmaster general with two deputies to look after the plantations. The deputy postmaster general residing in New York had general supervision of the distribution of mail in the American continental possessions. In 1753 Benjamin Franklin became one of the deputy postmasters general for America, and made some important improvements in the service. By having night as well as day shifts for the riders he reduced, by one half, the time required for carrying letters from Boston to Philadelphia. Under his wise management the income from the business was in excess of the cost of administration.

Fur trading was an important business throughout the entire *Fur trading* colonial period, and during the seventeenth century constituted the only commerce of any importance between the interior and the older settlements in the East. Some of the furs were obtained directly by the white hunters and trappers, but the greater amount was bought from the Indians. The skins of a number of animals were procured, but beaver was the most valuable of them all. As has already been seen (see p. 68), New York early became the leading center of the beaver trade. The Hudson and Mohawk Rivers afforded a waterway to the heart of the Iroquois country, where furs in large amounts could be obtained. The Iroquois sold to the colonial traders, not only the furs collected by their own hunters and trappers, but also many which had been brought in by the Indians living farther to the west. By the beginning of the eighteenth century the number of fur-bearing animals in the colonies north of Pennsylvania had become relatively scarce and so the trade in beaver was declining.

In the lower South beaver hides were not of so good a quality as they were in the North, and so the beaver trade was never as important in the former section as in the latter. In the Carolinas, however, in both the seventeenth and the eighteenth centuries, an extensive trade was carried on in deerskins. Trains of pack mules, sometimes as many as eighty in number, would bring the hides from the interior to the seacoast towns and carry back trinkets and goods for the purchase of skins.

Significance of the fur trade

Furs furnished the colonials with a valuable export. There was always a great demand for them in Europe and they could be easily transported abroad, for the cargo space required was small in proportion to value. Fur trading also aided in the exploration and occupation of the interior. As the clearing out of the lands in the East gradually forced the fur-bearing animals into the forests of the West, the traders had to go farther and farther into unexplored regions in search of furs. In this way a knowledge of the wilderness was acquired which proved valuable to the settlers who came after the hunters and traders. Furthermore, many of the trading posts afterwards became centers of permanent settlement. Finally, fur trading was a factor in causing the friction which led to the conflict between the French and the English (see p. 109, note).

Foreign commerce

The trade of the colonies with foreign countries gradually grew in importance until by the end of the era it constituted a substantial part of the commerce of the British empire. Most of this trade was carried on with England, although it also extended to other European countries and to Africa. At the beginning of the eighteenth century the balance of trade between England and the continental colonies was slightly in favor of the former, and by the end of the colonial period the value of the goods brought into the continental possessions from England was considerably above that of the products exported from them to England. The chief imports from England to America were woolen and linen goods and other manufactures. The most valuable of all the exports from America to England was tobacco. Other important exports to Britain in the eighteenth century were rice, indigo, and naval stores.

Trade between the continental colonies and the West Indies *The West* was also of real consequence. This commerce was at first confined *Indian trade* to an interchange of commodities between the mainland possessions and the British islands, but it soon widened out to include the French, Dutch, and Spanish West Indies. While all the plantations on the mainland had a share in this trade, the greater part of it went to the Northern and Middle colonies. From these two sections were shipped fish, grain, lumber, and other articles in exchange for Spanish coins, bills of exchange, slaves, and such commodities as sugar, molasses, rum, ginger, and other tropical products. It was on this outlet that the New England and Middle colonies were mainly dependent for the disposal of their surplus grain, fish, and other food products, for these commodities were excluded from the British markets by the high import duties which Parliament had imposed on foodstuffs.

The thriving rum industry of New England was dependent upon *The "trian-* the West Indian trade for the molasses from which rum was made. *gular trade"* This industry, the slave trade, and the commerce with the sugar islands were linked together to form what was known as the "triangular trade." The rum manufactured in New England was taken to the west coast of Africa and there exchanged for Negro slaves; these slaves were shipped to the West Indies and sold for molasses and other commodities; and the molasses was carried to New England to be manufactured into rum.

There was considerable coastwise trade between the Northern *Coastwise* and Southern colonies. This consisted in an interchange of goods *trade* between the two sections and the distribution of imports from abroad. There were only a few towns on the American coast to which goods from Europe were brought directly and from which colonial products were taken overseas. Smaller vessels would sail along the coast distributing foreign goods landed at these centers and bringing to them home products for export. Most of this trade, as well as the commerce between the colonies and the West Indies, Africa, Spain, and Portugal, was carried in American ships, while the greater part of that between the possessions and England was conveyed in English bottoms.

During the first three quarters of the eighteenth century foreign commerce was beset with many dangers. For a good portion of this time war was going on between England and France and their American dependencies. In this troublous period piracy and priva-

THE WEST INDIES AFTER 1763

teering flourished, as the naval powers were too busy fighting each other to police the seas. Merchant vessels, therefore, ran the almost constant risk of seizure either by enemy warships or by pirates and privateers. Despite these drawbacks, however, commerce grew in importance and shipowners prospered. With no cables or radios to assist them, warships had difficulty in locating merchant vessels which were on the alert.

Scarcity of metallic money

There was always a scarcity of metallic money in the colonies and the inconvenience caused by this shortage of specie was not remedied by the use of credit instruments, for there were no banks on which checks could be issued. This lack of gold and silver coin was due mainly to the following causes: (1) The value of the products sent from the Northern colonies to England was considerably less than the value of the manufactured goods brought in from the homeland, and this difference had to be met with gold and silver. There was thus a constant drain on the meager supply of metallic money in America. (2) A great many of the colonials were in debt to English capitalists for money which had been borrowed for the purpose of erecting dwelling houses, barns, and other buildings and equipping farms with tools and livestock. Payments on interest and principal of this indebtedness contributed heavily to the continuous stream of specie which was flowing from America to Europe. (3) The cheap paper money, to which all the colonies in time resorted, tended to run out of circulation the more valuable metallic money.

The Spanish dollar

There was little or no English money in use in the continental possessions. About the only money in actual circulation consisted of Spanish, French, and other foreign coins, brought in by foreign commerce. Some of these coins were of gold, but most of them were of silver. The monetary unit in all the colonies was the Spanish silver "piece of eight" (eight reals), which after 1728 was coined as a milled dollar. The Spanish dollar was thus the ancestor of the American dollar. When Congress adopted (1786) the dollar as the monetary standard of this country it was only giving legal recognition to a practice which was deeply rooted in colonial experience. For small change the colonials used the Spanish fractional currency, which ranged in value from one fourth of a real to four reals (the half-dollar). As the English monetary terminology was used in financial transactions, foreign coins had to be evaluated in pounds, shillings, and pence. A good deal of confusion was caused by the practice of using the money of one country and the monetary nomenclature of another, for there was no uniform system in adapting the foreign currency to English values. For example, the proper rating of the "piece of eight" was four and a half shillings, but the actual value accorded it in the various colonies ranged from four shillings eight pence to eight shillings.

Substitutes for metallic money

The scarcity of specie led to a resort to various substitutes for metallic money. In the early years wampum was so used in the Northern colonies,[1] since the Indians would receive it in exchange for furs. Farm products, such as wheat, tobacco, rice, and other grain were also used in the various colonies to take the place of money. This system of regulated barter was not only inconvenient but also brought about a very unsteady medium of exchange, since the prices of these commodities were subject to serious fluctuations. In Virginia (after 1724) planters could store their tobacco in the public warehouses and obtain certificates entitling the holders to the

---

[1] Wampum was made by stringing shell beads of cylindrical shape on strands of hemp or the tendons of animals, or by working them into a kind of embroidery on strips of deerskins.

quantity and quality of tobacco specified in the receipts. These certificates, which were known as "crop notes," circulated in the community and thus served as a sort of redeemable paper money. In Pennsylvania a similar plan was used with reference to wheat.

Paper money   Farm products did not prove satisfactory as a medium of exchange and the colonies turned to paper as a solution of their financial problems. The first paper money was issued by Massachusetts in 1690 to meet the extraordinary expenses incurred by an abortive military campaign against Quebec. The other colonies followed the example of the Bay Colony, and in time all of them were making an extensive use of paper money. If these bills of credit had been restricted in amount and adequate provision had been made for their redemption, they might have been kept at or near par, and in this way the monetary needs of the people might have been partially met. This was not done, however, and everywhere the paper money depreciated.

As a rule, the business interests and the creditor class advocated such a regulation of paper money as would prevent its depreciation. But many, probably a majority, of the common people were in debt and wanted a cheap money. The pressure they were able to bring upon the popular branches of the assemblies prevented the adoption of such restraints on the issue of bills of credit as the wealthier class desired. In New England the latter group appealed to Parliament and secured the enactment of a measure (1751) which restricted the use of paper money in that section. Later (1764) by an act of Parliament the further issuance of paper money was prohibited in all the American possessions.[1] The controversies over paper money, and the interference of Parliament with it, aggravated the ill feeling between the common people (the debtor class) and the wealthy merchants (the creditor class) and increased the opposition of the former group to Parliamentary rule.

*"Pine-tree   Except for imposing these restraints on the use of paper money,
shillings"*   the British authorities did nothing to solve the monetary problems of the colonials. The only effort to increase the supply of metallic money in the colonies was the operation of a mint in Boston from 1652 to 1684. At this mint "pine-tree shillings" (so called because the picture of a pine tree was stamped on them) and smaller coins were turned out. The "pine-tree shillings," although their value was lower than that of the English shillings, were, like other metallic money, drained away in the channels of foreign commerce.

---

[1] For an excellent brief discussion of the currency controversies see C. P. Nettels, *The Roots of American Civilization*, 530-537. A fuller account can be found in *The Money Supply of the American Colonies* by the same author.

INDUSTRY

Industry in the colonies was mainly of a primitive character. *Primitive character of colonial industry* Neither the supply of capital and skilled labor nor the currency and transportation systems were adequate for the large-scale production of advanced, or secondary, manufactures. On the other hand, the abundance of raw materials was favorable to primary manufactures, which changed the original form of these materials but little. Furthermore, laws were passed by the British Parliament which tended to encourage the latter and discourage the former type of manufactures (see p. 178 and note).

Manufacturing received greater attention in the Northern and Middle colonies than it did in the Southland. In the North there were no great agricultural staples for export as there were in the South and so the necessity of supplementing farming with other occupations was greater. Furthermore, the laborers in the former section were more skilled than the slaves of the South and were therefore better adapted to manufacturing.

Colonial industry consisted largely in the spinning and weaving *Household industries* of flax, hemp, coarse wool, or cotton into cloth, the tanning of hides, and the making of farm tools, furniture, shoes, and other similar articles. As these activities were carried on in connection with farming and many of them in the home, they are known as the household industries. These side-line occupations were pursued in all sections of English America. In the South this type of work was done on the big plantations by the slaves and on the small farms by the members of the family. To these extra tasks the yeoman farmer, both in the North and the South, often devoted his energies on rainy days and at other odd times.

Clothmaking was the most important of all the household industries. In every community there were several looms and in nearly every home there was a spinning wheel. Among the yeomanry it was the custom for the women to do all the spinning and much of the weaving, though they were often assisted in the latter task by the men. In the seventeenth century nearly all the cloth made in the home was used by the families producing it; but during the eighteenth century the output of the spinning wheel and loom was in many households sufficient not only to supply their own wants but also to furnish a surplus for sale in the community or even for export to other colonies. Besides, in many communities in the Northern and Middle colonies small factories had grown up to house the industry. The textiles produced in the colonies were of a coarse grade, and the finer fabrics were all brought over from England.

In all the colonies many of the small farmers made or repaired the shoes of their own families, and on the large plantations some of the slaves devoted all their time to this trade. In every community, however, there were shoemakers who made shoes on advance orders for their neighbors. They generally worked without help; but by the middle of the eighteenth century it had become the practice in some places for the shoemaker to employ a few journeymen and apprentices. Although some shoes were exported from Massachusetts from the middle of the seventeenth century on, the manufacture of shoes for export was exceptional in the colonies.

Lumbering

The most important of all the colonial manufactures was lumber. There was a great demand everywhere for timber for housebuilding and the making of furniture and farm tools. In the beginning each settler usually obtained this supply from his own woods or those of a neighbor. He would hew some timbers into shape for the framework of a building and split others into boards for the roof. It was not long, however, before practically every settlement was supplied with a sawmill, which was often operated in connection with a gristmill. These sawmills not only aided greatly in the preparation of lumber for local needs but also led to its successful production for commercial purposes. In due time, therefore, lumber became a valuable export. A large amount of sawn lumber was exported to the West Indies, much of it in the form of staves, hoops, and heads for barrels.

Naval stores

Another industry based on the forests was the production of naval stores—pitch, tar, rosin, and turpentine. These commodities were made from the white pine of the North and the yellow pine of the South. Naval stores were produced mainly in those localities which were at a distance from navigable streams or water power. These products were much in demand in England because they were necessary for the building and repairing of the vessels of the English navy and merchant marine. To encourage the production of these much-needed articles the British Parliament passed a law (1705) offering a liberal bounty on tar, pitch, rosin, and turpentine, sent over from America, and next year put these products on the enumerated list (see p. 179). By these inducements a considerable stimulus was given to the manufacture of naval stores in the possessions, especially in North Carolina, where pine trees were most numerous.

Shipbuilding

One of the oldest of American industries was shipbuilding. In Massachusetts and New Plymouth this industry was nearly as old as the colonies themselves. New England took the lead in shipbuilding though the Middle colonies, especially Pennsylvania, were close competitors. It was not until about the middle of the eighteenth century that this business had attained importance in Virginia and the Carolinas. By this time it had been discovered that live-oak—found in this region—was the best kind of timber for the construction of ships, and now shipbuilding became important in this section. New England's primacy in this industry was due in part to the fact that there was near the coast an abundance of timber suitable for building ships. The demand for ships for fishing and commerce also stimulated the industry. Shipbuilding in America was likewise promoted by the monopoly of the Anglo-American carrying trade, granted British and American shipping by the navigation laws. Ships could be built at less cost in New than in Old England, and so about one third of the British merchant vessels were built in America.

Conditions were favorable in the colonies for the manufacture of crude iron, as iron ore could be found in all the colonies and wood for making charcoal used in smelting was easy to obtain. A successful attempt at iron manufacture was made in New England about the middle of the seventeenth century (1643), and at the outbreak of the Revolution a line of furnaces and forges extended from New Hampshire to South Carolina. A large part of the output of these ironworks consisted of pig iron and bar iron, much of which was shipped to England to be used as raw materials by the British iron manufacturers. There were also turned out some finished iron products, such as wire, cannon, iron and steel work for carriages, farm implements, pots, and other household utensils. Bar iron was flattened into sheets, some of which were in turn slit into narrow strips. These sheets and strips were hammered into nails, horseshoes, and farm implements in the blacksmith shops which were found on all the farms of any consequence. *The iron industry*

There were numerous other industries which were carried on in connection with farming or as independent businesses. These included milling, the making of furniture, candles, and bricks, and the distillation of liquors from grain and fruits. The manufacture of rum from molasses was an important industry in New England, especially at Newport, Rhode Island. Glass works were also established in some of the colonies, but this industry had made little advance by the end of the colonial period. *Miscellaneous industries*

By the beginning of the eighteenth century the manufacture of beaver hats had become a prosperous industry in the North. Beaver could be obtained more easily in America than in Europe, and so the colonial hatmakers had a considerable advantage over their English competitors. The latter feared that they might be driven out of the European and West Indian markets by their American rivals, and to prevent this, induced Parliament to pass as a measure of protection the Hat Act of 1732 (see p. 178, note).

Fishing

Fishing came second to farming as a colonial occupation. It was carried on in all the colonies to meet local demands, but only in New England was fishing for export an important business. The waters along the New England coast were excellent fishing grounds and the Grand Banks of Newfoundland were the finest in the world. The New Englanders were well supplied with ships and the numerous harbors and inlets which indented the shore line served as convenient bases for the prosecution of this industry. Of the many varieties of fish taken, the most valuable were cod and mackerel, the former being especially important as an export. The harvesting of oysters was a profitable occupation in the Middle colonies, especially Virginia and Maryland.

The catching of whales was an important branch of the fishing business. At first the whalers confined their operations to near-by waters but later ventured into the polar regions. Whales were valuable because from them were obtained ambergris, used in the manufacture of perfume; blubber, from which oil was procured for lubrication and candlemaking; and whalebone, much in demand for manufacturing the stays needed for women's garments.

Fishing played an important part in the economic development of New England. It promoted shipbuilding and commerce and served as a training school for seamen. It provided the people with a much-needed export, which served as the basis of the valuable trade with the West Indies (see p. 131).

Mining

Mining was not a leading occupation in the colonial era. The rich stores of gas and oil, now so highly prized, were not dreamed of, and the deposits of coal, iron, and copper which have made the United States the leading industrial nation of the world were either unknown or slightly worked. The few metals which were obtained came from sources which are not now exploited. Bog ore was obtained from the peat bogs of eastern Massachusetts and the coastal plain region in the Middle and Southern colonies. Rock ore, which was of a better quality than bog ore, was mined in the "uplands from the Connecticut River, in a circle north of New York City, through northern New Jersey and eastern Pennsylvania southward."[1] Lead mines were worked in southeastern Missouri after 1720 and in Pennsylvania and Virginia in the Revolutionary period. At Symesburg, Connecticut, a copper mine was run with intermittent success from about 1707 to 1773, and also one in Hudson County, New Jersey, for a number

---

[1] V. S. Clark. *History of Manufactures in the United States*, I, 76.

of years in the eighteenth century. Small amounts of copper were also mined in several of the other colonies.

AGRICULTURE

Farming was the chief occupation in the English continental possessions during the entire colonial period. In all sections there was an abundance of fertile land which could be profitably exploited without a large outlay of capital. *The importance of agriculture in colonial days*

The settlers were taught by the Indians how to raise the native plants, such as corn, tobacco, squashes, gourds, pumpkins, beans, peas, and sweet potatoes.[1] No time or effort was lost in experimenting with these crops, as the Indians had already learned how and where they could be most profitably cultivated. *Native plants*

A good deal of experimentation was needed, however, in adapting foreign plants to the new conditions of soil and climate. This testing process led in some instances to costly failure, as for example, the efforts to raise cotton, rice, and indigo in New England, and the West Indian fruits, such as lemons, pomegranates, and ginger, in Virginia. By this method of trial and error it was determined what old world plants were suited to the colonies and the regions in which each would thrive. This was the most important contribution made by the colonials to the progress of agriculture. So well did they perform this service that very few important plants were added to their list until after the beginning of the twentieth century. *Experimentation with foreign plants*

The most valuable of all the farm products was maize, or Indian corn. It was raised in all the continental colonies and was everywhere the chief reliance for food. The yield per acre for corn is greater than that of any other grain, and of all the cereals it is the easiest to grind. The time for harvesting it is much longer than that of wheat and so all that was raised could be gathered. The grain, as well as the husks and fodder, served as excellent feed for livestock. Without this food product, it has been said, the infant settlement at Jamestown would have died in the cradle. *Indian corn*

Next to corn in importance came tobacco, though the culture of the latter was not nearly so widespread as that of the former. Tobacco was an important crop in North Carolina and the principal one in Virginia and Maryland, but was not grown elsewhere to any considerable extent. It had high value in proportion to bulk and was therefore easily transported to foreign markets. Most of the large plantations were located on navigable streams, having wharves at *Tobacco*

---

[1] The white, or Irish, potato, which was a native of South America, was carried to Europe and from there was brought to the English continental colonies.

which ocean-going vessels took on cargoes. There was always a demand in Europe for tobacco, though at times the market was so glutted that prices were very low. However, tobacco soon became, and continued throughout the entire colonial period to be, the most valuable of all colonial exports.

Other farm products

Wheat was raised in all sections but with special success in the Middle colonies (New York, New Jersey, Pennsylvania, and Delaware), which were known as the "Bread Colonies." Other grains that had a wide range of cultivation were oats, barley, and buckwheat. Rice and indigo were the great staples of the Carolinas and Georgia. The culture of indigo had been introduced into South Carolina as a result of some experiments carried on in the seventeen-forties by Mrs. Eliza Lucas Pinckney. Its production was stimulated by the bounty paid by the British government. Hemp and flax were also grown throughout the colonies, and cotton in small amounts was cultivated in the Southern and Chesapeake provinces.

Land tenure in the Chesapeake and Southern colonies

In the Chesapeake and Southern colonies (which have been termed the plantation area) numerous large land grants were made to individuals. A good deal of this land was held for speculative purposes and was sold from time to time to actual settlers. A large part of it, however, was held by the grantees and made into great plantations manned with numerous slaves. To be profitable, slave labor had to be supervised by highly paid white overseers. This supervision was less expensive if the overseer had a considerable number of laborers under his management. Besides, the great staples, tobacco, rice, and indigo, could be produced most profitably on a large scale. For these reasons there were many large plantations in the South and the Chesapeake region, though the small farmers even in this area were greatly in the majority. The English law of primogeniture was in effect in this section, and so these large landed estates were often passed on intact from father to son.

Landholding in New England

In New England the usual method of disposing of land was for a group of people to receive from the colonial assembly the grant of a small area, usually from eight to ten square miles, which would serve as the basis of a new town. Near the center of the grant the village would be laid out. Certain lots would be reserved for the church, the minister's house, the school, and the public square, and the remainder of the village lands would be divided up as house lots among the citizens. The arable ground and the hay fields would also be allocated to the citizens; but the forests and pasture lands would be held in common for the joint use of all the people. In this system were combined many of the advantages of both individual and communal ownership.

While these allotments were not made on the basis of equality, in the beginning no single grant was very much above the average in size. Later, however, the energetic and prosperous settlers, by purchase and exchange, enlarged their holdings at the expense of the less provident. Furthermore, in time speculators acquired large tracts of land in New England as they did elsewhere. Despite these trends toward large landholding, there was never a great number of big plantations in New England and the inequalities in land ownership were never as great there as they were in the South. In the Middle colonies farms were, as a rule, larger than they were in New England but smaller than the big estates in the plantation area.

Size of farms in the Middle colonies

The colonial farmer, whether he lived in New England or Georgia, was seldom skilled in farm management. He overworked his horses and did not provide the proper feed or shelter for his livestock.[1] Consequently, in America cattle, hogs, horses, and sheep were generally smaller than they were in the homeland. Horses and cattle were allowed to run at large and so there was nothing to prevent an intermingling of stocks. There was, therefore, no opportunity for segregating and improving the breeds.

Livestock

The implements used on the colonial farm were not much in advance of those employed by the ancient Egyptians. The plow was made of wood, except that the point was of iron and frequently the moldboard was covered with iron strips. Other tools in general use were the spade, the wooden fork, and the harrow, the teeth of which were often made of wood, but sometimes of iron. Grain was cut with a reap hook, or sickle, and was threshed with a flail or by having oxen tread it out, as was done in the time of Moses.

Farm implements

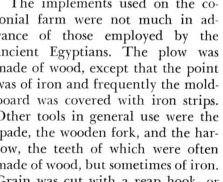

Courtesy of the New-York Historical Society, New York City

FLAX WHEEL.

American, early nineteenth century.

---

[1] The German farmers in Pennsylvania were an exception to this rule, for they properly housed their stock in the big barns which had been built on most of their farms.

*"Earth
butchery"*

As land was easily obtained, the farmer made little or no effort to preserve the fertility of the soil. His failure to do so was due in part to his conservatism—his reluctance to depart from the practices ordained by tradition—but mainly to the belief that it was more profitable to clear new than to improve old land. Therefore, after cultivating a field until its productivity was greatly depleted, he abandoned it and cleared another fresh plot from the forest. In this way he inaugurated the practice of "earth butchery" and put a curse on American agriculture which has not yet been entirely removed.

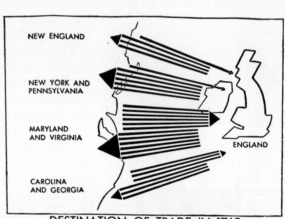

COLONIAL TRADE WITH ENGLAND

DESTINATION OF TRADE IN 1763

VALUE OF VISIBLE EXPORTS TO ENGLAND

NORTH | SOUTH

VALUE OF VISIBLE IMPORTS FROM ENGLAND

NORTH|SOUTH

Each symbol represents £100,000 worth of goods

COLONIAL TRADE WITH ENGLAND.

Pictograph Corporation. "The United States: A Graphic History."

CHAPTER X

Social Life in the Colonies

GOVERNMENT AND LAW

*T*HE political institutions established in the colonies were similar to those of the homeland. The American constitutions were not, however, close imitations of the British constitution, and in some cases the divergences from the British prototype were considerable. It was in Virginia that political life showed the closest correspondence to that of England. So much was this the case that one of her governors once spoke of the Old Dominion as having been created "from a rib taken from Britain's side."[1]

The chief official in each of the colonies was the governor. In the royal provinces he was appointed by the king, in the proprietary provinces he was chosen by the proprietor, and in the self-governing colonies he was elected by the voters. His powers were in many respects like those of his successor of today. In the royal provinces he was commander-in-chief of the army, made certain appointments, and performed other executive functions. He could call, prorogue, and dissolve the assembly; veto acts passed by it; and pardon all criminal offenses except treason and willful murder and grant reprieves even for these high crimes.[2] The place of the governor in the colonies thus corresponded roughly to that of the king in the mother country. *The governor*

The governor always had the assistance of a group of advisers, usually consisting of about a dozen of the most prominent men of the colony. In the self-governing colonies of New England this body was known as the board of assistants; in the other provinces it was called the council, or council of state. In the royal provinces the councillors were appointed by the king, usually on the nomination of the governor. In the proprietary provinces they were generally appointed by the proprietors, and in the self-governing commonwealths they were elected by the voters for a period of one year. In all the colonies the members of the council, or the board of as- *The council*

---

1 *Journal of the (Va.) House of Burgesses, 1712-1726*, 250.
2 In the self-governing republics of New England the governor did not have as much power as he exercised in the royal and most of the proprietary provinces.

sistants, because of their high standing, usually exerted considerable influence in the government.

The assistants and councillors acted as advisers to the governor in administrative affairs, and in some instances the governor was compelled to accept their advice. In addition to performing these executive duties they also constituted the upper house of the legislature and usually the highest court in the colony. The council in America, therefore, corresponded to some slight extent to the Privy Council and the House of Lords in England.

The assembly   By the end of the seventeenth century there was an assembly of two houses in every one of the continental colonies, but at the beginning of the eighteenth century (1701) the Pennsylvania assembly was changed to a body of one house. At the outbreak of the Revolution, every assembly was bicameral except this one. As has just been seen, the upper house consisted of the governor and his council or the governor and the board of assistants. The lower house was made up of representatives chosen by the voters. In organization and procedure the provincial assembly tried to follow the practices of Parliament, and in the view of the colonials the American assembly was a close counterpart of the British Parliament.

Local government:
The county   In Virginia, Maryland, and North Carolina the county was the one important unit of local government, and the county court was the principal agency of administration in the county. In Virginia, where the system was first developed, the county court was made up of a group of justices of the peace, meeting in a body, sometimes monthly and sometimes bimonthly. The justices were appointed by the governor, often if not generally, with the advice and consent of the council, and the selections were usually made from among the leading citizens. The justices could try minor criminal and civil cases, acting singly, and when they came together as a county court could decide more important civil and criminal cases. The county court also looked after administrative affairs and made, or helped to make, bylaws for the county. It ordered the opening of new roads and the making of repairs on old ones; licensed taverns and fixed the prices at which drinks could be sold; issued certificates for land grants; and apportioned the county levy among the taxpayers.

The county system of administration was later extended to all the other colonies, though it did not become effective in South Carolina until near the end of the colonial period. In New England the town was well established as the main unit of local government before counties were formed. In this section, therefore, the county held a place of secondary importance in local affairs. It was employed, however, as a militia unit and as the basis for the organization of a lower court.

The parish was a unit for the organization of the Anglican Church. *The parish* In a sense it was a subdivision of the county, but a parish might include a whole county and, in Virginia, would sometimes overlap two counties. The governing body in the parish was the vestry, usually a group of twelve of the leading men in the community. They looked after church affairs, collected dues for the ministers, repaired the church, and performed other minor administrative duties.

In New England the town or township was the principal unit, *The town* and the town meeting the chief agency in local government. The town meeting consisted of all the adult male citizens assembled in a mass meeting. These meetings were convened once a year for the election of local officials and the town's representatives in the General Court. Other sessions were held from time to time to look after other important affairs such as levying taxes, enacting bylaws, making distributions of land, and adopting regulations for the schools and churches. The details of administration were delegated by the town meeting to the selectmen, a body ranging in number from three to twenty-one or more. The selectmen were, however, responsible to the town meeting and could perform only such duties as had been imposed upon them by that body.

At the end of the colonial period there were in the English colonies *City* only four cities (Boston, New York, Philadelphia, and Charleston) *government* which deserved the name. There were, however, a number of towns which were regarded as cities and had been organized as such. The system of government for these municipalities was not uniform. Every city outside of New England had a mayor, recorder, board of aldermen, and common council. In a few instances the people chose all of these officials; in others, the common council only; and in some, the people had no voice in the selection of their rulers.[1]

The common law was brought by the settlers from England to *The common* America. In the seventeenth century, however, it did not form a very *law in the* important part of the legal system of the colonies. The common law *colonies* had been adapted to an old and well developed society, whereas the plantations in the seventeenth century were all more or less in the pioneer stage. Such a legal system could not, therefore, be easily

---

[1] The government of Williamsburg was typical of the last-named group of cities—those in which the people took no part in the choice of their rulers. In this little city the king chose the first mayor, recorder, and aldermen, who selected twelve councilmen to hold office for life or good behavior. When vacancies occurred they were filled by a vote of these officials.

grafted on to the new society. Furthermore, owing to the prejudice against lawyers, there were in this century very few persons who had had legal training. Most of the judges were not learned in the law, nor were they able to secure the advice of trained practitioners. Consequently, they were frequently ignorant as to the principles of the common law and had to resort to common sense to direct their decisions.

In the eighteenth century, however, development in America had gone so far that conditions in a number of places were similar to those in England at that time. The common law was, therefore, suited to these advanced communities. Then, too, the judges were now better informed as to legal principles and practice than they had been in the previous century. During the latter half of this century, a number of prominent American lawyers were trained in England. For these reasons the common law had a more prominent place in colonial justice in the eighteenth than it had had in the seventeenth century.

Suffrage   There never was at any one time universal manhood suffrage in all the British American possessions. For certain periods in the seventeenth century some of the colonies granted the right to vote to all free adult males; but with these few exceptions there was always a limitation of one sort or another on the voting franchise. Either property or religious qualifications were usually required. Certain religious groups, such as the Catholics, Quakers, Baptists, and Jews were at times deprived of the right to vote. In the eighteenth century the possession of a certain amount of property was the most usual requirement. As a rule, the qualification for the suffrage was higher in this century than in the seventeenth. It could be met in some cases by the ownership of either personal or real property, and in others by that of real estate alone. The suffrage, however, was broader in the colonies than in England because it was easier to acquire the property needed to qualify one to vote in America than in England.

INTELLECTUAL LIFE

The English   The school system in use in the colonies was borrowed from Eng-
school system land, though not without some important modifications. At the beginning of the colonial era there were in the homeland a number of primary and secondary schools, as well as the flourishing universities of Oxford and Cambridge. The government assumed no responsibility for the support of education but exercised the right to license teachers. The object of this restriction was to protect the people from dangerous ideas which might be taught in the schools. From Britain also came the aristocratic notion that education is for the privileged few and not for the masses.

In New England, schools were more numerous than in other sec- *Schools in*
tions. There the settlers lived in villages and towns, whereas in the *colonial*
New England
South, and to some extent the Middle colonies, they were scattered
on isolated plantations or farms. Furthermore, in New England, except Rhode Island, the great majority of the people belonged to one
religious denomination; in other sections there was a greater diversity
of religious beliefs. For these reasons co-operation on the part of any
community for the establishment of schools was easier in the New
England commonwealths than it was in the other colonies.

In 1647 the General Court of Massachusetts passed a law requiring
every town of fifty families to support a primary school for the teaching of reading and writing. Every town having one hundred or more
families was to maintain a Latin grammar school to prepare students
for college. Towns not complying with these requirements were to be
fined. Laws similar to this one were passed in all the New England
colonies except Rhode Island. The law, however, was ahead of its
time and was more of an ideal than an actual practice. While some
schools were established in the various New England communities,
these acts were not generally enforced. Many small towns, especially
those on the frontier, felt that the plan was too expensive for them.
Some of these would rather pay the fines than incur the expense of
providing for schools; while others were overlooked by indulgent
officials.

Schools were divided with reference to their financial support into *How schools*
three different classes. The private school, which had a place in all *were sup-*
ported in the
the colonies, was maintained by tuition fees paid by the pupils. A *colonies*
second type of school was the one in which support was partly by tuition fees and partly by funds derived from taxation or endowments.
Poor children were allowed to attend such schools free of charge,
whereas other pupils were required to pay a tuition fee. Schools of
this class were also scattered throughout all the colonies. A third kind,
less common than the other two, was the free school, which was supported entirely by public funds or benefactions made by churches or
philanthropists. All pupils attending these schools were admitted
free of charge. Public, or free, schools were more numerous in New
England (except Rhode Island) than elsewhere, but there were a few
in some of the other colonies. The number of free schools in the South
was comparatively small, although South Carolina had by the end of
the colonial era made considerable progress in establishing schools
of this type.

In colonial America, as in England, there were primary schools, *Primary*
Latin grammar schools (and later academies), and colleges. In the *schools*
primary schools the subjects usually taught were reading, writing,

and arithmetic, though in some cases the range was much wider. In New England there were numerous dame schools, in which instruction of a very elementary character was given. The dame school was one in which a woman taught the alphabet and sometimes reading and writing to small children. The teacher was frequently the mother or a maiden aunt in the family and seldom had more than a very rudimentary training. In the South the common schools were often located in old fields and were therefore called old field schools. These schools, however, were not concerned exclusively with the primary grades, for in them were sometimes taught, in addition to the elementary branches, more advanced subjects, occasionally including even Latin and Greek.

Tutors

Another agency for education in the South was the tutorial system. It was the custom for big planters to employ tutors for their sons and daughters. An outbuilding would be used as the schoolroom, in which would be taught not only the children of the planter but sometimes those of neighbors and friends and relatives from a distance, who would come to live on the plantation. The tutor, as well as the teacher of the old field school, might be an Anglican minister, a graduate of Oxford or Cambridge, or an indentured servant.

The Latin school

The Latin grammar school was established in all sections during the colonial era. In this school the primary aim was to prepare students for college. Emphasis was therefore placed on the study of Latin, although other branches were also taught. The Latin grammar school, however, was not well adapted to a new country, where Latin

The academy

was not much in use and, in time, it was superseded by the academy. The academy made its appearance at the end of the colonial era but did not reach full importance and become the chief agency of secondary education until after the Revolution.

Textbooks

The textbooks generally used in the seventeenth century were the Hornbook,[1] the A. B. C. manual, the primer, and the *Book of Manners*. During the greater part of this century nearly all of the textbooks were brought over from England. In 1690 the *English Protestant Tutor* was reprinted in New England under the title of the *New England Primer*. This took the place of the Hornbook, the A. B. C. manual, and the ordinary primer. It had a very wide use until after the Revolutionary War, when it was superseded by Webster's *Blue Back Spelling Book*.

The colonists, true to their aristocratic ideas as to education,

---

[1] The Hornbook was a sheet of paper mounted on a flat board which was rounded into a handle at one end. On this paper was printed the alphabet, the Lord's Prayer, some scriptural verses, and sometimes marginal pictures. The paper was covered by transparent horn to protect it against wear.

*Courtesy of the New-York Historical Society,
New York City*

INCREASE MATHER.

Courtesy of Essex Institute, Salem, Mass.

EARLY HARVARD.

*Colonial
colleges:*

Harvard

*William
and Mary*

Yale

made a greater effort to provide for higher education than for the training of the masses on the lower level. Consequently, the college outran the common school in development. The object was to train the few for leadership rather than the many for the ordinary activities of life. The first of the colleges was Harvard, founded in 1636, when an appropriation for it was voted by the General Court of Massachusetts. Two years later a generous bequest was made to the college by John Harvard, and the infant institution was named in his honor. Other endowments were received and the Massachusetts assembly was liberal in its appropriations. Some of the bequests were very small. At one time every family in the colony was asked to contribute at least a peck of corn toward the support of the college. With these aids Harvard enjoyed a steady growth and soon gave promise of becoming a prosperous institution. It was housed "in a fair and comely edifice, having in it a spacious hall and a large library with some books in it." Students were seated in classes and arranged at commons according to social position. Each tutor taught all subjects until 1776, when departmental instruction began.

The second of American colleges, William and Mary, was founded at Middle Plantation (now Williamsburg) under a charter granted in 1693 by the joint sovereigns for whom it was named. It owed its origin mainly to the energetic efforts of Commissary Blair, the encouraging support of Governor Nicholson, and the patronage of the king and queen. An endowment fund, started by private contributions, was increased by the grant of the quitrents which had accumulated in Virginia. Appropriations for the maintenance of the college were also made both by the crown and the Virginia assembly. James Blair, the founder and first president, remained at the head of the institution for fifty years. One of the leading objectives of the college was to train candidates for the Anglican ministry, and in the beginning all the professors were members of the Anglican Church and many of them were clergymen. After a period of struggle William and Mary entered upon a prosperous career, and during the greater part of the eighteenth century served as an important agency for higher education in the Old Dominion. Many of the Virginians who took a prominent part in the Revolution were educated there.

By the end of the seventeenth century the Congregationalists of Connecticut began to feel that they should have a college nearer than the one at Cambridge (Harvard). Furthermore, dissatisfaction had arisen among the conservative church leaders over the liberalism which was growing up at Harvard. If a new college were organized in western New England on an orthodox basis it would be convenient for the people of that region and would be free from the

Courtesy of Huestis Cook

JAMES BLAIR.

COLLEGE OF WILLIAM AND MARY.

From Lyon G. Tyler's "The Cradle of the Republic."

taint of heresy. This feeling led to the founding of a college in Connecticut, which was chartered in 1701 by an act of the legislature of
that colony. Efforts toward establishing the institution, however, had
been made a year earlier, when some Congregationalist ministers
met and gave a small collection of books for the support of a new
college. For a number of years the college had no settled place of
abode but moved around from one place to another. At one time
instruction was carried on at three different places. Finally at the end
of fifteen years it settled down at New Haven (1716). Two years
later it assumed its present name of Yale in appreciation of a substantial bequest from Elihu Yale, a wealthy New Englander who
had been an official of the East India Company.

Other colleges   There were by the end of the colonial period six other colleges.
Of the later institutions of higher learning Princeton was Presbyterian, and Brown, Baptist. The only one of the colonial colleges
not under religious influence was the "Academy," which afterwards
became the University of Pennsylvania. The "Academy," which
opened its doors in 1751, was nondenominational, and paid more
attention to English than did the other colleges. For this nonsec-
tarian character and more liberal attitude as to curriculum, Benjamin
Franklin was mainly responsible.[1]

Life in the   In the college curriculum emphasis was placed on the dead lan-
colonial   guages, Latin, Greek, and Hebrew, and in the eighteenth century
college   elementary French was added to the list. Other subjects taught were:
arithmetic and geometry; history, politics, logic, and ethics; the
Bible; rhetoric, composition, and oratory; and elementary physics,
astronomy, and botany (nature of plants). Students were held up to
a strict discipline by the college authorities, and upper classmen
domineered freshmen as they do today. In the early years, breaches
of the college rules at Harvard were punished by flogging and
after 1734, by fines. Since many of the students were very young,
a certain measure of discipline was badly needed. These restraints,
however, were carried too far, and by them the individuality of the
students was unnecessarily hampered. Intercollegiate athletics were
unknown, and very few other extracurricular activities were engaged in. There were no fraternities, but literary societies took their
place to some extent.

While most families in the colonial era had a few books, home

---

[1] The last of the colonial colleges to be established was Dartmouth. It began as
an Indian school and was originally located at Warren, Connecticut. It was moved to
its present seat (Hanover, New Hampshire) in 1770. The other colleges were: King's
College (now Columbia), chartered 1754, Anglican; Queen's College (now Rutgers),
Dutch Reformed, established in 1766.

libraries of considerable size were very rare. The largest private col- *Libraries* lections of books were those of Cotton Mather in Boston, and of the Byrd family at Westover in Virginia. In the latter library the number of titles in 1788 was estimated at nearly four thousand. One useful endeavor of the Anglican Church was to make good books accessible to the people. In keeping with this purpose, Dr. Thomas Bray, when Commissary of Maryland, established a library in nearly every parish in the province. A number of parochial libraries were likewise founded in Virginia and the Carolinas by the Venerable Society. Some of the towns and cities also had libraries for the use of the general public. The first provincial library for the people was established by South Carolina (1700) and the first public city library, by Philadelphia (1731) through the efforts of Benjamin Franklin. Good use was made of the few well-selected books which were available, and the people were thus nurtured on serious literature. One masterpiece which was widely read was the King James version of the Bible.

There were no law schools in the colonies. Near the end of the *Professional* period two medical schools were established. One was the Medical *schools* College of Philadelphia (founded in 1765), which afterwards became a part of the University of Pennsylvania. The medical department of King's College was organized two years later. Prior to that time the colonial doctor had had very little training. As a rule the young man who expected to practice medicine would serve as an apprentice to an older doctor. He would gather herbs for him and perform other errands while doing some reading on the side. With this inadequate training he would be turned loose on an unsuspecting public which was unmindful of his limited skill and knowledge. Only a few colonial doctors were educated in England.

The first newspaper in English America was *The Boston News* *Newspapers* *Letter,* published by William Campbell, beginning in 1704. Fifteen years later another newspaper appeared, and by the middle of the century there were a number of weekly publications throughout the various colonies. During the quarter-century preceding the Revolution, the newspapers by discussing political questions played an important role in preparing the psychological background for revolt against the mother country.

Very little literature worthy of the name was produced in the *Paucity of lit-* English American possessions before the pre-Revolutionary decade. *erature in the* A number of books were written in this earlier period, some of *colonial era* which are of value as sources of historical information, but most of them are not characterized by the originality of thought or beauty of expression which are the marks of real literature. The lack of good writing in the seventeenth century is explained by the fact that living conditions in that pioneering era were such as to leave little or no time for any activities other than those concerned with making a living. This explanation does not, however, apply to the eighteenth century. As this century advanced and the frontier was gradually pushed farther and farther toward the west, in each of the older plantations there grew up a wealthy class which had considerable leisure to devote to intellectual pursuits. This group was small and its members were as a rule closely associated with the civic and religious life of their respective communities. Their extra-vocational interests, therefore, found expression in political rather than literary activity. Moreover, the frontier, on retiring from the older settlements to push into the western wilderness, had left as a cultural sediment a utilitarian view of life unfavorable to the nurture of the contemplative idealism on which literature is based.

Jonathan Edwards

There was not, however, a complete dearth of letters in the colonial era, since there were two authors whose writings deserve to be classed as real literature. These were Jonathan Edwards and Benjamin Franklin. Edwards was the author of several works, but his fame rests mainly on the treatise, *On the Freedom of the Will*. This is a brilliant presentation of the Calvinistic doctrines as believed in by conservative New England Puritans of his day. It is probably the most masterly exposition of Protestant theology which has appeared since the publication of Calvin's *Institutes*. In closely-knit logic and clarity and forcefulness of expression, this work is a masterpiece and has won for its author the distinction of being America's greatest metaphysician.

Benjamin Franklin

Franklin owes his reputation as a literary man mainly to his *Autobiography* and *Poor Richard's Almanac*. The *Autobiography* was published in the post-Revolutionary period and so does not properly belong to the colonial era. For twenty-six years the *Almanac* came out annually under the name of Richard Saunders. In addition to the calendar and other items usually found in an almanac, these little pamphlets contained a collection of wise sayings, which were expressed in a simple, forceful, and epigrammatic style, not unlike that of the Proverbs of Solomon and the apothegms of Francis Bacon. The philosophy of *Poor Richard's Almanac* was not original with Franklin, but had been handed down by tradition from the past. He did, however, give it a clever phrasing and adapted it to American ideals. These crisp sayings inculcated thrift, industry, and the other virtues which had a high practical value in a new country. They, therefore, made a wide appeal to the people generally and so the *Almanac* was more widely read in colonial days than any other book, with the possible exception of the King James version of the Bible.

The worldly wisdom of Franklin's sayings was in marked contrast to the otherworldly teachings of Jonathan Edwards. Franklin, in language which all could understand, gave advice as to how the good things of this life might be obtained. He was "less concerned with the golden pavements of the city of God than that the cobblestones of Chestnut Street in Philadelphia should be well and evenly laid."[1] Edwards, on the other hand, wrote learnedly on abstruse subjects, and his ideas and the hair-splitting logic employed in presenting them did not appeal to the masses but only to the intellectual aristocracy. For his discussions were concerned not with the piling up of wealth in this world but with the laying up of treasures in Heaven.

Reproduced from THE PAGEANT OF AMERICA,
Copyright Yale University Press

OLD SOUTH MEETINGHOUSE, 1729.

THE COLONIAL CHURCH

State churches

In the colonial period there were three religious denominations which were united with the state and supported by taxation. These were the Anglican, the Congregational, and the Dutch Reformed churches.

The Anglican Church

The Anglicans had the distinction of introducing Christianity into the English colonies. The first church in British America was the one which was established at Jamestown in 1607. The company had sent over as the first chaplain of the emigrants the Rev. Robert Hunt, an Anglican clergyman of excep-

---

[1] V. L. Parrington, *The Colonial Mind,* 178.

tional piety, serenity of temper, and sacrificial spirit. In his efforts to minister to the religious needs of the settlers he earned the right to be considered one of the most saintly of American ministers. There were other Anglican preachers in the early years who, amid the trying experiences of pioneer life on the James River, proved themselves worthy of their high calling.

The later development of the Anglican Church was not in keeping with this promising beginning. By the end of the seventeenth century this denomination had been established in Virginia and Maryland but had not gained any considerable following in the other colonies. Outside of the Chesapeake plantations, what few churches had been established were confined mainly to the four leading cities, Boston, New York, Philadelphia, and Charleston. A turn for the better took place, however, at the beginning of the eighteenth century (1701), when a missionary society was founded in England to promote the Anglican cause in America.

JERUSALEM CHURCH,
Ebenezer, Georgia.
From E. M. Coulter's "History of Georgia."

The Vener-
able Society
This organization was known as the Society for the Propagation of the Gospel in Foreign Parts, or the Venerable Society. At its head was the Archbishop of Canterbury and it numbered among its sponsors King William III and other high dignitaries. It raised funds and sent out missionaries to America, primarily to teach Christianity to the Negroes and Indians and to establish churches in those communities where there was a dearth of opportunities for worship. The missionaries were generally earnest men and carried out their duties faithfully. They did not, however, confine their activities to preaching to the Indians and Negroes, but in some places they aroused the opposition of the dissenters by endeavoring to convert them to Anglicanism. The work of the Venerable Society was successful, in the main, and it proved an important agency in strengthening the Anglican Church in America.

It was the intention of the British government to make the Anglican the established church in all the royal provinces. This purpose, however, was not realized in every case. At the end of the colonial period the Anglican was technically, though not really, the state church in New York and was established by law in Maryland, Virginia, the Carolinas, and Georgia, although the number of churches in Georgia was very small. In all of these five jurisdictions the Anglican Church had the support of the government and was assured of a certain income; but despite this advantage and all the efforts made by the British government and the Venerable Society to promote its growth, in the greater part of these colonies it was not deeply rooted in the life of the common people.

How the Anglican Church was affected by its union with the state

The union with the state proved to be a disadvantage rather than a help. The income from taxation was small and in many cases was paid with reluctance. The obligation to support the established church aroused the antagonism of those taxpayers who were not friendly to the Anglican cause. The state church, it is true, enjoyed a greater social prestige than did the dissenting denominations, owing to the fact that the governor and ruling class were affiliated with it. This social prestige, however, was too often associated with a worldliness which caused a decline in spiritual tone. Then, too, the dependence of the church upon the state for its income rendered the ministers less bold in their championship of righteousness and holiness, and less free in their criticism of injustice and worldliness, for in many cases their salaries, if not tenure of position, were held at the pleasure of an official group whose good will they were tempted to cultivate.

The lack of progress made by the Anglicans in the colonies was due in part to the failure of the church authorities to send a bishop to America. Since no one but a bishop could ordain ministers and confirm applicants for membership in the church, these ceremonies, which were of vital significance to devout Anglicans, could not be performed on this side of the Atlantic. This apparent indifference to the needs of the church was caused to some extent by the opposition to the plan waged by the dissenters in America; for they felt that the Anglican cause would be strengthened and their own relatively weakened by the support which a local bishop would be able to give to the former.

Need of a colonial bishop

The Congregational Church, as has already been seen, was brought to America by the Pilgrims in 1620. From New Plymouth it spread to Massachusetts and then to the other Puritan colonies. It soon became the state church throughout New England, except in Rhode Island, in which commonwealth there was never an established church. At first these churches were financed by the voluntary contributions of their members, but after about the middle of the century (1657) they were supported by taxation. For some time taxes were levied on all the people, whether they were or were not

The Congregational the state church in New England

members of the Congregationalist denomination, but before the end
of the first third of the eighteenth century exemption from taxation
for church purposes was allowed in Massachusetts to Anglicans, Baptists, and Quakers. To enjoy this exemption, however, taxpayers had

Courtesy of Virginia Conservation Commission, Richmond, Va.

BRUTON PARISH CHURCH.

to present certificates of membership in one or the other of these
denominations. Members of these groups were at times apparently
unable to procure such certificates and so were forced to pay taxes
for the support of the establishment. In New England (except
Rhode Island) church and state remained united until beyond the
end of the colonial era.

*The Dutch
Reformed
Church*

The Dutch Reformed was the state church of New Netherland as
long as it was under Dutch rule. The adherents of this denomination
held views similar to those of the Congregationalists, but their attitude toward so-called worldly amusements was more liberal than
that of the Puritans of early New England.

*Other de-
nominations*

The Baptists began to come to New England at an early date. The
first church of this denomination was organized at Providence,

Rhode Island, in 1639, by Roger Williams and one of his associates. It later spread until by the beginning of the great revival (see p. 162) it had churches in all the colonies. It was especially strong in Rhode Island, New Jersey, and Pennsylvania because there was religious freedom in these colonies.

Reproduced from THE PAGEANT OF AMERICA, *Copyright Yale University Press*

JEWISH SYNAGOGUE, Newport, R. I., 1763.

The Quakers came early to Massachusetts, where, as has been shown, they met with very severe persecution. In time, however, they became well established in Rhode Island, New Jersey, Pennsylvania, and North Carolina.

By the middle of the seventeenth century there were some Presbyterians on Long Island. This denomination, however, made little headway until 1683, when Francis Makemie came to America to spread the Presbyterian doctrine. He was earnest in his efforts and conducted missionary tours in all the colonies from New York to South Carolina. As a result of these activities, a number of Presbyterian churches were established, but the denomination did not receive any strong impetus until the Scotch-Irish immigration began in the second decade of the eighteenth century.

The Lutheran and German Reformed Churches were the leading denominations among the Germans. The Swedes of Delaware also belonged to the Lutheran Church. Other sects among the German settlers were the Moravians, Dunkards, and Mennonites.

Religious toleration in the colonies

In the seventeenth century the English American colonies were in advance of the European countries in respect to religious toleration. There were so many varieties of theological opinion among the colonials that a policy of give and take as to religion was the only one by which neighborly relations could be maintained. Besides, emigrants were not willing to brave the hardships of pioneer life unless they could enjoy the right to worship without molestation. The colonies which had the finest record for religious toleration were New Jersey, Pennsylvania, Delaware, and Rhode Island, for in these jurisdictions church and state were never united. After the enactment by Parliament of the Toleration Act of 1689, the right of freedom of worship was granted, theoretically at least, to Protestant dissenters both in England and the American possessions. There was some question, however, as to whether this act applied to the colonies as well as to the homeland, but its principles were re-enacted by a number of the colonial assemblies and in general were accepted throughout the possessions. After 1689, therefore dissenters were legally exempt from persecution.

Religious persecution

Of the Protestant denominations the chief victims of persecution were the Baptists and the Quakers. It has already been shown how they were persecuted in Massachusetts in the seventeenth century. The Quakers were fined, whipped, and imprisoned in other colonies besides Massachusetts, notably in Connecticut, Virginia, and New Netherland. Even in Maryland under the mild policy of Lord Baltimore, the Quakers were expelled from the colony. The Baptists were also fined and whipped in New Netherland. Despite the fact that religious toleration was granted by law to all dissenters soon after the Revolution of 1688, there was some persecution of Baptists in Virginia and Massachusetts as late as 1774. In the Old Dominion a few Baptist ministers were in that year imprisoned because they had been unable to comply with the technicalities of a law requiring the licensing of places of worship. The refusal to obey the Massachusetts law for church taxes had about the same time caused the imprisonment of some Baptists in the Bay Colony.

Restrictions on Catholics

The number of Catholics in the colonies was never large. There were more in Maryland than in any other jurisdiction, but they were not numerous there in the seventeenth century, and in the eighteenth century they were decidedly in the minority. Owing to their wealth and position in the government, however, they exerted an influence much greater than would be expected from their number. Pennsylvania had more Catholics than any of the other English plantations except Maryland, but in this Quaker province they constituted only a small proportion of the entire population. Outside of these two provinces there were no Catholics to speak of in the Thirteen Original Colonies, except a few in New York during the reign of James II, a handful each in New Jersey and northern Virginia, and a straggler here and there at other places.

The Toleration Act of 1689 did not give any relief to the Catholics and they remained under the censure of the laws until the end of the colonial era. They were excluded from New York and New England and were restricted in their rights in other colonies. The severity of the anti-Catholic laws in New York and New England was due to the proximity of this section to Canada. There was a constant fear—though an unfounded one—that if Catholics were allowed in these jurisdictions they would intrigue with the French Catholics in Canada and the Catholic Indians against their Protestant neighbors.

Except for these drastic measures, during the eighteenth century greater restraints on the liberties of Catholics were imposed in Maryland than in the other provinces because they were more numerous there than elsewhere. They were allowed to engage in public worship but under very troublesome restrictions. In the later years of the colonial era sentiment relaxed with reference to Catholics throughout the American possessions and the unjust measures against them were not rigidly enforced anywhere; but the right to vote was denied them in Maryland and in some of the other colonies until the end of the colonial period.

THE GREAT AWAKENING

The eighteenth century was an age of reason rather than of faith. In some quarters in America the old attitude toward religion was being assailed by the skepticism and deism which had seeped in from Europe. In New England there arose during the early decades of the century a new liberalism which refused to accept the doctrine of election and predestination. The liberals contended that salvation is not confined to the elect but is open to all who are willing to accept it. This doctrine is called Arminianism. There had also grown up in the older settlements a prosperous leisure class which had time and money for the enjoyment of worldly amusements and felt cramped by the restraints imposed upon them by

Religious conditions in the first third of the eighteenth century

*The great
revival*

*Edwards and
Whitefield*

*Revival
methods*

*Results of
the revival*

Puritanism. In New England, as well as in other sections, wealth had mixed worldliness with religion, and worship was too often characterized by cold formalism rather than by emotional fervor. A realization of this condition caused a yearning on the part of church leaders for a genuine revival of religion.

At this juncture there swept over the colonies a series of revivals which were known as the Great Awakening. The revivals started in 1734 at Northampton, Massachusetts, where Jonathan Edwards was threatening the unsaved with the torments of eternal punishment. After a lull of a few years, the revival began anew, this time under the preaching of George Whitefield, a zealous evangelist from England. Whitefield traveled throughout the colonies preaching to great audiences which were often too large to be accommodated by the churches and had to be assembled in groves or in fields. At these meetings people by hundreds professed conversion.

By conversion, Whitefield and Edwards meant a religious experience which was the gateway to the Christian life. The first stage of this experience was characterized by a deep realization of his sinfulness on the part of the one who was under conviction, accompanied by a terrible fear of eternal punishment. This fear was accentuated by the evangelist's vivid portrayal of the tortures of the damned. The next step was one in which the penitent suddenly became conscious of the forgiveness of his sins and his heart was filled with a sense of peace, joy, and love. So ecstatic was this feeling that the convert would often yield to the impulse to shout aloud his thanks for redemption.

By his deep piety and fervent oratory, which was supplemented with unconventional and dramatic gestures, Whitefield made a most effective appeal to the masses. There were some, however, particularly among the intellectuals, who differed from his views and objected to his spectacular methods. As a rule, the Anglican ministers were not in sympathy with the movement, whereas the Baptist leaders were generally enthusiastic in its support. Many of those who opposed Whitefield's methods joined the Anglican Church, while many of his ardent adherents left their own denominations to unite with the Baptists.

As a result of the Great Awakening, large additions were made to the membership of the churches. To what extent these accessions represented a permanent improvement in spiritual conditions was then and is still a matter of dispute. It has been held by both contemporary and later students of the movement that the drain on the emotions made by the mass excitement caused a later indifference to religion. Even Edwards admitted that many of the converts were not permanently faithful to their profession. Writing in 1751, he expressed the opinion that the proportion of the true converts to those who were mistaken might be "truly represented by the proportion of blossoms on a tree, which abide and come to mature fruit, to the whole number of blossoms in the spring."[1] But after taking due account of backsliders and admitting that much seed failed to take deep root in shallow, unprepared hearts, it seems evident that as a result of the movement the church as a whole was inspired with a joyous hope and an active zeal and was thus raised to a higher spiritual level.

A new interest in higher education was also aroused by the revival, and this led to the founding of four new denominational colleges.[2] As the Great Awakening was a revival of Calvinistic theology, as well as religion, it widened the breach that had already started between the conservative and liberal elements in the Congregational Church. It also gave the common man a larger participation in church affairs; for it was held that all converted persons were equal in the sight of God. By this theory the ignorant and humble members of the church were put on a spiritual equality with the educated and wellborn. Such a democratic idea as to religion was favorable to the trend toward democracy in government. As Whitefield was comparatively free from narrow denominational prejudices and advocated freedom of belief, the revival tended to promote religious tolerance. From the emotional upheaval caused by the spiritual awakening there emerged a feeling of sympathy for the underprivileged and the desire for their betterment. This feeling gave an impetus to humanitarianism, led to a better treatment of servants and slaves, and aroused a new zeal for the conversion of the Indians to the Christian faith.[3]

---

[1] S. E. Dwight, *Life of President Edwards*, 298 f.

[2] These colleges were the College of New Jersey at Princeton (Presbyterian), Brown (Baptist), Dartmouth (Congregational), and Rutgers (Dutch Reformed).

[3] Efforts to Christianize the Indians had been made from time to time in all sections of the country almost from the beginning of the colonial period. The Reverend Alexander Whitaker, of the Anglican Church, was zealous in his efforts to evangelize the Indians in the Jamestown vicinity, and numbered among his converts the Princess Pocahontas. Of the early missionaries to the natives in New England the most noted was the Reverend John Eliot. Beginning about the middle of the seventeenth century (1646), he labored among the natives for more than forty years and finally translated the Scriptures into the Massachusetts dialect of the Algonquian language. For his faithful service to the red men he is properly called the "Apostle to the Indians." The Venerable Society through its missionaries also made a zealous effort to teach Christianity to the natives. Schools for their education were established in various sections by this society and other organizations. One of the Indian schools afterwards became Dartmouth College. The results of these efforts to educate and evangelize the Indians were disappointing, mainly because of the ill feeling caused by the bitter wars between the two races and the exploitation of the natives by the whites.

MODE OF LIVING

Colonial cities and towns

At the end of the colonial period there were a number of thriving trade centers in the colonies. Of these, four—Philadelphia, Boston, New York, and Charleston—had attained a wealth and population which placed them in the class of the European cities of that day. There were also smaller towns, several of which—notably Annapolis and Williamsburg, capitals of their respective provinces—enjoyed a political and social importance out of proportion to their size.

Philadelphia

The largest American city was Philadelphia, which had a population of about thirty thousand. Well located as to water transportation and connected by comparatively good roads with a fruitful wheat-growing hinterland, it had had a steady and continuous growth and was now basking in a comfortable prosperity. Large houses made of brick fronted on well-paved streets, which were bordered with sidewalks and lighted by lamps at night.

Boston

Boston was next to Philadelphia in size and importance. The city, situated on a rocky peninsula, was curved about the crescent-shaped harbor, with green fields and a leafy forest in the background. On the two-thousand-foot wharf were warehouses for storage purposes and near it, retail shops. Farther back were located the large houses of the merchant princes, each of which was surrounded by a shady lawn and flower and vegetable gardens.

New York

New York was also a thriving city but as yet gave no promise of becoming the metropolis of the world. In both New York and Boston the streets were narrow and crooked, though the more important ones were generally paved.

Charleston

Charleston was the largest city in the South and was the only town of any size in South Carolina during the entire colonial period. It was located on the finest harbor south of Virginia and had become an important commercial center. Thanks to the sea breezes, it enjoyed a partial immunity from malaria, especially in the early years. The wealthy planters usually spent the hottest months in the city, partly to take advantage of the social opportunities it afforded and partly to escape the discomfort and disease to which they were subjected on their mosquito-infested country estates. It was therefore the social and political, as well as the economic, metropolis of the province. So much was this the case that South Carolina more than any of the other colonies was in the nature of a city state.

Life in the colonial city

As commerce rather than manufacturing was the mainspring of urban life, the colonial city was not so dirty or noisy as the industrial centers of today. Sensitive nerves were never upset by screaming whistles, and housefurnishings were not begrimed with coal soot. On the other hand, the city dwellers had to do without certain conveniences and comforts which we look upon as necessities. There was no running water in the houses, no plumbing, and therefore few bathing conveniences. Water was supplied by surface wells, which could easily be polluted by disease germs. There was no arrangement for the disposal of garbage. Ashes and refuse were piled up in the alleys and on vacant lots. Hogs wandered around the streets picking up food remnants and other kinds of garbage. In Charleston a like scavenger service was performed by buzzards.

Classes of people

While the colonials, in the main, came from the middle and lower classes in Europe, they brought with them old world notions as to class distinctions. In New England social lines were deepened by the practice of seating the people in the churches and arranging the names of students in college catalogues according to social standing. With the wide prevalence of such undemocratic ideas, the rise of an aristocratic order was inevitable. Accordingly, there soon grew up in America an aristocracy which fenced itself off from the common people by social barriers. This patrician group was made up of the provincial officials, the Congregational ministers in New England, the wealthy merchants of the cities, and the owners of large landed estates, mainly in Rhode Island, New York, and the Southern provinces. In every colony the economic, political, and social life was dominated by the members of this privileged class. To them alone was the term gentleman applied, and they were distinguished by costly wearing apparel, which in the early years was forbidden the yeomanry by law.

The middle class constituted the bulk of the population in all the colonies. This class was made up of the small farmers, artisans, and tradesmen. Associated with these were the hired laborers, who by energy and thrift could easily win full membership in the middle class. The line separating the yeomanry from the aristocracy was not an insuperable barrier, and was often crossed by an ambitious plebeian who had acquired sufficient property to qualify as a member of the patriciate.

The colonial house

Colonial architecture was borrowed from Europe. The English, Dutch, Swedish, and German settlers brought to the new world the architectural ideas of their respective homelands. Modifications of these plans had to be made, however, to adapt them to climatic conditions and so there was no slavish imitation of the European patterns. Since paint and glass were scarce, painted houses were

From Thomas E. Tallmadge's "The Story of Architecture," W. W. Norton, Inc.

THE PARSON CAPEN HOUSE, TOPSFIELD, MASSACHUSETTS, 1683.

Courtesy of the New-York Historical Society, New York City

SENATE HOUSE, Kingston, N.Y.

very uncommon in the seventeenth century, and oiled paper often took the place of glass in windows. Late in this century the log cabin appeared in the colonies, the idea probably having come over from Sweden. It became the usual type of dwelling for the poor whites and Negroes in the South and the frontiersmen in the West.

Reproduced from THE PAGEANT OF AMERICA, *Copyright Yale University Press*

NEW JERSEY FARMHOUSE, 1676.

As a rule, housing conditions were much better in the eighteenth than in the seventeenth century. In the former era the typical house in Virginia was a story-and-a-half structure, weatherboarded with unpainted planks. Sometimes there was an added wing and a small front porch and nearly always a lean-to kitchen. The houses of the prosperous middle class in the North were often two stories high with gambreled roofs and dormer windows. Among the Dutch of New York, a popular type of dwelling was a story-and-a-half building with the gable end fronting the road or street. Of the low-ceilinged rooms on the first floor the most important were the kitchen and the parlor. The floor of the latter was covered over with sand on which flowered figures were made by the housewife.

About 1720 the Georgian style of architecture was introduced in the continental colonies and was generally used by the wealthy, in all sections, in the construction of their imposing mansions. This type of house was one of wide halls and large rooms, wainscoted to the high ceiling and adorned with carved mantels and beautiful staircases. In the South the mansion house was usually surrounded by a number of outhouses such as barns, granaries, laundry, schoolroom, office, poultry houses, etc. One noted mansion, Nomini Hall (late eighteenth century, Virginia), had sixty-two such outbuildings. These mansions were usually built of wood or brick.

House-furnishings

In the early years the average family had to get along with meager household furnishings. The tableware consisted mainly of tin vessels, wooden platters, pewter dishes, and a little earthenware, but no forks or chinaware and few knives. In the eighteenth century, forks and chinaware came into general use among the common people and silverware among the wealthy. During this later period stoves were used for heating purposes in some sections, especially among the Germans of Pennsylvania. The success of the heating stove was greatly increased by an invention made by Franklin in 1742. Despite the advantages of the open Franklin stove, the vast majority of colonial families, both rich and poor, still relied upon the fireplace for the heating of their houses, throughout the entire colonial period. The roaring wood fire everywhere seen in the wintertime imparted a cheery comfort to the colonial home which largely compensated for its shortcomings as a heating arrangement. For the lighting of their rooms the people generally had to rely on pine knots or candles, though on exceptional occasions lamps, supplied with sperm or lard oil, were used in the houses of the well-to-do.

Amusements

In colonial days the common people, as well as the aristocrats, were fond of amusements, but the former were restricted in their enjoyment of them by a lack of leisure. So much exertion was needed to make a living that a good deal of recreation had to be a combination of work and play. The working parties, therefore, afforded a wholesome type of amusement for the farmers, both old and young. This was the case, not only in New England, but in all sections (see p. 124).

The muster was everywhere an occasion of relaxation. Young and old would assemble at some central point in the community to participate in or witness military drills and the practice of marksmanship. Picnic dinners were served and there was always time enough for pleasant social intercourse. In all the colonies the church, the tavern, and the village or crossroads store were also centers at which farmers could meet for rest and conversation. Political gatherings, such as town meetings in the North and county courts in the South, likewise brought the people together and afforded opportunities for pleasant social contacts.

Courtesy of the New-York Historical Society, New York City

VAN CORTLANDT HOUSE.

Courtesy of the New-York Historical Society, New York City

SHIRLEY ON THE JAMES RIVER, Virginia.

In the seventeenth century some restraints were imposed on amusements in New England by the religious beliefs of the Puritans. By the beginning of the next century these restrictions had begun to relax and there was greater freedom in recreation, especially among the wealthy class. Dancing was engaged in and even plays were at times permitted in Boston. One form of amusement in which the New Englanders took delight was the weekly lecture on some religious topic, usually given on Thursday. Although these exercises were sometimes four or five hours long, they attracted large audiences. Additional interest was lent to the occasion by the punishing of criminals, the publishing of wedding banns, and the making of other announcements.

The observance of Christmas and Thanksgiving

The orthodox Puritans of New England objected to the observance of Christmas on the ground that this was a Catholic custom. Accordingly, except in Rhode Island, Christmas was not celebrated in New England at any time during the colonial period. The place of Christmas was taken by the Thanksgiving season. The custom of offering public thanks for material blessings, which had its origin in Europe before the Reformation, was first observed in English America in the fall of 1621, when the Pilgrims celebrated their first harvest by several days of feasting and thanksgiving. From time to time in the seventeenth century a day was set aside for thanksgiving by the Puritans, and by the end of the century there had grown up in Massachusetts and Connecticut the practice of observing Thanksgiving regularly once a year. This holiday usually lasted about a week and was a time of festivity as well as one of religious observance. It is thought that Thursday was finally chosen as Thanksgiving day because of its popularity as lecture day. In the other colonies, Christmas held an important place in the recreational life of the people. Among the Dutch of New York, May Day and New Year's were also celebrated as festive occasions. At these times visits were interchanged among friends and family reunions held.

Kinds of recreation

In New York both the Dutch and the English were fond of amusement and were not restrained by their religion from the enjoyment of many forms of recreation, such as picnics, private theatricals, and dancing, sleighing, and fishing parties. Not only in New York but also in the Chesapeake and Southern provinces the people devoted a good deal of time to recreation. Everywhere, except in those localities in which there was considerable Quaker and Puritan influence, cockfighting, cardplaying, and fox hunting were common sports. The most popular of all the amusements in the South was dancing. The waltz was unknown among the colonials, and their

Courtesy J. B. Lippincott Company

MOUNT PLEASANT, ON THE SCHUYLKILL. THE RIVER FRONT.
Built by Captain James Macpherson, 1761.
From Eberlein & Lippincott's The Colonial Homes of Philadelphia.
House was once owned by Benedict Arnold but he never occupied it as a residence

Courtesy of Huestis Cook

DRAYTON HALL ON THE ASHLEY RIVER, South Carolina.

dances were confined to jigs, square dances, and the Virginia
reel.

Visiting

Visiting among friends was another means of social enjoyment,
especially in the South. In this section all classes, the poor whites
as well as the rich planters, were noted for their hospitality. Strangers
were cordially received and well treated, and friends and relatives
were entertained in royal fashion. Many of the great families were
related or connected by marriage, and there was an easy camaraderie
between the patricians that made social intercourse natural and
delightful. Friends had to make long journeys to visit one another
and they generally went in large numbers, as several servants as
well as members of the family usually composed the party. An
ordinary visit, therefore, was something like a modern house party.
The exchange of hospitality in those days did not subject the lady
of the home to the strain which such social functions would impose
upon the modern housewife. Food was cheap and plentiful and
the numerous slaves stood ready to do the work. The exercise of
hospitality relieved the loneliness which would otherwise have
settled down on the plantations, widely scattered as they were.
Anyone coming in from the outside and breaking the tedium of
isolation was a welcomed guest, whether he was a patrician friend,
a plebeian stranger, or even a peddler.[1]

*The colonial
theater*

The colonial theater was borrowed from the mother country.
With a few important exceptions, all the plays given in America
were written by English authors and performed by English actors.
Just when the theater came to the colonies we can only conjecture.
It is known, however, that by the beginning of the eighteenth century (1702) an English actor was performing in New York, and in
1716 a playhouse (the first in America) was erected in Williamsburg. It was not, however, until about the middle of the eighteenth
century that the theater got a permanent footing in the colonies.
The transfer from the homeland to the continental possessions
was effected through the agency of two English joint-stock companies which toured the country and gave performances at important towns and cities.

In the last half of the eighteenth century the English drama,
although it had sloughed off much of the filth with which it had
been besmirched in the Restoration era, was still not entirely free
from the taint of licentiousness. For this reason and also because
it was a worldly amusement, religious leaders among the Puritans

---

[1] This entire paragraph and one on page 173 are taken from O. P. Chitwood's
A History of Colonial America. See pp. 593-594, 596. This courtesy was extended by
Harper and Brothers.

and Quakers were opposed to the theater. As a concession to this feeling, laws banning the theater were passed in the following colonies: Massachusetts (1750), Pennsylvania (1759), Rhode Island (1761), and New Hampshire (1762). By this time, however, the wealthy class in the North had assumed a more liberal attitude toward recreations and were disposed to accept the theater as a proper type of amusement. These laws were, therefore, probably not enforced and apparently were intended as appeasing gestures toward the Puritan sentiments of the middle and lower classes. On one occasion at least a clever playwright got around the prejudice against the drama by advertizing his performances in a New England town (Newport) as "Moral Dialogues."

Theaters were rude structures in New York in the early days. They were usually log rooms, accommodating about three hundred people. They were not heated except by a stove in the anteroom, and the audience in cold weather would usually crowd around it in the intervals between acts. Foot warmers were used as in church, and candles were employed for light and for footlights. Sometimes in the midst of a love scene or exciting tragedy the stagehand would interrupt the scene by snuffing the smoking candlewicks of the footlights. In Williamsburg it was the custom to have servants go to the theater about four in the afternoon to hold the seats of their masters for the performance, which usually began about six.

| Cavalier | Puritan | Hollander | Quaker |

COSTUMES OF THE EARLY SETTLERS.
From drawings by Darley for Lossing's "Our Country."

PART II

The American Revolution, 1763=1783

CHAPTER XI

From Controversy to Conflict

IMPERIAL SUPERVISION OF THE COLONIES

WHEN the English settlements in North America were first *The colonies* made they were placed under the authority of the crown. The king *under authority of* had the sole power to issue patents for lands and charters conferring *the king* governmental authority. In the early years, Parliament had no part in the supervision of the overseas possessions, but during the Commonwealth period it took over the management of the American plantations. With the Restoration, the crown was again put in control of colonial administration. Parliament did not, however, entirely surrender the power which it had acquired in the Interregnum. It continued to pass navigation and other laws affecting the colonies, and its activity in this kind of legislation gradually increased.

During the entire colonial era the authority of the crown in *The Privy* overseas affairs was exercised through the Privy Council, which *Council* the king appointed. This body had final authority in outlining policies for the plantations, in making appointments to office, and in issuing instructions to officials. The Privy Council, however, had a great many other duties to perform and could not look after the details of colonial administration. It had therefore to rely mainly on the advice of committees. At times special committees were appointed to make investigations and recommendations in specific cases; but the usual practice was to employ permanent commissions as advisory agencies. Of these permanent commissions the most important was the Board of Trade, established in 1696. From that *The Board* time until the end of the colonial period this Board was the domi- *of Trade* nant influence in the administration of the colonies. Its recommendations, to be effective, had to be endorsed by the Privy Council, but in nearly every instance the policies outlined by the Board were accepted.

Laws passed by the colonial assemblies and signed by the colonial *Review of* governors were sent to England to be accepted or rejected by the *colonial* Privy Council. In all the royal provinces the governors were in- *legislation* structed as to the procedure in submitting such laws. The charters of some of the proprietary colonies had provisions covering this procedure; but even in those colonies whose charters made no mention of the right of veto, laws passed by the assemblies were subject to disallowance by the Privy Council. The royal veto was applied usually to acts which were not in harmony with the Eng-. lish common law, violated the prerogative of the crown, or were unauthorized by the charters. This practice of submitting colonial legislation to the Privy Council for review became the established tradition in colonial America; and this tradition gave rise to the practice in the American judiciary of allowing the courts to pass upon the constitutionality of acts of the state and Federal legislatures.

Appeals from colonial courts

Appeals were also carried from the highest colonial courts to the Privy Council. Such appeals were usually not taken except in civil cases involving large amounts, or in criminal cases of importance. The reason for this limitation was the cost of prosecuting hearings across seas.

Policy of Mercantilism as applied to the colonies

In the seventeenth and eighteenth centuries England, like the other countries of Europe, was basing her economic policy on the theory of Mercantilism. According to this doctrine, each nation should endeavor to make itself as wealthy and strong as possible, with the view to self-preservation in an age of aggression. England felt that to protect herself against her ambitious neighbors she must have a strong army and a powerful navy, and be in a position to feed her population in time of war and supply her armies with the necessary equipment. If these results were to be achieved, there would have to be a continued growth in population to furnish the man power needed for security. The support of this increased population would demand the promotion of agriculture and manufacturing. If the navy was to be able to protect the homeland against attack and keep open the channels of trade to the outside world, it would have to have as an ally a strong merchant marine.

Imperial policy with reference to colonial industry

The colonies could help in this program, if they would buy from England finished manufactured products and sell to her such raw materials as she needed for her manufactures. Accordingly, laws were passed restricting the production of cloth, hats, and hardware in the plantations with the expectation that the American dependencies would purchase these commodities from the homeland. On the other hand, the colonials were encouraged by Parliamentary enactments to procure furs and produce pig iron for the use of British hatmakers and iron manufacturers, respectively.[1]

---

[1] The manufacture of woolen cloth in the possessions was discouraged by an act (1699) which forbade the exportation of wool or woolen cloth from one colony to another or to foreign countries. In like manner, colonial hatmakers were prohibited by

Navigation laws were also passed for the purpose of stimulating shipbuilding throughout the empire. By acts of Parliament passed from 1651 on, American, British, and Irish ships were given a monopoly of the trade between England and the colonies. Also certain commodities which the British manufacturers needed, as raw materials or for home consumption, were put on the "enumerated" list. This was a list of those exports from the British possessions which could not be sent directly to any country except England and her colonies. They could be transhipped to European ports only after they had been landed in England and, in most cases, a duty had been paid. This policy gave England the preference in the purchase of these articles, enabled the government to derive a revenue from them, and afforded the merchants an opportunity to make a middleman's profit. *Navigation laws*

The British merchants were also granted special privileges with reference to European goods sold to the colonials. One of these laws (the Staple Act of 1663) provided that, with a few exceptions, all European products sent to America would have to pass through English ports.

The most unjust of all of these laws was the Molasses Act of 1733. It placed excessively high duties on sugar, molasses, rum, and some other commodities which were shipped from the foreign West Indies to the American continental colonies. If the law had been enforced it would have seriously crippled the trade between the northern plantations and the French, Spanish, and Dutch West Indies; but it did not have this effect for the reason that the English colonials disregarded the law and continued their trade by smuggling. *The Molasses Act of 1733*

A DECADE OF DISCONTENT

The British plan of administering the American possessions which was in effect between 1660 and 1763 is usually known as the old colonial system. The restrictions on the dependencies rested on the unfair purpose of advancing British at the expense of American interests; but the regulations as actually carried out worked no serious hardship on the colonies. Some of these laws were favorable to the plantations and those which were unfavorable *The old colonial system*

---

the Act of 1732 from selling their hats outside of the colony in which they were produced, and each hat manufacturer was limited to two apprentices. The English hatters were guaranteed a monopoly of the American supply of raw material, as furs had been put on the enumerated list (1722). The manufacture of iron goods in the plantations was discouraged by the law of 1750, which prohibited the erection in America of any new steel furnaces or slitting or rolling mills.

were generally disregarded; for the home government was lax in the enforcement of its colonial policy. This ineffectiveness of imperial management was due partly to the fact that there was no sharp line separating the duties of Parliament in colonial affairs from those of the crown, or the powers of one group of administrators from that of another. This division of authority was attended by a lack of responsibility. Effective administration was also rendered impossible by the ignorance and corruption of the inferior officials who were in charge. Furthermore, for a good part of this period the home government pursued a policy of indifference or salutary neglect, as it was called, with reference to the possessions. The result was that the limitations on the rights of the colonials were more theoretical than actual, and they were allowed to manage their own affairs without much hindrance. On the whole, therefore, the American people were prosperous and loyal to the mother country until 1763.

The new colonial system

This year, however, proved to be an important turning point in the relations between England and her colonies. Her successes in the Seven Years' War had made Britain the leading power of Europe. She was not only mistress of the seas but also the owner of a world-wide empire. This enviable position had been purchased at a great cost, however, for her national debt had been doubled and the tax burdens of her people had been greatly increased. Industry in the homeland was rapidly advancing, and British manufacturers were more anxious than ever to use the possessions as a source of raw materials and as a market for their finished products. To attain this objective it would be necessary (it was thought) to tighten the bonds which held the various parts of the empire together. The restrictions on colonial industry and commerce should be carried out more effectively and the plantations should be required to assume their share of the imperial tax burden. In short, the mother country was to impose upon the adult colonies a rigid discipline which had not been attempted in their childhood.

This would have been a dubious experiment if conditions had remained as they had been before the French and Indian War. But owing to recent changes in the American situation, the colonies were desiring a looser rather than a closer association with the empire. They were now less dependent than formerly upon the British government for protection, since the defeat of the French and the Indians had relieved them of the French menace and to a great extent of the danger from Indian attack.

The dozen years which followed the Treaty of Paris (1763) proved to be the most critical period in the entire history of Anglo-

American relations. The difficult problems of that era, which called *Political* for a statesmanship of the highest order, were handled with blunder- *conditions in* ing ineptitude. George III had come to the throne (1760) with an *England* ambition to restore the kingship to a position of real authority. He was not satisfied to be a figurehead, as had been his two immedi- ate predecessors, and political conditions at the time were favorable *George III* to his purpose. The Whig Party still had a large majority in Parlia- ment but was broken up into a number of factions. A working Cabinet could not be formed without bringing together representa- tives of several discordant groups. The chance to make the com- binations necessary for Cabinet organization gave George III a power over the Cabinet and the House of Commons which his successors have not enjoyed. Furthermore, there was a group in Parliament, known as the King's Friends, on whose support he could always count because they had been bound to him by bribery and gifts or promises of office.

If the king had been a capable ruler this increase in authority might have served the empire in good stead. George III, however, had neither the ability nor the temperament needed to meet grave responsibility, and so this accession of power proved to be a costly liability rather than a valuable asset. Furthermore, during the greater part of this trying period the king did not have wise coun- sellors to lean on. William Pitt was the most capable statesman in the empire, but he did not enjoy royal favor and was not a member of the Cabinet except for a few years. Even then he was prevented by ill-health from taking advantage of his opportunity for leadership.

The responsibility for inaugurating the new colonial policy was *Grenville's* placed on George Grenville, who became prime minister in the *policy* spring of 1763. Although he was not without ability, Grenville was unequal to this difficult task, for he was not conversant with conditions in America. His first effort was to increase the revenue derived from the colonial trade by putting a stop to the leaks due to smuggling. The commissioners of customs were held up to a stricter performance of their duties and were granted the assistance of warships in their campaign against smuggling.

The trade between the continental colonies and the West Indies *The Sugar* was to be put on a revenue basis. As the Molasses Act of 1733 had *Act of 1764* never been effectively enforced and some of its rates were too high for revenue purposes, it was superseded by the Sugar Act of 1764. The new measure, as well as the old one, placed a duty on sugar, molasses, and other products brought into the continental American colonies from the foreign West Indian plantations. One purpose behind both acts was that of discouraging trade with the Spanish and French West Indies, but an additional objective of the Act of 1764 was the collection of revenue. By it the importation of rum and spirits was prohibited and the duty on sugar was raised, but that on molasses was lowered by one half. As an encouragement to the indigo business, which under the stimulus of the bounty was getting a good start in South Carolina and Georgia, a tax was placed on indigo brought into the colonies. The net revenue obtained from the Sugar Act was to be used "toward defraying the necessary expenses of defending, protecting, and securing" the colonies.

Since the rum industry in New England was dependent upon the molasses obtained from the West Indies, the lowering of the duty on molasses was a greater concession to the colonials than the raising of the tax on sugar was an objection. It would seem therefore that the new bill would be more acceptable than the old. This was not the case, however, for the reason that there were now provisions for the collection of the duties, whereas the old law had been largely disregarded.

Restriction on the use of paper money

The complaints against the Sugar Act came mainly from the wealthy merchant class, and the masses showed no serious concern about it. In this same year (1764), the common people were also provided with a grievance by an act of Parliament prohibiting the colonies from issuing any more paper money. This law did much toward enlisting the poorer and debtor class in opposition to the British government. The effort to make the colonies live up to a sound financial policy was very unpopular, because the desire for an inflated currency was widespread. There was very little metallic money in the colonies, and for them, therefore, the choice as to a medium of exchange was largely between barter and paper money. The institution of a sound financial policy did not go along with the prohibition of an unsound one.

A military force to be stationed in America

During the intercolonial wars the demands made on the various colonies by the British military authorities for men and supplies were seldom if ever fully complied with. The requisition system had thus proved to be a failure, and there was need of a more effective plan of defense. It was therefore decided to leave a force of ten thousand men in America. These troops could be used for keeping the Indians quiet, curbing any restlessness that might arise among the French Canadians, and bolstering the authority of the royal governors in their efforts to put down smuggling and uphold imperial authority. The colonists had not asked for this little army and apparently did not want it, especially if they had to bear the expense of supporting it.

The new commercial policy was expected to yield more revenue than had heretofore been collected but not enough to finance the proposed military arrangement. To find money for this extra outlay was another problem which confronted the prime minister. He felt that all of this expense should not be saddled upon the tax-payers of the homeland, who were already bowed down by heavy tax burdens. He therefore decided to raise some of this needed revenue by a tax on the Americans. Accordingly, he announced a year in advance that the stamp tax would be extended to the American possessions, but promised that if the colonials would suggest some other plan for securing funds he would give it due consideration. Objection to the proposed tax was widely expressed in the colonies, but no substitute was presented except the discredited requisition system.

The Stamp Act

Grenville had no difficulty in getting Parliament to pass the Stamp Act (1765), which required the placing of revenue stamps on newspapers, playing cards, legal documents, and many business instruments. All the revenue accruing from the purchase of these stamps was to be used for "defending, protecting, and securing" the colonies.

At first the colonials seemed inclined to submit to this tax, and Americans of good standing agreed to serve as agents in the selling of the stamps. It was not long, however, before this attitude of acquiescence gave way to one of aggressive antagonism. The first important step toward arousing opposition was taken by the House of Burgesses in Virginia. In this body, resolutions offered by Patrick Henry were passed which declared that the General Assembly of Virginia had the exclusive power to levy taxes on the people of that colony. These radical resolutions were opposed by some of the members, and in the heat of the discussion Henry made use of some fiery expressions. "Caesar," he said, "had his Brutus; Charles the First, his Cromwell; and George the Third (at this point he was interrupted by numerous cries of 'Treason!') may profit by their example."

Opposition to the Stamp Act

As these resolutions were quickly circulated throughout the colonies, they played an important part in stirring up feeling against the Stamp Act. This opposition was expressed in, and intensified by, resolutions of town meetings, discussions in newspapers, and various other ways. In several of the northern states there were agreements among merchants not to import any more goods from England until the objectionable measure was repealed.

As a step toward united action, the legislature of Massachusetts invited all the colonies to send delegates to an intercolonial con-

The Stamp Act Congress

gress. In response to this invitation, the Stamp Act Congress met in New York (October, 1765). In it sat representatives from nine colonies. This body drew up a bill of rights and a statement of colonial grievances and sent petitions and memorials to the king and Parliament. In accordance with the principle of no taxation without representation, it held that, as the dependencies were not and could not be represented in Parliament, they could not be taxed except by their own assemblies. Parliament had therefore exceeded its authority in passing the Stamp Act and had acted unjustly toward the colonies in imposing on them burdensome trade restrictions.

*Sons of
Liberty*

Opposition to the stamp taxes also took the form of mob violence, the worst exhibition of which was the burning and looting of Chief Justice Hutchinson's house in Boston. Organizations known as Sons of Liberty were active throughout the colonies in enforcing the nonimportation agreements or compelling the stamp agents to resign. Public indignation was aroused to such a pitch that the stamp agents declined to serve and the law was largely disregarded. Furthermore, British merchants were losing trade on account of the boycott on their goods and were afraid that the continuance of strained relations between the colonies and the mother country would prevent the collection of the money due them by their American debtors. Influenced by petitions from these merchants in favor of repeal, and confronted with the undeniable evidence of its failure, Parliament wisely voted to rescind the act (March 17, 1766).

*The Declar-
atory Act*

When the Stamp Act was repealed Parliament passed the Declaratory Act affirming its right to make laws binding on the colonies. The colonials, however, overlooked the objectionable principle embodied in this measure and accepted the repeal of the stamp law with joy and expressions of loyalty. A further concession was made to the colonials by a favorable modification of the Sugar Act.[1]

*The Town-
shend Acts*

The period of harmony which followed the repeal of the Stamp Act was short-lived. It came to an end the following year when on the recommendation of Charles Townshend, Chancellor of the Exchequer, Parliament passed some other unpopular laws. A new Cabinet had been formed in the summer of 1766 at the head of which was placed William Pitt (now Earl of Chatham). This was a coalition ministry made up of Whigs, Tories, and King's Friends,

---

[1] The duty of threepence a gallon on molasses imported into the continental possessions from the foreign West Indian colonies was superseded by an impost of one penny a gallon on all molasses brought in, whether from the British or the foreign plantations.

representing discordant political factions. Furthermore, it was not long before Pitt was forced by ill-health to withdraw from active service, and so this heterogeneous group was left without the proper leadership. This situation gave the Chancellor of the Exchequer the opportunity to act as the head of the Cabinet and carry out his policy with reference to the American possessions.

In their discussions regarding the Stamp Act, the colonial agitators had drawn a line between an internal tax, which was levied inside the country, and an external tax, which was collected at the ports. Townshend therefore concluded that an external tax would be accepted, and so he induced Parliament to pass a law (the Townshend Duty Act) imposing a duty on glass, tea, lead, and paper imported into the colonies. A part of the revenue thus raised was to be used for paying the salaries of the colonial judges and governors. In the royal provinces these officials were appointed by the king and held their places at his pleasure. In most of the provinces, however, they had hitherto been dependent partially or wholly upon the assemblies for their salaries. As one branch at least of every colonial legislature was chosen by the voters, these royal appointees were thus indirectly accountable to the people. But if their salaries were paid out of this proposed fund these officials would be entirely independent of the assemblies and might become the willing tools of the king. Another objectionable feature of the act was the provision authorizing the courts to grant writs of assistance, or general search warrants. These writs enabled the imperial officials, in their effort to put down smuggling, to search any house or ship which was suspected of harboring smuggled goods.[1]

By another of the objectionable Townshend Acts a board of customs officials was established in America, which was expected to promote trade between England and the plantations and aid in the enforcement of the commercial regulations. A still more unpopular measure was the one passed by Parliament (June, 1767) which suspended the New York Assembly because it had declined to make satisfactory arrangements for the quartering of the British troops which were to be stationed there. The colonials regarded this act as a step toward the undermining of the foundation of their liberties. They contended that the position of the assemblies in the colonies was similar to that of Parliament in England; and that if one colonial legislature could be suspended by an act of Parliament all of them could be suspended or abolished.

---

[1] James Otis had first come into prominence when in 1761 he boldly opposed the granting of writs of assistance, contending that the practice was unconstitutional.

"Letters of a Pennsylvania Farmer"

Strong opposition to the Townshend Acts was voiced by able American lawyers who had studied in the homeland and were well informed as to the principles of the English constitution. Of the legal arguments presented by them, the ones which had the greatest influence were embodied in a series of articles published by John Dickinson of Pennsylvania under the title of "Letters of a Pennsylvania Farmer." These articles were clearly and forcibly expressed and were widely read throughout the colonies. Dickinson maintained that the Townshend Acts were contrary to English law and practice, and should not be accepted by the colonials. "We are only as much dependent on Great Britain," he boldly asserted, "as one perfectly free people can be on another."[1]

Nonimportation agreements

The burdens of the Duty Act were especially heavy on the commercial class, which took an important part in organizing the opposition to the measure. The merchants of the principal cities, together with some of the southern planters, entered into agreements not to import any more English commodities until the objectionable laws were repealed. As a result of this second boycott, there was a considerable decline in the importation of British goods, especially into New England and the Middle provinces. The British merchants felt the pinch from this loss of business, for in their case the sensitive nerve which runs from the pocketbook to the heart had been painfully touched. For a second time, therefore, they urged Parliament to remove the cause of their trouble by rescinding laws which were unacceptable to the colonies.

The "Boston Massacre"

There was so much unrest in Massachusetts that the British authorities transferred two regiments of soldiers from Halifax to Boston. The presence of these troops was resented by the townsmen, and on one occasion a clash occurred between a mob of citizens and a group of seven soldiers (March 5, 1770). In this street fight, for which both sides were about equally to blame, four citizens were killed. This unfortunate tragedy, improperly called the "Boston Massacre," aroused the people of Massachusetts to a fever of excitement. A distorted account of the affair went out to the other colonies and helped to stir up a general feeling of bitterness against the British.

During the first year, the amount of revenue realized from the Duty Act was very slightly in excess of the cost of collection. This

---

[1] On February 11, 1768, the Massachusetts House of Representatives adopted some resolutions protesting against the recent tax law. A *Circular Letter* written by Samuel Adams was sent to the legislatures of the other colonies urging them to join in this protest. Of the favorable responses to this appeal made by other colonial assemblies, the most noted was the Virginia Resolves of 1769, offered by George Washington and adopted by the assembly of the Old Dominion.

meager return and the opposition in England and America showed that the law was a failure both in a financial and a political sense. It was therefore repealed (April, 1770), except that the duty on tea was continued. The tax on tea was retained to save the principle that Parliament had the authority to tax the dependencies. *Partial repeal of the Townshend Duty Act*

The partial repeal of the Townshend Duty Act led to the abandonment of the nonimportation agreement except as to tea, and the pledge regarding it was not strictly kept. The merchants and conservatives generally were now in favor of putting a stop to agitation and settling down to peace and quiet. They sensed a danger in the radicalism which had been aroused among the masses by opposition to British policy. For some time there had been among the common people a growing antagonism to the aristocratic clique that ruled Massachusetts, and the quarrel with the mother country gave added strength to this feeling. The conservatives feared that the wind of peaceful opposition to British policies started by them would grow into the whirlwind of mob violence. Furthermore, if revolution were once begun the upper class might lose its privileged position in the rule of the province. And there was ground for this uneasiness, for agitation did not cease with the partial repeal of the Duty Act. *A lull in the controversy*

In the early stages of opposition to British policy, Massachusetts enjoyed the brilliant leadership of James Otis. Not only had he taken a bold stand against the writs of assistance (1761), but in 1764 he had written a pamphlet in which the rights of the British colonists were ably upheld. A few years later he was assaulted by a British revenue official, on account of an article which he had published, and was dealt a sword cut which brought on insanity. Otis now had to drop out of the fight, but his mantle fell on Samuel Adams, a capable politician, who became the leader of the Massachusetts agitators. *James Otis*

Adams was sincere and earnest in his convictions and prejudices, and upheld them with courage and zeal. Having a clear and straightforward style, he was convincing as a writer and very effective as a public speaker. He had borrowed from Locke some advanced liberal views, which he was ever ready to uphold with perfect fearlessness. His influence with the masses was due partly to his active championship of their rights and partly to the support he received from a powerful political organization. At this time he, more than any other leader in the Bay Colony, acted the role of tribune of the people. During the two years following the partial repeal of the Duty Act he continued his agitation against the alleged tyranny of the imperial government by publishing forty anti-British articles in the radical *Samuel Adams* press. In this way he nursed the wrath of the people, keeping it warm until another blunder of British administration caused it again to flare up.

Committees of corre- spondence

One important achievement of Adams during the period of comparative quiet was the formation of committees of correspondence. At his suggestion Boston appointed (November, 1772) a committee to correspond with the committees to be selected by the other towns of Massachusetts. These committees were to formulate the rights of the people and announce their action to the outside world. There was a prompt response to this suggestion, and soon the various communities of the province were bound together in an extralegal organization. This plan of communication was soon extended to other provinces, and by the middle of the following year six colonies were tied together by committees of correspondence. After the Boston Tea Party other colonies were brought into the system by action of the assemblies. In this way the groundwork was laid for co-operative effort.

The Tea Act

The period of comparative quiet following the partial repeal of the Townshend Duty Act was brought to an end by the enactment by Parliament of another unpopular measure, the Tea Act (effective May, 1773). The main purpose of this act was to relieve the British East India Company of the financial straits into which it had fallen. This company had the exclusive right to supply England with tea, but had to pay a tax of twelve pence a pound on all that was imported. At this time it had a large amount of tea stored in its warehouses in England for which it could find no sale. If America could be induced to buy this surplus the company might be spared the threat of bankruptcy. With the view to bringing about this desirable result the new law provided for a rebate of the twelve-pence tax on all tea reshipped from England to America. The only tax which tea would have to pay in America was the three-pence import duty originally imposed by the Townshend Duty Act.

Owing to the higher tax collected in the homeland, the price of tea there was about twice as high as it would be in America. Cheap tea, it was thought, would be so acceptable to the colonials that they would buy it in large amounts. In so doing they would also be acquiescing in the import duty, for they would be drinking down the tax with their low-priced tea. In this way the East India Company would be saved from bankruptcy and the legality of the tea tax would be accepted by the Americans.

The company could dispose of its tea through its own agents in America and save what would otherwise go to middlemen. It was therefore able to offer tea to the Americans at a price with which the colonial merchants could not compete. The latter were strongly opposed to the monopoly granted the East India Company and joined in with the radicals who had all along been agitating against "British oppression." The company took advantage of its privilege by sending ships loaded with tea to all the important American ports. When these vessels arrived at New York and Philadelphia there was no one to receive the consignments, for the agents appointed by the company had resigned under pressure of public opinion. The vessels therefore returned to England without making any effort to land their cargoes. At Charleston the tea was received and stored in public warehouses. Later during the Revolutionary War it was sold and the money received was used to aid the patriot cause.[1]

While other colonies were opposed to the Tea Act, it was in Massachusetts that the controversy assumed its most violent form. The agents of the company in Boston (a nephew and two sons of Thomas Hutchinson, the unpopular governor) refused to resign, and the governor would not give the tea vessels clearance papers so that they could return to England. It looked therefore as if the tea would be landed and sold. To prevent this, two meetings were held in the Old South Church in both of which Samuel Adams took a prominent part. After the second meeting (December 19, 1773) a mob of fifty or sixty men dressed in the garb of Indians, boarded the ships and threw the tea overboard. While this "Boston Tea Party" was taking place a great crowd of people looked on in silent approval. Evidently the action of the mob was endorsed by public sentiment, and no effort was made by either the city or provincial authorities to punish the offense.

The "Boston Tea Party"

Among the radicals of the other colonies there was a disposition to rejoice over the bold action taken at Boston, though there were quite a number of moderate men, such as Franklin, who regretted this display of mob violence. Public sentiment in England was greatly aroused by this destruction of private property, and even advocates of the American cause, like William Pitt, condemned "the late illegal and violent proceedings at Boston." The "Boston Tea Party" was thus a turning point in the controversy between America and England; it was the event which changed the family quarrel into an irrepressible conflict.

Effect of the "Boston Tea Party"

To punish the obstreperous Bay Colony and discipline her into obedience, Parliament now passed some coercive measures which the colonials termed "Intolerable Acts." These were: the Boston Port

The "Intolerable Acts"

---

[1] When another consignment of tea was sent to Charleston it was thrown into the Cooper River (November, 1774). The arrival of a tea ship at Annapolis, Maryland, caused a great deal of excitement, which led to the burning of the vessel by a mob.

Bill, which closed the harbor of Boston to all trade except bare necessaries until the people had paid for the tea which had been destroyed; the Massachusetts Government Act, by which the upper house of the assembly was made appointive by the crown instead of elective by the assembly as heretofore, and the towns were restricted in their right of self-government; and the Administration of Justice Act, which provided that appointees of the king in Massachusetts, accused of capital offenses in the discharge of their official duties, could be sent to other colonies or England for trial provided they could not, in the opinion of the governor, receive a fair hearing without a change of venue. A fourth measure was a new Quartering Act, which applied to the colonies generally but was intended primarily for Massachusetts. This law gave the provincial governors authority to requisition, with due compensation to the owners, inns, alehouses, and unoccupied buildings which might be necessary for the proper housing of the British troops.

The Quebec Act

The Quebec Act, passed in the same year as the coercive measures, was regarded by the colonials as one of the "Intolerable Acts." This law was not, however, intended to be punitive, but was enacted for the purpose of giving the French settlers in Canada and the Illinois region a better form of government than they had had for the past decade. The province of Quebec was widened out so as to include the region between the Ohio and Mississippi Rivers and the Great Lakes. Civil suits were to be decided in accordance with French law, in which there was no provision for trial by jury. The French Catholics were to enjoy religious freedom, and their priests were given authority to collect tithes from their parishioners. As the province was sparsely populated and the French inhabitants had been accustomed to autocratic rule, there was no provision for a representative assembly, and so the people were to have no voice in the government of the province.

In the older English colonies in the East objection was made to this new arrangement in the West for several reasons. It deprived Massachusetts, Connecticut, and Virginia of western territory which they claimed under the sea-to-sea clauses of their charters. Englishmen would, it was held, be deprived of the right of trial by jury, and the establishment of an autocratic regime on the borders of other colonies would be a challenge to their right of self-government. The alleged privileges granted to the Catholic Church—notably the right of its clergy to levy tithes—aroused the anti-Catholic prejudices of the masses and revived the bogey of papal domination.

General Gage, who now became governor of Massachusetts, was given four regiments of soldiers to enable him to carry out the coer-

cive acts. He obeyed his instructions literally and enforced the objectionable measures so vigorously as to arouse opposition in all the
other colonies; for there was a general feeling that the punishment
meted out to Massachusetts was too severe for her offense.

General Gage as governor of Massachusetts

The Virginia House of Burgesses showed its sympathy with Boston by a resolution designating June 1 (the day the Boston Port Bill
was to go into effect) as a day of fasting and prayer. Governor Dunmore regarded this action as an impudent challenge to British
authority and dissolved the assembly. The burgesses then met unoffi-
cially at Raleigh Tavern and issued a call to the other colonies to
send delegates to a general congress with the idea of formulating a
united plan of resistance.

The First Continental Congress

In response to this invitation, representatives from all the thirteen
colonies except Georgia assembled at Philadelphia September, 1774.
A few of the delegations had been chosen by the colonial assemblies,
but most of them had been appointed by so-called conventions or
other irregular bodies. The full membership of the First Continental Congress was fifty-six, and in it were included some of the ablest
statesmen of America. The congress did not rest on any legal basis
and could only express opinions and make recommendations. The
representatives were divided into two main parties, the radicals and
the conservatives. The former, who were in the ascendency, following the leadership of the able delegates from Virginia and Massachusetts, advocated resistance to British aggression.[1]

The conservatives were in favor of conciliation and hoped for an
agreement whereby American rights would be safeguarded. It was in
line with this expectation that the conservatives, under the leadership of Joseph Galloway of Pennsylvania, offered a plan of union
for the continental colonies. This plan was similar to the one which
had been presented by Franklin at the Albany Congress. By the Galloway Plan the affairs of the union were to be managed by a president general appointed by the king and a grand council made up of
delegates chosen by the colonial assemblies. No law relating to the
colonies as a whole could be effective until endorsed both by Parliament and this general council. This latter body was thus to be a sort
of federal assembly and was to act as a shock absorber in easing the
jolts, if there should be rough sledding, in the relations between the
colonies and the homeland. This proposal was defeated by one vote.

The Galloway Plan

The congress adopted a conciliatory tone in expressing loyalty to
the king and in requesting him by petition to redress their griev-

---

[1] The Virginia delegation included in its membership Patrick Henry, Washington,
and Peyton Randolph, the last-named being chosen president of the congress. The
leading representatives from Massachusetts were John and Samuel Adams.

The "Declaration of Rights and Grievances"

ances; but in voting a "Declaration of Rights and Grievances" it announced a bold determination to uphold colonial rights. These resolutions stated that the rights of the colonials "to life, liberty and property were secured by the principles of the British Constitution, the unchanging laws of nature, and their colonial charters." The right of Parliament to tax the colonies was denied, but its authority to regulate their external commerce was conceded, provided that in this regulation there was no "idea of taxation, external or internal."

SAMUEL ADAMS.   PATRICK HENRY.

The Association

Another important act of the congress was the signing of the Continental Association. This was a nonintercourse agreement entered into by the members on behalf of themselves and their constituents. A solemn pledge was made not to import any more goods from Great Britain and Ireland after December 1, 1774, nor to send any of their products (except rice) to the British Isles or the British West Indies after September 10, 1775, unless in the meantime their grievances had been redressed. Local committees for the enforcement of the boycott were to be appointed in all the communities. This was done in every colony except Georgia. As the nonintercourse policy was strongly supported by public opinion it was generally well enforced. Wherever serious opposition showed itself, tar and feathers or other instruments of mob violence were called into requisition.

In Massachusetts the coercive acts had brought about a critical *Battles of* situation and the people were on the verge of an outbreak. Feel- *Lexington* ing against England had been raised to a white heat by the agita- *and Concord* tion of Samuel Adams and other radical leaders. The authority of General Gage, the royal governor, was no longer accepted. To take its place, a revolutionary government had been organized and an army had been collected. On being informed that the insurgents were assembling military supplies at Concord, a village

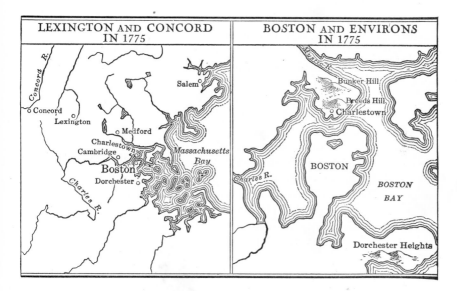

about eighteen miles from Boston, Gage dispatched a small band of soldiers to seize these stores. By early morning, April 19, 1775, Gage's redcoats had advanced as far as Lexington on their march. Here they found a small force of armed colonials which seemed ready to challenge their further progress. When the British commander ordered the Massachusetts men to lay down their arms they refused to do so. A shot was fired (but whether by an insurgent or a British redcoat, no one knows) and a skirmish ensued in which eight of the Massachusetts soldiers were killed and two were wounded. The British continued their march to Concord and destroyed the stores there; but in the meantime the report of the encounter at Lexington had been spread throughout the community, and a number of volunteers rushed forward to attack the British on the return march. From Concord to Boston the redcoats had to face an almost continuous fire leveled at them from behind trees and rock fences.

In this way began the fighting of the Revolutionary War. The exciting news of bloodshed flew rapidly, and soon armed forces from all parts of New England were hurrying to Boston to assist in besieging the British troops. In the other colonies too the people were aroused to a high pitch of excitement, and throughout the entire country patriotic resolutions were passed and war preparations were pushed forward.

The Second Continental Congress

Three weeks after the events at Lexington and Concord, the Second Continental Congress met at Philadelphia (May 10, 1775). In this assembly there were representatives from all of the thirteen continental colonies, though some of those in attendance at the first session had been chosen by only a small minority of the people whom they represented. The governors had been prohibited by royal instructions from allowing the regular election of these representatives, and therefore many of them had been chosen by revolutionary conventions. After the state governments were organized, the members of Congress were elected by the state legislatures. The Second Continental Congress continued until 1781, when the Articles of Confederation went into effect. During this time it had entire control of Federal affairs.

Washington made commander-in-chief of the Federal army

Of these early delegates, the radicals were in the majority though the conservatives, led by John Dickinson of Pennsylvania, showed considerable strength. It was due largely to the influence of the latter group that an immediate break with the mother country was prevented and an address professing loyalty to the king was voted. The radicals, however, succeeded in carrying through some measures which were a virtual declaration of war on Britain. The troops which had assembled in front of Boston were taken over by Congress and made into a Federal army, which was to be enlarged by new recruits from other colonies. On the nomination of John Adams, George Washington was chosen commander-in-chief of the Federal forces.

The selection of Washington was due in part to the wish of the Massachusetts leaders to win the South to the cause of resistance. This was a very fortunate choice. Probably no man in America was better suited to the difficult task now assigned him. He had had less practice in the art of war and enjoyed less military prestige than some of his subordinate officers, but his high moral qualities made up for any shortcomings in this respect. Possessed of remarkable self-control, he had his emotions so well-disciplined that he could present an unruffled exterior under the most discouraging circumstances. His stout optimism and firm faith in the ultimate

success of the cause gave him poise and serenity in times of gloom
and inspired his men with hope and confidence. "He was often
anxious but never despondent."[1]

1 C. H. Van Tyne, *The American Revolution*, 43-44.

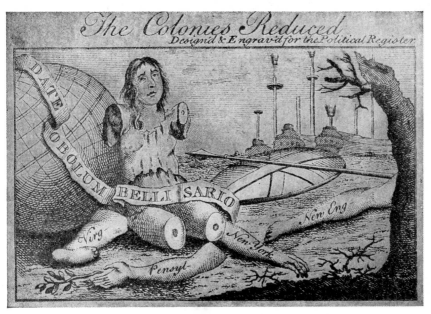

FRANKLIN'S FAMOUS CARTOON MADE AT THE TIME OF THE STAMP ACT.

From Fay's "Franklin, The Apostle of Modern Times,"
Little, Brown and Company.

CHAPTER XII

Separation from the Empire

A FAMILY QUARREL

Washington assumes command of the army

WASHINGTON was prompt in assuming the duties of commander-in-chief of the American forces. On July 3, 1775, at Cambridge, Massachusetts, he took command of the troops which had assembled in front of Boston. There were sixteen thousand of these farmer-soldiers, and soon three thousand recruits were added from Pennsylvania, Maryland, and Virginia.

The situation was anything but encouraging to the Patriot cause. The men were untrained and undisciplined, their zeal was flagging, and many of them were leaving at the end of their short terms of enlistment. There were petty jealousies among the officers, and no unified plan had been worked out for gaining accessions to the army and furnishing it with the proper supplies. Washington's first task was to bring order out of this confusion. The soldiers were trained and disciplined and the leaks due to desertions were largely stopped. When his raw troops had been molded into an efficient fighting force, Washington hoped to oust the British from Boston. To do this it would be necessary to seize and fortify one of several hills from the top of which the town could be bombarded.

Battle of Bunker Hill

Before Washington's arrival the Patriots had already had a stiff encounter with the British in an effort to realize this aim. The Americans under the command of Colonel William Prescott had seized and fortified Breed's Hill in Charlestown, north of Boston. Since this hilltop commanded Boston, Gage, the British commander, determined to drive the rebels from it. With the reinforcements which had come in to him, his troops numbered about ten thousand. With such a force he could have entrapped the Patriots by seizing the narrow isthmus at their rear. Instead of doing this he decided to attack them in front. The first two assaults were repulsed by the defenders with heavy losses to the assailants; but when the third was made the Americans had exhausted their ammunition and so had to withdraw. This, the first serious encounter of the war, is usually known as the battle of Bunker Hill, although it took place (June 17) on the adjacent height of Breed's Hill.

Washington did not have enough powder to bombard Gage's position, and as the enemy would not give battle, for some months he was forced to pursue a policy of watchful waiting. The scarcity of munitions was remedied when he received a supply of guns, including cannon, which had been captured from the British at Forts Ticonderoga and Crown Point, on Lake Champlain. Ethan Allen and Seth Warner had seized these two posts and with them a considerable amount of arms and ammunition. From these forts cannon were brought over the snow on sleds to Boston. This additional equipment enabled Washington to fortify Dorchester Heights to the south of Boston (March, 1776). He was now in a position to shell the British troops, and Howe, who had succeeded Gage, hurriedly evacuated the town. His army, along with nine hundred Loyalists, was put on shipboard and conveyed to Halifax, Nova Scotia. *Capture of Ticonderoga and Crown Point*

The British withdraw from Boston

The capture of Forts Ticonderoga and Crown Point opened the gateway to Canada. In the fall of 1775 the Patriots took advantage of this opportunity by sending two expeditions into Canada, which were under the command of Richard Montgomery and Benedict Arnold. It was hoped that the French Canadians would welcome their fellow Americans and would join in the revolt against British authority. Montgomery was able to capture Montreal and then join Arnold, who, after a march of terrible suffering, had appeared before Quebec. An unsuccessful assault was made on Quebec by the joint commands, in which Montgomery was killed. Arnold held his position in front of Quebec during the winter but in the spring was pushed southward by a British force under Sir Guy Carleton. Owing to the strong resistance offered by Arnold in his retreat, the advance of Carleton was slowed down and he was kept from joining Howe in New York. *The expedition against Canada*

The controversy between the mother country and her colonies brought about a division of sentiment in both England and America. In the early stages of the quarrel some of the leading Whigs in the homeland, such as the Earl of Chatham and Edmund Burke, upheld the American position, while the conservative Tories as a rule had no sympathy with the American cause. The colonials were also divided into liberals, or radicals, and conservatives. During the decade of controversy the former were aggressive in their opposition to British policies while the latter were in favor of acquiescence in or of moderate opposition to them. At first the issue between the radicals and the conservatives was a debatable one. With the outbreak of hostilities, however, and especially after independence was declared, the line which divided the advocates *Whigs and Tories* from the opponents of the revolutionary movement became a wall that separated the sheep from the goats. Those who upheld the American cause were known as Patriots, or Whigs; those who remained loyal to the empire were called Loyalists by the British and Tories by the Americans. Some of the Loyalists had joined in the protests against the objectionable acts of Parliament but were unwilling to carry their opposition beyond the limits of legal resistance. Others believed that the safety and welfare of the colonies were bound up with their membership in the empire. The Loyalists were doubtless as honest in their convictions as the Whigs.

Harsh and unjust treatment was meted out to the Loyalists with the purpose of converting them or punishing them for their fifth-column activities. Their property was seized by the state officials; while some of them were sent into exile, others were made the victims of tar and feathers, and a few were hanged as traitors. Those who were expelled from the country took refuge in England, the West Indies, Canada, or some American city under British control. A large number of them joined the British army and aided in the fight against their fellow countrymen. The persecutions to which they were subjected aroused in the Loyalists a feeling of intense bitterness, and whenever they had the opportunity they repaid their Whig enemies in kind for the sufferings which they had been forced to endure. Notable examples of Tory atrocities were the massacres and depredations perpetrated by them and their Indian allies in Wyoming Valley, Pennsylvania (July, 1778), and Cherry Valley, New York (November, 1778).

There were Tories in all sections, and in some of the states they were in the majority. John Adams estimated that a third of the population of the thirteen colonies and a larger proportion of the upper class were opposed to the Revolution. In the North the conservatives generally came from the wealthy and educated classes. The radicals, on the other hand, were recruited mostly from the lower and middle classes, though in the list of zealous supporters of the Revolution were included some of the merchants and others of the aristocracy. Most of the radicals from the lower and middle classes had not enjoyed the right of suffrage and had not had any voice in the provincial government. Their dissatisfaction with the rule of the aristocratic cliques which dominated the provincial governments was behind much of their opposition to British policy; for they felt that the power of the privileged aristocracy at home was propped up by imperial authority. A direct thrust at the latter would therefore be an indirect blow to the former.

Most of the large landowners of the Chesapeake and Southern

colonies were ardent revolutionists. As a rule, they were stout in-dividualists and resented the new colonial policy of Britain as an unjustifiable restraint on their political rights. There was consider-able Loyalist sentiment among the backwoodsmen of the Carolinas and among the Scotch Highlanders living on the Cape Fear River. The Scotch-Irish of the Carolina hill region were, however, as strongly in favor of the Whigs as the Highland Scotch were against them; but some of the Carolina frontiersmen were Tories. Most of these Tories were still nursing the grievances against the ruling clique of the East which had led to clashes between the Regulators and the provincial authorities, culminating in the battle of Alamance Creek (see p. 101). It was largely on account of their ill feeling toward the Tidewater aristocrats, who were generally Whigs, that these upland folk had remained loyal to the mother country.

The British government overestimated the strength of Loyalist feeling in the Carolinas and hoped quickly to bring these two rebel states back under imperial control. In furtherance of this aim a British fleet under Sir Henry Clinton was sent to Southern waters to co-operate with the Loyalists in stamping out revolt; but before these ships arrived at the coast of North Carolina the Tories had been badly defeated by the Whigs at Moore's Creek Bridge (Febru-ary 27, 1776). This victory yielded the Patriots nine hundred prison-ers and valuable booty in the form of gold and munitions of war. *Battle of Moore's Creek Bridge*

Clinton's squadron of warships did not arrive at the mouth of the Cape Fear River until about six weeks after the battle of Moore's Creek Bridge. After waiting for some weeks and conclud-ing that no further action could be expected from his Tory allies in the back country, Clinton sailed for Charleston. By taking this city the British would have a strong rallying-point for the Loyalists of South Carolina. The defense of the city was entrusted to Colonel Moultrie. He stationed his army of about six thousand militia on an island which commanded the entrance to the harbor. His men were protected by sand banks and a fort made of green palmetto logs. From behind this shelter they poured raking broadsides into the British ships without suffering much from the return fire, for most of the cannon balls hurled from the enemy fleet sank harm-lessly into the sandbanks or the soft logs of the fort. *British naval attack on Charleston repulsed*

SEPARATION FROM THE EMPIRE

When hostilities began between England and America a ma-jority of the colonials were opposed to separation from the empire. They hoped that the fight would be a brief one and would end in

Sentiment in favor of independence develops in the colonies

a recognition of their rights by the British government; but feeling between the mother country and the thirteen colonies grew in bitterness as the war progressed, and in America there rapidly developed a desire for independence. The growth of this feeling was greatly promoted by the policy of the English government. In August, 1775, the king declared America to be in a state of rebellion, and later, Parliament passed an act forbidding all commercial intercourse between the homeland and the continental colonies for the duration of the rebellion. Under such circumstances it was both inconsistent and unwise for the colonies to continue their membership in the British empire. To profess loyalty to a government against which they were waging war was to continue to sit on the limb at which they were sawing. At this juncture the only sensible course was either to quit sawing or get off the limb. America chose the latter alternative.

Early in 1776 there was, throughout the entire country, a strong sentiment for separation. By declaring their independence the colonies might be in a position to form military alliances and commercial agreements with the continental European powers and secure from them recognition of their rights as belligerents. No such possibility would be open to them as long as they professed allegiance to the British empire. All that was needed to whip up this feeling into active enthusiasm was a little propaganda of the right sort. And this propaganda was abundantly supplied by a pamphlet,

Common Sense

entitled *Common Sense,* published by Thomas Paine, an Englishman who had been living in America for the past year. Written in a clear but colorful style, this brilliant essay made a great appeal to the people and was widely read in all sections. It argued convincingly in favor of independence and pointed out the folly of America's looking for direction to a government three thousand miles away.

The Declaration of Independence

The sentiment on the part of the people in favor of independence was reflected by their leaders in Congress, and by the middle of the year that body, now in control of the radicals, was ready to take a definite stand in favor of separation. The delegates in Congress from North Carolina were instructed (April 12, 1776) to unite with the other representatives in a declaration of independence, and like instructions were received by the delegates of other colonies. Before Congress had taken action, however, Virginia, the oldest and one of the most important of the provinces, had announced her separation from the homeland. The hesitating colonies were encouraged by this bold step to follow her example. The delegates of the Old Dominion were also directed (May 15) to offer a resolution in favor of independence. In compliance with this mandate Richard Henry Lee moved (June 7, 1776) that the thirteen colonies be declared "free and independent states." This motion was ably supported by John Adams, who was called the "Atlas of Independence." Action on Lee's proposal was delayed, however, and it was not adopted until July 2.

In the meantime a committee composed of Thomas Jefferson, John Adams, Benjamin Franklin, Roger Sherman, and Robert R. Livingston had been appointed to draw up a declaration of independence. The original text of the Declaration was prepared entirely by Jefferson, except for a few slight changes suggested by Franklin and Adams. When the document was presented to Congress, John Adams made an earnest appeal for its acceptance. On July 4, 1776, the Declaration was adopted by Congress by a vote of twelve colonies, but not before a few rather important revisions had been made in the original draft. The text of the Declaration was afterwards neatly inscribed on parchment and signed by the members. On August 2 all who were present attached their signatures to the famous document, and the others signed it later in the session.

The Declaration of Independence was hailed with joy and enthusiasm by a large proportion of the people in all the colonies. There were numerous demonstrations such as the ringing of bells, the booming of cannon, and other modes of rejoicing. Among conservatives, however, there was a strong feeling of regret that the bonds holding the colonies to the mother country had been finally severed. America, as they considered, owed its safety and security to imperial authority, and without this protection it would become the scene of internal strife and bloodshed. Even some of the Whigs were saddened by the thought that the old homeland would henceforth be a foreign country.

In the Declaration of Independence are set forth certain "self-evident" truths regarding the natural rights of man and the powers and limitations of government. It is stated that all persons are endowed "with certain unalienable rights, that among these are life, liberty and the pursuit of happiness"; and all governments derive "their just powers from the consent of the governed." Then follows a long list of grievances which the colonials had suffered at the hands of the king. These acts of misrule, it is asserted, justify a secession of the colonies from the empire, and therefore Congress declares that "these United Colonies are, and of right ought to be, free and independent states." *Nature of the Declaration*

The doctrines embodied in the Declaration were not original

with Jefferson but were borrowed largely from John Locke, especially from his "Second Essay on Government." These ideas had been widely discussed by the radical leaders and were therefore not new to the members of Congress. Jefferson's merit in writing the Declaration lies in his skill in organizing these ideas and giving them clear and forceful expression. He was very clever as a phrase-maker, and was able to cast popular concepts into a form which makes the Declaration of Independence a literary masterpiece.

AN INTERNATIONAL CONFLICT

Relative strength of the belligerents

The division of sentiment in America was a weighty obstacle to the success of the revolutionary movement. The weakness of the general government was also a serious drawback. The Continental Congress, which had charge of Federal affairs, could not raise revenue by taxation and in other ways was not an efficient governing body. On the other hand, Britain was the richest nation in the world. Its government had good credit and a tax system which was in fine running order. Adequate funds for prosecuting the war could therefore be easily obtained by taxes and loans; but an efficient management of the war was prevented by corruption among responsible officials. There was also considerable disagreement in the mother country over the quarrel with America. In England the war was opposed by some liberal statesmen, a good portion of the merchants, and the ministers of the dissenting denominations. Besides, the masses had no relish for the fight against their kinsmen across seas. The unwillingness of the English people to enlist in the army caused the military authorities to make use of a good many mercenaries hired from German princes.

The American army

The Patriot forces included two classes of soldiers—the Continental army and the militia. The regular army varied in size, since the periods of enlistment were short and the men often left the army at the end of their terms of service. Seldom was the total strength of the fighting force in excess of sixteen thousand men at any one time, and at Valley Forge Washington's command was reduced to two thousand. It was difficult to keep the army supplied with the necessary recruits, despite the offer of bounties to volunteers and the attempts at conscription made late in the war in several states. The soldiers were poorly clad and the small pay promised them was often in arrears, whereas industry and trade were holding out tempting offers in the form of high wages and large profits.

There was also a great deal of unnecessary suffering among the men due to a lack of proper care of the sick and wounded; for the hospital service was "badly organized, ill-supplied, [and] dishonestly administered."[1] As the personnel of the army was constantly changing, it was impossible to maintain a high standard of training and discipline. The military situation would have been hopeless but for a small nucleus of regulars who remained in continuous service. They were devoted to the cause and never yielded to discouragement, even under the most adverse circumstances.

The militia

At times the Continental army received the assistance of the state militia. This arm of the service was far from satisfactory. The citizen soldiers who constituted the militia were little, if any, better than raw recruits, as they had generally had only a few days' training a year. They were undisciplined and often cowardly. In times of crisis some of them would not prolong their short terms of service to save the cause. They were therefore almost useless for long and sustained campaigns; but since they were good marksmen and familiar with the terrain of their own localities, they often performed useful service in defending their home communities.

The British handicapped by distance

The British were at a great disadvantage in prosecuting a war three thousand miles from the home base. In that day of small vessels the transportation of a large army and its needed supplies was a difficult task even for the Mistress of the Seas. There was no single strategic center, the capture of which would lead to the collapse of American defense. On the contrary, if the Patriots were to be defeated, a wide expanse of territory would have to be seized and held. This necessitated the division of the British forces into small units and their dispersion throughout the country. Such a strategy ruled out large-scale operations. Furthermore, the British army in America was never strong enough to cope with the difficult military situation, although Clinton's forces at one time (1781) aggregated thirty-four thousand men.

Officers in the American army

In the American army the officers of the lower ranks were as a rule very inefficient. In speaking of them in 1776 Washington said that "except in a few instances [they were] not worth the bread they eat." Some of the higher officers, however, such as Greene, Montgomery, and Arnold, were efficient. Washington also had the assistance of a few foreign officers who were capable leaders. Prominent among these were the Prussian general, Baron von

---

[1] Quoted by C. H. Van Tyne, *England and America*, 141.

Steuben,[1] and two French generals, the Marquis de Lafayette and Count Rochambeau. The best-known, though probably not the most efficient, of these was Lafayette. Although he was possessed of wealth and high social prestige, this young nobleman sacrificed his bright prospects of preferment at home and came to America to offer his services to the Continental army. Ablaze with youthful enthusiasm, he regarded the struggle in which Washington and his ragged soldiers were engaged as a battle for the ideals of freedom preached by Rousseau and other French philosophers. He was cordially received by Washington and was given high rank in the army.

British military leaders

The British army was unfortunate in its leadership. Howe's heart was not in the fight against his kith and kin, and on more than one occasion he failed to follow up and make the best of an advantage which he had over the Americans. Whether these mistakes were due to his lack of interest in the cause or to his ineptitude as a commander, we are unable to say. The policy of Clinton, Howe's successor, was also dilatory and hesitating.

Howe attacks New York

Howe remained at Halifax for only a short time and then moved his army to New York. If he could take and hold this town he would be able to divide the northern part of the American confederacy from the southern and might be able to control the Hudson-Champlain approach to Canada. The Loyalists were numerous in New York, and Howe was counting on their support in carrying out his plans. Washington also realized the strategic value of New York and had stationed his forces there before the British arrived. He threw up fortifications and hoped to hold the enemy in check.

British victories around New York

Early in the summer of 1776 Howe appeared off Sandy Hook. With an army of thirty-two thousand men and with the co-operation of the British fleet under command of his brother, Admiral Richard Lord Howe, General Howe was ready for an attack on Washington's greatly outnumbered forces. In the first engagement at Brooklyn Heights on Long Island (August 22) a part of the Patriot army under General Putnam was badly defeated. If Howe had at once pressed his advantage he could have captured nine thousand of Washington's entrapped soldiers; but his delay and the friendly aid of a dense fog enabled Washington to effect their escape by transferring them to safety on Manhattan Island.

---

1 Before offering his services to Washington, Steuben had earned and received distinction in the wars of Frederick the Great. The most useful service performed by Steuben was that of drilling the American soldiers and thus giving them a measure of training in military tactics. Other foreigners who won distinction as leaders in the American army were the French officers, Thomas Conway and Johann Kalb; and the Polish commanders, Thaddeus Kosciusko and Count Pulaski, who were noted for their courage and ability.

The British won other victories around New York. In one of these they captured (at Fort Washington) twenty-eight hundred of Washington's finest troops. These successes gave the British control of New York, which was retained by them to the end of the war. The city now became a haven for persecuted Tories who hurried from all quarters to this safe refuge. Upon the few Whigs who remained there they wreaked a vengeance as harsh as that which had been dealt out to them.

The British government was anxious to come to an understanding with the insurgents and had authorized the Howe brothers to offer terms of conciliation. The role of peacemaker was a very acceptable one to them, for they had always had a kindly feeling toward the Americans, and Lord Howe had spoken in Parliament in advocacy of their rights. After the battle at Brooklyn Heights the admiral met three commissioners from Congress in an effort to work out a formula of peace. The Declaration of Independence had just been voted, and the American commissioners were instructed to urge the recognition of the independence of the states as a necessary condition of agreement. Howe was not authorized to make so great a concession, and so his well-intentioned efforts ended in failure. *An unsuccessful effort for peace*

The Patriot army was demoralized and disorganized after the defeats around New York. It was also dwindling away because many of the men were leaving when their terms of enlistment expired. Washington's only hope now was to take his remnant of an army to a place of safety. Accordingly, he withdrew rapidly through New Jersey and across the Delaware River. The British who were hot on his trail were stopped at the Delaware because the Americans had seized all the boats. Washington's army had now been reduced to about three thousand "ragamuffins," and only the stoutest optimists were hopeful of success. The people of Philadelphia were stricken with terror, and Congress fled to Baltimore. *Washington retreats across New Jersey*

This condition of discouragement was greatly relieved by two successful ventures of Washington. On Christmas night (1776) he recrossed the Delaware and made a surprise attack on the British troops at Trenton. The enemy force (composed of Hessian mercenaries) was badly defeated and a thousand prisoners were taken. Shortly afterwards (January 3, 1777) he won another victory over the British at Princeton. The Patriots were greatly encouraged by these successes and new recruits began to come in. Congress conferred upon Washington dictatorial powers for a period of six months. He stationed his army at Morristown for the winter and during this time devoted his efforts toward reorganizing it. *American successes at Trenton and Princeton*

In the spring of 1777 Howe transferred the greater part of his

Battle of
Brandywine

army from New York to Philadelphia. He seemed to think that the seizure of their capital would lower the morale of the rebels. His soldiers were put on shipboard and under convoy of Lord Howe's fleet were sent up to Elkton, Maryland, at the head of Chesapeake Bay. Washington moved below Philadelphia with the view to preventing the enemy's approach to the capital. A battle was fought at Chadd's Ford on Brandywine Creek in which the Patriot

Philadelphia
taken by
Howe

forces were badly defeated. Philadelphia was then taken by the British. Congress had in the meantime fled to Lancaster, Pennsylvania.

The capture of Philadelphia was hailed by the British as a great victory for their cause and a severe blow to American prestige, but it made no material change in the military situation. On the other hand, it cost Howe the opportunity of participating in an ambitious project for compassing the downfall of the insurgent movement.

The British
plan an
elaborate
campaign

By this plan Burgoyne was to march southward from Canada by way of the Lake Champlain route to join Howe, who was to come up from New York. Colonel St. Leger was to advance from Oswego down the Mohawk Valley and join forces with Burgoyne and Howe around Albany. These plans woefully miscarried. Howe, as has been seen, was tied up with the Pennsylvania campaign and could not send aid to Burgoyne. The latter therefore failed to receive the much-needed reinforcements which he had a right to expect. Nor was St. Leger able to carry out his part of the assignment. He encountered such strenuous opposition from the Patriots at Fort Schuyler (Fort Stanwix) and Oriskany that he returned to Canada.

Burgoyne's
difficulties

Burgoyne therefore had to bear alone the responsibility of performing this arduous task, and he was beset with almost insurmountable obstacles. His line of march was over a difficult terrain interspersed with swamps and forests, and progress had to be slow. These difficulties were aggravated by the many large trees which the American soldiers had felled to impede his advance. His army grew smaller as he moved forward because of the necessity of stationing troops at certain points to guard his communications with his base in Canada. His force was still further depleted by the de-

Battle of
Bennington

feat of two detachments, composed of German and Indian troops, which had been sent to destroy the military stores at Bennington. This ill-starred venture cost the British more than nine hundred men in killed, captured, and wounded.

Two battles
at Freeman's
Farm

Burgoyne's advance was opposed by an American army consisting of both regulars and militiamen. It was commanded at first by General Schuyler and later by General Horatio Gates. Reinforcements kept coming to Gates until he had an overwhelming superiority over his opponent. Two battles were fought at Freeman's

NORTHERN CAMPAIGNS
OF THE
REVOLUTIONARY WAR
——— St. Leger's route
– – – Arnold's route
• • • • Burgoyne's route
–·–·– Baum's route

HAGSTROM CO., INC.

Farm, near Saratoga (on September 19 and October 7, 1777). The first of these was indecisive, but the second was an important victory for the Americans. A leading part in both these encounters was taken by Benedict Arnold. Not long after the second battle Burgoyne was surrounded and forced to yield to the superior strength of his antagonist. On October 17, 1777, his entire command of fifty-eight hundred men surrendered at Saratoga. This was easily the most outstanding victory scored by the Americans up to this time and proved to be an important factor in the final outcome of the contest. An immediate result of great significance was that by it France was induced to form an alliance with the Americans.

THE HORSE AMERICA, *throwing his Master*

Reproduced from THE PAGEANT OF AMERICA, *Copyright Yale University Press*

"THE HORSE, AMERICA, THROWING HIS MASTER."

CHAPTER XIII

The Winning of Independence

THE FRENCH ALLIANCE

*A*T the outbreak of the American Revolution the government of France was an absolute monarchy, with young Louis XVI on the throne. Louis leaned heavily on the advice of Count de Vergennes, Secretary of State for Foreign Affairs. Vergennes had no sympathy with the liberal ideas of the Declaration of Independence but was disposed to encourage the Americans in their revolt against the mother country. He was smarting under the humiliation inflicted upon his country by Britain as a result of the Seven Years' War and he was anxious to even scores with France's traditional enemy. *Why France sympathized with the United States*

He hoped that the uprising in America would subject England to a long and costly war and possibly lead to the loss of her overseas possessions. In either event England's prestige and power would be lessened and France's position in the family of European nations would be relatively strengthened. Furthermore, he feared that if Britain should succeed in putting down the rebellion she might then seize the French and Spanish dependencies in America. On the other hand, if the American insurgents should be successful without having received aid from France and Spain they might feel free to appropriate these French and Spanish possessions.

Vergennes, therefore, wished to aid the Americans, but was unwilling to take the chance of a war with Britain until he had reasonable assurance as to the success of the revolt. Owing to his doubts regarding the outcome of the war, he refused for a time to recognize the independence of the colonies. He did, however, give secret aid to the Americans in the form of loans and gifts of money. Supplies were furnished the Patriot army by the French government through the agency of a fictitious mercantile establishment in Paris.

In the meantime the Continental Congress had been making efforts to cultivate the friendship of France and other European powers. Even before independence was declared, Silas Deane had been sent to Paris as the agent of Congress. In the fall of 1776 Arthur Lee and Franklin were commissioned to act with Deane as envoys *Franklin in France* at Paris. As they were not officially received, their negotiations with the foreign office were carried on in an indirect way. Franklin took the leading part in presenting the claims of his country, and Deane was afterwards recalled (December 8, 1777). Franklin at once became the lion of French society. His fine common sense, his terse and epigrammatic sayings, his reputation as a scientist and author, and the Quaker-like simplicity of his taste in dress, marked him out as a philosopher of the highest rank. Indeed, to the French people he looked as if he might have stepped out from one of Rousseau's treatises on the simple life.

Reproduced from THE PAGEANT OF AMERICA,
Copyright Yale University Press

BENJAMIN FRANKLIN.

The Franco-American alliance

The surrender of Burgoyne at Saratoga led Vergennes to believe that the Patriots would win the war. He was now willing to risk a break with England and form an alliance with the American states. On February 6, 1778, two treaties were signed between France and the United States. One of these was an agreement for mutual commercial advantages and the other was a treaty of alliance. France recognized the independence of the new republic and gave a pledge of military and naval support in upholding this independence. The two allies were to co-operate in the war which was expected to break out between England and France, and neither of them was "to conclude either truce or peace with Great Britain without the formal consent of the other first obtained." France agreed to make no effort to regain the possessions on the mainland of North America which she had lost to England, but reserved the right to appropriate any of Britain's West Indian islands which she might be able to conquer. Each party guaranteed to the other all the American territory which it then had or might acquire as a result of the war.

France at once entered the war on the side of her ally. The following year Spain also declared war on Britain, but not as an ally of the United States. Making an alliance with England's revolting colonies would have been setting a bad example for her own American dependencies. Sentiment among the non-belligerent powers of Europe was also against England. In 1780 Denmark, Sweden, the Netherlands, Portugal, and Russia entered into an agreement known as the League of Armed Neutrality. This alliance was a gesture of rebuke to British naval practices, for behind it was a declaration of the rights of neutrals, some of which England had been violating. A controversy arose between Britain and the Netherlands which led to war in the latter part of this year. *The Anglo-American war widens into a European struggle*

The quarrel between England and her American colonies had thus become a European struggle, and England's naval superiority was greatly reduced. This change in the naval situation was a prime factor in deciding the final outcome of the war. The French soldiers did not take an important part in military affairs in continental America except at the battle of Yorktown, but some of the French officers did good work in training the American troops for service. The Patriot cause was also greatly aided by the money lent to the United States by the French government. These loans made possible the purchasing of much-needed supplies for Washington's army. Later (1782), through the efforts of John Adams, the government of the Netherlands recognized the independence of the United States and signed a treaty of commerce with the new confederacy. A loan of two million dollars was also secured from Dutch bankers.

WINNING INDEPENDENCE

During the winter of 1777-78 Washington's army was quartered at Valley Forge. While here the soldiers were subjected to extreme hardships owing to a shortage of food and clothing. These sufferings could have been avoided if proper arrangements had been made for bringing in supplies; for there was an adequate stock of food in the country. The failure to meet the needs of the army was due mainly to a lack of transportation facilities, and this handicap was aggravated by the inefficiency of Congress. Another cause was the depreciated paper money. British gold enabled Howe's army in Philadelphia to live in luxury, whereas the Pennsylvania farmers refused to supply Washington's soldiers with food in exchange for their cheap paper money. Over this scene of unnecessary distress, Washington's grandeur of character shed the one bright gleam of splendor. He was daily confronted with the sufferings of a justly *Washington's army at Valley Forge* complaining army, the intriguing efforts of some of his subordinate officers to displace him, the impotence of the government, and the unconcern and lack of patriotism exhibited by the civilian population. In this atmosphere of envy and selfishness he stood erect and exhibited a faith and composure which stamped him as one of the world's noblest characters.

Philadelphia evacuated by the British

When news of the French alliance reached America it brought cheer to the hungry Patriots at Valley Forge and disappointment to the British at Philadelphia. With the aid of the French fleet the new allies might now block the river approach to Philadelphia and thus deprive the British army of its water-borne supplies. In the spring the English army was ordered to evacuate Philadelphia and return to New York. While Sir Henry Clinton, who had succeeded Howe in command of the English forces, was advancing across New Jersey, Washington arranged to strike at him at Monmouth. The attack was led by General Charles Lee and gave every promise of success. But, owing either to cowardice or treachery, Lee gave the command to retreat when an advance would probably have meant victory. Washington arrived on the scene in time to check the retreat but too late to prevent the escape of the enemy. For his action on this occasion Lee was severely reprimanded by Washington and later court-martialed and suspended from the army.

Battle of Monmouth

The French and Americans fail in an attack on Newport

The British were now stationed in force at New York and Newport, Rhode Island. A French fleet under the command of Count D'Estaing appeared before Newport to co-operate with American troops in an assault on the town. After some maneuvering, D'Estaing, feeling unable to cope with Lord Howe's fleet, withdrew and sailed to Boston, much to the chagrin and regret of the American soldiers who were eager for the attack. From this time until the end of the war the other engagements in the North were only of a minor character.

Congress rejects the peace offer of the British government

The defeat of Burgoyne indicated that the Americans could not be subdued, and commissioners were sent over by the British government to offer peace and pardon on generous terms. Everything short of independence which the Patriots had demanded was now to be conceded. This second attempt at peace failed, however, because Congress refused to consider any offer which did not include independence. Furthermore, the treaty of alliance with France had already been signed, and no agreement could be honorably made with England without the consent of the French government.

The settlements in western Pennsylvania and western Virginia.

including those in Kentucky, were in constant danger from Indian attack. Colonel Henry Hamilton, who commanded the British post at Detroit, was inciting his Indian allies against the frontiersmen and buying the scalps they brought in. For this reason he was known as the "Hair-buyer." Colonel George Rogers Clark felt that the best way to protect the western settlers was to take from the British the posts which they held in the Northwest. He therefore obtained authority from Governor Patrick Henry of Virginia to lead an expedition against the forts in the Illinois region. With a force

Expedition of George Rogers Clark

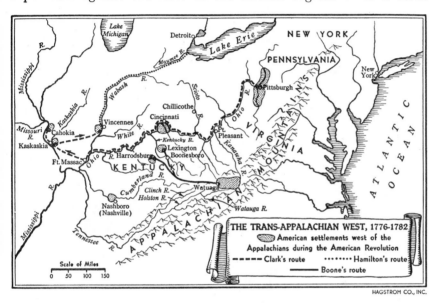

THE TRANS-APPALACHIAN WEST, 1776-1782
American settlements west of the Appalachians during the American Revolution
----- Clark's route ········· Hamilton's route
——— Boone's route

HAGSTROM CO., INC.

of one hundred and seventy-five men he floated down the Ohio River to the mouth of the Cumberland and marched overland to Fort Kaskaskia. This post was taken by surprise and easily captured. The few French settlers who lived in the Illinois villages were indifferent as to whether the country was under British or American control. When they learned that France and the United States were in alliance they readily gave their allegiance to the latter country. Clark therefore had no difficulty in taking over the entire Illinois country, including Vincennes on the Wabash (1778-79).

In an effort to regain the French forts, Hamilton marched down from Detroit and recaptured Vincennes. His plan was to remain here until the winter was over and then move against Clark at Kaskaskia. Instead of awaiting this attack, Clark led an expedition in February (1779) against Vincennes, marching over flooded prairies with the men at times wading in water up to their necks. Taken by surprise and outnumbered, Hamilton surrendered and was sent as a prisoner to Williamsburg. Virginia's claim to the Northwest, originally based on her colonial charters, was now reinforced by conquest. The legislature signalized its authority over the region by organizing it into the County of Illinois.

Part played by the American navy

The American navy was too small to play a leading part in the conflict with the Mistress of the Seas. Congress did have, however, a number of small men-of-war at its command, and every state, except New Jersey and Delaware, had some warships, which were used mainly for home defense. There were also a number of privately-owned vessels which had been commissioned by Congress to prey upon enemy merchant ships. These privateers, as they were called, were able both to serve the Patriot cause and enrich their owners by seizing British ships and their cargoes. France, being friendly, opened her ports to American war vessels and privateers, and from these safe bases they could operate, before as well as after the signing of the treaty of alliance.

John Paul Jones

The greatest of the Revolutionary naval heroes was John Paul Jones. After winning in a number of lesser encounters, in which he had exhibited unusual boldness and skill, he was entrusted with a squadron of five vessels, four of which had been supplied by the French government. While searching for prey on the east coast of Scotland he encountered a convoy of forty merchantmen escorted by two British men-of-war. He engaged the two war vessels in battle and captured both of them.

Savannah captured by the British

After the repulse of the French-American attack on Newport the British made the South the chief scene of the war. The Tories were numerous in Georgia and South Carolina, and it was expected that they would co-operate with the invaders. At the very last of the year (December 29, 1778) a British force landed near Savannah and at once captured the town. A few months later Charleston was besieged by the British commander (May, 1779). The Patriots, however, put up such a strong opposition that the siege was raised.

The British repulse a Franco-American attack on Savannah

Later in the same year (September, 1779) Count D'Estaing appeared off Savannah with a strong fleet and transports loaded with troops. General Lincoln came to his assistance, and the American and French land forces numbered about six thousand. After laying siege to the town for a while they unwisely attempted an assault. This was beaten off by the British with great loss to the assailants (October). D'Estaing now sailed away and gave no further aid to the Americans. Encouraged by this great success, Clinton sailed from New York and again made an attack on Charleston. The

Charleston captured by the British

city was captured, and General Lincoln, who was in charge of the defense, had to surrender his entire army of five thousand men (May, 1780).

The British were now free to run at large throughout South Carolina and Georgia. For some time the only resistance they encountered came from guerrilla bands skillfully led by such bold leaders as Francis Marion and Thomas Sumter. By making surprise

Guerrilla warfare

SOUTHERN CAMPAIGNS IN THE REVOLUTIONARY WAR

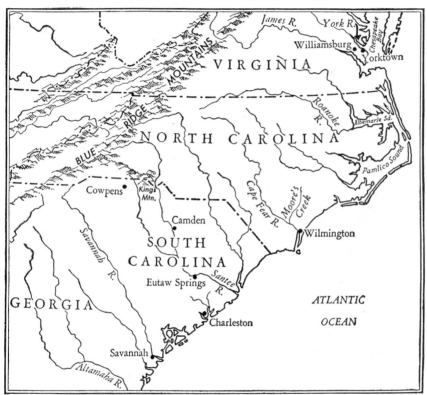

attacks on small detachments and then escaping through the swamps to safety these leaders were able to cause the enemy considerable annoyance.

To aid the Whigs in their one-sided contest, Congress sent General Gates to the south with an army composed of regulars and militia in about equal numbers. At Camden, Gates unexpectedly encountered a British force under Lord Cornwallis and was badly defeated (August, 1780). The Patriot army lost in casualties and captures about two thirds of its entire number.

Battle of Camden

A partial offset to the rout at Camden was a noted victory gained

Battle of King's Mountain

by the Americans at King's Mountain. On this wooded elevation on the border of the two Carolinas, a British force of two thousand men under the command of Colonel Ferguson was attacked by a numerous band of American militia. The terrain was ideal for the kind of fighting for which the backwoodsmen were best suited. From the shelter of trees and boulders they could in comparative safety use their fine marksmanship with telling effect. The British were defeated and forced to surrender after having sustained heavy losses in killed and wounded. The morale of the Patriots was greatly heightened by this victory, which proved to be a turning point in the southern campaign. The partisan leaders were now stirred to greater activity than ever.

Greene in command of the American forces in the south

Some months after the debacle at Camden, Nathanael Greene was put in command of the remnant of the army in the south. He was an efficient officer and was able to inspire his men with hope and confidence. With such a small force he could not act on the offensive and more than once suffered defeat at the hands of the enemy. Reinforcements soon began to come in, however, and with the aid of the guerrilla leaders and his able subordinates he succeeded in putting up a fine fight. Owing to his skill in conducting a retreat and his knack of wresting from defeat the fruits of victory, he made an efficient use of his little army.

Battle of Cowpens

The one outstanding victory scored by southern troops after King's Mountain, was won by Daniel Morgan's men at Cowpens, in northwestern South Carolina. Morgan stationed his men on the banks of the unfordable Broad River and invited attack by Tarleton (January, 1781). Although the British had a slight superiority in numbers they suffered a defeat which cost them more than three fourths of their entire force.

A period of gloom

In the fall of 1780 the fortunes of America had reached a very low ebb. To the discouragements growing out of military defeats in the south were added those arising from the inefficiency of Congress, the worthlessness of the Continental currency, and the war-weariness of the people. The soldiers in Washington's army were poorly fed and clothed, and many of them were deserting and joining the forces of the enemy. Never were American affairs blacker than during the year which preceded the surrender of Cornwallis. Even Washington had almost ceased to hope.

The treason of Benedict Arnold

In this time of gloom the Patriots had to steel themselves against another sore disappointment. This was the treachery of one of their ablest generals. After the British had withdrawn from Philadelphia, Benedict Arnold was put in command of the American troops in the Quaker City. During this time of relaxation (following periods of extreme hardship) he lived in luxury and entered upon some unwise monetary ventures which brought him into financial straits. A claim for expenditures which, as he alleged, had been made in connection with the Quebec expedition was not allowed by Congress, and he was on the verge of bankruptcy. He had succeeded in winning as his second wife an attractive young lady who belonged to a prominent Loyalist family. This connection and the social contacts he had made with persons of Tory leanings rendered him unpopular with some of the Whigs. Taking advantage of this hostile feeling, his enemies preferred charges of misconduct against him. He was cleared of all the serious accusations by a committee of investigation, but was found guilty by a court-martial of certain trivial offenses for which he was to be reprimanded by the commander-in-chief. Washington performed this unpleasant duty as considerately as he could, and by dwelling on Arnold's brilliant past record made his reprimand sound like a eulogy.

Embittered by the treatment he had received, Arnold decided to sell out his country and go over to the enemy. Since Washington's confidence in him was unimpaired, the important post of West Point was entrusted to him. After receiving command he arranged with Clinton to turn over this strategic position to the British. The plan was thwarted by the capture of Major André (who was the go-between in the negotiations) and the seizure of his papers. Major André was hanged as a spy, but Arnold, having received warning in time, made his escape to the British lines. As a reward for his treason he received a large sum of money and the rank of brigadier general in the English army.

Arnold believed, so his apologists contend, that the best interests of America demanded that she accept the generous terms offered by Britain and retain her membership in the empire. By going over to the British he would aid in bringing the war to a speedy conclusion and would thus advance the highest interests of his country; but even the mantle of charity is not broad enough to cover the crimes of bribery and perfidy to a friend. If this unhappy Quisling could have remained true to his first love for a year longer his name would probably now have a place next to that of Washington in the list of Revolutionary heroes.

Cornwallis felt that the war could not be brought to an end *Cornwallis in* until Virginia was conquered. To attain this objective he moved *Virginia* northward from the Carolinas and joined ranks with Arnold (May, 1781), who had been harrying the Old Dominion for some months. Opposed to the British was a force under the command of Lafayette. It was too small to cope with the enemy and could do little more than entice him into bootless pursuit marches. Perceiving the uselessness of these long chases, Cornwallis marched eastward and took position (August 2) at Yorktown, near the mouth of the York River. Here he could keep in touch with Clinton and would be in reach of land reinforcements and naval aid. Lafayette also moved eastward and remained within easy distance of his antagonist. Cornwallis did not seem, however, to be in any immediate peril, for the river at his back was only a mile wide and his cannon commanded its entire width.

Cornwallis surrenders at Yorktown

About the time Cornwallis was settling down at Yorktown, Washington received a message from the French Admiral, Count de Grasse, offering to bring his fleet from the West Indies to Chesapeake Bay to co-operate with the land forces in an attack on the British. Washington accepted this proposal and made plans to join Lafayette in Virginia. For about a year there had been a French army and a squadron of French warships at Newport, Rhode Island, which had been evacuated by the British in 1779. The land troops under the command of Count Rochambeau now left Newport and marched overland to join Washington, while the naval unit later sailed to Chesapeake Bay to reinforce Count de Grasse's fleet.

Leaving a considerable force near New York to watch Clinton, Washington started early in August (1781) on his long march to Virginia with about six thousand men, the greater portion of whom consisted of the French reserves from Newport. For a while Clinton considered the movements in the American camp as preliminary to an attack on New York. He was so preoccupied with plans for meeting this expected attack that he did not discover Washington's real purpose until the advance southward was well under way. In due course the American and French soldiers from the north joined their comrades in Virginia, and Cornwallis with seven thousand men was now besieged by an army more than twice as large.

Early in September Count de Grasse came into Chesapeake Bay with a fleet of twenty-eight ships of the line. He was now in a position to prevent Cornwallis's escape by water. The fate of the British army at Yorktown was therefore sealed unless the British navy could gain superiority in Chesapeake Bay. Clinton made an effort to save Cornwallis by dispatching Admiral Graves with his war vessels to the Chesapeake. A battle was fought between the two fleets at the entrance of the Bay (September 5) in which the British fleet sustained the greater losses. Five days later the French fleet was strengthened by new arrivals which gave it an overwhelming superiority over its antagonist. The British admiral, therefore, sailed for New York and left the French fleet in undisputed control of the Virginia waters. In a second effort to save Cornwallis, Clinton left

New York for Yorktown (October 19) with an army and forty-four British ships; but when the expedition reached the mouth of the Bay he learned that Cornwallis had surrendered nine days earlier.

Cut off as he was from all outside assistance, Cornwallis soon realized that his position had become critical. With the capture of two redoubts by the French and Americans he gave up all hope of escape and on October 19, 1781, surrendered his entire army. This victory was a decision in favor of the success of the Franco-American allies in the war, though it was more than a year before hostilities ceased and nearly two years before the definitive treaty of peace was signed.

PEACE NEGOTIATIONS

Negotiations for peace began in the spring of 1782. Before the victory at Yorktown Congress had appointed five commissioners who were to go to Paris and carry on negotiations with British representatives. The active members of the commission were John Adams, Benjamin Franklin, and John Jay.[1] Congress had acted with its accustomed timidity in giving instructions to these envoys. They were to ask for the Mississippi as the western boundary of the United States, but were not to insist upon this request as an absolute condition of agreement. They were instructed to keep Vergennes informed of all their actions; to undertake nothing in the negotiations for peace or truce, without his knowledge and consent; and ultimately to govern themselves by his advice and opinion.

American commissioners; their instructions

The first steps in the negotiations were taken by Franklin, who in the spring of 1782 was in communication with Lord Shelburne, British Minister of the Colonies. As a result of this correspondence, Lord Shelburne decided to send a special representative to Paris to treat with Franklin. For this important service he chose Richard Oswald, a Scottish merchant who had financial interests in America and was on cordial terms with Franklin. At this time Adams was at the Hague engaged in what proved to be successful negotiations with the Dutch government, and Jay was at Madrid chafing under the difficulties he was encountering in his futile attempt to win Spanish recognition of American independence. Franklin began at once to confer with Oswald, and a good start toward the formulation of peace terms had been made before Jay and Adams arrived at Paris.

Negotiations begun by Franklin

The American commissioners were resolved to make a strong fight for the Mississippi River as the western boundary of the United

---

[1] Thomas Jefferson and Henry Laurens were also included in the list of commissioners, but neither of them took part in the negotiations. Jefferson did not go to Paris, and Laurens, who had been captured by the British and later released, did not arrive at Paris until two days before the preliminary treaty was signed.

States. This purpose ran counter to the plans of Spain, which had designs on a portion of the western territory. Count Vergennes, French foreign minister, was therefore in the embarrassing position of having to decide between the conflicting claims of the allies of France. His private secretary offered as a solution of the problem the division of the trans-Allegheny region into two parts—the portion north of the Ohio River to go to England and that south of it to remain in the possession of the Indians. Some of this Indian territory would be under the protection of the United States and the remainder under that of Spain. This proposal was very unsatisfactory to the American commissioners, who were unwilling to accept the Allegheny Mountains as the western boundary of their country. One motive which prompted Vergennes to make this suggestion was the wish to satisfy the claims of Spain. Another possible incentive was the fear that the new republic in possession of the western lands might become a menacing rival of France. On the other hand, Lord Shelburne, the English prime minister, was willing to allow the claims of the United States to the Northwest. Affairs had thus taken the strange turn of placing America's enemy in support of her demands and her ally in opposition to them.

Owing to his unhappy experiences in Madrid, Jay had come to Paris with a bad taste in his mouth and with a prejudice against European courts in general. Out of such a feeling there easily grew up in his mind a suspicion as to the motives of Vergennes, and this distrust was aggravated by the apparent preference for Spain which the French minister had shown on the western question; for Jay saw in the proposal of Vergennes' secretary a willingness to sacrifice American to Spanish and French interests. He was resolved, therefore, to disregard his instructions and enter upon secret negotiations with the English authorities. Adams was in hearty accord with the plan and Franklin gave reluctant assent to it, although he did not share Jay's suspicions regarding Vergennes.

The British foreign office gladly seized this opportunity to encourage dissension between the two allies, and soon came to an agreement with the United States. A preliminary treaty was signed (November 30, 1782), but it was not to go into effect until after France had come to terms with England. After this had been done the final treaty was signed (September 3, 1783). The definitive treaty was substantially the same as the preliminary treaty except that the latter contained a secret clause not found in the former. This clause provided that if some power other than England should receive the Floridas in the final treaty the boundary between the United States and West Florida should be the thirty-first parallel; but if England should get West Florida the boundary between it and the United States would be a line drawn due east from the mouth of the Yazoo River to the Apalachicola River.

The two points on which the most serious controversy turned were the question of the debts due English creditors by American debtors and the problem of the Loyalists, or Tories. The British commissioners stoutly contended that there should be a clause in the treaty providing for the payment of all pre-Revolutionary debts due Englishmen by American debtors. This demand was not fully accepted by the American representatives, but a compromise was agreed upon whereby "creditors on either side shall [should] meet with no legal impediment for the recovery of the full value in sterling money of all *bona fide* debts heretofore contracted." As has already been shown, the Loyalists had suffered during the war from the confiscation of their property and from a general violation of their rights. The British representatives insisted that the treaty should make provision for the return of the property of the Loyalists and the restoration of their other rights. The American commissioners held that it was not within the province of Congress to provide effective relief for the Loyalists and that that question would have to be decided by the states. The problem was finally solved by a compromise whereby Congress was pledged to recommend to the state legislatures such action as would restore the legitimate rights of the Tories and safeguard those rights for the future.

By the terms of the treaty, the independence of the American republic was recognized and it was given a generous allotment of territory. Under the boundaries specified in the treaties the United States would extend from the Atlantic on the east to the Mississippi on the west; and from the Canadian border on the north to the northern boundary of East and West Florida on the south. Unfortunately, however, the young confederacy was cut off by the Spanish possessions from the Gulf of Mexico and the mouth of the Mississippi River. The Mississippi was to be open to both English and American ships; but as Spain owned both banks of the river in its lower reaches there was no guarantee that this provision could be carried out. American fishermen were given the right to ply their trade on the banks of Newfoundland and in the Gulf of St. Lawrence, as they had done in colonial days.

In winning such liberal terms for their country the American envoys could claim a great diplomatic victory, for they had secured virtually all their demands. They had, however, positively disobeyed their instructions in signing a separate treaty without the knowledge and consent of Vergennes. They had also violated the spirit of the

Franco-American alliance, though they had kept within the letter of the agreement with France in that the preliminary treaty would not go into effect until France and England had signed a treaty. In a letter of protest to Franklin, Vergennes indicated his displeasure at the way in which the American commissioners had acted. Franklin in a weak reply contended that since the preliminary treaty was not to be effective until England and France had made peace, no commitment had been violated and that he and his colleagues had been guilty only of a failure to observe the proprieties.

Attitude of Congress toward the treaty

The treaty was ratified by a unanimous vote of Congress. A majority of the members, however, were inclined to blame the commissioners for having disregarded their instructions in signing the preliminary treaty without the knowledge of Vergennes. The inclusion of a secret clause in the provisional treaty was also widely condemned.

"THE HOWES ASLEEP IN PHILADELPHIA."

A caricature drawn forth by the Doings of Revolutionary Privateers.

(The cow represents British commerce; while the American cuts off her horns, a Hollander milks her, the Frenchman and Spaniard help themselves to the milk, the British merchant wrings his hands in despair, and the British Lion sleeps through it all. In the background are two Howes asleep, and the *Eagle* high and dry, the rest of the fleet being nowhere visible.)

From Spears' " History of Our Navy," Vol. I.

CHAPTER XIV

Political and Social Aspects of the Revolution

POLITICAL CHANGES

W ITH the breaking of the bonds which held them to the home- *The new state* land, the colonies—now commonwealths—had to put their political *governments* systems on a new basis. Even before independence was declared, steps had been taken toward the adoption of state constitutions, and by the spring of 1777 every state had organized a commonwealth government. In Connecticut and Rhode Island the liberal colonial charters were accepted as state constitutions and the new govern- ments were a continuation of the old. In every other case a new constitution was adopted. The differences between the new and old governmental systems were less than their similarities. In each case the colonial framework was used and the changes made were mainly in the nature of repairs. Such innovations as were brought in were based on experience and the ideas advanced by the French and Eng- lish philosophers, especially Montesquieu and Locke.

From John Locke and the French writers was derived the idea *Bills of* that all persons are entitled to certain natural rights which cannot be *rights* infringed by government. These, together with the prescriptive rights enjoyed by all Englishmen, include the right of trial by jury, the enjoyment of freedom of the press and worship, and exemption from unjustifiable search, unreasonable bail and fines, and cruel punishments. In most of the constitutions these principles were listed in bills of rights which appeared as prefaces to or as separate articles in the constitutions. If all the liberal doctrines of the declara- tions of rights had been actually realized, important reforms in the political and social order would have been made. While these high ideals were not fully realized they did exert some influence on actual government. It was probably due to the democratic principles proclaimed in the bills of rights that there was in some of the states a slight lowering of the qualifications for voting, but in none of the original thirteen commonwealths was universal manhood suffrage allowed at this time.

223

*Weakness of
the executive*

In the new state constitutions the legislature was given a more important place than the executive. In a majority of the commonwealths the governor was appointed by the legislative assembly and was thus to some extent dependent upon it. "Ten states limited his term of office to a year; in eleven states he had no veto. A number of states contrived a council of state to advise the governor. The legislature, as a rule, chose this council and the civil officers upon whom the governor must depend for administrative service."[1]

This increase in the power of the legislature at the expense of the executive was due to the feeling that the latter was more disposed to abuse its authority than the former. In the controversies immediately preceding the Revolution the assemblies had generally championed the rights of the people, whereas the royal governors had upheld the privileges of the crown. There was therefore a general impression that the interests of the people would be safer in the hands of the legislature than in those of the executive. The framers of the state constitutions seemed to overlook the fact that administrative officials if made responsible to their constituencies would be no more likely than legislators to abuse their powers. As a guarantee therefore that the new governor would not follow the example of the old, he was so restricted as to authority that he was usually able to perform very little efficient service.

*The Second
Continental
Congress*

The fight against the mother country called for the co-operation of all the thirteen colonies. This co-operation could not be secured unless a government for the united colonies or states was established. Such a government was created when, at the beginning of the war, the Second Continental Congress was organized. This body was the organ of the Federal government from May, 1775, to March, 1781. This congress was a revolutionary body and did not rest on a constitutional basis. What authority it was able to exercise it owed to the willingness of the states to yield certain of their powers to the union.

*The Articles
of Confeder-
ation framed
and adopted*

The exigencies of war called for a closer union than was possible under a general government which was not supported by constitutional authority. Early in the struggle, therefore, it was felt that a Federal constitution should be adopted. With Lee's resolution for independence, offered on June 7, 1776, there was coupled the motion "that a plan of confederation be prepared and transmitted to the respective Colonies for their consideration and approbation." A few days later a committee of thirteen, one from each colony, was chosen

---

[1] C. H. Van Tyne, *The American Revolution*, Harper and Brothers, 144.

to draw up a constitution. On July 12 the committee, of which John Dickinson, now of Delaware, was chairman, reported to Congress a scheme of government.

The proposal of the committee was taken up by Congress and debated from time to time, with the result that some changes were made in the original draft. The plan as thus amended was agreed to on November 15, 1777. This delay was due to the stress of other business and the interruptions caused by the war. The new frame of government, known as the Articles of Confederation, was submitted to the states with the provision that it would go into effect when accepted by the legislatures of all of them. Most of the states ratified it within the following year, but Maryland withheld her assent until March 1, 1781. She had refused to act more promptly because of her apprehensions regarding the states which had claims to western territory. If the western lands were retained by the states which claimed them, these states would soon become so important that those not favored with such possessions would be dwarfed into comparative insignificance. A political union composed of commonwealths differing so greatly in area and population would be a partnership of giants and pygmies, and the latter might fare badly from the association. By March, 1781, Maryland's fears on this score were abated, because New York had surrendered to the Confederation her claims to western lands, and it was expected that the other six states which had rights in the West would follow her example.

Reasons for the delay in ratification

The union was not materially strengthened by the adoption of the Articles of Confederation. The states retained their sovereignty and were insistent upon their rights, while the Federal government had only such authority as was delegated to it and was not implemented with sufficient powers. The states as the successors of the colonies were rooted in historic tradition, whereas the Confederation was a new and artificial arrangement. Besides, it was in defense of their right of local autonomy (states' rights) that the colonies had separated from the British empire. The people, therefore, were resolved not to run into the same danger by placing the states under the control of a new empire of their own making.

Nature of the government under the Articles of Confederation

The framers of the Articles of Confederation were not unmindful of the fact that much of the friction between the colonies and the mother country had grown out of the attempt of the latter to tax her dependencies and regulate their commerce. The authority exercised by the royal governors was another cause of strife. To avoid similar trouble in the future it was provided that in the new government the power to levy taxes and regulate commerce should be retained by the states and that there should not be a separate executive department. Congress could make requisitions on the states for money contributions but could not compel them to meet their quotas. In foregoing the right of laying import duties and regulating commerce, as well as that of levying direct taxes, the Confederation was surrendering sources of revenue and forfeiting powers which are necessary for effective government.

Administrative departments

As all executive, as well as legislative and judicial, functions were to be performed by Congress and its agents, there were no specific provisions for the enforcement of Federal laws, but Congress was free to create such administrative machinery as it might deem necessary or useful. During the greater part of the war, the executive authority of Congress was exercised largely through committees. But this procedure proving unsatisfactory, in the early part of 1781 provision was made for the creation of four administrative departments. The heads of these new departments were the Superintendent of Finance, Secretary of War, Secretary of Marine, and Secretary of Foreign Affairs. This plan was continued after the adoption of the Articles of Confederation, and in this way the foundations were laid for the executive departments, the heads of which now constitute an important part of the Cabinet.

Amendments

Under the Articles of Confederation each state had one vote in Congress, and all important measures required the assent of nine states. Amendments to the constitution proposed by Congress could not go into effect until ratified by the legislatures of all the states.

The Committee of the States

A committee, known as the Committee of the States, composed of one representative from each state, was to act during a recess of Congress and perform such minor duties as that body by a vote of nine states should impose upon it. Representatives of the states were to be chosen and paid in such manner as their legislatures should prescribe.

Powers of Congress

The powers of Congress included the "right and power of determining on peace and war"; "of sending and receiving ambassadors; entering into treaties and alliances"; of establishing rules for deciding upon the legality of captures on land and water and the manner of disposing of prizes taken by the land and naval forces; of "appointing courts for the trial of piracies and felonies committed on the high seas"; and of establishing admiralty courts for the trial of appeals from state admiralty courts in all cases of captures. There was also an awkward arrangement for the settlement of disputes between the states. These last-mentioned clauses constituted the only provision in the Articles for the establishment of a Federal judiciary.

ECONOMIC ASPECTS OF THE REVOLUTION

One of the most serious problems that confronted Congress in the *How the war* management of the war was that of raising the funds necessary for *was financed* its support. Money for financing the war was raised from four main sources: bills of credit; requisitions on the states; domestic loans; and foreign aids and loans.

Since Congress could not raise revenue by taxation, it called on *Requisitions* the states from time to time for specified contributions. These requi- *on the states* sitions were only partially met, and the total amount so raised was about six million dollars (as measured in specie). In 1780 requisitions were made on the states for army supplies, such as corn, hay, and beef.

Funds were also obtained by the sale of bonds to the American *Loans* people; but as there was very little free capital in the country, no great amount was realized in this way. The total amount brought in by the sale of domestic bonds was less than nine million dollars in specie. The army officers at times took over food products and wagons and other means of transportation at an assessed valuation. As payment for these supplies was to be made in the future, these requisitions were in the nature of forced loans.

Before entering into an alliance with the United States, the French government had granted about two million dollars as aids to the insurgents, and the Spanish government had furnished a small amount. These advances were virtually gifts and were regarded as investments to encourage the rebels to continue the struggle with Britain. After the Franco-American Alliance was made, Spain lent to the United States a small sum, and France, about six million dollars. When victory seemed certain (1782), Dutch bankers made loans aggregating more than a million dollars.

From these various sources there was derived about one third of *Continental* the total amount spent on the war. For the remaining two thirds, *currency* Congress had to rely on bills of credit, or Continental currency. In June, 1775, bills of credit were issued to the amount of two million dollars. This amount was greatly increased by later issues, and finally the figure of 241,000,000 was reached. Besides, the states issued an additional two hundred million dollars. The states were asked to raise a fund for redemption, and the obligation to redeem the Continental currency was apportioned among them according to population. Slight heed was paid to this demand, and the amount actually redeemed was inconsiderable. With such a volume of irredeemable paper money in circulation, rapid depreciation was a foregone conclusion. So great was the decline that by the middle of 1781 the Continental bills of credit had ceased to have any value and were no longer used as money.

In the meantime, the general government had adopted a policy of virtual bankruptcy by calling in the paper money at one fortieth of its value. In 1780 Congress offered to receive the Continental currency for government dues in lieu of silver at this rate.[1]

Inflation

With the decline in the value of paper money there went a corresponding increase in the cost of goods. There was thus a constant rise in prices, which promoted extravagance and speculation. The state legislatures all passed laws making the Continental currency a legal tender, receivable in the payment of bills and debts. By repudiating its obligations, the general government set an example in financial dishonesty which too many people were inclined to follow. Dishonest debtors would pursue their fleeing creditors and pay them "without mercy." Cheap money was also very unfair to all who were dependent upon salaries for support. Although the paper money gave rise to the usual evils of inflation, it was a necessary evil. For without it the means of financing the war could not have been obtained.

Effect of the war on commerce

The war had an important effect on commerce and industry. While hostilities were going on, the British government made a vigorous attempt to prevent trade between the United States and other countries. In the early years this effort met with such success that intercourse between the new republic and Europe was greatly hampered, and the supply of goods which the Americans were accustomed to get from foreign lands was markedly curtailed. The country as a whole suffered from these deprivations, and the soldiers especially were subjected to hardships by the shortage in imported woolen cloth.

As the war progressed, American and neutral ships learned how to evade the British patrols and thus some of the channels of trade were kept open. But this foreign trade had to follow circuitous routes and was subject to numerous British attacks. Owing to these hazards and inconveniences, the insurance and freight rates were high. Despite these drawbacks, however, by 1777 foreign commerce had revived and was carried on to a considerable extent until the end of the war.

---

[1] In 1780 Congress, after calling in the old bills of credit, issued a new lot of notes ($4,400,000 in amount) which were to bear six per cent interest and be redeemed in six years. It was hoped that these pledges would keep up the value of the new tenor notes, but this expectation was disappointed. The new notes, as well as the old ones, became worthless. When Federal finances were put on a sound basis by the funding act of 1790, the new tenor notes were received in small amounts for government stock and in this way were redeemed. The old currency was also accepted for government securities at the rate of one cent on the dollar.

Soon after hostilities began, the country went through a period of *Effect on* hard times. Owing to the activity of the British fleet, fishing and *industry* shipbuilding, which had been important businesses in the North, could not be carried on profitably. Certain types of agriculture were also discouraged. The bounty on indigo was withdrawn, and the foreign market for tobacco and the British market for pig and bar iron were closed by the war.

On the whole, however, the war helped rather than hindered industry. Owing to the decrease in the supply of foreign goods, the home market was in large measure reserved to the American manufacturer. The war also greatly increased the demand for certain manufactures, such as shoes and socks, woolen clothing, canvas for tents, and guns and ammunition. As the paper money was constantly declining in value and prices were steadily rising, goods always found a ready sale. Furthermore, American industry had thrown off the restraints imposed on it by the imperial government and so was free to develop along natural lines. Manufacturing was stimulated by these favorable circumstances and new industries were established throughout the country. Prominent among the industries which now grew into importance was the production of salt. Nearly all the salt consumed in the colonies had been imported from southern Europe and the Canary, Madeira, and West Indian Islands. When the war clogged up these channels of supply, there was a scarcity of this much-needed article and a corresponding increase in price which greatly stimulated domestic production.

With the Revolutionary War there came the independence of the *A new postal* colonial postal system. The American postal system had, since 1707, *system* been a branch of the British imperial mail service. In the period just preceding the outbreak of the Revolution there was a good deal of complaint against the high rates of postage and the arrogance of the employees of the Royal Mail Service. When friction arose between the colonies and the mother country, after the passage of the Stamp Act, dissatisfaction with the postal system was greatly increased, for private letters were frequently "opened by the postal authorities and information obtained from them was transmitted to the English authorities."[1]

War could not be carried on with any degree of success with the chief means of communication under the control of the enemy. Congress therefore soon realized the necessity of creating an independent postal system. Accordingly it passed an act (July 26, 1775) creating a postoffice department which would have charge of the

---

[1] J. C. Fitzpatrick, *The Spirit of the Revolution*, 237.

distribution of mail throughout the country. Benjamin Franklin, who had for many years successfully administered the colonial postal system, was made Postmaster General, with headquarters at Philadelphia. Postal rates and the salaries of employees were fixed by law, and Congress assumed financial responsibility for the management of the system. On assuming this new task Franklin acted with his accustomed energy and efficiency, and when at the end of 1776 he left the country for France the new postal system was well established.

The Royal Mail Service continued in operation for some months; but the anti-British feeling was so strong among the Patriots that very little mail was entrusted to it. Besides, the carriers were sometimes attacked by the rebels who would rifle the mails. So insecure was the business, and so small were the returns, that the British authorities formally closed the Royal Mail Service, on Christmas Day, 1775.

EFFECT ON SOCIAL LIFE

The American Revolution not a violent social upheaval

The revolution in America did not lead to such an upheaval in the social order as was caused by the French Revolution. It did, however, bring about some important changes not only in the political and economic system but also in the institutions and ideals of the people. It had an unfavorable effect on education in that schools and colleges were forced to suspend their activities. It gave rise to an anti-slavery sentiment which, together with favorable economic conditions, resulted in the immediate or gradual abolition of slavery in a large portion of the country.

Effect of the Revolution on land policy

The Revolution brought about some important changes in land policy. It abolished quitrents (small fees which had been imposed on landowners by the proprietors and the king) and thereby relieved the landowners of payments amounting to about one hundred thousand dollars a year. Public lands which had hitherto belonged to the crown were taken over by the states. A large portion of this land, as well as a number of great estates which had been seized from the Tories, was broken up into small tracts and sold to yeoman farmers. In this way the number of moderate-sized farms was considerably increased. Within a few years of the close of the Revolution, the practice of entailing land had been prohibited in most of the states and the law of primogeniture repealed in all of them.[1] These re-

---

[1] An entail was an estate that was limited to a particular class of heirs, and the holder of it could not sell or give it away. Under the law of primogeniture all the landed property of a father who died without a will went to the oldest son.

forms prevented the tying up of estates for several generations and favored the equal distribution of landed property among all the children of a deceased parent. The effect of these changes was therefore to check the concentration of landownership in the hands of a few men and to forward the trend toward the subdivision of large estates into small farms.

One significant result of the Revolution was its effect on religious conditions. At the end of the colonial era, church and state were united in nine of the thirteen colonies. The Anglican was the state church in New York, Maryland, and the four Southern provinces, and the Congregational was the established church in three of the New England colonies. With the Revolution, however, there came a strong demand for a complete separation of church and state. In New York, Maryland, the Carolinas, and Georgia the church was disestablished early in the war. In New England[1] and Virginia separation was effected only after a long fight. The cause of religious equality was ably championed by such statesmen as Madison and Jefferson. A statute providing for complete separation of church and state was written by Jefferson and presented to the Virginia assembly where Madison made a vigorous fight for it and succeeded in winning its passage at the end of 1785. This was a great victory for religious freedom, and established a principle which in a few years was embodied in the Federal Constitution in the form of the First Amendment.

Effect on religious freedom

The Revolution resulted in the ecclesiastical as well as the political independence of the American states. The Congregational Church at the time of its organization in America had severed the bond that held it to the mother country, and now other religious bodies broke their British connections. In the case of the Methodists the breaking of the home ties led to the formation of a new denomination. The Methodists did not begin religious activity in America until the pre-Revolutionary decade, but so great was their zeal that by 1771 their following numbered nearly five thousand. Most of the preachers were Englishmen sent over as missionaries by John Wesley, the founder of the movement. Wesley, however, had come out against the Revolution and was greatly disliked by the Patriots. Hence the Methodists were regarded as enemy aliens or Tories and were subjected to fines, whippings, or imprisonments. All the missionaries returned to England except Francis Asbury, and he had to go into hiding for a time. In the beginning the Methodists were members of the Anglican Church, and for some time the movement

The Methodists in America

---

[1] Entire separation of church and state came in New Hampshire in 1817; in Connecticut, in 1818; in Massachusetts, in 1833.

was kept within the framework of that denomination. After the Revolution, however, the American Methodists broke away from the mother church and formed a separate ecclesiastical organization with Francis Asbury as their first bishop.

Effect of the Revolution on religion and morality

The American Revolution had a disastrous effect on morality and religion. While all religious denominations suffered a decline, the Anglican Church was dealt the most serious blow. Not only was there a decided lowering of its spiritual fervor and influence, but it also sustained losses of a more tangible character. By disestablish-

Courtesy of the New-York Historical Society, New York City

CLOTH LOOM.

United States, early nineteenth century.

Mortise and tenon and pegged construction.

ment it had lost its main source of revenue. Moreover, many of its ministers had fallen into disfavor because of their adherence to the British cause. In a number of places churches were closed, and some of the rectors were unable to continue their work. Besides, the missionaries sent out by the Venerable Society were recalled and their activities were discontinued. The Anglican Church had therefore suffered a great loss in prestige and membership throughout the entire country. Even in Virginia, which had been one of its few strongholds, the outlook was so discouraging that such prominent

Episcopalians as Bishop Madison and John Marshall thought that the church was too far gone ever to be revived.

The dissenters had also suffered greatly—both spiritually and materially—from the ravages of war. The armies had destroyed many of their houses of worship and desecrated others. There had been a decided cooling off in religious fervor among the Methodists, Congregationalists, Presbyterians, and Baptists. Semple, the historian of the Virginia Baptists, spoke of his coreligionists as follows: "With some few exceptions, the declension was general throughout the state. The love of many waxed cold. Some of the watchmen fell, others stumbled, and many slumbered at their posts."

PART III

The Federal Period, 1783=1860

CHAPTER XV

The Period of the Confederation

WHEN the Articles of Confederation were put into effect the strain of actual practice revealed certain defects of a serious nature. These were virtually all due to a lack of authority on the part of the general government, which did not rest directly on the people but on the states. Some of the weaknesses which soon appeared were the dependence of the inadequate executive on the legislature, the absence of a well-organized Federal judiciary, and the inability of Congress to levy taxes and regulate interstate and foreign commerce. These imperfections, however, could have been remedied, but for the unwise provision for changing the constitution, which virtually ruled out the possibility of amendment. All amendments proposed by Congress failed of ratification—in one case by the adverse vote of only one state legislature.[1]

No amendments to the Articles of Confederation

The framers of this imperfect instrument expected the union under it to be permanent, whereas it lasted less than a decade. If a temporary government had been set up with a suitable plan for future adjustments it might have become permanent; but this attempt to fit a changing society into a fixed mold was doomed to failure. To the growing young republic the constitution soon became a strait jacket instead of a comfortable suit of clothes.

DIPLOMATIC PROBLEMS

An important problem confronting the new nation after independence was that of making the proper adjustments with foreign powers. The peace treaty had in itself the germs of controversy. To England the promise had been given that Congress would earnestly recommend to the state legislatures the enactment of such provisions as would lead to the restoration of the just rights of Tories, or Loyalists, whose property had been confiscated. English creditors were also to meet with no legal impediment to the full recovery of all

Relations with England: Controversy over the terms of the peace treaty

---

[1] In 1781 an attempt to amend the Articles for the purpose of giving Congress power to levy an import tax of five per cent to pay the national debt was defeated by the action of Rhode Island.

debts hitherto contracted in America. Congress made the promised recommendation as to Tories, but only a few of the states endeavored to obey the injunction and these only to a limited extent. It was not until after the war of 1812 that all the laws against Tories had been repealed.

The pledge as to prewar debts was at first clearly violated. Laws were passed by state legislatures by which the collection of such debts was hampered. Congress sent a circular letter to the states urging them to repeal these statutes, and by 1789 most of the states had complied with this request. At that time all state laws in violation of the treaty were annulled by the new Constitution. The courts were now open to British creditors and nothing but legal delays stood in the way of collection. These delays were so great, however, that it was considered necessary to insert in Jay's Treaty (1794) a clause providing for a mixed commission to pass upon all uncollected debts. This commission failed to agree, and a final settlement was made in 1802, when our government paid the British creditors a lump sum of 600,000 pounds "in complete satisfaction" of all debts, principal and interest.

Britain had promised in the treaty to withdraw her garrisons from American soil "with all convenient speed." In direct violation of this pledge she maintained for twelve years seven military posts in the Northwest, south of the Canadian border. The excuse offered for the noncompliance with a plain commitment was that the Americans had violated the terms of the treaty—notably as to English debts and the treatment of Loyalists. But probably the real reason was the desire of the British traders to use these posts as centers for the promotion of the Canadian fur trade and for the control in their interest of the western Indians.

Adams'
unsuccessful
mission

In 1785 John Adams was appointed American minister to England. He repaired to London with the hope of negotiating a commercial treaty with the British government, of persuading it to withdraw its troops from the western posts, and of securing an indemnity for slaves seized in America after the treaty had been signed. He was cordially received by the king, but was unable to make any progress with the foreign office toward these objectives. In response to his urgent request that the British posts be removed, he was told that this would not be done until the debts had been paid. In these negotiations the British ministers did not cushion their refusal of American demands with diplomatic suavity; but Adams was not overawed by their attitude, and was a match for them in blunt candor.

Since it seemed impossible to make a dent in British self-complacency, Adams returned home in 1788 without having attained any of the three objectives. He felt that the failure of his efforts in London had been due largely to the weakness of our Federal government. As Congress did not have power to regulate foreign commerce, the British authorities considered it useless to sign a commercial treaty which, as they thought, could not be enforced. They knew also that the American government was not able to offer any inducements for a liberal treatment of its citizens nor to retaliate if their rights were infringed. There was, therefore, nothing to be gained for Britain by the acceptance, and nothing to be lost by the refusal, of a treaty of commerce with the United States.

Out of the peace treaty there also developed disputes with Spain. In the treaty between England and the United States it was stated that the boundary between Spanish West Florida and the United States should be the thirty-first parallel and that the Mississippi River should be free for the use of the nationals of both England and the United States. Spain did not consider these terms as binding upon herself, contending that Great Britain had exceeded her authority in making such promises. During the war West Florida had been seized by Spain, and so was in her possession at the time the peace treaty was signed. Spain contended therefore that England had no right to dispose of West Florida or any part of it. Spain still held the region up to the mouth of the Yazoo River and claimed virtually all the territory west of Georgia and south of the Cumberland River. This overlapping of the claims of the two countries was a source of considerable trouble to the American settlers in the Southwest. The disputed area was occupied by powerful Indian tribes, which were encouraged by the Spanish authorities to exclude American traders and settlers from the region. Consequently, on the entire southwestern frontier there was the constant menace of Indian attack.

Relations with Spain: Causes of dispute

Spain was in unquestioned possession of both sides of the Mississippi for two hundred miles above its mouth and claimed the land on both sides to a greater distance to the north. She was thus in a position to control navigation on the "Father of Waters." The United States contended for the right to navigate the Mississippi. Spain did not close the river to the Westerners but allowed them to use it only as a *privilege* to be granted under such terms and regulations as her own policy might dictate. For a while this privilege was allowed only to certain individuals, like James Wilkinson, who were expected to promote Spanish interests in the West.

Negotiations between the United States and Spain, looking to a settlement of these disputes, were begun in the summer of 1785, when Don Diego de Gardoqui, the Spanish chargé d'affaires, arrived at Philadelphia. The American government was represented by John Jay, the Secretary for Foreign Affairs. Jay had been instructed to use his best endeavors to induce the Spanish minister to agree to a commercial treaty, accept the thirty-first parallel as the northern boundary of West Florida, and grant to our citizens the right of free navigation of the Mississippi River. In exchange for these large demands Jay had nothing of commensurate value to offer, nor could he frighten Gardoqui by the threat of war. Had he attempted this the Spanish representative would have realized that he was bluffing.

Jay's proposal   Jay, thinking that a partial success would be preferable to a complete failure, asked Congress for new instructions authorizing him to make a more acceptable offer. He felt that if a favorable commercial treaty could be agreed upon between the two countries, the United States could afford to waive its claim to the thirty-first parallel as the southern boundary, and suspend for twenty-five or thirty years its demand for the right to navigate the Mississippi. In response to this request it was proposed in Congress that Jay be instructed to make the concessions which he had suggested. After a heated debate the proposal was defeated by a sectional vote, with the Northern states voting for and the Southern states against it. The Southern states opposed the proposal because they still had western lands and their representatives realized, more fully than did Jay and the Northerners generally, how impossible it would be to exclude the Westerners from the use of the Mississippi as an outlet for their produce. In the North, where commerce was important, it was felt that a commercial treaty with Spain would greatly benefit that section and the country as a whole. To secure this advantage the Northern representatives in Congress were willing to forego, for the time being, the right to navigate the Mississippi River.

HARD TIMES

Prosperity during the war   During the war the American people enjoyed a considerable measure of prosperity, except in those regions which were overrun by the troops of the enemy. The needs of the American, French, and English armies created a home market for manufactures and farm products. Privateering was a source of profit for many shipowners and was thus a partial compensation for the loss of commerce. The gold and silver brought in by French and British soldiers furnished a plentiful currency. It was thought that still better times would be ushered in by peace. As a result of this expectation there came a brief period of prosperity and with it a season of extravagance. This artificial prosperity in a short time gave way to financial depression and times were hard until about 1787.

The long war had thrown the economic machinery out of gear and subjected the country to a severe financial strain. Commerce, agriculture, and industry had to adjust themselves to peace and independence. The break in the connection with a great commercial empire could not be effected without economic loss. Nor could the return to peace be made without a dislocation of the channels of business. Certain ports in the French and Spanish West Indies were open to American products and ships, but trade with these islands was handicapped by tax restrictions.

Causes of hard times after the war

The greatest blow, however, to the prosperity of the new republic was struck by the commercial regulations of the British government. Fish oil and whale products were excluded from England, and this virtually ruined the American whaling industry, for England had hitherto been the only market for these articles. Worse still were the new barriers to trade between the United States and the British West Indies. Prior to the Revolution the continental colonies found a ready market in the English and foreign sugar islands for their fish, lumber, grain, and other products. In exchange for these they received English and foreign coins, sugar, molasses, and other commodities not produced at home. Molasses was manufactured into rum, which was sold to the Indians for furs and to slave dealers on the east coast of Africa for Negroes. Therefore, the prosperity of the grain grower, the fur trader, the fisherman, the lumberman, and the slave trader were all bound up to some extent with this trade. When this interchange of goods was hampered all of these businesses suffered.

Restrictions on trade between the United States and the British West Indies

After the American colonies ceased to be a part of the British empire, the British navigation laws in the main operated against the States as they did against other foreign nations. By a royal proclamation of July 2, 1783, imports into and exports from the British West Indian Islands were forbidden unless transported in British ships. These ships, however, were not allowed to carry lumber, livestock, grain, vegetables, and certain other articles from American ports to the islands nor to take certain products—including rum, sugar, and molasses—from the islands to the States. The object of this policy was to give the British merchants a monopoly of the carrying trade between the United States and the British West Indies, and to exclude from the latter all products that would compete with Canadian exports. The damage to American commerce caused by this policy was lessened by the easy access enjoyed by American seamen to the Dutch and Danish West Indian Islands, for these places were used by smugglers as back doors to the English islands.

That this narrowing of the West Indian outlet would hurt agriculture as well as commerce and fishing goes without saying. Agriculture was also discouraged in other ways. The home market, which had been expanded by war needs, was now contracted to prewar dimensions. The stoppage of the bounty on indigo, and the annulment of the favors shown in England to tobacco grown in colonial America, led to a lowering in price of those articles. The infant manufacturing industries were crippled by the competition of the cheap foreign goods with which the country was now flooded.

Prosperity returns; reasons

The darkest period of the depression was reached in 1786. Next year conditions took a turn for the better and hard times soon gave way to prosperity. The people had adjusted themselves to the new political and economic situation. Commerce had found its way back into the old channels and a new trade had been opened up with the west coast of North America, China, and the East Indies. A shortage of crops in France created a greater demand in that country and in her West Indian colonies for American farm products. Agriculture was thus restored and even industry revived and prospered.

Alleged responsibility of the government for the hard times

The government of the Confederation was not responsible for the hard times. It had not produced them, nor could the best government in the world have removed them. The fact, however, that the depression came under this government caused many people then, and some historians of later times, to blame the government for it. It was held that if the general government had been stronger it could have forced from foreign powers more favorable treatment in the form of trade concessions. Interstate commerce could have been regulated, and by a uniform tariff policy the infant industries might have received some protection against the products dumped upon the country by English manufacturers. While there may be some basis for this opinion, the economic shortcomings of the government of the Confederation have been greatly exaggerated. The new government under the present Constitution was fortunate enough to start off in a time of prosperity. It has, therefore, received too much credit for the good times, and the old government too much blame for the bad times.

PAPER MONEY

The demand for paper money; reasons

By the end of the war, as has already been shown, the Continental currency had depreciated until it ceased to circulate as money. The country was, therefore, on a specie basis except in those states which still issued bills of credit. In the short boom period that came with peace, the extravagant buying of foreign goods by our people drained the country of much of its specie. Money, therefore, became scarce and prices fell. Farmers, who had contracted debts when their produce brought a high price, had now to pay these debts when their commodities were a drug on the market. By this condition of deflation, as it is called, creditors were benefited and debtors were injured and exploited.

During the period of hard times farmers, laborers, small tradesmen, and debtors generally were unable to pay their debts and the heavy taxes that had been imposed upon them. Numerous foreclosures of mortgages resulted and a great many people lost all their property, while many were thrown into prison for debt. From this distressed portion of the population there went up a cry for relief. The malcontents demanded "stay laws," which would declare a moratorium on debts; reforms in the courts which would make the dispensing of justice less costly; and paper money, which would have the effect of scaling down debts by depreciation. Under pressure of the masses seven states decided to issue paper money.

Of all the states which entered upon a policy of inflation, the experiment attempted by Rhode Island commanded the greatest attention. The paper money issued in this little state was made a legal tender and creditors were forced to receive it. There was later a provision making it a penal offense to refuse paper money in ordinary business transactions. Out of this provision there grew a noted legal case, that of *Trevett vs. Weeden*. A butcher of Newport, John Weeden, refused the paper money offered by John Trevett in payment for meat. The former was brought before the supreme court of the state on the charge of having violated the law. The court freed him of the accusation on the ground that the law violated by the defendant was unconstitutional and therefore void. This was one of the first cases (and the most noted of them all) in which a court decided that an act of a state legislature could be set aside on the ground of unconstitutionality.

Paper money in Rhode Island

In six of the states, the class of property owners and prosperous business men dominated the legislatures to such an extent that the demands of the radicals for paper money were disregarded and the policy of deflation was continued. The issuance of paper money meant inflation and by it debtors were able to rob their creditors, whereas a continuance of deflation allowed creditors to exploit their debtors. The proper remedy was a monetary system so regulated as to insure justice to both groups, but such a plan was not worked out in any of the states.

*Shays'
Rebellion*

In Massachusetts the evils of deflation seem to have been greatest. Farmers, owing to the narrowing of the West Indian outlet, could not find a market for their produce and were staggering under unbearable debt burdens. Creditors were demanding their pound of flesh. Justice was slow and costly "and lawyers were more grasping than usual." The privileged class which controlled the state government had shifted too great a proportion of the tax burden to the shoulders of the farmers and laborers. Some of the money so raised went to pay off the state's indebtedness and thus found its way into the pockets of speculators who had bought up the state's paper at a low figure. The debtor and poorer class was becoming desperate.

A feverish discontent arose among the common people, which expressed itself in town meetings, county conventions, and petitions to the legislature. They asked for a scaling down of the public debt, a lessening of the privileges of the propertied class, reforms in the judiciary and tax systems, and relief for debtors in the form of paper money. The legislature refused to accede to these demands and mob violence was the result. Courts were prevented from holding their sessions by infuriated groups of farmers, laborers, and mechanics. The insurgents, led by Daniel Shays, a veteran of the Revolutionary War, were suppressed in the winter of 1787 by troops sent out by Governor Bowdoin under command of General Benjamin Lincoln.

Shays' Rebellion, and lesser disorders of a similar character in other states, filled the conservatives with a dread of radicalism. They were now more anxious than ever to have a strong central government which could assist the states if necessary in maintaining law and order—a government which would uphold the sanctity of property, guarantee the observance of contracts, and put a stop to the use of irredeemable paper money.

THE WESTERN PROBLEM

*State claims
to Western
territory*

The lands west of the Appalachian Mountains were claimed by the states of Massachusetts, Connecticut, New York, Virginia, North Carolina, South Carolina, and Georgia. The right of New York to a share of the western area was based on her suzerainty over the Iroquois, who had at times exercised a sort of authority over some of the Indian tribes as far west as the Mississippi. The other states traced their titles to the grants made to them by royal charters when they were colonies. Since these grants overlapped, the claims of some of the states conflicted with those of others. These titles were of doubtful validity, because the British government by extending the limits of Quebec down to the Ohio (1774) had virtually repudiated

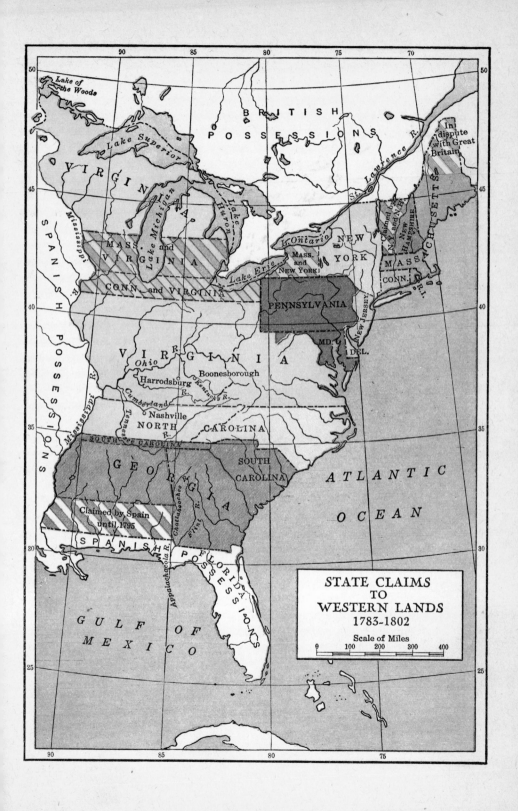

STATE CLAIMS
TO
WESTERN LANDS
1783-1802

Scale of Miles

0   100   200   300   400

them. For this reason France and Spain, during the Revolution, took the position that these claims had been cancelled by the Quebec Act. Virginia, however, had strengthened her title by the conquest of the Northwest under the leadership of George Rogers Clark, as this expedition had been sent out by her authority. Maryland, on the other hand, contended that Clark's success was made possible by the joint action of all the colonies in opposing the British forces in the East and therefore that the West should belong to all the colonies jointly.

In 1780 New York yielded to the Confederation her shadowy rights in the West. The other states followed her example, though it was not until 1802 that all the cessions were made. With the acquisition of these Western lands there arose two new problems for Congress. First, it had to decide upon a policy for the disposal of the land to individuals; and second, it had to devise a plan of government for the settlers. In meeting these responsibilities two committees were appointed and Thomas Jefferson was chosen as chairman of each. Acting on the report of one of these committees, Congress adopted a scheme for the government of the entire West. This was the Ordinance of 1784. It would become effective when all the lands had been ceded to the general government; but before this had happened this ordinance had been superseded by the Ordinance of 1787. *The Ordinance of 1781*

The other committee framed a plan for disposing of the land to settlers. It was accepted by Congress and is known as the Land Ordinance of 1785. According to this plan considerable areas were to be surveyed from time to time and divided into rectangular tracts of six miles square, each tract to be known as a township. Each township was to be divided into thirty-six squares (or sections) of 640 acres each, the sixteenth section in every township being reserved for the use of schools. After surveys had been made, the land was to be put up at auction and sold to the highest bidder. The minimum amount that could be bought was one section and the minimum price was to be one dollar per acre, which was to be paid in cash. To buy the minimum amount of land required therefore at least $640 in cash. As few actual settlers could raise such a large sum, little land was sold except to speculators, who could cut up their holdings into small tracts and sell them to settlers on credit. *The Land Ordinance of 1785*

The government was sorely in need of money and was eager to dispose of as much land as possible. It was willing, therefore, to sell large amounts to companies at bargain prices. Of the groups of buyers who took advantage of this situation, the most noted was the Company of Ohio Associates, made up of Revolutionary veterans *Land sale to the Company of Ohio Associates* from New England who held certificates of indebtedness issued by Congress. The Reverend Manasseh Cutler, as agent for the company, bought from Congress about a million and a half acres for one million dollars, to be paid in certificates of indebtedness worth about twelve cents on the dollar. To get the measure through, it was necessary to link this company up with a land-grabbing group, the Scioto Company, in which some members of Congress had an interest. The latter company received at the same time an option on several million acres of land.

A settlement made at Marietta

The Ohio Company at once proceeded to occupy its vast domain. In the spring of 1788 General Rufus Putnam went forward to plant a settlement. When he and his followers arrived at the Youghiogheny River, they constructed a boat, the *Mayflower,* and in this vessel of hallowed name and others of smaller size, they floated downstream to their new home. Landing at the mouth of the Muskingum River (1788), they started to build the town of Marietta, the first authorized settlement in the present state of Ohio. True to the New England tradition, they made provision for education and religion by reserving one section in every township for the support of schools and one for the support of churches.

The Ordinance of 1787

Before the land sale to the Ohio Company had been consummated, Congress had passed a new act for the government of the West, the Ordinance of 1787. This new measure applied to the Northwest Territory—a vast area lying between the Ohio River and the boundary of Pennsylvania on the east, the Mississippi on the west, the Ohio on the south, and the Canadian border on the north. The ordinance consisted of governmental provisions and a bill of rights. The latter was similar to the bills of rights in the constitutions of the old states. The inhabitants were guaranteed freedom of worship, the benefits of the writ of habeas corpus and trial by jury, and exemption from unusual and excessive punishments. Private contracts were not to be interfered with, judicial proceedings were to be in accordance with the common law, and no one was to be deprived of life, liberty, or property "but by the judgment of his peers or the law of the land." There was to be no slavery or involuntary servitude in the entire territory.

The bill of rights

Governmental provisions

The whole region was to be governed temporarily as one district but later was to be divided into not less than three, nor more than five, prospective states. The Territory was to pass through three governmental stages. In the first stage, laws were to be made and administered by a governor and three judges, who would be appointed by Congress. There was also to be a secretary appointed by Congress. The people would have no voice whatever in the government during this first stage, but this period of autocratic rule was to last only until the district should attain a population of 5000 adult males. Then there would be a legislature, consisting of a lower house chosen by the people, and an upper house, the members of which would be selected by Congress on nomination of the lower house of the territorial legislature. At this stage the Territory could send a delegate to Congress, who could not vote but could take part in the deliberations of that body.

Whenever there should be, in any one of the three or five districts into which the Territory was to be divided, a free population of 60,000, that district was to be admitted into the Union as a state with all the rights and privileges of the older states.

The Ordinance of 1787 inaugurated a policy in the government of our territories which has been followed in principle ever since. It was a decision to treat the new area not as a colonial dependency but as an integral part of the country. It meant that the settlers in the West were to have from the beginning all the rights of citizenship enjoyed by the inhabitants of the older states, and that ultimately the new states to be carved out of the Territory would be put on the basis of political equality with the Original Thirteen. This wise decision settled at once—and in the right way—the problem as to whether the United States should or should not have a colonial system.

The Land Ordinance of 1785 and the Northwest Ordinance of 1787 were the most noted pieces of legislation enacted by the Congress of the Confederation. When the latter measure was passed by Congress meeting in New York, a convention in session in Philadelphia was framing a constitution to supersede the Articles of Confederation. The old Congress was in its last years and had fallen into decrepitude. Many of the members had lost interest in its proceedings and were absenting themselves from its sessions. When the Northwest Ordinance was passed only eighteen members were present and only eight states were represented.

The enactment of these two ordinances was a remarkable achievement for so weak a body. Indeed it is surprising that the old Congress was able to prop itself up on its deathbed and pass these two important measures.

THE CREATION OF NEW STATES IN THE WEST

No new states were admitted into the Union during the Confederation period, but steps were taken which later led to the formation of three new commonwealths. The first of these was Vermont. *Vermont*

About 1763, pioneers from Massachusetts, New Hampshire, and Connecticut began to move into the Green Mountain region, and by the outbreak of the Revolution the emigrants that had gone there numbered thirty thousand or more. They occupied lands which had been granted by the governor of New Hampshire. Both New Hampshire and New York claimed jurisdiction over these settlers, and the claim of the latter was confirmed by the Privy Council in England.

When the colonies separated from the mother country the "Green Mountain Boys," as the Vermont frontiersmen were called, determined to form a new state. This movement was led by Ethan Allen and his brothers, who felt that their large landholdings would be more secure under separate statehood. In 1777 a democratic constitution was adopted and a government was organized for the new commonwealth, which was appropriately called Vermont (*Vermont* means *green mountain*). For fear of antagonizing New York, Congress refrained from recognizing the new state during the Confederation period; but after New York had surrendered her rights (1790), the Federal Constitution was ratified by the legislature and Vermont became the fourteenth state (February 18, 1791).

Discontent in Watauga and Transylvania

During the Revolutionary War the settlements in east Tennessee (Watauga) and central Kentucky (Transylvania) had grown in numbers and importance. Watauga was brought under the jurisdiction of North Carolina, and Transylvania under that of Virginia; but in each case these western communities were separated from the eastern portion of the state by mountain barriers and wide stretches of wilderness. Under such conditions it was virtually impossible for the seaboard authorities to provide them with a just and efficient government. The frontiersmen complained that too much of the land had been monopolized by land-grabbers, that adequate measures for defense were not provided, and that in general the laws under which they lived were not suited to local conditions. They, therefore, wanted the right to govern themselves, and this desire took the form of a demand for separate statehood.

Virginia more than once generously offered Kentucky permission to separate from the mother state. But partly because state consciousness developed slowly in this western country, and partly because of obstacles that arose from time to time, the offers were not promptly accepted, and it was not until 1792 that Kentucky was finally admitted into the Union as the fifteenth state.

In the later years of the Confederacy James Wilkinson, who had held the rank of brigadier general in the Revolutionary army, came to Kentucky to trouble the waters in order that he might fish a fortune out of them. He was a man of ability, with a glib tongue and a ready pen. In the use of his gifts he was not hampered by principles, and his selfish ambition had free play. Soon he began to earn the reputation he afterwards gained of "being the most finished rascal in American annals." *James Wilkinson, a disturbing factor in Kentucky*

The Kentuckians, as well as the Tennesseans, felt that the use of the Mississippi as an outlet to market was necessary to prevent the strangulation of their economic life. Farm products, whiskey, and other articles that the people had for sale were loaded on flatboats and floated down the tributaries of the Ohio and then on that stream and the Mississippi to New Orleans. Here the commodities were sold or stored for export and the flatboat was broken up and disposed of for lumber. Most of the products of the Westerners were too bulky and heavy to be transported across the mountains on pack horses to eastern towns, and for such wares New Orleans was the only accessible market. The Westerners, therefore, insisted on the free use of the Mississippi, and the failure of Congress to secure this right from Spain caused great dissatisfaction among them. *The Westerners insist on the right to use the Mississippi*

When the report came to them that the Northern members of Congress had voted for Jay's proposal regarding the closure of the Mississippi, they felt that the Federal government was disposed to sacrifice their rights in order to promote the commercial interests of the East. This report, which had been distorted before it reached them, caused the Westerners to distrust the Federal government. This distrust was still alive when the new Constitution was submitted to them for acceptance. It was largely because of their fear that their rights would not be upheld by the Federal government that they voted against ratification in 1788.

The dissatisfaction aroused in the West by Jay's proposal gave Wilkinson the opportunity to use his skill in intrigue. He made the Spanish authorities at New Orleans believe that he could and would utilize this discontent to the advantage of their country. If the right to navigate the Mississippi were given exclusively to him and his allies they could use this monopoly as a club to frighten the frontiersmen into the right attitude toward Spain. With such an argument he could easily persuade them that secession from the Union and an alliance with Spain would gain for them access to the New Orleans market, while loyalty to the American Union would result in a loss of this valued privilege. By such misrepresentations he was able to procure for a few years the coveted monopoly and with it the tickling of his palm with Spanish gold. *Wilkinson's intrigues*

The Spanish governor at New Orleans was deceived by this trickster, for a majority of the Kentuckians had no thought of seceding from the Union. They would be satisfied with separate statehood within the Union. Nor did Wilkinson himself while in Kentucky agitate for anything more. With the admission of Kentucky as a state (1792) the possibility of secession vanished and she took her place as a loyal, if not enthusiastic, member of the Union.

The settlers of east Tennessee became state conscious more quickly than did those of Kentucky. This feeling was encouraged by the Ordinance of 1784. One of the proposed states under this

Reproduced from THE PAGEANT OF AMERICA, *Copyright Yale University Press*

PITTSBURGH IN 1796.

plan covered approximately the area of the east Tennessee communities. North Carolina in 1784 ceded her western lands to the Union on certain conditions. As these conditions were not complied with by Congress she recalled the cession and re-asserted her authority over the Watauga settlements.

In the meantime the people here, under the leadership of John Sevier, had organized a separate government and given their new state the name of Franklin. North Carolina regarded this movement as an act of rebellion and made a vigorous effort to put a stop to it. After considerable difficulty her authority over the obstreperous pioneers was restored, but in 1789 the territory was for a second time ceded to the Union.

In the meantime other settlements had been made. Nashboro (Nashville) on the Cumberland River had been founded by James

Robertson (1779), and Knoxville was established a decade later. *Tennessee admitted into the Union* The Southwest Territory was organized in 1790 and William Blount was appointed by Washington as its first governor. Blount had jurisdiction in theory over Tennessee and that vast region extending southward as far as the 31st parallel. The Spaniards still held their post at Natchez, and thus Blount's authority was virtually confined to the Tennessee settlements. Population grew rapidly in the Southwest Territory, and by 1796 the state of Tennessee was carved out of it and admitted into the Union.

CHAPTER XVI

The Creation of a New Government

THE FRAMING OF THE CONSTITUTION

*The
Annapolis
Convention*

*D*URING the half-decade following the close of the Revolutionary War there was a growing dissatisfaction with the government
of the Confederation owing to the commercial and financial confusion and the general instability of conditions throughout the
country. This discontent was strongest among the upper classes,
who dominated economic, social, and political life in the states.
There soon arose, therefore, among the leaders of these classes
an agitation in favor of giving more power to the Federal government. This propaganda was carried on by means of private correspondence and the circulation of printed pamphlets. Prominent
among those who took part in the movement were Alexander Hamilton, James Madison, Pelatiah Webster, and George Washington.

The first important step toward converting this sentiment into
action was taken by the Annapolis Convention. Through the influence of Madison, the legislature of Virginia issued an invitation
to all the states to send commissioners to Annapolis to consider
in joint meeting the problem of uniform commercial regulations
among the states. At the appointed time (September 11, 1786)
commissioners from five states appeared at Annapolis. In view
of the meager representation, the convention declined to take
any action except to make a recommendation to the states. It was
unanimously agreed by the commissioners present that all the
states should appoint delegates to a convention to be held at Philadelphia on the second Monday of May, 1787, "to devise such further
provisions as shall appear to them necessary to render the constitution of the Federal Government adequate to the exigencies of the
Union."

*The Consti-
tutional
Convention:
Membership*

Virginia, the first state to accept the invitation issued from
Annapolis, chose seven delegates to attend the proposed convention. Other states followed the example of the Old Dominion,
and the movement soon made such headway that Congress decided
to take action. Accordingly, it passed a resolution (February 21,
1787) calling a meeting at the time and place suggested by the

252

Annapolis Convention, "for the sole and express purpose of revising the Articles of Confederation." All amendments that might be offered by this convention were to be reported to Congress and the various state legislatures for their acceptance or rejection.

The states which had not already acted (except New Hampshire and Rhode Island) promptly chose delegates to the proposed convention. New Hampshire did not appoint her delegates until late in June, hence they did not arrive at Philadelphia until July 23, after most of the controversial questions had been settled. No deputies were ever chosen by Rhode Island and this little state had no share in the work of constitution-making. The total number of delegates selected for the Convention was seventy-four, but only fifty-five were in actual attendance. Some of these were absent for a good portion of the time, and only thirty-nine signed the finished document.

In choosing representatives, Virginia set a high standard by naming her most distinguished sons. Her example was emulated by the other states, and therefore the list of appointees included most of the outstanding leaders of the country. It was considered a great honor to be appointed a delegate, and the state legislatures in making their selections were able to skim the cream of American statesmanship. Thomas Jefferson, then in Paris, was deeply impressed with the roster of names and, with an exaggeration which he probably later regretted, spoke of the Convention as "an assembly of demigods." Most of the deputies were college-trained, and a few, like Franklin, were self-educated. A large majority of them had had practical experience in governmental affairs as administrative officials or as members of Congress or state legislatures.

The delegates in the main belonged to the wealthy and educated classes, and were aristocratic in their political opinions. They held the view, then generally accepted by the ruling class, that one of the most important functions of government is to protect property rights. Furthermore, a considerable portion of them owned Federal and state bonds,[1] the value of which would be greatly enhanced if a strong general government were established. Then, too, a stabilized government, state and Federal, would be favorable to the growth of commerce and industry and would therefore promote

---

[1] C. A. Beard, in his *An Economic Interpretation of the Constitution of the United States,* gives a long list of members of the Convention who presented Federal bonds for redemption in 1791. Just how many of these bonds were purchased after 1787 and how many belonged to clients whom these former deputies to the Convention represented, it would be difficult to determine. But after making all due allowances, it is quite probable that a considerable number of the deputies owned state or Federal paper while they were sitting in the Convention. A discussion of the economic interests of the deputies is given in Chapter V. For a good brief summary, see pp. 150-151.

the prosperity of the wealthy classes and the people generally.

To what extent the framers were influenced by these selfish considerations it is impossible to say. It is more than likely, however, that they acted from higher and more patriotic motives. They were doubtless firm in the conviction that what was good for their group would be good for the country as a whole. The belief of the deputies in the sanctity of property, together with their aristocratic notions, was a guaranty that the actions of the Convention would be characterized by conservatism. Their idealism had been tempered by experience in actual government, and they were therefore able to differentiate between the desirable and the attainable. Moreover, their conservatism had been accentuated by Shays' Rebellion and other recent disorders. They were therefore in general agreement as to the desirability of establishing a political system which would not only safeguard liberty but would also protect property.

Washington The most illustrious member of the Convention, Washington, headed the Virginia delegation. He preferred not to serve, but was induced to overcome his reluctance and accept the appointment. He was at the height of his fame at that time, and was easily the most noted man in the Western Hemisphere. He was looked up to with awe and reverence by the American people, and if his great prestige could be linked with the movement it would inspire respect for the Convention and give assurance that its work would be for the good of the country. As he was president of the body, he did not participate in the debates. He spoke only once or twice on the floor, but he took a deep interest in the proceedings and voted as a member of the Virginia delegation. Furthermore, it was charged, perhaps falsely, that his attitude on important measures was shown from the chair by smiles of approval or frowns of disapproval.

James Madison Although less conspicuous than some of his colleagues, James Madison proved to be the most effective member of the Convention. He was thirty-six years of age, and had had considerable experience in the art of government as a member of Congress and the legislature of Virginia. For some time he had been advocating an increase in the power of the general government, and had qualified as a conservative by successfully opposing the issuance of paper money in Virginia. While not a brilliant orator, he was a clear thinker and a logical debater. As a preparation for his work in the Convention, he had studied the experiments in federation made by the ancient Greeks, and was thus armed with historical information as well as the knowledge that comes from experience.

Next to Madison in the work of the Convention came James

Wilson of Pennsylvania. Of Scotch birth and education, he had *James Wilson*
lived in this country long enough to become one of the best lawyers in America. He had served a number of years in Congress,
had signed the Declaration of Independence, and now at the age
of forty-five was in the prime of life. More brilliant than Wilson
was his young colleague in the Pennsylvania delegation, Gouverneur
Morris. Clever, aristocratic in his views, and gifted with a fine
style, Morris played a more conspicuous than useful part in the
proceedings.

All of the above-mentioned leaders were ardent advocates of a *William*
strong Federal government.[1] The opponents of nationalism could *Paterson*
also point to able leaders. Members of this group who deserve particular mention were: William Paterson of New Jersey, a good
debater, who had been a member of the Continental Congress, a
signer of the Declaration of Independence, and for eleven years
attorney general of his state; and Roger Sherman, an able politician
of sound judgment, who had been in succession a shoemaker, al-
manac-maker, lawyer, and judge.

These and the other leaders who stood out against nationalism
did not act merely as obstructionists but performed a valuable service in the framing of the Constitution. By their opposition they
kept the trend toward centralization from going to such lengths
as to sacrifice unduly the powers of the states. Their insistence upon
the rights of the states led to certain compromises but for which
the Constitution might never have been accepted.

Two other names that have a high place in American history *Franklin and*
should be mentioned. These are Benjamin Franklin and Alexander *Hamilton*
Hamilton. The former could look back to an illustrious career
and the latter forward to a brilliant record in the service of his
country; but neither of them exerted any considerable influence
in the Convention. Franklin's more than fourscore years had taken
toll of his vigor, and his temperament—always conciliatory—had now
been softened by age. He therefore did not take an aggressive stand
on the questions at issue. His chief service consisted in pouring oil on
the troubled waters when controversy reached the danger point.
Hamilton's extreme nationalism handicapped his usefulness, for
the majority of the members were unwilling to create a govern-

[1] Among the others who belonged to the strong-government party should be mentioned the following: Rufus King of Massachusetts, who because of unusual personal
charm, marked ability, and a fine voice, impressed the Convention as a pleasing orator
and successful debater; Edmund Randolph, the handsome and polished governor of
Virginia, who was a successful lawyer and a good debater; George Mason, a Virginian
of the old school, author of the constitution of his state and one of the ablest debaters
in the country; and Charles Pinckney of South Carolina, who was only twenty-nine
years of age and the youngest member of the Convention.

ment as highly centralized as he suggested. His two colleagues from New York were especially opposed to his views and he was usually outvoted in his delegation. Furthermore, he was absent from the sessions for a good part of the time.

Conspicuous for their absence were John Adams and Samuel Adams of Massachusetts, and Thomas Jefferson and Patrick Henry of Virginia. John Adams and Jefferson were on foreign missions, the former at London and the latter at Paris. Samuel Adams was not chosen as a delegate. Patrick Henry's name was put on Virginia's list next to that of Washington, but he declined the appointment since he was not in sympathy with the trend toward nationalism. His reason for not going to Philadelphia, as given by him later, was that "he smelt a rat."

Organization of the Convention

By May 14, the time set for the opening of the Convention, only a few of the deputies had reached Philadelphia, and it was not until eleven days later that delegations from a majority of the states had arrived. The Convention was then organized (May 25) with Washington as the unanimous choice for president. Rules of procedure were adopted, one of which pledged the members to the strictest secrecy. The debates were thus free from the influence of outside clamor. Each state had one vote, which was determined by the voice of a majority of its representatives. Important questions were thoroughly debated and opinions were molded by discussion to a greater extent than is customary with parliamentary bodies. The comparative smallness of the Convention and the absence of the motive for speaking for the effect on listening constituencies made for efficient debating.

Sources of information regarding the work of the Convention

Owing to the secrecy of the sessions, the newspapers were unable to record information as to the proceedings. The secretary was not efficient and the record kept by him was meager and unsatisfactory. Fortunately we have a much fuller and better account in the *Notes* taken by Madison. He chose a seat in front of the president's chair, with the other members at his right and left hand, and so was in a position to hear all that was going on. It was his custom to take down in abbreviated form what was said and done, and to write up his notes in full between sessions. His manuscript was thus completed in a few days after the last meeting of the Convention. This account is by all odds the fullest and best we have of the work of the Convention. The statements are clear and fair and not colored by feeling. Motions and the votes on them are recorded, and also the arguments for and against them.

Next in importance to the notes of Madison are those which were taken by Robert Yates. There has also recently come to light the journal of his colleague in the New York delegation, John Lansing, Jr.[1] In addition to these we have brief accounts by other delegates[2] and scraps of information gleaned from the letters and speeches of members.

While waiting for latecomers to arrive, the Virginia delegation had daily meetings and agreed upon a set of resolutions which were to be offered as the basis of the new constitution. These resolutions, which were probably written by Madison, were presented to the Convention by Randolph, who made a brilliant speech showing the need of a strong government. The scheme of government embodied in them was known as the Virginia, or Randolph, Plan. It provided for an effective general government, one that would be favorable to the large states, since there was to be proportional representation in both houses of the Federal legislature. This plan was discussed at great length and a number of important revisions and additions were made in the original resolutions. The Randolph Plan, after having been thus hammered into shape, was accepted by the Convention and became the Constitution of the United States.

The Virginia Plan

The delegates from the small states were opposed to the Randolph Plan, contending that it would confer too much authority on the general government and give the large states an undue influence in Federal affairs. So dissatisfied were the small-state representatives with the Randolph Plan that they proposed as a substitute another scheme of government. This proposal was embodied in a series of resolutions offered by William Paterson of New Jersey and is known as the Paterson, or New Jersey, Plan. It proposed to amend the Articles of Confederation and to give Congress greater powers but not to clothe the Federal government with sovereignty. It continued the old system of raising money by requisitions on the states, but made it more effective by giving Congress power to direct the collection of an assessment whenever a state failed to comply with the requisition within a specified time. The acts of Congress and Federal treaties were to be the supreme

The New Jersey Plan

---

[1] Lansing's notes were edited and published (1939) by Joseph R. Strayer under the title of *The Delegate from New York*. They give a brief account of the proceedings of the Convention until July 9, the day before Yates and Lansing withdrew from the body.

[2] Of the delegates, other than those already mentioned, who have left brief accounts, the following should be mentioned: King, Paterson, McHenry, Hamilton, Charles Pinckney, Mason, and Pierce. The notes of the last-named are valuable because of the character sketches of delegates given in them. In 1819 the seal of secrecy was broken, when by order of Congress the official account of the secretary was published. Madison's *Notes* were published in 1840. These and the other sources mentioned above (except Lansing's *Proceedings*) can all be found in Max Farrand's *The Records of the Federal Convention of 1787* (3 volumes, 1911).

law of the land, and the state courts were to be bound by them.
There was a provision for the use of force to compel the states to
obey the treaties and laws of the United States.

For three days (June 16, 18, 19) it was warmly debated whether
the Paterson Plan should supersede the amended Randolph Plan.
This was a crucial period in the deliberations. The larger states
wanted a stronger Federal government than would be provided
for by the Paterson Plan. As the strong-government party had a
majority over the states' rights group, the Paterson Plan was rejected.
The victory of the large states was not complete, however, since
the small-state party put up a vigorous fight against nationalism
and was able to secure important modifications of the original
Randolph Plan.

*The Great
Compromise*

In the fight between the two parties the issue which caused the
greatest controversy was that of representation. It was decided,
with little opposition, that the Federal legislature should consist
of two houses. Next came the question of apportioning representation in the lower house. The large-state group insisted that membership in this house should be based on proportional representation. The small-state party demanded equal representation. Each
side was so unyielding that a hopeless deadlock seemed to have
been reached. It was at this critical juncture that Franklin offered
his motion that "prayers imploring the assistance of Heaven . . .
be held in this Assembly every morning." The proposal was not
accepted. One objection urged against it was that the introduction
of this practice so late in the session might cause the people on the
outside to feel that the Convention was on the verge of a dangerous
crisis. Indeed, a situation so serious as to cause politicians to resort
to prayer might quite properly alarm the general public. Probably
the real reason, however, for not engaging the services of a chaplain
was that the Convention had no funds with which to pay one.

The danger passed and it was decided "that the rule of suffrage
in the first branch ought not to be according to that established
by the Articles of Confederation." This was, in awkward phrase-
ology, the virtual acceptance of the principle of proportional
representation.

The large-state party having won the victory as to representation
in the lower house, the small states made an able second-line fight
for equal representation in the upper house. Their delegates contended that proportional representation in both houses would put
the small states entirely at the mercy of the large states. The latter
would combine into a predominant party and thus completely
control Congress. In reply Madison argued ably to show that party

lines in the future would be drawn not with reference to the size of states but in accordance with geographical and economic conditions, the large and small states of one section combining against those of another. Furthermore, he pointed out the injustice of allowing the people of a small state the same voice in the government as those of a large one. To do this would be to give each citizen of a small state a voting power several times as great as that enjoyed by a citizen of a large state.

The vote on this heated question resulted in a tie, five to five, with Georgia divided. To break the deadlock a committee of one from each state was chosen and instructed to report a plan of compromise. The plan suggested by the committee was that the upper house should be made up of two Senators from each state, and the lower house, of representatives apportioned among the states according to population. There was also a provision that all bills for raising and appropriating money and for fixing salaries must originate in the lower house and such bills could not be amended by the upper house. This clause was added to ease the forebodings of the large-state delegates, who were afraid that the small states, acting through the upper house, would impose unnecessary tax burdens upon the country. This provision was afterwards changed so as to read as follows: "All bills for raising revenue shall originate in the House of Representatives; but the Senate may propose or concur with amendments as on other bills."

This proposal of the committee, known as the Great Compromise, was warmly debated for a week, being strongly opposed by the large-state delegates. Finally, it was accepted by the narrow vote of five to four, with Massachusetts divided. The vote of New York was not counted, as two of her delegates had left the Convention.

The Great Compromise was a concession to the small states, and they gave no further trouble. The other provisions regarding the legislature were adopted without controversy. The first and second branches of the new Congress were to be known respectively as the House of Representatives and the Senate. Representatives were to be elected by the voters, and Senators by the state legislatures. All persons in each state who could vote in the election of members of the lower house of the state legislature could vote in the election of Representatives in Congress. In the enactment of laws, the voting in both houses of Congress was to be by individuals and not by states. *Other provisions relating to the legislature*

The new Congress was to have the powers exercised by the old Congress, namely: those of borrowing money, coining money and regulating the value thereof; establishing post offices and post roads; punishing piracies and felonies committed on the high seas; declaring war and granting letters of marque and reprisal; raising and supporting armies; and providing and maintaining a navy.

In addition to these, certain other powers were granted to the new legislative body that were not exercised by the Congress of the Confederation. Prominent in this list were the right to "lay and collect taxes, duties, imposts, and excises, to pay the debts and provide for the common defense and general welfare of the United States"; to regulate interstate and foreign commerce; to exercise exclusive legislation over the territories and the Federal district in which the seat of government should be located; and "to make all laws which shall be necessary and proper for carrying into execution of the foregoing powers, and all other powers vested by this Constitution in the government of the United States, or in any department or officer thereof."

All laws required the assent of both houses, and the two houses were equal in other respects, with a few important exceptions. To the House was granted the power to impeach certain delinquent Federal officials and to elect the President of the United States when the Electoral College should fail to make a choice. The Senate had the right to accept or reject the more important appointments to office made by the President; to try officials that had been impeached by the House; and to elect the Vice-President when the Electoral College should fail to agree upon a candidate. All treaties negotiated by the President required confirmation by a vote of two thirds of the Senate.

Minor com-
promises
While some of the minor disputes were in progress, sectionalism showed its ugly visage. Gouverneur Morris contended that the West should not be put upon an equality with the East in the government of the republic. Madison and Mason strongly opposed any discrimination against the West. They wanted the new states to be admitted into the Union on the same terms with the original states. Morris, though he did not entirely succeed in his endeavor, was able to prevent the embodiment of such a guarantee in the Constitution. Instead, this rather vague clause was agreed upon: "New States may be admitted by the Congress into this Union." Whether Congress could limit the power of new states by prescribing conditions on their admission was left as an open question for later decision.

Slavery also figured, though not importantly, as a cause of sectional dispute. Some of the delegates from the far South contended that all slaves should be counted when determining the basis of representation. Certain Northern members, on the other hand, were opposed to counting any of them. The fact that the slaves were property strengthened the argument in favor of counting them, as there was a feeling that property should be one of the bases of representation. By coupling taxation with representation, a plan was found which was acceptable to both sides. It was agreed that in apportioning representation and direct taxation, three fifths of the slaves would be counted.

Sectionalism also figured in the discussions over the question of giving Congress the power to regulate commerce. Southern delegates feared that if Congress, by a mere majority vote, could pass navigation laws it might require all American exports and imports to be carried in American bottoms. Such a monopoly would mean high freight rates for agricultural products sent abroad from the South and thus favor the Northern shipowner at the expense of the Southern farmer. Burdensome duties might also be imposed on Southern exports, such as tobacco and rice.

The South, therefore, contended that navigation laws should receive the assent of two thirds of both houses of Congress. This proposal was opposed by the Northern delegates, who maintained that one of the principal reasons for calling the Convention was to give Congress the right to regulate commerce. The situation was further complicated by the demand in Georgia and the Carolinas for more slaves. The deputations from these states insisted that the Federal government should not have the power to prohibit the importation of slaves.

Evidently these different points of view could be reconciled only by a policy of give and take. To relieve the South of the fear that their staples would be overburdened with taxation in their passage to foreign markets, it was voted that Congress be prohibited from levying export duties.

It was not so easy to settle the question raised by the far South regarding the slave trade. Representatives from this section declared that their states would not ratify the Constitution if their demands were not met. The delegations from the middle region were opposed to further importation, while some of the New England deputies were willing to allow the continuance of the traffic rather than jeopardize the acceptance of the Constitution. The result was a compromise whereby Congress could not prohibit the slave trade prior to January 1, 1808, but could levy an import duty of $10 each on all slaves imported. After these concessions were made to the South it was agreed that navigation acts, like other laws, could be enacted by a majority vote of both houses of Congress, with the consent of the President.

The creation of a Federal executive

One of the knottiest of all the problems which confronted the Convention was that of providing for an adequate Federal executive. At one time a plural executive was advocated by some of the delegates, but the general feeling was in favor of a single executive, who should be independent of the legislature and should be clothed with large powers. Accordingly, it was agreed that there should be a chief executive with the title of President, who was to be commander-in-chief of the army and navy; was to have power, "by and with the advice and consent of the Senate, to make treaties, provided two thirds of the Senators present concur"; and with the advice and consent of a majority of the Senate, to appoint judges of the Federal courts, ambassadors, ministers, and consuls, and other important public officers. He was also to have considerable legislative authority. He was to keep Congress informed as to the state of the Union and recommend measures for its consideration. He could exercise a suspensive veto on any bill passed by Congress, this suspensive veto to be final unless the vetoed bill were reconsidered and passed by a two-thirds majority of both houses of Congress.

To devise a method of selecting an officer of such powers and responsibilities proved to be a most difficult task. Many plans were offered and rejected. If the President were appointed by Congress he would be dependent upon that body, and the principle of the separation of powers would be violated. The delegates were not democratic in their notions, and a majority of them felt that the people were not qualified to make so important a choice. Even George Mason, though more liberal than many of his colleagues, thought that to call upon the people to elect the President would be like asking a blind man for a judgment as to colors.

Finally, it was decided that the President would be chosen by electors, and these electors would be selected in such manner as the state legislatures might prescribe. Each state was to have the same number of electors as it had Representatives and Senators in Congress. The electors were to meet in their respective states and vote for two persons for President. These votes were to be sent in a sealed package to the president of the United States Senate. In a joint session of the two houses of Congress the president of the Senate was to count the votes. The candidate who had received the highest number of votes would be declared President, provided the number received by him was a majority of all the votes cast. The candidate receiving the next highest number of votes would be accepted as Vice-President. In the event that no candidate should receive a majority in the Electoral College, the House of Representatives should make a selection from a list of the five candidates who had received the highest vote. The election in the House would be by states, each state having one vote.

In the provision for electing the President there cropped out again the idea of compromise between the large and small states. It was thought that a majority of the electors would seldom agree on a candidate and that more often than not the House of Representatives would be called upon to act. In such cases, the large states, due to their predominance in the Electoral College, would make the preliminary slate, while the small states would have a strong voice in the final election by the House owing to their over-representation in that body whenever it should act as an electoral assembly.

The Convention was proud of the scheme devised by it for the election of the President and Vice-President. In fact, it was one of the few original features of the Constitution. But the provision did not work out as the Fathers had expected. Soon the electors, instead of acting independently in the selection of the President and Vice-President, became rubber stamps, obediently registering the will of their respective parties. After the plan had been tried a decade and a half, it was modified by the Twelfth Amendment.

One of the clearly apparent weaknesses of the Articles of Confederation was the lack of a strong Federal judiciary. The Convention was, therefore, in general agreement that such a judiciary should be established. There was also no difference of opinion as to the jurisdiction of the Supreme Court of the United States. A dispute arose, however, as to whether inferior Federal courts should be established. Some of the delegates firmly maintained that such tribunals should not be created but that the state courts should be used as such, with appeals from them to the United States Supreme Court. The Convention sidestepped the question by declaring that "the judicial power of the United States shall be vested in one Supreme Court, and in such inferior courts as the Congress may from time to time ordain and establish." As this clause gave Congress an option rather than an obligation, the final responsibility as to inferior courts was imposed upon that body.

The Federal judiciary

The power of the Federal judiciary was to extend "to all cases affecting ambassadors, other public ministers, and consuls; to all cases of admiralty and maritime jurisdiction; to controversies to which the United States shall be a party; to controversies between two or more States; between a State and citizens of another State; between citizens of different States; between citizens of the same

State claiming lands under grants of different States and between a State or the citizens thereof, and foreign States, citizens, or subjects."

Sources of the ideas embodied in the Constitution

The Constitution was not a new creation. It did not spring full-armed from the brain of the Jovian Fathers, as Mr. Gladstone once indicated. Nearly all its provisions were borrowed from one source or another. The work of the framers was, therefore, mainly one of selection, adaptation, and organization. Most of the stones had been shaped by experience before they found a place in the new structure. The principles embodied in the Constitution came from a variety of sources. Among them the following should be mentioned:

(1) The Articles of Confederation and the experience of the general government under them. A considerable portion of the old constitution was transferred to the new, much of it word for word. Some of the most important of the new provisions were added because experience under the Articles revealed the desirability of such changes.

(2) The state constitutions and the lessons learned from actual government under them. The similarity in the framework of the government of the Union and that of the states was due, not to a coincidence, but to conscious borrowing. As the states had been running their own affairs for more than a decade, the strong and weak points in their political institutions were clearly apparent. The framers of the Federal Constitution were able, therefore, to distinguish between the good and the bad in the state constitutions and to find in these siftings useful ideas to be embedded in the new organic law.

(3) Colonial practice. The state governments were generally modeled after the colonial governments, and so the principles taken from the former were indirectly borrowed from the latter. Furthermore, certain colonial practices had grown into traditions, which were perpetuated in the Federal and state governments. To this source, for example, we are indebted for the idea that bills for raising revenue should originate in the lower house of the assembly and that enactments of legislative bodies should be subjected to judicial review.

(4) The English constitution. As the colonial governments were more or less imitations of the British government, many of the political ideas contributed by the former came indirectly from the latter. Besides, some of the features of the American Constitution were borrowed directly from the British Constitution. For example, the division of governmental functions between the Union and the

states was quite similar to the distribution of power between the British colonies and the homeland.

(5) Political theories current at the time. There were embodied in the Constitution some ideas which the Fathers had gleaned from the writings of English and French philosophers. Especially marked was the influence of Montesquieu, whose doctrine of the separation of powers and of checks and balances was generally accepted in America.

Provision for amendments

The Fathers did not regard their handiwork as a perfect instrument of government. The infallibility attributed to them by later generations would doubtless have made a strong appeal to their sense of humor. The Constitution was a bundle of compromises, and few if any of its framers approved of it in its entirety. It was, however, the best scheme available by which a real union and an effective general government could be established, and they accepted it for that reason. It was hoped that the imperfections could be worked out in the future by the amending process.

Amendments could be proposed in two ways. First, by Congress, by a two-thirds vote of both houses; and second, by a national convention called by Congress. The call for a national convention must be issued by Congress whenever the legislatures of two thirds of the states should by petition ask it to do so. The framers probably thought that the national convention would be used at times not only to offer amendments but also to give the Constitution a thorough overhauling. Such has not been the case, for no second national convention has ever been held.

After an amendment has been proposed it has to be ratified by the legislatures of three fourths of the states or by conventions of three fourths of the states. Congress decides which method of ratification shall be employed. So far (to 1944), only one amendment (the twenty-first) has been ratified by state conventions; all the others have been ratified by state legislatures.

General character of the new government

In creating the new government the framers of the Constitution were performing a noble experiment. Two governments were established, each of which rested directly on the people. The problem was to make the Federal government strong enough to take care of general interests and at the same time leave to the states such authority as was needed for the safeguarding of local interests. This attempt to create a political machine made up of wheels within a wheel was no easy task. The difficulty was to keep all the wheels running smoothly without any jamming of cogs. Certain powers were allocated to the Union and others to the states. But the line that separated the one group of powers from the other was not sharply drawn, and for seven decades there was more or less controversy as to the locus of this dim line.

The vagueness of the constitution in this particular, and in other respects, has given rise to important differences of opinion as to its meaning. For the settlement of these differences numerous appeals have been made to the Federal judiciary. In these decisions the courts have at times stretched and even changed the Constitution to make it fit new conditions. Because these opinions have been accepted as fundamental law, the Supreme Court has been able virtually to make amendments to the Constitution by judicial interpretation.

It is not clearly stated in the Constitution whether sovereignty, or supreme authority, resided in the states, as it did under the Articles of Confederation, or in the Union, as it does today. It took a terrible fratricidal war to settle this mooted question. And yet the Fathers are not to be severely criticized for this vagueness. If it had been clearly and definitely understood in 1787 that the new Constitution had created a national government, such as we have today, in all probability it would have been rejected by the state conventions.[1] On the other hand, if it had been generally conceded that the states were still sovereign, the Federal government might never have gained the power needed to meet the problems with which it has had to cope.

Shortcomings of the Constitution

Some of the shortcomings of the original Constitution were doubtless due to inadvertence. Cases in point were the failure to confer upon the Union any definite authority to acquire new territory or any power to regulate manufacturing. These may have been oversights, *casa omissa,* as Jefferson afterwards termed them. At that time commerce was more important than industry. The confusion which arose from state control of commerce demonstrated the necessity of giving the general government the power to regulate foreign and interstate commerce. It could not then be foreseen that industry would become nation-wide in scope and would, as much as commerce, demand national regulation.

Not all of the omissions in the Constitution, however, can be attributed to inadvertence. In one case, at least, the Convention

---

[1] This view is ably contested by Professor McLaughlin, who is firmly of the belief that it was "the intention of the framers to establish a national government and to abandon a Confederation of sovereign states." Furthermore, it was, he says, clearly pointed out in the discussions in the state conventions and in the controversial literature of the period that the acceptance of the Constitution would mean the end of state sovereignty. That such arguments were frequently used in the conventions and in the newspaper discussions cannot be denied. It does not follow, however, that these views were generally accepted at the time. A. C. McLaughlin, *The Constitutional History of the United States,* 214-216.

consciously refused to grant the Federal government a power which has since been considered one of its proper functions. A motion was made by Franklin to give Congress authority to construct canals, and Madison suggested that the general government be allowed to issue charters of incorporation for the purpose of encouraging internal improvements. These proposals were defeated.

The Constitution did not at first contain a formal bill of rights, but in a few particulars the rights of the individual were protected against governmental interference. The privilege of the writ of habeas corpus was not to be suspended "unless when in cases of rebellion or invasion the public safety may require it." No bill of attainder or *ex post facto* law could be passed by either the Federal or a state legislature.

The states were also forbidden to "coin money; emit bills of credit; make anything but gold and silver a tender in payment of debts; . . . or [pass any] law impairing the obligation of contracts." These latter restrictions were placed on the states for the protection of the propertied interests. By these clauses creditors were insured against the scaling down of their debts or the payment of them in cheap money. With these provisions should be classed the following clause: "All debts contracted and engagements entered into, before the adoption of this Constitution, shall be as valid against the United States under this Constitution, as under the Confederation." This was a guarantee that holders of United States bonds would be paid in full. It is this clause especially on which rests the charge that the Fathers (those of them who owned government paper) were looking out for their own selfish interests. But if the indebtedness of the old government had not been assumed by the new, the credit of the country would have been greatly impaired. *Limitations on the powers of the states*

In recent years much has been said of the undemocratic features of the original Constitution. That the Fathers were members of an aristocratic class which had little confidence in either the wisdom or the virtue of the masses cannot be doubted. On the other hand, the regulation of the suffrage was left to the states and nothing was done to limit the exercise of this privilege. Furthermore, the people had either direct or indirect control of all branches of the government.

On September 17 the Constitution, which had been put into final form by Gouverneur Morris, came up for adoption. A few of the members were unwilling to sign it, and so the document could not go out with the unanimous approval of the delegates. In order that the action of the Convention might have the semblance of unanimity, the resolution of adoption was, on motion of Franklin, *Adoption of the Constitution* worded as follows: "Done in Convention by the unanimous consent of the States present. . . . " This resolution was adopted and the engrossed copy of the Constitution was then signed by all but three of the delegates present.

THE RATIFICATION OF THE CONSTITUTION

Provision for ratification

The Constitution contained this provision for its ratification: Conventions were to be held in the states, and as soon as nine of these conventions should ratify the new instrument of government, it would go into effect as between such states as had accepted it. Those states were to be left out in the weather which were unwilling to come under the "New Roof," as the Constitution was called. The launching of the new government under such an arrangement would, therefore, be an act of revolution. Under the old constitution changes in the fundamental law could be made only with the consent of the *legislatures* of *all* the states. The important innovations suggested by the proposed Constitution were to be effective when accepted by *conventions* of *some* of the states. Furthermore, the Articles of Confederation declared that the old union was to be perpetual; it was now to be destroyed by the secession of the ratifying states.

The Constitution submitted to state conventions

The new frame of government was sent to Congress with the request that it be submitted to the state conventions for their acceptance or rejection. The old government was thus invited "to light its own funeral pyre." At first, Congress was by no means enthusiastic over the new plan; but despite objections raised by some of the members, it was voted unanimously by the eleven states present to submit the new instrument to the state conventions for action. In so doing the old government was virtually proclaiming its own abdication.

Federalists and Antifederalists

The Constitution, now before the people, was the issue between the two political parties which had been promptly formed. Those who favored ratification called themselves Federalists. This term was a misnomer, as most of the advocates of ratification were not in favor of a federation of states but of a strong general government. The word "nationalist" would more nearly have defined their views. But the latter term was in disfavor with the people, and so the friends of the new system appropriated the more acceptable name of Federalists. There was left then for the opponents of ratification nothing but the designation of "Antifederalists." They were therefore under the disadvantage of having to wear a label which had only a negative connotation.

In some of the states there were heated contests between the supporters and opponents of ratification. These disputes were not confined to the state conventions, but were carried on in state legislatures, on the stump, and in the press. Numerous articles on both sides, over Latin or fanciful pseudonyms, appeared in the newspapers. These discussions were not always kept on the high plane of principle, but frequently degenerated into personal abuse and appeals to prejudice.

Objections to the Constitution

The basis of the opposition to the Constitution was the contention that it gave the Federal government too much power and left too little to the states. It had, so the Antifederalists maintained, changed a confederation into a consolidated government and reduced the states to a position of undue subordination. It would give the President and Congress greater power over the states than that formerly exercised by king and Parliament over the colonies. The Federalists, on the other hand, denied that a consolidated national government would be created and that the states would be deprived of any rights needful for the control of their legitimate interests. The new union would be a cross between a league of states and a consolidated nation.

Breaking down their general objection into specific complaints, the Antifederalists pointed out a number of features in the new Constitution to which they objected. Throughout the country there was pretty general agreement among them that the absence of a bill of rights was a serious shortcoming. Owing to this omission there was no guarantee that religious freedom, freedom of the press, and other natural rights of the individual would be respected by the new government. No provision had been made for trial by jury in civil cases in the Federal courts. Among debtors there was objection to those provisions which prevented the states from impairing the obligation of contracts and issuing paper money. Class feeling also figured as a cause of opposition to the new plan of government. The land speculators, merchants, manufacturers, lawyers, and persons of wealth in the coast towns were, as a rule, for ratification. These favored classes were in some localities cordially hated by their poorer neighbors in the towns and by the small farmers of the interior. The advocacy of any measure by the former group—usually termed with a spice of malice the "well-born"—tended to arouse the suspicion, if not the opposition, of the latter.

Early ratifications

The Constitution was readily accepted by the small states, and it was promptly ratified by them with little or no opposition. The large state of Pennsylvania also signified its acceptance at an early date (December 12, 1787) although the Antifederalists put up a vigorous fight in opposition. Before the middle of January, 1788, ratification had been voted by the states of Delaware, Pennsylvania, New Jersey, Georgia, and Connecticut, in the order named. The vote in Delaware, New Jersey, and Georgia was unanimous. In Pennsylvania it was two to one, and in Connecticut more than three to one. Then came ratifications by Massachusetts, Maryland, South Carolina, and New Hampshire. By the action of New Hampshire (June 21) the new union was assured, as she was the ninth state to accept the Constitution.

The contest over ratification in Massachusetts

The opposition offered by the Antifederalists was particularly strong in Massachusetts, New York, and Virginia. In Massachusetts there was left as a hang-over of Shays' Rebellion a feeling of bitterness, on the part of the small farmers of the interior and the poorer classes generally, toward the merchants, lawyers, and others among the "well-born" in the East. This less fortunate group was inclined to oppose ratification because the prosperous classes were supporting it. Moreover, the two most popular of the Revolutionary leaders, John Hancock and Samuel Adams, did not at first throw the weight of their influence in favor of ratification. Hancock was late in putting in his appearance at the state convention, although he had been elected its president. An attack of gout was given as the excuse for his absence. The real reason, however (in the opinion of some), was that he was waiting to see which way the wind of public opinion was blowing before hoisting his sails. Later he took his place in the convention, and after it had voted to recommend certain amendments to the Federal Constitution which had been proposed by him, he fell in line with the advocates of ratification. The Federalists, it has been said, had appealed to his vanity by dangling before him the Vice-Presidency of the new republic. Samuel Adams was at first opposed to ratification; but when the shipwrights and mechanics of Boston adopted resolutions in its favor, he gave up his opposition and climbed on the band wagon. Finally the Antifederalists were defeated, and the Constitution was accepted by a vote of 187 to 168.

In Virginia

In the Virginia convention the Antifederalists had a number of able leaders, such as George Mason and Patrick Henry. At the head of the Federalist delegation were James Madison and John Marshall. The contest was a battle royal between giants. The eloquence of Henry, who was the most polished orator in America, was not a match for the clear reasoning of Madison, who was no orator but an able debater. In this body of intellectuals Henry's ability to stir the emotions of his hearers did not make so effective an appeal as did Madison's skill in marshalling arguments. In the Old Dominion and elsewhere Washington's influence in favor of ratification was a great aid to the Federalist cause, although he was not a member of the Virginia convention. In a private letter which had been printed in the newspapers he said: ". . . and clear I am if another Federal Convention is attempted, the sentiment of the members will be more discordant. . . . I am fully persuaded . . . that it [the Constitution] or disunion, is before us. If the first is our choice, when the defects of it are experienced, a constitutional door is open for amendments and may be adopted in a peaceable manner without tumult or disorder."[1] After a long and earnest discussion, the Constitution was ratified by a vote of 89 to 79.

The New York convention was at first under the control of the *In New York* Antifederalists. George Clinton, who was strongly opposed to ratification, was president of the body. Hamilton, though not satisfied with the Constitution because it did not go far enough toward nationalism, was one of the outstanding leaders of the Federalists. The Antifederalists could by prompt action have defeated ratification; but they hesitated to assume this responsibility, and a heated discussion, characterized by abusive speeches, was carried on for two weeks. They lost their opportunity by this delay; for before a final decision was reached news had been received of the favorable action of New Hampshire and Virginia. The union was now a certainty, and New York would be forced to come in or be subjected to the great difficulty of maintaining a separate political existence in the middle of the new republic. Accordingly, ratification was voted, but only by a very narrow majority.

The convention of North Carolina adjourned without accepting *Attitude of* the Constitution, deciding to await further developments. Rhode *North Carolina and* Island declined even to call a convention. The new union, there-*Rhode Island* fore, went into effect with a membership of eleven instead of thirteen states.

The most important of the newspaper articles which figured in *The* the propaganda for and against ratification was a series of learned *Federalist* essays in support of the Constitution which is known as *The Federalist*. These essays were published in certain New York papers in the period from October, 1787, to August, 1788. All of them bore the signature of "Publius." The authors who used this pen name were Hamilton, Madison, and John Jay. These essays were distinguished from the ordinary newspaper discussions of the day by

1 See W. C. Ford, ed., *Washington's Writings*, XI, 210-211, note.

the absence of abuse and personal allusions. Sound arguments were logically arranged and expressed with a clarity which rendered an abstruse subject understandable to the ordinary citizen. *The Federalist* is an interpretation of the Constitution by able contemporaries and is the best commentary we have on that document. Furthermore, it is, in the opinion of an eminent historian, "one of the greatest works ever written in the realm of political science."[1]

JAMES MADISON.

Was the Constitution made by the people?

In the preamble of the Constitution is the statement, "We the people of the United States . . . do ordain and establish this Constitution." The people did not, however, as individuals participate directly in either framing or ratifying the Constitution. In both steps they acted through their respective states. All votes on the various questions which arose in the Philadelphia Convention were by states and all ratifications were by states. It was, therefore, by the states, rather than by the people, that the Constitution was ordained and established. Besides, the majority of the people did not share even indirectly in the building of the "New Roof." Owing to the limitations then imposed on the suffrage, a good portion of the adult male population was not allowed to vote, and a majority of those who were qualified refused to exercise the privilege. It is estimated, therefore, that "no more than one-fourth of the adult

---

[1] A. C. McLaughlin, *The Confederation and the Constitution* (Harper and Brothers), 308.

white males in the country voted one way or the other in the elections at which delegates to the state ratifying conventions were chosen."[1]

1 A. C. McLaughlin, *A Constitutional History of the United States* (D. Appleton-Century Company) , 220-221; and C. A. and Mary R. Beard, *The Rise of American Civilization* (Macmillan) , I, 332.

CHAPTER XVII

Washington at the Helm

LAUNCHING A NEW GOVERNMENT

*T*HE last work of the old Congress consisted in making plans for ushering in the new government. It was decided that the new Congress should meet at New York on March 4, 1789. At the appointed time only a few Representatives and Senators were in attendance, and it was about a month before both houses could muster a quorum. This delay was due in part to poor roads, inclement weather, and the shortness of the period that had elapsed since the members of Congress had been elected, though lack of interest in the new government doubtless also figured as a cause.

When the president of the Senate counted the votes of the Presidential electors (April 6) he found that Washington had been unanimously elected President. Of the several candidates listed as second choice, the name of John Adams appeared more often than that of any of the others and so he became Vice-President.

Washington and Adams were both promptly notified of their election. Adams arrived at New York first and at once took over his duties as president of the Senate. Two days after receiving formal notification, Washington left home for his new responsibilities. His journey to New York was one continuous ovation. He was escorted from city to city by guards of honor and was complimented with dinners and eulogized by speeches. Women and children paid their respects to the Father of the Country by strewing flowers along the road. When he landed on Manhattan Island he was greeted with the wildest expressions of joy.

It was with genuine reluctance that Washington gave his consent to serve as the country's first Chief Magistrate. As a statesman he could hardly hope to add to the prestige which he already enjoyed as a warrior. On the other hand, he ran a serious risk of losing much of the high esteem in which he was held by the people. Besides, he was tired of public life, and his naturally vigorous physical constitution needed rest and recuperation, while his private affairs, after long neglect, demanded his attention. For several years he had been experiencing the delights of country life in his beautiful home on the bluffs of the Potomac, and was living the kind of life which he preferred.

The inauguration was a festive occasion in New York and an immense crowd assembled to witness the ceremony. The oath of office was administered to Washington on the balcony of Federal Hall, which had just been completed and was considered one of the finest structures in America. At the end of this ritual the crowd below greeted its elected chief with rousing cheers. Washington then returned to the Senate Chamber where, with his paper shaking from embarrassment, he read his inaugural address.

One question which gave the congressional leaders some concern was that of the title which should be used in addressing the President. John Adams thought that it would give added dignity to the Chief Magistrate if he were designated by some high-sounding title. After considerable debate, however, Congress decided that inasmuch as the chief executive is by the Constitution termed "President of the United States" no title should be employed in addressing him. *The "republican court"*

Another problem which demanded an early solution was that of the etiquette which should govern the President's contacts with others and the social relations at the executive residence. If no general system were adopted the Chief Executive's time would be frittered away in receiving guests. Furthermore, the public appearances of the President should be characterized by sufficient dignity as to command respect, but should not smack of pomp, which might arouse the opposition if not the ridicule of the plain people. Washington felt that this was important, especially as he would be setting a precedent which might be more or less binding on his successors. After consulting with some of his leading advisers he decided upon a plan by which his official and social relations would be kept on a high plane of dignity and decorum without resort to undue ceremony.

While Congress was in session, the President and Lady Washington gave levees—or formal receptions—every Tuesday afternoon. On such occasions Washington wore a black velvet suit, with knee and shoe buckles. He held in his hand a cocked hat adorned with a cockade, and carried at his side a sword in a scabbard of white leather. His powdered hair was tied behind in a silk bag. Visitors, when presented to him, were greeted not with a handshake but with a bow, which was often rather stiff. On Friday evenings there were parties of a less formal nature, known as "drawing-rooms." At these parties Washington would unbend to some extent and try to appear as a private citizen rather than as a public functionary. Formal dinners were also given from time to time to foreign ministers, members of Congress, and high officials of the government. Washington arose early in the morning, sometimes by four o'clock. He, therefore, retired early, generally at nine o'clock, and so the informal "drawing-rooms" ended at that time.

When the President drove out he used a coach of state imported from England. It was drawn by four, and sometimes six, horses and attended by two outriders, who were dressed in livery, with cocked hats over their powdered hair. The horses were meticulously groomed and their hoofs were blackened and polished and even their teeth were scoured. His drives to church, which he attended regularly every Sunday, were characterized by less state.

The organization of a new government

The question of etiquette, though taken seriously by Washington, was of minor importance as compared with other problems which confronted him. The great task before Congress and the executive was to build a government around the Constitution. The document generally known as the Constitution was only a blue print plus a framework; brick and mortar had to be added to make it a finished structure. While this filling-in process has been going on continuously from the beginning to the present time, more of it was done during Washington's two terms than in any other period of equal length. There was little in the practice of the old government to serve as a basis for the new. Washington and his colleagues therefore had to build from the ground up. The new Congress was predominantly Federalist, and so the Constitution was in the hands of its friends. The Antifederalists who had been chosen to seats in the legislative branch also accepted the Constitution as a finality. They were in disagreement with the Federalists only as to the interpretation of the fundamental law. The new regime was thus not hampered by the obstructionist policies of a group of irreconcilables.

In the beginning, Madison was the leader of the House of Representatives and spokesman of the President. Prior to the creation of his Cabinet, Washington leaned heavily upon him for advice. At this time Madison and Hamilton were on very friendly terms, and these brilliant young statesmen were often seen walking the streets together.

Creation of executive departments

The Constitution made no definite provision for the creation of executive departments. This responsibility was left to Congress. To give the President proper assistance in the discharge of his administrative duties, laws were passed establishing the departments of State, War, and Treasury, and the office of Attorney General.

It was some months before these measures were enacted, and during the period of waiting the executives of the old government carried on in their respective positions. John Jay, who had been Secretary of Foreign Affairs under the Confederation, continued in the performance of his duties until a new official (now called Secretary of State) was designated as his successor.

Jefferson was asked to assume this responsible task, for which no *Heads of departments* man in the country was better qualified. His wide experience as minister to France had acquainted him with the technique of diplomacy. Besides, he was held in high esteem in France, and it was important that our foreign affairs should be managed by one who was *persona grata* to our ally. Jefferson preferred to hold his place as minister but yielded his preference and accepted the post. General Henry Knox had been Secretary of War under the old government and was given the same position in the new. Hamilton was placed at the head of the Treasury, which at that time was the most important of all the executive departments. Ex-Governor Edmund Randolph was made Attorney General.

Washington's inexperience in government made him feel deeply the need of official advice. The Constitution does not state what body shall act in an advisory capacity to the President. It was thought, however, that the Senate would perform that service, as the council of state had done in colonial times, and this expectation was an argument in favor of limiting the size of the Senate.

The Senate proved impracticable as an advisory body, and Washington fell into the practice of calling together the heads of the *Origin of the Cabinet* three executive departments for advice. Owing to the legal aspects of Cabinet discussions, the Attorney General was also later included in these meetings. In this way the Cabinet grew up. Jay, the Chief Justice, was also invited to attend these sessions. But, since as a member of the Supreme Court he might be required to pass on a question considered in Cabinet meeting, he very properly declined the invitation. The Vice-President was also requested to be present, but Adams did not take advantage of this opportunity. These refusals became precedents, and no Chief Justice has ever sat in the Cabinet, and no Vice-President ever served regularly in that capacity, until Calvin Coolidge broke the precedent by accepting a seat in Harding's Cabinet.[1]

The few general provisions in the Constitution regarding Federal *Organization of the judiciary* courts left large powers to Congress in the establishment of the judiciary. Congress was to decide as to the creation of inferior courts and determine their organization and jurisdiction. It could also decide upon the number of judges in the Supreme Court and the

---

[1] While McKinley was President, Vice-President Hobart occasionally attended the sessions of the Cabinet.

salary of all judges. In discharge of this responsibility it passed the first Judiciary Act in September, 1789. By it the Supreme Court was to consist of a Chief Justice and five associate justices, and there were to be thirteen district courts, with a judge to preside over each. Between the Supreme Court and the district courts there were to be intermediary tribunals known as circuit courts. The law provided for three circuits and specified that "there shall be held annually in each district of said circuits two courts which shall be called Circuit Courts, and shall consist of any two justices of the Supreme Court and the district judge of such districts, any two of whom shall constitute a quorum."

In the organization of the judiciary the question of states' rights came to the fore. One group of Congressmen, which advocated states' rights, was opposed to the creation of inferior Federal tribunals and wanted the state courts to act as such with appeals to the United States Supreme Court. This effort was unsuccessful and a Federal judiciary entirely independent of that of the states was voted.

The first tariff act

One of the most urgent of the needs of the new government was that of a source of revenue. The treasury was empty and the national debt was constantly rising. The House of Representatives, under the leadership of Madison, began to discuss a revenue bill within a week after it had been organized and before Washington was inaugurated. Madison wished this measure, which imposed a low tariff on certain imports, to pass as early as possible, since the government was in such dire need of money. But through the influence of the merchants of Philadelphia, Baltimore, New York, and other places, the act was not passed until July and did not go into effect until August 1. The reason for this delay was that these merchants, in anticipation of the tariff, had made large orders abroad and were desirous of having their goods landed before the tariff became effective.

Amend-ments

The Antifederalists, though loyal to the new political regime, were insistent upon the adoption of amendments to the Constitution. A large number of amendments had been suggested by the various ratifying state conventions, and Madison had promised his constituents that he would sponsor an attempt to have changes made in the Constitution. The Antifederalists of his district were now clamoring for a redemption of this pledge. Accordingly, he selected a number of amendments from the seventy-eight suggested by the various states and presented them to the House. Seventeen of these passed the House, but the number was reduced to twelve by the Senate. Ten of this dozen were ratified by the states.

These ten amendments were in the nature of a bill of rights and were intended as a protection of the people and the states against *The Bill* encroachments upon their rights by the Federal government. By *of Rights* them Congress was restrained from making any law respecting an establishment of religion; or abridging freedom of worship, freedom of speech, freedom of the press, or the right of petition. The people were to be secure against excessive bail and unreasonable search, and were guaranteed the right of trial by jury in criminal and important civil cases. Article X was as follows: "The powers not delegated to the United States by the Constitution, nor prohibited by it to the States, are reserved to the States respectively, or to the people."

By the addition of a bill of rights the Constitution was made *North Caro-* acceptable to North Carolina, and in the fall of 1789 she held a *lina and* second convention and voted to come into the Union. Rhode Island *Rhode Island* did not accept the Constitution until the following spring, and then *enter the* not until after Congress had threatened to cut off trade with her. *Union* The Union was now complete, as it included all of the Original Thirteen states.

HAMILTON'S FINANCIAL MEASURES

The adoption of a wise financial policy was one of the most urgent needs of the new government. A huge indebtedness had been piled up during the war by both the Union and the individual states. The general government had been unable to pay the interest on its obligations, "and many of the states had been unwilling, or unable, to do any better." With such a record, credit—both state and Federal—was at a very low ebb. The revival of public credit was thus a matter of immediate concern for both the executive and the legislative branches of the government.

This situation gave to Alexander Hamilton, the Secretary of the *Alexander* Treasury, an opportunity to perform his greatest service to his *Hamilton;* country. Although only thirty-two years old, he had already shown *personal* exceptional interest and ability in public finance. He had played *traits and* a conspicuous part in the events that had led to the framing and *views* ratification of the Constitution, and was now ready to give up a lucrative law practice to assist in the organization of a strong government. Out of the brilliant mind of this handsome and well-groomed young man there issued forth both the conservatism of maturity and the optimism, enthusiasm, and boldness of youth. He was still cherishing the aristocratic notions which had crippled his influence in the Philadelphia Convention. The new political system could not, as he believed, have the requisite stability unless it could enlist the support of the rich and wellborn. Accordingly, he advocated a financial policy that would promote the welfare of merchants, manufacturers, and capitalists generally, and bind up their interests with the success of the Federal government. With such support the new regime would rest on a firm basis and could disregard the complaints of the common people.

Courtesy of Boston Museum of Fine Arts

ALEXANDER HAMILTON.
By John Trumbull.

It was in the spirit of this philosophy that Hamilton entered with alacrity upon his difficult task. In response to requests from Congress, he made four reports to that body, in which were embodied his financial measures. These were as follows:

Funding the national debt

(1) The funding of the debt of the general government. The United States owed to foreign creditors, chiefly the French government, about twelve million dollars. To domestic creditors it owed an amount in excess of forty-four million dollars. Hamilton's proposal was to fund this indebtedness—that is, allow creditors, both foreign and domestic, to exchange their depreciated paper for interest-bearing bonds now to be issued. The latter would be as good as specie, since they would be guaranteed by a strong government with a revenue adequate to meet interest and other payments. In this

way public credit was expected at once to rise to a high level. The owners of these bonds would have a private stake in the government and would exert their influence in favor of perpetuating and strengthening the Union and of promoting the interests of the Federalist Party.

(2) The assumption of the debts of the states. The unpaid indebtedness of the states, incurred in carrying on the war, was estimated at about twenty-five million dollars. Hamilton proposed that these obligations, up to twenty-one and a half million dollars, be assumed by the Federal government. The credit of the country could not be restored, he maintained, as long as the states had outstanding bonds which they could not or would not pay. Furthermore, these debts had all been incurred in a common cause, and should therefore be paid by the country as a whole. Another reason (but one which, of course, he did not give in his report) was that assumption would mean the issuance of more Federal bonds. The purchasers of these would be bound by their interests to the Union rather than to the states. This would be an additional means of strengthening the Federal government by identifying the wealthy class with it.

Assumption of the debts of the states

There was little or no opposition to the funding of the foreign debt. The fight began on the proposal to fund the domestic debt and pay the holders of government certificates at par. Many of the original holders of these certificates had been forced to sell them to speculators at a great discount, some at twenty-five and some as low as ten cents on the dollar. The speculators naturally made a strong fight for Hamilton's proposals. The galleries of the House of Representatives were crowded by them when these measures were under consideration. Most of the original owners of these certificates who still held them lived in backward rural communities, and were not informed as to what was going on at New York. A few days after Hamilton's report was made, speculators and their agents hurried to these places (which were mostly in the South) to buy up the remainder of this paper at a reduced figure. Two fast-sailing vessels were sent by a member of Congress to the South for the purpose of purchasing Federal bonds. Agents of speculators drove as rapidly as possible behind horses that were lashed into a fast pace.

Opposition to Hamilton's measures

The opponents of the plan argued that it would rob the original owners of the paper and enrich the speculators. Many of the former were Revolutionary soldiers and small farmers, whose necessities brought on by the failure of the old government to redeem its pledges had forced them to sell at such low figures. These same victims would now have to pay taxes so that the speculators could reap their ill-gotten gains.

Madison's proposal

Madison remained silent in the early stage of this fight. Finally, however, he aligned himself with the opposition. In lieu of the proposal of Hamilton he suggested that the domestic debt be funded at par, but that the present holders be paid the market price of the paper at the time the discussion started and the original holders be given the balance. Madison's motion was defeated, and Hamilton's plan was accepted. The arguments against Madison's proposal were that only by paying off those who then held the certificates could the government meet the pledges originally given. If this were not done the public credit would suffer, for the "security of transfer" is "an essential element of public credit." Furthermore, in many instances it would be very difficult, if not impossible, to find out who the original grantees were. As a result of this, the first disagreement of Madison with the Federalists, he ceased to act as spokesman of the Administration and was read out of the party.

The fight against assumption

There was a strenuous fight against the assumption of the debts of the states. Those states that had little indebtedness were opposed to it, while those with large indebtedness were in favor of it. Virginia, for example, had paid off the greater portion of her debt by the sale of western lands. If assumption were carried, her people would be taxed by the Federal government to assist in the discharge of the debts of other states. She was therefore opposed to assumption.

Another argument against assumption was that it would transfer the interests of the holders of state bonds from the states to the Union. This would strengthen the Federal government and weaken the authority of the states. Madison, reflecting the sentiments of his constituents, declared against the proposal. The bill for assumption was defeated in the House of Representatives by the narrow majority of two.

Hamilton did not accept this adverse vote as a final defeat. On the contrary, he began to lay plans for a reconsideration of the measure. Jefferson had lately returned from France and had entered upon his duties as Secretary of State. On one occasion he and Hamilton happened to be at the President's residence at the same time. On leaving they walked up and down the street arm in arm for half an hour discussing the question of state debts. Hamilton convinced his older colleague that the failure of assumption might disrupt the Union, as some of the states would, he said, secede from the Union if their debts were not taken over by the Federal government. So convincing were his arguments that Jefferson agreed to use his influence in favor of Hamilton's proposal.

Hamilton's plan could not be carried out without a change in the votes of a few Representatives. If these changes were to be effected a bargain would have to be struck. A log-rolling agreement was entered into at a dinner party given by Jefferson, to which Madison and Hamilton had been invited. The South wanted the permanent capital located on the Potomac River. Hamilton was indifferent as to the site of the capital and so was willing to accede to the wishes of the Southern Representatives on this point if by so doing they would agree to vote for assumption. Accordingly, he agreed to secure enough votes for the Potomac location if Madison would see that a few more votes were obtained for assumption. This agreement was carried out; and the indebtedness of the states (or rather, nearly all of it) was assumed by the Federal government. Twenty-nine of the sixty-four members of the House were security holders. Of these twenty-nine, twenty-one voted for and eight against assumption. *The log-rolling agreement as to assumption*

The enactment of the assumption measure was the signal for another mad scramble by the speculators. Quick action was necessary if state paper was to be bought at low prices before its owners heard of the action of Congress. Jefferson's account of the "base scramble" was as follows: "Couriers and relay horses by land, and swift-sailing pilot boats by sea, were flying in all directions. Active partners and agents were associated and employed in every state, town, and country neighborhood, and this paper was bought up at five shillings, and even as low as two shillings in the pound, before the holder knew that Congress had already provided for its assumption at par. Immense sums were thus filched from the poor and ignorant, and fortunes accumulated by those who had been poor enough before." *The "base scramble" of speculators*

(3) The excise act. The financial obligations imposed upon the government by Hamilton's measures called for a greater revenue than the tariff would yield. Another tax, therefore, was devised. In his second report, Hamilton proposed an internal tax on distilled liquors. This tax would fall rather heavily upon the frontiersmen of western Pennsylvania and the upland regions of the South; but (as Hamilton doubtless felt) their opposition could safely be disregarded as long as the government could count on the support of the wealthy merchants and manufacturers. Indeed, the power of the Federal government might be increased by the successful assertion of its right to tax the small farmers of the backwoods. *The excise act*

To the people of these isolated regions the proposal appeared unjust. Owing to a lack of transportation facilities, they could not market their surplus farm products to any advantage. Whiskey, distilled from corn, was an important export for them. It had high value in proportion to bulk and could be easily transported. The tax would, therefore, hamper a leading frontier industry and place upon the people an unjust burden. It was regarded as the same in principle as the internal taxes of the British government against which their fathers had revolted. Moreover, the enforcement of the objectionable law would involve a system of espionage and the invasion of the privacy of their homes. Despite these objections, however, Congress went ahead and passed the bill.

The establishment of the Bank of the United States

(4) The establishment of a national bank. In his fourth report Hamilton recommended that a national bank be created. A bill providing for such an institution was brought forward and was passed after a brief but sharp discussion in the House (1791). By the charter thus granted, a corporation was to be formed with a capital stock of ten million dollars. One fifth of this stock was to be subscribed by the government and the other four fifths by private individuals. A bank controlled by this corporation was to be established at Philadelphia, with branches in the leading financial centers throughout the country. The Bank was to carry on an ordinary banking business and have power to issue notes. These notes, as long as they were redeemed in specie, were to be received in payment of government dues. The Bank was also to serve as a repository for government funds. The charter was to run for twenty years and during this period the Bank was to enjoy a monopoly of the privileges granted.

Such a banking system, thought Hamilton, would serve as an invaluable aid in putting the finances of the country on a proper basis. The facilities thus afforded would be a great convenience to business and the notes would furnish the people with a sound paper currency. The notes of other banks, except those which were redeemable in gold and silver, could not compete with the national bank notes. In this way a salutary restraint would be put on the issuance of notes by the state banks. The Bank through its branches could assist the government in the distribution of currency throughout the country and aid it in other ways. And last, though not least, the corporation would afford an excellent opportunity for the investment of money. It would thus serve as an additional ligament to bind the wealthy and the powerful to the general government.

Madison was opposed to the measure and he put up an able fight against it in the House of Representatives. It was attacked mainly on the ground that it was unconstitutional. In the Constitutional Convention an attempt had been made to confer on Congress the power to grant charters of incorporation. This proposal was voted down, although Madison himself had favored it.

When the bill came before Washington, after having passed both houses of Congress, he asked the members of his Cabinet for an opinion in writing as to its constitutionality. Knox and Hamilton argued in favor of, and Randolph and Jefferson against, the right of Congress to pass such a measure.

Hamilton, although he admitted that the authority to grant charters of incorporation was not in the list of powers expressly delegated to Congress, contended that a delegated power carries with it by implication the right to employ such means as are useful in the proper exercise of such power. "If the *end* be clearly comprehended within any of the specified powers, and if the measure have an obvious relation to that *end,* and is not forbidden by any particular provision of the Constitution, it may safely be deemed to come within the compass of the national authority." The obligation to coin money and regulate the value thereof is expressly placed upon Congress. A national bank is a means that Congress can employ to great advantage in meeting this responsibility. Therefore, the right to use such an agency is implied in the specific grant of power. This is the doctrine of implied powers. *Hamilton's arguments in favor of the measure*

Jefferson maintained that the bank bill was not constitutional. He did not rule out implied powers altogether, but restricted their use to the narrowest limits. In the exercise of implied powers, Congress could employ only such means as were necessary, not those that were merely convenient. The incorporation of a bank is not one of the enumerated powers of Congress; a bank is not necessary as a means for carrying out any enumerated power; therefore, the bill creating it is unconstitutional. He was thus contending for a strict construction of the Constitution—one that would limit the authority of the general government and leave large powers to the states. *Jefferson's arguments against it*

Hamilton favored a loose construction of the Constitution, with a liberal use of implied powers. He looked toward a strengthening of the Federal government, with a corresponding weakening of the state governments. He was for nationalism and against localism, or particularism, as it is sometimes called.

Washington seems to have been perplexed at first as to which was the correct view. His advisers were equally divided, and he finally decided in favor of the Hamiltonian theory, on the ground that the measure concerned his department more directly than any other, and the Bank of the United States was established. *Washington's decision*

In his fourth report (December, 1791) Hamilton presented able arguments in favor of the adoption of a tariff system which would afford protection to American industry. This proposal was not carried out at the time except that certain increases were made in the duties by the act of 1792.

A mint established

At Hamilton's suggestion, Congress enacted a law establishing a mint at Philadelphia (April 2, 1792). Gold and silver were to be coined at the ratio of fifteen to one. Prior to this time no coins had been struck by the general government except copper cents. Hamilton proposed that the coins be stamped with the head of the President in whose administration they should be minted. There was considerable opposition to this device because it was thought to savor too much of monarchy. It was decided to use the head of the goddess of liberty instead of that of the President.

Hamilton's success

Hamilton was remarkably successful in putting his program in effect and he was justly proud of the result. His influence over Congress had been like that of a British prime minister over Parliament. Thanks to his policies, the public credit had been suddenly restored. To quote the colorful language afterwards used by Daniel Webster, he had "touched the dead corpse of public credit and immediately it sprang to its feet." Along with this achievement he had succeeded in tying up the wealthy class with the government by bonds of economic interest. This class was vigorously supporting his economic and political program and was serving as a bulwark to the Federalist Party. His followers held the strategic positions in the economic and social life of the country and were organized for political victory. From surface indications it appeared that he held an impregnable position in the government of the country.

A careful examination would, however, have revealed certain weaknesses in his position. He was not a good politician and was not adept at pulling wires. He overestimated the importance of the privileged few and underestimated the strength of the unorganized masses. Handicapped by some un-American notions, he did not realize that there was an undercurrent of democracy which was soon to come to the surface. His conservatism had narrowed his vision and blinded him as to some of the forces that were destined to mold the future.

FEDERALISTS AND REPUBLICANS

The controversy over the establishment of a national bank caused a permanent breach between the supporters and opponents of Hamilton's financial measures. The latter, under the leadership of Jefferson and Madison, were gradually organized into a party of opposition. The followers of Hamilton retained the name of Federalist, while the new party assumed that of Republican, with the view to implying that the Federalists were monarchists. The Federalists likewise tried to discredit the Republicans by calling them Democrats, as a term of reproach; for owing to the excesses to which the popular party had gone in France, democracy was regarded by many Federalists in about the same light in which Russian Bolshevism was viewed by American conservatives of the Coolidge era.

Behind the political controversies over the Bank and other measures favored by Hamilton there was a clash of economic interests between the classes and sections, which was the real basis of the new party alignment. Hamilton's policies would promote the commercial and manufacturing, rather than the agrarian, interests. It was not easy to convince the small farmers, who constituted the great bulk of the population, that these measures would be of value to them. Madison and Jefferson were championing the cause of the farmers, and were contending that as a result of Hamilton's nationalistic policies their rights would be infringed in order that the wealthy might enjoy special privileges. They further argued that legislation unfair to the masses was more apt to be enacted by Congress than by the state legislatures. For this reason the authority of the Federal government should be kept within the limits prescribed by a strict construction of the Constitution and the states should be powerful enough to act as a curb on the general government. The Republicans, therefore, were opposed to nationalism and advocated the doctrine of states' rights. *Economic basis of the political division*

Hamilton, on the other hand, felt that his policy was not only favorable to the upper classes but also good for the public generally. If this policy was to be realized the general government must be strong and not hampered by the interference of the states. His party, therefore, advocated nationalism and opposed localism, or the doctrine of states' rights. Later, the Federalists and Republicans reversed their positions on the question of localism and nationalism.

Jefferson's advocacy of agrarianism was a matter of conviction and not merely of political expediency. He believed that farming was the occupation which would best serve as the basis of our economic and social order. Every citizen should be a landowner. Land should be granted by the state to those who were unable to purchase it. The country would thus be made up in the main of yeoman farmers, among whom there would be no great inequalities of wealth. Substantial economic equality would supply the proper conditions for political equality. In such a society it would be safe to confer the right of suffrage upon all, and political democracy would thus be superimposed upon economic democracy. Under such a regime, liberty and individuality would be preserved, and law and order secured. He objected to Hamilton's policy of stimulating commerce and manufacturing by governmental help, partly because it would impose an unfair tax burden upon farmers. Furthermore, he felt that a desirable social order could not be built on these occupations. A rapid development in industry would give rise to gross inequalities in wealth and a division of the people into employers and employees, with conflicts between labor and capital. With such an economic aristocracy political democracy would be impossible.

Disagreement as to foreign policy

The Republicans and Federalists were sharply divided on foreign policy. The former were pro-French; the latter, pro-English. The Republicans hailed the French Revolution as a movement to give to the French people the liberty won for Americans by their Revolution; the Federalists saw in the excesses of the Parisian mobs and the cruelties of the Reign of Terror the unleashed forces of anarchy and brutality. The Republicans were firm in their advocacy of the French alliance and in their criticism of Jay's Treaty, which they considered a humiliating surrender to Great Britain (see p. 297). The Federalists regarded the French alliance as an embarrassing encumbrance, and Jay's Treaty as a necessary price to pay for the peace and prosperity of the country.

Jefferson and Madison as political leaders

The Republican Party included in its membership most of the Antifederalists and some of those who had favored the ratification of the Constitution. At first, as has already been seen, Madison was the leader of the party, but soon Jefferson became the general of the movement and Madison served as an able lieutenant. Seldom have political yokefellows pulled together more loyally and efficiently than did these two noted Virginians. They were united by mutual affection and congeniality of intellectual interests, and their work was not marred by any feeling of jealousy or envy. Often the tall sandy-haired premier could be seen walking along the streets of Philadelphia with the short Congressman. The difference between them in size and age caused the younger Madison to look upon Jefferson as a father.

Jefferson; personal traits and views

To the casual observer it might seem strange that Jefferson should ever have become the founder of a political party. When he gave up his post in Paris to become Secretary of State he seemed to have had no relish for politics and never dreamed that he would one day become a great political leader. And yet he had many qualities that the politician always finds useful. He could gauge public sentiment with uncanny accuracy. Not only did he know which way the winds of public opinion were blowing at any particular time, but he could frequently chart in advance the currents of popular sentiment. In the history of our country there have been few statesmen who could equal him in reading aright the signs of the times.

Much of his success as a political leader was due to effective organization. By extensive correspondence he kept in touch with his lieutenants, from whom he received loyal and energetic support. Never dictatorial in manner, he led his followers, never drove them. As he treated everyone with kindness and courtesy, he inspired his partisans with a feeling of affection for their leader.

Jefferson was fortunate both as to heredity and environment. His father, Peter Jefferson, was a man of literary tastes and exceptional ability. He belonged to the prosperous upper middle class, while Jefferson's mother was a scion of the proud Randolph family. There were thus united in the blood of young Jefferson the best plebeian and patrician strains. Reared in the upland region of Virginia, his childhood was subjected to frontier influences. But he was educated at William and Mary College, and there he was brought in contact with the charming social life of the colonial capital. To his patrician heritage and the brilliant social opportunities of his youth he probably owed the naturalness and simplicity of his manners. He also came by his democracy honestly. From his sensible father he doubtless imbibed a correct view of the common people, which was reinforced by his early frontier environment. This faith in the common man and the liberal philosophy that grew out of it were accentuated by his acquaintance with the writings of Locke and Rousseau.

WHITNEY'S COTTON GIN.

CHAPTER XVIII

Domestic and Foreign Affairs

DOMESTIC PROBLEMS

The Whiskey Rebellion

HAMILTON'S view as to the minor importance of the plain people was destined to receive a rude shock. It was not long before the despised common man gave warning that he would have to be reckoned with. The objectionable excise tax aroused a storm of opposition in the frontier regions of Pennsylvania and the states to the southward. In southwestern Pennsylvania discontent went from protests to a defiance of the law. Stills of those who paid the tax were broken up and threats of violence were made against the tax collectors. Indignation meetings were held at which disobedience to the law was urged. Some of these meetings were attended by Albert Gallatin, who later played a prominent part in the history of the country. His voice was raised in favor of moderation and against violence, but unfortunately his counsel was not heeded.

Hamilton wanted the Federal government to use this uprising as an occasion for displaying its power. Accordingly, he advised Washington to send a large army against the insurgents. Washington fell in with the plan and issued a proclamation announcing his intention to enforce the law. An army of over twelve thousand men, made up of militiamen from Pennsylvania, Maryland, and Virginia, was sent against the rebels. Before it reached the scene of action, the malcontents had decided to yield. A number of the leading troublemakers were tried for treason and two of them were convicted. These were pardoned by Washington.

In putting down the revolt so easily the Federal government had won an apparent victory. It had impressed the country with its power and its ability to maintain law and order. But the size of the force sent out was very much greater than was needed, and this gave rise to the feeling (not confined to the malcontents) that the Federalists, who were responsible for this punitive expedition, were encouraging a dangerous trend toward militarism. Moreover, the discontent behind the revolt was not allayed by this show of force. In these western districts there remained in the hearts of the people a feeling of bitterness toward the party which had enacted this unpopular law and had pinned it down with bayonets. The Federalist Party was thus weakened and the Republican Party strengthened by the excise law and its aftermath, the so-called Whiskey Rebellion.

The advance of settlements north and west of the Ohio reawakened the perpetual Indian danger. The Indians were exploited by the land-grabbing frontiersmen, and the Federal government had not been able to punish such unjust practices or to prevent the Indians from retaliating against this unfair treatment. The British posts in the Northwest were also used as centers of propaganda against the American settlers. Unrest among the Indians was incited by Canadian officials and fur traders. Under such conditions a conflict between the natives and the Westerners was inevitable. *Indian troubles in the Northwest*

The Indians living along the Maumee and Wabash Rivers gave trouble, and troops were sent to reduce them to submission. The expedition was unsuccessful and, by its failure, the savages were emboldened to greater hostility. Thereupon General Arthur St. Clair, Governor of the Northwest Territory, led a strong force against them. He was a brave man and a good fighter in a subordinate position, but did not have the initiative and originality needed in this crisis. With a force of about two thousand men he left Fort Washington (at Cincinnati) and marched northward. As he advanced, his numbers were greatly reduced by desertions of the militia. Stopping for encampment on the eastern fork of the Wabash River, he was surrounded and attacked (November 4, 1791). Taken completely by surprise and unable to see their concealed assailants, his men were badly defeated with a loss that mounted to more than nine hundred killed and wounded. St. Clair acted with unusual courage but all to no avail. This was the worst military defeat that the Americans had ever suffered at the hands of the Indians. *St. Clair's defeat*

When the news of the terrible rout was reported to Washington he was entertaining company at dinner. After reading the dispatches he rejoined his guests and acted as if nothing out of the ordinary had happened. At the evening party which followed, his cordial greetings to visitors showed no signs of an emotional upset, but at ten o'clock after the guests had all left he gave way to his feelings. Walking back and forth in his room, he expressed his great grief and sore disappointment as follows: "It's all over! St. Clair is defeated—routed,—the officers nearly all killed—the men by wholesale,—the rout complete,—too shocking to think of,—and a surprise into the bargain! ... O God, O God, he's worse than a murderer! How can he answer it to his country!"

In fairness to St. Clair it ought to be added that his conduct was investigated by a committee of Congress and he was cleared of all wrongdoing. He resigned his command of the military forces but retained his position as governor.

The battle of Fallen Timbers

General Wayne, "Mad Anthony" of Revolutionary fame, was now put in command of the little army in the West. Despite his reputation for rashness, he was a coolheaded leader and took plenty of time to make ready for his task. Before attacking the enemy he put his soldiers through a long course of training, which made them into a body of disciplined troops.

By the summer of 1794 Wayne was ready for the advance against the Indians, whose fighting edge had been sharpened by the encouragement given them by Canadian officials. While proceeding down the Maumee River in August of that year, he was attacked by a band of thirteen hundred redskins who were crouching behind fallen trees. His men fought bravely and forced the enemy to retreat. The battle of Fallen Timbers was thus a decided victory for the whites.

Wayne remained in the Indian country to destroy villages, crops, and other property. Soon the foe asked for peace terms and the Treaty of Greenville was signed (August 4, 1795). By this treaty the Indians relinquished their claims to a large area of land in central Ohio and a strip in southeastern Indiana. This treaty, and the removal of the British posts the following year, brought peace to the Northwest.

RELATIONS BETWEEN THE UNITED STATES AND FRANCE

The French Revolution

Soon after Washington's inauguration the great revolution started in France. The government was liberalized and important changes were made in the economic system. It was not long, however, before liberalism gave way to radicalism. In September, 1792, a republic was proclaimed and King Louis XVI was later executed (January, 1793).

At the beginning of the French Revolution all classes in the United States welcomed it as a struggle for the same principles for which the American people had fought in their conflict with Great Britain; but the execution of the king and other radical measures had aroused among Federalist leaders a strong opposition to the new regime in France. Jefferson and the Republicans, however, still acclaimed the French Revolution, and their belief in its doctrines was not destroyed by the excesses of the Reign of Terror, since they were hopeful that these excesses would be temporary and the reforms permanent.

War in Europe

The ideology of the French Revolution clashed with the political and social views of the other European countries. This conflict of opinion, coupled with the determination of each party to support its beliefs aggressively, led to serious strife in Europe. France, therefore, soon found herself at war with her neighbors, England among them.

The United States government was now in an awkward position. While a great many people strongly sympathized with France, Washington wanted to avoid a war with England. But by our treaties with France (signed in 1778) we had made pledges to that country the fulfillment of which might bring us into war with Britain. By the terms of this alliance we were bound to help France if her West Indian possessions were attacked. Prizes captured by French privateers could be received in our ports but those taken by English privateers were not to be so favored. As we had no navy, the obligation to aid France in the protection of her West Indian colonies could not be carried out and was not pressed by France; but the provisions regarding the hospitality of our ports to French privateers became a source of trouble. *Attitude of the United States toward the European war*

Washington asked the advice of his Cabinet on the difficult questions raised by the war between England and France. Should the United States receive the minister sent by the new republic? Was the treaty of alliance still binding? If so, should a proclamation of neutrality be made? Hamilton argued that the American treaty had been made with the French king, not the French nation. The execution of the king and the change to a republic had therefore cancelled all these treaty obligations. Jefferson, on the other hand, rightly maintained that the treaty was with the French people and was binding, regardless of the form of government the latter might adopt. This view was accepted by Washington, but it was unanimously agreed by the Cabinet that the United States should remain neutral in the contest. Accordingly, Washington issued a proclamation (April 23, 1793) warning American citizens against taking part in the war. It was also decided to receive the new French minister.

The minister who had been commissioned by the French government was Edmond Charles Genêt, an enthusiastic supporter of the doctrines of the Girondin party, which was in control in France at that time. He allowed his zeal for the new cause to run away with his judgment, and his behavior further complicated the relations between the two republics. Genêt arrived in the United States two weeks before Washington's proclamation was issued. His ship had been swerved from its course by storm, and he had landed at Charleston, South Carolina, instead of Philadelphia, as he had intended. His head was turned by the fervid cordiality with which he was re- *The Genêt episode* ceived in Charleston and by the great ovation accorded him on his later overland journey to Philadelphia.

Emboldened by this attitude of the people, he entered upon a policy based upon a liberal interpretation of the treaty of alliance. He contended that inasmuch as the treaty gave to French privateers the right to bring their captures into American ports they could also sell them there. Furthermore, by declaring that an enemy of France could not fit out privateers in the United States, the treaty indicated by implication that France could exercise this privilege. Accordingly, he fitted out in Charleston, with Governor Moultrie's approval, four privateers and sent them to prey on British commerce.

At Philadelphia Genêt was received by Washington with formal politeness, but not with the warm cordiality to which he had been accustomed. He was not, for example, kissed on both cheeks by the "Father of the Country"; but the President by his policy, more than by his manners, threw cold water on the high aspirations of the enthusiastic Frenchman. He decided that Genêt could license privateers in American ports, as such a procedure was in accordance with the practice of the day, but that the prizes taken by French privateers could not be sold or refitted for war purposes in American waters. Washington would not comply with Genêt's request for advanced payments on the United States bonds which the French government held, for the reason that to do so would be to compromise American neutrality.

Genêt wanted these funds to finance the expeditions which he was planning to send against Spanish American possessions. One expedition was to go from South Carolina and Georgia against Florida. He had also accepted an offer from George Rogers Clark to lead a band of Kentuckians down the Ohio and Mississippi to attack Louisiana. These plans failed because of a lack of funds. After Genêt's recall, Washington learned of the proposed expedition against Louisiana and directed the Governor of Kentucky to prevent it. Besides, the new French minister issued a proclamation against it and this was the end of the attempt. The intended expedition against Florida was also abandoned.

Although Washington had ruled that American ports could not be used by French privateers as bases of operation against English ships, Genêt—in violation of a virtual promise to Jefferson—refitted and sent out a captured British ship, *The Little Sarah,* as a French privateer, whose name he had changed to *The Little Democrat.* Such impudence was too much for the patience of the President, and he demanded the recall of the conceited French minister. In the meantime the Girondin party had lost power in France, and the new and more radical government was ready to order him home. At the same time the French government requested the removal of Gouverneur Morris, American minister at Paris, whose royalist sympathies had made him obnoxious to the new regime. Washington complied with this request and sent James Monroe to Paris as Morris' successor. Monroe was effusively welcomed by the French National Convention and was held in high esteem by the government and people during his entire stay in Paris.

RELATIONS WITH ENGLAND AND SPAIN

Washington's policy of neutrality toward France did not prove a guarantee against tension between England and the United States. The refusal of the British government to evacuate the military posts held in the West was for a number of years a constant source of complaint by the American people. The part played by Canadian traders and officials in inciting the Indian troubles had aggravated this grievance. To these old causes of friction were added new ones growing out of the war between England and France. Britain's control of the seas was her greatest asset in this contest, and she was determined to make the best possible use of her advantage; to respect the rights of neutrals on the high seas would be to dull her sharpest weapon. Restrictions on neutral commerce were therefore carried out which the American people regarded as a serious infringement of their rights. Their vessels were seized by British warships, and their passengers and crews subjected to indignities and even brutalities.

American grievances against Britain

The British and American governments were also in disagreement as to the practice of visit and search. It was generally agreed that a belligerent warship had the right to stop a neutral vessel on the high seas and search it for contraband. The method by which this practice should be carried out was the point at issue. The American contention was that the search should go no farther than an examination of the vessel's papers. The British insisted on examining the cargo, maintaining that otherwise the search would be of no avail owing to the use of false papers by shipowners.

The British authorities also asserted and practiced the right to stop merchant vessels on the high seas and take off sailors of English birth, even if they had become American citizens, and force them into the service of the British navy. The United States government protested against this impressment of American seamen, although at this time this grievance was not emphasized so much as some of the others; but in later years it figured prominently as a cause of strife (see pp. 338-339) .

It was hard for a proud people to submit to these violations of their rights, and the feeling of resentment in the United States kept growing. By 1794 it had reached such dimensions as to threaten war. But it would have been foolhardy for the infant nation to challenge to combat the leading power of the world. With the West in an attitude of doubtful loyalty and the national sentiment weak in all sections, a declaration of war against the Mistress of the Seas would have been suicidal. Washington wisely considered that the cement which held the new union together must have time to dry before the political structure should be subjected to such a strain. He felt that a twenty-year period of peace was necessary for the new nation to consolidate its strength. At the end of that time he hoped it would be strong enough to compel respect for its rights. He, therefore, resolved to agree with the adversary if possible, even at the cost of his popularity with the general public.

It was decided that a special envoy could best handle the difficult problems then troubling the relations of the two countries, and for this responsible mission Washington selected John Jay, the Chief Justice of the Supreme Court, who had had wide experience in dealing with foreign governments. He was instructed to secure the withdrawal of the British posts; to get compensation for the slaves that had been taken away and for the ships which had been illegally seized; and to arrange a treaty of commerce. There was to be a plain recognition of the rights for which the American government had been contending. Jay was expressly charged to agree to nothing that would infringe upon American treaty obligations to France. If the British government should prove unwilling to make reasonable concessions he was to co-operate with the representatives of the northern European countries in a joint effort to protect the rights of neutrals.

After four months of negotiation an agreement was reached between the two powers (1794). Jay had not obeyed his instructions and had conceded much and obtained little. He overestimated the strength of his opponent's hand in the diplomatic game and, therefore, was not as bold in his demands as he might have been. He seemed oblivious of the fact that Great Britain would be willing to yield to just demands rather than jeopardize peace and friendship with the United States. While engaged in a war which was heavily taxing her resources, England could not afford to lose the profitable American trade or add to the list of her enemies a rising young nation which had recently put its finances on a firm basis and showed other signs of vigor and strength.

Furthermore, an indiscretion committed by Hamilton enabled Jay's opponent to trump his highest card. Denmark and Sweden had invited the United States to join them in a League of Armed Neutrality to uphold neutral rights. This proposal was considered by Washington's Cabinet and rejected, on the ground that it would involve this country in an entangling alliance. Hamilton very unwisely reported this decision to the British minister. In this way Jay was deprived of a means of pressure which he might have employed to advantage in the negotiations. That the United States and other neutrals might unite in such a league had been a possibility which the British government viewed with grave concern; but now this argument had lost its force.

Under such conditions only a policy of appeasement could be expected, but the American public was surprised and shocked at the one-sided terms of the treaty when they were made known. The one outstanding provision in America's favor was the promise that all British posts would be evacuated by June 1, 1796. The United States government guaranteed the payment of pre-Revolutionary debts due British creditors by American citizens in all cases in which the collection of such debts had been prevented by legal impediments. The amount and justice of these claims were to be determined by a joint commission. The British government agreed to make compensation for irregular and illegal seizures of American property on the high seas. Reparation by the American government was also to be made for improper seizures of the property of Englishmen. Another joint commission was to pass upon all claims presented under these clauses. Nothing was said about impressment or the payment for slaves taken from the United States by British soldiers during the Revolution. The principles of international law for which the American government had been contending were not mentioned. Food supplies were listed as contraband but with the understanding that when seized on American vessels payment should be made for them. American vessels were, under certain restrictions, given the right to carry on trade with the British East Indian possessions.

Provisions of Jay's Treaty

Washington was by no means satisfied with this unfair treaty, but accepted it in preference to war. He therefore declared it in effect on February 29, 1796. The people throughout the country were in the main strongly opposed to the acceptance of the treaty, and Jay became the most unpopular man in America. He was burned in effigy a number of times, and Hamilton on one occasion was stoned for attempting to defend the treaty. The Republicans made a bitter fight against the treaty. After it had been ratified by the Senate they tried to defeat it in the House of Representatives by refusing to appropriate the small sum of money needed to carry out its provisions. So strenuous was the opposition in the House that the motion to

Opposition to the treaty

refuse the appropriation was lost in the committee of the whole only by the casting vote of the chairman.

Washington showed sound judgment in accepting this treaty, despite its serious objections. Although bold diplomacy might have won better terms from the British foreign office, to reject the agreement might have led to war. The young republic was not in a condition to take such a risk, and at that time peace at almost any price was preferable to war. Washington decided that it was better to sacrifice our pride than to menace our independence.

The treaty with Spain

One favorable result of Jay's Treaty was that it paved the way for an agreement with Spain. For the two years preceding 1795 Spain had been joined with England in the coalition against France. This association gave her a sense of security as to her American possessions. Hence she was more or less unconcerned about the efforts made by our commissioners to settle the differences which had arisen between her government and that of the United States. In this year Spain made peace with France and the alliance with England came to an end. Having now no guarantee against encroachment upon her territory in the new world, Spain was deeply concerned over the treaty between England and the United States. She was afraid that it was a forerunner of an alliance between the two countries and that such an alliance might place her possessions in North America at the mercy of either or both of these powers. To forestall this danger she was willing to make liberal concessions to the United States. In this way she hoped to win the favor of the latter country and prevent a coalition between it and Great Britain. Thanks to this more favorable attitude, Thomas Pinckney was able to negotiate a treaty (1795) by which Spain agreed to the thirty-first parallel as the northern boundary of West Florida, and granted to the American people the right to navigate the Mississippi River to its mouth and have for three years a place of deposit at New Orleans.[1] The treaty also contained the pledge that the privilege of using a place of deposit either at New Orleans or elsewhere would be renewed at the end of the three-year period.

WASHINGTON'S FAREWELL ADDRESS

Why Washington served a second term

Washington was possessed of a growing desire to exchange the cares of public office for the enjoyments of private life. He, therefore, had decided to retire at the end of his first term and, with the aid of Madison, had in 1792 prepared a farewell address. But owing

---

[1] By a place of deposit was meant a space on which goods could be unloaded, stored, and reloaded for reshipment.

to the precarious condition of American relations with foreign nations and the difficulties which had arisen in connection with domestic affairs, it was the general opinion of the leaders of the day that he should not retire at that time. The government was still in the experimental stage. The different sections of the country were not yet firmly bound together, and there was danger that the Union might fall apart. The prestige of Washington was needed to save the country from these threatening dangers. So Republicans, as well as Federalists, urged his continuance in office. In a letter to him Jefferson said: "The confidence of the whole Union is centered in you. . . . North and South will hang together if they have you to hang on." Yielding to these entreaties, Washington agreed to accept a second term and again was unanimously elected. The Republicans, however, were opposed to Adams and gave their fifty electoral votes to George Clinton of New York for Vice-President. Adams was supported by the Federalists, and the seventy-seven electoral votes cast by them insured his re-election.

Washington's attitude toward political parties

Washington was not able to carry out his original plan of administering the government without regard to partisan politics. The feeling in favor of party government was so deeply fixed in the consciousness of the people that it could not be set aside even by the Father of the Country. His social instincts and political views were more nearly in accord with the conservatism of Hamilton than the liberalism of Jefferson. Accordingly, in his second term, his administration was allied with the Federalist Party. After the resignation of Randolph in 1795, his Cabinet was composed entirely of Federalists. Washington's acceptance of Federalist principles led to violent attacks on the Administration by the Republicans. These assaults accentuated his longing for release from the responsibilities of public office. He now came to a final decision to retire at the end of his second term. To announce this intention and to give some salutary advice to his fellow countrymen, Washington issued a Farewell Address to the American people (September, 1796).

For the wording of this paper Hamilton was chiefly responsible, as he put the finishing touches on it. It is quite likely, too, that Washington was indebted to Hamilton for some of the ideas it contained. On the other hand, the sentiments of the Address were those of Washington, and as such they have exerted a marked influence on the policies of the Federal government throughout its entire history.

His reasons for not running for a third term

The Address begins with the announcement of his decision to retire from office at the end of his second term. He could now indulge his yearning for the quiet and repose of private life without any dereliction of duty. The reasons given for retirement were these personal considerations; nothing was said about the danger to the country of a President's remaining in power too long.

His advice as to foreign relations

In the Address the benefits of union and the dangers of sectionalism were pointed out. Party spirit was deprecated. In the conduct of its foreign relations the young republic was advised to maintain a policy of strict neutrality and isolation. ". . . permanent, inveterate antipathies against particular Nations, and passionate attachments for others should be excluded. . . ." Instead, "just and amicable feelings towards all should be cultivated." While there should be a strict observance of commitments already made to foreign powers, American policy in the future should be "to steer clear of permanent alliances with any portion of the foreign world," as "we may safely trust to temporary alliances for extraordinary emergencies." In giving reasons for such a foreign policy, Washington made a strong appeal for the doctrine of isolation, which was now formulated for the first time.

Washington's achievements as President

Because of Republican agitation, Washington had less popularity at the end than at the beginning of his term of office. He had, however, deserved well of his country. Under his leadership an effective government had been organized, federal finance put on a solid basis, rebellion subdued, Indian uprisings quieted, maritime commerce encouraged, and foreign occupation of American lands ended. Furthermore, he had kept the country out of war during a period of European strife. He had had able advisers to assist him in the handling of these difficult problems, but in every case his was the responsibility of a final decision. In making these decisions he displayed the courage, sound judgment, and integrity which were characteristic of him as a military leader. Many of the practices initiated by him served as precedents which have been almost as binding as principles imbedded in the Constitution. It was fortunate for the country that these "conventions of the Constitution" were started by so wise a statesman.

The election of 1796

With Washington out of the running, the race for the Presidency developed into a hotly contested party battle. The Republicans entered the fight with strong hopes of victory. Jefferson, the leader of the party, was selected to head the ticket, and Aaron Burr, an astute politician of New York, was named for second place. The financial measures of Hamilton and the suppression of the Whiskey Rebellion had arrayed the common people against the Federalists, particularly in the South and West. The Federalists were also the butt of the antagonism aroused by the measures of eight years of constructive policy. The unpopularity of Jay's Treaty allowed the Republicans to capitalize and appropriate the anti-British and pro-French feeling. They were also able to turn to their account the opposition of the states' rights group to Hamilton's nationalist measures. To the other troubles of the Federalists was added that of internal dissension, for their most outstanding leaders, Hamilton and Adams, were not pulling together in the party harness.

"CITIZEN" EDMUND CHARLES GENÊT.

Oil painting by Ezra Ames (1768-1836), from
Collections of the Albany Institute of History and Art, Albany, N. Y.

As an offset to these drawbacks the Federalists could point to a conspicuous record of achievement. The policies of the outgoing Administration were approved by conservatives in general, and the commercial and industrial classes in particular. The Federalists were aided by the unwise interference of Adet, the former French minister at Philadelphia, who was still residing in this country although he had been officially recalled. His efforts to influence the people in favor of the Republicans aroused resentment in many voters and caused them to support the Federalist ticket. Besides, as a protest against the Jay Treaty, the French government was interfering more extensively than ever with the rights of Americans on the high seas. For these reasons, the anti-French feeling in this country was growing, to the detriment of the Republican, or pro-French, Party.

For its origin and early development the Federalist Party was indebted to Hamilton more than to any other one person. He was not, however, selected as its standard-bearer in the campaign of 1796 for the reason that his ultraconservatism and personal unpopularity negatived his availability as a candidate. The Federalist members of Congress met in caucus and nominated John Adams for the Presidency, and Thomas Pinckney of South Carolina for the Vice-Presidency. Hamilton's dislike of Adams caused him to intrigue against him and to try to bring in Pinckney for the first place. When the scheme was discovered, a few of Adams' friends among the electors refused to vote for Pinckney. The result was the election, by a close vote, of Adams to the first and Jefferson to the second place. In consequence of this intrigue, the Federalists, although they won the election, lost the Vice-Presidency to their opponents.

CHAPTER XIX

The Administration of John Adams

THE second President was a man of unusual ability, and his virile *Adams; per-* intellect had been developed by a good education. He was coura- *sonal traits* geous, patriotic, and thoroughly honest. The major part of his life had been spent in the service of his country, and so he was well qualified by experience for the great responsibility he was now assuming. With these fine qualities were coupled some defects of character which proved a decided drawback to his success as Chief Magistrate. He was vain, irritable, self-opinionated, and lacking in tact. His faults were on the surface and, therefore, easily discernible, while his virtues were more deep-seated and had to be discovered. These imperfections roughened the exterior of his personality and often caused needless friction in his contacts with others. Even his virtues were sometimes a liability rather than an asset; for his stubborn honesty, allied as it was with undue self-confidence, frequently prevented an adjustment of his principles to party expediency. All of which goes to show that he was not a good politician.

When a member of the Second Continental Congress, Adams was classed as a liberal, if not a radical. He had fought valiantly for the democratic doctrine of the Declaration of Independence; but now he was conservative and aristocratic in his political views. As he came from a middle class family, these aristocratic notions seemed a little out of place, and the profession of them gave his enemies the opportunity to dub him a self-made aristocrat.

Adams took over Washington's Cabinet without change, which *His Cabinet* was a serious mistake. The members were all Federalists, but they looked upon Hamilton, and not their chief, as the leader of the party. He did not, therefore, receive from them that disinterested loyalty which a President has a right to expect from his official advisers.

FRANCO-AMERICAN RELATIONS

The most difficult problem with which Adams had to contend *Effect of* was that of adjusting the relations between his country and France, *Jay's Treaty*

303

which had been strained by Jay's Treaty with England. The French government regarded this treaty as a violation of American commitments to it and an effort to aid England. Although the treaty stipulated that nothing in it was to "operate contrary to former and existing public treaties with other sovereigns or States," its terms were contrary to the spirit of the alliance of 1778. Furthermore, by listing food supplies and naval stores as contraband, Jay's Treaty violated the letter of the commercial treaty of 1778, which declared that such articles were not to be so classed.

The French government contended that a neutral must protect its rights against a belligerent, and that the failure to do so constitutes a breach of neutrality. According to this view, America's acquiescence in British methods gave France the right to indulge in the same practices against our ships. Food supplies were therefore seized as contraband by French as well as English vessels. Despite these violations of our rights, the Republicans still advocated adherence to the French alliance and opposition to Jay's Treaty.

Monroe as minister to France

James Monroe, who had been sent to succeed Gouverneur Morris as American minister at Paris, was an ardent Republican and an enthusiastic supporter of the French alliance. Dissatisfied at heart with Jay's Treaty, he had difficulty in defending it before the French foreign office, although he argued in its favor in his formal correspondence. He was accused by Washington's Federalist advisers of having failed to make as good a case for the treaty as he might have done. Washington also suspected his loyalty to the Administration. For these reasons he was recalled and C. C. Pinckney, a stanch Federalist, was sent to Paris to take his place. The latter was not received by the French government. The French minister also withdrew from the United States, and thus diplomatic relations were severed between the two republics.

The XYZ Affair

As a final effort to prevent a rupture, Adams sent a commission of three distinguished men to Paris with the hope that they might come to an agreement with the French government. Although Pinckney had been forced to leave France by the authorities there, he was put on this commission, and with him were associated Elbridge Gerry and John Marshall. Gerry was a Republican and Marshall a Federalist.

When the envoys arrived at Paris, French administration was in the hands of a Directory of five men. The most outstanding member of this group was Talleyrand, Minister of Foreign Affairs. As his later career showed, he was the ablest diplomat of his generation. The American commissioners were not formally received by Talleyrand, and intercourse with him was conducted through three of his agents. It soon developed that his itching palm would have to be soothed if the negotiations were to proceed. The American envoys were told that they would be received only on the condition that their government would make a loan to the French government and tender a *douceur* to Talleyrand. To this brazen request for a bribe Pinckney warmly replied, "No, no, not a sixpence." The two Federalist members now left France, and Gerry was afterwards recalled by the President.

Adams was justly incensed by this highhanded policy. In his messages to Congress he strongly condemned these proceedings and recommended that preparations be made for war. No other minister would ever be sent to France, he declared, "without assurances that he will be received, respected, and honored as the representative of a great, free, powerful, and independent nation." The correspondence between the American envoys and Talleyrand's agents was submitted to Congress and then made public. Before these documents were sent to Congress the names of the intermediaries were deleted and the letters X, Y, and Z were put in their places. For this reason this diplomatic incident is known as the XYZ Affair.

The country was aroused by the publication of these documents, and both Congress and the people readily responded to Adams' suggestions to put the country on a war basis. Pinckney's spirited reply to Talleyrand's intermediary—changed into "millions for defense, but not one cent for tribute!"—was widely circulated to arouse patriotic fervor. The navy was strengthened by the building of a number of new vessels and the Department of the Navy was created. Privately owned American vessels were armed for defense and a considerable number were commissioned as privateers and armed for offense. The President was authorized to raise an army of ten thousand volunteers, and the treaties of 1778 were annulled.

As a result of these strained relations the two countries engaged *Naval warfare* in naval hostilities for two and a half years. American vessels, both warships and privateers, gave a good account of themselves, and eighty-five French vessels, nearly all of which were privateers, were captured, with the loss of only one American vessel. Unarmed French merchantmen were not attacked, since no war had been declared and technically the two countries were still at peace.

Fortunately, the new army was not called into active service, but the provision for its organization was the cause of much annoyance to the President. The act provided for a commander-in-chief and "a suitable number of major generals." Adams selected Washington as commander-in-chief, and wished to appoint as major generals, Henry Knox, C. C. Pinckney, and Hamilton, to be ranked in the order named. Washington, however, insisted that Hamilton should have the first place, although in the Revolutionary War he had been outranked by both of the others. As Washington was not expected to take the field, under this arrangement Hamilton would be the real commander-in-chief. The President finally yielded to this request; but the extreme reluctance he showed in complying with it widened the breach which was dividing the Federalist Party into two factions.

The controversy settled The turn which events had taken alarmed Talleyrand, and the anti-French feeling which his policy had aroused in America caused him to assume a more conciliatory attitude toward the United States since he did not wish to add that nation to the list of his country's enemies. Accordingly, he approached the American government with a peace offering. William Vans Murray, American minister at The Hague, was assured by Talleyrand that if a minister were sent to Paris he would be properly received. Adams thereupon nominated Murray as minister to France, to the surprise and chagrin of the Hamilton faction of the Federalist Party. At the suggestion of the Senate, three commissioners were sent instead of one minister, and so Oliver Ellsworth and W. R. Davie were joined with Murray to form the commission.

When the envoys reached Paris, Napoleon had superseded the Directory in the management of French affairs. He had decided upon a new American policy, and therefore the commissioners were able to secure his assent to a new treaty (1800). By this agreement the treaties of 1778 were abrogated, and the United States was freed from its only entangling alliance with a European country. Thanks to Adams' wise handling of a difficult foreign problem, the United States was kept out of a declared war.

THE ALIEN AND SEDITION ACTS

The Alien acts The war scare was the occasion of some unwise legislation. War hysteria gave rise to the feeling on the part of the Federalists in Congress that the government should be protected against the assaults of disloyal American citizens and of resident foreigners. In pursuit of this aim, four laws were passed which were particularly objectionable to the Republicans. One of these was the Naturalization Act, which extended the period of residence required of aliens before being naturalized from five to fourteen years. Two others that applied to foreigners were the Alien Act and the Alien Enemies Act. By the Alien Act the President was given authority for two years to send out of the country all aliens whom he might deem "dangerous to the peace and safety of the United States" or might have reason to suspect of plotting against the government. By the Alien Enemies Act he was granted power in time of war to imprison or remove from the country all subjects of an enemy power or impose upon them (if allowed to remain in the United States) such restrictions as he might consider necessary for the public safety.

The most unpopular of all of these measures was the Sedition Act, since it was intended mainly as a curb on disgruntled American citizens. It was an effort not only to preserve the dignity of and respect for the government, but also to shield the Federalist rulers from uncomfortable criticism. The law made it a criminal offense, punishable by fine and imprisonment, for any persons unlawfully to combine or conspire to oppose any legal measure of the government, to "advise or attempt to procure any insurrection," or publish "any false, scandalous and malicious writing . . . against the government of the United States, or either house of the Congress, . . . or the President of the United States, with intent to defame [them] . . . or bring them, or either of them, into contempt or disrepute." Persons charged with a violation of this law were to be allowed trial by jury. The act was to expire at the end of Adams' term. *The Sedition Act*

The Republicans contended that the Sedition Law was unconstitutional since it was an infringement of the freedom of the press and thus a violation of the First Amendment. Furthermore, the Constitution does not confer upon the Federal courts any common-law jurisdiction. The misdemeanors defined in the act were common-law offenses and, therefore, cognizable in the state courts only. At that time the Federal courts rendered decisions under the law and thereby accepted by implication its constitutionality; but in 1882 the Supreme Court decided that the Federal courts have no jurisdiction in common-law cases. *Opposition to these measures*

The Alien laws were probably enacted to frighten objectionable aliens away from American shores or into good behavior, for there were no convictions under these laws. This was not the case with the Sedition Act. A number of indictments were brought under it, and ten editors and printers, all Republicans, were tried and convicted. It was charged, with a considerable show of reason, that partisanship figured in these trials and that the verdicts were not characterized by due impartiality. This unpopular law was thus made more objectionable by an unfair method of enforcement.

THE VIRGINIA AND KENTUCKY RESOLUTIONS

The Republicans saw in the Alien and Sedition Acts an infringement of the rights of the individual, as guaranteed in the Bill of

Rights, and a usurpation of power on the part of the general government. They felt that these and other measures sponsored by the Federalists were rapidly pushing the government toward centralization
at the expense of states' rights. The increase in the size of the army
and the war spirit which had been aroused were causing them great
anxiety. They were, therefore, deeply discouraged, and some of them
advocated a dissolution of the Union. Prominent in this latter group
was John Taylor, a brilliant political philosopher of Virginia, who
suggested to Jefferson that Virginia and North Carolina should secede from the Union.

Jefferson, however, was not so pessimistic. He regarded the objectionable Federalist measures as temporary evils which the people
would later correct. He was opposed to a resort to secession, but felt
that the state legislatures should express disapproval of these acts. In
pursuit of this aim he and his friend Madison each drew up a set of
resolutions which were adopted respectively by the legislatures of
Kentucky and Virginia (1798). In both sets of resolutions the Alien
and Sedition laws were denounced as unconstitutional and the compact theory of the Union was upheld.

According to this theory, the Union is a compact between the
states, the terms of which are specified in the Constitution. By this
agreement certain powers are delegated to the general government
and others are reserved to the states. If the general government un-
dertakes to exercise a power not so delegated, such an assumption of
authority is a usurpation and the acts resulting from it are null and
void. In passing the Alien and Sedition laws Congress had assumed
powers not delegated to it by the Constitution. These laws were,
therefore, null and void.

According to the Kentucky Resolutions, the Federal government
"was not made the exclusive or final judge of the extent of the powers delegated to itself"; "but that as in all other cases of compact
among parties having no common Judge, each party has an equal
right to judge for itself, as well of infractions as of the mode and
measure of redress." In one of the resolutions it was declared that
Kentucky would "submit to undelegated and consequently unlimited powers in no man or body of men on earth."

In the Virginia Resolutions, which were not so radical as those of
Kentucky, it was stated that "in case of a deliberate, palpable, and
dangerous exercise of other powers not granted by the said compact, the states, who are parties thereto, have the right and are in
duty bound to interpose for arresting the progress of the evil." Regret was expressed at the tendency of Congress "to consolidate the
states by degrees into one sovereignty."

Both sets of resolutions were sent to the other states for their consideration. The legislatures of the Northern states, all of which were controlled by the Federalists, replied that they were opposed to the resolutions. Those of the Southern states, in which Federalism had recently made important gains, sent no replies, doubtless considering as unwise an action which might lead to further agitation. It would seem, therefore, that Jefferson and Madison had failed in their effort to arouse opposition to Federalist measures. Not so, however; for the action of Kentucky and Virginia had led to a nationwide discussion of the protests and the unpopular laws which had incited them. It was in this way that the Alien and Sedition laws were made the main issue in the Presidential campaign of 1800. *Reaction of the states to the resolutions*

The Resolutions of '98 (as the Virginia and Kentucky Resolutions were sometimes called) were a vigorous assertion of states' rights and gave a new importance to this doctrine. They served as storehouses from which all later champions of localism in government drew their ablest arguments. The political philosophy expressed by them was the basis of the later doctrines of nullification and secession. When Calhoun elaborated his theory of nullification he contended that it embodied the same principles as those enunciated by Madison and Jefferson. Madison, who was still living at the time, denied that the conclusions of Calhoun could properly be deduced from the Resolutions; but many unprejudiced readers encounter less difficulty in accepting Calhoun's claim than Madison's denial. There is, however, enough vagueness in the Resolutions of '98 to afford a loophole of escape from the charge that they justify nullification. *Significance of the resolutions*

THE CAMPAIGN OF 1800

Before Congress adjourned in May, 1800, the Republican and Federalist members of Congress had each held a caucus and nominated candidates for the Presidency and Vice-Presidency. The Federalists chose Adams, and C. C. Pinckney of South Carolina; the Republicans, Jefferson, and Aaron Burr of New York. The chief issue in the campaign was the Alien and Sedition laws, the Federalists endorsing and the Republicans opposing them. *Party nominees*

The Federalists entered upon the campaign with a number of handicaps. Many of the measures for which they had been responsible, especially the Alien and Sedition laws, were unpopular with the masses. Believing as they did that "men of information and property" should hold the reins of authority, they had acted (in the opinion of many of the common people) as if government should *Reasons for opposition to the Federalists* be not only by but also for the privileged class. The war spirit, which had been so helpful to the Federalists in 1798, had now cooled down and anti-French feeling was of little or no use to them. On the other hand, there was a growing feeling against England on account of the policy of impressment and other restrictions on American commerce. As the Federalists were the pro-British party this anti-British sentiment was a source of weakness to them.

There were other reasons for opposition to the Federalists. The undeclared war with France had cut down imports and reduced the revenue from the tariff. At the same time, war preparations had led to increased expenditures. The result was a deficit in the Federal treasury of three and a half million dollars, which had to be met by a loan at a very high rate of interest. This gave the Republicans the opportunity to accuse the Federalists of extravagance. The enlargement of the army and navy lent color to the charge of militarism which was also brought against them.

The Federalist Party divided

The difficulties of the Federalists would not have been quite so serious if they had presented a united front against their opponents. But this they were unable to do. The split in the party had widened into a dangerous breach. Early in the campaign Adams had accepted the resignation of McHenry and dismissed Pickering from the Cabinet. Their places were filled respectively by Samuel Dexter of Massachusetts, and John Marshall of Virginia. These dismissals were fully justified, since both McHenry and Pickering, as allies of Hamilton, had been disloyal to their chief; but their removal served to widen the breach in the party.

The ill feeling between Adams and Hamilton was aggravated by exhibitions of bad temper on both sides. Adams accused Hamilton of belonging to a pro-British faction. Hamilton hotly resented the charge and wrote an elaborate pamphlet to disprove it. In this pamphlet he attacked Adams' record and represented him as unfit for the Presidency. The pamphlet was sent by him to a few of his intimate friends, and through the agency of Burr some of its contents were made public. Thereupon Hamilton was forced to publish the whole pamphlet. This, of course, was grist for the Republican mill.

Burr and Jefferson tie in the electoral vote

Adams' ineptitude as a politician also worked against the Federalists. The Republicans, on the other hand, had in Jefferson and Burr two of the most astute politicians that the country has ever produced. In the election the Republican candidates had a majority of the electoral votes, but as Jefferson and Burr received an equal number, the election went to the House of Representatives for a final decision.

The election returns were referred, not to the newly elected House which had received a fresh mandate from the people, but to the old, or "lame duck," House, which had been in large measure repudiated. In selecting the President the choice was confined to Jefferson and Burr, and the representation from each state had one vote. The Republicans were for Jefferson for the first place. The Federalists, who had decided in caucus to support Burr, were strong enough to prevent a choice.[1] Two of the Federalist Representatives, however, voted for Jefferson and the score stood eight to six in favor of Jefferson, who thus lacked only one vote of having the necessary majority. *The final decision by the House of Representatives*

The deadlock continued for thirty-five ballots and it seemed that no choice would be made by the end of Adams' term. The Republicans accused their opponents of trying to prolong the deadlock until after March 4, with the hope of then making John Marshall or some other Federalist President. The Republicans were determined to prevent this, even if they had to resort to force. At this juncture Hamilton came to the rescue. Although he regarded Jefferson as unfit for the Presidency, he considered him less dangerous than Burr, whom he dubbed the "Cataline of America." He, therefore, urged a few of his Federalist friends in the House to abstain from voting. This they did on the thirty-sixth ballot, and Jefferson was chosen President and Burr became Vice-President.

This election, together with the one of 1796, showed that the plan for choosing the President as outlined in the Constitution was unworkable. There arose, therefore, a demand for a change. This led to the adoption of the Twelfth Amendment, which provides that the electors shall ballot separately for President and Vice-President. One unhappy result of the election was that it started the quarrel between Hamilton and Burr, which culminated in the duel by which the former lost his life. *The Twelfth Amendment*

After their defeat the Federalists pushed through a measure which was very objectionable to the Republicans. This was the Judiciary Act of 1801. Prior to this time the judges of the Supreme Court had been going on circuits, each sitting with district judges in circuit courts. The Supreme Court had very little business and therefore its members had plenty of time for this extra duty; but an overfondness for work was not one of the faults of these early jus- *The Judiciary Act of 1801*

---

[1] Of the sixteen delegations eight voted for Jefferson from the beginning. The delegations of Maryland and Vermont were equally divided and so these two states did not vote. Out of deference to the sentiments of their constituents, one Federalist from North Carolina and the sole Representative from Georgia (who was a Federalist) voted for Jefferson. This made the vote eight to six. J. S. Bassett, *The Federalist System*, 291.

tices, and so they were averse to serving as circuit judges. Besides (so ran the argument) it was not proper for a justice to sit as a member of a circuit court on a case on which he would be required to give an opinion in the Supreme Court. It was on these alleged grounds that the Judiciary Act of 1801 was passed by the repudiated Federalist Congress. The main reason, however, for the new measure was probably the desire to create a number of good offices for Federalist leaders. The Federalist Congressmen felt that if they did not pass such a law the incoming Republicans would do so and would then fill the new offices with men of their own party.

The act provided for the creation of a new judgeship for each of the sixteen circuits and the number of clerks, marshals, and attorneys was considerably increased. These places were all filled by deserving Federalists. It is doubtful if the measure was justifiable, but even if it had been, the motive which prompted its enactment was quite indefensible. John Randolph characterized the new court as "a hospital for decayed politicians."

JOHN ADAMS.

CHAPTER XX

A Republican New Deal

DEMOCRATIC SIMPLICITY

Jefferson's inauguration

*E*ARLY in the morning of March 4, 1801, John Adams, the retiring President, left Washington for his home in Massachusetts. By so doing he escaped the humiliation of having to participate in the ceremonies which dramatized his own defeat and the victory of his political rival. Although he had earnestly longed for re-election, he doubtless took keen pleasure in shaking from his feet the dust of the little town that was hidden between the Potomac and the surrounding forest.

Courtesy of the New-York Historical
Society, New York City

THOMAS JEFFERSON (1743-1826).
By Rembrandt Peale (1778-1860).
Painted from life at Washington, D. C.
in 1805.

While the carriage of the ex-President was jolting along the rough Maryland roads his successor was preparing with pleasurable excitement for the installation exercises. About noon Jefferson left his boardinghouse and walked the short distance of two squares to the unfinished Capitol. He was accompanied by an escort of militia, two members of Adams' Cabinet, and some political friends. The oath of office was administered in the Senate Chamber by John Marshall, the new Chief Justice, whom Jefferson disliked personally and whose political principles he detested.

When Jefferson read his inaugural address it was done in such a low tone of voice that only a small portion of his audience caught its meaning. When printed, however, this inaugural proved to be a very important state paper. It was couched in a brilliant literary style and, in the main, expressed sentiments with which few would find fault. It contained such generally accepted principles as "free-

313

dom of religion," "freedom of the press," "freedom of person under the protection of the habeas corpus"; "equal and exact justice to all men"; and "absolute acquiescence in the decision of the majority." The government should "restrain men from injuring one another," "leave them otherwise free to regulate their own pursuits of industry and improvement," and "not take from the mouth of labor the bread it has earned." The foreign policy of the country should be one of "peace, commerce, and honest friendship with all nations, entangling alliances with none."

In the address Jefferson showed no symptoms of party rancor, despite the fact that the Presidential campaign had been characterized by great bitterness of feeling. Instead of a policy of proscription, he indicated one of reconciliation toward his Federalist opponents. He pointed out that "every difference of opinion is not a difference of principle." "We have," he said, "called by different names brethren of the same principle. We are all Republicans, we are all Federalists." Strange doctrines these to come from the lips of a man who had been represented as a narrow, bitter partisan and a dangerous radical! Many Federalists had expected and probably hoped that the new incumbent would assail the ears of his hearers with foolishly extreme pronouncements which would place him in a bad light before the country. They were, therefore, surprised at the mildness and sanity of the inaugural.

The Cabinet   Jefferson was fortunate in the selection of his Cabinet. For the important posts of State and the Treasury he was able to secure men who were eminently suitable. That Madison would be made Secretary of State was a foregone conclusion. Not only were he and Jefferson warm personal friends, but they had generally seen eye to eye on political questions, and had co-operated perfectly in the organization and development of the Republican Party.

For Secretary of the Treasury, Albert Gallatin was the logical choice.[1] Gallatin was born in Geneva, and his foreign origin, evidenced by an accent in his speech, was used as a point against him; but he was well educated and had taught at Harvard. As a member of Congress he had proved himself an able critic of Hamilton's financial measures and had demonstrated a greater knowledge of financial affairs than anyone else in the party. The high expecta-

---

[1] Other members of the Cabinet were General Henry Dearborn of Massachusetts, Secretary of War, and Levi Lincoln of the same state, Attorney General. Jefferson had difficulty in filling the place of Secretary of the Navy, and at one time facetiously remarked that he would have to advertise for candidates. Finally, General Robert Smith of Maryland was appointed to the position. Gideon Granger of Connecticut was made Postmaster General. The incumbent of this office did not, however, at this time have a seat in the Cabinet.

tions raised by his previous record were abundantly realized by his administration of the Treasury Department.

With the accession of Jefferson there came a decided change in the social customs at the Executive Mansion. The formal etiquette of the Federalist regime was discontinued, and one of democratic simplicity took its place. Jefferson was familiar with the usage of European courts and complied with it when he was in France; but he did not like such artificialities, or even the conventionalities of American high society, and decided not to adopt them for the White House. The levee introduced by Washington was accordingly discontinued, and only on the Fourth of July and New Year's Day did Jefferson have formal receptions. On these occasions the reception rooms at the White House were open to all who wished to come. "Diplomats rubbed shoulders with grocers," and in the bestowal of his courtesies, Jefferson made no distinction between Senators and barbers. Even among ministers representing foreign countries he did not recognize any precedence at his dinner parties. He was, however, cordial to visitors and the White House was open to callers at all times. *Social practices at the White House*

Despite their informality, the social functions at the White House were greatly enjoyed by those who participated in them. Jefferson was a delightful host, one who exerted himself to please his guests and put them at ease. The versatility of his tastes, his interest in the affairs of other people, and his conversational ability made him interesting to all classes. As Mrs. Jefferson had died some years prior to his election, there was no First Lady to direct social affairs. His two daughters were married and were able to spend only a part of each year with their father. At times, therefore, social activities at the White House were not under the efficient management of a mistress of ceremonies. Fortunately, in the discharge of his social responsibilities, Jefferson had the assistance of one of the most charming social leaders that this country has ever known. This was the wife of the Secretary of State, Mrs. "Dolly" Madison. She was now entering upon her long and remarkable career as the leader of Washington society, and the President often called upon her to preside on important social occasions.

Jefferson was wrongfully accused of being careless and even slovenly in dress, and of carrying democratic simplicity beyond the limits prescribed by official decorum. It is true that his clothes, although made of the finest material, were plain and sometimes old-fashioned and that he was not always strict in the observance of what he considered unreasonable conventions. But his simplicity never degenerated into vulgarity, nor his friendliness into undue *Social informality* familiarity. At times, too, he probably showed too great an aversion to formality, notably when on one occasion he received the British minister in heelless slippers. Although the minister was in other respects treated with marked cordiality, he felt that he had not been accorded due consideration. Jefferson was not, however, unmindful of the dignity of his office, and maintained a standard of living worthy of the high place he held. When he drove out with his family his carriage was drawn by four beautiful bay horses. In going back and forth between Washington and Monticello, and in making short trips in and around the capital, he often rode his fine saddle horse, "Wildair."

Washington at the beginning of the century

The country town which had recently been made the nation's capital afforded a better setting for Republican simplicity than for Federalist formality. The stiff and dignified etiquette of the Federalist regime did not appear so incongruous to the old and wealthy families of Philadelphia as it would have seemed to the few newcomers who were domiciled in the wilderness city. Washington had been laid out on a magnificent scale by the Frenchman, Major L'Enfant; but, as has been said, at this time the only appearance of magnificence was its distances. No one dreamed that one day it would be one of the world's most beautiful capitals. Here and there were clusters of houses separated from each other by fields and connected by unpaved roads which served as streets. A large swamp near Capitol Hill was a breeding place for myriads of mosquitoes and a source of malaria.

At Jefferson's accession there were no churches in Washington, though religious services were held sometimes in the Treasury Building and almost every Sunday in the Hall of the House of Representatives. At these services the President was a regular attendant, generally going on horseback. Despite the uncouthness in outward appearances of the little city, its society was gay and interesting.

REPUBLICAN REFORMS

Republican hopes and Federalist fears

The defeat of Adams is often designated as the "Revolution of 1800." In the campaign of 1800 the danger of and the need for such a revolution were stressed by Federalists and Republicans respectively. Even Jefferson afterwards declared that the defeat of the Federalists was a peaceable revolution. The significance of the change was not such, however, as to justify so high-sounding a term. Owing to this agitation there were raised among Republicans exaggerated hopes of reform, and among Federalists unwarranted fears of destructive change.

Some of the Federalist leaders (those who were most ardent in their opposition) saw, or pretended to see, in Jefferson a Jacobin[1] in politics, an advocate of free love in morals, and an atheist in religion. From such a ruler they could expect nothing short of a subversion of the political and social order. Democracy in government, laxity in morals, and skepticism in religion would be the result. The prophets of evil were especially vociferous in New England, and some of the Congregational ministers in that section were earnest and serious in proclaiming these jeremiads. Fisher Ames, one of the New England pessimists, defined democracy as "a troubled spirit, fated never to rest, and whose dreams, if it sleeps, present only visions of hell." The Rev. Theodore Dwight said: "We have now reached the consummation of democratic blessedness. We have a country governed by blockheads and knaves." The peace, prosperity, and security enjoyed by the people during Jefferson's first term showed how false were these gloomy prophecies. It must have afforded the President gleeful—indeed, almost sinful—satisfaction to be able thus to heap coals of fire on the heads of his enemies.

The gloomy forebodings felt, or professed, by the Federalists were matched by a hopeful exultation displayed by the Republicans, who maintained that their victory had saved the country from monarchy and militarism. There is no basis for this contention. There had never been any danger of monarchy, and the tendency toward militarism which got under way during the French crisis had been arrested by Adams' peace policy. All that the Republicans could reasonably claim in the way of change was a new deal of a rather mild character.

Jefferson's program of reform included the clearing away of what he considered the rubbish of Federalist misrule and the adoption of constructive policies which would be beneficial to all the people. This objective could not be attained without the co-operation of Congress. He was fortunate, however, in having a Congress that was sympathetic with his aims. In both houses the Republicans had a majority and the leaders stood ready to give hearty support to his plans. The Speaker of the House, Nathaniel Macon, and the chairman of the Ways and Means Committee, John Randolph of Roanoke, were both firm adherents of the doctrine of states' rights and advocates of reform.

The Republicans control Congress

Randolph, leader of the Administration forces in the House, was brilliant but erratic. Physical suffering caused by ill-health prodded a sensitive spirit into bitterness, which gave a sharp barb

John Randolph

---

[1] The Jacobins were the extreme democrats of France who were responsible for many of the excesses of the French Revolution, especially the Reign of Terror.

to his intellectual acumen. He was a master of sarcasm. A natural gift for forceful expression had, by study and wide reading, been trained and polished into a beautiful literary style. His knowledge of history and world literature was a storehouse from which he drew apt illustrations and pertinent allusions. His leadership would have been more effective, however, had he been less sarcastic and more conciliatory toward Federalists and recalcitrant Republicans. As it was, fear played a greater part than personal loyalty in maintaining party discipline.

The "Quids"   Randolph was never quite comfortable in the harness of party regularity. By temperament he was a nonconformist and felt most at home when in opposition. Besides, he, Macon, and a few others stood consistently by the doctrines of '98, while the Administration was moving toward nationalism. He was also opposed to Madison, whom Jefferson was grooming for the succession. For these and other reasons he and Macon in a few years had ceased to be in accord with the Administration and had become leaders of a small group of insurgents. They regarded themselves as Old (or states' rights) Republicans, but were dubbed "Quids."[1] This irregularity cost them the influence that they had been wielding in Congress. Macon lost the speakership, and Randolph ceased to be leader in the House.

Jefferson sends messages to Congress instead of making addresses   Jefferson's objectives were set forth in his first message to Congress (December, 1801). The delivery of this message was in itself an innovation, as a copy was sent by messengers to each house instead of being read to both houses in joint session. The reason given for this break with custom was the convenience of Congress and the economy of its time. Probably a more important consideration with him was the fact that he was not an impressive speaker and could present his plans more effectively in writing than by oral expression. Doubtless, too, he felt that the formal address before Congress was too much like the speech from the throne of the English king before Parliament. By sending written messages to both branches of the legislature, Jefferson set a new precedent which was followed by his successors for more than a century, until broken by his noted disciple, Woodrow Wilson.

The most objectionable of all the Federalist measures were the Alien and Sedition laws. These acts expired by limitation at the end of Adams' term and therefore the Republican Congress took no action regarding them. The Naturalization Law was changed so as to require five instead of fourteen years of residence for foreign-

---

[1] *Quid* is a Latin word meaning *what?* The term was intended to convey the idea that they did not know what they stood for.

ers as a prerequisite to citizenship. The residence requirement was thus made the same as it had been before the accession of Adams.

Another Federalist measure to which the Republicans were strongly opposed was the Judiciary Act of 1801. They attacked it on the ground that the new judges and officers created by the act were not needed and, therefore, an unnecessary expense had been incurred. They maintained that this increase in the number of Federal courts would lead to greater activity in the Federal judiciary and would thus weaken the power and influence of the state courts. In this way the general government would be strengthened at the expense of the state governments. The Federalists contended that to repeal the act and deprive the judges of their offices would be to violate that clause in the Constitution which declares that judges shall hold office for life or during good behavior. The answer of the Republicans was that what Congress can create, it can destroy. Repeal was carried, but by the narrow majority of only one vote in the Senate.

Repeal of the Judiciary Act of 1801

An improvement in the management of the finances was a reform which both Jefferson and Gallatin were anxious to accomplish. Their purpose was to lower taxes and at the same time reduce the public debt. This would mean strict economy in government. Minor economies could be effected by lopping off unnecessary offices, but the chief saving could be obtained by the lowering of appropriations for the army and navy. This reduction would involve the weakening of our defenses. But as the world was enjoying a temporary peace, the President felt that the danger of war was remote. Furthermore, to keep the army and navy on a small footing would accord with his antimilitaristic sentiments. The lull in hostilities in Europe was, however, only a truce and Jefferson's policy proved to be ill-timed if not unwise. Under it the little standing army was made smaller, and if this policy had been fully maintained, the navy also would have been crippled; but the Tripolitan War led to an increase in the efficiency of the navy, and it was stronger at the end than at the beginning of Jefferson's administration.

Financial reforms

The one important step toward the lowering of the taxes was the repeal of the internal revenue act. By repealing this unpopular measure the Republican Party gained additional strength in the frontier regions, where the manufacture of brandy and whiskey was an important supplement to farming. It took away a considerable amount of revenue, however, and might have proved a source of embarrassment to the Treasury. Fortunately, the European situation took such a turn as to increase greatly the volume of American foreign trade. This meant an increase in tariff receipts, and so the

Repeal of the internal revenue act

government had enough income to meet current expenses and also to make large payments on the public debt.

*Improve-
ments in the
method of
handling
public funds*

On the recommendation of Gallatin, Congress instituted the practice of making specific, instead of general, appropriations—a change which lessened the power of the Secretary of the Treasury. Heretofore, appropriations had been made in lump sums, which were broken down into specific items by the Treasury Department. Gallatin also introduced improvements which simplified the method of handling the public moneys.

*Patronage
under
Jefferson*

One of the problems with which Jefferson had to contend early in his administration was that of the patronage. When he took over the government he found that the civil service was manned almost exclusively by Federalists. It had been the policy of both Washington and Adams to give no important offices to Republican opponents of the Administration. After his defeat Adams was especially active in filling all possible vacancies with his political friends. He was charged by the Republicans with having been busy until midnight on March 3 signing commissions, and therefore his latest appointments were known as "midnight appointments."

The new President was soon besieged by a crowd of hungry Republicans, who pressed upon the pie counter with appetites which had been whetted by long waiting. To satisfy them meant the removal of Federalist officeholders. The philosopher-politician was thus put in an embarrassing position. The politician in him was suggesting that he yield to the demands of his followers and give them the offices, while the philosopher was urging him to put the civil service on a nonpartisan basis. The result was a compromise between idealism and opportunism.

The principles which at first guided him in making appointments to office were as follows: All "midnight" appointees, all marshals and attorneys for the Federal courts, and persons who had been guilty of misconduct in office should be removed and, as a rule, Republicans put in their places. The reason given for the removals of marshals and attorneys was that all the officials of the Federal courts, including the judges, were Federalists. The judges could not be removed, and but for the new marshals and attorneys, the Republican party, which represented a majority of the people, would have had no voice whatever in the administration of the Federal judiciary.

If removals had been confined to these cases, Jefferson would have exhibited a generosity toward political opponents which no other President has shown; but practical politics, as he later considered, demanded a wider basis of action. Vacancies were slow in occurring, for, as he said, "those by death are few; by resignation none." He, therefore, removed some for offensive partisanship and others for the purpose of giving Republicans a proper share in the offices. Under these latter principles the spoils system had an inning, and the pressure put upon him by politicians led to a number of changes. And yet, considering all the circumstances, his policy regarding the patronage was one of moderation. At the end of his first term the number of Federalists still in office exceeded that of the Republicans; but by the end of his second term the ratio was preponderantly in favor of the Republicans.

The mild spirit of Jefferson's Inaugural Address and the generosity he was practicing toward Federalist officeholders proved that he was not the dangerous radical who had figured in the Federalist imagination. His moderation is explained in part by the fact that he had a streak of conservatism which had been developed by the responsibilities of power. Then, too, it was good politics to falsify the gloomy pre-election prophecies made by Federalist pessimists. He felt that a large portion of the rank and file of the Federalists were Republicans at heart and had only been deceived by their leaders. A sane constructive policy, tempered by a sensible conservatism, would appeal to them and enable him to lead them into the Republican fold. He needed these new recruits, for in the beginning the Republican majority was narrow in the Senate. Besides, factional differences in New York and Pennsylvania were weakening the party in those states. If the New Englanders could be won over, it would be carrying the war into Africa and would render the Republican victory complete. *Jefferson's moderation*

From the beginning of his public career Jefferson had been opposed to the slave trade. In his first draft of the Declaration of Independence, in a clause which was deleted from the document by Congress, the King of England was severely arraigned for forcing slaves upon the American colonies. The Constitution forbade the prohibition of the slave trade prior to January 1, 1808. Jefferson in his annual message of December, 1806, recommended an act of repeal. This suggestion was accepted by Congress and a law forbidding the importation of slaves after January 1, 1808, was passed (1807). The penalties for violating the act were not severe and it did not entirely stop, but did greatly reduce, the traffic. *Importation of slaves prohibited*

The Ordinance of 1785, which inaugurated the American public land policy, was slightly modified in Washington's administration (1796). Later (1800) at the request of William Henry Harrison, delegate in Congress from the Northwest Territory, the land policy of the government was liberalized in favor of the actual settler. Tracts of three hundred and twenty acres were offered for sale, only *Changes in the public land acts* one fourth of the purchase price to be paid in cash, the other three fourths to be met in four annual installments. In 1804 a new act reduced the minimum limit of purchase to one hundred and sixty acres. Since only eighty dollars were now needed for the first payment, homesteads out of the public domain were in reach of the masses.

Ohio admitted as a state

These changes in the public land policy were favorable to emigration to the West and the organization of new states and territories. The first of the states carved out of the Northwest Territory was Ohio, which was admitted into the Union in 1803. The unsold public lands within her limits were retained in the possession of the Federal government. Also Ohio promised not to tax for five years any lands which had been sold by the United States. As a compensation for these concessions, the act of admission contained two important pledges: (1) that one section in every township sold would be granted to the inhabitants for the maintenance of schools; and (2) that five per cent of the proceeds from the sale of public lands in Ohio would be used for constructing roads from the eastward flowing navigable waters to the Ohio River and in the State of Ohio. The funds arising from these sales were used to build the Cumberland Road, or National Turnpike, from Cumberland to Wheeling, Virginia. In this way the foundation of the system of internal improvements was laid—and that by a Congress and President who professed a rigid adherence to the doctrine of states' rights.

THE FIGHT BETWEEN JEFFERSON AND THE FEDERAL JUDICIARY

Reasons for the conflict between the executive and the judiciary

Like a later New Dealer, Jefferson was confronted at the outset by an antagonistic Federal judiciary. In attempting to cope with this obstacle, both New Dealers learned that a fight with the judiciary is a difficult if not a dangerous undertaking. After the Federalists had lost control of the legislative and executive branches of the government they were still impregnably intrenched in the judiciary. All the judges were Federalists, and the Chief Justice, John Marshall, was a bitter personal and political enemy of the President. A month before the latter's inauguration he had entered upon his career as Chief Justice, and for more than a third of a century he was the dominating personality of the Supreme Court.

The basis of the conflict between the executive and judicial departments was a disagreement as to the interpretation of the Constitution. The Federalist judges held to the doctrine of nationalism, and the Republican President and many of his followers in Congress, to that of states' rights. But this academic dispute was heated by the ill feeling that existed between Jefferson and Marshall. Further-more, the Republicans generally regarded Associate Justice Chase as a "Bloody Jeffreys." He had won this unflattering designation by his overbearing manner in presiding at trials under the Sedition Act.

The Administration led the attack, and in the repeal of the Judiciary Act of 1801 won the first victory. The next year, however, the Supreme Court assumed the offensive when it rendered its decision in the case of *Marbury vs. Madison*. William Marbury had been named by Adams as one of the justices of the peace for the District of Columbia. His appointment had been confirmed by the Senate, but the commission had not been delivered to him. In obedience to instructions from Jefferson, Madison had refused to deliver this commission and the others which had been made out to the "midnight" appointees. Marbury applied to the Supreme Court for a writ of mandamus to compel the Secretary of State to deliver the commission.

The case of Marbury vs. Madison

In handing down the decision of the Court, Marshall declared that Madison had no right to withhold the commission, but that the Supreme Court could not issue a mandamus to force him to deliver it. In refusing to grant the petition of the plaintiff, which should have been presented to a lower Federal court, Marshall reasoned as follows: The Judiciary Act of 1789 provides for the issuance of writs of mandamus by the Supreme Court as an exercise of its original jurisdiction. But the Constitution, in listing the cases in which this tribunal has original jurisdiction, does not include that of issuing a mandamus. Therefore, the Act of 1789, in conferring such jurisdiction on the Supreme Court, is contrary to the Constitution and null and void as to that particular provision.

This was the first time that the Supreme Court had ever declared an act of Congress unconstitutional, and it was more than a half-century before it again asserted this authority (in the Dred Scott Decision, 1857). The idea of judicial review, however, was not new to the American people. In colonial days the right of the Privy Council in England to pass upon the constitutionality of colonial legislation was generally accepted. During the period of the Confederation there were a few instances in which state courts had assumed the right to review the acts of state legislatures. There was some doubt, however, as to whether the Constitution had conferred upon the Federal judiciary this power over Congress.[1]

Significance of the decision

[1] The clauses on which the alleged authority was based were these: "This Constitution and the laws of the United States which shall be made in pursuance thereof, and all treaties made . . . under the authority of the United States, shall be the supreme law of the land." "The judicial power [of the United States] shall extend to

The action of the Supreme Court in this case was bitterly resented by Jefferson and his friends, who contended that the legislature would cease to be an independent branch of the government if its acts could be set aside by the judiciary. They denied that the right of judicial review could be deduced from the clauses cited; but their main ground of complaint was the attempt made by the Chief Justice to show up the Administration in an unfavorable light. Apparently, the Court had gone out of its way to lecture the President and Secretary of State; for if the Court had no jurisdiction in the premises (as they contended) it should not have given an opinion as to the merits of the case. This decision, therefore, increased the tension between the executive and the judiciary.

Fuel was also added to the flames by an act of imprudence on the part of Justice Chase. Before Jefferson's resentment over the Marbury decision had cooled off, Justice Chase, in a charge to a grand jury in Baltimore, made a foolish harangue in which he warned against the dangers of universal suffrage and deprecated the evils of democracy. It was virtually a stump speech against the political ideals of the Administration. This exhibition of partisanship by a member of the Supreme Court helped Jefferson in his attack on the judiciary. It gave him a good opportunity to try out the weapon of impeachment in his fight with the judges.

This method of disposing of an objectionable judge had recently been used with success. Judge William Pickering, of the New Hampshire District Court, had been impeached and removed from office for drunkenness on the bench, though his improper conduct was doubtless due to insanity. At Jefferson's suggestion, charges were now brought against Chase and he was impeached by the House by a strict party vote; but in the Senate the necessary two-thirds majority for conviction could not be secured and therefore the attempt at removal failed. The majority of the Republican leaders took the position that to remove a judge under impeachment procedure it was not necessary to convict him of crime but only to show that he held dangerous opinions. This view, however, was not sustained by two thirds of the Senators, since all the Federalist and a few of the Republican Senators insisted that conviction of an indictable offense was necessary for removal. They held that partisanship, though a gross offense, was not a crime.

all cases in law and equity, arising under this Constitution, the laws of the United States, and treaties made, or which shall be made, under their authority." The courts, therefore (so argued Marshall), must consider the Constitution as well as a law whenever the former applies to a case before them. If there is a conflict between a constitutional provision and a statute the former must take precedence over the latter since it is the paramount authority.

If the former view had been accepted and Chase had been ousted, other removals for objectionable partisanship would perhaps have followed. The President and the Republican Congress might have been able to "purge" the judiciary and remake it to their liking; but such a victory would have been purchased at the cost of the independence of that branch of the government. It was, therefore, fortunate that Chase was not convicted. Happily, the fright to which he had been subjected acted as a wholesome restraint on him and other judges and made them more moderate in their subsequent homilies.

THE TRIPOLITAN WAR

The "mosquito fleet"

Jefferson's wish to save money, together with his pacifistic leanings, caused him to rely for home defense largely upon a number of small vessels which he had had constructed and placed in the harbors along the coast. In time of emergency these were to be manned by the citizens of the surrounding country. This "mosquito fleet," as it was called, could not be used successfully in rough water and so proved of little or no value.

The European powers pay tribute to the Barbary States

As has already been seen, fortunately for the navy, the President's program of retrenchment regarding the navy was considerably modified by the demands created by the Tripolitan War. This war arose from the acts of the rulers of the Barbary States of northern Africa—Morocco, Algiers, Tunis, and Tripoli—whose ships had for many years been preying on the commerce of European countries. Instead of chastising these corsairs, the European powers had been purchasing immunity by paying an annual tribute. The tribute paid by the British government also protected American ships in the colonial period. But soon after the close of the Revolutionary War, these pirate states had come to realize that the United States was no longer a part of the British empire. They, therefore, began to make attacks on American commerce and continued the practice during and after the Confederation period. To protect American sailors, Washington adopted the usual plan of making payments to the rulers.

Cause of the Tripolitan War

Jefferson did not approve of this policy, as he considered it more costly than a vigorous assertion of American rights. He was confirmed in this opinion by the demand of the Pasha of Tripoli for more tribute. When the Tripolitan ruler declared war on the United States (May 10, 1801), Jefferson decided to use coercion rather than persuasion in upholding the interests of his country. Accordingly, ships were sent to blockade the Tripolitan coast with the view to bringing its ruler to reason. These vessels performed feats of valor, and with some degree of success; but the difficulties were great and a decisive victory was not in sight even after four years of hostilities.

Results of the war

In the meantime the American consul at Tunis had induced the brother of the Pasha to invade the latter's dominions with a troop of about five hundred men. This invading force was making rapid headway, when the Pasha offered terms of peace. A treaty was signed (June 4, 1805) between Tripoli and the United States by which about three hundred American sailors were released from bondage on the payment of sixty thousand dollars by the United States. No mention was made of tribute, but it was understood that the American government would send to the Pasha by each newly appointed consul a present of not more than six thousand dollars.

While this was not a glorious ending of a long and vexatious contest and did not put a stop to all trouble with the Barbary corsairs, the activity of the American navy had inspired them with respect for the new republic. The most significant result, however, was the effect the fighting had upon the navy. The engagements in the Mediterranean increased its morale and gave the officers a training which proved valuable in the war soon to come with England.

THE PURCHASE OF LOUISIANA

The territory included in Louisiana

The greatest achievement of Jefferson's administration was the purchase of Louisiana. The term "Louisiana" is a difficult one to define, as the boundaries of the region so named were for a long time not definitely marked. At the beginning of the nineteenth century the territory included the Isle of Orleans (a long narrow island east of the southern reach of the Mississippi River) and a vast expanse of land between the Mississippi River and the Rocky Mountains. Whether it also included West Florida and Texas was a disputed point.

The Treaty of San Ildefonso and events leading to it

Louisiana was settled by the French and held by them until 1763, when it was ceded to Spain, who retained possession of the territory until the end of the century. At that time there were in the region which centered at New Orleans about forty thousand inhabitants, including slaves. There was also a small settlement at St. Louis. These two places were connected by scattered garrisons and trading posts along the western shore of the Mississippi. A few posts had also been established on the Red River. The province was not self-sustaining but was a drain on the resources of the homeland. For this reason the Spanish government did not appreciate the value of this undeveloped empire.

Napoleon was trying to build a French colonial empire in America. He had no expectation of regaining Canada, but was hopeful of obtaining other lands as a compensation for what had been ceded by France at the end of the Seven Years' War. Of the few possessions left to France in America, the western part of Santo Domingo was easily the most important. It was the center of a profitable trade in tropical products, but it did not raise sufficient food for its own people. Louisiana would serve as a source of supply for food and lumber and would, therefore, be a valuable complement to Santo Domingo. These and other considerations induced Napoleon to repossess Louisiana.

Shortly after his great victory at Marengo, while flushed with overconfidence as to his power and importance, he sent to the king of Spain a request which was virtually a demand for the retrocession of Louisiana. The Spanish king, Don Carlos IV, had no alternative but to accept the offer; but he seems to have yielded with little, if any, reluctance, thinking apparently that he was getting a just *quid pro quo* for the cession. Accordingly, Louisiana was ceded to France by the Treaty of San Ildefonso (October 1, 1800). The agreement was kept secret for some time, and for more than three years Spain retained possession of the territory. Napoleon promised to make the son-in-law of Don Carlos king of Tuscany (to be called the Kingdom of Etruria), and not to dispose of Louisiana to any power other than Spain.

At the time of his accession Jefferson knew nothing of the Treaty of San Ildefonso and was on very friendly terms with the French government. When at a later date he learned of the agreement for the transfer of Louisiana to France, his attitude suddenly changed, for he considered French ownership of Louisiana a grave menace to the prosperity and security of his country. As long as this province was owned by a weak power, friendly to the United States, he did not seriously fear that the Mississippi would be closed to western trade; but with Louisiana in the possession of a strong and aggressive power like France, the situation would be quite different. His deep concern over the cession was expressed in a letter to Robert R. Livingston, American minister at Paris, as follows: "There is on the globe one single spot, the possessor of which is our natural and habitual enemy. It is New Orleans, through which three eighths of our territory must pass to market. . . . France placing herself in that

Jefferson opposed to the acquisition of Louisiana by France; reasons

door assumes to us the attitude of defiance. . . . The day that France takes possession of N. Orleans . . . we must marry ourselves to the British fleet and nation."

A few months later the news came that the Spanish authorities had withdrawn the right of deposit, an act the responsibility for which was erroneously attributed to Napoleon. The Westerners on learning of the retrocession and the withdrawal of the right of deposit were aroused to a warlike attitude. There was a danger that they might make an unauthorized attack on New Orleans, or arrange terms with France and withdraw their allegiance to the United States. Jefferson now felt that something unusual should be done. Accordingly, he sent James Monroe as minister plenipotentiary to France to co-operate with Livingston in negotiating an agreement with Napoleon.

Instructions of the American envoys at Paris

The instructions of these envoys covered several alternative proposals. They were to make a liberal offer for the Isle of Orleans and the Floridas. If these regions could not be obtained they were to try to get enough land on the east bank of the Mississippi for a port. If all efforts to purchase land on the lower Mississippi should fail, they should as a final effort press for a perpetual guarantee of the free navigation of the Mississippi together with the right of deposit. If this last demand should be refused and France should force a war by closing the river to American trade, then Livingston and Monroe were to enter into communication with the British authorities with the view to forming an alliance with them.

Napoleon wishes to sell Louisiana; reasons

By the time Monroe arrived in France Napoleon had changed his mind as to a colonial empire and had decided to sell Louisiana to the United States. There were several reasons for this reversal of policy. One of these (and one which had considerable weight with him) was the failure of his attempt to put down the insurrection in Santo Domingo. The slaves there had revolted against French rule and, under the leadership of a remarkable Negro, Toussaint L'Ouverture, had set up an independent black republic. Napoleon's effort to regain his authority, though successful at first, ended in disastrous failure. After sacrificing fifty thousand soldiers in one year on this far-off island, Napoleon decided that the cost of its reconquest was greater than its worth. The loss of control over Santo Domingo broke the strongest link in the chain of his American plans and lessened the value of Louisiana to him.

Besides, he felt that the war with England would soon be renewed and if so, Louisiana could be taken over by the Mistress of the Seas. Then, too, the purchase money would furnish sinews for the coming war. A secondary consideration was that in doubling the territory of the United States he was raising up a great power to be a rival of Britain.

Therefore, before Monroe reached Paris, Talleyrand asked Livingston how much his country would give for all of Louisiana. *Negotiation of the purchase* Livingston was so surprised that he could hardly believe his ears. He concealed his enthusiasm, however, and waited until Monroe's arrival before closing the bargain. A treaty was then signed (dated April 30, 1803) by which France ceded to the United States all of Louisiana for 80,000,000 francs (about $15,000,000), one fourth of which was to be applied to the payment of American claims against France.

According to a very probable tradition, Livingston, after signing his name to the treaty, rose and while shaking hands with Monroe and the French foreign minister said: "We have lived long, but this is the noblest work of our lives." He had a right to be proud of this achievement, for by it the area of his country was doubled and the territorial basis formed for its becoming a great world power.

The boundaries of Louisiana were not clearly indicated in the treaty. There was a clause, however, which defined the land purchased as "Louisiana with the Same extent that it now has in the hands of Spain, and that it had when France possessed it." Whether it included West Florida or Texas or both was not clear. When Livingston asked for a more specific statement as to boundaries, Talleyrand evaded the question by replying: "You have made a noble bargain for yourselves, and I suppose you will make the most of it." But in his instructions to the first French governor he had given, as boundaries of Louisiana, the Iberville River on the east and the Rio Grande on the west. According to this interpretation, Louisiana did not include West Florida but did include Texas. *Boundaries vague*

On receiving information that this great bargain had been made, Jefferson was delighted and was resolved that the agreement should be consummated. He felt, however, that the authority to make the purchase was not granted by the Constitution, which had no specific provisions regarding the acquisition of new territory. This was, he thought, an oversight of the Fathers. The authority to acquire new territory could be derived, therefore, only by resorting to the doctrine of implied powers, of which he had been the arch-opponent. He was, therefore, placed in an awkward position. It looked as though he might have to sacrifice either his consistency or a great opportunity to serve his country. *Jefferson's view as to the constitutionality of the purchase*

To get around the difficulty, he first suggested that Congress propose an amendment conferring upon the general government power to acquire new territory. Livingston, however, was urging

prompt action and indicating that delay might be dangerous, as
Napoleon might change his mind. The idea of an amendment was
accordingly dropped. In signing the treaty Jefferson stretched his
states' rights conscience and sacrificed consistency to patriotism.
The treaty was ratified by the Senate and the purchase money voted
by Congress by overwhelming majorities.

Later decision
of the Su-
preme Court

The acquisition of Louisiana was not a violation of the Constitution. Later (1828) the Supreme Court decided that the power conferred upon the general government to make treaties includes by
implication the authority to acquire new territory by treaty.

French law in
Louisiana

The French had not taken possession of Louisiana at the time
the treaty was ratified. It was not until the last of November (1803)
that the transfer to France was made. Twenty days later the United
States was formally invested with the ownership of the province.
In this short period of French occupation the *Code Napoleon* was
introduced, adding further complications to an already confused
legal system in Louisiana.

Federalists
oppose the
purchase

The purchase of Louisiana was strongly opposed by the Federalists. They admitted the constitutional right of the government to
acquire territory by purchase, but branded this treaty as unconstitutional because of the pledge that the inhabitants of Louisiana
should be "incorporated into the Union of the United States and
admitted as soon as possible . . . to the enjoyment of all the rights,
advantages, and immunities of citizens of the United States." They
contended that the authority of Congress to admit new states into
the Union was limited to states carved out of territory belonging
to the United States in 1787.

The Lewis
and Clark
expedition

In January, 1803, before Louisiana had been purchased, Jefferson
asked Congress for an appropriation for an exploring expedition
up the valley of the Missouri River and on to the Pacific. Since these
explorations would be in territory not belonging to the United
States, they might be considered as an intrusion upon the domains
of other nations. As an offset to this objection, the motive given in
the request was to extend the internal commerce of the country.
Whether Jefferson intended the expedition as one to spy out the
land of friendly states with the view to later invasion, or whether
he sent it to gratify his scientific curiosity, we cannot say with certainty. Congress voted the necessary money, and by the time the
expedition was ready to start, Louisiana had been transferred to
the United States. All objections to the venture which might have
been urged were thus removed.

Captain Meriwether Lewis was in charge of the exploring party

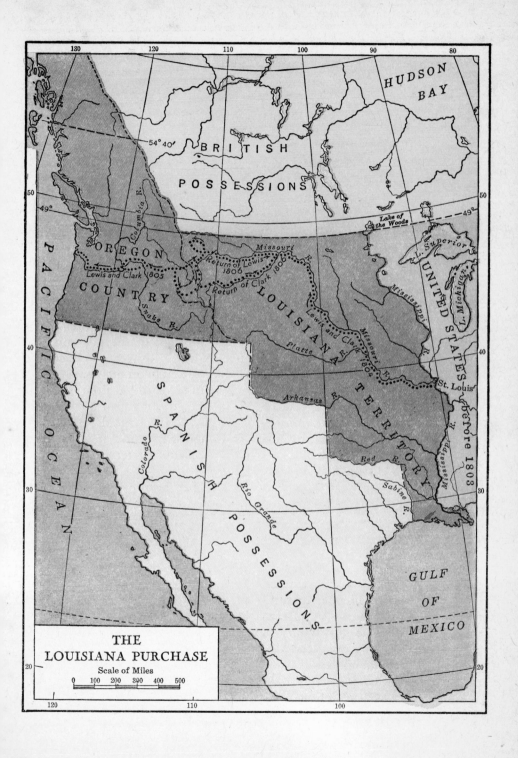

THE
LOUISIANA PURCHASE
Scale of Miles
0   100   200   300   400   500

and he associated with himself William Clark, a younger brother of George Rogers Clark. With them went twenty-three other persons, all of whom were enlisted in the regular army. After six months of severe training and rigid discipline in preparation, the detachment was ready to start on the perilous journey. It left St. Louis in May, 1804. Difficulty was encountered in ascending the Missouri River, owing to the rapidity of the current in some places and the shallowness of the stream in others. By laborious effort the explorers could usually make only about ten miles a day. After six months of strenuous exertion they arrived at the present site of Bismarck, North Dakota, near which they spent the winter. Resuming their progress in the spring, they reached the Pacific Ocean in the fall (1805). Here they spent another winter and then journeyed back to St. Louis, reaching this place in September, 1806.

As a result of this exploring venture, much new geographical information was gained regarding the Northwest. The location of rivers and mountains, the lay of the land, the nature of the soil, and the disposition of the Indians were noted. In the accounts the Indians were reported as friendly, but Lewis and Clark did not consider the land suitable for settlement. Its only value, in their opinion, lay in the possibilities for trade. The exploration of the Oregon country strengthened the claim of the United States to that region.

Not only were the Federalists strongly opposed to the purchase of Louisiana, but they were also alarmed at the growing strength of the Republican Party, which was even making dangerous inroads in New England, a region sacred to Federalism. So great was their disappointment that a small group of them concocted a scheme for breaking up the Union. They were accused of a plan to induce the New England states and New York, and possibly New Jersey and eastern Pennsylvania, to secede and form a northern confederacy. Some of the Canadian provinces might, with British consent, come into this new union. *A disunion plot*

The political situation in New York, they thought, was favorable to this scheme. Burr was running for governor as an independent Republican, against the regular nominee of the party, and was anxious to receive the endorsement of the Federalists. The would-be disunionists hoped that Burr might be used in furtherance of their aims. A conference was held with him at which their plans were discussed. Burr made no promises of support, but was cordial in his attitude toward these leaders. Accordingly, on their own hopes rather than Burr's pledges, they based the expectation that he would aid them in their project. Furthermore, the loyal Federalists felt that the election of Burr would be a heavy blow to the regular Republicans. The Federalists of New York, therefore, decided to support him although, owing to the influence of Hamilton, they did not give him a formal caucus endorsement. The secessionists hoped that, after he became governor, Burr would take New York out of the Union and would figure as a prominent leader in the new confederacy.

Burr, however, failed of election and with his defeat there came the collapse of the secession plan. The project never gave promise of success and was not formidable enough to furnish real cause for alarm. The great majority of the people of New York and New England—including a majority of the Federalists—were not in sympathy with it.

*The Hamil-
ton-Burr duel*

Burr considered that an important factor in his defeat had been the opposition of Hamilton, who in the campaign had denounced him as a "dangerous man." Burr's post-election mood was aggravated by despair, for not only were his political prospects ruined, but he was also financially bankrupt. While in this dangerous frame of mind, he sent a letter to Hamilton asking him to retract the offensive expression. In the correspondence which ensued neither side showed a very conciliatory spirit. The quarrel, therefore, resulted in a challenge sent by Burr to Hamilton. The latter was opposed to duelling and decided not to return Burr's fire if called out; but, as he thought that a refusal to accept the challenge would cost him all his influence, he picked up the gauntlet thrown down by his enemy. Early on a July morning they faced each other at Weehawken for a final settlement of their quarrel. Burr fired the fatal shot and Hamilton was carried away with a mortal wound.

*The election
of 1804*

As Jefferson's first term approached its end he could view the achievements of the period with marked satisfaction. His domestic policy had pleased his original supporters and brought in numerous recruits from the camp of the enemy. By doubling the national domain he had given success a bright tinge of glory. This was, as he said, the harvest time of his public career. It is true that he had aroused the bitterest enmity among some of the leaders of his old political opponents, who, prodded by their prejudices and unfounded fears, were willing to break up the Union rather than have him rule over them; but they could do little more than bite their nails in futile rage.

Jefferson's reputed popularity received the stamp of certainty in the election of 1804. He was nominated by the Republican caucus, with George Clinton of New York as his running mate. The Federalists held no caucus but agreed among themselves to support

Charles C. Pinckney for the Presidency. The results showed that Jefferson had received all the electoral votes but fourteen. Even Massachusetts was found in the Republican column, and only Connecticut was solid in its opposition to the President.

Reproduced from THE PAGEANT OF AMERICA, *Copyright Yale University Press*

THE WHITE HOUSE IN 1805.

CHAPTER XXI

The Difficulties of Neutrality

DOMESTIC AFFAIRS

*T*HE outstanding achievements of Jefferson's first term, except the acquisition of Louisiana, which was a happy accident, were in the realm of home affairs. During his second term, his greatest difficulties were bound up with the foreign relations of the country. He had been remarkably successful in handling the situation at home, but the foreign problems now confronting him demanded a type of leadership which had not been called into requisition by domestic affairs. Whether the President would measure up to the new responsibility was a question on which there was ground for misgivings. And certainly the prospect of retaining his popularity was far from promising. The role which fate had assigned him was that of holding his country to a policy of neutrality in a time of war. The belligerents were playing the leading parts in the world drama, and the minor roles assigned to neutrals could hardly be acted in such a way as to win applause.

The "conspiracy" of Aaron Burr

Not all of the President's attention during his second term was turned to foreign affairs. There were important happenings at home as well as complications abroad. Among the former, probably the most exciting was the trial of Aaron Burr and the events which led to it. After the fatal duel with Hamilton, Burr became a social outcast in the North. He had for some time been at odds with the Republican leaders, and by running for governor against the regular nominee he had sacrificed what little standing he had had with the party. Being both politically and financially bankrupt, he doubtless felt that for him the only road to success and glory lay through some adventure of exceptional boldness. Nor was he in the mood to be restrained by ethical considerations from any scheme toward which ambition might beckon him.

The acquisition of Louisiana had resolved all doubts as to the loyalty of the West, but the feeling against Spain was still intense in that section and might be stirred into belligerence by the right leaders. To Burr, therefore, the West and Southwest seemed to offer a fine opportunity for a profitable adventure. Accordingly, he and his lieutenants organized a plot to carry out his ambitious plan. Just what this plan really was it is now impossible to say, since the scheme as unfolded by him to his various associates was not always the same. Some of them thought that he was planning an expedition against Spanish Mexico, and others that he was trying to establish a buffer state between Louisiana and Mexico. To others still, his purpose seemed to be that of creating a southwestern confederacy to be composed of territory taken from Spain or from the United States or both.

Prominent among his associates was Harman Blennerhassett, a well-to-do Irishman who was living in comfort in the most beautiful surroundings on an island in the Ohio River just below Parkersburg (now West Virginia). The owner of this paradise and his wife became eager converts to the scheme, being tempted by the promise of the opportunity to make a great fortune in land speculation in Louisiana. The prospect of representing the new state as minister to the Court of St. James was also dangled before Blennerhassett. Fired by these hopes, he contributed money, boats, and supplies for the enterprise.

When Burr's arrangements were consummated, an expedition of thirteen flatboats and sixty men embarked from Blennerhassett Island for New Orleans. Burr joined them farther down on the Ohio. General James Wilkinson was in command of the American forces at New Orleans at the time. He had been in communication with Burr and seems to have been a party to the plot; but to what extent he was involved is not clear. Wilkinson was a past master of intrigue and could successfully cover his tracks. The trail he left behind in the Burr "conspiracy" is, therefore, not sufficiently marked to enable one to decide with absolute certainty how far he went along with Burr. Before Burr's expedition reached its destination Wilkinson had decided to desert his cause and turn informer. The report sent by Wilkinson to Washington caused the President to bestir himself against the movement, although hitherto he had been so certain of the loyalty of the Westerners to the Union that he showed little or no concern over Burr's preparations.

When Burr with his little flotilla reached Natchez he learned that *Burr arrested* Wilkinson had betrayed him. He thereupon gave up the expedition *and tried* and fled for safety, leaving his followers to their fate. He was soon afterward arrested and sent to Richmond, Virginia, for trial.

His case came up before a United States circuit court, presided over by Chief Justice Marshall. The trial was protracted to great length and became one of the most noted in the annals of legal history. Personal rancor and political feeling played too great a part in it. Jefferson was anxious for the conviction of the former Vice-President and urged the prosecution in a way unbecoming the high office he occupied. On the other hand, Marshall allowed his enmity to Jefferson to influence his attitude to such an extent as to subject him to the charge of bias. He had Jefferson summoned as a witness in the trial. The President refused to obey the summons, contending that the independence of the executive would be destroyed if its highest official could be ordered to attend the Federal courts. Marshall's rulings in the case were favorable to Burr, and with the instructions issued to it the jury felt obliged to render a verdict of not guilty.

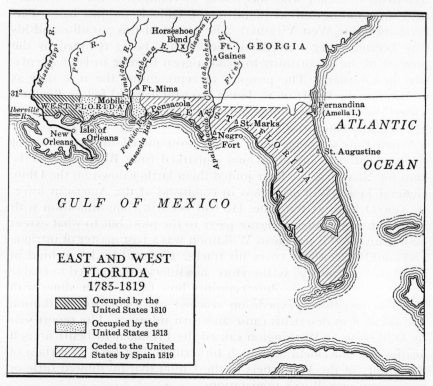

EAST AND WEST
FLORIDA
1783–1819

Occupied by the
United States 1810

Occupied by the
United States 1813

Ceded to the United
States by Spain 1819

The annexation of West Florida

The Westerners were eagerly desirous of gaining possession of West Florida because within its limits were Mobile Bay and the mouths of several rivers flowing into the Gulf of Mexico. They were disappointed that the possession of this territory did not go along with Louisiana. As a concession to this feeling, Livingston advanced a theory whereby the coveted land could be obtained. He contended that the eastern boundary of Louisiana was the Perdido River, and Jefferson and Madison were easily induced to accept this view. This would mean that Napoleon, in ceding Louisiana, had given the United States a claim to West Florida.

Jefferson was extremely desirous of obtaining West Florida. In furtherance of this aim he sent Monroe to Madrid with instructions to negotiate a treaty which would cover American claims against the Spanish government and settle the dispute as to Florida. Napoleon, however, would not allow the Spanish government to make any concessions as to either the spoliation claims or Florida, and Monroe's mission ended in failure. Further efforts on the part of Jefferson to bring Spain to an agreement were unsuccessful and the Florida problem was passed on to his successor.

Not long after Madison's accession there came to him the opportunity of seizing the land which Jefferson had been unable to obtain by negotiation. Spanish authority in the Floridas was weak and the population was mixed and turbulent. Incited by the spirit of revolution then abroad in Spanish America, the inhabitants in the northwestern part of West Florida (a large majority of whom were Americans) rose in revolt and captured Baton Rouge (1810). A convention of the insurgents declared the independence of West Florida and asked that it be annexed to the United States. Taking advantage of this opportunity, the President seized a good portion of the province. At the end of that same year (December 7, 1810) Governor Claiborne, of the Territory of Orleans, took formal possession of the land as far east as the Pearl River. During the war with Great Britain, military necessity was given as a pretext for an act of Congress (February 12, 1813) by which the President was authorized to take over the remainder of West Florida, and shortly thereafter General Wilkinson occupied the land to the Perdido River.

FOREIGN AFFAIRS

Early in Jefferson's first term there was for a brief period a lull in the European conflict. War was renewed in 1803 and continued (with one short break) until Napoleon was sent to St. Helena a dozen years later. The United States again had to adjust itself to a situation of international strife. As had been the case under Washington and Adams, the war was in some respects favorable to American economic interests. It increased the demand for American food products and other raw materials. The belligerent nations did not have enough ships for both war and commercial purposes, and American ships were therefore actively engaged in the carrying trade. This meant high prices for farm products and large profits for shipowners. Agriculture, commerce and shipbuilding, and allied industries were, therefore, reaping a rich harvest.

Effect of the European war on the United States

There was, however, one serious drawback to this artificial prosperity. England and France, the leading belligerents, were trying to starve one another into submission. In furtherance of this aim each tried to prevent neutral trade with its enemy. Accordingly, both governments imposed restrictions on commerce which violated the rights of neutral powers. The United States was the most important of the commercial neutrals and, therefore, protested most strongly against these restraints. The measures of France were in principle just as violative of American rights as those practiced by England; but the latter country enjoyed a great naval superiority over her rival, and therefore instances of interference by her were more numerous than those by France. For this reason, feeling in the United States was more bitter toward England than toward her enemy. The problem of the American government was to protect the interests of its people without being drawn into the conflict. The country wanted to warm itself by the European fire without being burned.

The French victories of Jena and Austerlitz, and the English naval victory of Trafalgar, clearly demonstrated the primacy of France on the land and of England on the sea. At one time Napoleon was in control of the whole western coast of Europe. Each of the contestants was determined to use its power to prevent its opponent from benefitting by the neutral carrying trade, and neither was willing to allow its best weapon to be dulled by consideration for the rights of neutrals.

A second grievance of the United States against England arose out of her impressment of American seamen. It had been the practice in England for a long time to send out press gangs to gather up deserters from the navy and force able-bodied seamen into the service. Merchantmen were searched and seamen taken off and put on warships. Now, as in the first part of the Anglo-French war, American vessels were stopped on the high seas, and British seamen were taken from them for service in the navy. While the intention was to impress only British subjects, nationals of the United States were by mistake sometimes included. In such cases proof of American citizenship secured a release, but an American forced to serve on an English man-of-war was not always in a position to present his case in a fair light. For this reason sailors born and reared in the United States were sometimes pressed into the British service.

Furthermore, the government of the United States did not agree with that of England as to the definition of citizenship. The former took the position that a foreigner, after five years of residence in this country, could if he elected to do so become a citizen of the United States in the same sense as a native-born American. The English authorities, on the other hand, were not willing to concede the right of expatriation to their subjects. "Once an Englishman, always an Englishman," was their contention. The government of the United States therefore protested against the seizure of its British-born subjects, whereas the English government contended that their impressment was a legitimate exercise of its rights.

To the British government the question of impressment was one of prime importance, for the practice was closely bound up with the efficiency of the navy. As the navy was their guarantee of independence and their only protection against starvation, the English people felt that no chance of crippling it should ever be taken. Impressment was necessary to stop the leaks due to desertion. For seamen in considerable number were deserting from the British warships and finding employment on American merchantmen, since the pay was higher and living conditions were better on them than on the English ships.

In connection with the impressment controversy there occurred an unfortunate event at sea which greatly aroused feeling in America. In the summer of 1807 the United States frigate *Chesapeake,* under Captain James Barron, sailed for the Mediterranean Sea. Her armament was new and the guns were not properly placed for action. Captain Barron expected to clear the decks and put the vessel in fighting order during the long voyage. There were on board with Barron three American citizens who had been impressed by the British and had escaped, and one British subject who had enlisted under an assumed name. When the *Chesapeake* sailed out between the capes at the mouth of Chesapeake Bay, she was followed by the British warship, the *Leopard.* When she overtook the *Chesapeake,* the *Leopard* hailed her and asked for the return of English deserters. Captain Barron replied that there were none with him and refused to muster his crew for inspection. Thereupon the *Leopard* fired a broadside into the *Chesapeake.* The latter could not use her guns and for fifteen minutes had to receive the attack without resistance. The *Chesapeake* surrendered, but not until three men had been killed and eighteen wounded. The four alleged deserters were removed to the *Leopard,* and the crippled *Chesapeake* returned to the harbor of Norfolk.

The affair of the Chesapeake

By this highhanded act the emotions of the American people were stirred, very much as they were a century later by the sinking of the *Lusitania.* Federalists were carried along with Republicans in the current of patriotic fervor. Jefferson would have had no difficulty in taking the country into war if he had wished to do so; but he did not want war, even with so good a pretext. He did, however, order all British public vessels away from American waters.

Although Canning, the British foreign minister, at once expressed regret and promised "the most prompt and effectual reparation . . . if the British officers should prove to have been culpable," it was not until 1811 that amends were made for this outrage. At that time the act was disavowed and reparation promised. The surviving American citizens were restored to the *Chesapeake* in dramatic fashion. Expiation came too late, however, to quiet the ill feeling that this grievance and others had aroused among the people of the United States.

The President's refusal to take a belligerent attitude toward the *Chesapeake* incident was branded by chauvinists as a sacrifice of national honor to a cowardly pacifism. This was, however, an unwarranted accusation. Jefferson's courage had been proved on other occasions, and his policy with reference to Tripoli shows that he did not adhere to the doctrine of nonresistance; but he did not favor a resort to arms when peaceable means were open. With him the costs of war in both money and human life were a strong argument against it. Furthermore, the spirit of war was opposed to that of democracy and might lead to tyranny. Then, too, he hoped to force the belligerents into an observance of neutral rights by peaceable coercion. But his unwillingness to make this outrage the occasion of vigorous action brought a sense of humiliation to many patriotic Americans who had no militaristic leanings. It also confirmed Canning in the belief that he could continue to violate American rights without incurring the danger of war.

Jefferson rejects a treaty negotiated with England

In their efforts to cut off supplies from France and the other countries dominated by Napoleon, the British authorities imposed restrictions on American commerce which the United States considered a violation of its rights as a neutral. In carrying out these regulations the English navy made numerous seizures of American vessels. These seizures, and the impressment of American seamen, caused Jefferson to take steps looking toward an understanding with England. A new treaty was especially desirable because the commercial clauses of Jay's Treaty would expire in 1807. Accordingly, William Pinkney was sent as a special commissioner to England to join Monroe, the regular minister there, in an effort to reach an agreement. As a result of their negotiations, a treaty was agreed to by the representatives of the two countries (1806). The terms, however, were less favorable to the United States than the instructions had prescribed. They were rendered absolutely impossible by an unreasonable condition imposed by the British foreign office. Jefferson refused to submit the treaty to the Senate and recalled Monroe.

In 1806 Charles James Fox became Minister of Foreign Affairs in England. He issued an executive order declaring the coast of Europe under blockade from the Elbe to Brest, but the blockade was not to be enforced except between Ostend and Havre. This order gave Napoleon a pretext to issue the Berlin Decree, by which he declared the British Isles under blockade and prohibited all trade with them. As his fleet had been all but driven from the ocean, this was a paper blockade with a vengeance. The British government replied by issuing three Orders in Council, which declared a blockade of the whole coast of Europe from Copenhagen to Trieste. Neutral ships were prohibited from trading at these blockaded ports, except those vessels which had stopped at a British port and paid "transit duties." A month later Napoleon retaliated against these orders by issuing the Milan Decree, which announced that any ship would be seized if it paid these duties, submitted to search by the British, or was found to be on the way to England. *British Orders in Council and the Berlin and Milan Decrees*

If these orders and decrees had been rigidly enforced all of Europe would have been closed to American trade except Russia, Sweden, and Turkey, and for a time Russia also would have been debarred. Napoleon, however, had scarcely any ships on the high seas with which to enforce his decrees, but he could seize offending neutral vessels when they touched at ports controlled by him.

It was hardly to be expected that a self-respecting power of the rank of the United States would tamely acquiesce in these infringements of its rights. The peace-loving President, however, felt that his country should fight for its rights with economic weapons and thus avoid the necessity of going to war. American trade, he thought, was so valuable to the belligerents that they could be frightened into an observance of neutral rights by a threat to withhold this trade from them. By this policy of "peaceable coercion" he proposed to force the warring powers into good behavior. *"Peaceable coercion"*

In keeping with this purpose Congress passed the Nonimportation Act in April, 1806, to become effective in November of that year; but negotiations were pending between the United States and Britain, and its operation was postponed until December 17, 1807. The act prohibited the importation of such British goods as could be obtained from other countries or produced in the United States. It was hoped that this measure would serve as a threat to England and so could be used as a trading point by American ministers in London in the negotiations with the British foreign office. They could offer its repeal for a concession from Britain. It was too weak a policy, however, to have much weight with England. John Randolph characterized it as "a milk-and-water bill! a dose of chicken-broth to be taken nine months hence!" *The Nonimportation Act*

Unfortunately, Randolph's opinion as to the inefficacy of the Nonimportation Act proved correct. As a threat, it had little or no influence on British policy, and by the end of 1807 it was evident that the *The Embargo Act*

American government would be compelled to adopt more vigorous measures or surrender its rights as a neutral. The President, therefore, recommended that Congress impose an embargo on American shipping engaged in trade with the outside world. It was in the middle of this same year that the *Chesapeake-Leopard* affair had occurred and feeling against England was still running high, for no reparation for this outrage had yet been made. Congress, therefore, promptly responded to the President's suggestion and passed the Embargo Act (December 21, 1807). This law prohibited all American vessels to leave port for foreign countries, and required American vessels engaged in the coastwise trade to give bond in a sum of double the value of the vessel and cargo to guarantee that the cargo would be relanded in some port of the United States. Foreign vessels (except those already loaded) could leave the ports of the United States only in ballast. If this law were enforced it would deprive American ships of all participation in foreign trade and would preclude all exports from the United States.[1]

The object of the measure was to deny the belligerents the assistance which they had been receiving from the American carrying trade and to deprive them of the food supplies and raw materials which had been going to them. Jefferson expected that these deprivations would cause a serious disturbance of the economic life of the warring powers and force them to respect American rights. For several reasons this expectation was not realized. In the first place, the law was not strictly enforced, despite the strenuous efforts put forth by the government. Many American vessels at sea at the time the act was passed refused to return to home ports. They could, therefore, continue their activity in the international trade without incurring the penalties of the law. Furthermore, the letter, as well as the spirit, of the measure was disregarded by some vessels, which smuggled goods out through Canada and Florida.

Effect of the act on France

The act did practically no harm to France. In a way it was an aid to Napoleon, for it was in line with his policy of cutting off neutral trade with England. It also gave him an excuse to perpetrate a new act of injustice on American shipping. By a decree issued at Bayonne, American ships in French ports were all seized by the French authorities. When a protest against this wrong was made by the American minister, Napoleon replied that under the Embargo Act American ships were not allowed in foreign ports and, therefore, these

[1] The Embargo Act did not prohibit the bringing in of imports by foreign ships. It discouraged importation, however, by the provision that these foreign ships could not carry a cargo on the return trip. Furthermore, the Nonimportation Act, which went into effect just before the Embargo Act was passed, prohibited the importation of certain English goods.

ships were really English vessels. He even had the effrontery to contend that he was helping Jefferson enforce the Embargo Act.

Nor did the embargo interfere with the economic life of England as much as had been expected. Owing to a shortage of raw materials, there was some suffering among the laboring classes, especially among the workers in cotton mills. But at this time, because of the friendship of Spain and Portugal, the South American ports were thrown open to England, and this trade was a partial compensation for the loss of that of the United States. Besides, the new restrictive policy was a positive benefit to English shipowners, since it lessened the competition of their American rivals and gave them increased opportunities in the carrying trade.

Effect on England

This self-denying ordinance was a two-edged sword. The edge which was expected to cut into foreign interests was dulled by the circumstances mentioned above. On the other hand, the edge which slashed into American rights was keen. American ships were tied up in the harbors, to the great loss of their owners. This inactivity struck a great blow to commerce, shipbuilding, and allied industries. The ban on exports deprived agricultural produce of its foreign market and caused a great decline in prices. Cotton, tobacco, wheat, and other farm products became a drug on the market.

Opposition in the United States

There was, therefore, strong opposition to the measure, much of which took the form of criticism of the Administration. The antagonism was greatest in New England, where the Federalists were most numerous and economic objection was reinforced by bitterness of partisan feeling. The opponents of Jefferson welcomed this opportunity to attack him, and in New England they even threatened nullification. The Virginia Republicans, on the other hand, out of loyalty to the party, accepted the act, although it was interfering with their interests. The Federalist legislature of Massachusetts pronounced the act oppressive and unconstitutional and advised the people of the state to unite to prevent its enforcement. The Federalist leaders in Congress denounced it with equal vehemence. The Federalists were now advocating the doctrine of '98, and Madison and Jefferson, the authors of this doctrine, were championing a measure as nationalistic as any proposed by Hamilton.

So great was the opposition to the embargo in the East that a number of Republican Congressmen from New England and New York co-operated with their Federalist colleagues against the President. Accordingly, the Embargo Act was repealed and the Nonintercourse Act substituted for it. On March 1, 1809, Jefferson, with apparent willingness but real reluctance, signed the new act and by so doing acknowledged the failure of a measure of peaceable coercion

Repeal of the Embargo Act

in the efficacy of which he had strongly believed. He always contended, however, that had the embargo been adhered to and rigidly enforced, war with England would have been prevented.

The election of 1808

The election of 1808 came at a time when the excitement over the embargo was running high. This measure furnished the Federalists with a much-desired issue and its unpopularity gave them hope of success. Their nominees were C. C. Pinckney and Rufus King, for President and Vice-President, respectively. Resolutions were adopted by several state legislatures urging Jefferson to run for a third term. In response to these requests he issued a statement announcing his decision not to be a candidate and giving his reasons. Old age was one of the reasons mentioned, but a more important one was the feeling that eight years was long enough for any President to serve. If Presidents were allowed to succeed themselves indefinitely the office might become one of life tenure and ultimately hereditary. In refusing a third term he set a precedent, or confirmed one set by Washington, in favor of limiting the Presidency to two successive terms. This precedent was closely followed from that time until 1940.

There were three prominent aspirants for the Republican nomination—Madison, Monroe, and George Clinton. Jefferson was outwardly neutral, but really used his influence in favor of Madison. This insured Madison's nomination. The Republicans in Congress held a caucus and nominated Madison for the first place and Clinton for the second. The friends of Monroe and Clinton were disgruntled at the rejection of their candidates, but Monroe's followers voted for Madison in the election. Clinton, however, received six electoral votes for the Presidency. Madison and Clinton were elected by a large majority of the electoral vote, though the Republican majority in Congress was considerably reduced. The Federalists carried every New England state except Vermont.

Appraisal of Jefferson's statesmanship

Jefferson's foreign policy in his second term cost him much of the popularity he had won by his domestic policy in the first, and during the last few months he was quite unhappy. The opposition to the embargo emboldened the Federalists to redouble their attacks, and his old enemies were given aid and comfort by insurgent Republicans, who were opposed to his policy of peaceable coercion. He, therefore, left Washington with a bad taste in his mouth. So far as his popularity was concerned, there was much truth in John Randolph's saying, that the four lean kine had eaten up the four fat kine. When he departed from the little capital never to return, his enemies doubtless felt that his Presidential career would be handed down to posterity as a failure. This, however, has not been the case; for after partisan feeling had cooled down and his achievements were viewed in the clear light of objectivity, many of them stood out as monuments of a wise and farseeing statesmanship.

His statesmanship combined in well-balanced proportions the three elements of opportunism, idealism, and practical politics. As an opportunist he could point to the great achievements of his first term—practical measures which met the needs of the day. When we consider his unswerving faith in the people and his ability to appraise correctly the present, to see into the future, and to inspire the co-operation of his lieutenants, we can readily understand why a grateful posterity has placed the name of the father of American democracy along with those of Pericles and the Gracchi in a list of the world's great tribunes of the people.

THE ADMINISTRATION OF JAMES MADISON: FOREIGN PROBLEMS

Personality of Madison

James Madison was the logical successor of Jefferson. For eight years he had served as the latter's premier and had been in entire agreement with him on all major issues. At the inauguration ceremonies Jefferson beamed with delight. This feeling was partly one of relief and partly one of anticipation—relief from the public cares of Washington and anticipation of the private joys of Monticello. But probably the highest satisfaction of the occasion came from seeing his protégé and warm personal friend elevated to the highest place in the gift of the people.

For the serious responsibilities with which he was confronted, the new President had some fine qualifications. With these were associated certain shortcomings which at times might prove a handicap. He was well educated and had probably given more study and thought to political science than any other American of his day. Furthermore, practically all of his adult years had been devoted to public affairs. As he was short of stature and not very robust in health, Madison did not have as forceful a personality as did his predecessors. A timidity which might easily be taken for weakness detracted somewhat from the impressiveness of his manner. Like the Virginia planters generally, his social habits were characterized by marked simplicity and informality. With a sense of humor to enliven his cordiality, he gave promise of being a success so far as the social side of his office was concerned. If, however, there had been any doubts on this score they would have been dispelled when it was recalled that the charming "Dolly" was to be mistress of the White House.

His Cabinet

Madison was hampered in the choice of his Cabinet by an unfortunate situation in his party. As the affairs of the Treasury were going on smoothly, he wanted to transfer Gallatin to the State Department. He felt, however, that the opposition of certain Republican Senators would prevent his confirmation for this place and therefore he retained him as Secretary of the Treasury. Prominent in the list of Gallatin's opponents were Senators William B. Giles of Virginia and Samuel Smith of Maryland. To placate this group Madison appointed as Secretary of State, Robert Smith, the incompetent brother of the Maryland Senator. He held this responsible position for two years although the President had to write all the important dispatches sent in his name. At the end of this period Smith's resignation was called for and James Monroe became Secretary of State. The other members of the Cabinet were men of ordinary ability.

The Nonintercourse Act

A few days before Madison's accession, the Embargo Act had been superseded by the Nonintercourse Act. By the latter measure all trade between the United States and England and France, including their colonies or dependencies, was suspended. If, however, either France or England should withdraw its restrictions on American commerce, intercourse with that power would be reopened by the President. It was expected that this law would be liberally interpreted and so would open up considerable trade to American shipping.

Nonintercourse with England suspended and renewed

Madison had been in office only six weeks when he came to an understanding with the British minister, D. M. Erskine, as to the commercial dispute. According to this agreement Great Britain would cancel the Orders in Council so far as American ships were concerned and the United States would renew intercourse with England. As the Nonintercourse Act would still apply to France, it would give England a decided advantage. For three months, trade between the two countries was open, much to the satisfaction of American merchants and shipowners. Then Madison received notice that Erskine had exceeded his instructions and the treaty was repudiated by Canning. Thereupon nonintercourse with Britain was revived.

Macon's Bill No. 2

The policy of peaceable coercion was weakened by the substitution of the Nonintercourse Act for the Embargo Act. This policy was still further attenuated when the former measure was repealed and Macon's Bill No. 2 was passed (May 1, 1810).[1] This act provided for the reopening of trade with both England and France, with the added provision that if one of these countries removed its restrictions on American trade and the other did not, nonintercourse would be revived with the power that refused to do so.

The new act gave Napoleon an opportunity to play a trick on the

---

[1] This measure was so called because the first bill offered by Macon had been defeated.

guileless American President. He had his Minister of Foreign Affairs, the Duke of Cadore, write to the American minister at Paris (August 5, 1810) announcing that the decrees of Berlin and Milan had been revoked but with the understanding that the English would cancel their Orders in Council. Madison accepted this as a pledge that France would rescind her decrees and overlooked the condition which was thereto attached. Therefore, on November 2, acting in accordance with the Macon Act, he announced the revival of nonintercourse with Great Britain. But American vessels were still seized in French ports, and the British foreign office was correct in contending that the French decrees had not been actually cancelled. The English government, therefore, refused to revoke its Orders in Council. *Napoleon's trick*

Relations between the United States and England were gradually becoming more menacing. The situation was aggravated by the presence off Sandy Hook of British cruisers, which were stopping American vessels to search them for deserters. An effort by the American navy to put an end to this practice led to a battle off the Virginia coast between the American frigate *President* and the British sloop *Little Belt* (May, 1811). After a fight of fifteen minutes the latter was disabled, with nine of her crew killed and twenty-three wounded. The incident aroused a spirit of exultation in the American people, who regarded it as a just requital for the *Chesapeake* insult. It also whetted their appetite for war. *Encounter between the President and the Little Belt*

DOMESTIC PROBLEMS

While foreign affairs presented the greatest difficulties of Madison's two terms, other problems arose which were of a purely domestic nature. One of the most important of these was that of providing the country with a sound and adequate financial system. The charter of the First Bank of the United States would expire in 1811 if it were not renewed. In 1808 the American stockholders of the bank petitioned for an extension of the charter. It was not, however, until the session of 1810-11 that Congress gave serious attention to the application. Gallatin urged the renewal of the charter and declared that the management of the bank had been sound and conservative. The constitutionality of the bank was assumed by him, as the charter had "for a number of years been acted upon or acquiesced in as if constitutional by all the constituted authorities of the nation." It was, he thought, a necessary means for the "exercise of legitimate powers of government." *An unsuccessful effort to recharter the Bank of the United States*

This opinion was not accepted, however, by all the Republican

Congressmen, for some of them still held to the old states' rights view as to a national bank. Others objected to it on the unreasonable ground that a large proportion of the shares was owned by Englishmen. Opposition also came from those who were interested in state banks; for if the operations of the national bank and its branches were discontinued, state banks would have a greater opportunity and would multiply rapidly. These more or less honest objectors, together with the enemies of Gallatin, were able to defeat the measure, but by a very close margin. The bank, therefore, went out of existence the year before the War of 1812 started. This was unfortunate, since the bank would have been a valuable aid to the government in financing the war.

The Territory of Orleans

In 1804 by an act of Congress the southern and most populous part of Louisiana was organized into the Territory of Orleans. At first the people had no voice in their own government since all their rulers were appointed by the President. Shortly afterwards, however, the territory was granted a representative assembly and the right to send a spokesman-delegate to Congress. Later (1810) the Territory of Orleans was enlarged by the addition of a part of West Florida which had been taken from Spain, and soon thereafter it asked for admission to the Union as the State of Louisiana with its present limits.

Louisiana admitted as a state: Opposition of the Federalists

It will be remembered that the Federalists had offered violent opposition to the purchase of Louisiana. A like attitude was shown by them toward the proposal that Louisiana be admitted into the Union. To admit this new state would be to establish a precedent which would lead to the formation of a number of trans-Mississippi commonwealths each having the same rights and privileges as the old states. If this were done New England and the older section in general would lose prestige and power in the councils of the nation. Federalist leaders in New England, therefore, contended that the creation of new states out of territory acquired after 1787 could not legally be done without the consent of all the original parties to the Constitutional compact (the Original Thirteen States). Their leader in the House, Josiah Quincy of Massachusetts, said: "If this bill passes, it is my deliberate opinion that it is virtually a dissolution of this Union; that it will free the States from their moral obligation, and as it will be the right of all, so it will be the duty of some, definitely to prepare for a separation, amicably if they can, violently if they must." The Republicans paid no heed to such Federalist arguments, and in accordance with the pledge made in the treaty of purchase (see p. 330), passed an act admitting Louisiana as a state on equal terms with the other states.

Westward expansion was threatening the Indians with the loss of all their lands. Out of the area reserved to the natives by the Treaty of Greenville (1795), large sections for settlement by the whites had been acquired by later treaties. William Henry Harrison, Governor of Indiana Territory, was encouraging these cessions and the Indian domain was gradually shrinking. Furthermore, contact with the white man was causing deterioration in the character of the Indians, who were copying the vices more readily than the virtues of the frontiersmen. Under such conditions it was only natural that friction should develop between the two races. *Indian troubles*

At this time the Indians of the Northwest had as their leaders Tecumseh and his brother, the Prophet. The former was an able statesman and patriot and wished to save his people from the unhappy fate to which they were hastening. In this aim he was greatly aided by the Prophet, who as a religious leader preached a moral reformation. His people were urged to throw off the white man's vices and return to the simple virtues of the olden time. Drunkenness was especially decried. The Prophet, therefore, presented the rare spectacle of a temperance leader among the Indians. Tecumseh's plan was for all the Indians, north and south, to unite into one great confederacy to prevent encroachment upon their lands. Land cessions in the future should be made only by the joint action of all the tribes. He preferred a policy of peace to one of war, but felt that his people should resist any effort to push them farther toward the west and should defend their rights by arms if necessary. *Tecumseh and the Prophet*

In 1811 he went to the south to enlist the aid of the Indians in that section. Taking advantage of his absence, Harrison led a force to the Prophet's town, located near the confluence of the Wabash and Tippecanoe Rivers. Here a battle took place in which the whites lost more heavily than the natives; but as the latter left the place next day and the whites burned the village, the engagement was hailed by the Westerners as a great victory. The Battle of Tippecanoe was the beginning of a war which continued in the form of depredations on the frontier until the Indian conflict merged into the War of 1812. *The Battle of Tippecanoe*

The occupation of the West by American settlers ran counter to the interests of the fur traders who were operating from the British posts in Canada. That these traders would gain greater profits if the western lands were held by Indians than if appropriated by white men cannot be doubted. It is also true that certain Canadians were selling arms and ammunition to the Indians. But whether the Canadian authorities were in any way responsible for these sales is a question on which American and British officials held contrary opinions. Governor Harrison contended that they were, since some of the guns and powder captured at Tippecanoe had come from the British post *The Canadian authorities charged with inciting the Indians* at Malden. Governor Brock of Upper Canada, however, denied that the Canadian government had had any part in inciting the natives. He admitted that individual British, as well as American, traders had sold arms and ammunition to the red men, but maintained that the government officials had had no agency in this traffic. On the contrary, they had, he maintained, tried to dissuade the Indians from hostilities.

In all probability the authorities of Upper Canada were opposed to an Indian war at that time. They foresaw that a premature attack on the settlers would result in defeat and that the loss of morale occasioned by such a defeat would weaken the natives and make them less valuable as possible allies. Whatever may have been the facts in the case, there is no doubt that the Westerners believed that the British government was inciting the western Indians against the Americans and was supplying them with arms and ammunition. The frontiersmen felt, therefore, that they could never enjoy security against Indian attack until American had superseded British control in Canada. The hope of taking Canada was, therefore, a strong motive for favoring war.

TECUMSEH.

CHAPTER XXII

The War of 1812

WAR IS DECLARED AGAINST ENGLAND

*I*N the mid-term election of 1810 strong opposition was expressed *The "War* toward the foreign policy of the Administration. About half of the *Hawks"* Congressmen who had voted for Macon's Bill No. 2 were defeated and a large number of seats were filled by new men. Prominent in the list of new members of the House of Representatives were Henry Clay of Kentucky, John C. Calhoun of South Carolina, Peter B. Porter of New York, and Felix Grundy of Tennessee. These leaders and others who worked with them were tired of what they considered the weak-kneed policy of peaceable coercion and clamored for war. John Randolph dubbed them "War Hawks." In the fall of 1811 they were in control of the House and chose as Speaker, Henry Clay, one of the most brilliant and belligerent of the group.

Clay was born in eastern Virginia but had gone to Kentucky in *Henry Clay* early manhood. Owing to the limited means of his family, he did not have in his youth good opportunities for education. He was fortunate, however, in being able to study law under Chancellor George Wythe, one of the ablest of the legal lights in the Old Dominion. Young Clay had not been long in his new home before his magnetic personality and brilliant oratory were marking out for him a promising career in politics. Although he was now only in his thirty-fifth year, he had been elected twice to the Kentucky legislature and had served for two short periods in the United States Senate. As presiding officer of the House, he established a new tradition in that body. Hitherto the Speaker had acted as an impartial moderator; Clay determined to use the great power of the office in favor of his war policy, and committee appointments were made with that in view.

Madison was for a while undecided as to what attitude he should *Madison's* take toward war. In time, however, he identified himself with the *attitude* war party. As a preliminary to war he advocated an embargo on *toward war* American ships, and Congress in April voted an embargo of ninety days. The purpose of this was to get American merchantmen home before hostilities started. In a message to Congress (June 1, 1812) he reviewed the grievances that the United States had suffered at the

351

hands of England. These aggressions, he declared, constituted a state of war on the side of Great Britain against the United States. "Whether the United States shall continue passive under these progressive usurpations and these accumulating wrongs" or shall oppose "force to force in defense of their national rights," he left it to Congress to determine. His message was thus a virtual, though not an actual, recommendation for war.

Just what arguments the War Hawks used in the conversion of the President are not known with absolute certainty. One of the traditional explanations is that Clay warned him that his nomination by the Republican caucus would be contingent upon his support of a war policy. There is no proof that Clay ever gave him this warning; but Madison knew that he would probably not be renominated if he did not satisfy the War Hawks as to his position. Whether he was influenced by such considerations no one can possibly say.

The declaration of war

Acting on the President's suggestion, the young hotspurs pushed through Congress a declaration of war on June 18, 1812. The vote in its favor, however, was not overwhelming. The Federalists of the Northeast opposed the declaration, and some Republicans either refused to vote or voted against it. One of the most bitter of the opponents of war was John Randolph of Roanoke. The War Hawks, he declared, repeated with "whip-poor-will" monotony the war cry "Canada! Canada! Canada!" The Southern and Western members, however, were almost unanimous for war. From the four frontier states of Vermont, Ohio, Kentucky, and Tennessee, only one vote against the declaration was cast. On the other hand, there was a feeling among many thoughtful Americans that England was fighting for the rights of self-determination and constitutional government, whereas Napoleon was trying to impose a dictatorship on Europe. By attacking the mother country the people of the United States were thus giving aid and comfort to a cause which they detested and were combatting one with which they were in sympathy.[1]

Why war was declared against England rather than France

One naturally wonders why the United States selected Great Britain rather than France for war, since its grievances against the latter power were in principle very much the same as those against the former. So strong was this feeling that Calhoun was in favor of declaring war on both England and France, and Madison seriously discussed with Jefferson the possibility of naming both belligerents

---

[1] It ought to be added that this view was not accepted by a majority of the American people. The Republicans, in the main, felt that the success of Napoleon would lead to the acceptance throughout Europe of many of the liberal principles of the French Revolution.

in the declaration. But to have fought on both sides at once would
have been the height of folly.

There were several reasons for the choice of England as the enemy
rather than France. As England had a strong navy on the high seas
and France did not, the complaints against the former country were
more numerous than those against the latter. Nor had any French
infringements of American rights been so dramatic and anger-stir-
ring as the attack on the *Chesapeake*. Blame for Indian troubles
could be placed on England but not on France. Probably, however,
the most important of all the considerations was that the Americans
could strike at England in her Canadian provinces and could not get
at the French possessions. Canada, it was thought, would be an easy
prey for the American forces. The small population there of about
a half-million was scattered over a long, narrow area, and it was not
expected that the Canadians would offer much resistance. Clay
boasted that the Kentucky militia alone could capture Montreal and
Quebec. Jefferson expressed the opinion that the taking of Canada
would be only a matter of marching. Great Britain was kept busy by
Napoleon on the other side of the ocean, and the Canadian provinces
were not strong enough to put up a vigorous unaided fight. It could
not be foreseen that after two years Napoleon would be defeated and
Britain would be free to turn her entire attention to the conflict with
the United States. Florida could also be seized, to balance the hoped-
for additions to the North, since the war would afford a good excuse
to attack Spain, the ally of England. This intention was expressed
by Clay as follows: "I feel anxious not only to add the Floridas to
the South, but the Canadas to the North of this empire." "The conquest of Canada is in your power. Is it nothing to extinguish the
torch that lights up savage warfare?"

While America was thus advancing toward war, conditions in *British Orders
in Council
withdrawn*
Europe were becoming more favorable to peace between the two
English-speaking nations. During the winter of 1811-12 the strain of
war was bearing heavily upon the British people. Napoleon's Continental System (the policy of closing the European countries to English trade) was at the height of its success, and British commerce was
excluded from all of western Europe. Commerce between the United
States and Britain was outlawed by the revival of nonintercourse. A
failure in the wheat crop in England had produced an unusual scarcity of food, and there were three hundred thousand English soldiers in Spain who were dependent upon the United States for most
of their food supplies. Nonintercourse was, therefore, greatly hampering the success of British arms in the Spanish Peninsula, as well

as producing a scarcity of food at home and economic distress in the manufacturing towns. Manufacturers could not find sale for their wares, and the closing of mills was causing riots among the workmen. Deputations from the manufacturing centers appeared before Parliament, urging the revocation of the Orders in Council as a means to the reopening of the American trade. Parliament was slow to act, but finally, on June 16, 1812, Lord Castlereagh announced in the House of Commons that the Orders in Council would be withdrawn immediately. This action came too late, however, for two days later war against England was declared by the American Congress.

Could an Atlantic cable have prevented war?

The question has often been asked whether an Atlantic cable could have prevented war. To answer this question in the affirmative would be to overlook some important factors. It is true that with the revocation of the Orders in Council there went a cancellation of all the measures in restraint of American commerce except those connected with impressment; but the continuance of this latter practice, together with the alleged incitement of the Indians by British officials, was considered by the War Hawks as adequate grounds for war. Furthermore, the ill feeling caused by a long period of increasing friction had aroused a spirit of belligerence in the minds and hearts of the people of the United States. The war therefore went on, with the slogan "free trade and sailors' rights."

The election of 1812

The Presidential election of 1812 gave the people an opportunity to register their attitude toward war. Madison was renominated by the Republican Congressional caucus, and Elbridge Gerry of Massachusetts was selected as his running mate. The New York Republicans, who had for some time been chafing under Virginia's dominance in the party, nominated DeWitt Clinton for the Presidency. He was endorsed by the Federalists and supported by the antiwar Republicans. The war thus became the issue in the campaign. A vote for Madison was a vote for continuing the struggle; whereas a vote for Clinton was a vote for coming to terms with England. In the election the sections lined up very much as their representatives in Congress had done on the declaration of war. Clinton received the support of all the New England states except Vermont, and all the middle states but Pennsylvania, with Maryland divided. All the western and southern states were for Madison. The majority for Madison in the Electoral College was not large, and the popular vote showed that sentiment in favor of war was far from unanimous.

LACK OF PREPAREDNESS

Lack of unity of spirit

The United States was unprepared for war in 1812 in practically every particular. In the first place, there was a woeful lack of that unity of spirit which usually characterizes successful war. Madison was aware of the opposition to the war on the part of certain sections, but he hoped that all coldness and indifference would give way to the heat of the contest. When the flag of the country was thrown forward, he said, "the people would press onward to defend it." He was, however, sadly disappointed in this expectation. As soon as war was declared, thirty-four Federalist members of Congress signed a protest against it, which was broadcast over the country. Nor did this opposition cease after the military campaign had warmed up. This attitude of protest was maintained by Federalist New England to the end, and the success of American arms was hampered by the positive and negative opposition of this section. National spirit was at a very low ebb. For a long time the rights of the states had been emphasized and the powers of the general government minimized by political agitators, and this propaganda had reversed the trend toward nationalism which had been started by the Revolutionary War.

To carry on a war with England, who proved herself in a few years to be the world's greatest power, the United States had a standing army of less than seven thousand men. Jefferson, like one of his disciples of a century later (W. J. Bryan), felt that a large standing army was unnecessary, as the people would spring to arms overnight in defense of their country whenever it was attacked. Republican policy, therefore, had been to rely mainly on volunteers and militia in time of war. Higher pay and land bounties were now offered to volunteers, but despite these inducements the number of recruits for the regular army were comparatively few. In the entire country there were about seven hundred thousand militiamen to be drawn from; but the requisitions on the states for militia were rarely if ever responded to with alacrity and in some cases were positively refused. Even after militia contingents had been mustered into the service, at critical times numbers of them refused to leave their states or the country at the command of their officers. Owing to these drawbacks only about fifty-six thousand men were enrolled in the American armies during the entire war—including regulars, volunteers, and militia. At no time did a commander have in his fighting line a force of more than six thousand men.

The army small and inefficient

The militiamen who entered the service had had no training to speak of, and they—as well as the volunteers—were, for all practical purposes, raw recruits. The molding of this raw material into a trained army called for efficient officers. But the officers of the little regular army were not equal to this task. Many of them were incompetent. Most of them had had no experience in commanding large bodies of men. Improvement in such conditions could come only from experience in actual fighting. It was not, therefore, until near the end of the war that the American soldiers had been disciplined into efficient troops.

The general management of the army was also in very poor hands. The ranking major general was Henry Dearborn, who had acted as a deputy commissary general in the Revolution. He was now sixty-one years old and was overcautious, dilatory, and incompetent in general. Above him was the Secretary of War, William Eustis, who was not fitted for the place. At the end of the first year he resigned, but his successor was not much, if any, better. It was not until 1814, when Monroe took charge, that the War Department had an efficient head. Furthermore, the President, who was properly characterized as a "master of arguments but not of men," was not a suitable person to direct the management of a war. The fortifications were old and inadequate, and many of them had been designed mainly for defense against the Indians. There was also a scarcity of supplies and munitions.

Small navy

The American navy was ludicrously small compared with that of the Mistress of the Seas. The number of men serving on British war-ships was thirty times as great as that on American public vessels, and in the number of ships the British navy had as great a preponderance. As an aid to the little American navy, there were over five hundred privateers, which were markedly successful in capturing enemy merchant ships. The fighting craft of the United States were well built and the crews were well trained. The American merchant and fishing vessels afforded a good school for the training of seamen, and from them valuable recruits could be drawn for service on warships and privateers. The Barbary wars had afforded officers experience in actual fighting and so there were a number of trained commanders. Consequently, the little navy gave an excellent account of itself.

Financial affairs poorly managed

The country was not in a proper financial condition to stand the economic strain caused by war. The refusal of Congress to continue the national bank had left Federal finances without the machinery needed in making loans. The stabilizing effect of a great financial institution was also lacking, and the state banks (which had increased rapidly in number) were released from much-needed disciplinary restraints. Partly because notes were overissued, and partly because the gold of the country gravitated toward New England, by the end of 1814 every bank in the country west of the Hudson River had suspended specie payment. As the government kept its money in state banks, it lost millions of dollars by this failure of the banks to meet their obligations. These losses helped to bring the Treasury into temporary bankruptcy.

Although the people were prosperous and Gallatin had paid off more than one half of the national debt, the public revenue was small, and even without war a deficit for the year was forecast. The war would greatly increase the amount of this deficit. The reason for this gloomy prospect was that the duty on imports was the chief source of revenue, and the restrictions which had been put on trade had greatly reduced imports. As John Randolph had complained, the country had been "embargoed and non-intercoursed almost into consumption." Gallatin recommended new taxes to finance the war and even suggested an internal tax, one which he had formerly denounced so loudly; but Congress was deaf to his wise advice and voted no new taxes for a year. Indeed, it was not until the last year of the war that it was willing to levy the necessary taxes.

Most of the money for financing the war had to be raised by borrowing. It was not easy to procure funds in this way, since the financial interests, located mainly in New England and New York, were not in sympathy with the war and were not disposed to lend financial assistance to its support. Bonds were sold below their par value although they yielded a high rate of interest (sometimes as high as seven and one-half per cent). Only about one third of the cost of the war was met by taxes, and the remainder had to be raised by loans and treasury notes.

The young republic had one great advantage in the struggle with its mighty antagonist. This was geographical position. The width of the Atlantic rendered difficult the transportation of men and supplies from England to the seat of war in the slow-sailing vessels of that day. The vast extent of its territory was also in favor of the United States. "The attempts of England to penetrate into the great interior would be like the blows of a sledge-hammer struck into a bin of wheat: a few kernels would be bruised or destroyed, but the iron would soon bury itself harmlessly just under the surface of the mass."[1] Besides, England was engaged in a life-and-death struggle with Napoleon and prior to his overthrow could expend only a minor part of her energies in the American war.

The advantage of geographical position

MILITARY EVENTS: "ON TO CANADA," 1812

The plan of campaign for the United States was to strike at Canada at three points. An expedition against Montreal was to be led by General Henry Dearborn, the senior commanding officer, who was to proceed by way of Lake Champlain; an attack on the Cana-

The American plan of campaign

---

[1] K. C. Babcock, *Rise of American Nationality* (Harper and Brothers), 82.

dian center was to be made across the Niagara River by Generals Stephen Van Rensselaer and Alexander Smyth; and in the west, Upper Canada was to be invaded by General William Hull, using Detroit as his starting point.

The execution of these plans involved serious difficulties. In the frontier regions where military operations would have to be performed there were no roads worthy of the name, and the obstacles to the transportation of men and supplies were very great. The Indians in the Northwest were aiding the British, and this added greatly to the difficulties of the invading troops. Furthermore, control of Lakes Erie and Ontario, especially the former, was a *sine qua non* of success. Against the advice of Hull, the Washington authorities decided to proceed with this program without first securing control of Lake Erie.

The plan would have been a good one if it had been executed efficiently. If the expeditions had gone forward simultaneously under capable leadership, the three armies would have converged on Montreal and gained possession of Canada. But there was no concert of action, and at the head of each army was a commander who was not fitted for his place.

The surrender of Detroit Hull had the misfortune to lead the first advance against Canada. He had marched to Detroit from Dayton, Ohio, with a force of two thousand men, made up of regulars and militia. Most of his troops were ill equipped, undisciplined, and insubordinate. A leader of strong character and winsome personality might have inspired their loyalty and commanded their obedience; but Hull was not such a leader. He had performed valiant service in the Revolutionary War, but by this time his sixty years had brought on a premature spiritual dotage. He was dilatory, overcautious, indecisive, and lacking in courage. On the other hand, Isaac Brock, the British commander, was one of the ablest of all the military leaders that figured in the war. He was now in early middle life and his faculties were at their best. In him were combined the wisdom of maturity and experience with the daring and resourcefulness of youth.

Leaving Detroit, Hull crossed the Canadian border and marched toward Malden. When he learned that the British were collecting a strong force at Malden and that Tecumseh and his Indians had joined the British, he was frightened into retreat and retired to Detroit. Brock followed up his advantage by threatening to attack Detroit. He demanded the surrender of the town, intimating that he might not be able to prevent atrocities on the part of his Indian allies if an attack had to be made. After some hesitation, Hull complied and surrendered not only Detroit but all of Michigan—and that without firing a shot (August 16, 1812).

General Hull was tried by court-martial and convicted of cowardice. He was sentenced to be shot but was pardoned by the President in consideration of his record in the Revolutionary War. In this way responsibility for this great defeat was laid upon this unlucky general. But Hull's incompetence and cowardice were not the only causes of this blunder. The failure of the War Department to push forward the other portions of the plan left Brock free to use the greater part of his forces against Hull. By leaving Britain in control of Lake Erie there was added another factor in this disgraceful performance. Under such conditions even a capable general might have failed.

The attack on Canada at Niagara proved almost as great a disaster *The Niagara* to the American cause as the surrender of Hull. General Van Rens- *campaign* selaer, who commanded the troops there, was, according to Monroe, "a weak and incompetent man with high pretensions." A part of his force crossed the river and secured a lodgment on Queenstown Heights. General Brock was killed in an effort to drive the invaders from this position. Reinforcements came to the British, and the Americans were outnumbered and defeated with a loss of more than a thousand in killed, wounded, and captured. While this battle was in progress, a thousand American militiamen looked on from the New York side of the river and refused to go to the aid of their fellow countrymen. The excuse given for this unpatriotic attitude was that their officers had no authority to lead them out of their own state into Canada.

Van Rensselaer resigned and was succeeded by General Alexander Smyth, who was more incompetent than his predecessor. After much foolish boasting, he made a weak effort to advance against the British, which was a grotesque failure. It was now too late in the season for another campaign, and so this abortive movement ended for the year the attempt at invasion at the center.

The Americans were disheartened by these defeats. Nor did any *The campaign* consolation come to them from the operations of their troops in *in the north* the north. The commander of this force, General Dearborn, did not advance promptly against Montreal, although he had at Platts- burg, on Lake Champlain, the largest and most promising army that had ever flown the Stars and Stripes. His delay was due in part to his incompetence and in part to certain negotiations looking toward peace which he had been carrying on with Admiral Warren. The prospect for peace faded, and in November he marched to the

Canadian border. His militiamen refused to go farther, and this refusal, together with his fear of an approaching British contingent, caused him to return to Plattsburg.

For the disastrous results of the land campaigns of the first year, the President and Secretary of War must bear a considerable share of the blame. Secretary Eustis' unfitness for his place was recognized and he was superseded by General Armstrong, who was also

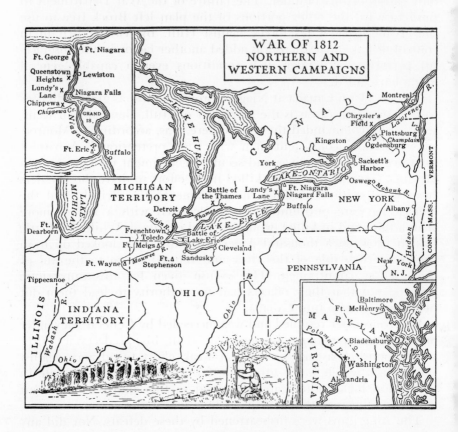

unequal to the task. The President was responsible for many of the bad appointments, since he knew personally a number of the incompetent generals that were selected. But it was difficult to judge as to the ability of prospective military leaders, for, as Jefferson properly said, "The Creator has not thought proper to mark those on the forehead who are of the stuff to make good generals." Furthermore, at first he had only poor materials from which to select the higher officers. When capable leaders were discovered, the Washington authorities were quick to recognize their ability and give them rank and responsibility.

NAVAL WARFARE

The American navy was so small that not much could be expected of it. The two hundred and fifty-seven gunboats, the "Mosquito Fleet," on which Jefferson had relied for coast defense, were unmanageable and therefore of little or no value. In each, the gun had to be put down in the hold before the boat could be launched. However, the few government frigates were better, ship for ship, than those of the British navy. They were faster, larger, better built, better manned, and better officered. The strength of this little navy was greatly underestimated by the British authorities. The record made by these frigates was, therefore, a surprise to both Englishmen and Americans.

The American navy small but efficient

Three days after the surrender of Detroit, Captain Isaac Hull, a nephew of the unfortunate commander in the west, won a great naval victory. His ship, the *Constitution*, engaged the British warship, the *Guerrière,* off the coast of Nova Scotia (August 19). The American vessel was larger than its British competitor and in other respects superior to it. The battle had lasted less than thirty minutes when the *Guerrière* had become a helpless wreck and seventy-nine of her crew had been killed or wounded. The *Constitution* had sustained slight injury and had lost only fourteen of her crew in killed and wounded. The news of the victory was received with the wildest exultation throughout the country. The chief significance of the triumph was the encouragement it gave to the American people. The gloom which had been settling upon them was now lifted and hope took the place of despondency.

The Constitution and the Guerrière

The American navy was successful in several other engagements of this year.[1] These victories had the effect of arousing pride in the navy, increasing morale both in it and in the army, and strengthening the zeal of the people in the contest. They also brought a burning smart to British pride. It was very humiliating to contemplate the blows dealt to the prestige of the Mistress of the Seas by a midget navy which had been the butt of British ridicule. Spurred on by this feeling, the British admiralty put forth greater efforts

---

[1] These victories were as follows: The American vessel, the *Wasp*, Captain Jacob Jones, defeated the *Frolic*; the *United States,* Captain Stephen Decatur, defeated the British *Macedonian*; and the *Constitution*, now commanded by Captain Bainbridge, won over the *Java*. In this latter engagement British bullets made so little impression on the *Constitution* that it gained the name of "Old Ironsides." Early in the next year the American *Hornet,* Captain Lawrence, came out victorious in a contest with the British sloop, *Peacock*.

to prevent a recurrence of such defeats. Consequently, the blockade of the American ports was tightened the next year. United States warships were now mostly shut up in the harbors at home. The few that roamed the seas confined their activities mainly to distant waters. Privateers were also not so successful after the first year, for they had great difficulty in bringing their prizes into home ports.

The Chesa-
peake and
the Shannon

The American navy did not, of course, have an unbroken record of victory. Among its reverses, the most conspicuous was the defeat of the *Chesapeake* by the *Shannon*. As a reward for his victory over the *Peacock,* Captain Lawrence had been put in command of the *Chesapeake,* the vessel which had been forced to strike her colors to the *Leopard* (in 1807). Captain Lawrence was challenged by the commander of the *Shannon* to a fight outside the harbor of Boston. His ship and crew were not ready for such a contest, but Lawrence unwisely accepted the challenge. After a bloody encounter of fifteen minutes Lawrence was defeated and killed. His dying words were: "Don't give up the ship." This advice could not be followed, however, and the *Chesapeake* was taken to Halifax as the prize of the *Shannon.*

"ON TO CANADA," 1813-14

Perry's victory

The most outstanding triumph of American arms in 1813 was Perry's victory on Lake Erie. Realizing that the advance into Canada from the northwest could never be successful as long as this lake was under British control, the authorities at Washington provided for the building of a squadron on Lake Erie. All materials used in the construction of the ships, except the timber, had to be hauled by horses and oxen over bad roads for several hundred miles. A number of vessels were hastily constructed and put under the command of Captain Oliver H. Perry, a young man in his late twenties. Bold and energetic himself, he inspired courage and loyalty in his men. His antagonist, Captain Barclay, fought bravely; but Perry's squadron was stronger than his, and after three hours of fighting Barclay was forced to surrender. In reporting the results of the contest Perry sent to Harrison this famous dispatch: "We have met the enemy and they are ours."

This victory gave Harrison his opportunity to defeat Proctor and thereby to regain the Northwest. Lake Erie remained under American control until the end of the war. For the first two years of the war there was a contest between the ships of both sides for supremacy on Lake Ontario, and at the end of that time the British fleet was left in possession.

After Hull's defeat, General William Henry Harrison was given command in the west. He had an army which was much larger than the one entrusted to Hull. Because of his victory at Tippecanoe, Harrison was considered an able leader by the Westerners. He made plans for a vigorous campaign against the British, but for a year his achievements fell far below expectations. This poor showing was due in part to the difficulties he encountered in transporting supplies and munitions, and in part to the lack of effective co-operation by the War Department. *Harrison in the Northwest*

The first engagement was near Frenchtown on the Raisin River. A portion of his force was badly defeated here (January 22, 1813) by the British and their Indian allies. The Americans lost about nine hundred men in killed and captured. After the battle Proctor, the British commander, made no effort to restrain his Indian allies, and many prisoners were massacred by them. *The American defeat at Frenchtown*

The Westerners were aroused by this massacre and other Indian atrocities and were determined to give the war a stronger support than ever. Harrison was able to hold Fort Meigs and Fort Stephenson against British attack, but could not proceed against Detroit as long as the enemy had control of Lake Erie. On September 12 he received Perry's famous dispatch announcing his victory on the lake. He then made ready to move forward. Proctor felt that Detroit and Fort Malden could no longer be held, and so he burned both places and retreated northward. Tecumseh was opposed to giving up these posts and reproached Proctor for not standing his ground. The latter was acting, he said, like "a fat animal that carries its tail upon its back; but when affrighted it drops it between its legs and runs off." *Proctor retreats into Canada*

Harrison moved his army across to the Canadian side and pursued the retreating enemy. Overtaking Proctor at the Thames River, he there attacked and defeated him (October 5). The success of this engagement was due in large measure to the Kentucky mounted riflemen under the command of Colonel Richard M. Johnson. The losses of the Americans were slight, and fifteen hundred prisoners were taken. Tecumseh was killed in the battle and his Indian confederacy was dissolved. The Northwest was thereafter relieved of all danger from British or Indian attack. Harrison retired to Detroit, and no further effort was made in the west to invade Canada. *Battle of the Thames*

In the spring of this same year (1813) General Dearborn attacked York (now Toronto), the capital of Upper Canada, and after a bloody contest captured the town. The public buildings were burned —but against the orders of Dearborn—and this gave a British gen- *Operations in the center and in the north* eral the excuse for burning the Capitol and the White House when he took Washington the following year.

Battle of Sackett's Harbor

In the Niagara region during this year the advantage in the fighting veered from one side to the other. One conspicuous victory for the Americans was the repulse of a British attack on Sackett's Harbor. An important result of this engagement was to bring into favorable notice General Jacob Brown, who had so efficiently led the American forces in the battle.

General Dearborn had repeatedly shown his incapacity as a military leader. His health was poor and he had for some time been anxious to retire from the service. His wish was now (July, 1813) complied with, and General James Wilkinson was selected in his place. This was a most unfortunate choice. In a long and unsavory public career Wilkinson had never shown any ability as a military leader, and had been notorious for intrigue and disloyalty to his associates. Winfield Scott characterized him in after years as an "unprincipled imbecile."

Lack of co-operation between American leaders

Major General Wade Hampton of South Carolina was put in charge of the army on Lake Champlain. The plan of the Secretary of War was for Wilkinson to attack Kingston and then descend the St. Lawrence to Montreal. Hampton was to proceed northward from Plattsburg and join Wilkinson in an attack on Montreal. He hated and despised Wilkinson, and hearty co-operation between the two generals was not easy to effect. Hampton, however, went ahead and reached Chateaugay in Canada. This was a dangerous position, but he waited here until he was satisfied that Wilkinson had no intention of joining him in an attack on Montreal that winter. Thereupon, he returned to Plattsburg.

Battle of Chrysler's Farm

In the meantime Wilkinson had been demonstrating his utter incapacity for military leadership. Leaving Sackett's Harbor (October 17), he sailed down the St. Lawrence toward Montreal. At Chrysler's Farm, two thousand of Wilkinson's regulars were defeated by eight hundred Britishers. The Americans lost almost four hundred in killed, wounded, and captured. Shortly afterwards Wilkinson learned that Hampton had withdrawn. This gave him an excuse to give up the attempt to attack Montreal.

Chippewa and Lundy's Lane

The failure of Wilkinson and Hampton to carry out their plans did not put an end to the "On-to-Canada" movement. In the summer of 1814 General Brown was in command of the American forces in the Niagara region, and he had as an able lieutenant, General Winfield Scott. With such leadership, much was expected of the army in this section and these expectations were not disappointed. Several battles were fought on the Canadian peninsula, in which the soldiers on both sides showed marked valor. The Americans won at Chippewa a victory over their British antagonists. At Lundy's Lane, a mile from Niagara Falls, a bloody contest raged for five hours. It was a drawn battle though the American forces retired from the field.

These encounters showed that the Americans, both men and officers, had learned how to wage war. Any country might well be proud of the spirit of bravery exhibited in these contests. British reinforcements gave the enemy a superiority which the Americans even under capable leaders could not hope to overcome. Accordingly, General Brown withdrew to the American side of the river and no further effort was made to invade Canada.

THE BRITISH OFFENSIVE

In December, 1812, the British government issued a proclama- *The blockade* tion closing Chesapeake and Delaware Bays by blockade. By later orders the blockade was extended until it covered the entire coast from New London, Connecticut, to the Florida coast. Since the greater part of New England was not at this time included, this section suffered less from the blockade than the rest of the country. This exception was made because of the opposition of the New Englanders to the war and the possibility of winning them back to their pre-Revolutionary allegiance to the British empire. But by a proclamation issued in May, 1814, all American harbors were put under blockade. British naval supremacy was sufficient to make this blockade effective, and American sea-borne trade was now reduced to very low limits.

By shutting off imports and exports the war brought considerable hardship to the American people. Such products as groceries and iron could be had only at high prices, while the farmer had difficulty in marketing his wheat, flour, tobacco, and cotton, even at low prices. To the merchants, seamen, and farmers of the Middle and Southern states the closing of the harbors proved a severe blow. The economic conditions caused by the blockade were an important factor in bringing the United States government to the verge of bankruptcy.

To enforce the blockade, a British fleet appeared in Chesapeake and Delaware Bays (1813), which alarmed and harassed the people dwelling near the coast. A few towns were looted and burned and even private houses were destroyed. Of these outrages the most outstanding was the pillage and destruction of Hampton, in Virginia.

Prior to 1814 the British were putting forth their main efforts in Europe in the life-and-death struggle with the forces of Napoleon and were not expending their best energies on the American war. But with the defeat of Napoleon in this year came the opportunity to push more vigorously the attack on the United States. The British government determined to make use of this opportunity by sending over ships and trained soldiers in sufficient numbers (as it thought) to ensure the defeat of the former colonials. If such efforts had been made in the beginning they might have been crowned with success; but by this time the American army had been trained into an efficient fighting machine, with brave and skillful leaders. The opportunity for success had thus been lost.

The vigorous offensive now planned against the United States was to include joint land and naval attacks at three points—Lake Champlain, Chesapeake Bay, and the Gulf of Mexico. The blockade of American ports was also to be tightened.

The invasion of New York by way of Lake Champlain was entrusted to General Sir George Prevost, who had at his command eleven thousand veterans. With him went a fleet under Captain George Downie. To contest the advance of the invaders, the Americans had a small land force under Brigadier General Macomb, who was entrenched at Plattsburg, and a naval squadron under Captain Thomas Macdonough in the harbor in front of the town. Macdonough was a young man of thirty who had received excellent training in the Barbary wars. He placed his fleet in such a way as to give him a decided advantage in a naval fight with his antagonist. The guns on his ships were of short range; those of the enemy, of long range. He, therefore, took a position in the small bay in front of Plattsburg under the protection of the American land batteries. Within this narrow space his short-range guns were quite effective; but if the battle had occurred out in the open lake, the American vessels would have been a target for British cannon without being able to deliver a telling fire in return.

If Prevost had first attacked Macomb, he could have captured his batteries, turned them on Macdonough's ships, and driven them out of the small bay into the open lake; for his force of trained veterans was twice as large as that of Macomb, which was composed largely of militia and second-rate regulars. But for some unaccountable reason, he threw away this advantage by attacking Macdonough instead of Macomb. The battle was therefore fought in the bay with the Americans winning the greatest and most important victory of the war (September 11). Every British warship was destroyed or captured. With the enemy in control of Lake Champlain, Prevost's communications with his base were cut and, believing that his position was untenable, he hastily retreated to Canada. A court-martial for him was ordered, but he died before the trial could be held.

In the summer of 1814, four thousand troops were sent over under the command of General Robert Ross. The men and officers of this force had played a worthy part in the victorious campaigns of the Spanish Peninsula, and much was expected of such well-trained troops. Ross was to co-operate with the British fleet in Chesapeake Bay in effecting a diversion on the coasts of the United States in favor of the British army in Canada. In pursuance of this plan it was decided to make an attack, first on Washington and then on Baltimore. *Plan of the British*

Although the British navy had been active in the region of the Chesapeake for a year and a half, nothing had been done to protect the national capital from attack. " . . . there was not a fort, a breastwork, a trench, or a battery, even on paper." Ross's troops were conveyed up the Patuxent River by the British ships and landed some distance from Washington. From this point to the capital they proceeded overland without opposition until they reached Bladensburg, five miles from the town. Here they were halted by a motley array of approximately seven thousand men under the command of General W. H. Winder, an incompetent leader. This force included about one thousand sailors and regulars, but the remaining portion of it was made up of militia of the rawest kind. *Battle of Bladensburg*

Owing to their superiority in number, the American troops were expected by the Washington authorities easily to defeat the British invaders. To witness this anticipated victory there went from Washington the President, some members of his Cabinet, and other prominent personages. But instead of victory they were obliged to observe a disastrous and disgraceful defeat. Although the Americans were in a good position for defense, the militia after firing a few shots broke and fled in great panic. The few regulars and seamen—the latter under command of Commodore Joshua Barney—fought bravely but were outnumbered and forced to yield. This battle has been called in ridicule the "Bladensburg Races."

The British then marched unopposed to Washington. In retaliation for the burning of the public buildings at York, Canada, by the Americans, they now burned the Capitol, the White House, and other public buildings. There was great panic in the little town and the government officials practically all hurried away. President Madison also fled, and so hasty was his departure that the dinner prepared for him and his family was left to be eaten by the British *The capture of Washington* officers when they took possession of the White House. Mrs. Madison, however, delayed her departure long enough to have Stuart's portrait of Washington removed to a place of safety.

Ross withdrew hastily from Washington and made plans for a joint naval and land attack on Baltimore. On September 11 the British were at the mouth of the Patapsco River just twelve miles from the city. The authorities of Baltimore had in the meantime been active and had made ready for an effective defense. Fortifications had been constructed and a force of about thirteen thousand men had been collected. The harbor was protected by Fort McHenry, which was adequately manned by regular troops, artillerists, and sailors.[1] A line of ships had been sunk in the channel, which kept the heavier British vessels at a distance from the city.

On September 12 the land force started its march to the city. The attempt to check it led to a skirmish in which the British were successful. This little victory was won at the cost of a considerable loss of men, including that of their general—Ross. The skirmish delayed the British advance, but by next evening they were in sight of the fortifications of the city. In the meantime the British fleet had, during the day and half the night, bombarded the forts and batteries that protected the harbor. Little damage was done, and as the larger ships could not get up into the harbor on account of the barrier, they decided to withdraw. The land troops were unwilling to make an unaided assault on the works of the city and they too withdrew and then embarked on the ships.

The Creek Indians in the Alabama region were aroused by Tecumseh in 1811, but they did not begin fighting until two years later. In 1813 they went on the war path and attacked Fort Mims, on the Alabama River, killing two hundred and fifty pioneers who had come together at the fort for protection (August 30, 1813). To avenge this defeat and quiet the Indians, Andrew Jackson was sent against them with a force of Tennessee militiamen. He made little headway against the red men until the spring and summer of 1814. During this time he had a number of engagements with them, the

most important of which was the battle of Horseshoe Bend. Here at least eight hundred and fifty Indians were killed. The Creeks now gave up the fight and ceded to the United States about two thirds of their territory.

---

[1] During the night of September 13-14 Fort McHenry was subjected to severe artillery fire from the British ships. This bombardment was watched with intense anxiety by Francis Scott Key, who on his return from a mission to the British admiral was detained on an American ship. Next morning he was so thrilled to see the flag still flying that he was inspired to write "The Star Spangled Banner."

In the meantime Jackson had been commissioned a major general in the regular army and put in control of the Mobile-New Orleans district. Pensacola was still in possession of Spain and was, therefore, a neutral port. The British seized it and planned to use it as a base of attack on the Americans. On learning this, Jackson, against instructions, captured the village and forced the British to leave.

Early in December General Jackson was in New Orleans getting ready to defend the town against an expected attack by a British force of nearly ten thousand veterans, then advancing under command of General Sir Edward Pakenham. Pakenham had seen twenty years of service in the British army and was regarded by the Duke of Wellington as one of the best of his generals. His troops had performed valiant service in the Peninsula campaign against the forces of Napoleon.

To meet these seasoned and well-officered battalions Jackson had a good-sized army (made up of militiamen, volunteers, and regulars), which was supported by a small naval force. He had reached New Orleans three weeks before the British soldiers appeared. It took Pakenham some time to disembark his troops and drag his cannon into position. Jackson made good use of this respite by putting forth every exertion to get in readiness for the attack.

The great battle occurred on January 8, 1815. Some of Jackson's men were stationed on the west shore of the river to prevent the enemy from getting behind his main column; but the greater part of his force was on the eastern side of the river, placed in a line that extended from the levee to a swamp. It was intrenched behind strong breastworks, in front of which was a deep ditch. A part of Jackson's force consisted of untrained and undisciplined frontiersmen. These proved good soldiers, however, as they displayed great courage and fine marksmanship. Pakenham underestimated their valor, for he seemed to have expected from them a behavior like that shown by the militia at Bladensburg. Accordingly, he threw away his usual caution and ordered an attack on Jackson's eastern line. In two brave assaults the British troops were mowed down by the fire of the Americans and were driven back in bloody defeat. A force was also sent against Jackson's column on the west side of the river. This flank movement was successful, but it came too late to prevent the failure of the main action.

This unwise assault on Jackson's entrenched forces cost the British the lives of three major generals, including Pakenham, and more than two thousand men, counting killed, wounded, and missing. Jackson's troops, sheltered behind strong earthworks, sustained

MAJOR GENERAL HARRISON.
From an engraving by W. R. Jones
after a painting by Wood.

OLIVER HAZARD PERRY (1785-1819).
Commodore, United States Navy.
Victor in the Battle of Lake Erie, 1813.
By Rembrandt Peale (1778-1860).

THOMAS MACDONOUGH.
From engraving after portrait by
J. W. Jarvis.

ANDREW JACKSON.
From an engraving by Charles Phillips
after a painting by Jarvis (1815).

(*Four portraits, Courtesy of the New-York Historical Society, New York City*)

only slight losses. The British retired after this defeat, and New Orleans and the Southwest were saved.

This great victory was most soothing to the hurt pride of the American people. It renewed their self-confidence and tended to make them feel that they had won the "Second War for Independence." It singled out Andrew Jackson as the outstanding hero of the war and gave him a prestige which later won for him the Presidency of the United States. It proved, however, to be an unnecessary sacrifice of human life; for before the battle was fought the treaty of peace had been signed at Ghent.

ATTITUDE OF NEW ENGLAND TOWARD THE WAR

Opposition of New England to the war

When war was declared by Congress, the Federalist members—most of whom represented New England constituencies—voted almost unanimously against it. The legislature of Massachusetts sent a protest to Congress against the declaration. After the fateful step had been taken thirty-four Federalist members of Congress issued an address to their constituents in which they severely attacked the Republicans on their war policy.

The militia question

New England's objection to the war was not confined to resolutions of disapproval. Opposition, both negative and positive, of a more dangerous character was made by this section. In the beginning some of the New England governors refused to obey the call of the War Department for militia, and such militiamen as did join the army refused to march into Canada, while others would not go outside the limits of their own states.[1]

Backward in loan subscriptions

The New Englanders also refused to assume their share of the financial burden of the war. The amount of money lent to the government by them during the struggle was far below their proportional share, although nearly all the specie of the country was held by them. Most of their ports were not blockaded until the last year of the war and nearly all the foreign trade passed through them. To purchase the products brought in from Europe, other sections poured their specie into New England. Even when foreign products

---

[1] The governors of Massachusetts and Connecticut refused to comply with the request for their quotas of militia on the ground that the Federal government had no authority under the Constitution to call out the militia at this time. The Constitution provides for the calling out of the militia to enforce the laws, quell rebellion, and resist invasion. As no invasion of the country had yet been made by the British, the Massachusetts and Connecticut authorities contended that there was no constitutional basis for the action of the President in calling out the militia. By a later decision of the Supreme Court (1827) it was declared that the President was by an act of Congress (1795) made the judge as to whether the contingency had arisen which demanded a requisition for the militia.

were excluded by the extension of the blockade to all American ports, these states still sold more to other sections of the country than they bought from them, for the infant industries which sprang up in the East were an important source of supply of manufactures for the agricultural regions. This difference in the balance of trade had to be made up by payments in gold and silver.

Trade with the enemy

Not content with these legitimate gains, many of the New Englanders (as well as some Southern merchants) were reaping a rich harvest by selling supplies to the enemy. British troops in Canada, and British seamen along the coast, were supplied with food products at immense profits. In August, 1814, a British officer wrote to the home authorities as follows: "Two-thirds of the army in Canada are at this moment eating beef provided by American contractors. . . ."

The Hartford Convention

The opposition of New England culminated in the Hartford Convention, which met on December 15, 1814. There were twenty-three delegates from Massachusetts, Connecticut, and Rhode Island, who had been chosen by their legislatures. Two representatives chosen by popular assemblies in New Hampshire and a representative of one county in Vermont were also admitted. Some of the leading Federalists in New England had, in letters and through the press, been threatening secession. It was feared, therefore, that steps looking toward a disruption of the Union would be taken by this body. The assembly, however, fell under the control of the less radical group, and the action taken was not as dangerous as had been anticipated.

Proposals of the convention

The proceedings were secret and it was not until 1833 that the journal was published. At the time of adjournment, however, the convention published a report stating the result of its deliberations. Using in part the exact language of the Virginia Resolutions of 1798, which had been written by Madison himself, the report declared that a state had the right and duty to interpose its authority for the protection of its citizens against unconstitutional acts of the Federal government. In line with this general principle, the states were urged to adopt measures which would protect their citizens from the draft; to pass laws which would enable the New England states to assist each other by the use of their militia; and to make an arrangement with the Federal government whereby the states would provide for their own defense and retain "a reasonable portion of the taxes collected within the said states." This last demand was in the nature of an ultimatum. If it were not accepted by the United States government, another convention was to be held in Boston on June 15, "with such powers and instructions as the exigency of a crisis so momentous may require."

Seven amendments to the Federal Constitution were also proposed. The changes in the national government outlined in these recommendations were as follows: Free persons only should in the future be counted in apportioning direct taxation and representation among the states; a two-thirds vote of both houses of Congress should be required for the admission of new states, a declaration of war, and the prohibition of foreign commerce; all embargoes should be limited to sixty days; no naturalized citizen was to hold a Federal civil office; and the tenure of the President should be limited to one term, and two Presidents could not come in succession from the same state.

While some of these proposals were wise, most of them were inspired by feeling against the Republican Party or jealousy of Virginia's predominance in the Federal government. If these principles were embodied in the Constitution, the representation of the South in the House of Representatives would be cut down; a Virginian could not succeed the hated Madison; and a man of foreign birth, like Gallatin, would not be able to sit in a future Cabinet.

A committee was appointed to present these resolutions to Congress. This committee proceeded to Washington to negotiate with the Federal government. Before anything could be done, news came of Jackson's great victory at New Orleans and of the signing of the treaty of peace at Ghent. This mission now seemed ridiculous as well as treasonable to the patriotic Republicans, who were rejoicing over what they considered victory. Accordingly, the representatives of the convention returned quietly to New England without mentioning the object of their journey. *A committee sent to Washington*

The Hartford Convention furnished the Republicans with a good weapon, which they used with telling effect against their Federalist opponents. It gave them the opportunity to charge the Federalists with sedition at a time when loyalty was especially needed. Every man who was connected with the movement was branded as disloyal. The whole party came in for criticism, for the Federalist leaders had in the main either endorsed or acquiesced in the movement. *Effect on the Federalist Party*

PEACE NEGOTIATIONS

Four days after the United States entered the contest against England, Napoleon declared war on Russia. As Russia was now an ally of England, she did not want the latter country to be hampered *Mediation offered by Russia* by an American war. Furthermore, Czar Alexander had shown a very friendly feeling toward the United States. He, therefore, was anxious to settle the quarrel between his ally and his friend. As a step in this direction he offered to mediate between the two belligerents. President Madison, assuming that the British government was favorable to the plan, hastily accepted the offer. To conduct the negotiations with the British government, James A. Bayard and Albert Gallatin were sent over as commissioners to co-operate with John Quincy Adams, American minister to Russia. Lord Castlereagh, the British Minister of Foreign Affairs, declined the Czar's offer of mediation but later indicated a willingness to enter upon direct negotiations with the United States. Thereupon Madison added Henry Clay and Jonathan Russell to the list of envoys.

The American peace commissioners

The American commission was one of outstanding ability. At the head of the delegation was John Quincy Adams. He was well-educated, experienced in diplomacy, and possessed of exceptional courage, patriotism, and ability. As a diplomat, however, he was somewhat handicapped by a cold exterior, a bad temper, and an untactful manner. Clay was in many respects his opposite in temperament. He was brilliant and bold, but the magnetism of his personality was sometimes overborne by the imperiousness of his temper. Since his ardent patriotism bore the western stamp and that of Adams was of the New England brand, a clash between two such aggressive characters could hardly be avoided. This situation gave Gallatin the opportunity to act as peacemaker in his own delegation as well as in the negotiations with the British representatives. His patience, even temper, sound judgment, and knowledge of European affairs made him the most useful member of the commission.

The British commissioners

The English envoys at Ghent, which was finally agreed upon as the place of meeting, were very commonplace men. At that time the most skilled British diplomatists were at the Congress of Vienna. Furthermore, Lord Castlereagh wished to keep the threads of negotiation in his own hands, and this he could not easily do with men of outstanding reputation. The British envoys were allowed little freedom of action, but had to await instructions from Castlereagh on all important questions. This handicap, together with their inferiority in ability to the American commissioners, gave the latter an advantage in the skillful game of diplomacy.

Terms laid down by the American commissioners

The American envoys were instructed to insist on the abandonment of the British practice of impressment, and if this demand were not met they were to return home. Other concessions were to be asked for, some of which were quite unreasonable. These included the cession of all or a part of Canada to the United States and the closure of the Great Lakes to British warships.

To the British government these conditions seemed absolutely impossible. There was a strong feeling in that country in favor of prosecuting the war to a glorious finish, on the ground that the hurt to British pride caused by the early victories of the American frigates could be soothed only by an undeniable defeat of the presumptuous Yankees. This could easily be done (it was argued), since the downfall of Napoleon and the end of the European conflict had released their armies and fleets for the American war. The British government, however, had the good sense to see that this was the wrong attitude. To continue the struggle would unnecessarily add to the great financial burdens under which the people were already staggering.

The first instructions of the British commissioners were just as unreasonable as those of the American envoys. They were not only to insist upon the continuance of the right of impressment but were to demand the creation of an Indian buffer state in the west out of territory taken from the United States; the cession of a part of Maine to England; the destruction of American forts on the Great Lakes; and the removal of all American ships from these waters. The right of the English people to navigate the Mississippi was to be continued, but the right of the Americans to engage in the Newfoundland fisheries was to be terminated. These drastic terms were refused by our commissioners, and it looked as if the negotiations would at once come to an end. *British demands*

When these impossible conditions were brought to the United States a cry of indignant protest arose from the people, indicating a firm determination to reject them and continue the war. The confidence of the people had been revived by the victories of Brown and Macdonough and there was no thought of accepting these humiliating terms. *Concessions made on both sides*

When Castlereagh was apprised of this feeling in the United States he decided not to push his demands, especially as he was having his difficulties at the Congress of Vienna. A continuance of the war with the United States would lessen the prestige of Britain and weaken his hand at Vienna. Accordingly, more reasonable terms were offered. In the meantime the American commissioners had been instructed not to insist on the abandonment of impressment as a *sine qua non* of agreement.

The treaty of peace was signed on December 24, 1814. It provided for a cessation of hostilities, a return of prisoners, a restoration of conquests, and the appointment of a commission to fix the disputed *Terms of the peace* boundary between Canada and the United States. Nothing was said about impressment or visit and search. It, therefore, conceded none of the rights for which the United States had fought. For both countries it was a peace without victory, but for both it was a peace with honor. It was so regarded by both groups of envoys, who celebrated the event by a joint banquet at which "everybody drank everybody else's health." James Gallatin, who had acted as his father's secretary, spoke of the occasion as follows: "The band played *God Save the King,* to the toast of the King, and *Yankee Doodle.* Congratulations on all sides and a general atmosphere of serenity; it was a scene to be remembered. God grant there may be always peace between the two nations."

*The treaty
unanimously
ratified*
The treaty was gladly received by the American people—both Republicans and Federalists. On February 14 it was submitted to the Senate and unanimously ratified.

*Results of
the war*
The toll of human life taken by the war was not heavy. The number of soldiers in the armies of the United States never exceeded thirty thousand, and the number in any one engagement was never much more than six thousand. It is estimated that less than fifteen hundred Americans were killed in the land battles during the conflict and that the entire losses on land, including wounded, captured, and missing, were under ten thousand.

Nothing in a material way was gained by either side as a result of the contest. Not one foot of land passed from one to the other belligerent. Not one of the questions at issue was settled. It would appear, therefore, that the war had been entirely futile. There were, however, certain spiritual results which were important. Because of the successes of the navy and the few victories on land, the American people were inspired with a new self-confidence and felt that they had won the war. The spirit of nationalism which had been on the decline since 1783 was revived and strengthened.

The war put an end to that condition of semi-colonialism which had existed since the Revolution. With political separation there had not come to the former British colonies economic and social independence. The new country had been dependent upon trade with England for the sale of many of its raw materials and the purchase of most of its finished manufactures. During the long period of strife in Europe it had had an important stake in overseas events, and so foreign affairs had held a prominent place in American policy. Party lines were drawn largely in accordance with sentiment for or against England or France. The cessation of strife in Europe removed many of the causes of conflict between the old and the new world. American interests were, therefore, not so vitally affected by European conditions now as formerly, and the energies of the government could be directed more toward domestic and less toward foreign affairs. The country now addressed itself toward the occupation and development of the empire acquired from France. The United States thus turned its back to the east and its face toward the west.

Although Madison had taken a belligerent attitude in 1812, after the war he made a successful effort to bring about a lasting peace between his country and the British empire. In obedience to an act

The Rush-Bagot Agreement

Bruin become MEDIATOR *or Negociation for* PEACE.

Courtesy of the New-York Historical Society, New York City

CARICATURE.

By Wm. Charles del et Sculp. 1812–1815.

of Congress, he ordered, in 1815, that all American war vessels on the Great Lakes be laid up or sold, except the small number needed in the revenue service. He then made a proposal to the British government, which was accepted by the British foreign office, and an agreement was negotiated under his successor (1817) between Richard Rush, acting Secretary of State, and Charles Bagot, British minister at Washington. By the Rush-Bagot Agreement neither power was to keep on the Great Lakes or Lake Champlain any armed vessels except a few revenue cutters. Either party to the understanding could denounce it by giving the other six months' notice. It has been in effect continuously from that time until the present.

This is the first instance known to history of the limitation of armaments by international agreement. It set a precedent in favor of breaking down military barriers between the United States and Canada, which since that time has been followed by both countries. After 1846 the few fortifications on the northeastern Canada-United States border fell into decay, and thereafter the entire transcontinental boundary remained unfortified, "a situation which has come to have the force of an unwritten treaty."

For the long period of peace between the United States and the British empire we are indebted, however, less to any formal agreement than to the strong desire for peace on the part of the two powers. The absence of any real clash of interests explains the continuance of an international friendship which, though strained at times, has lasted for a century and a quarter. If the Canadians had persisted in their desire for a buffer Indian state in the northwest and the Americans had persisted in their desire for the annexation of Canada, there doubtless would have been sufficient ground for frequent strife. But fortunately these foolish ambitions were not revived after the end of the war.

CHAPTER XXIII

The Revival of Nationalism

T HE new spirit of nationalism which was so much in evidence immediately after the war was not based on mere sentiment. It rested on a foundation of new economic conditions. These new conditions were closely associated with the Industrial Revolution which started in England and spread to the United States and other countries.

THE INDUSTRIAL REVOLUTION IN ENGLAND AND AMERICA

At the beginning of the eighteenth century the methods used in manufacturing textiles in Europe were not much in advance of those employed in ancient Babylonia and Egypt. Cotton and wool were spun in the home on the old-fashioned spinning wheel and woven into cloth on the hand loom. This method of producing cloth was radically changed by a series of inventions made in the latter half of the eighteenth century. By the invention of the "spinning jenny" (1764) and the power loom (1785), the making of textiles was put on a machine basis and the amount of the output was greatly increased. One drawback, however, in the manufacture of cotton cloth was the difficulty of separating the cotton fiber from the seed. This difficulty was solved by Eli Whitney's invention of the cotton gin (1793). Another important step in the progress of the textile industry was the substitution of steam for water power in operating the machines. This step was taken in 1769 when James Watt made improvements on the steam engine which enabled it to be harnessed to the new machines.

Important inventions

As a result of these inventions the textile industry was taken out of the home and put into the factory. This change from the domestic to the factory system was sudden enough to be regarded as a revolution. It has, therefore, been properly designated as the Industrial Revolution. These inventors were all Englishmen, except Eli Whitney, who was an American. The British government tried to prevent a knowledge of the machines from spreading to other countries. Laws were passed prohibiting the export of the machines,

Rise of the factory system

379

the copying of plans, and the emigration of workers who had acquired skill in the mills.

Primacy of England in industry

While it is impossible permanently to confine ideas within a geographical area, the English people were able to enjoy a monopoly of the new processes for a number of years. In this way they got the start of the rest of the world in industry. Other circumstances favorable to the growth of manufactures in the British Isles were: an abundance of capital available for investment; an adequate supply

*Courtesy of the New-York Historical
Society, New York City*

SAMUEL SLATER.
From engraving by Wm. H. Dunnel after a painting by Cole.

of labor; plenty of coal and iron; and the possession of colonies which could supply raw materials and purchase finished products. For these reasons British manufacturers could underbid their competitors in all other countries.

American industry after the Revolution

As has already been shown, the American Revolution acted as a stimulus to manufacturing in the United States. The progress in industry during the next quarter-century was not, however, in keeping with this promising start. American manufactures were discouraged by the high cost of labor and the scarcity of capital. With such a handicap the budding industries in the new republic could not compete on equal terms with their British rivals, who were enjoying the exceptional advantages indicated above. Furthermore, the European wars greatly increased the demand for American food products and the opportunity for American shipping. Cheap lands in unlimited amounts were also a spur to activity in farming. For these reasons the energies of the American people, during the quarter-century that ended in 1807, were devoted more to agriculture and commerce than to industry, and manufactured articles were in large measure imported from England.

The passage of the Embargo Act (December, 1807) marks the beginning of a new era in the economic history of the United States. *The Restrictive Period (1807-1815)* This measure, the nonintercourse policy of the American government, and the British blockade during the War of 1812, imposed serious restrictions on the trade between Europe and the United States. Foreign manufactures were to a large extent cut off and their place had to be supplied by home production. The export of farm products was also greatly curtailed. Commerce and agriculture therefore languished, and capital available for these pursuits was seeking better employment. At the same time commercial restrictions, by prohibiting foreign competition, were giving American industry a monopoly of the home market. Manufacturing had thus become profitable and was attracting to itself much of the capital which would otherwise have been devoted to agriculture and shipping. Numerous small industries sprang up to supply the home demand.

During the Restrictive Period, American industry was carried on *The beginning of the factory system in America* mainly according to the domestic system. By the end of this period, however, the factory system had made a beginning. The spinning jenny was in operation in Philadelphia as early as 1775, and a cotton factory was established at Beverly, Massachusetts, in 1787. Two years later Samuel Slater erected a mill at Pawtucket, Rhode Island, in which he used the new textile machinery. He had worked for the Arkwright firm in England and while so doing had committed to memory the plans for the spinning machinery. He was thus able to reproduce the English machines and use them for his own benefit. In 1814 Francis C. Lowell brought the power loom to this country. He set up at Waltham, Massachusetts, a factory in which all the processes of both spinning and weaving were carried on under one roof. This was the beginning of the factory system in the United States. The factory system developed rapidly, especially in New England, because in that section there were ample water power and a considerable amount of free capital seeking investment. Factories were also numerous in the other Northern and in the Middle states, especially Pennsylvania, for in this state there was an abundance of coal and iron.

NATIONALISM PROMOTED BY THE POLICY OF RECONSTRUCTION

The Republican Party nationalized

In his annual message of December, 1815, President Madison recommended that Congress make provision for the adequate defense of the country and establish a uniform national currency, a tariff which would protect the infant industries, a system of roads and canals, and a national university. He indicated that if constitutional objections were urged against internal improvements these obstacles could be removed by an amendment to the Constitution. The adoption of this forceful program of reconstruction involved the acceptance of the old Federalist view of nationalism; but all these proposals except the last were enacted into law by Congress.

It hardly seems credible that a Republican President would propose, and a Republican Congress would accept, such nationalistic measures. For the Republican Party owed its origin to a vigorous protest against such policies. An indication as to how much times had changed and men had changed with them is seen in the fact that Madison was now advocating what he had once opposed, and the followers of Hamilton were opposing what they had formerly advocated. The Republicans had thus pushed the Federalists off their own platform and ensconced themselves on it. The Federalists had no alternative but to climb up on the deserted Republican platform and profess a comfortable adjustment to their new situation. So the Federalists were now the champions of states' rights and the opponents of centralization in government, while the Republicans were advocating the assumption of large powers by the Federal government and trying to identify nationalism with patriotism.

The Old School Republicans

The nationalization of the Republican Party had been a gradual development. Even Jefferson, the apostle of localism, was in the camp of the nationalists when he sponsored such measures as the purchase of Louisiana and the Embargo Act. The occasional lapses into nationalism under Jefferson had become a habit under Madison; but this change in the character of the party was not accepted by all its members. There was a conservative minority which still adhered to the original doctrine of states' rights and stood out consistently and persistently against the trend toward nationalism. This faction is known as Old School Republicans. They were ably led by two brilliant Virginians, John Taylor of Caroline and John Randolph of Roanoke. The nationalists were, however, the dominant element of the party. Since its outstanding leaders were young men, such as Clay and Calhoun, the members of this group were termed Young Republicans.[1] With the acceptance by Congress of one nationalist measure after another, the breach between the two factions grew wider and wider. In this way the Old School Republicans became an insurgent minority which gave considerable annoyance to the majority. They voted with the Federalists against such policies as a national bank, the protective tariff, and internal improvements.

The importance of defense realized

The war had punctured some of the theories as to defense upheld by the early Republicans. It had demonstrated the inefficiency of the militia and the value of the navy as a means of defense against invasion. Gone was the traditional fear that a strong standing army would be used by the executive to destroy American liberty. In its place was the feeling that an efficient standing army was the guardian of American liberty. Accordingly, the navy was kept at its full war strength, with some slight additions. The peace-time strength of the army was put at ten thousand men.[2]

Financial reform badly needed

From the tangled condition of its finances during the war the country learned some valuable lessons in monetary affairs. The demise of the First Bank of the United States (1811) left the field open for state banks. They took advantage of this opportunity and greatly increased in number. Each was chartered by a state legislature and was a bank of issue as well as of deposit and discount. Many of them went far beyond the limits prescribed by sound business in putting out their notes. To make matters worse, most of the gold and silver of the country was gravitating toward New England. Under such conditions the banks could hardly be expected to withstand the stress of war, and so before the end of 1814 all the banks outside of New England had suspended specie payment. Their notes, however, still circulated as money, though they were not legal tender. The reason for this was that there was not enough gold and silver in circulation to supply the monetary needs of the people. Since some banks were safer than others, there were wide differences in the val-

---

[1] It must not be inferred, however, that all the prominent young leaders were Young Republicans. For example, John Tyler, when he entered the House of Representatives in 1816, was one of the youngest members of that body; and yet he was a stanch Old School Republican.

[2] Soon after the treaty of peace the navy found other work of importance to engage in. The Dey of Algiers, taking advantage of the war, had captured American ships and enslaved American sailors. In May, 1815, Captain Stephen Decatur was sent to the Mediterranean Sea in command of ten ships to bring the haughty African ruler to terms. After destroying a frigate and a smaller vessel, Decatur appeared at Algiers and forced the Dey to sign a treaty renouncing all claim to tribute, returning all prisoners without ransom, and promising good conduct for the future. Decatur was also able to secure restitution for the violation of American rights from the rulers of Tunis and Tripoli.

ues of these notes. This lack of uniformity was confusing and inconvenient and put serious obstacles in the way of business transactions.

A national bank, it was thought, would be a great aid in remedying this situation. By issuing notes it would supply the country with a sound and uniform currency. It would also serve as a curb on state banks and help to keep their issues within the limits of safety. For only the notes of sound state banks could compete with those of the national bank. Like the First Bank of the United States, it would be a repository for government moneys and would serve as a valuable agency in the collection and disbursement of government funds. For these reasons the Republican Congress waived whatever constitutional scruples it may have had and passed an act (April, 1816) providing for the creation of the Second Bank of the United States.

This bank was closely modeled after the one established in 1791, except that its capital stock of $35,000,000 was three and a half times as great as that of the First Bank of the United States. Only one fifth of this stock was owned by the Federal government, the other four fifths being in the hands of private individuals, states, corporations, or companies. Government funds were deposited with the bank and no interest was paid for their use. Moreover, the notes of the bank were accepted in payment of all dues to the government, a provision which virtually made them a legal tender. For these privileges the bank gave the government a bonus of $1,500,000. The parent bank, located at Philadelphia, and the branches scattered throughout the country engaged in ordinary banking business besides issuing notes. Four fifths of the directors were appointed by the private stockholders and the other fifth by the President with Senate confirmation. The bank was thus mainly a private institution as far as its management and ownership were concerned, while it enjoyed many of the privileges of a governmental agency.

John C. Calhoun, who in later years was the great protagonist of states' rights, was now the arch-advocate of the bank measure. He was chairman of the committee which reported the bill to the House and he argued ably in support of it. He felt no doubt as to the constitutionality of the measure; for Congress (he contended) had power to regulate the currency, and a national bank was a necessary means for the proper exercise of this power. Henry Clay, who had again become Speaker of the House, also gave the bill his ardent support, although he had held in 1811 that a national bank was unconstitutional. To explain this change of position he maintained that in 1811 a national bank was not necessary for the regulation of the currency but had become so by 1816. Webster, who afterwards became a strong advocate of a national bank, was now against it. His opposition was not based on constitutional grounds but on the contention that gold and silver should be used as the money of the country. If nothing but specie were accepted in payment of dues to the government, the problem, he held, could be solved without difficulty. Webster's influence in Congress was not great at this time, and Clay and Calhoun, supported by other nationalist Republicans, were able to secure a charter for the establishment of the Second Bank of the United States (1816).

To force the state banks to resume specie payment, the Secretary of the Treasury, acting on a joint resolution of Congress, announced that on and after February 20, 1817, the Federal government would not accept in payment of public dues the notes of any state banks except those that were redeeming their notes in specie. This policy had the desired effect, and at the appointed time all banks which were in a sound condition were redeeming their notes in specie.

Resumption of specie payment

Another nationalist policy sponsored by the Young Republicans was that of protection. With the end of the war the infant industries which had sprung up lost the virtual protection that they had enjoyed during the Restrictive Period. They now had to face the competition of old and well-established English factories, which had for some time enjoyed unrivalled advantages. Furthermore, the British manufacturers had on hand a large surplus of products which they proceeded to "dump" upon the American market. These articles were sold at prices too low to be met by American producers. If something were not done the infant industry of the United States would be smothered in its cradle; for the new manufacturing businesses which had been propped up by the commercial restrictions and by the war felt unable to stand alone. They therefore clamored for a protective tariff which would check the inflow of English goods until they could get firmly on their feet.

Reasons for protection

But to save the vested interests of those who had risked capital in the new plants was not a valid reason for the country's launching upon a policy of protection. A measure which would raise the prices of goods to consumers throughout the country could not be justified on such grounds. The argument used in favor of protection was, therefore, that of economic self-sufficiency. The war had shown the danger and inconvenience of having to rely on European countries for manufactures. Madison in his annual message of December, 1815, recommended that Congress, in selecting industries to be favored with protection, give special preference to such "as will relieve the United States from a dependence on foreign supplies" and to "articles necessary for the public defense or connected with the primary wants of individuals." Those manufactures which were based on farm products as raw materials were also to be particularly favored. By the aid of a protective tariff, industries would be developed to such an extent that in time of war the country could be supplied with clothing, munitions of war, and other necessary supplies even if it should be cut off from the outside world, and in this way would gain and keep its economic independence.

The Tariff Act of 1816

The tariff had been gradually raised since the beginning of Washington's administration until by 1812 it had reached a general level of about twelve and a half per cent. During the war the rate had been raised to about twenty-five per cent, with the expectation that it would be lowered with the coming of peace. An act was now passed (1816) which retained the war rate and even raised it on some articles.

Calhoun and Clay were ardent in their support of the new policy. Calhoun urged it on the ground of economic independence. He also contended that home manufactures would supply the farmer with a home market, and this dependence of one class and one section upon another would strengthen the bonds of union. Webster, who was representing a commercial district in Massachusetts, was opposed to the new tariff act on the ground that it would discourage commerce. Before the end of the next decade Calhoun and Webster had reversed their positions on the tariff, the former having become a strong opponent and the latter a warm advocate of protection.

Internal improvements

The war had also revealed the need of better means of transportation. The military campaigns had been greatly hampered by a lack of good roads. Better facilities for travel and transportation were also called for in order to tie the West more closely to the Union. President Madison, in strongly recommending the construction of roads and canals by the Federal government, suggested the proposal of an amendment to the Constitution to remove any constitutional obstacles which might be encountered. Clay and Calhoun contended that such an amendment was unnecessary, as the government already possessed the requisite authority. According to Calhoun, Congress is empowered by the Constitution to levy taxes to "provide for the common defense and general welfare." As roads and canals were necessary for the common defense and general welfare, Congress could provide for their construction.

The Bonus Bill

Calhoun offered a bill in the House providing that the bonus paid the government by the Bank, and the income from the government's bank stock, be appropriated for the construction of roads and canals. This was pushing nationalism too far for the Old School Republicans and they and the Federalists voted against it. Despite this opposition, however, the bill passed and went to the President just before the end of his second term. Madison's old states' rights principles had revived within him sufficiently to cause him to veto the measure, which therefore did not become a law.

NATIONALISM ADVANCED BY THE FEDERAL JUDICIARY

The judiciary was the last of the three departments of the Federal government to come into prominence. In the early years the Supreme Court did not give promise of its later importance. Its decisions were of a strictly legal character without any leanings toward politics. Comparatively few cases came before this high tribunal, and the principal work of the justices was that of attending the circuit courts. Nor was a place on the supreme bench considered as great a distinction as it has since become. John Jay resigned the Chief Justiceship to become Governor of New York, and John Rutledge declined a seat on the supreme bench to accept the chief justiceship of South Carolina. *The Supreme Court in the beginning*

Early in the nineteenth century, however, the Federal judiciary began to take its place as an important branch of the government. It owed its new significance largely to the influence of John Marshall, who became Chief Justice in February, 1801. This honor came to Marshall after he had spent a number of years in the public service and had won a reputation for unusual ability as a lawyer. He was born and reared in Fauquier, a county on or near the Virginia frontier. His mother was a Randolph, and closely connected with the Tidewater aristocracy. He seems, however, to have been influenced more by the environment of the West than by the heredity of the East; for he imbibed the nationalism of the uplands rather than the particularism of the lowlands. With him, therefore, Federalism was bred in the bone. Washington was his patron saint and Jefferson his pet aversion. *John Marshall*

Marshall was not a hard student or a wide reader. Consequently, he owed his success as a lawyer more to originality of thought than to study. Since he did not waste his energies by overwork or smother his originality with the ideas borrowed from reading, he usually brought an unwearied and unfettered mind to his tasks, and his strong intellect was able to function in full vigor. He had a clear and forceful style and was a master of the art of reasoning. The Supreme Court at that time afforded a better opportunity for the display of such intellectual gifts than it does today; for very few precedents had been established by it, and decisions could be based chiefly on principles.

When the Republicans came into power, all the Federal courts

The Supreme Court nationalized were manned by Federalists with nationalist opinions. Appointments by Republican Presidents gradually changed the character of the Supreme Court until by 1811 the majority of the justices were Republicans; but the nationalist movement which had captured the Republican Congress had had a like influence on the Republican judiciary, and so the Supreme Court had been nationalized. Marshall's forceful and magnetic personality had also been a marked influence in this nationalization of the Republican part of the Supreme Court. Under such conditions it was reasonable to expect that the interpretation given to the Constitution by the Supreme Court would be of a nationalistic character. There were, therefore, a number of outstanding decisions which put the stamp of judicial approval upon the national legislation of the day.

Noted decisions: Marbury vs. Madison

One of the earliest of the noted decisions of the Court was in the case of *Marbury vs. Madison,* in which the Court assumed the right to declare an act of Congress unconstitutional and void (see p. 323).

Fletcher vs. Peck

The right to pass upon the validity of an act of a state legislature was asserted in the case of *Fletcher vs. Peck* (1810). This case arose from the sale by the Georgia legislature in 1795 of 35,000,000 acres of land to four companies for $500,000. It was undoubtedly a fraudulent transaction, and every member of the legislature but one had a private stake in the deal. On learning of this disgraceful performance the people of Georgia raised an outcry, which caused the next legislature to repeal (1796) the former act of sale. The act of 1795 was publicly burned and all evidence of it expunged from the records. In the meantime, however, one of these companies had disposed of its tract to another company, and portions of it had gone to innocent purchasers.

This reversal of her action on the part of Georgia led to a suit over a land title which finally reached the United States Supreme Court. The decision in this court was based on the contention that the act of 1795 of the legislature was valid despite the fraudulent procedure connected with its passage. The validity of the act was not affected by the motives of the legislators. This act was a contract between the state of Georgia and the purchasing companies. The later act (of 1796) invalidated this contract and was, therefore, null and void; for the Constitution declares that no state shall pass any law impairing the obligations of contract.

Dartmouth College vs. Woodward

The doctrine of this decision was carried still further in the opinion handed down by the Court in the case of *Dartmouth College vs. Woodward* (1819). In 1769 a charter was granted to Dartmouth College by the royal Governor of New Hampshire in the name of the

king. In 1816 the legislature of New Hampshire passed a law changing the management of the college. The old board of trustees opposed the change and brought suit against the new trustees on the
ground that the act of the legislature was unconstitutional. Daniel
Webster, an alumnus of the college, as counsel for the old trustees,
ably upheld their contention. His point of view was accepted by the
Court and the decision was that the charter of the college was a
contract and that money had been given to the college under the
terms of the charter. The act of the legislature annulling some of
the provisions of the charter impaired these contracts and was therefore void.

This decision gave additional sanctity to contracts and charters *Effect of the*
and increased the popularity of the corporation as a form of business *decision*
organization. By depriving the state legislatures of the right to regulate these chartered corporations, it exempted the latter from needed
regulation and enabled them to abuse the extensive privileges which
they enjoyed. In later years the states regained some of this lost authority by reserving the right when issuing corporation charters to
revise and amend them. In subsequent decisions, too, the Supreme
Court has declared that a state cannot by charter commitments or
otherwise divest itself of its power to protect its citizens in their
health and security, that is, a state cannot waive its right to exercise
its police power. In this way the states have been able to curb some
of the abuses which have rested on the principle originally enunciated in this case.

The interpretation given to the Constitution by the two last- *Martin vs.*
named cases was contrary to the doctrine of states' rights. This doc- *Hunter's*
trine also received quite a setback in the two decisions of *Martin vs.* *Lessee*
Hunter's Lessee (1816) and *Cohens vs. Virginia* (1821). In these
opinions the Court asserted the right to hear appeals from the highest state courts in cases involving Federal rights.

One of the most important decisions handed down by Marshall *McCulloch*
and his associates was the one given in the case of *McCulloch vs.* *vs. Maryland*
Maryland (1819). The legislature of Maryland had taxed the note-
issuing business of the Baltimore branch of the Bank of the United
States. McCulloch, the cashier, refused to pay the tax on the ground
that the Maryland act imposing the tax was unconstitutional. The
Maryland courts decided in favor of the validity of the act and it
was brought to the Supreme Court of the United States. In the decision of this court two important points were involved: (1) Was the
act of Congress creating the bank constitutional? (2) If so, was the
act of the Maryland legislature taxing the bank constitutional?

In answer to the first question the Court came out squarely in favor of Hamilton's view as to implied powers. The Constitution, it argued, gives Congress the power to regulate the finances of the country. In the exercise of this power it can employ all means which are appropriate and plainly adapted to that end unless such means are prohibited by the Constitution. A national bank is such an agency, and, therefore, the act chartering it is constitutional. A state legislature cannot kill what Congress has authority to create. But if a legislature can tax the business of a branch of the bank it can destroy such a branch; for the power to tax is the power to kill. Therefore, the act of the Maryland legislature is unconstitutional and void.

Gibbons vs. Ogden

The Supreme Court gave a broad interpretation to that clause in the Constitution which confers upon Congress the power to regulate interstate commerce. In the case of *Gibbons vs. Ogden* (1824) the Court declared that the right of Congress to regulate interstate commerce applies to navigation, as well as to buying and selling. Congress can also regulate navigation within a state when such navigation is a part of an interstate journey.

The American Insurance Company vs. Canter

A later decision of importance was that of the *American Insurance Company vs. Canter* (1828). In this case the Court decided that inasmuch as the Federal government has the power to declare war and make peace and conduct negotiations with foreign powers, it can in the exercise of this power acquire territory by war or negotiation. Territory so acquired comes within the jurisdiction of the United States, and Congress can legislate for it, since it is granted the power to make all needful rules and regulations for the territories.

The election of 1816

The Republicans felt sure of success in the campaign of 1816. The Federalists had no issues on which to make a fight and their attitude in the war had made them unpopular. Their party had thus been reduced to a helpless minority. In accordance with the usual practice, the Republican members of Congress held a caucus in Washington to make nominations for the Presidency and Vice-Presidency. This method of naming candidates was objectionable to some of the leaders, as it gave Congress too strong a voice in selecting the President. Owing to this criticism, some Republican Congressmen declined to attend the caucus.

The two names considered by the caucus were William H. Crawford and James Monroe. Crawford was the representative of the Young Republicans and, therefore, had a strong following. Monroe, however, received the support of the Administration, and his availability was enhanced by the fact that he had not participated in the factional quarrels. He won the nomination over Crawford, but only by the narrow majority of 65 to 54. In the election he had an easy victory over his Federalist opponent, Rufus King. King carried the three states of Massachusetts, Connecticut, and Delaware, and Monroe all the rest.

Madison had the unusual experience of retiring from the Presidency in a happy frame of mind. The ravages of war were being rapidly repaired, and other problems were being solved one after another. The country was prosperous, and instead of a deficit in the Federal treasury there was now a surplus. When he turned over his high office to a hand-picked successor, he retired to his country estate, where he could indulge both his love of rural life and his interest in public affairs without being worried with the responsibilities of office.

CHAPTER XXIV

The "Era of Good Feeling"

JAMES MONROE AS PRESIDENT

*T*HE eight years of Monroe's Presidency was an interlude of comparative peace in an age of political bitterness. The Federalist Party was too weak to put up an aggressive fight, and factionalism in the Republican ranks had not yet gone the lengths of extreme bitterness. For this reason the period is often referred to as the "Era of Good Feeling." This designation, however, is misleading in that it implies an entire absence of political strife; for within the bounds of party solidarity there was room enough for personal bickerings and differences in principle among politicians.

Monroe; personal traits As a rule the President stood apart from these disagreements and was able to exert a moderating influence on them by virtue of the suavity of his manner and the serenity of his temper. He was, therefore, one of the most popular of all our Presidents, and when he came up for re-election in 1820 he received every electoral vote but one. One elector threw away his vote for the whimsical reason that he did not want any other man to receive the honor which had been accorded Washington of being unanimously elected to the Presidency. Monroe had had a long career in the public service and was experienced in legislative, executive, and diplomatic affairs. A youthful flair for radicalism had been tamed down by age and experience into prudence and conservatism. Of unquestioned integrity and patriotism, he had the dignity which has the appearance of greatness. Furthermore, he was not handicapped by the brilliancy that advertises shortcomings. The country was passing through a transitional stage and needed in its leadership the caution and sound judgment of mediocrity rather than the hazardous daring of genius. It was a time, however, when questions of serious import were raised and policies of real significance were initiated. While the President had to make some very important decisions, his responsibility with reference to some of the new policies was chiefly that of attending properly to the incubator while they were hatching. Circumstances had thus created a niche in the public service into which he could fit perfectly. And so while in no sense a superman, he was a safe and successful President.

Monroe was exceptionally fortunate in the selection of his Cabi- *His Cabinet*
net. For Secretary of State he chose John Quincy Adams, son of the
second President. The younger Adams had spent a good deal of time
representing his country abroad and was therefore well trained by
experience for handling the foreign affairs of the nation. It was as
Secretary of State that he performed his greatest service to his country, and it is doubtful whether his superior as a premier has ever had
a place in an American administration. Crawford was continued as
Secretary of the Treasury. Clay was offered the Secretaryship of War
but declined it because he was disgruntled at not being made Secretary of State. Calhoun thereupon became Secretary of War.

The short-lived prosperity which came at the end of the war led *The Panic of*
to speculation and extravagance, which brought on panic. In the *1819:*
East a reaction from the self-denial imposed by the war caused an *Causes*
indulgence in extravagant luxuries. The high price of cotton and
food products raised the price of land and encouraged wild speculation in western lands. The numerous state banks which had sprung
up, all of which were issuing notes, made credit easy. Even the
United States Bank, which went into operation at the beginning of
1817, at first pursued a lax policy and encouraged speculation.

The land policy of the government had also promoted speculation.
By the act of 1800 one fourth of the cost of the land sold by the government had to be paid at the time of purchase, or a few months
thereafter, and the remaining payments could be met within a period of four years. Under this plan speculators would buy up large
areas with the hope of selling them in small tracts at a profit before
the later installments became due. Actual settlers who purchased
directly from the government would make the first payments and
borrow from the banks for the later installments. In this way there
arose a feverish boom in western lands. Government sales mounted
to more than 5,000,000 acres in 1819, and prices were run up by
competitive bidding to unheard-of heights. Behind this "orgy of
speculation" was a system of easy credit which kept expanding in an
ever-widening circle. It was inevitable that the bubble would ultimately burst.

In the pricking of this bubble the Bank of the United States had
an important part. After a short period of loose management, which
brought it to the verge of failure, the Bank was reorganized and put
on a sound and conservative basis. In order to save itself, it adopted
a stringent policy toward the state banks and individual creditors,
with little or no regard for their rights or the interests of the country
as a whole. All state bank notes received by it were sent in for redemption. To secure specie for these payments the state banks had

to call in their loans and limit discounts. Debtors found it impossible to meet these demands without great financial sacrifice. To make matters worse, the European countries had got back on their feet and were producing more and more of their needed food supplies. The demand for American farm products, therefore, declined and prices fell. There were numerous bank failures, and merchants, manufacturers, and farmers, as well as speculators, were unable to meet their obligations and were forced into bankruptcy. Imports fell off and the revenue of the government was greatly curtailed. The panic, which reached its height in 1819, brought on hard times which lasted for several years, and it was not until 1822 that prosperity returned.

Effect of the panic on manufacturing

The financial crisis had also brought distress to the manufacturers. In the boom period industrial plants had been constructed beyond the needs of the country, and more goods were produced than could be sold. The manufacturers, therefore, again held out their hands to the government for help. In response to this appeal a tariff bill was proposed which would have afforded a greater degree of protection. The bill passed the House of Representatives, but was defeated in

Tariff Act of 1824

the Senate by one vote. In 1824, after the Presidential election, a tariff measure similar to this one was enacted by Congress, though by a narrow majority in each house. By this act a duty of 25 per cent was put on hemp, and the rates on raw wool, iron, lead, glass, cotton bagging, and cotton and woolen goods were raised.

Feeling against the Bank

Another result of the panic was to make the Bank of the United States unpopular in the South and West. The Bank not only reduced discounts and circulation, but was also ruthless in foreclosing mortgages. As a result of this selfish policy property was sold at auction and bought in by the Bank at figures far below its true value. In this way much of the real estate of western towns came into possession of the Bank. "All the flourishing cities of the West," said Benton, "are mortgaged to this money power. They may be devoured by it at any moment. They are in the jaws of the monster! A lump of butter in the mouth of a dog—one gulp, one swallow, and all is gone!"

THE ACQUISITION OF EAST FLORIDA

Anarchy in Florida

East Florida (the present state of Florida) was still in nominal possession of Spain at the end of the War of 1812. At that time, however, the Spaniards had no control over the territory except at St. Augustine, St. Marks, Pensacola, and some minor points. The rest of the province was a refuge for criminals, runaway slaves, and former British soldiers. In this region there were also quite a number of Indians belonging to the Seminole and other Creek tribes. The anarchy prevailing in Florida was a menace to the good order of the neighboring territory of the United States, and afforded our government a plausible excuse for attempting to get possession of the province. Taking advantage of this opportunity, Secretary Adams entered into negotiations to this end with the Spanish minister at Washington. The negotiations had not gone far before they were suspended by General Jackson's invasion of Florida.

A war with the Seminole Indians had broken out in southern *Jackson in* Georgia at the end of 1817, and Jackson was put in command of the *Florida* expedition against them. Responding eagerly to this order, he quickly organized his forces, and by spring was on the Georgia frontier ready for action. He was instructed to pursue the Indians into Spanish territory if it should prove necessary. He was anxious for the acquisition of Florida and was ready to effect it if he should be so instructed by the Administration. Accordingly, he wrote to the President (so he stated) saying: "Let it be signified to me through any channel (say Mr. J. Rhea)[1] that the possession of the Floridas would be desirable to the United States, and in sixty days it will be accomplished." No answer to this letter was received and Jackson considered that silence gave consent. Moreover, he afterwards declared that he had received through Rhea direct approval of his plans from the President. Monroe denied having issued any such orders and declared that he had not read Jackson's letter until a year later. While there is still some doubt as to the exact facts behind this misunderstanding, it seems to the impartial student of history that Jackson had ground for assuming that an occupation of Florida by his forces would be quite acceptable to the government.

With the directness and thoroughness which were characteristic of the "Old Hero," he marched into East Florida and quickly brought the Seminoles to terms. He also seized the Spanish posts of St. Marks and Pensacola (June, 1818). Two British subjects, Alexander Arbuthnot and Robert Ambrister, were executed by his order after having been found guilty by court-martial of inciting the Indians to revolt.

This campaign added greatly to the prestige of Jackson, who was *Effort to cen-* already considered the hero of the War of 1812 because of his victory *sure Jackson* at New Orleans. By occupying East Florida and quieting the frontier he had achieved two objectives which the South and West had long been pursuing. The people of these two sections, therefore, hailed this twice-crowned hero as their idol. And yet he had brought embarrassment to the government. The territory of one friendly power

---

[1] Mr. Rhea was a member of the United States House of Representatives from Tennessee.

had been invaded and two subjects of another had been executed. The insult to Spanish pride might endanger the success of the negotiations which Adams was conducting with the Spanish minister, and there was danger of more serious trouble with the British government.

For a while it looked as though the American government, to appease England and Spain, would have to censure Jackson and disavow his acts. On the other hand, the attempt to discipline a popular hero, especially one with a fiery temper, was fraught with hazards which prudent politicians were loath to incur. A Cabinet meeting was held to determine what policy should be pursued in this delicate situation. Calhoun, the Secretary of War, was in favor of censuring Jackson publicly because he had exceeded his orders. Adams was opposed to this, contending that Jackson's course in Florida was in line with his duty. This view prevailed, and the decision of the President was to return the captured posts to Spain but at the same time sustain Jackson.

Adams' firm attitude

Adams was able to convince the British foreign office that the conduct of Ambrister and Arbuthnot had been such as to forfeit all claim to British protection. To the Spanish authorities he justified Jackson's action on the ground that it had been necessary to protect the United States against Indian incursions from Florida. Instead of assuming a conciliatory tone he expressed strong disapproval of Spain's weak policy in Florida and made it clear that his government would not put up with it any longer. "The United States," he said, "can as little compound with impotence as perfidy, and Spain must immediately make her election, either to place a force in Florida, adequate at once to the protection of her territory and to the fulfillment of her engagements or cede to the United States a province of which she retains nothing but the nominal possession, but which is in fact a derelict, open to the occupancy of every enemy, civilized or savage, of the United States, and serving no other earthly purpose than as a post of annoyance to them."[1]

Of the two alternatives offered to Spain by this bold declaration only one was within her reach—that of ceding Florida to the United States, for she was unable to restore order in the province. Spain had been frightened by Jackson's invasion and felt that Adams' ultimatum was not an idle threat. Besides, none of the war-weary European powers was willing to come to her assistance. Spain, therefore, signed a treaty with the United States in February, 1819.

The treaty of 1819

By this treaty Spain ceded East Florida to the United States and recognized the latter's right to West Florida. The United States

[1] C. F. Adams, ed., *Memoirs of John Quincy Adams,* IV, 107-115.

agreed to pay the claims of its citizens against the Spanish government to the amount of $5,000,000 and gave up her claim to Texas. Whatever rights in the Oregon country north of the forty-second parallel Spain may have had were by this treaty granted to the United States.

The treaty was promptly ratified by the United States Senate, but Spain delayed ratification for two years, hoping that by this delay the American government would be induced to make a pledge not to recognize the independence of the revolted Latin American states. As President Monroe showed no sign of yielding on this point, Spain gave way and ratifications were exchanged in 1821.

THE MISSOURI COMPROMISE

The most important question which came before Congress during Monroe's incumbency was that of the admission of Missouri into the Union. When the southern part of the Louisiana Purchase was organized into the Territory of Orleans (1804) the rest of that vast region was created into the District of Louisiana. In 1812 this district was granted full territorial rights and was given the name of Missouri. Slaveholding had been established by custom in all the settled portions of Louisiana while it was under French and Spanish control. Nor had the United States government done anything to interfere with slavery since it had taken over the province. Missouri was, therefore, slave territory in 1818 and would continue so unless Congress or a territorial legislature should pass laws prohibiting it.

Missouri Territory

By 1819 that part of the Missouri Territory comprised within the present state of Missouri had attained a population which entitled it to admission into the Union. Accordingly, a bill providing for its admission as a state was offered in the House of Representatives. To this bill an amendment was added by James Tallmadge of New York, which provided that the further introduction of slavery into Missouri should be prohibited, and that all children of slaves born within the state after its admission into the Union should be free at the age of twenty-five.

Missouri asks for admission to the Union

The Tallmadge Amendment

This resolution precipitated a debate in Congress which lasted a year. During this time that body was keyed up to a high pitch of excitement, and into the controversy all the prominent members of both houses were ultimately drawn. Besides, the country at large shared in this excitement, and the debates in Congress were echoed by state legislatures and mass meetings throughout the land. This was the first serious controversy over the slavery question which had arisen under the present Constitution, and it was an earnest of the great and awful struggle which occurred in the 'sixties.

Arguments in favor of slavery restriction

In defense of this restriction the antislavery advocates urged that the amendment was both constitutional and expedient. The Constitution, they contended, says that "Congress may admit new states into this Union." That implies that it is left discretionary with Congress as to whether any new state shall or shall not be admitted. Inasmuch as Congress has power either to admit or refuse to admit any new state, it has the right by implication to prescribe the terms on which the admission will be allowed.

The restrictionists also contended that the opening up of the new state to slavery would exclude the small farmers of the North and East from land which had been purchased by the country as a whole; for their system of free labor could not compete successfully with the system of bond service. Besides, if slavery were to be legal in the new states the slaveholding section would be given an undue voice in the Federal government; for by the three-fifths provision in the Constitution the South was allowed more representatives in the House in proportion to white population than was the North.

Arguments against restriction

The Southern leaders maintained, on the other hand, that it was both unconstitutional and inexpedient to impose this restriction on Missouri. Even ,if Congress had discretionary power in the admission of new states, this discretion was limited—it could either admit or refuse to admit, but could not impose conditions. On this point the ablest argument was offered in the Senate by William Pinkney of Maryland. In a speech of great length he argued with forceful logic and literary ability against the constitutionality of imposing restrictions on new states. If Congress can impose this restriction it can impose any restriction. As the old states did not have restrictions placed upon them they would be on a different basis from the new ones. A union made up of states, some of which had more powers than others, would not be a union of equals but one of giants and pygmies.

To the Southern leaders it seemed unfair that the planters of their section should not be allowed to take their laborers with them into territory for which they had helped to pay; for to them the exclusion of their labor system from this territory virtually meant the exclusion of the Southerners from it. This territory, it was said, was purchased out of the common purse, and the North and the South were joint tenants of it. To oust one section to the advantage of the other would be an act of gross injustice.

Southern Congressmen contended that the continuation of slavery in Missouri would not encourage the importation of more slaves into the country from Africa, but would alleviate the condition of those already here by preventing the overconcentration of them in the old states. The opening up of new markets for slaves would increase their value, and the more valuable they became the more it would be to the interest of the owners to treat them kindly. The evils of slavery would thus be mitigated by diffusion.

The House passed the Missouri Bill with the Tallmadge Amendment incorporated in it (February, 1819). The Senate refused to accept the amendment and so the measure was lost. *The House and the Senate deadlocked*

The question came up again at the next session of Congress, but for some time the House and Senate were unable to agree on the terms for the admission of Missouri. In the meantime Maine, with the permission of Massachusetts, had adopted a constitution and asked to come into the Union as a free state. A bill for the admission of Maine passed the House (January, 1820) and was sent to the Senate. The Senate joined the Maine Bill to the Missouri Bill and voted to admit Maine as a free state and Missouri as a slave state. The Senate bill also included an important additional clause which Senator Thomas of Illinois had offered as a compromise amendment. It provided for the exclusion of slavery from the remainder of the Louisiana Purchase north of the parallel of 36° 30′. *The Maine-Missouri Bill* *The Thomas Amendment*

The House refused to accept this plan and again there was a deadlock. Thereupon a conference committee was appointed and its recommendations were accepted by both houses. By the terms of this final agreement, Missouri was to be admitted to the Union as a slave state, and slavery was to be excluded from the remainder of the Louisiana Purchase north of the parallel of 36° 30′. These proposals were accepted by both houses, and so they were adopted as a settlement of the controversy (1820). Maine in a separate bill was also admitted as a free state. *Terms of the final agreement*

Since President Monroe signed the bill, the controversy was now apparently settled, but the agreement proved to be only a truce. About the middle of the year 1820, Missouri adopted her constitution, which contained a clause prohibiting the immigration into Missouri of any free Negroes and mulattoes. When this constitution was presented to Congress in November as a basis for the admission of Missouri as a state, objection to it was raised on the ground that this paragraph was in violation of the Constitution of the United States. In some states, it was contended, Negroes were citizens, and to exclude them from Missouri would be to violate that clause in the Federal Constitution which says that "the citizens of each State shall be entitled to all the privileges and immunities of citizens in the several States." *The second Missouri Compromise*

The controversy was now reopened and a long and acrimonious debate followed. Meanwhile Clay had assumed the management of the case. He suggested a formula which after slight modification was finally agreed upon by both sides. By this second compromise Missouri was admitted to the Union under a promise given by her legislature that no law would ever be passed by it which would deprive any citizen of another state of any rights to which he was entitled under the Constitution of the United States.

The second Missouri Compromise was nothing more than a face-saving device, as the condition imposed was difficult, if not impossible, of enforcement. It was only a pledge on the part of the legislature, and, of course, could not limit the future action of the state.

Jefferson's apprehensions as to the Missouri question

With the acceptance of the Missouri Compromise there came a temporary lull in the fight over slavery. But the bitter controversy, and the principle of agreement which grew out of it, laid the foundations for serious trouble in the future. Thomas Jefferson, with prophetic instinct, spoke of the portents of evil which would emanate from this historic quarrel as follows: "This momentous question, like a fire bell in the night, awakened and filled me with terror. I considered it at once as the knell of the Union. It is hushed, indeed, for the moment. But this is a reprieve only, not a final sentence. A geographical line, coinciding with a marked principle, moral and political, once conceived and held up to the angry passions of men, will never be obliterated; and every new irritation will mark it deeper and deeper."[1]

THE MONROE DOCTRINE

The American background

In 1808 the Spanish American colonies revolted against the authority of Napoleon, who had deposed Ferdinand, the Bourbon King of Spain, and taken over the government. These colonies returned to their allegiance to the home country when Ferdinand was restored (1814); but the effort on the part of the Spanish government to restore the restrictions on colonial commerce was strongly resented in the American dependencies, and in 1817 they were again in revolt.

Attitude of Britain toward the Spanish American rebels

In the meantime an extensive trade, beneficial to both sides, had grown up between England and Latin America. British manufacturers were procuring valuable raw materials from South America and selling their finished products to great advantage in the

---

[1] P. L. Ford, ed., *The Works of Thomas Jefferson*, 12 vols. (The Federal Edition, 1904-1905), XII, 157, 158

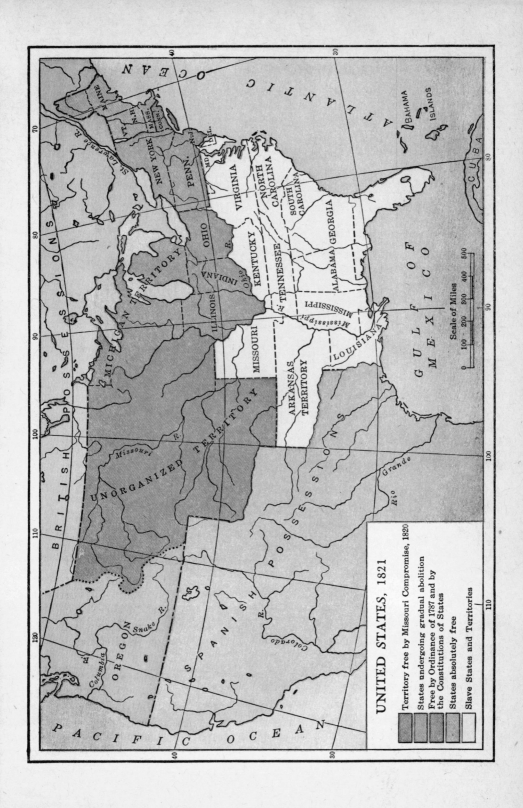

UNITED STATES, 1821

Scale of Miles
0   100   200   300   400   500

Territory free by Missouri Compromise, 1820
States undergoing gradual abolition
Free by Ordinance of 1787 and by the Constitutions of States
States absolutely free
Slave States and Territories

rebel states. The suppression of the revolts and the consequent renewal of Spanish commercial restrictions would put an end to this lucrative trade. The British government, at that time in the hands of the Tories, had no sympathy with rebellion and was opposed to the ideology of the insurgents. But the jingling of the guinea made such a loud and pleasant sound that it drowned the still, small voice of Tory principles. Accordingly, the British government gave moral, and English citizens actual, support to the rebel cause. Spain was not able to cope with the situation, and in a few years had lost all her continental possessions in both Americas.

In the United States, the people—especially those in the West— strongly sympathized with the Latin American patriots. They regarded their struggle for the right of self-determination as a movement similar to the one by which our independence was gained. The most brilliant champion of this sentiment was Henry Clay. He made a great speech in the House (May, 1818) in which he earnestly supported his motion providing for the recognition of the insurgent states by the American government. He contended that by such recognition the new republics would be encouraged to preserve their rights and liberties and would be bound to the United States by close commercial ties and would follow its lead in diplomacy and foreign policy. In this way our country would achieve a moral leadership and a sort of political hegemony throughout the Western Hemisphere. Such a position would greatly aid us in winning economic independence and security against outward attack. This foreign policy was one phase of the American System which he so ardently championed. *Attitude of the United States* *Clay's position*

Apparently Monroe was at first inclined toward Clay's views, but Secretary Adams insisted that his country should not sacrifice its interests to the dreams of idealism. To him the Latin Americans seemed too turbulent and inexperienced in political affairs to set up permanent governments. Furthermore, recognition of the independence of the rebel states might get us into trouble with European powers. Action with reference to recognition should, therefore, be taken only in conjunction with England and possibly with other European nations. Another objection—and probably the main one— was that Adams had his heart set on the acquisition of East Florida. If his government should recognize the independence of the South American states it would antagonize the Spanish government and jeopardize the success of his efforts to secure this territory. *Attitude of Adams toward the Latin American patriots*

This latter objection was removed by Spain's ratification in 1821 of the Florida treaty. By this time there was no doubt that some of the Latin American states had won their freedom. In the follow-

Independence of the Latin American states recognized

ing year, therefore, both the President and Congress indicated a willingness to recognize the independence of some of the new republics, and others were added to the list later.[1]

At the time the United States was gaining territory in the southeast by the purchase of Florida, it was threatened with a loss of its possessions in the northwest. In 1821 the Russian Czar issued a ukase laying claim to the Pacific coast of North America as far south as the parallel of 51°. The authority of Russia was asserted over all waters within one hundred Italian miles of the coast, and the nationals of other countries were not allowed to fish or trade in them. In protest against this decree, Secretary Adams (July, 1823) declared to the Russian minister at Washington that the United States government did not recognize Russia's claim to this territory or *any other* territory on this continent. "We should assume distinctly," he said, "the principle that the American continents are no longer subjects of any new European colonial establishments." In contesting Russia's right to any territory in North America, Adams was taking a more advanced position than he could maintain; but the principle that America was not open to new colonization was virtually accepted by Russia when she signed (1824) a treaty giving up all claims to land south of the parallel of 54° 40'.

The European background: The European Concert

At the end of the Napoleonic era Europe was sick of war and was anxious for an agreement whereby the nations would be forced to keep the peace. In November, 1815, therefore, the Allies—England, Prussia, Russia, and Austria—concluded a quadruple alliance, pledging themselves to the preservation of "public peace, the tranquillity of states, the inviolability of possessions, and the faith of treaties." European congresses were held from time to time to enforce this policy. France too (from 1818 on) took part in these meetings, and so there was in effect a sort of league of nations. This league, including as it did all the great powers of Europe, is known as the Concert of Europe.

The Concert subsequently (1820) declared in favor of intervention to put down insurrections in the various states of Europe and carried out this policy by sending troops to stamp out revolutions in Spain and Italy. The Tory government of Great Britain, although not in favor of revolution or even liberalism, was unwilling to assume responsibility for regulating the internal affairs of other

---

[1] President Monroe formally received diplomatic representatives from Mexico in December, 1822; from the Empire of Brazil in May, 1824; and from the Central American Confederation in August, 1824. Diplomatic representatives were sent from the United States to the United Provinces of La Plata (Argentina) and Chile in January, 1823, and to Peru in May, 1826. S. F. Bemis, *A Diplomatic History of the United States*, 201.

countries. It therefore dissented from this interpretation of the treaty of alliance. The Concert was now dominated by Prince Metternich, foreign minister of Austria, who was the dean of the reactionaries. Under his guidance the Concert made an effort to strike down revolution and liberalism wherever they raised their heads.

The Congress of Verona

The European Concert (or Holy Alliance[1] as it is generally known) was next called upon to intervene in Spain. A revolt had broken out in that country, and the king, Ferdinand VII, had been forced to accept a liberal constitution. He chafed under the restrictions on his power imposed by the new constitution and began to intrigue with foreign rulers to free himself from them. In response to these requests an international congress was held at Verona in 1822 to consider the question. Against the protest of England this congress decided to have France intervene to restore Ferdinand to his old authority, and this policy was carried out.

The possibility of intervention in America by the Concert

Ferdinand also wanted the European allies to send ships and men to America to help him reconquer his rebellious colonies. Another European congress was to be held, and at this meeting intervention in the Western Hemisphere might be discussed. The British government was frightened by this prospect. For if Spain were restored to her old place in America the commercial restrictions would be revived, and English merchants and manufacturers would lose the profitable trade which they had lately been enjoying. Furthermore, by intervening in America, France would increase her power and prestige and get a foothold across seas that might be highly prejudicial to British interests. Later investigation has shown that Russia, Prussia, and Austria had no intention of intervening in America, as they could have gained nothing by assuming such a responsibility; but they might have been willing to give France a free hand in the Western Hemisphere.

Canning's proposal

England, being no longer in agreement with her former allies, was in a position of dangerous isolation in Europe, and was also menaced with the loss of her trade in America. To strengthen the

---

1 In 1815 the rulers of Austria, Prussia, and Russia, at the suggestion of Czar Alexander, entered into an agreement to govern their subjects and conduct their foreign relations in accordance with the principles of the Christian religion. This understanding is known as the Holy Alliance. If its *professed* intentions had been realized the millennium would have come to Europe. But the alliance was not implemented in any way and was merely a pious, harmless gesture, although most of the powers of Europe, to humor the whim of the Russian Czar, joined it. For some reason, hard to understand, historians speak of the activities of the European Concert in the eighteen-twenties as those of the Holy Alliance. They intimate, but do not clearly state, that the Holy Alliance had been changed and made the basis of the Concert. If this view is correct the Holy Alliance was holy in its professed objectives in the early years, but was not an alliance; in the later period it had become an alliance but had lost its holiness of purpose.

position of his country in both the old world and the new, Canning, the British foreign minister, began to look about for an ally. The United States was likewise opposed to intervention in Latin America by the European allies. Such intervention might not only put a stop to its new trade with South America but might menace its safety; for the danger of attack on the United States would be increased if the European powers should get a strong hold on the Western Hemisphere. Canning, therefore, saw in the youthful republic a possible ally that might co-operate with England in the pursuit of their common interests. Accordingly, he suggested that the two governments issue a joint statement pledging themselves against taking any of Spain's American possessions and declaring their opposition to any transfer of Spanish American territory to any other power.

Monroe declines Canning's offer

When Monroe received Canning's proposal he was at first favorably disposed toward it. He consulted Jefferson and Madison as to the offer. Both advised acceptance and Jefferson was enthusiastic over the proposition. He felt that if Canning's invitation were accepted, England would throw the weight of her power into the scale and "emancipate a continent at one stroke." And this from the man who coined the phrase "no entangling alliances"!

John Quincy Adams, the able Secretary of State, did not agree with the venerable ex-Presidents as to the proposal. He advised that it be declined, since he was opposed to our government tying itself up with a European power. It should act alone, he thought, in protesting against European interference in South America and not "come in as a cock-boat in the wake of the British man-of-war." Furthermore, he was unwilling to give the pledge that the United States would never take over any Spanish territory, for he expected that at some future day Cuba would be added to the American domain.[1]

The Doctrine as enunciated by Monroe

Monroe accepted the suggestions of his Secretary of State and embodied them in his annual message to Congress in December, 1823. In this message he gave the attitude of his government toward any possible intervention in Latin America by the European powers and toward Russia's claims with reference to the Northwest. These statements constituted the Monroe Doctrine. They are in brief as follows:

(1) The American continents "are henceforth not to be considered as subjects for future colonization by any European Power. . . ."

(2) "In the wars of the European powers, in matters relating to

---

[1] C. F. Adams, ed., *Memoirs of John Quincy Adams*, VI, 179, 194, 199-212.

Malady of Love

Refused a divorce on evidence that she was allergic to her husband, Mrs. Joyce Holdridge, 27 of Los Angeles, had her marriage annulled on the grounds that she could not perform her wifely duties. "Every time I was near him I would break out in a rash from head to toe," she testified, and "physicians and psychiatrists finally told me I would have to leave him."

This is not the first time love has broken out in a rash or made one sick. The Greeks defined love as a malady and one of its symptoms is an outward inexpressibility of an inward alloverishness. Like an itch or hayfever, it upsets the victim's emotional, physical and chemical equilibrium.

Hollywood, where incompatibility and mental cruelty are so often given as legal substitutes for that keener competition that prevails there, will now suffer an epidemic of new allergies. Temperamental screen stars suffering with eccentricities so easily work themselves into itches, urges and rashes.

A Mrs. Eleanore Croze, 31, of Detroit, was granted a divorce from her husband, Robert, after she testified that he refused to let her kiss him because of fear of germs and would not permit her to sit on his lap because it put new creases in his pants.

Microbes and "your-crobes" have a contagious affect upon the spread of what the Greeks diagnosed as that dangerous but not incurable malady of love.

Salem Switcher
Says He's Richer

SALEM, Mass.—"I switched to Ca[l]vert," says Ralph Raymond, loc[al] painter, "because I think Calvert's [a] better buy. It *always* tastes milder an[d] mellower . . . that's why I say, penn[y] for penny, it's the *only* one for me."

CALVERT RESERVE Blended Whiske[y] —86.8 Proof—65% Grain Neutral Spirit[s] Calvert Distillers Corp., New York Cit[y]

Call WA. 6565 for Want Ad[s]

---

themselves, we have never taken any part, nor does it comport with our policy, so to do."

(3) The political system of the Continental European powers is essentially different from that of America, and we should consider any attempt to extend this system "to any portions of this Hemisphere, as dangerous to our peace and safety."

(4) "With the existing Colonies or dependencies of any European power we have not interfered, and shall not interfere."

(5) But with the governments that have declared and maintained their independence and whose independence we have acknowledged, "we could not view any interposition for the purpose of oppressing them, or controlling in any other manner, their destiny, by any European power, in any other light, than as the manifestation of an unfriendly disposition towards the United States."

The immediate effect of this pronouncement was slight. None of the European powers, with the possible exception of France, had any intention of intervening in America. If France had had any such purpose it had been dispelled two months earlier by the strong stand against intervention which Canning had taken in a note to the French minister in London. The declaration did, however, hold "up a hand of warning to Europe, a hand which in 1823 was little, but later was to be seen by everybody."[1] *The immediate effect of the pronouncement*

The historic importance of this statement lay in its future rather than in its contemporary significance. It was a formulation of policies which had grown out of American foreign relations during the half-century of independence. Washington in his Farewell Address and Jefferson in his First Inaugural had come out vigorously for a policy of isolation—"no entangling alliances" with foreign powers. Opposition to the transfer of American territory from one European power to another was strongly shown by Jefferson in his attitude toward the cession of Louisiana to France by Spain. In the handling of the Florida question Jefferson and Madison had shown that the United States had an interest greater than that of any other country in the affairs of the Western Hemisphere. Thus the doctrine of isolation, opposition to transfer of colonial possessions, and the paramount interest of the United States in cis-Atlantic affairs had already been embodied in American practice. These doctrines were now all clearly and forcefully declared. To these older doctrines was added the new one that the political ideology and practice of the old world were not to find a lodgment in the new. *Policies out of which the Doctrine had grown*

The Monroe Doctrine as first enunciated was only a part of a

---

[1] S. F. Bemis, *A Diplomatic History of the United States.* 204-205.

*Significance
of the
Doctrine*

Presidential message. It did not call for or receive any action from Congress. It had, therefore, technically no legal standing whatever but it became the basis of the most important element in American foreign policy.[1] To prevent European nations from extending their power and influence in the Western Hemisphere became the cardinal principle in American policy of public defense. This policy is as deeply rooted in the minds of the American people as any that rests on constitutional sanction. The Monroe Doctrine is thus a part of the unwritten constitution of the nation.

[1] It was not until recently that Congress gave legal recognition to the Monroe Doctrine. In June, 1940, it adopted a resolution declaring that our government will not recognize the transfer of any American territory from one European power to another.

Courtesy of New York Central Railroad

PASSENGER PACKET BOAT ON THE ERIE CANAL IN 1820.
Speed six miles per hour.

CHAPTER XXV

Sectionalism in Politics

THE WESTWARD MOVEMENT (1815-1830)

*D*ESPITE the revival of nationalism which resulted from the *The sections* War of 1812, sectionalism began in the early eighteen-twenties to play an important part in American politics. The country was divided into the three regions of the Northeast, the South, and the West. So different in their economic interests were these three sections that the term "economic empire" has been suggested as the proper one to characterize the United States at this time. It is true that each region was subdivided into smaller economic areas with conflicting interests; but in each of the three sections there was one outstanding occupation which dominated the economic life of the entire region and gave to it a large measure of solidarity. In the Northeast, manufacturing had before the end of this period become the predominant interest, although commerce had until lately held the primacy; in the South the production of cotton, tobacco, and rice by the use of both slave and free labor was the leading factor in economic life; while in the West the growing of grain on small farms with free labor was the chief occupation.

Of these sections the one which developed most rapidly after the *Economic* War of 1812 was the West. The main reason for the rapid growth *conditions a* of the West was the existence there of a seemingly unlimited amount *factor in* of unoccupied land to match the land hunger of the farmers in the *expansion* older settlements. The advantages of this section had been advertised by the war; for the soldiers who participated in the frontier campaigns observed the fertility of the soil of the unoccupied regions and noted the fine opportunities they offered for agriculture. Western expansion was also considerably influenced by economic and social conditions in the East.[1] The war and the events immediately

---

[1] According to the contention of the earlier students of the westward movement, hard times in the East encouraged immigration to the West. The difficulty of finding employment and earning a livelihood in the older communities caused the people to seek their fortunes in a new land. Later scholars have taken issue with this view and have convincingly shown that hard times in the East retarded the westward movement, because in times of panic it is difficult for would-be emigrants to procure the means needed for the trek westward. For a discussion of the later view see Murray Kane, in the *Mississippi Valley Historical Review*, XXIII, 169-188; XXVII, 379-400.

preceding it had caused economic dislocations which gave rise to discontent among those groups in the East that had difficulty in making adjustments to the changed conditions. The restrictions on foreign trade which preceded and accompanied the War of 1812 proved a great drawback to the shipping and commercial interests of the North. This meant unemployment for sailors and others engaged in seafaring occupations. Nor was the gap thus created bridged over by the infant manufacturing industries which had sprung up; for the new jobs were filled mainly by women and children. The tiller of the soil in New England was suffering from the competition of the farmers on the rich lands of the then-settled West. He was thus inclined to leave his rocky hillsides and seek more productive lands on the frontier.

Occupation of the Northwest   At first the New Englanders, on leaving the older settlements, moved to the frontier regions of their own section and to western New York. It was not long, however, before many of them were going into Ohio, and after the completion of the Erie Canal (1825) a considerable number moved on into Indiana and Illinois. There also poured into the Northwest a large stream of emigration from the middle states, especially Pennsylvania and New Jersey. Into the region north of the Ohio came many settlers from Kentucky, Tennessee, and the older southern states. So numerous were these Southern emigrants that at the end of this period they constituted the predominant element in the population of Indiana and Illinois. Some of these Southerners belonged to the wealthier families and were attracted by the bright economic prospects and the opportunities for political leadership in the new section. They took their slaves with them, keeping them in bond service by technical contracts of indenture. Most of the Southerners, however, who went to the Old Northwest were yeomen, who owned few or no slaves. Many of them were affiliated with religious denominations, such as the Baptists and the Quakers, which opposed slavery.

The Southwest   But to the Southerner, the Southwest offered the finest field for expansion. After the War of 1812, and especially from 1830 on, emigrants from the South advanced rapidly into this section. Those who sought out this favored land included big planters and small farmers, a good part of the latter going from Tennessee and the upland regions of the older states. The soil in the Atlantic coastal plain was wearing thin, and the rich lands of the Southwest were most inviting to the cotton grower. The Industrial Revolution had put in rapid motion the wheels of the cotton mills in both Old and New England, and there was a great demand for cotton. The invention of the cotton gin made it possible to meet this demand by the cultivation of larger areas. The journey westward by the big planter was more like a picnic excursion than a trek into the wilderness. Riding with his family in his carriage, serenaded by a lively pack of hounds, he could enjoy ease and comfort while his slaves drove forward numbers of horses, cattle, hogs, and sheep.

While economic opportunities in the older states were declining, conditions in the West were becoming more inviting. Room for new settlers was made by securing more and more land from the Indians. As a result of the military activity of Jackson in the Southwest and of Harrison in the Northwest, the natives had been subdued and forced to surrender much of their territory. By a series of treaties almost all of the desirable land in both the Northwest and the Southwest had been surrendered by them before the end of this period. *Circumstances favorable to western migration*

Improvement in the means of transportation also made it easier for pioneers to reach their destination. The construction of turnpikes, notably the National Turnpike (which reached the Ohio River in 1818), rendered the approaches to the Ohio less difficult. The steamboat had been in use on the Ohio since 1811, and by 1820 was taking cargoes both up and down the Mississippi and its tributaries. Later the completion of the Erie Canal afforded a convenient route for Northern emigrants.

It was also easier now to obtain land in the new country than it had been heretofore. The Land Law of 1820 was more favorable to the settler than the earlier acts had been. Prior to this time the minimum amount that the government would sell was one hundred and sixty acres and the minimum price was $2.00 per acre. One fourth of this had to be paid in cash and the remainder in four installments extending over a period of four years. By the act of 1820 the credit system was abolished, but the minimum amount which could be bought was reduced to eighty acres and the minimum price to $1.25 per acre. As one hundred dollars would now buy a homestead, the land was put in reach of the actual settlers. Next year a provision was added for the relief of purchasers under the old plan who could not meet their payments. By this act persons who had fallen behind in their payments could retain such portions of their tracts as they had paid for and return the others to the government. *The Land Act of 1820*

Before the Erie Canal was opened the settlers made their way to the Ohio River over wagon roads, some of which were turnpikes. The most widely used of these turnpikes was the National Road, which ran from Cumberland, Maryland, to Wheeling (now West Virginia). Pioneers from Kentucky, Tennessee, and the older South- *Routes of travel to the West* ern states, on their way to the Northwest or to Missouri, passed through the gaps of the Alleghenies to the Ohio. On reaching that river the emigrant either took a steamboat or loaded his family and belongings on a flatboat and floated down stream to the point of debarkation. A typical trip of this kind as described by a contemporary (1820) was as follows: "Today we passed two large rafts lashed together, by which single conveyance several families from New England were transporting themselves and their property to the land of promise in the western woods. Each raft was eighty or ninety feet long, with a small house erected on it; and on each side was a stack of hay, round which several horses and cows were feeding, while the paraphernalia of a farm-yard, the ploughs, waggons, pigs, children, and poultry, carelessly distributed, gave to the whole more the appearance of a permanent residence, than of a caravan of adventurers seeking a home."[1]

Settlers going into the Southwest from the South Atlantic states followed the two upcountry routes running from Fredericksburg, Virginia, to a point near Milledgeville, Georgia. Here these roads converged to form the "Federal Road," which terminated at New Orleans. Some of the emigrants, however, left these roads at such points as Columbia, Greenville, and Athens and crossed the mountains to the road leading southwestward along the Great Valley. From this road and its branches settlers moved into interior Mississippi and West Alabama by the Jackson Trace and the Natchez Trace, or by the Coosa River.

Stages of development in the West

At the point of destination the emigrant unloaded his few household goods and proceeded through the wilderness to the site of his new home. Here he cleared out a small area and with the aid of neighbors erected a rude log cabin. Still ruder structures were also built to shelter his stock. A small acreage was prepared for cultivation by clearing out the underbrush and deadening the trees. This latter process consisted in cutting a circle through the bark around the tree at its base to prevent the sap from rising through the trunk to the branches. Some of the trees—those freest from knots and limbs—were split into rails for the zigzag fences. Other tree trunks when they fell or were cut down were rolled together and burned. This work was so heavy as to require the assistance of the neighbors. A logrolling, like a house-raising, was an important co-operative activity and despite the arduous work, an occasion of enjoyment, for it usually brought forth generous supplies of food and drink. The first settler cultivated only a small amount of his land. His

---

[1] Quoted by E. L. Bogart and C. M. Thompson in *Readings in the Economic History of the United States* (Longmans, 1917) , 352.

cattle and hogs were allowed to wander in the woods, the one feeding on the buds and the grass of the treeless spots and the other picking up acorns and nuts dropped by the trees. By the aid of his long-barreled rifle the pioneer could supplement the supplies gathered from garden and field.

This primitive method of living did not last long. After a few years the pioneer had developed into a successful farmer or had sold his clearing with its improvements to a newcomer from the East. More lands were now brought under cultivation, orchards were planted, and more comforts were enjoyed. Sawmills and gristmills were erected and weatherboarded houses took the place of log cabins. Small villages grew up at which were located retail stores, and in some cases schools and churches. Itinerant preachers passed through and stopped long enough to carry on revival meetings.

It was not long before the West reached another stage in its development. Villages grew into towns and cities; numerous schools, churches, and some small colleges were established; and life in these more advanced communities assumed the pattern of the old settlements in the East.

The difficulties encountered in the occupation of the New West *Personal* were very much the same as those generally experienced by frontiers- *traits and* men. The hardships and severities of the early years tended to de- *ideals of fron-* velop a type of character universally found under pioneer condi- *tiersmen* tions. Courage and coolness in the face of danger, self-reliance, and inventiveness were highly prized virtues. Life in the untamed wilderness also brought forth certain ideals, such as a belief in the worthiness of the common man and a distrust of experts. The frontiersman was therefore usually a rugged individualist with strong democratic leanings both in his social relations and in his political views. On the frontier there was no great inequality as to the ownership of wealth, a condition which was conducive to social and political equality. Frontier conditions in other respects were also unfavorable to the promotion of aristocratic ideas. Aristocracies are usually based either on wealth or family prestige; most of the backwoodsmen had neither. Even the few who could boast of distinguished lineage were so far removed from their family connections that they could not touch base and thereby gain an advantage over their neighbors.

Along with these good qualities were developed some characteristics which were not so attractive. Owing to the scarcity of schools and churches the frontiersmen were backward in intellectual, artistic, and spiritual culture and, therefore, often exhibited a rawness of personality which was anything but desirable. Self-confidence too often lapsed into braggadocio, and individuality into conten-

LIFE ON THE FRONTIER: THE FIRST CRUDE CABIN.

LIFE ON THE FRONTIER: THE LAND CLEARED FOR FARMING.

(BOTH) From Woestemeyer & Gambrill's "The Western Movement,"
D. Appleton-Century Company, Inc.

LIFE ON THE FRONTIER: THE FARM DEVELOPED.

LIFE ON THE FRONTIER: THE FAMILY HOMESTEAD ON A LARGE TRACT.

(BOTH) From Woestemeyer & Gambrill's "The Western Movement,"
D. Appleton-Century Company, Inc.

tiousness. There was also an inadequate appreciation of the beautiful and too great a tolerance of ugliness. Under the new environment the customs of the old settlements were somewhat relaxed, and this exemption from restraint was favorable to the development of originality and inventiveness. But a disregard of some of the conventions deprived social relations of many pleasant amenities and tended to promote boorishness.

Was there homogeneity in the West?

At first the whole Mississippi Valley was characterized by a marked homogeneity. The settlers, whether they lived in the northern or southern part, had much in common. The problems of pioneer life and economic and social conditions were very much the same throughout the entire region. The Mississippi River was also a strong bond to hold both sections together. But by 1830 a line of demarcation had appeared between the northern and southern West. In the region north of the Ohio River the people were engaged in raising grain and livestock on small farms with free labor, and had begun to take an interest in manufacturing and town life. Their trade routes, economic interests, and social ideals tended to bind them to the older Middle and Northern states. On the other hand, the rapid growth of cotton culture and the spread of the plantation in the southern West was binding that region to the eastern South. The interests of this newer South were closely assimilated to those of the older South. These divisive trends were destined in time to split the new region into a northern and southern West, as they had already divided the seaboard into a northern and southern East. By 1830, however, this trend had not gone very far, and so at that time there was still considerable homogeneity in the West.

Transportation in the West

The main problem of the West was transportation. How to get needed supplies from the East and find an outlet for their farm surplus was a matter of deep concern for the frontiersmen. During the latter half of this period merchandise from the East was brought across the mountains over the Pennsylvania turnpikes and the Cumberland Road. Companies using four-horse wagons made a business of transporting freight from the eastern cities to the interior. In the year 1820 more than three thousand wagons were driven from Philadelphia to Pittsburgh conveying merchandise valued at eighteen million dollars. Freight that was particularly heavy could not be transported in this way except at prohibitive costs and was usually brought to the interior by steamboat up the Mississippi and its tributaries. But western Georgia, Alabama, and eastern Mississippi were served by the rivers flowing eastward and southward and by the roads leading from Charleston, Savannah, and Mobile. The Coosa-Alabama-Tombigbee River system was particularly useful in the transportation system of Alabama and eastern Mississippi, and the Chattahoochee was important in west Georgia.

How to get the surplus of the western farms to market was also a problem. Livestock could be driven to eastern markets, and mules and horses were sent to the southern plantations in this way. Hogs and cattle in great numbers were also driven across the Appalachian Mountains. Travellers in this period report seeing droves of hogs numbering four and five thousand.

Courtesy of the New-York Historical Society, New York City

JOHN QUINCY ADAMS (1767-1848).

United States Minister to the Netherlands, Prussia, Russia, and Great Britain, Secretary of State under Monroe and Sixth President of the United States. Painted from life in 1834 by Asher B. Durand (1796-1886).

But the chief outlet for western produce was the Mississippi River and its navigable tributaries. Down these streams were floated cattle, flour, bacon, whiskey, and other products of the farm on all kinds of river craft—including rafts, flatboats, keelboats, skiffs, and steamboats. The steamboat had the advantage over all its rivals not only because of its greater speed but also because of its being able to carry a cargo upstream as well as down. Before the invention of the steamboat a few barges conveying small cargoes made, with great difficulty, one trip a year from New Orleans to Louisville.

It took about ninety days for this strenuous pull upstream, whereas the steamboat as early as 1822 could make the trip in sixteen days.

On reaching New Orleans some of the western products were transshipped to the Atlantic seaboard and some to foreign countries. A good part of them, however, was distributed among the settlers of the Southwest. The rapid extension of cotton culture in this region greatly enhanced its importance as a market for food supplies produced in the northern West.

The admission of new states

The westward movement led to the rapid addition of a number of new states to the Union. Before 1812 three of these, Kentucky, Tennessee, and Ohio, had been admitted. From 1812 to 1821 six more were added—Louisiana (1812), Indiana (1816), Mississippi (1817), Illinois (1818), Alabama (1819), and Missouri (1821).[1] The gain in population in these new commonwealths from 1820 to 1830 was nearly a million and a half, an advance of more than sixty-five per cent. Besides, there had been a large increase in the population of the frontier districts of the older states. This growth in population gave the West a marked increase in its representation in Congress. This section had therefore by the end of this period a strong voice in the councils of the nation.

REALIGNMENT OF POLITICAL PARTIES

Conflict of interests between the sections

The conflict of interests between the sections impelled statesmanship to concern itself more and more with the problem of making the proper adjustments between their conflicting interests. The first serious clash between the sections was the dispute which arose over slavery when Missouri applied for admission to the Union. While this controversy was settled by the Missouri Compromise, the slavery question was connected, either directly or indirectly, with most of the other disputes which afterwards arose between the sections.

Attitude of the various sections toward protection

Among the sectional issues that figured in the decade of the 'twenties, internal improvements and protection played a prominent part. The manufacturers of the Northeast were clamoring for a higher tariff, which would raise the prices of their products and thus protect home industry against foreign competition. They also advocated the construction of roads and canals at Federal expense. The Southerners could not share to any considerable extent in the benefits of protection, since manufacturing was not an important occupation in the South. Furthermore, a protective tariff would raise the price of the goods they would have to buy and thus saddle

---

[1] During this period one eastern state, Maine, was also admitted into the Union (1820).

an unnecessary burden upon them. The home-market argument did not appeal to them, since the great staples of the South—tobacco, cotton, and rice—found a ready sale in foreign countries. A high tariff, by restricting imports, would also discourage exports. For if the European countries were hampered in the sale of their goods in the United States they would be less likely to buy Southern and other American products.

Nor did the Southern planters and farmers favor the construction of internal improvements at the expense of the Federal government. Such a policy would impose extra taxes upon them without giving them adequate compensating advantages. The Appalachian mountain system formed a barrier between the Southern coastal plain and the West which could be crossed by turnpikes only with great difficulty and could be pierced by canals only at a few places, if at all. The eastern South could, therefore, hardly hope for a proportional share of the roads and canals which would be constructed in carrying out a national program of internal improvements. Furthermore, the doctrine of states' rights, which the Tidewater South had embraced, was contrary to the nationalism involved in a policy of internal improvements by the Federal government. *Attitude of the sections toward internal improvements*

By the use of the steamboat and the completion of the National Turnpike to the Ohio, and later by the construction of the Erie Canal, transportation facilities for the Westerners were greatly improved. These means of transportation were not, however, adequate to the needs of a rapidly increasing population. The Westerners therefore clamored, in the early days, for government aid in the construction of canals and favored Clay's policy of internal improvements. They also believed that a protective tariff by promoting manufactures would greatly aid in creating a home market for agricultural produce. Factories would be established in the West, as well as in the East, and towns would grow up around them. The employees in these industrial centers would be consumers of farm products and the farmer would be able to sell his commodities at home. The home-market argument in favor of a protective tariff therefore made a strong appeal to them. Thus on the questions of tariff and internal improvements they were nationalists.

It was only in the Northwest, however, that this nationalism persisted. For after the Southwest had become closely affiliated economically and socially with the southern East, the newer South took up the states' rights views of the older South. Nor did the nationalism of the Northwest extend to the money question. Since many of the small farmers of this section were in debt, they wanted a cheap and abundant currency. Such a currency would be afforded by the state banks, provided there was no national bank to curb them in their issue of notes. So they were opposed to a national bank.

The election of 1824: Political factions

The era of good feeling ended with the close of Monroe's second term. The Federalist Party was no longer a factor in national politics, and the Republican Party, which had controlled the national government for nearly a quarter of a century, had begun to break up into factions. Each of these factions was led by an aspirant for the Presidency. The party was embarrassed with a superabundance of Presidential timber, and the problem of making a choice was a difficult one.

Opposition to the Congressional caucus

Since the national convention had not yet come into existence, the only machinery available for uniting on a single standard-bearer was the Congressional caucus. This had been the agency previously employed (since 1796); but with only one party in the field a nomination by the caucus would be equivalent to an election. The President would thus be an appointee of Congress and the executive would become dependent upon the legislative branch of the government. There was therefore widespread opposition to the Congressional caucus as a means of selecting the Presidential candidate.

Candidates for President

Despite this objection, there was still considerable support for the old plan, and in February, 1824, a caucus was held to choose the Republican candidate. Only sixty-six members of Congress attended the meeting, which declared almost unanimously for William H. Crawford, Secretary of War, for President, and Albert Gallatin for Vice-President. The reason for the smallness of the attendance was that the friends of the other candidates, all of whom had declared against a caucus, had refused to take part in the proceedings. If earlier precedents had been followed, this recommendation would have been accepted as a party nomination; but the action of a rump caucus weakened rather than strengthened the claims of Crawford. It identified him with an unpopular cause and gave his opponents the opportunity to use against him the slogan, "Down with King Caucus."

The refusal of the leaders to abide by the Congressional caucus left the way open to the state legislatures to make nominations. Accordingly, several names were so presented. It was in this way that Clay, Adams, and Jackson were brought forward. In the beginning Calhoun was also a candidate, but early in the campaign, realizing that his time had not yet come, he withdrew from the race to make sure of the Vice-Presidency. Many of his friends now lined up behind Jackson.

In this four-cornered contest personalities played a more prominent part than principles. It is true that the views of the candidates were widely divergent on the questions of the day, such as the tariff, internal improvements, and the financial policy of the government; but so successful were they in concealing their opinions that the voters had difficulty in knowing where they stood. Both sectionalism and political issues did, however, figure to some extent in the campaign.

Early in the campaign (September, 1823) Crawford suffered a *Crawford* paralytic stroke and his recovery was slow and gradual. Despite this handicap he had a strong following among the Old School Republicans in the South. In New York his forces were ably led by Martin Van Buren, a politician of exceptional astuteness. Clay's oratorical *Clay* powers, his brilliant record in Congress, and his magnetic personality had drawn to him a personal following throughout the country and particularly in the West. Moreover, by his able championship of a protective tariff he had won favor with the manufacturing interests in the East.

Jackson's position with reference to the issues of the day was not *Jackson* generally known, but in the matter of personal popularity he had the advantage of all his competitors. His military record—the conquest of the Creek Indians, the victory at New Orleans, and the invasion of Florida—made a strong appeal to the hero worship of the masses, and in the West his popularity was even greater than that of Clay. In the fall of 1821 he had resigned the office of Governor of Florida and returned to his home in Tennessee. Retiring to his plantation of more than a thousand acres, located eight miles from Nashville, he again took up the life of a Southern planter. At the Hermitage, a pretentious brick mansion recently erected, he dispensed a hospitality which was worthy of the finest traditions of the Old South. He and Mrs. Jackson—the beloved Rachel—were rejoicing over the release from public duties and were looking forward to a long period of enjoyment in this rural paradise.

But the sweets of private life and the delights of fame seldom hold together for long. The Old Hero had been too much in the public eye to fall into obscurity at the age of fifty-four. Accordingly, his friends began to groom him for the Presidency. At first he ridiculed the idea, declaring that he was not fit for so exalted a position. Later he stated in a letter to a friend that he would "neither seek nor shun" the Presidency. His supporters accepted this statement as consent for the use of his name, and they proceeded to prosecute a vigorous campaign in his behalf. Thanks to the skillful management of Major William B. Lewis and other Tennessee friends, the prospects of "Old Hickory" grew brighter as the canvass advanced, and when it ended he was leading the race.

No choice by the Electoral College   The election returns showed that Jackson would receive 99 electoral votes, Adams 84, Crawford 41, and Clay 37. Calhoun was elected Vice-President by a very large majority. As no one of the four candidates for the Presidency had a majority, the final decision would be made by the House of Representatives, to which only the three highest names could be submitted. Clay therefore could not be considered. The chances were also against Crawford, partly because of his physical condition and partly because of the smallness of his electoral vote. The race was, therefore, between Jackson and Adams.

Adams elected   Clay was Speaker of the House of Representatives and thus wielded a great influence in that body. His friends held the balance of power, and this gave the popular Kentuckian the role of President-maker. An alliance with him was, therefore, courted by the supporters of both candidates. He had had bitter personal differences with Jackson and had opposed some of the policies which Adams as Secretary of State had tried to carry out. To Clay, therefore, neither of the two candidates was entirely satisfactory, although he was in accord with Adams on the leading issues of the day. While he kept his own counsel except to intimate friends, he decided some time before the House entered upon the election that he would throw his influence to Adams. With this support and that of a vacillating Representative from New York (whose vote put that state in the Adams column) Adams was elected on the first ballot by a bare majority of one (February 9, 1825).

Why Clay supported Adams   Jackson's friends were sorely disappointed over the alliance between the Kentuckian and the New Englander; but no other decision could have been expected in the light of all the circumstances. Clay doubtless felt that he could best advance his political prospects by joining forces with Adams rather than with Jackson; for if Jackson were elected, the next President would come from the South or East, as the West could not hope to furnish two Presidents in succession. On the other hand, an alliance between Clay and Adams would probably secure the election of the latter, and at the end of his administration his friends in the East would line up with Clay for the succession. With this accretion of strength, Clay would have the coveted prize within his grasp. Moreover, he could salve his conscience with the conviction that patriotism as well as prudence called for the election of Adams. Jackson was uneducated, comparatively inexperienced in civil affairs, and had, it was said, an uncontrollable temper. Adams, on the other hand, was well educated, had had a long and successful career in the service of his country, and usually kept his emotions under restraint.

These reasons, however, were not accepted by all of Jackson's *The charge of a "corrupt bargain"* friends as a satisfactory explanation of Clay's action. More unworthy motives were attributed to him by some of them. In the latter part of January (1825) there was published in a Philadelphia newspaper an anonymous letter in which Clay and Adams were charged with having entered into a corrupt bargain. Clay was to throw his influence to Adams and in return was to receive the Secretaryship of State. Clay bitterly denied the accusation, the author of which, as was afterwards learned, was George Kremer, a Representative of no prominence from Pennsylvania, whose only claim to notoriety so far had been a rustic manner and an eccentricity displayed in wearing an oddly-cut leopard skin coat. Despite the humble origin of this accusation, Clay was not able to brush it aside with furious denials. Some of the leading politicians of the day, including Calhoun, believed or pretended to believe it. Jackson would not credit it until Clay became Secretary of State, and then he too joined the ranks of those who were repeating the charge of "corrupt bargain."

This indictment was unfair both to the President and his Secretary of State, but the suspicion aroused by it was kept alive by the opposition during Adams' entire term and was used as a sharp weapon against him in the next campaign. It is true, however, that from their conferences with Adams, Clay's friends doubtless received the impression that their leader would be offered a prominent place in the Cabinet. Indeed, one would naturally have expected this if no understanding had been reached; for gratitude would dictate the offer of the premiership to the President-maker. There is, however, no proof that any bargain had been entered into between the two statesmen, although the accusation was believed by a good portion of the people.

THE ADMINISTRATION OF JOHN QUINCY ADAMS

Adams therefore entered upon his duties under very unfavorable *Adams; personal traits and previous career* auspices. He had a feeling that two thirds of the American people were opposed to his choice. His election by the House of Representatives also made him the victim of the prejudice which had been aroused against the Congressional caucus as a means of nominating candidates for the Presidency. His selection over a candidate who had received a greater electoral vote than he accentuated this prejudice and enabled his enemies to represent him as the beneficiary of Congressional intrigue. Despite these adverse appearances, the younger Adams, like his father, was thoroughly honest and was one of the ablest and most patriotic of all our Presidents. He had been well trained by education and experience for the great responsibilities now assumed. He was a graduate of Harvard and at one time was a professor in that college. During a long diplomatic career he had served in turn as minister to the Netherlands, Portugal, Prussia, and Russia. At the time Jefferson was urging the adoption of the embargo, Adams was representing Massachusetts in the United States Senate. He supported this measure and thereby antagonized his Federalist constituency. Owing to this disagreement with his former political supporters, he resigned from the Senate and thereafter was affiliated with the Republican Party. As has already been seen, he was afterwards one of the leading members of the peace commission that negotiated the Treaty of Ghent. His record as Secretary of State gave additional prestige to an eminently successful career.

Despite his high character and fine qualifications, Adams was not able to win a strong popular following. The Puritanism which had descended to him had retained all of its uncompromising sternness but was not characterized by that charity "which suffereth long and is kind." Cold in manner, with a suspicious attitude toward others and a temper which was easily ruffled, he found it difficult to practice good fellowship. The iron in his nature was not covered over with a gracious politeness and was thus not cushioned against unpleasant contacts with other political leaders. His virtues were jewels, but they were unpolished and he could not "sell" them to the public at their real value.

The division of the Republican Party

In his first message to Congress, President Adams suggested a broad program of progressive legislation. Among the measures advocated were the construction of roads and canals, the establishment of a national university, and the enactment of laws for the promotion of agriculture, manufactures, and commerce, the "encouragement of the mechanic and of the elegant arts, the advancement of literature, and the progress of the sciences, ornamental and profound." The realization of these plans would involve a loose construction of the Constitution and the assumption of large powers on the part of the general government. He thus put himself in the class of the ultranationalists and at once became anathema to the states' rights planters of the South.

In the beginning the President and his Secretary of State had a strong following in Congress and so the younger Adams was not a President without a party. His political adversaries soon began to unite and thus form an anti-Administration party. Jackson was the standard-bearer of this group, and the campaign in favor of his candidacy went on during practically the whole of Adams' term. All of these various factions still professed adherence to the Republican

Party; but the Republicans were now virtually divided into two parties. One, the followers of Clay and Adams, were the pro-Administration party, which afterwards took the name of National Republican; the other, the anti-Administration element, were pro-Jackson men and were afterwards known as Democrats.

This new pro-Jackson party included, in addition to the original Jackson men, the followers of Calhoun and Crawford. In the North the outstanding leader of the Crawford group was Martin Van Buren of New York, one of the most experienced and skillful politicians of the day. After some hesitation and delay he threw in his lot with the Old Hero and proved a tower of strength to his cause. The Crawford men of the South also went over to Jackson although their support of the latter's candidacy was not characterized by marked enthusiasm. To them he was an unknown quantity opposed to an objectionable known quantity. Adams' extreme nationalism rendered him utterly impossible to them, whereas Jackson, being a Southerner, might be expected to favor the interests of his section. Senator Tyler of Virginia (afterwards President of the United States) doubtless voiced the general sentiment of the planter aristocracy of the South when he said: "Turning to him [Jackson] I may at least indulge in hope; looking on Adams I must despair."

Adams' one great advantage in the contest with his opponent was the power he had in making appointments to office; but he threw away this advantage by refusing to use the patronage in the interest of his own candidacy. With too rare exceptions, officeholders were re-appointed when their terms expired. In this way incompetent and unworthy officials were retained in the civil service. Many of the Federal employees used the influence of their positions to further the claims of his opponent and weaken Adams for the succession. This disloyalty even found a place in his own political household. The Postmaster General, who held the most strategic political position in the Cabinet, used his great power to promote the interests of Jackson. Adams' advisers warned him against this suicidal policy, but his strict principles would not relax enough to permit of his swerving from his beliefs.

One of the first problems which confronted the President was that *The Panama* of deciding what should be the attitude of his Administration toward *Congress* the Panama Congress. Plans had been made for a congress of all the Latin American states to be held at Panama (1826), and the United States was invited to send representatives to this body. In the invitation no clear statement was made as to what was the purpose of the meeting. It developed later, however, that the plan was to form a union of the former dependencies of Spain, with the idea of united action against any effort of Spain to restore her authority over them and against any attempt of any other power to interfere with their rights.

Clay saw in the congress an opportunity to enhance the power and influence of his country in the Western Hemisphere and urged acceptance of the invitation. Adams was at first disinclined to send delegates to the meeting; but he finally decided to do so and announced this intention in his first message to Congress. He appointed two delegates and sent their names to the Senate for confirmation and asked Congress to make the necessary appropriation for their expenses. This proposal gave the opponents of Adams their first opportunity for united action, and they argued against the Panama meeting. Despite this opposition, however, both houses of Congress voted in favor of sending delegates to Panama. But nothing was accomplished by the mission. One of the representatives died on the way to Panama and the other arrived there only after the congress had adjourned.

Internal improvements

Adams was not able fully to carry out his plans for the construction of roads and canals, although expenditures for internal improvements were greatly increased during his term. In 1824 Congress passed the General Survey Act, which authorized the President to have surveys made for prospective roads and canals. Adams used this power extensively by sending army engineers to make numerous surveys looking to the construction of future canals and turnpikes. But the most important achievement of his administration in internal improvements was the impetus given to the extension of the National Turnpike. From 1825 on, liberal appropriations were voted by Congress for the extension of this highway across central Ohio, Indiana, and into Illinois.

The "Tariff of Abominations"

The year in which the President of the United States is chosen has always been an awkward time for Congress. The members of Congress in making speeches and casting their votes always have to consider the effect that their action may have on the coming election. They may be pulled in one direction by loyalty to the best interests of the country and in an opposite direction by considerations of party expediency. This effort to serve two masters subjects honest men to a severe strain and creates for weak and unscrupulous politicians temptations which they are seldom able to overcome. Senators and Representatives, by attempting to look to their duties at Washington and at the same time to visualize political conditions in their states and districts, often become cross-eyed and fail to view correctly questions of fundamental importance. At such times farsighted measures cannot be expected from our national legislature. Indeed, the country is lucky if it is spared legislation that is positively bad.

The campaign of 1828 was a notable confirmation of this rule. The mid-term elections (1826) had favored the pro-Jackson party and given it control of both houses of Congress. The leaders of this party in Congress decided to make use of the tariff issue in the fight for the succession. They felt that if they were committed in favor of a protective tariff the South would vote against the Old Hero, whereas Pennsylvania would be against him if they should oppose a protective duty on iron. To frame a tariff bill which would avoid both horns of this dilemma was the problem. Their plan for meeting the difficulty was to propose a protective measure and have it defeated by the friends of Adams. Accordingly, they offered a bill which in its final form provided not only for the protection of manufactures but also for high duties on hemp, wool, iron, and molasses. Since these commodities were largely in use as raw materials by Northern manufacturers, a high tax on them would raise the cost and lower the profits of manufacturing. Congressmen who represented the industrial interests of New England were, therefore, expected to vote against the bill. Indeed, the objectionable features of the measure were inserted largely for that purpose. The enemies of protection, as one of them declared, wished to inject enough poison into the bill to kill it. The opposition of the New England Congressmen and that of their Southern colleagues, it was thought, would defeat the measure, and the South would rejoice over the outcome. The Jacksonians could placate Pennsylvania and the West by posing as advocates of protection and putting the blame for the failure of the bill on Adams' friends in New England.

But to the surprise of these politicians, a considerable number of the New Englanders swallowed the bill even with these objectionable features, "abominations," as they were called. They voted for it because it would prolong the life of the protectionist principle, and they felt that it would not be long until they could revise the objections out of the act. The measure also received the strong support of the Middle States and the West and was passed, despite the almost unanimous opposition of the South and the Southwest. In this way the "Tariff of Abominations" was foisted upon the country.

THE CAMPAIGN OF 1828

For Adams the executive chair had proved to be a very uncomfort- *Presidential* able seat. He had scarcely become ensconced in his high position *candidates* when a vigorous campaign was launched to defeat him in the next

election. The opposition party did all it could to discredit him and
to bring Jackson into popular favor. Public measures were supported
or opposed mainly with the view to their effect on the coming election. Early in 1828 party feeling, which had been at a high tempera-
ture during his entire term, broke into white heat. Both Adams and
Jackson had been nominated by a number of state legislatures, and
politicians were waging a relentless war of abuse in the name of their
champions.

Mudslinging   The campaign was a disgraceful exhibition of partisan hate and
unfair tactics. Mudslinging was indulged in to an unusual extent,
even for American politicians. Slander and vituperation were much
in evidence. Not only was the policy of the President attacked but
his motives and character were also assailed. His opponents rang the
changes on "bargain and corruption" and tried to convince the
masses that their leader, Jackson, had been cheated out of the Presidency by political chicanery.

But the Democrats were not the only offenders in this campaign
of hate and misrepresentation. The pro-Administration leaders also
did their best to asperse the character of Jackson. His conduct in the
Creek War and the War of 1812, it was charged, had been arbitrary
and overbearing. He was termed a ruffian, a duelist, a gambler, a
murderer, and an adulterer. Handbills were circulated giving the
names of persons who had been killed by him in duels and executed
by his orders as a military leader, with the picture of a coffin above
each name. Much unjust publicity was given to the technical irregularity of his marriage. The basis for this unfair accusation was the
fact that Jackson had married Mrs. Rachel Robards before the proceedings for divorce from her former husband had been consummated. These ugly stories cut deeply into his feelings and aroused
within him the most vindictive hatred of his foes.

The real issue   In the campaign, personalities played the major role and principles only a very minor part. Little attention was paid to the questions of the day, such as the tariff, internal improvements, and foreign policy. But underneath all the slander and loud talk of the campaign leaders there was a real issue at stake—democracy versus aristocracy. As Jackson was the idol of the western democracy and the
champion of the masses in other sections of the country, a vote for
him was a vote to take the Federal government out of the hands of
the upper classes and turn it over to the plain people. "Shall the
people rule?" might, therefore, be properly regarded as the issue of
the campaign. The Jackson men contended that Congress in 1825 by
selecting Adams over "Old Hickory," who had received a plurality of
the electoral votes, had thwarted the wishes of the people. To elect

Jackson now would be (so they maintained) to vindicate the right of the people to choose the President.

The campaign had not advanced far before it became apparent *Jackson elected* that the odds were strongly in favor of Jackson. Adams was unable and unwilling to practice the arts of the politician. Furthermore, his supporters in upholding his cause were actuated more by a sense of duty than by a feeling of personal loyalty. Behind Jackson's candidacy, on the other hand, there was an efficient political organization and an enthusiastic personal following. He was a military hero with a grievance, and such a combination is invincible.

The outcome of the election showed that Jackson had received more than twice as many electoral votes as his opponent. The West and South had gone solidly for him, and he had also carried Pennsylvania and won a majority of the electoral vote of New York. Adams had received a part of the vote of New York and Maryland and every electoral vote in New England but one. He also carried Delaware and New Jersey.

To celebrate his victory Jackson's Tennessee friends arranged for *The death of* a great banquet, reception, and ball to be given at Nashville. When *Mrs. Jackson* the time set for this notable occasion arrived Jackson was in no mood for festivities of any sort. On the contrary, he was passing through the greatest sorrow of his entire lifetime. The beloved Rachel was dead. She had been in poor health for some time and had died of a heart attack, which Jackson always believed was the result of the worry caused by the slanderous assaults made on her character in the campaign. She had, as he said, been "murdered by slanders that pierced her heart." In this way there was given a tinge of sacredness to his hatred of the opposition leaders.

CHAPTER XXVI

Democracy in the White House

THE ACCESSION OF ANDREW JACKSON

The progress of democracy

THE United States was not a political democracy when it started out as an independent nation. In none of the old states was there universal manhood suffrage, and the people who had the right to vote usually recognized the leadership of the upper classes. The Revolution, to be sure, released some radical ideas, as can be seen in the Declaration of Independence; for such phrases as "All men are created equal" cannot be repeated without producing an effect, and so some progress toward democracy was made at the time we separated from the mother country. But despite these new ideas, our national government for the first four decades of its existence was a political aristocracy.

In the meantime, as has been seen, democracy had been growing up and developing a vigorous activity in the West, and the leaven of democracy produced in the West was destined to leaven the whole lump of American government. Not only had democracy captured the West, but it was also gaining strength in the East. The plain people in the older states began to tire of the leadership of their patrician neighbors and to clamor for a larger share in the government. In response to this demand constitutional changes were made in a number of the older states which widened the suffrage and in some cases gave the right to vote to all adult white males. This democratic movement gained in momentum until by 1828 it had become stronger than the forces of the aristocracy and so captured the national government.[1] The election of Jackson, therefore, marks an important turning point in our development.

The personality of Jackson

It was not an accident that Jackson became the leader of the plain people of the East and most of the people of the West in their struggle for supremacy, for he was eminently fitted by both character and temperament for this service. He had an unwavering faith in the people, which was never shaken during his entire lifetime. His democracy was thus ingrained in his nature and had in it no element

---

[1] For excellent maps showing the trend toward a broadening of the suffrage from 1780 to 1860, see Clifford L. and Elizabeth H. Lord, *Historical Atlas of the United States*, 54-57.

of make-believe. The people, therefore, were guided by a true instinct when they regarded him as their faithful friend and aggressive champion.

Moreover, he was the most typical Westerner to be found in the country at that time. The greater portion of his life had been spent on the frontier, and he had been an important actor in all the stirring and tumultuous events of his day. He was born in the South Carolina uplands and had spent his boyhood in the Carolina backwoods. When a young man he had gone to Nashville, then a small settlement surrounded by a vast wilderness. So deeply was he imbued with Western ideals that it may properly be said that he was the very incarnation of the spirit of the West. He had many of its shortcomings and most of its virtues, and in both his virtues and his vices he outwesternized the average Westerner. In addition to the fine qualities that he owed to the frontier, he had also acquired a dignity and poise of manner which a cultivated Easterner might well have emulated. If the West, therefore, had wished to create a god in its own image it could not have done better than copy the personality of Andrew Jackson.

Jackson's election in 1828 was a great victory for the West over the East, and of the plebeians over the patricians. Democracy had captured Washington, and on the fourth of March took up its domicile at the White House. Washington society awaited the new social order with amusement mingled with a modicum of disgust. Prophetic jokes were circulated as to what would happen at the White House. The inauguration must have been a disappointment to the soreheads who had made these prophecies, for Jackson conducted himself during the ceremony with rare dignity and good sense, and nothing was said or done with which anyone could find fault. Attended by a group of friends, he walked the short distance from his hotel to the Capitol. He was greeted with vociferous cheers by the immense crowd that had assembled for the ceremonies. The President-elect, advancing erectly with his white head conspicuous above those of his associates, looked worthy of the part he was called upon to play as the ruler of a vigorous young republic. The oath of office was administered by John Marshall, the aged Chief Justice, who probably felt apprehensions for his country similar to those experienced when he performed the same service at the installation of Jefferson.

The inauguration

The dignity which characterized the inaugural ceremony was not in evidence at the reception given at the White House, and here the wildest expectations of the most pessimistic of the aristocrats were fully realized. Democracy was not yet versed in drawing-room eti-

The reception at the White House

quette and had not learned good table manners. Consequently, the President's reception soon became an unruly mob. From fifteen to twenty thousand people rushed into the reception rooms to shake hands with the President and partake of the refreshments. They stood with muddy shoes on the damask chairs, and jostled the incoming waiters in their efforts to get at the refreshments. The jam was so great that the people inside could get out only by jumping out the windows. Finally, tubs of punch were sent out on the lawn and that to some extent relieved the pressure of the crowd.

It must not be inferred, however, that the social life of the White House was characterized by such pandemonium during the entire period of Jackson's administration, for this was not the case. Mrs. Andrew J. Donelson, the wife of Jackson's private secretary, was mistress of the White House, and she discharged the duties of her responsible position with the proper dignity and decorum.

The Cabinet   In choosing his Cabinet the President had to recognize the claims of the different factions which had united to form the Democratic Party. The list of appointees included three of Calhoun's supporters and two of Jackson's political and personal friends. The latter were Senator John H. Eaton of Tennessee and John M. Barry of Kentucky, who became respectively Secretary of War and Postmaster General. The Crawford group was represented by Martin Van Buren, who was made Secretary of State. This able politician had performed yeoman's service for the party in New York, and Jackson's victory in that state was due largely to his capable leadership. He was the only man of outstanding ability in the Cabinet. So mediocre were the others that a leading Democrat pronounced the President's official advisers "the most unintellectual Cabinet we ever had."

The "Kitchen Cabinet"   On such a Cabinet the President could hardly be expected to lean heavily for advice. In the early part of his Administration little or nothing was asked of most of the members except the performance of the administrative duties of their respective departments. The practice of holding Cabinet meetings was discontinued after a few weeks. For advice the President looked to a group of intimates whom he consulted informally whenever the occasion arose. This little coterie of unofficial advisers was known as the "Kitchen Cabinet."[1]

---

[1] It included two members of the regular Cabinet, Eaton and Van Buren; three newspapermen—Amos Kendall, who had edited a paper in Kentucky, Isaac Hill, former editor of a New Hampshire paper, and Duff Green, then editor of the *United States Telegraph*, a pro-Administration publication; William B. Lewis, an old personal friend and promoter of Jackson's political fortunes; and Andrew J. Donelson, nephew of Mrs. Jackson and secretary to the President. When Duff Green began to show leanings in favor of Calhoun he dropped out of the President's confidence and his place was taken by Francis P. Blair, editor of the *Washington Globe*, a pro-Administration paper.

Before Jackson's accession there had grown up in some of the *The spoils*
states—notably New York and Pennsylvania—the practice of making *system ex-*
tended to the
appointments to office on the basis of political loyalty rather than on *Federal*
merit. The theory was that "to the victors belong the spoils." Ac- *government*
cordingly, when a party won in a state election it rewarded its adherents by giving them the offices which had been made vacant by
turning out such incumbents as belonged to the opposing party. This
practice is known as the "spoils system."

The spoils system was extended to the Federal government by
President Jackson. The principle had been employed to some extent
by his predecessors, however, as all of them had been influenced to
a considerable degree by party loyalty in making appointments; but
under Jackson there were more removals than there had been under
any other President. Many of the discharged persons had grown old
in the government service, and the loss of their positions left them
in a number of cases without any means of support. This phase of the
policy gave it the appearance of a heartless cruelty, which raised a
great outcry from the opposition. While Jackson removed more persons from office than had any of his predecessors, the number was not
as large as the noisy criticism of his enemies indicated. During his
two terms, changes in personnel were made in about one fifth of the
Federal positions. These included voluntary resignations and removals by death and for misconduct in office, as well as those for
partisan reasons. The vacancies so caused were all filled with deserving Democrats.

In support of the spoils system Jackson used the following argu- *Jackson's*
ments: (1) No citizen has any more right to a public office than an- *arguments in*
favor of rota-
other and therefore the removal of an official involves no impairment *tion in office*
of a vested right. (2) The loss to the public service resulting from the
displacement of experienced by inexperienced men is more than offset by the gain that accrues from bringing in fresh blood. The feeling of security which comes with life tenure in office tends to promote an indifference to and a neglect of duty which leads to inefficiency and sometimes malfeasance in office. On the other hand, the
duties of the public service are so simple (or should be made so) that
an industrious person of ordinary capacity can soon learn to perform them. (3) The participation of a citizen in governmental activities gives him a greater interest in and knowledge of public
affairs. Rotation in office makes it possible for a large number of people to receive this training. In this way democracy is promoted.

The spoils system was continued by Jackson's successors, and from *Later history*
his day until the present it has been deeply intrenched in the Federal *of the spoils*
system
government. It has been an important factor in the development of
machine politics. The practice of distributing offices to advance par-

tisan interests has given rise to a large group of professional politicians, made up of actual and prospective officeholders. These politicians by virtue of their effective organization and unity of action wield an influence in the government out of proportion to their number and importance. And too often this power is used to advance their own private interests rather than the public good; for they are inclined to fight valiantly for their own party, whether that party is right or wrong. The evils of the spoils system have been mitigated but not eliminated by the civil service reform measures adopted since the War for Southern Independence.

Veto of the
Maysville
Road Bill

At the time of his accession Jackson's position as to internal improvements was largely a matter of conjecture. While he was in the Senate he had more than once supported measures for internal improvements. Later, however, he seems to have adopted the states' rights view as to the propriety of Federal expenditures for roads and canals. All doubt as to his attitude on this question was resolved by his action with reference to the Maysville-Lexington Road Bill.

In May, 1830, Congress passed a bill authorizing the Federal government to take stock in a company which was planning the construction of a turnpike from Maysville to Lexington, Kentucky. The advocates of the bill contended that the road was national in character because it was to be linked up with other roads and thus form a part of a great national system. One of these roads went from the Ohio opposite Maysville to Zanesville on the National Highway; and another from Lexington to Nashville and thence on to Florence, Alabama. The opponents of the measure contended that by such reasoning any road could be declared of national character, for every road is connected directly or indirectly with some thoroughfare.

Despite the opposition of the states' rights advocates, the bill was passed by both houses of Congress and sent to the President. After due deliberation Jackson decided to veto the measure. His objections were based on both practical and constitutional grounds. The proposed road, he contended, was not a project of national importance but only of local interest as it began and ended in one state. Moreover, there was still doubt in his mind as to the constitutional power of Congress to construct and maintain public improvements. He suggested, therefore, that an amendment to the Constitution be proposed which would clearly define the powers of Congress on this question.

Henry Clay, who was sponsoring the bill in the Senate, felt that the veto would cost Jackson much of his popularity and lessen his chances for the succession. The road of sixty miles in length was to run through a district which was favorable to the President, and his opposition to the project might cost him the support of this section and cause him to lose Kentucky in the next election. Clay's prophecies as to Kentucky proved true, but the veto did not arouse popular feeling throughout the country. It was especially pleasing to those Democrats who were ardent believers in states' rights.

Jackson did not oppose the aid that was voted by Congress for continuing the Cumberland Road, and he also accepted a bill appropriating money for a road in Alabama. With these exceptions, however, he showed opposition to appropriations for roads and canals in the states. Road building in the territories and the improvement of navigable streams and harbors did not in his opinion present the same constitutional difficulties, and so he signed a number of bills making appropriations for such purposes. Jackson's stand on internal improvements had the effect of putting a decided check on the construction at Federal expense of roads and canals in the states.

The general attitude of Jackson toward internal improvements

INDIAN AFFAIRS

One of the difficult problems which Jackson had to solve was that of the relations of the Indians and the whites. In the Northwest the natives were being gradually pushed back and their lands taken by the settlers. In Georgia and the Southwest there were about fifty-three thousand Indians, with vast landed possessions which were coveted by the whites surrounding them. Among the southern Indians the leading tribes were the Creeks, the Choctaws, the Chickasaws, and the Cherokees. These tribes had abandoned their savage mode of life and were gradually accepting the Christian religion. Farthest advanced in civilization of these tribes were the Cherokees, most of whose landholdings were in northwestern Georgia. Having settled down into successful agriculture, they had orchards, had built roads, were cultivating cotton, grain, and other farm products, and were engaging in the manufacture of wool and cotton cloths. With this prosperity had come an increase in population and a stronger confidence in themselves.

The Cherokees

When Georgia ceded her western lands to the Union it was with the understanding that the Federal government would extinguish the Indian claims to land within the state "as early as the same can be peaceably obtained upon reasonable terms." At the time of Jackson's accession, the Cherokees still held more than five and a quarter million acres of land in Georgia. A large portion of this great area was not under cultivation and was used only as hunting grounds. As a result of the rapid expansion in the growth of cotton this unused

The controversy between Georgia and the Cherokees

land was increasing in value and arousing the cupidity of the white planters. The discovery of gold in the Cherokee territory in 1829 increased the hunger of the white Georgians for the land of their Indian neighbors.

In 1827 the Cherokees adopted a constitution and declared themselves an independent sovereign nation. This action was in accordance with treaties with the Federal government (going back as far as 1785) which recognized the Cherokees as a nation, with power to make war and peace and to govern its own citizens by its own laws. For the Georgians to recognize the Cherokee state would, in their opinion, be contrary to their economic interests and political theory. The legislature thereupon passed a law (1828) providing for the annexation of the Cherokee lands to the adjacent counties and declaring that after June 1, 1830, the laws of the state should apply to the Cherokees as well as to other citizens of the state.

Jackson's proposal

There was thus a deadlock between the state of Georgia and the Cherokee state within its borders. The dispute could be settled only by action of the Federal government. The Federal executive was the first to act. The President in his message to Congress (December, 1829) expressed the view that the Cherokees did not have the right to create an independent jurisdiction within the limits of Georgia. He proposed that they emigrate to the region west of the Mississippi and settle on lands set apart for the Indians. Here they could maintain their tribal government, and the Federal authorities would not interfere except to preserve order on the frontier and peace between the tribes. Their removal to the West should be voluntary, but if they did not emigrate they were to retain only such of their lands as they could use and would have to obey the laws of the state in which

Creation of the Indian Territory

they resided. In accordance with the President's recommendation, Congress passed a bill (May, 1830) providing for the exchange of Indian lands in the East for lands west of the Mississippi River and appropriating money to defray the cost of removal. A later act (1834) created an Indian territory in the West.

Decisions of the Supreme Court

The Cherokees refused to emigrate, and the Governor of Georgia issued a proclamation (June 3, 1830) asserting that the title to their lands was vested in the state. The dispute went to the Supreme Court of the United States, and decisions against Georgia were handed down. In one of these, the case of *Worcester vs. Georgia,* the court declared that the Cherokees were a nation and that the laws of Georgia had no force over them. Georgia ignored the decisions and

Jackson's attitude toward these decisions

the President declined to enforce them. He is reported to have said: "John Marshall has made his decision; now let him enforce it."

By taking such a stand Jackson was supporting Georgia in her nul-

lification of the treaties of the Federal government as interpreted by
the Supreme Court, although shortly afterwards he regarded South
Carolina's nullification of an act of Congress as treason. It is hard to
explain this inconsistency. He believed, however, that Georgia was
right and South Carolina was wrong in the position each had taken.
The fact that the Supreme Court had given a contrary decision in the
case of Georgia made no difference; for, as he considered, the executive had as much right to interpret the Constitution as the judiciary
—that his oath bound him to uphold the Constitution as he interpreted it and not as John Marshall interpreted it. The fact that in
sustaining the action of Georgia and in opposing that of South Carolina he was antagonizing John Marshall and Calhoun respectively—
two men whom he violently hated—may have had some influence
on his attitude.

In pursuance of his policy of removal Jackson signed ninety-four *Removal of*
treaties with the Indians, most of which provided for land cessions. *Indians to*
lands west of
His policy was so successful that by December, 1835, all the major *the Missis-*
groups of Indians east of the Mississippi from Lake Michigan to the *sippi River*
Gulf of Mexico had been removed to the west of that river except
the Cherokees, the Seminoles, and two small bands living in Ohio
and Indiana. In that same month a treaty was signed with the Cherokees by which they surrendered their lands east of the Mississippi for
a grant in the Indian Territory, five million dollars in money, and
the expense of transferring them to their new home. But despite this
agreement, force had to be resorted to in the removal of some of
them.

The Sac and Fox Indians in the Northwest were loath to leave *The Black*
their lands in Illinois and Wisconsin, and under the leadership of *Hawk War*
their brave chieftain, Black Hawk, put up a strong fight in defense
of their rights (1832). In this bloody war many Indians, including
women and children, were cruelly killed.

The Seminoles of Florida also resisted removal and a long war re- *War with the*
sulted, with Osceola as their leader. This war lasted from 1835 to *Seminoles*
1842 and came to an end only after most of the Seminoles had been
destroyed.

THE BREACH BETWEEN CALHOUN AND JACKSON

In the campaign of 1828 the friends of Calhoun supported Jackson *Calhoun's*
with the expectation that the noted Carolinian would have the en- *hopes for the*
succession
dorsement of the President for the succession. This hope was encouraged by the cordial relations which then existed between these
Southern leaders. "Old Hickory" was expected to serve only one
term and then Calhoun's turn would come. It was not long, however,

before the President's friends began to talk of a second term and Jackson did not discourage the suggestion. Calhoun's hopes for election in 1832, therefore, soon began to wane. In the meantime a formidable rival had arisen who might jeopardize his chances in 1836. This was the " Little Magician," Martin Van Buren. As leading member of the Cabinet he had a better opportunity to ingratiate himself into the good opinion of his chief than did the Vice-President.

The Eaton Affair

Luck seemed to be against Calhoun in this contest with Van Buren, who was able to turn incidents of comparative unimportance to his own benefit. One such incident was the "Eaton Affair." Just before the inauguration, Major Eaton had married Mrs. Timberlake, an attractive young widow, often known as "Peggy O'Neill," since she was the daughter of William O'Neill, the proprietor of a tavern in Washington. Jackson had known her in childhood when he as a Senator boarded at her father's hotel, and he and Mrs. Jackson had become quite fond of this agreeable young person. Peggy had not always been careful in observing the strait-laced conventions laid down for womanhood in that day. Consequently, gossip busied itself against her reputation and began to pull down her good name.

The marriage of Peggy to Major Eaton, soon to be a member of the Cabinet, gave these stories national significance. Owing to these rumors Mrs. Calhoun and the wives of several Cabinet members would not recognize her socially. This aroused the ire of Jackson, who regarded Peggy as the victim of a cruel and unwarranted ostracism. Believing her innocent of the scandalous charges which had been brought against her, he called his Cabinet together and urged them to induce their wives to change their attitude toward Mrs. Eaton. It is doubtful whether the members of the Cabinet attempted the impossible task of dictating to their wives as to their social relations. Or if they made the effort, nothing came of it, and Mrs. Eaton gave up the endeavor to enter Washington society.

Van Buren cordially assisted the President in his attempt to secure proper recognition for Mrs. Eaton. As he was a widower with no women in his family to restrain him, he was always free to offer courtesies to her and never lost an opportunity to show her a kindness. In so doing he won the favor of the Old Hero. On the other hand, Mrs. Calhoun was a leader of the group which was unwilling to accord proper recognition to Mrs. Eaton. This was displeasing to Jackson and was a factor in disturbing the friendly feeling that had existed between the President and the Vice-President.

The Jefferson Day banquet

Relations between Jackson and Calhoun were also subjected to a severe strain by the brusque behavior of the former at the Jefferson

Day banquet. The Democrats had arranged for a dinner on Jefferson's birthday (April 13, 1830) at which Jackson was to be present. Since he was a Southerner and was thought to have states' rights leanings, the South Carolina Democrats hoped that his attitude on this occasion might be favorable to the doctrine of nullification. Being warned in advance of these hopes, he determined to dash them violently to the ground. This was done with more boldness than courtesy when, looking Calhoun in the face, he offered this toast: "Our Federal Union—it must be preserved!"

The expression of this sentiment was not only an indication of the President's disapproval of nullification but it was also an insinuation that Calhoun and his followers were disloyal to the Union. With a feeling of chagrin and resentment at this implied indictment, Calhoun made the best of the situation by replying with the following toast: "The Union—next to our liberty, the most dear! May we all remember that it can only be preserved by respecting the rights of the states and distributing equally the benefits and the burdens of the Union."

While the incidents just related were disturbing influences in the friendship between Jackson and Calhoun, they alone would probably never have led to a breach. More important was the leak of a Cabinet secret for which Crawford was responsible. When Jackson's action in invading Florida without instructions was considered by Monroe's Cabinet in 1818 (see p. 396) Jackson received the impression that Calhoun had defended him in the Cabinet meeting. In 1830 a letter written by Crawford was sent to Jackson which showed that Calhoun instead of defending had censured his conduct in Florida. Jackson wrote to Calhoun and received an unsatisfactory reply. He thereupon branded Calhoun a traitor and ended his last letter to him with the phrase, "Et tu Brute!" This terminated the personal friendship and the political alliance between the President and the Vice-President. *The Crawford Letter*

After the break with Calhoun, Jackson reorganized his Cabinet by getting rid of the pro-Calhoun members and accepting the voluntary resignation of Van Buren. In the new Cabinet Edward Livingston of Louisiana was made Secretary of State; Louis McLane of Delaware, Secretary of the Treasury; and Roger B. Taney of Maryland, Attorney General. *The Cabinet reorganized*

Van Buren was appointed minister to England during the interim of Congress and at once proceeded to London to assume his duties. When his name came before the Senate his political opponents made a fight against his confirmation. The accusation brought against him was that while Secretary of State he had issued improper instructions *Van Buren rejected as minister to England* to McLane, the American minister to England (see p. 456). Calhoun as Vice-President cast the deciding vote against his opponent, feeling that his rejection by the Senate would mean the political death of his rival. But in all these calculations Andrew Jackson was not taken sufficiently into account. "Old Hickory" resented this slight to his protégé and determined to leave no stone unturned to promote the fortunes of the "Little Magician." As a result of this determination on the part of Jackson, Van Buren soon became Vice-President and thus president of the body that had tried to disgrace him. Thomas H. Benton was one of the Senators who foresaw that the effort to discredit Van Buren would lead to his advancement. "You have broken a minister," he said (at the time of Van Buren's rejection), "but made a Vice-President."

JOHN C. CALHOUN.

THE DOCTRINE OF NULLIFICATION

Calhoun's writings

Before Calhoun and Jackson had come to the parting of the ways the former had ceased to be a nationalist and had become the leading advocate of states' rights. Following his theory of states' rights to its logical conclusion, he had arrived at the doctrine of nullification. This doctrine was first stated at length in a paper known as the "South Carolina Exposition," which he had prepared for the consideration of the legislature of South Carolina as a protest against the Tariff Act of 1828. In the "Exposition" and his later writings, notably "A Disquisition on Government," Calhoun clearly and logically explained his views as to nullification. While his doctrine has never been widely accepted, in his discussion of it he won for himself a place in the top rank of America's original thinkers in the field of political philosophy.

Personal traits of Calhoun

At his accession to the Vice-Presidency (1829) Calhoun's intellectual gifts were at their best. He had already made a brilliant record in public life and was looking forward to still greater political preferment. Like several other noted statesmen of his day, he was a perennial candidate for the Presidency; but this ambition seems never to have swerved him from a faithful adherence to his principles. It is true that immediately after the War of 1812 he was an ardent champion of the nationalist measures then adopted, including the protective tariff of 1816. At that time he believed that a policy of protection would aid in making the country economically independent and would bind the various sections together into a closer bond of union. Now, however, he felt that a high tariff was unfair to the agricultural South and was promotive of sectionalism.

CHIEF JUSTICE MARSHALL.

Calhoun was able to bring to his advocacy of public measures a vigorous personality which added force to his arguments. Descended from a Scotch Presbyterian ancestry and reared under semifrontier conditions, he naturally imbibed a serious view of life. This seriousness was accentuated in appearance by deep-set eyes, heavy eyebrows, and bushy hair and was not relieved by a sense of humor. However, he had a gentle and kindly manner that attracted the good will of others and imparted an unusual magnetism to his personality. As a debater he was noted for force of argument, clarity of expression, and flawlessness of logic. He did not, however, employ the flowery style of oratory which was so popular in his day.

According to Calhoun, the doctrine of nullification, if generally accepted, would not cause but rather prevent the disruption of the Union (to which he was ardently loyal) by furnishing an antidote to secession. In justifying his doctrine and pointing out its practical implications, he argued as follows:

The doctrine of nullification in theory

The Union was formed by a compact between the states. The states had entered into a covenant with each other and the terms of this covenant are embodied in the Constitution. By the Constitution, provision was made for a division of powers between the states and the Federal Union. There was, however, no such division of supreme authority, or sovereignty, for sovereignty is one and indivisible and rests entirely with the one or the other. Now the states were undoubtedly sovereign in the old union under the Articles of Confederation. They did not surrender their sovereignty when the new union was formed in 1789, and so they were still sovereign. As the Union is the creation of the states and not the states of the Union, it stands to reason that the former will be subordinate to the latter in case there is a dispute as to respective powers; for the creator is always greater than the creature.

Since the Federal government is not supreme, it can exercise only such powers as are delegated to it by the Constitution. If it exceeds those powers and enacts measures which are unconstitutional, such measures are null and void.

The question now arises, How shall it be decided as to whether a measure under dispute is or is not constitutional? The power to make such decisions resides in the several states and not in the United States. For the acid test of sovereignty as applied to any political entity is its power to judge its own competence. The Supreme Court of the United States cannot be an arbiter in such disputes, for this court is an agency of the Federal government. To allow the claim that a branch of the Federal government can pass on such controversies would be to concede that the general government is a judge of its own competence and therefore sovereign; and this is not the case, since sovereignty resides in the people of the states.

In practice   The procedure for putting the theory of nullification into actual practice as outlined by Calhoun was as follows: If Congress should pass a law which is unconstitutional and flagrantly unjust to any state, such state would have the right to suspend the operation of said law within its own limits pending a final decision as to its constitutionality. Such action, however, should never be taken by any state for light cause but only as a last resort in the protection of its rights. In thus passing upon the constitutionality of a law of the Federal government the state should act only in its sovereign capacity, that is, through a convention called for the express purpose of considering this question; for this is the only way in which the people of a state can give expression to their sovereign will. If the convention after due consideration should declare the act null and void its operation would be suspended within the limits of the state until a final decision could be reached.

At this stage Congress should come in by offering an amendment expressly authorizing the power which had been contested. Such an amendment after having passed both houses by the customary two-thirds majority would be sent to the various states for ratification or rejection. If the necessary ratifications were not obtained the decision would be in favor of the complaining state, and the suspension of the law would become a final annulment of it, not only for that state but for the whole confederacy. On the other hand, if the amendment were ratified the power under dispute would then be clearly within the authority of the Federal government. In that case the dissatisfied state would have to yield. Or if the new amendment was contrary to the whole tenor and spirit of the Constitution, the nullifying state could withdraw from the Union, but it could not remain in the Union without accepting this amendment.

In this way, Calhoun contended, the final arbiter in all disputes regarding the authority of the Federal government would be the same power that created the original Constitution and added the amendments. The decision in such a case would be final, and no state would ever claim the right of further appeal. By this procedure, secession could be prevented; for rarely, if ever, would a state pursue her grievance to the point of secession after three fourths of the states had pronounced against her. Furthermore, the trouble and expense incurred by going through the process of nullification, coupled with the fear that her action would be rebuked by the other states, would restrain any state from resorting to nullification except in extreme cases.

The doctrine of nullification was vigorously assailed and vigorously defended in the most dramatic debate ever staged in the United States Senate. This noted forensic contest was, however, an accident. In December, 1829, Senator Foot of Connecticut offered a resolution which suggested the advisability of limiting for the time being the sale of public lands to those which had already been surveyed and put up at auction. Benton, the champion of a liberal land policy, saw in this proposal an effort to check the development of the West and so he argued strongly against it. Nothing came of the measure as it was tabled later on in the session. In the meantime, however, it had served as a curtain raiser to the great debate between Daniel Webster of Massachusetts and Robert Y. Hayne of South Carolina. *The Foot Resolution*

The South was anxious to have an alliance with the West and to win over that section to its own political views. Such a union would insure the Southern planters and Western farmers against objectionable measures advocated by Northern manufacturers and would give them a controlling voice in the Federal government. It was doubtless this hope that prompted Hayne to sustain Benton in his opposition to the Foot Resolution. On January 19, 1830, Hayne spoke against Foot's proposal. In the course of his speech he made a *The Webster-Hayne debate* vigorous attack on New England Federalism and severely arraigned that section for its disloyalty in the War of 1812. This indictment brought Webster into the fray, for he felt called upon to defend his state and section. In this way began the noted debate which took up most of the time for the rest of the month.

Nationalism vs. state sovereignty

In this intellectual bout the doctrine of state sovereignty measured lances with that of nationalism, and the champion of each cause was probably the ablest that could be found in the entire country. Both statesmen were at the zenith of their illustrious careers and were well primed for the encounter. Webster was an able constitutional lawyer and America's greatest orator. His speeches were so well organized and

Daniel Webster

couched in such beautiful language that they would have been eloquent even if poorly delivered. On the other hand, he had an exceptionally attractive personality, made impressive by a large head, a noble countenance, flashing eyes, a stately bearing, and a deep and sonorous voice. His appearance

DANIEL WEBSTER.

was so commanding and his delivery so effective that a commonplace production sounded oratorical when presented by him. Hayne

Robert Y. Hayne

was also an able lawyer, a finished orator, and a skillful debater. In personality and character he typified what was best in the South Carolina aristocracy. He was favored with a tall and well proportioned figure, graceful carriage, and cordial and unaffected manners. With the exception of Calhoun, he was the ablest advocate of its doctrines that the Tidewater South could furnish.

As was to be expected in an age when political contests were highly relished by the people, this joust between two brilliant speakers attracted wide attention. The little Senate chamber was crowded to capacity and beyond the limits of comfort. At one time so many Representatives had left their seats to listen in on the debate that the House could not carry on its business.

Hayne defended with logic and eloquence the theory of nullification as it had been outlined by Calhoun. So well did he do this that *Position of Hayne* the Vice-President could not keep from smiling his approval from the chair despite his effort to pose as a neutral moderator.

Webster with equal or greater skill upheld the doctrine of na- *Webster's arguments* tionalism. He contended that the Constitution is law and that the Union was created by the people. Sovereignty was divided between the states and the Union, and the Federal government had received the same warrant from the people as had the states. The formation of the Union created a government, not a league of nations. The states had no right to declare an act of the Federal government null and void and no legal right to secede from the Union. If a dispute should arise between a state and the Federal government it should be referred to the United States Supreme Court as the final arbiter. Webster closed his great speech in a burst of eloquence which ended in the oft-quoted phrase—"Liberty and Union, now and forever, one and inseparable."

Courtesy of the New-York Historical Society, New York City

ROBERT Y. HAYNE.
From engraving by J. B. Forrest, 1835. After a drawing from life by J. B. Longacre.

This historic debate had the ef- *Significance of the debate* fect of clarifying the issue between localism and nationalism. It inked the line which separated those who favored states' rights from those who advocated a strong national government. It furnished both groups with able arguments and thus accentuated the ardency with which each supported its cause.

THE ELECTION OF 1832

By the end of his first term Jackson had consolidated his followers *Political parties* into a united group which was known as the Democratic Party. His vigorous measures, however, had aroused violent opposition as well as enthusiastic support. This opposition had crystallized into a new party, the National Republican, led by Henry Clay. This latter party included the greater part of those who were opposed to the President's policies—his support of Georgia in the Indian controversy, his resort to the spoils system, and his attitude toward internal improvements, the tariff, and the Bank.

In the meantime there had come into being a third political group, the Antimasonic Party. The mysterious disappearance in 1826 of William Morgan, of Batavia, New York, who was thought to have made public the secrets of Freemasonry, aroused the suspicion that he had been murdered by the Masons. The feeling against this secret order was so strong that it led to the formation of an antimasonic party in New York. It soon spread to several other states and in the election of 1828 was able to play a minor part in support of Adams. In 1830 this new party was organized on a national basis, and a call was issued for a convention to be held the following year to nominate a candidate for the Presidency.

Origin of the national convention

After the Congressional nominating caucus fell into disfavor in 1824 the state legislatures were the only agencies left for nominating candidates for the Presidency and Vice-Presidency. This method was satisfactory in 1828 as there were only two outstanding candidates in the field. But the situation in 1832 was more complicated. The Democrats were united on Jackson for the Presidency but had to make a choice between several aspirants for the Vice-Presidency. Clay was also the generally accepted choice of the National Republicans, but a national convention was needed to name a Vice-Presidential candidate and consolidate support for the ticket. Among the Antimasons there was no generally recognized leader, and so it was necessary for them to get together and outline a program of national action. To meet these conditions the national party convention was called into existence. As the national convention brought Presidential candidates closer to the people, its introduction was another forward step in the democratization of the Federal government.

Nominees for President

The Antimasonic Party held its convention at Baltimore, September 26, 1831, and nominated William Wirt of Virginia for President. This was the first national nominating convention ever held by a political party in this country. In December of the same year the National Republicans met in Baltimore and selected Henry Clay for the Presidency and John Sergeant of Pennsylvania for the Vice-Presidency. In May of the next year a convention of young National Republicans was held at Washington. At this meeting Clay and Sergeant were endorsed as candidates and a platform was adopted. This the first platform enunciated by a national political party declared against the policies of Jackson and in favor of a protective tariff and internal improvements. The Democrats held their convention in Baltimore in May, 1832. Jackson was unanimously endorsed, and Van Buren was nominated for the Vice-Presidency by a large majority. A rule was adopted that a two-thirds majority would be necessary for the choice of either candidate. This rule, except for one break, was in effect for more than a century.

As had been the case in 1828, the campaign was characterized by bitter feeling and loud abuse. In it the political cartoon was first used to any considerable extent. The President's veto of the Bank bill made that the leading issue. Jackson received a large majority of the popular vote and an overwhelming majority of the electoral vote. The victory won by the Democrats in the election was due partly to the opposition of the masses to the Bank, but mainly to their loyalty to the Old Hero. The Antimasons carried only one state (Vermont), and this poor showing sealed their fate as a national party. They exerted considerable influence in the two succeeding campaigns, but never again did they offer a candidate for the Presidency.

Result of the election

Reproduced from THE PAGEANT OF AMERICA, *Copyright Yale University Press*

CITY OF WASHINGTON IN 1834.

CHAPTER XXVII

Democracy Becomes Aggressive

TARIFF AND NULLIFICATION

The tariff act of 1832

IN his message to Congress (December, 1831) Jackson recommended a revision of the tariff, as the revenues of the government were in excess of the expenditures and the national debt was being paid off rapidly. The South and Southwest strove for revision downward; but the Northeast and Northwest were in favor of continuing the policy of protection. The friends of protection won in the contest, and under the leadership of Henry Clay in the Senate and ex-President John Quincy Adams in the House succeeded in getting a protective measure through Congress in July, 1832. This act was in some minor respects an improvement on the one of 1828, as the "abominations" were removed and the general level of duties was slightly lowered; but the reductions were made almost entirely on products not competing with American manufactures and so the protective feature was hardly touched.

Discontent in South Carolina

At the time the tariff act of 1832 was passed, South Carolina was not receiving her share of the prosperity which the country as a whole was enjoying. For her unfavorable economic plight she blamed the policy of protection, which forced her to buy in a high market and sell in a low one. While the high tariff was undoubtedly a real grievance it was not the sole cause of her failure to keep pace with other sections in the increase of wealth. Her soil had become thin as a result of long years of cotton culture and was not able to compete on equal terms with the fresh lands of the new Gulf states. For this latter condition there was no immediate remedy, but an effort could be made to lessen the burdens of an unjust tariff policy.

The Ordinance of Nullification

According to her leading statesman, Calhoun, the best way to meet this grievance was to invoke the principle of nullification. Since Congress had by the tariff act of 1832 committed itself in favor of a high tariff as a permanent policy, South Carolina felt that the time had come for resorting to nullification. Accordingly, a state convention was called and it promptly passed an ordinance of nullification (November 24, 1832). By this ordinance the tariff acts of 1828 and 1832 were declared unconstitutional and therefore null and void.

446

No enforcement of these laws was to be allowed in South Carolina after February 1 of the coming year. Warning was also given that if force were used by the Federal government to compel the obedience of the state, South Carolina would sever her connection with the Union.

In obedience to instructions from the convention the legislature met and passed laws for the enforcement of the ordinance. State officials were required to take an oath to carry out the ordinance. It also passed the Replevin Act. This act enabled an importer in South Carolina whose goods should be seized by a Federal customs official because of a failure to pay the duties of the act to recover double their value by a writ of replevin, said writ to be issued by a state court. *The Replevin Act*

The President met the crisis created by the boldness of his native state in true Jacksonian fashion. Although he had two years earlier been a party to nullification himself in that he had supported Georgia in her refusal to accept a decision of the Supreme Court, he now showed no patience with the action of South Carolina. He issued a proclamation (December 10, 1832) in which he took a strong stand in favor of nationalism. In this paper he declared that the Constitution formed a *government,* not a league, and that this government "operates directly on the people individually, not upon the states." The power to annul a law of the United States by one state was, as he considered, "incompatible with the existence of the Union, contradicted by the letter of the Constitution, unauthorized by its spirit, inconsistent with every principle on which it was founded, and destructive of the great object for which it was formed." He regarded the Union as a nation and therefore no state had the right to secede from it. "Disunion by armed force is treason." "The laws of the United States must be executed. I have no discretionary power on the subject; my duty is emphatically pronounced in the Constitution." *Action of the President*

The Proclamation

The Proclamation was the ablest state paper which ever came from Jackson's pen. For its constitutional arguments and its high literary quality the Secretary of State, Edward Livingston, is entitled to the chief credit; but to Jackson is due the credit for its nationalistic sentiments and the vigor and firmness with which they are expressed. This Proclamation and the energetic measures adopted by the President to suppress nullification won the enthusiastic approval of such nationalists as Webster. It is needless to say, however, that this policy alienated many of the President's political supporters who adhered to the doctrine of states' rights.

The dire threats of the Proclamation were accompanied by acts which were just as menacing. Seven revenue cutters and a ship of war

Measures taken to compel the obedience of South Carolina

were sent to Charleston with orders to be ready for instant action. Soldiers were also dispatched from Fortress Monroe to strengthen the garrison there, and General Scott was put in command of the defenses. On January 16, 1833, Jackson sent a special message to Congress in which he reviewed at length the situation in South Carolina and recommended the enactment of such measures as would enable the executive to cope fully with the situation.

The Compromise Tariff Act

Along with the sword, the President bore the olive branch. In his annual message to Congress (December 4, 1832) he referred to the early extinction of the national debt and recommended a gradual reduction of the tariff. After an unsuccessful attempt of the Democrats to carry out this suggestion, Clay offered in the Senate a compromise tariff measure. By this bill there was to be a gradual reduction of the tariff until 1842, at which time the rate would not exceed twenty per cent on any article. This compromise was the result of an agreement between Clay and Calhoun, who had resigned the Vice-Presidency to take his seat in the Senate. With such backing the measure was easily put through Congress and was accepted by South Carolina.

The "Force Bill"

Congress sustained the President in his determination to uphold the authority of the Federal government in South Carolina. A bill, known as the "Force Bill," was passed which authorized him to employ the army and navy in carrying out the laws. He could also change the location of customs houses if he deemed it necessary. This measure was very objectionable to the South Carolinians, who termed it the "Bloody Bill." Calhoun, however, feared that continued opposition to this bill would jeopardize the success of the Compromise Tariff, and so he did not oppose it in its final passage, although he had characterized it as a tyrannical measure. When the vote was taken in the Senate he and other states' rights advocates had withdrawn from the chamber, and it was passed with only one negative vote. This was cast by John Tyler of Virginia, who had waged a strenuous opposition to the whole policy of coercion.

Final settlement of the controversy

When the compromise measure was passed the South Carolina Convention rescinded the Ordinance of Nullification. At the same time, however, it reasserted its principles by declaring the Force Act null and void.

With the ending of the controversy both sides claimed the victory. The nationalists contended that the authority and dignity of the Federal government had been upheld by the vigorous policy of the President and Congress. South Carolina, on the other hand, maintained that nullification had proved an effective remedy as it had secured a redress of her grievance. But the refusal of the other Southern states to lend moral support to South Carolina's action showed that nullification was not practicable as a method of protest against Federal usurpation. Nullification was therefore never again attempted in the South, and the extreme states' rights party in that section thereafter looked to secession as the best method of defense against what it considered injustice at the hands of the national government.

JACKSON AND THE BANK

The alliance between Jackson and Webster and other nationalist leaders was a short-lived affair and could not withstand the strain to which it was subjected by the subsequent policy of the Administration. It was not long, therefore, before Jackson was engaged in a bitter fight with the nationalists over the question of rechartering the Second Bank of the United States.

It will be recalled that the Bank in the early years of its history *Opposition to the Bank in the West and South; reasons* had been very unpopular in certain sections, especially in the West and South. The people there had looked upon it as "a rapacious, greedy, oppressive, and destructive monopoly." Some of the states opposed the Bank because they regarded it as an agency for weakening their authority and strengthening that of the Federal government. At Jackson's accession there were still quite a number of political leaders who considered the act establishing the Bank as unconstitutional, but this opinion was not so widely held as it had formerly been.

In his first message to Congress Jackson spoke in a complimentary *References to the Bank in Jackson's early annual messages* way of the Bank's useful service to the Treasury, but in his recommendations he showed undoubted hostility to the institution. He suggested that, inasmuch as the charter would expire in 1836, Congress take under consideration the question of a recharter "in order to avoid the evils resulting from precipitancy in a measure involving such important principles and such deep pecuniary interests. . . ." "Both the constitutionality and the expediency of the law creating this bank," he said, "are well questioned by a large portion of our fellow-citizens, and it must be admitted by all that it has failed in the great end of establishing a uniform and sound currency."

In his second and third messages he showed that he had not changed his attitude toward the Bank, but seemed disposed to place upon Congress the responsibility for any further action. McLane, Livingston, and other members of the Cabinet, as well as some members of the "Kitchen Cabinet," were favorable to the Bank, and if

wise diplomacy had been used the storm might have been safely
weathered.

McLane and most of the other Democratic friends of the Bank
were of the opinion that Jackson could be won over if no application
for recharter were made until after the election. But if a move toward
a renewal of the charter were made in Congress before the election
the President would take it as a challenge and would veto the bill.
The National Republican leaders, on the other hand, were in favor
of bringing up the measure before Congress and thus making the
Bank an issue in the Presidential campaign. If a bill for recharter
were passed and vetoed by Jackson, Pennsylvania would (they
hoped) go against him, while a failure to veto such a bill would
cause him to lose votes in the South and West. Nicholas Biddle, president of the Bank, was at first inclined to follow the advice of his
Democratic friends, but unfortunately for the Bank he was later convinced by the National Republican leaders that he should act before
the election. Accordingly, application was made for a renewal of the
charter, and a bill for rechartering the Bank was passed by Congress
in the summer of 1832.

The President vetoed the bill and returned it to the Senate with
his objections. Indeed, by raising the question when and as he did,
Biddle practically forced Jackson to veto it. By putting his Bank into
politics against the wishes of Jackson and his friends he divided the
Democratic Party into two factions—Bank and anti-Bank men—and
gave the opposition a welcome issue. Jackson eagerly accepted the
challenge. An effort to override the President's veto failed in the
Senate, and so the bank measure was finally defeated.

In his veto message Jackson expressed opposition to the bill on a
number of grounds. Certain provisions were regarded by him as
unconstitutional. He admitted that the Supreme Court had decided
in favor of the power of Congress to charter a national bank. In doing
so, however, it had not covered the whole ground, but on the contrary had indicated that Congress has a responsibility in deciding
whether the particular features of a banking measure "are *necessary*
and *proper* in order to enable the [proposed] bank to perform con-
veniently and efficiently the public duties assigned to it as a fiscal
agent."

But even if "the opinion of the Supreme Court [had] covered the
whole ground of this act, it ought not to control the co-ordinate authorities of this Government." The President and each member of
Congress when they take the oath to support the Constitution swear
that they will support it as they understand it and not as it is understood by others. It is as much the duty of Congress and of the Presi-

dent to decide upon the constitutionality of any bill or resolution which is presented to them for passage or approval as it is of the Supreme Court when it is brought before it for judicial decision.

Objections of a practical nature were also pointed out in the message. The charter, he continued, created a monopoly and conferred special privileges upon a favored few. By virtue of this monopoly the price of the stock would be greatly enhanced. Of the stockholders a large number lived abroad, and most of the others resided in the Eastern states. On the other hand, the West was greatly indebted to the Bank and the interest paid by these debtors was contributing largely to its profits. The Bank was thus an agency for draining away from the West its money and pouring it into the coffers of Eastern and foreign capitalists. Owing to a certain clause in the bill, the stock would be worth from 10 to 15 per cent more to foreign than to American holders. Not only would the government be granting a bonus of millions of dollars to foreign stockholders, but the possibility that the control of the Bank might fall into the hands of foreigners owning the major part of the stock would in time of war constitute a danger more formidable "than the naval and military power of the enemy."

The appeal of the message to the masses

Political scientists of today regard his constitutional arguments as having little or no foundation, while economists laugh at most of his economic reasoning. The message, however, made a deep impression on the people and proved to be an invaluable campaign document. It appealed to American prejudice against England; to the jealousy of the West toward the East; and to the hatred of the poor for the rich. The ignorant masses were truly convinced that the Bank was an agency for making "the potent more powerful" and the poor poorer, as well as a means for putting the United States at the mercy of England. Just how the ownership of stock in an American corporation by citizens of England would give that country an advantage in time of war was not easily explained, but to many ill-informed voters—already obsessed by a prejudice against England—this bugaboo was none the less frightening because of the lack of a sufficient explanation.

The National Republicans had used poor strategy in bringing in the Bank as the chief issue of the campaign of 1832. It is true that in ridiculing the veto message and in arguing for the Bank they were on solid ground with the few who were in sympathy with the moneyed interests, but such tactics carried little or no weight with the masses. On the other hand, the appeal to deep-seated and long-standing prejudices made by the message found a ready response in the hearts of the plain people. Jackson was therefore elected by a large majority.

*Jackson
decides to
withdraw gov-
ernment
funds from
the Bank*

Jackson interpreted his victory of 1832 as a plebiscite in favor of his opposition to the Bank. The fight against the Bank had therefore been won, and it would cease to operate as a national bank in 1836. There was a danger, however, that if the Bank should wait and close up its business suddenly at the end of the period of its charter, loans would be called in such large volume as seriously to contract credit and possibly bring on a financial panic. There would then be an outcry for a continuance of the Bank, and Congress might yield to this pressure and pass a bill for recharter even over the President's veto. Biddle would thus in the end win over his powerful antagonist. Moreover, Jackson did not consider the Bank a safe repository for government funds. He was afraid too that if they were allowed to remain in the custody of the Bank they would be used to bribe members of Congress to pass a recharter over his veto.

These dangers could be averted if the business of the Bank were gradually reduced. To bring about such a result Jackson decided that no more government funds should be deposited with the Bank or its branches and that those which were already on deposit (approximately $9,000,000) should be drawn out gradually to meet the current expenses of the government. In the future the Federal funds would be placed in certain state banks.

*Cabinet
changes*

There was, however, one impediment in the way of carrying out this policy. The charter of the Bank provided that the money of the United States should be deposited in the Bank or its branches unless the Secretary of the Treasury should otherwise direct. In case the Secretary of the Treasury should make such a change in the deposits he must notify Congress and give the reasons for his action.

McLane, who was Secretary of the Treasury, was friendly to the Bank and would not, of course, issue such an order. Moreover, he was too influential to be removed from office. Accordingly, he was promoted to the post of Secretary of State, made vacant by the appointment of Livingston to the English mission. William J. Duane of Pennsylvania was promptly selected for the headship of the Treasury, with the expectation that he would carry out the President's wishes. Duane, however, had made no promises as to the removal of the public funds, and he too refused to order their withdrawal from the Bank. Jackson thereupon removed him and transferred Roger B. Taney from the office of Attorney General to that of Secretary of the Treasury. Taney was an ardent supporter of the President's bank policy, and, it is thought, wrote his veto message. He therefore at once (September 26, 1833) ordered his subordinates to cease making deposits of government money in the Bank or its branches.

*Taney dis-
continues
government
deposits*

Before the new policy was inaugurated the Bank had begun to

restrict its loans. These reductions were caused partly by the hostile relations that existed between the Bank and the Administration and partly by the alleged necessity of insuring the safety of the Bank. There followed as a result of this contraction the panic of 1833-34. This depression lasted for less than a year and conditions had returned to normal by the middle of the summer of 1834. Jackson and his friends contended that it had been brought on by Biddle, who wanted to discredit the Administration, and that it affected only speculators. Whether the charge against Biddle is well-founded it would be difficult to say. There was a feeling, however, that he had reduced discounts to a greater extent than was necessary and public sentiment forced him to renew lending. *A brief depression*

When Congress assembled in December, 1833, Secretary Taney reported to both houses his action in withholding deposits from the Bank of the United States and its branches with the reasons that prompted his action. By this time the banking question had become the main issue between the political parties. The regular Democrats had lined up behind Jackson in opposition to the Bank, while the National Republicans were virtually a unit in its support. Working with the latter were some former Democrats, but they had been read out of the party. *The Senate resolution condemning the President*

Clay opened the attack on Jackson's bank policy. He offered two resolutions of censure which were adopted by the Senate. Taney's appointment as Secretary of the Treasury was also rejected by the Senate. In their final form Clay's resolutions declared that the reasons given by Taney for the removal of the deposits were "unsatisfactory and insufficient" and that the President in removing them had "assumed upon himself authority and power not conferred by the Constitution and laws but in derogation of both."

Jackson sent a protest to the Senate declaring that this body did not have the right to censure the policy of the executive. If he had acted illegally the proper remedy, he contended, was impeachment by the House and trial by the Senate. This protest the Senate refused to receive. *Jackson's protest*

Immediately after the resolutions of censure were passed, Benton announced his intention to make a continuous effort to have them expunged from the journal. Accordingly, a motion to cancel the objectionable resolutions was offered at the opening of each session of Congress, with the determination to keep the question before the Senate and the country until his proposal was accepted. Benton's perseverance in support of his measure was finally rewarded with success, as it was passed by the Senate early in the last year of Jackson's second term. *The expunging resolution*

*End of the
Bank*

The Bank of the United States ceased to operate under a national charter in 1836. It had in the meantime secured a charter from Pennsylvania and so for a few years continued as a state bank. Biddle caught the fever of the new era of uncontrolled "wildcat" banking and launched his bank into the speculative mania of the time. With such mismanagement the bank went down into final failure in 1843. With its downfall there went the loss of Biddle's reputation for financial ability and integrity. Jackson was thus avenged of his adversary and had realized his purpose of taking "the strut out of Nick Biddle."

PUBLIC LANDS AND THE DISTRIBUTION OF THE SURPLUS

"Pet banks"

With the withdrawal of the public moneys from the national bank and its branches the government funds were deposited in certain state banks which had met specified requirements for safety. Banks chosen for deposit were called "pet banks." There were at first only twenty-nine of them, but before the end of 1836 the number had increased to eighty-nine. With these increases in their deposits the "pet banks" were able to extend their loans and note issues. This meant a considerable expansion of credit, and to a certain extent inflation.

*The Specie
Circular*

As times were flush and credit was easy, there was a great demand for public lands during the latter half of Jackson's second term. So great was this demand that the sales of government lands jumped from six million acres in 1834 to twenty million in 1836. Speculators and settlers were paying for the lands bought from the government with the notes issued by state banks. Some of these banks were on an insecure basis. When the limit of credit expansion should be reached these banks would not be able to redeem their notes, and the government would have on hand large amounts of depreciated paper. To prevent this, Jackson decided to put a stop to the acceptance of bank notes for public lands. Accordingly, the Secretary of the Treasury issued (1836) a circular of instructions to Federal land agents, known as the Specie Circular, directing them to receive only gold and silver in payment for public lands.

*The debt of
the Federal
government
paid*

Early in Jackson's second term it became apparent that the public debt would soon be paid. This expectation was realized in 1835, and for a short period the general government was free from debt. During the boom years revenue was pouring into the Federal treasury from two sources, the tariff and the sale of public lands. Each stream had been swollen by the prosperity of the time and the Treasury was overflowing with funds. The surplus which was emerging was large enough to become a real problem. Extravagance begotten by pros-

*A surplus in
the Treasury*

perity was enlarging the volume of imports and thus increasing the income from tariff duties. Activity in the sales of western lands was swelling the revenue from this source. The problem was how to relieve the Treasury of an embarrassment of riches. The tariff could not be changed prior to 1842 without violating the Compromise of 1833, and it was not considered proper to do this. Nor could the money be used for the building of roads and canals; for in vetoing the Maysville Road Bill the President had shown that he was a faithful watchdog of the Treasury and opposed to this type of expenditure.

Clay's solution of the problem was to distribute the proceeds of *The Distri-* the sale of the public lands among the various states. This would *bution Act* remove the possibility of a reduction of the tariff, and so the prin- *of 1836* ciple of protection would not be further disturbed. Jackson was opposed to this policy, and a distribution bill passed by Congress in 1832 was killed by his pocket veto. The question was still agitated, however, and was settled by the Distribution Act of 1836. By this act all funds in the Treasury above five million dollars, from whatever source derived, were to be distributed among the states in quarterly installments in proportion to their representation in both houses of Congress. To overcome Jackson's constitutional scruples, the distribution was to be technically (though not actually) in the form of a loan. The measure was quite popular and so would help Van Buren's chances for the succession. The President, therefore, signed the bill, though with evident reluctance.

The first two installments and one half of the third were distributed, when the panic came and converted the surplus into a deficit. The Treasury still carries these amounts on its books as debts due by the states; but it was understood at the time that no repayments would ever be made. The amounts received by the states encouraged some of them to still greater activity in unwise expenditures for internal improvements and thus aggravated a tendency that had already gone too far.

FOREIGN AFFAIRS

Unlike most of his predecessors, Jackson prior to his accession had *"Shirt-sleeve* had no experience in diplomacy. Not only was he unacquainted with *diplomacy"* the conventions that govern diplomatic relations, but his forthright manner ruled out the finesse of diplomacy. Furthermore, owing to the spoils system, most of his subordinates who were responsible for the conduct of foreign affairs were new at their tasks and had not had time to learn the niceties of international usage. And yet, despite his practice of "shirt-sleeve diplomacy," he was able to score victories in foreign relations where his experienced predecessors had failed.

Successful negotiations with England regarding the West Indian trade

One such victory was the agreement with England regarding the West Indian trade. This trade had been a most lucrative one in colonial days, and the restrictions on it had cut off an important outlet for American products. Our government from the end of the Revolution on had been trying to come to an understanding with England whereby the direct trade with her West Indian colonies would be opened to our ships. These efforts had in recent years aggravated the situation, and when Jackson came into power both British and American ships were prohibited by law from engaging in the direct trade between American and British West Indian ports.

Negotiations were begun by McLane, Jackson's first representative at London. By his instructions he was authorized to say that sentiment in the United States had changed and that the new Administration was prepared to consider favorably the terms of an offer previously made by the British government. This reference to the political change in the United States was bringing party politics into foreign affairs. For such a violation of the traditions of diplomacy Van Buren, the Secretary of State, was severely criticized by his enemies. This departure from precedent was seized upon by them as an excuse for effecting his rejection by the Senate when he was afterward appointed minister to England to succeed McLane (see pp. 437f).

The trade agreement with England

Congress supported the President in his endeavor by authorizing him to open the ports of the United States to the ships of England whenever the government of that country should admit American vessels to British colonial ports without discrimination. The British authorities were already inclined toward a more liberal commercial policy, and so they welcomed the new attitude of the American State Department. Consequently, Jackson announced (October, 1830) that an agreement for mutual trade had been entered into. By this treaty American vessels could with certain restrictions carry imports to and exports from the British colonial ports. As a result of this understanding, the value of the imports to the United States from the British West Indies was in 1831 more than eight times that of the previous year, and the value of the exports from the United States to the British West Indies had increased from $140 to $1,439,593.

Relations with France

A like success rewarded the efforts of Jackson to come to terms with France over the claims against that country held by citizens of the United States. These claims had grown out of injuries to American commerce during the Napoleonic regime. Although they had been the subject of negotiation ever since 1815, no understanding had been reached at the time of Jackson's accession. William C. Rives was now sent as minister to France with instructions to arrange for a settlement if possible. The French government, thanks to the patience and tact of Rives, was finally won over to an acknowledgment of the legality of the American demands. In the meantime, however, the French foreign minister had brought up counter demands against the United States for losses sustained by France's nationals during the troublous times of Jefferson and Madison. Finally, a treaty was signed (July 4, 1831), by which the claims of the nationals of each country against the government of the other were to be paid. The claims of France based on alleged violations of the Louisiana Purchase treaty were offset by a reduction of the duty on French wines imported into the United States.

The Franco-American agreement

The treaty between France and the United States did not by any means settle the controversy. The money to meet the stipulated payments had to be voted by the French Parliament, which had declined to make the necessary appropriations. Livingston, who had succeeded Rives as minister to France, felt that a show of force would be necessary to bring the French Parliament to terms. He therefore suggested to the President that he assume a firm tone in his next message to Congress. Jackson took up the suggestion quite readily and in his annual message to Congress (December 1, 1834) recommended that a law be passed authorizing reprisals upon French property in case provision should not be made for the payment of the debt at the approaching session of the French Chambers.

France refuses to make the stipulated payments

Jackson's bold stand

The House of Representatives voted unanimously to uphold the President in his bold policy with reference to France. The Senate, however, under the lead of Clay refused to take action. A great deal of excitement was aroused in France by Jackson's statement, and each government recalled its minister. The French Parliament for a time persistently refused to vote the money due the nationals of the United States. Finally (April, 1835) it made the necessary appropriation with the stipulation that it was not to be paid until Jackson had made a satisfactory explanation of the language used in his previous annual message.

In response to this action the President declared in his next annual message (December, 1835): "The honor of my country shall never be stained by an apology from me for the statement of truth and the performance of duty." In a later message he recommended as a measure of reprisal that French products and French ships be forbidden to enter our ports. The French government had put itself in an awkward position and was doubtless looking for a face-saving excuse for backtracking. Such an excuse it found in a statement by Jackson in his annual message to the effect that he had shown no "intention to menace or insult the government of France." An offer of mediation

Settlement of the dispute

on the part of Great Britain also helped, and so the French government announced its intention to meet the payments.

The Texan question

When Louisiana was purchased from France in 1803 some of our
American statesmen, among them Henry Clay and John Quincy
Adams, contended that Texas was included in the grant. But in the
treaty (1819) by which East Florida was ceded to the United States
by Spain, the Sabine River was agreed upon as the southwestern
boundary of the Louisiana Purchase. In this way the United States
yielded to Spain whatever right she may have had to Texas. When
Mexico won her independence from Spain (1821) Texas became a
part of this new southern republic.

Early efforts to secure Texas

There was a feeling in the minds of some of our political leaders
that Texas had been unduly relinquished and should be regained
at the earliest opportunity. Accordingly, an effort was made (1827)
under President Adams by Clay, Secretary of State, to buy a portion
or all of Texas. The price which he was willing to pay was small,
however, and the American minister, realizing how reluctant the
Mexican authorities were to alienate any portion of their country's
domain, did not make the proposal, as he was instructed to do, and
so nothing came of the attempt. The next move to purchase Texas
was made when Jackson was President and Van Buren, Secretary of
State. This attempt was also unsuccessful, although Jackson and
Van Buren were willing to pay a much higher price for the territory
than that suggested by Adams and Clay.

Texas colo- nized by Anglo-Ameri- cans

The failure of these two efforts to secure Texas by purchase indicated that Mexico was unwilling to part with this prized possession.
But in the meantime events had taken such a turn as to open up the
possibility of winning Texas by peaceable penetration, since numerous emigrants from the United States had settled in Texas. The
initiative in this colonization movement was taken by Moses Austin,
originally from Connecticut but lately from Missouri. Just before
Mexico became independent he obtained from the Spanish authorities a large grant of land on condition that he would settle on it three
hundred Catholic families. His death soon afterward imposed upon
his son Stephen the task of carrying out his plan.

Stephen Austin

In the meantime Mexico had declared her independence and
Stephen Austin had his grant confirmed by the Mexican ruler. His
princely domain was located in the favored region between the
Brazos and Colorado Rivers. In January, 1822, he established at San
Felipe de Austin the first authorized settlement of Anglo-Americans
in Texas. Immigrants were attracted by his liberal grants of land at
the nominal price of twelve and a half cents an acre and in the course
of eight years he had established a prosperous colony. The settlers

had come in from Tennessee, Mississippi, and Louisiana and were typical frontiersmen of the better sort.

The young republic of Mexico was anxious to fill up the vast empty spaces in Texas with settlers from the outside and offered large grants of land at low cost to immigrants. Each married colonist could obtain 4428 acres for about $200. Since 1820, sales of public lands in the United States had been on a cash basis and the minimum price was $1.25 an acre, with fertile cotton lands bringing a much higher price. The opportunity of obtaining good cotton and grain lands in Texas at a nominal figure thus made a great appeal to would-be settlers. So many immigrants came in from the United States that by 1835 there were in Texas about twenty thousand Anglo-Americans to three thousand Mexicans.

This influx of population was a part of that westward movement which has extended the area of settlement across the continent. Land hunger was the main motive that prompted it. The American abolitionists, however, saw in this natural trek to the Southwest a conspiracy on the part of the slaveholding interests to stake off new lands for their hated institution. This opinion was reflected by politicians and historians, and the charge has been so often reiterated that for a long time this view was generally accepted. *Relation of slavery to the colonization of Texas*

Scholars now hold that slavery was not the cause of this expansion although it was closely associated with it. There were virtually no free laborers in Texas, since all white settlers could easily become landowners. For this reason slaves were considered necessary for the development of the new land. The emigrants, the great majority of whom were from the South, would be more inclined to go to Texas if they were allowed to take their labor system with them. The promoters of colonization therefore favored the bringing in of slaves, and Stephen Austin, who was personally opposed to slavery, shared this view and made every effort in favor of the legalization of slavery.

By 1830 the Anglo-American immigration had reached proportions which were alarming to the Mexican government. The colonists were different from the Mexicans in race, language, religion, and social customs. Under such conditions an amalgamation of the two diverse groups could not be effected so as to insure the dominance of the weaker native element. If this trend toward peaceable penetration continued, Texas would soon be ripe fruit, ready to drop from the Mexican tree into the open basket of the northern republic. Fearing this outcome, the Mexican government adopted a policy of discouraging, and finally preventing, further immigration from the United States. A decree issued by the Mexican president (1829) provided for the abolition of slavery throughout the country. *Immigration discouraged by the Mexican government*

The purpose of the decree was to discourage colonization in Texas by Anglo-Americans. Later (December, 1830) the decree was modified so as to permit the continuance of slavery in Texas; but the further introduction of slaves was prohibited there as in other portions of the Mexican domain. This restriction on slavery, along with the constant fear of emancipation which it led to, was a chronic cause of dissatisfaction.

Texas closed to further immigration from the United States

A more drastic measure was one passed by the Mexican Congress (April, 1830) prohibiting further immigration from the United States to Texas. To enforce this act and prevent smuggling, troops were stationed in Texas, much to the annoyance of the Anglo-Americans.

Other griev- ances of the Texans

The colonists were also dissatisfied with their system of local government. Texas had been united with the more populous Coahuila to form a state. Representation in the legislature was so apportioned as to give Coahuila a marked predominance in the state government.

Another grievance, though of lesser importance, was the fear of religious intolerance. The Catholic was the only church recognized by the government, and since there was no legal toleration of other religions there was among Protestants a constant apprehension that they might become the victims of persecution. This was not, however, an acute grievance, but, like the slavery question, "was a dull, organic ache and not an excruciating pain."[1] Also among the minor causes of complaint was the tariff imposed on articles coming into the country. More serious was the inadequate judicial system which permitted long delays in the trial of criminal cases.

Mexico adopts a policy of conciliation

In 1834 the Mexican government adopted a policy of conciliation toward the Anglo-Americans in Texas. The anti-immigration measure of 1830 was repealed; a better judiciary system was provided for; and Texas was given an additional representative in the legislature of the joint state. With these reforms there went the declaration that no one would be molested for religious views provided he did not disturb the public peace.[2] These reforms had the desired effect of lulling opposition, and during the first half of 1835 sentiment in Texas was overwhelmingly in favor of avoiding a breach.

Latent causes of friction

Below the surface of this outward calm there were, however, latent causes of friction which might easily be brought to the surface by some unwise measure of the Mexican authorities. The Mexicans feared that some day the Anglo-American colonists would aid their former fellow countrymen to appropriate Texas, and these appre-

---

1 E. C. Barker, *Mexico and Texas, 1821-1835,* 86.
2 *Ibid.,* 130.

hensions had been aggravated by the efforts of Presidents Adams and
Jackson to buy Texas. Ill feeling between the two groups of settlers
was also increased by the disposition of the English-speaking colonists to look down upon the Mexicans as their inferiors. Owing to
the unstable character of the general government, the Anglo-Americans had lost respect for it and did not greatly fear its power.

In the fall of 1835, events suddenly took an unfavorable turn. *The outbreak*
Santa Anna, who had been brought into power by the liberal, federalist party, having changed his attitude, had centralized the government and made himself a virtual dictator. The Texans were
opposed to this consolidation of authority in violation of the constitution, and Austin, who had hitherto advocated conciliation, now
went over to the revolutionists. The garrisons which had been stationed in Texas in 1830 had been removed two years later. Now for
the second time soldiers were sent to Texas and two prominent Texans were arrested and imprisoned. In this way the revolution was
precipitated.

The Texans rose in revolt (October 2, 1835) and soon drove out *Mexican*
the Mexican forces. Santa Anna marched against the insurgents with *atrocities*
a force numbering 3000 men and defeated them in several minor
engagements. These victories were attended with atrocities which
were greatly to the discredit of the Mexican leader. At the Alamo in
San Antonio, 183 Texans held off for thirteen days a greatly superior
attacking force. All the men except a small remnant of sick and
wounded were killed and these were massacred after the capture of
the fort (March 6, 1835). On March 20, 371 Texans were captured
by the Mexicans, and a week later all of them were shot except twenty
who had made their escape.

The heroic defense of the Alamo aroused the bitter enmity of the *Sympathy in*
insurgents against Mexico and inspired them with the determination *the United*
to fight to the finish. "Remember the Alamo" became the battle *States for*
slogan. Owing to the barbarities practiced by the Mexican troops *the rebels*
and the fine courage displayed by the rebels, public sentiment in the
United States was strong against the former and warmly in favor of
the latter, and men and supplies poured in to aid the Texans.

Of all the Americans who went to Texas to take part in the *Sam Houston*
struggle for independence, the most noted was Sam Houston, a great
admirer and close personal friend of President Jackson. Fortune had
been somewhat fickle with him at home. It had pushed him up to a
seat in the United States House of Representatives and the guber-
natorial chair in his home state of Tennessee. Then, taking a sudden
turn against him, had robbed him of his popularity and sent him

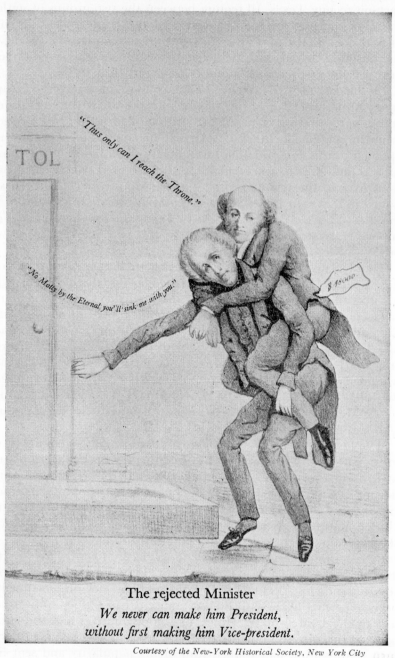

The rejected Minister

*We never can make him President,
without first making him Vice-president.*

into voluntary exile.[1] The Texan revolt came at a time when fortune was frowning upon him. Here was an opportunity to fish in troubled waters which made a strong appeal to a spirit that liked to gamble for high stakes. Ending his exile among the Cherokee Indians, he went to Texas and became the leader of the rebel troops. Again fortune smiled on him, and he defeated the Mexican forces at San *Battle of* Jacinto (April 21, 1836) and captured their commander, Santa *San Jacinto* Anna, the President of Mexico. By this battle the independence of Texas was virtually won.

Shortly before this victory Texas had declared her independence *Texan inde-* (March 2, 1836) and had asked that it be recognized by the United *pendence* States. As recognition might complicate relations with Mexico, Jackson hesitated to comply with this request, and he tried to throw upon Congress the responsibility for this important step. Congress was not afraid to act, and the independence of Texas was recognized at the end of Jackson's second term (March, 1837).

---

[1] A sudden and mysterious separation from his young wife (he was married in January, 1829), who belonged to a prominent Tennessee family, had caused sentiment in the state to turn strongly against him. While under this cloud he resigned the governorship and went to live with the Cherokee Indians.

CHAPTER XXVIII

Van Buren and the Panic of 1837

Rise of the Whig Party

BY the spring of 1834 the National Republicans had united with other anti-Administration groups to form a new party, which had assumed the name of "Whig." By thus appropriating a term which had been applied to the patriot party in the Revolution they were able to designate their opponents as Tories. With the National Republicans there were associated Antimasons and anti-Administration Democrats. Jackson's vigorous measures, notably his attitude toward the nullification policy of South Carolina and his removal of the Bank deposits, had given serious jolts to the Democratic Party and had shaken out a number of dissenters who had joined the ranks of the opposition. The Southern members of the new party who adhered to the doctrine of states' rights looked to Calhoun for leadership. In uniting these Southern Democrats with Northern National Republicans, politics was certainly making strange bedfellows.

Whig nominees in 1836

The new party first tried out its national strength in the Presidential campaign of 1836. With so many diverse elements, agreement as to a platform or even a candidate was not possible and so no national convention was held. The strongest faction in the coalition was the National Republican element, and in the main it endorsed William Henry Harrison, a hero of the War of 1812. In Massachusetts, however, the National Republicans supported Webster, and he received the vote of that state. The states' rights Whigs of the South (except the Nullifiers of South Carolina) supported as their candidate Judge Hugh L. White of Tennessee, who "was a strict constructionist of the purest type." The Whigs had two candidates for the Vice-Presidency, John Tyler of Virginia and Francis Granger of New York.

Democratic nominees

At the request of Jackson the Democrats nominated Van Buren for the Presidency, and Colonel Richard M. Johnson of Kentucky was named for the Vice-Presidency.

Result of the election

The Whigs did not expect that any one of their three candidates would receive a majority in the Electoral College, but they hoped that enough votes would be drawn away from Van Buren to prevent his receiving a majority. The election would then be thrown into the House of Representatives, where a Whig would have a chance to be chosen. Thanks to the popularity of Jackson and the effective support which he gave Van Buren, the latter received a good majority over all his competitors and was declared elected. Johnson received a plurality but not a majority of the electoral votes. The Senate was, therefore, called upon to make a choice between him and Granger, his closest competitor. Johnson was chosen on the first ballot.

MARTIN VAN BUREN AS PRESIDENT

Martin Van Buren (1782-1862) was of Dutch descent and was born and reared at Kinderhook, a village in eastern New York. What formal education he received was obtained in the common schools and an academy in his native town. This rather meager training was supplemented, however, by a wide course of reading which he systematically pursued in later life. After a long period of preparation he entered upon the practice of law and quickly achieved a brilliant success in the profession. With a deep interest in public affairs, he was soon drawn into the stream of active politics. He had, therefore, before entering Jackson's Cabinet as Secretary of State, held a number of important offices, among them those of United States Senator and Governor (for a short time) of New York. To this record had been added the prestige gained by his success as Secretary of State and Vice-President. By thus working faithfully at the oars he had qualified himself for the place at the helm of the ship of state. *Van Buren; previous career and personal traits*

Unlike his immediate predecessor, Van Buren did not have a picturesque personality. With a cheerful manner, a courteous demeanor, and an optimistic outlook, he was pleasing rather than colorful in his social contacts and official relations. An erect posture and dignified bearing atoned for a shortness of stature, which, combined with his rare intellectual acumen, won for him the sobriquet of "Little Magician." He was well endowed with the solid virtues of courage, sincerity, and honesty, but not with those which appeal to the popular imagination, and so he could not dramatize his achievements as Jackson had been able to do. In a long public career he had learned the difficult art of dealing with men and enlisting their aid in the furtherance of his purposes. In short, he was a very successful politician—probably the most skillful of his day and generation. His genius for political manipulation had been trained into effectiveness in the school of New York politics—the finest institution for such purposes in the country.

In his inaugural address Van Buren indicated his agreement with the principles of his illustrious predecessor. Jackson's Cabinet was retained except that Joel R. Poinsett, the anti-nullification leader of South Carolina, was made Secretary of War in place of Lewis Cass, who had gone as minister to France. The President declared his "inflexible and uncompromising" opposition to any attempt on the part of Congress to interfere with slavery in the states or to abolish it in the District of Columbia. Such views had the ring of conservatism, and he doubtless thought that he would be able to move safely and securely along the paths that the Old General had so clearly marked out. If he indulged such fond hopes he was soon shaken out of his comfortable complacency by the financial storm which burst upon the country.

Like some of the other panics of the nineteenth century, that of 1837 was caused by overspeculation in land and overexpansion in banking and transportation. The hopeful prospects held out to farmers were attracting great numbers of them to the fertile lands of the Northwest, while the high price of cotton was causing a rapid extension of the plantation system in the Southwest. These movements pushed the demand for government lands to unusual heights. The tendency was accentuated by the action of speculators in buying up large amounts of public land with the hope of reselling them at a profit. The revenue received by the government from the sale of its lands was stepped up from $2,000,000 a year before 1830 to $25,-000,000 in 1837. Credit was easy because state banks had multiplied greatly and were pouring out a large volume of bank notes which were circulating as money. The feverish activity of this boom period was stimulated by Jackson's policy of depositing the public moneys in state banks ("pet banks") because it increased the amount of funds available for loans. The success of the Erie Canal had started a craze for canal building which reached its height at the time the panic broke. More canals were constructed than the country needed and many of them were located at places where they could not be used to advantage.

A boom cannot keep itself aloft without continually advancing. Whenever it stops going forward it falls backward and becomes a depression. If a feverish prosperity is maintained, prices must keep rising and credit keep expanding. Such a condition cannot go on indefinitely and whenever the upward movement stops, a reaction of panic and depression sets in. In this case the bubble of overinflated credit would have burst eventually even if it had not encountered any adverse conditions.

By 1837, however, several unfavorable circumstances had arisen which combined in pricking the bubble and causing it to collapse. Business failures in England in 1836 lessened the demand for cotton and caused a drop in the price of this important export. These failures also led to the sale of American securities held by English investors, which resulted in the transfer of specie from the United States to England. Then, too, in the years 1835 and 1837 there were crop failures, which led to a decline in the export of food products and left many American farmers unable to meet their obligations.

The panic was precipitated by two measures of Jackson, the Specie Circular and the Distribution Act. When the Federal land offices began to demand gold and silver in payment for lands (p. 454), the speculators and other buyers presented their notes to the banks for redemption in specie. This run on the banks forced those which had overissued notes ("wildcat" banks) to suspend payment in gold and silver and caused the sound banks to call in their loans and make drastic curtailments in discounts. The distribution of the Federal funds among the states suddenly took large amounts of specie from the "pet banks" in which these funds were deposited. To meet this emergency they also had to call in their loans. These drains on the banks, both strong and weak, caused the failure of many, especially the weak ones, and a general contraction of credit resulted. *How the panic was precipitated*

There was a great shrinkage in bank note circulation and the sale of public lands was reduced to a very low level. By May of 1837 specie payments had been suspended by every bank in the country. Most of the states that had borrowed money from English capitalists for internal improvements were unable to meet their obligations. As taxes could not be raised in such a time of depression, some of the states repudiated these debts, much to the disgust of British creditors. Later, some of the bankrupt states paid off a part or all of their indebtedness though a few allowed their repudiation to become final. *Repudiation of debts by the states*

Cotton, which had been eighteen cents a pound, now fell to eight. Large numbers of men were thrown out of employment, and the promising growth of the new movement in favor of the organization of labor was halted. According to an estimate of Horace Greeley (1837), one fourth of all connected with mercantile and manufacturing interests were out of business. Times were hard and remained so until well into Tyler's administration (about 1842). *Hard times*

Fortunately the unoccupied West offered a way of escape to many of the victims of the depression. Lands in the surveyed areas were open for sale at the price of $1.25 an acre, but many would-be emigrants were unable to raise the $100 needed to purchase the minimum tract of eighty acres. Some of these went into the regions which had not been opened for sale and there established themselves as *Pre-emption acts* squatters in plain violation of the land laws. Public sentiment in the West would not permit the eviction of these trespassers on the public domain, and so the government acquiesced in and encouraged the practice by the enactment of pre-emption laws.

By these measures squatters who had occupied and made slight improvements on unsurveyed government lands were granted pre-emption rights to the tracts on which they had settled. The holder of such a claim could buy the land covered by it (not to exceed 160 acres) at the minimum price. From 1830 on, a number of pre-emption laws were passed which applied only to settlements already made. At the end of Van Buren's term a bill, known as the "Log-cabin" Bill, which provided for general prospective pre-emption, was put through the Senate but was defeated by the opposition of the Whigs in the House of Representatives. Later in the same year, after Tyler had acceded to the Presidency, the Whig leaders in Congress gave up their opposition to pre-emption in order to gain votes for their policy of distribution. Pre-emption was thus adopted (1841) as a permanent policy and was to apply to future, as well as to past, settlements.

Pre-emption was one of the few measures adopted by either the Whigs or the Democrats to aid the country in its recovery from its economic ills. It had the effect of stimulating emigration to the West and especially to the new Northwest. In the territories of Iowa, Minnesota, and Wisconsin there was much productive land which had not been disturbed by the surveyor and into this favored region went many pre-emptioners.

The Independent Treasury plan The rapid decline in imports and the scarcity of gold and silver in circulation reduced to a low figure the income of the government derived from the tariff and from the sale of public lands. By this loss of revenue the surplus of the Treasury was soon changed into a deficit. To meet the crisis Van Buren called Congress in extra session in October. In response to his recommendation it voted to stop the distribution of money to the states and to replenish the Treasury by issuing treasury notes. The President also suggested a new plan for handling the government moneys. The use of both state and national banks had, he maintained, proved unsatisfactory. The Treasury should not deposit its funds in banks but should provide for their safekeeping and disbursement through its own agencies. By so doing its funds would be secure and could not be used by banks to stimulate speculation or be manipulated so as to cause a contraction of credit.

A bill embodying these suggestions was offered, but for some time it could not muster the support necessary to get through Congress.

It was opposed not only by the Whigs but also by some conservative Democrats, mainly in New York and Virginia. Finally, in 1840 the plan, with modifications, was accepted under the title of the Independent Treasury Act. It provided that the government should keep its money in the Treasury at Washington and in subtreasuries in five other cities (Boston, New York, Philadelphia, St. Louis, and New Orleans). There was also a provision that after the first of July, 1843, only gold and silver should be received for all government dues.

In their arguments against the Independent Treasury, or Subtreasury, Bill, as it was called, Clay and the Whigs contended that it would ultimately put the country on a gold and silver basis, and the exclusive use of metallic money would lower prices and add great weight to the burdens which debtors were bearing. In the campaign of 1840 the Whigs were noncommittal on most points but were definite in their opposition to the Subtreasury scheme. Consequently, when they came into power they repealed the act (1841). Five years later, with the Democrats again in power, the measure was for a second time adopted but with the omission of the provision regarding specie payments, and from that time (1846) until 1913 the government kept its money in its own vaults.

Later history of the Independent Treasury

RELATIONS WITH ENGLAND

Van Buren not only had to contend with financial difficulties at home, but he was also confronted with some knotty problems in foreign affairs. These were connected with the relations between the United States and England and grew out of an effort on the part of some Canadians to throw off British rule.

Rebellion in Canada

In 1837 a rebellion broke out in Canada against the authority of the English, and the demands of the insurgents for self-government found a sympathetic response in the United States. Americans along the border gave aid to the rebels and furnished them with arms and ammunition. Van Buren enforced a policy of strict neutrality at the cost of losing, along the border, votes which were badly needed in the next Presidential race. The situation was so intense that incidents could easily arise which might threaten the peaceable relations of the two countries. One such incident was that of the *Caroline*.

The *Caroline* was an American vessel which had been aiding the Canadian rebels in 1837. While this vessel was lying on the American side of the Niagara River, an expedition from Canada came over, cut the moorings of the ship, set her on fire, and allowed her to drift over Niagara Falls. In the encounter an American citizen named Durfree was killed. The British authorities justified this action of the Cana-

The Caroline incident

dians on the ground that it was a necessary means of defense. The American government would not accept this explanation, contending that the act was unwarranted because it had been committed in American waters. It was not until July, 1842, that an agreement was reached. At that time Webster and Lord Ashburton, special minister from England to the United States, came to an understanding which was acceptable to President Tyler.

The McLeod affair

In the meantime there had grown out of the *Caroline* episode another cause of friction between England and the United States. This was the McLeod affair. Alexander McLeod, a Canadian, had come over to New York, and while in his cups had boasted that he had killed Durfree when the *Caroline* was destroyed. He was arrested (November, 1840) and later brought up for trial in a New York state court. The British government strongly protested against McLeod's arrest, contending that persons engaging in a transaction of a public character could not incur private or personal responsibility. Webster, who was then Secretary of State, agreed to this view but was unable to secure McLeod's release, since the New York authorities insisted on holding him for trial. The difficulty was finally solved when the prisoner was declared not guilty by the New York court.

To prevent such an embarrassing situation from arising in the future, Webster, with Tyler's approval, drafted a bill to cover such eventualities, which was passed by Congress in August, 1842. By this act the Federal courts were given jurisdiction in all cases in which aliens had been charged with crimes committed under authority of a foreign government.

"TIPPECANOE AND TYLER TOO"

Whig nominees for President and Vice-President

Early in December,1839, the Whigs met in a national convention at Harrisburg, Pennsylvania, to select candidates for President and Vice-President. Clay was the ablest and best known of the candidates whose names were before the convention. But during his long career in Congress he had taken a decided stand on public questions about which there was marked disagreement among the Whigs; for this reason it was difficult for the diverse elements in the party to unite on him. On the score of availability, therefore, he was thought by some of the leaders to be the weakest of the aspirants.

Clay's strongest competitor for the honor was General William Henry Harrison, who had made a creditable record in the War of 1812 and might properly be considered a military hero of a mild type. Moreover, he had won the sobriquet of "Tippecanoe" by having fought the Indians at a place by that name, and this word would sound well in a campaign slogan. His career as a civilian in public affairs had been an inconspicuous one. To the great mass of the voters, therefore, his attitude on public questions was unknown, and he was not associated in the public mind with any policy that would arouse violent antagonism. For these reasons the politicians who controlled the convention selected him as the standard-bearer of the party, considering his availability a better bet than the ability of the brilliant Kentuckian.

For Vice-President the convention named John Tyler of Virginia, who was a strong states' rights man and an ardent supporter of Clay. Having been a candidate for the same office on the Whig ticket in the campaign of 1836, he was well known to the voters of the South. His nomination was a recognition of the Southern states' rights element of the party and a peace offering to Clay's followers.

The Whigs have no platform

No effort was made in the convention to adopt a platform. The coalition which went by the name of the Whig Party was composed of groups of such diversified views that there was no possibility of an agreement on the important issues of the day. A straightforward statement of principles would have destroyed the unity of the party and invited defeat.

Clay's disappointment

The action of the convention was a sore disappointment to Clay. When notified of his defeat he gave vent to his feelings by exclaiming: "My friends are not worth the powder and shot it would take to kill them. . . . If there were two Henry Clays, one of them would make the other President of the United States. . . . It is a diabolical intrigue, I now know, which has betrayed me for a nomination when I, or any one, would be sure of an election."

Democratic nominees

The Democratic Party held its national convention early in May (1840) in the city of Baltimore. The meetings were characterized by exceptional harmony, and Van Buren was renominated unanimously. No agreement, however, could be reached as to a candidate for the Vice-Presidency. There were several aspirants for the second place, and the convention decided to make no choice between them, hoping that as the campaign advanced, some one of the number would develop sufficient strength to cause the others to withdraw from the race. This expectation was realized, for Colonel Richard M. Johnson, the incumbent of the office, showed signs of running ahead of his competitors and they, one after the other, retired from the contest.

The Democrats were hopeful of victory, as they were presenting a united front to the enemy. For twelve years this party had controlled the Federal patronage and also that of most of the states. Another valuable asset was the prestige and popularity of Andrew Jackson. There was, however, one dark cloud on the horizon. Times were still hard, and, of course, the Administration received the blame for this unfortunate state of affairs. Moreover, the Democrats allowed their opponents to outplay them in the game of dealing out buncombe to the voters. By a mistake in tactics they gave the Whigs an opportunity to create a great wave of popular enthusiasm and harness it to their cause.

Slogans and campaign methods

Soon after the Harrisburg Convention the Baltimore *Republican*, a Democratic paper, published an unwise statement of its Washington correspondent to the effect "that upon condition of his receiving a pension of two thousand dollars and a barrel of cider, General Harrison would no doubt consent to withdraw his pretensions, and spend his days in a log cabin on the banks of the Ohio." The Whigs seized upon this indiscreet utterance and used it to the very best account. It enabled them to represent their candidate as being a simple farmer belonging to the class that drank cider and lived in log cabins. As a great many of the farmers at that time, especially in the West, lived in log cabins, it made a very favorable impression on the masses.

The Whigs already had one good slogan—"Tippecanoe and Tyler too," and this gave them another—"Log Cabin and Hard Cider." The log cabin and cider barrel also lent themselves very appropriately to the dramatics of the campaign. At every great political rally a log cabin with a cider barrel in front and a coonskin tacked on the door—the latchstring of which was always on the outside—served as headquarters for the various delegations. Log cabins were also transported long distances to these meetings and were borne in the processions.

In contrast to the plebeian farmer of North Bend, Van Buren was represented as an aristocratic epicurean living in the greatest luxury and extravagance in "the Palace," as the White House was termed. This soft and self-indulgent monarch (it was loudly proclaimed) walked across royal Brussels and Wilton carpets "deep enough for a good loco-foco Democrat to bury his foot in"; reclined on costly Turkish divans; and ate in the "court banqueting room," where gold spoons and gold and silver plate were used. Of course, there was no foundation in fact for the charge that Van Buren was living in extravagance and luxury. He was not responsible for the furnishings of the White House, which had been bought by the Committee on Public Buildings. Nor were these furnishings beyond the requirements of such a pretentious mansion. Moreover, Van Buren was a self-made man of middle-class parentage, whereas Harrison and Tyler were both scions of old and aristocratic families and could boast of the proudest patrician blood.

THE NORTH BEND FARMER and HIS VISITORS.

CARTOON, THE CAMPAIGN OF 1840.

Campaign dramatics

Despite the mudslinging engaged in by the leaders, this was a frolicsome, as well as dramatic, campaign. Political gatherings were made attractive by barbecues and long processions enlivened with the blaring of numerous brass bands. Singing also played a prominent part, and one Whig leader said that "General Harrison was sung into the Presidency."

The Whigs noncommittal on important issues

Since the Whigs had no platform and the component factions of the party were not in agreement on most of the major issues of the day, their speakers in the campaign generally took a noncommittal attitude on important questions. Common to all the Whigs was a feeling of opposition to some of the major policies of Jackson or Van Buren and to the alleged executive usurpation which was behind these policies. They were especially united in their disapproval of the financial measures of Van Buren. There was, however, no such unanimity as to the remedies which should be employed to cure the monetary evils of the day, and certainly no decided general stand was taken for or against a national bank. There is, therefore, no warrant for assuming that Tyler or anyone else was honor-bound to support a national bank or any other particular policy (except the repeal of the Independent Treasury Act) as a result of commitments made during this burlesque campaign. Indeed, if we should judge the wishes of the people in this contest by their demonstrations and by the speeches of the politicians, we would be inclined to agree with the facetious statement of Silas Wright that the only clear mandate received by the Whigs was to tear down the Capitol and erect a log cabin in its place.

Result of the election

When the returns had all come in, it was found that the Whigs had won, though Harrison's plurality over Van Buren was not overwhelming, being only 145,914. In the Electoral College, Harrison and Tyler each received 234 votes to 60 for Van Buren.

CHAPTER XXIX

A President Without a Party

HARRISON'S SHORT TERM

Wᴵᴸᴸᴵᴀᴍ HENRY HARRISON (1773-1841) was born in *Harrison;* Virginia at "Berkeley," a mansion overlooking the broad and lazy *previous ca-* James River. His father, Benjamin Harrison, a signer of the Decla- *reer and per-* ration of Independence and afterwards governor of Virginia, was one *sonal traits* of a number of progenitors who had been prominent in the political and social life of the Old Dominion for several generations. At the age of twenty-one young Harrison enlisted in the army and was sent to Ohio to take part in the campaign against the Indians. This was the beginning of a long career in which civil duties alternated with military activity. As has already been shown, he had in the course of his military career won a victory over the Indians at Tippecanoe and played a worthy, though not a brilliant, role in the War of 1812.

Before his accession to the Presidency he had also held a number of responsible civilian positions, including those of Governor of Indiana Territory, Ohio State Senator, member of both houses of Congress, and minister to Colombia. In none of these offices had he achieved any marked distinction, but he had made a creditable record, except that his mission to Colombia was to some extent ill-starred.

He brought to his high office a sound common sense, fine principles and high ideals, and a reputation for sterling integrity. With simple and unassuming manners, he was easily approachable and able to win the affection of those who were associated with him. Before aspirations for the Presidency began to disturb his serenity Harrison was living the wholesome and comfortable life of a country gentleman at his residence near the village of North Bend, about fourteen miles below Cincinnati. Here in a large house overlooking the Ohio River he dispensed a hospitality worthy of the ancestral mansion on the James.

Leaving this pleasant retreat, he arrived at Washington on his *His Cabinet* sixty-eighth birthday to assume, a few weeks later, a burden that was too heavy for his years. His first serious responsibility was that of naming his Cabinet. Daniel Webster was made Secretary of State.

475

Clay had been offered any place in the Cabinet to which he might aspire, but declined office because he preferred to remain in the Senate, where, as he considered, he could "most effectually serve the new administration, and be ready to enter the field four years hence." He influenced the President to call an extra session of Congress and in other ways showed an inclination to dictate the policies of the Administration. So high were his assumptions of authority that Harrison had to remind him that he, not Clay, was President.

Illness and death

Harrison's routine of living was disturbed by social dissipation, and his peace of mind was upset by the importunities of hungry office seekers. When, therefore, he was attacked by pneumonia on March 24 he was unable to put up an effective resistance to the disease and succumbed to it on April 4, only one month after his accession.

Tyler was promptly notified of Harrison's death by messengers sent by the Cabinet, and so hurriedly did he make the journey from his home at Williamsburg, Virginia, that he was in Washington in time to take part in the funeral ceremonies of the deceased President.

THE ACCESSION OF JOHN TYLER

Tyler; previous career and personal traits

Harrison and Tyler were both born and reared in Charles City County, Virginia, and their fathers were personal friends and at times political rivals. John Tyler (1790-1862) belonged to an old family whose representatives had since the middle of the seventeenth century been leaders in the plantation life of central Tidewater Virginia. His father, also named John, took a prominent part in public affairs and held a number of responsible offices, among them that of Governor of Virginia. The elder Tyler was a warm personal and political friend of Thomas Jefferson, and so young John imbibed in childhood an ardent admiration for the great champion of democracy. The future President was educated at William and Mary College and after taking a course of reading in the law was at the early age of twenty admitted to the bar.

Although he was not long in building up a paying legal practice, he entered politics almost as soon as he attained his majority. During his public career he served a number of years as a member of the Virginia legislature, was twice elected governor of the state, was a member of the Virginia Constitutional Convention of 1829-30, and was in Congress for about fourteen years, serving first as Representative and later as Senator. In all this period he had never lost an opportunity to reaffirm his adherence to the particularistic views enunciated by Jefferson and vigorously to oppose a national bank, a protective tariff, and the construction of internal improvements by the Federal government.

The tenth President was favored with an attractive personality, which was enhanced by the naturalness, simplicity, and cordiality of his manners and the excellence of his conversational powers. He was a wide reader and was thus in possession of a good store of the kind of information which enriches conversation. Unlike many of the statesmen of the day, he did not harbor bitter enmities toward his opponents. He was noted for his poise and dignity, his kindliness toward men, and his gentleness and gallantry toward women. And yet this affable Virginian, whose social graces were an ornament to any drawing room, was the center of the most violent storm that ever raged in American politics.

As Harrison was the first President to die in office, there was no precedent to indicate whether the Vice-President should be accorded all the power and dignity of a regular Chief Magistrate or be regarded only as an acting chief executive. Some of the leaders in Congress, both Democrats and Whigs, were at first inclined to look upon him as a Vice-President upon whom had devolved the duties but not the office of the Presidency. Tyler, however, took the position that he was President in the full sense of the term and Congress accepted this view. The precedent set by Tyler has been followed in every subsequent case in which a Vice-President has succeeded to the Chief Magistracy. *Tyler's difficulties: President or acting-President?*

The first problem of the new incumbent was that of deciding as to the Cabinet inherited from Harrison. The members of this body, except Webster and Francis Granger, Postmaster General,[1] were all partisans of Clay and were determined to use their influence in favor of his succession to the Presidency four years later. Such an attitude was not consistent with the fullest co-operation with the Chief Executive. Tyler, therefore, should have had a new Cabinet chosen on the basis of loyalty to him and his principles. But to call for the resignation of the heads of the departments would have caused a serious breach in the party. He, therefore, went along for a time with advisers who were not in entire sympathy with him. With such an official family the outlook was not bright either for harmony or efficiency. *The Cabinet*

Another serious drawback to the success of his administration was the inability of the President to take over the leadership of his party. A President cannot expect much in the way of achievement unless *Clay, not Tyler, leader of the Whig Party*

---

[1] The other members of the Cabinet were: Thomas Ewing of Ohio, Secretary of the Treasury; John Bell of Tennessee, Secretary of War; George C. Badger of North Carolina, Secretary of the Navy; and J. J. Crittenden of Kentucky, Attorney General.

he is recognized as the actual as well as the nominal head of his party. In the case of John Tyler, all the circumstances were against his assumption of such control. As the Vice-Presidential candidate, he had played an inconspicuous part in the campaign, and so neither the politicians nor the people had looked upon him as an important leader. Nor had Harrison's mantle, when it fell upon him, endowed him with the power to control the Whigs. If the different groups that composed the Whig coalition were to be fused into a united party, the strongest faction must dominate the weaker ones. Since the nationalists among the Whigs greatly outnumbered the particularists, it was hardly to be expected that the former would accept a leader from the latter group. Therefore, in the contest for party supremacy, Clay, the champion of nationalism, had every advantage over Tyler, the advocate of localism.

Tyler mis-judged by Clay

Nor did Clay fail to take full advantage of all the circumstances in his favor. He promptly assumed the leadership of the Whigs and determined to put through a program to his liking. Tyler's tactful method in dealing with his colleagues sometimes left the mistaken impression that he did not have much backbone. Clay was one of those who mistook courtesy for weakness. He failed to understand that while the President was exceptionally pleasant in his relations with others, he was unyielding when his convictions were involved. He did not realize that a gloved hand may easily become a clenched fist.

THE BANK CONTROVERSY

Clay's aggressive leadership

The Whigs were in control of both branches of Congress, and Clay began to assert his authority in the Senate with little or no regard for the sensibilities of the states' rights President. Clay was now at the height of his power, and the Whig majority in Congress—except for a handful of Tyler supporters known as the "Corporal's Guard"— accepted his pronouncements as law and gospel. However, his ambition to be President was a serious handicap to his usefulness at this time. The Presidential bee was buzzing so loudly around his ear that he did not always hear the still, small voice of wisdom or the loud noise of public opinion. If his ambition as to the succession in 1845 were to be realized, Tyler would have to be eliminated as a possible competitor for the Whig nomination. To what extent Clay was influenced by this consideration it is impossible to say, but his actions afforded Tyler's friends the opportunity of giving it as the chief motive for his unyielding attitude toward the Administration.

Early in the extra session (June 7) Clay offered six resolutions as a plan of work for the session. These resolutions provided for the repeal of the Independent Treasury Act, the establishment of a *Clay's program of legislation* national bank, an increase in the import duties to provide an adequate revenue for the government, the distribution of the proceeds from the sale of public lands, and other measures of minor importance. This program was strictly in accord with the principles of the nationalist wing of the Whig party and revealed his intention to override the scruples of a President whom he chose to regard only as a sort of regent.

The first item on Clay's agenda made no difficulty. Tyler in cam- *Repeal of the Independent Treasury Act* paign speeches and in his message to Congress had expressed opposition to the Independent Treasury Act, and when a bill for its repeal was passed by Congress he willingly signed it. This reversal of a major policy of the previous administration caused great rejoicing among the Whigs of Washington. In celebration of this event a large group of them marched in procession up Pennsylvania Avenue accompanied by a hearse bearing a coffin labeled "The Sub-treasury Plan."

This apparent harmony was deceptive, for a conflict between the President and Senate leader was imminent, and it broke out in violent form as soon as the former was asked to put aside his states' rights scruples and endorse the bank policy of the latter. Tyler was willing to accept a plan which would provide for a central bank in the District of Columbia with branches located in the several states with their consent. In creating this bank Congress might be considered as acting not in its national capacity but as the legislative body of the District of Columbia. This would do away with the constitutional objection to the creation of the central bank. The provision that no branch be located in any state without its consent would remove the constitutional objection to the establishment of branches.

Clay offered a bill for chartering a bank by Congress acting in its *A bank bill passed by Congress and vetoed by the President* capacity as the legislature of the whole country and not of the District of Columbia. The parent bank was to be located in Washington because of the alleged financial advantages that would accrue from the proximity of the bank to the government. In its final form the measure provided that the consent of the states was to be required for the establishment of the branches; but such assent was to be presumed in respect to any state whose legislature at its first session after the passage of this act did not unconditionally express its dissent to the establishment of a branch within its limits. The amended bill was passed by Congress and sent to the President, who after due deliberation returned it with a veto. His objections were based partly on practical, but mainly on constitutional grounds.

The action of the President aroused violent opposition among the supporters of a bank. A mob assembled at the White House late at night and insulted the President with cries of "Huzza for Clay!" "A Bank! A Bank! Down with the Veto!" Clay made a long speech in the Senate in which he excoriated the President for his rejection of the bill, charging him with disloyalty to Whig principles. No commitment, however, on the bank question had been made by the Whig Party in the campaign, and so Tyler was as free to oppose the measure as Clay was to support it.

A second bank bill passed and vetoed

The bill could not be passed over the President's veto, and the Whig leaders therefore decided to come to terms with him on the question of the bank. Accordingly, the Whig caucus sent two emissaries to confer with Tyler and find out what kind of a measure would be acceptable to him. He would not discuss details with them but gave in a general way his views on the points at issue. Two members of the Cabinet—Webster and Ewing—also discussed the question with the caucus representatives and indicated the type of bill which, in their opinion, would meet with the approval of the President.

On the basis of these understandings a second bank bill was framed and offered in the House of Representatives. Under this plan there was to be a central bank in the District of Columbia with branches in the states, establishd without the consent of the states. There was no provision authorizing the central bank or the branches to engage in local discounts; but according to the opponents of the bill, local discounts could and would be permitted under the clause allowing the bank to deal in bills of exchange.

The sponsors of the measure contended that the bill had been framed in accordance with Tyler's wishes, and some of them declared that he had seen and approved the text of the measure before it was presented in the House. These assertions were stoutly denied by Tyler. Furthermore, soon after the bill appeared in the House he notified members of that body that he could not accept it unless it were modified. No heed was paid to this warning, and the measure was rushed through both houses of Congress without amendment. As might have been expected, it also was vetoed by the President.

Tyler read out of the Whig Party

This second act of defiance placed Tyler beyond the pale of Whig forbearance. Accordingly, a caucus attended by some fifty or more Whig members of Congress was held on Capitol Square and resolutions were adopted which virtually expelled the President from the party. Henceforth Tyler was a President without a party.

Effect of the vetoes on the bank question

These vetoes ended the attempt to establish a national bank. Although Tyler's action had occasioned loud outcries among the Whig leaders, it was probably acceptable to the country as a whole, for a majority of the people seem to have been indifferent or opposed to a national bank. No further effort to ally the banking business with the Federal government was made for more than a score of years.

After his veto of the second bank bill all the members of Tyler's *Cabinet changes* Cabinet except Webster resigned in protest. The vacancies so created were quickly filled and the nominees were promptly confirmed by the Senate. The new appointees were all Whigs who had originally been Jackson men and had, like Tyler, left the Democratic Party because of their disagreement with some of Jackson's policies. They were all, or nearly all, men of ability, though most of them were not well-known nationally.

The resignation of his former colleagues left Webster in an awkward, not to say embarrassing, position. If he held on to his place he could be charged with party irregularity, as the great majority of the Whigs sided with Clay in this controversy. He would also be identified with a discredited administration. On the other hand, to follow the lead of his colleagues would be to forfeit unnecessarily an honored place, for he had seen no sufficient reason for the dissolution of the Cabinet. Moreover, to resign at that juncture would be to give up all hope of succeeding his chief in the Presidency. For a break with Tyler would mean a tie-up with the tail of Clay's kite. Then, too, he had entered upon diplomatic negotiations with the British minister which gave promise of yielding new laurels to his fame. He, therefore, remained at the head of the State Department until 1843, when he was succeeded after a short interval by Abel P. Upshur of Virginia. Upshur was killed by the explosion on the *Princeton*,[1] and soon thereafter Calhoun was appointed Secretary of State.

A PRESIDENT WITHOUT A PARTY

Tyler's veto of the second bank bill aroused a storm of opposition *Unpopularity of the President* among Whig leaders throughout the country. Hundreds of letters were received threatening him with assassination. "The fires of a thousand effigies," he afterwards wrote, "lighted the streets of the various cities." "Indignation meetings were everywhere held; . . . and a universal roar of Whig vengeance was heard in every blast." The *Lexington* (Ky.) *Intelligencer*, Clay's special organ, was quoted as saying: "If a God-directed thunderbolt were to strike and annihi-

---

[1] On February 22, 1844, the government warship, *Princeton*, took a party on a pleasure excursion from Washington to Mount Vernon and return. The list on board included the President, members of the Cabinet, and other political and social leaders. On the return trip the firing of a big gun stationed on the bow of the vessel caused an explosion which killed a half-dozen or more people, including Secretary Upshur and T. W. Gilmer, Secretary of War.

late the traitor all would say that 'Heaven is just.' " The Whigs persisted in their hatred of the President until the end of his term.
Later vetoes by him fed their rage and they kept up their efforts to
vilify and discredit him. When an epidemic of influenza swept over
the country it gave them the opportunity of disparaging the President by calling it the "Tyler Grippe." Whig editors inked their pens
with venom when writing about him.

For the President this bitter fight had ended in defeat, vilification,
and expulsion from his party. The only gain that had accrued to him
from it was a feeling of self-respect and a consciousness of honesty
and integrity, with the hope of an ultimate vindication by history.
The outcome would have been very different if he had swallowed
his constitutional scruples and accepted the nationalist policies of his
powerful opponent. By so doing he would have recognized Clay as
mayor of the palace and accepted for himself the futile but honored
place of *roi fainéant*. In that event he would have enjoyed peace and
popularity, and, to all outward seeming, his administration would
have been a success. However, the Presidential chair into which he
would have been comfortably ensconced would not have been a seat
of the mighty but the high chair of an infant.

The tariff and   As has already been seen, the third item on Clay's program was the
distribution   raising of an adequate revenue by the imposition of tariff duties.
acts of 1841   The fourth was the prospective distribution among the states of the
proceeds from the sale of public lands. A strong reason for raising
the tariff duties was the need of getting an increase of revenue to
balance the budget. It was estimated that the deficit in the Federal
treasury at the end of the year 1841 would be more than eleven million dollars. If this deficit was to be wiped away and the budget bal-
anced, an increase in tariff duties would have to be made. The
distribution of the proceeds from the public land sales would be a
great boon to the states, many of which were staggering under debt
burdens too heavy for them in a period of hard times.

With the view to attaining these objectives two bills were passed
by Congress during the extra session (1841). The first of these provided for the distribution among the states of the proceeds from the
sales of Federal lands. To this act was attached the condition that
the distribution was to be suspended whenever the tariff duties
should exceed the twenty per cent level. The bill also included a
provision granting pre-emption rights to settlers who had occupied
and improved unsurveyed public lands or should do so in the future
(see pp. 467 ff.) . The second of these acts provided for an increase in
the revenue by an extension of the tariff. The measure was not inconsistent with the Compromise, as the increase in the duties was

made by imposing the twenty per cent rate, the ultimate maximum, on articles then on the free list or taxed less than the maximum. Tyler signed both of these measures and in so doing went along with the Whig Party although it had repudiated him.

In his report to Congress (June, 1841) the Secretary of the Treas- *The Tariff* ury had estimated that these tariff increases would provide more than *Act of 1842* enough revenue for the running expenses of the government. The proceeds from the sale of the public lands could, therefore, be used for other purposes. Unfortunately the hoped-for prosperity on which this prophecy was based was slow in arriving, and when Congress assembled in December for the regular session the condition of the Federal finances was anything but promising. In order to meet the expenses of the government and provide for adequate national defense it would be necessary to put the tariff rates above the twenty per cent maximum on some important articles.

To meet the difficulty Congress passed an act (August, 1842) which raised the tariff rate above the twenty per cent level and also provided for the unconditional continuance of distribution.[1] The President vetoed this bill because, he said, it proposed to give away a fruitful source of revenue at a time when the Treasury was in a state of extreme embarrassment and the government had not only to lay additional taxes, but to borrow money to meet pressing demands. Such a proceeding he regarded "as highly impolitic, if not unconstitutional."

The Whig leaders and the Whig press again raised a savage outcry against the President, charging him with treason against his party. To talk of a President's disloyalty to a party from which he had been expelled would under ordinary circumstances have appealed irresistibly to the sense of humor of politicians. But by this time the hatred which the Whigs had for Tyler seems to have paralyzed their risibles, and in all seriousness they undertook to flay him for his political irregularity. They succeeded in getting through the House of Representatives by a narrow majority some resolutions that severely arraigned the President for his alleged misdeeds.

Despite all the noise made by them, the Whigs in Congress realized that they dared not return to their constituents without having enacted a revenue measure. So they were forced to yield to Tyler and present another bill without the objectionable distribution clause. Accordingly, such a measure was passed and signed by the President (1842). The tariff act raised the general level of duties to

---

[1] Congress had in June of this year passed a temporary tariff measure whose provisions were of the same character as those of this bill. This temporary bill had been vetoed by the President.

that of 1832, and was quite satisfactory to the protectionists throughout the country. It was objectionable, however, to the low-tariff
advocates, especially those in South Carolina.

RELATIONS WITH ENGLAND

Causes of ill feeling between England and the United States

When Tyler acceded to the Presidency, American relations with
England had assumed a threatening aspect. In the unwelcome legacy
left to him by his predecessor were three causes of dispute between
the United States and Great Britain. These were: (1) the *Caroline*
case and the McLeod incident that grew out of it (see pp. 469-470,
note) ; (2) a disagreement as to the location of the northeastern
boundary; and (3) the question of the right of visit and search in
connection with the suppression of the slave trade. These issues had
aroused a feeling of bitterness, which in each case had been intensified rather than alleviated by the discussions which had rotated
around them.[1]

There were other reasons, more or less intangible, for the growth
of misunderstanding between the two kindred peoples. Some of the
states had repudiated their debts, and as a result English creditors
had lost heavily. The rebellion against British authority which had
broken out in Canada had not yet entirely subsided, and some of our
citizens were in sympathy with the rebels. British fears exaggerated
the activities of these American sympathizers with the insurgents
and saw in them a feeling of hostility to England on the part of our
people in general.

The northeast boundary dispute

Of the controversies with Great Britain the most serious was the
one over the northeastern boundary. This dispute was as old as the
nation itself and owed its origin to the vague or inaccurate wording
of the treaties of Paris (1782, 1783) . By 1798 the northeastern boundary of the United States had been fixed from the mouth to the source
of the St. Croix River, but the rest of it was still under dispute.
Before the accession of Tyler the location of the line ceased to be
merely a question for academic discussion but had become the occasion of a dangerous practical controversy. The citizens of Maine and

---

[1] Another cause of friction was the *Creole* case, which arose soon after Tyler's accession. The *Creole*, an American vessel, had sailed (October, 1841) from Hampton Roads,
Virginia, for New Orleans, with a cargo of slaves and merchandise. When she got out
to sea some of the slaves revolted, overpowered the officers and crew, and forced the
mate to steer for Nassau, a British port in the Bahama Islands. Here the slaves that
had participated in the mutiny were kept in custody and the others were liberated by
the authorities. Secretary Webster protested against this highhanded act, but the
British government was slow to make amends for it, and the dispute was not settled
until 1853.

those of New Brunswick came to blows in the disputed area, the *The "Aroos-took War"* Aroostook Valley. These clashes (1838-1839), sometimes called the "Aroostook War," might easily have led to international strife. General Scott was sent to the frontier by Van Buren and through his agency the friction was temporarily suspended. Efforts at arbitration made in 1840 were futile, and therefore the disagreement over the northeastern boundary was one of the most pressing problems left to Tyler by his predecessor.

In the spring of 1842 Lord Ashburton was sent over as a special *Negotiations between Webster and Lord Ashburton* envoy to adjust the controversy. He was kindly disposed toward the United States and was very anxious to cement and prolong the friendship between the two English-speaking peoples. He was quite tactful and conciliatory in all his relations and was cordially received by social and official Washington.

The negotiations between Webster and Lord Ashburton were carried on in the main by informal conferences rather than by formal notes. Despite this free and easy procedure, at one time the negotiations seemed doomed to failure, and Ashburton was so discouraged that he was on the verge of ending his mission and returning home. The terrific heat of a typical Washington summer was making inroads on his comfort and strength and causing him to long for a change of climate. Webster's nerves were also frayed by ill-health and the heat, and he found it difficult to maintain the poise and composure necessary for success in diplomacy. It was at this juncture that the President was able to give the most effective aid. He realized that if this attempt to settle the controversy failed, relations between the two powers would be more strained than before. A conference was held between Tyler and Lord Ashburton at which the latter was impressed with the importance of continuing the negotiations and induced to remain at his post. The situation was one which called into requisition the President's suavity of manner, conversational ability, and familiarity with the amenities employed in diplomacy.

By a policy of give and take, Lord Ashburton and Webster were *Provisions of the Webster-Ashburton Treaty* able to iron out their differences, and in due time an agreement was reached as to all the disputed portions of the American-Canadian boundary from the source of the St. Croix River to the Rocky Mountains. Under the terms of this treaty the United States received about seven of the twelve thousand square miles in dispute. This compromise was quite a concession on the part of the United States; for in the light of later evidence it appears that the boundary originally claimed by the American government was the same as the one agreed upon by the commissioners in 1782.[1] But this unconscious sacrifice of a few thousand square miles of land was in the nature of a peace offering, and was a small price to pay for the adjustment of a dispute which had menaced the amicable relations of two great powers for two generations.

The African slave trade

After having settled the boundary dispute, the peacemakers turned their attention to the question of the slave trade. At that time slave vessels could go from the coast of Africa and deliver their cargoes at a West Indian or South American port without much fear of molestation. To put a stop to this practice the British government suggested that all the great powers allow each other to exercise a limited right of search, or at least of visitation. Some of the leading nations of Europe were willing to grant this privilege, and the United States was asked to accede to the arrangement.

The feeling in our country against visit and search, owing to the abuse of the practice by the British prior to the War of 1812, was so strong that Webster would not agree to discuss it; but a practical plan for putting a stop to the slave trade was adopted. It was agreed that each nation would "maintain on the coast of Africa . . . a naval force . . . of not less than eighty guns to enforce, separately and respectively, the laws . . . for the suppression of the slave trade." Each squadron was to be independent of the other, but the officers of each were to receive from their respective governments such instructions as would enable them to co-operate whenever the exigencies should demand it.

The treaty ratified

The treaty was duly ratified by the Senate, and thus ended a most important chapter in the history of American diplomacy. Both the President and the Secretary of State were justly proud of their success in settling this long-standing dispute. Of this achievement Tyler later wrote as follows: "The peace of the country when I reached Washington on the 6th day of April, 1841, was suspended by a thread; but we [Webster and he] converted that thread into a chain cable of sufficient strength to render that peace secure."

Better times

The accession of Tyler was preceded by a quadrennium of depression, and times were still hard. Recovery was on the way but had not yet peered around the corner. The Federal government was unable to balance its budget, and the deficit Tyler inherited kept piling up. Even with this excess of expenditure over income, the pay of the

---

[1] Old maps with the northeastern boundary marked in accordance with the understanding of 1782 have come to light since this treaty was signed. One of these was discovered in the archives of Spain as late as 1933. The marking on these maps shows that the Maine-New Brunswick boundary, as laid down by the treaty of 1782, was the same as that which the United States had contended for all along. See S. F. Bemis, *A Diplomatic History of the United States*, 263-264.

army, the navy, and the civil list was at times suspended, owing to the utter destitution of the Treasury. Under such conditions the credit of the government naturally fell to an unusually low level, and it was with great difficulty that loans were floated. In March, 1842, the New York *Herald* said that the Federal treasury was empty, the nation bankrupt, several states bankrupt, and almost every city in debt. Owing to this lack of funds, the home squadron of the navy was lying idle, and the workmen in the navy yards and arsenals were grumbling because they had not been paid.

In time, however, the depression passed and commerce and industry revived. The income of the government increased and the deficit was wiped away. National credit was raised and by September, 1842, government bonds were selling at par and some were being held at a premium.

From THE CHRONICLES OF AMERICA
Copyright Yale University Press

SAM HOUSTON.

CHAPTER XXX

Expansion and Conflict

THE ANNEXATION OF TEXAS AND THE CAMPAIGN OF 1844

Offers of annexation by Texas refused by the United States

*A*FTER the United States had recognized the independence of Texas (March, 1837), England, France, and other European powers followed her example. The people of Texas, who were mainly emigrants from the United States, were desirous of having their new republic incorporated into the union of their fellow countrymen. This wish was shown unmistakably when in the plebiscite (September, 1836) on their constitution they gave an overwhelming majority in favor of annexation to the United States. Texas, therefore, as early as December, 1836, asked to be annexed. This request and one made the next year (August, 1837) were declined by the government of the United States. This refusal of the Washington authorities to accept the offer of Texas was the result of opposition to annexation on the part of a good portion of the American people. This opposition was due in part to the fear that annexation would lead to war with Mexico. There was also in the North a strong objection to such an increase in the slaveholding area of the country, since it would greatly strengthen the cause of slavery and enlarge the influence of the South in the Federal government. The Texas question had thus become a sectional issue.

This repulse to her advances was disappointing and humiliating to the debutante republic. Having failed to win the desired suitor by leap-year diplomacy, she retired into maidenly reserve and resolved to await overtures from Uncle Sam as the next step in the courtship. Accordingly, the offer was formally withdrawn the next year by order of President Houston. No other proposal for annexation was made by Texas until after Tyler's accession.

Tyler was strongly in favor of acquiring Texas, and yet twice in the year 1842 he declined an offer of annexation made by Houston. His refusal to accept the proposal was due to the belief that a treaty of annexation would at that time have been rejected by the Senate. In August of the next year the tender was withdrawn.

Texas flirts with England

Houston now took a new tack. He instructed Van Zandt, Texan chargé d'affaires at Washington, to leave all further action looking to annexation to the initiative of the United States. He also began to encourage closer relations with Great Britain and paraded every incident that pointed to an understanding between Texas and England. Whether this was a flirtation to arouse the fears of the United States and awaken at Washington a greater concern for annexation or whether it was a *bona fide* effort to enlist the aid of England in securing the independence of Texas is a matter of dispute. Houston afterwards said that he had "coquetted a little with Great Britain" in order to make the United States jealous. His plan was to play upon the fears of the Senate and make it realize the danger of allowing the prize to slip from its grasp. Tyler, however, regarded Houston's "billing and cooing with England" as a real love affair, as serious "as any in the calendar." If the desire to arouse in the United States a greater interest in Texas was the main purpose behind Houston's "flirtation" with England, he certainly made a correct appraisal of American sentiment and discovered the proper method of harnessing this feeling to his purposes.

The retirement from the Cabinet of Webster, who was against annexation, and the transfer of Abel P. Upshur from the Department of the Navy to that of State gave Tyler a premier who was enthusiastically in favor of the acquisition of Texas. Shortly after this change was made Tyler definitely decided to take steps looking toward annexation. The final decision was precipitated by fear of the influence that England might gain over Texas if the latter were not soon taken into the United States. Financial and social conditions in the new republic had gradually become worse, and by the end of the year 1842 it looked as if it could not continue its separate existence unless there was some strong outside power on which it could lean. England, it was thought, stood ready to serve as a prop to this tottering state. *Tyler and Upshur fear British influence in Texas*

Such a connection, however, between the two countries would be fraught with danger to the United States. Its commercial and naval supremacy over the Gulf of Mexico would be menaced if Texas were brought under the protection of Great Britain. Moreover, if this great power, already in possession of Canada on the north, should get a firm grip on Texas, the United States in a war with England would be between the upper and the nether millstone. Such were the fears which disturbed Tyler and Upshur, and therefore they favored annexation on the broad ground that it was conducive to national security. They also felt that the acquisition of Texas was necessary to protect slavery in the South; for the British government was strongly opposed to slavery, and an alliance between England and Texas might result in the abolition of slavery in the latter country.

This would be a great blow to slavery in the South. If there should be a large area of free territory contiguous to the slave states, slave property in the border Southern states would become insecure. Fugitives would be constantly escaping to free Texas and efforts to regain them by their masters would cause continuous strife.

A treaty of annexation negotiated

Spurred on by these fears, Upshur proposed the opening of negotiations for the annexation of Texas. After receiving the assurance from Upshur that two thirds of the Senate could safely be counted on for ratification, Houston decided to accept this offer. Accordingly, negotiations were begun and were progressing hopefully when they were suspended by the sudden death of Secretary Upshur (see p. 481). Calhoun took matters up where Upshur left off, and soon a treaty of annexation was agreed upon by the representatives of the two republics (April 12, 1844).

Terms of the treaty

By the terms of the treaty Texas would be incorporated into the Union as a territory and its citizens would be admitted, as soon as consistent with the provisions of the Federal Constitution, "to the enjoyment of all the rights, privileges, and immunities, of citizens of the United States." The public lands of Texas were to be ceded to the United States, which was to assume the debt of Texas, amounting to ten million dollars. Not a word about boundaries is found in the treaty.

The treaty rejected by the Senate; reasons

Much to the disappointment of Tyler and Calhoun the treaty was rejected by the Senate by a vote of 16 yeas to 35 nays (June 8, 1844). Although, generally speaking, the North opposed and the South favored annexation, this unfavorable vote was given on partisan rather than sectional grounds. The national conventions had been held and the Texan question was considered not on its merits but only as a factor in the political situation. Clay, the Whig nominee for President, had come out against annexation, and so the Whigs both in the North and the South opposed it. The Democrats had nominated Polk and declared in favor of annexation. They could, therefore, be expected to vote for ratification; but they were in the minority in the Senate and some of them were disgruntled over Van Buren's defeat. Seven of these and all the Whigs but one voted nay. All the other Democrats who were present and the lone Whig voted yea.

The campaign of 1844: Clay and Van Buren opposed to annexation

The next important stage in the development of the Texan situation was the Presidential campaign of 1844. In the early spring of this year it seemed certain that Clay would be nominated for the Presidency by the Whigs and Van Buren by the Democrats. Both were opposed to the immediate annexation of Texas and in April each published a statement giving reasons for this attitude. As these pronouncements came out on the same day it was thought that the two leading candidates had come to an agreement which in their opinion would eliminate this troublesome question as an issue in the approaching campaign. If such was their purpose they were doomed to sad disappointment.

A serious objection to annexation as given by both was that it might lead to war between Mexico and the United States. Clay also thought that Texas should not be added to the Union against "the wishes of a considerable and respectable portion of the confederacy." Later on in the campaign, seeing that this stand would cause him to lose votes in the South, he made another statement, which was less unfavorable to annexation. This modification of his original position cost him Northern votes and left the people uncertain as to just where he stood on the question.

Clay, however, was unanimously nominated by the Whigs, who *Clay the Whig* had assembled in national convention on May 1 in Baltimore. Theo- *nominee for* dore Frelinghuysen of New Jersey was named for the Vice-Presidency. *President* The platform had much to say in praise of the candidates but made no mention of Texas or a national bank. Otherwise, it reaffirmed the regular Whig position in favor of protection and internal improvements.

On May 27 the Democratic convention met in Baltimore. A ma- *The Demo-* jority of the delegates had been instructed for Van Buren, but owing *crats nominate* to his anti-Texan pronouncement most of the Southern delegates *Polk; reason* were opposed to his nomination. To provide them with a way of escape from their commitment in his favor the two-thirds rule was renewed, despite the ardent opposition of Van Buren's supporters. As was intended, a deadlock was produced, for although Van Buren received a majority of the votes on the first ballot he could not get the required two thirds. His vote declined on subsequent ballots, and finally the deadlock was broken on the ninth ballot by the choice of James K. Polk of Tennessee. To soothe the wounded feelings of Van Buren's adherents, Silas Wright, his warm personal and political friend, was nominated for the Vice-Presidency. Wright promptly declined the nomination, and George M. Dallas of Pennsylvania was then named for second place on the ticket.

The platform declared for the "re-annexation of Texas and the *The Demo-* re-occupation of Oregon." By the use of the prefix "re" the effort was *cratic* made to remove from a policy of expansion the taint of imperialism, *platform* the implication being that the United States was only trying to regain territory which it had formerly held. Furthermore, since accessions were to be made in the northwest as well as the southwest the desire to extend slavery could not be ascribed as the motive for expansion.

Part played by Tyler in the campaign

If Texas was to be the main issue of the campaign—as in fact it was—Tyler was the logical person to lead the annexation forces since he had done more than anyone else to bring the question to the fore. But he could not expect the Democrats to choose him as their standard-bearer and he could not hope to win with the following which he could command. He could, however, head an independent movement which might force the Democrats into a proannexation policy and compass the defeat of the Whigs. With this purpose in mind he accepted the nomination for President which was unanimously tendered him by a convention at Baltimore representing his friends and supporters throughout the country. The annexation of Texas was the one policy advocated by this party, and Tyler accepted the nomination for the sole purpose of promoting this objective. Later, deciding that Polk's election was the only hope of immediate annexation, he withdrew in favor of the Democratic nominee. The support received by Polk from Tyler's following was an important, if not a decisive, factor in a few close states.

The Liberty Party

The Liberty Party, made up of Abolitionists, for a second time nominated James G. Birney of Michigan for President. It declared strongly against slavery and was violently opposed to any extension of the slave area. Clay's hedging on the Texan issue turned some of the antiannexationists against him and caused them to vote for Birney. With this help the Liberty Party was able to poll about sixty thousand votes, more than a fourth of which were cast in New York. If half of the antislavery vote of New York had gone to Clay he would have carried this state and have been elected. Thus by giving this indirect aid to Polk the Liberty Party was in actual practice supporting immediate annexation, a policy to which it was strongly opposed. Polk was elected by an electoral majority of sixty-five; but in the popular vote his plurality over Clay was only forty thousand.

'olk elected

The annexation of Texas the main issue

Seldom is a Presidential campaign won on any single issue. For this reason it is difficult to determine the verdict of the people as registered by their polls in a regular quadrennial national election. This campaign was, to a considerable extent, an exception to this rule. Texas was the one outstanding issue and the election of Polk indicated that a majority of the voters of the country were in favor of annexation.

The joint resolution in favor of annexation

Tyler did not give up the fight for annexation even after his treaty was rejected by the Senate. He was greatly encouraged in his persistence by the election of 1844, which, he declared, was a plebiscite in favor of annexation. When Congress met in December, 1844, he recommended that the provisions of the rejected treaty be accepted by Congress in a joint resolution. This procedure was suggested because a joint resolution, requiring a bare majority of each house, could be obtained more easily than a confirmation of the Senate, which required a two-thirds majority.

Although Tyler had no party to support him, his recommendation regarding Texas could not well be ignored. The endorsement of annexation by the people in the recent campaign had given the question a new importance. Even if the Congressmen had been inclined to sidestep the issue, they would have been forced into action by pressure from their constituents. For petitions from individuals and resolutions adopted by state legislatures showed that the people considered the subject a matter of outstanding importance.

Congress, therefore, soon began to attack the knotty problem. After several resolutions had been offered and considerable discussion carried on in each house a bill proposing annexation was passed by both houses. The terms offered in the joint resolution were more favorable to Texas than were those of the original treaty. By the former she was to be admitted as a state without going through the territorial period. New states, not exceeding four in number, could with her consent be created out of her territory. Such new states if north of the 36° 30′ line were to be admitted without slavery. If south of that line they would come in with or without slavery as their citizens might desire. Texas was to pay her own debt but was to retain her public lands. *Terms offered Texas under the joint resolution*

The joint resolution for annexation reached President Tyler on March 1, 1845, and at once received his approval. Next day, acting on the unanimous advice of his Cabinet, he decided to send the proposal at once to Texas. As he had only two more days to serve, it was expected that he would leave to his successor the duty of forwarding the joint resolution. Delay was dangerous, however, and therefore Tyler showed good judgment in acting promptly. *Tyler signs the joint resolution and sends the proposal to Texas*

The action of the United States government came just in time to save the cause of annexation, for events were moving in the opposite direction in the south. Thanks to the good offices of the British and French chargés at the Texan capital, a treaty had been drawn up between Texas and Mexico providing for the recognition of the independence of Texas by Mexico on condition that the former would promise never to consent to union with another country. If this agreement were carried out all hope for annexation to the United States would be blasted. The preliminary treaty was accepted by the Mexican authorities and ratified by the Mexican Congress. It was now incumbent upon the government and people of Texas to decide *Texas accepts the offer* whether they preferred independence and peace with Mexico or annexation to the United States. The convention called to consider annexation declared (July 4) for it with only one dissenting vote. The Texan Congress had already voted unanimously in favor of rejecting the Mexican treaty and accepting the offer of the United States. In October the people ratified the act of the convention by an overwhelming majority. This was the crowning event in a movement by which there was added to the national domain, peaceably and honorably, without money and without price, a region vastly greater in extent than areas which European powers have been willing to purchase at the cost of lavish expenditure of blood and treasure.

THE PRESIDENCY OF JAMES K. POLK

Polk; previous career and personal traits

James Knox Polk (1795-1849) was the first "dark horse" to be nominated for the Presidency. By repeating the question "Who is James K. Polk?" the Whigs tried to brand him with an obscurity which was denied by a long and successful, though not a brilliant, career in the public service. After graduating from the University of North Carolina he studied law and was soon enjoying a lucrative practice at Columbia in his home county in Tennessee. Entering politics at an early age, he served for two years in the state legislature and fourteen years as a member of the United States House of Representatives. During the last four years of this period he was Speaker of the House. In 1839 he became governor of Tennessee, which office he held for two years.

The eleventh President made no claim to brilliancy and was not a fervent orator, though he was a logical and convincing debater. His strong points were sound judgment, firm determination, strict integrity, and an unlimited capacity for work. By persistent effort and rigid self-discipline he always kept his powers in a high state of efficiency. Not knowing how to play, he denied himself needed recreation and considered all time devoted to amusement as lost. So punctilious was he in the performance of duty that he is said never to have missed a recitation while in college. His health was impaired by overwork while President and the strain would have been still greater but for his Sunday rest, for he was regular in his observance of the Sabbath. As he was lacking in magnetism he never had many close personal friends. A stern sense of duty, a dignified demeanor, and a secretive, if not suspicious, attitude were qualities which did not lend themselves to spectacular action, and he never was a popular idol.

Polk took his politics as seriously as a Puritan did his religion. To

him the Democratic Party was the sole keeper of the oracles of po- *Polk as a*
litical orthodoxy, and Whigs were at best honest heretics and at worst *politician*
unscrupulous demagogues. He was a firm believer in the doctrines
of Jefferson and was an earnest admirer of Jackson. While the latter
was President, Polk did yeoman service for his chief in the bank fight
and was rewarded with the strong personal friendship and political
support of the Old Hero. To this support he was largely indebted for
his elevation to the Presidency. As long as he was a private in the
ranks he served his party with exceptional loyalty and regularity; but
on going to the White House he regarded himself as the general-in-
chief and acted accordingly. So while President he frequently
accepted advice but never orders from party leaders. It was distinctly
understood that he and not someone else was the real President.

In the selection of his Cabinet Polk chose new men except that *His Cabinet*
John Y. Mason of Virginia, who had been Secretary of the Navy
under Tyler, was made Attorney General. R. J. Walker of Mississippi became Secretary of the Treasury, and James Buchanan of
Pennsylvania, Secretary of State. The latter was not in entire accord
with the President on some questions and had some minor defects
in character which at times irritated his chief. Regarding his premier,
Polk in his *Diary* made the following comment: "Mr. Buchanan is
an able man, but is in small matters without judgment and sometimes acts like an old maid."

In making his Cabinet selections the President was anxious to satisfy the friends of Van Buren. Accordingly, the first offer of a place in
the Cabinet was made to Silas Wright, who was asked to become
Secretary of the Treasury. He declined on the ground that he had
been elected governor of New York on a pledge that he would serve
if elected. B. F. Butler, another Van Burenite, was offered the port-
folio of War, which he declined. Polk then appointed William L.
Marcy of New York, Secretary of War. As Marcy belonged to the
opposing wing of the party his appointment was objectionable to
Van Buren and his friends.[1]

President Polk went into office with four definite objectives in *Polk's pro-*
mind. These were: to lower the tariff and put it on a revenue basis; *gram:*
re-enact the Independent Treasury plan; settle the Oregon dispute *The Inde-*
with England; and secure California. Since the Democrats controlled *pendent*
both houses of Congress the first two of these measures were enacted *Treasury plan*
in 1846. The Subtreasury system was restored but with the omission *restored*
of the provision requiring all payments to the government to be
made in specie.

---

[1] George Bancroft, the historian, became Secretary of the Navy, and Cave Johnson
of Tennessee, a close friend of Polk, was made Postmaster General.

A tariff measure, framed in accordance with Secretary Walker's recommendations, and known as the Walker Act, was passed by Congress and signed by the President (1846). It lowered the general level of import duties to a strictly revenue basis and increased the number of articles on the free list. The protectionists contended that it would cripple manufactures and reduce the income of the government. On the contrary, manufacturing prospered under it and the revenue of the government increased.

THE OREGON QUESTION

Oregon was originally claimed by Spain, England, the United States, and Russia. Spain based her claim on priority of discovery, Russia on the activity of her fur traders, and England and the United States on the rights conferred by their fur traders and explorers. England could point to an expedition under Captain Cook (1778) which touched at points on the coast of Oregon, and the United States to two expeditions by Captain Gray (1788, 1792), who traversed the coast of Oregon and sailed into and named the Columbia River. The American title was also strengthened by the explorations of Lewis and Clark.

By the treaty of 1819 Spain yielded to the United States all her rights in this region north of the forty-second parallel. A few years later Russia by a treaty with the United States (1824) and with England (1825) gave up her claim to the region south of the parallel of 54° 40′. Oregon now had definite boundaries. These were the crest of the Rocky Mountains on the east; the Pacific on the west; the parallel of 42° on the south; and that of 54° 40′ on the north.

England and the United States were now the sole claimants and for quite a while no friction arose over their disputed titles. The reason for this was that in the first quarter of the century British interests were confined almost entirely to fur trading, and American interests, to fur trading and commerce with China. The question of ownership remained an academic one until settlers began to come in in considerable numbers.

In 1818 the two countries entered into an agreement of joint occupation for a period of ten years. This convention was renewed indefinitely in 1827 with the stipulation that either party could terminate it by giving the other a year's notice. No serious friction resulted from this joint occupancy, since the few American settlers were located mainly in the region south of the Columbia River and the British in that to the north of it.

In the eighteen-thirties. due to accounts given out by Methodist and Presbyterian missionaries, American settlers pushed into Oregon in increasing numbers, being attracted by the report of fine farming lands. This stream of emigration grew in volume in the 'forties, and in 1843 at least one thousand pioneers trekked westward into this distant land. In that year the settlers organized a provisional government and asked that the American government assume authority

American settlers organ ize a provi- sional government

THE OREGON
CONTROVERSY

_____ Line proposed by American
Negotiators, 1818-1846

.... Line proposed by British
Negotiators, 1824-1846

- - - - Line of Buchanan-Pakenham
Treaty, June 15, 1846

over them. This made it necessary for the United States to come to an agreement with Britain as to the ownership of the territory.

By this time there had grown up a strong feeling in the West in favor of American control of Oregon. The Democrats saw an opportunity to capitalize this sentiment and so declared in their platform of 1844 for the "re-occupation of Oregon." All of Oregon, it stated, rightfully belonged to the United States and it should lay claim to the whole region. This plank in the platform gave rise to the catchy slogans, "All of Oregon or none" and "Fifty-four forty or fight."

Oregon as a campaign issue, 1844

Despite the commitment of his party to the policy of taking over all of Oregon, Polk instructed Buchanan to propose (July, 1845) to Pakenham, the British minister at Washington, a settlement by extending the boundary along the forty-ninth parallel to the Pacific. This concession was made, he said, out of consideration for the action of his predecessors; for in 1824 and again two years later the United States had suggested the forty-ninth parallel as the line of division and both offers had been rejected by the British government, which each time made the counter offer of the Columbia River. It was, however, the probability of war with Mexico rather than respect for precedent that really caused the President thus to disregard the pledges of the Democratic platform. He wanted to be free from the danger of a conflict with England over Oregon before entering upon hostilities with Mexico.

*The proposal
rejected by
the British
minister;
Polk's bold
recommen-
dation*

Pakenham declined Polk's proposal and couched his refusal in language which was not very polite. Furthermore, he did not take the trouble to forward the offer to the British government. Polk's fighting spirit was aroused by this cavalier treatment and the offer was withdrawn. He was in favor of acting boldly in the assertion of American rights. "The only way," he said, "to treat John Bull was to look him straight in the eye" and "a bold and firm course on our part [was] the pacific one." In line with this policy he recommended to Congress, in his annual message of December, 1845, that notice be given at once of the intention of the American government to terminate the joint agreement at the end of twelve months; that the laws of the United States be extended over Oregon; and that forts be erected along the route to Oregon. The people of the West vociferously upheld the President in his bold stand and again was raised the cry of "fifty-four forty or fight." Congress after much discussion authorized the President to give the notice at his discretion, and this was done in May, 1846.

Seeing that the action of the President was sustained by Congress and the country, the British government realized that a concession on its part would have to be made if conflict was to be averted. It felt that Oregon was not worth a war with a kindred people and so showed a willingness to reopen negotiations. Disapproval of Pakenham's refusal to consider Buchanan's proposal was expressed and an effort made to have this offer renewed. Polk declined to take the initiative in further negotiations but intimated that if a proposition like that of Buchanan's were made by the British foreign office it would be considered. Thereupon the British government sent in as its proposal the draft of a treaty which embodied Polk's suggestions in slightly modified form.

To shield himself against the criticism of Western leaders who *The treaty*
were clamoring for all of Oregon, the President forced the Senate to *accepted*
share with him the responsibility of a decision by asking it to advise
him as to what action should be taken with reference to the proposed
treaty. As the Senate voted by a very large majority in favor of acceptance he signed the treaty and it was promptly confirmed. By the
terms of the treaty the boundary was extended along the forty-ninth *Terms of*
parallel from the Rocky Mountains to the straits that separate Van- *the treaty*
couver Island from the mainland and through the middle of this
channel to the ocean.

THE MEXICAN WAR

When Texas was annexed, Mexico promptly broke diplomatic *Causes*
relations with the United States. She had never recognized the independence of Texas although this independence had been maintained
for more than eight years, and during that time no attempt (except
sporadic incursions by raiding parties) had been made to assert
authority over the rebel state. Nevertheless in annexing Texas the
United States had seized territory belonging to Mexico, according to
the view held by the government of the latter country.

Another cause of dispute between the two republics was the claims *Slidell's*
against Mexico held by American citizens. Polk was also anxious *mission*
about the influence that Britain might exert on the Mexican government with the view to getting California. With the hope of ironing
out the differences between the two countries and of counteracting
foreign influence in Mexico, the President sent John Slidell on a
special mission to the southern republic. Slidell was also instructed
to endeavor to come to an agreement as to the boundary dispute between Texas and Mexico and to purchase New Mexico and California. To attain these objectives the American government would be
willing to assume all claims held by its citizens against Mexico and
pay her a liberal sum of money in addition.

Slidell was not received by the Mexican authorities and therefore
this plan failed. Polk was now resolved to bring Mexico to terms
through military pressure, and decided to recommend a declaration
of war. Mexico played into his hand and enabled him to score on her
in the game of make-believe. By acting prematurely she allowed him
to put the mask of self-defense over the policy of aggression which he
had already decided upon.

In the summer of 1845 General Zachary Taylor was sent with an *General*
army into Texas with instructions to take a position on or near the *Taylor sent*
Rio Grande. He did not, however, advance that far at first, but for *into Texas*

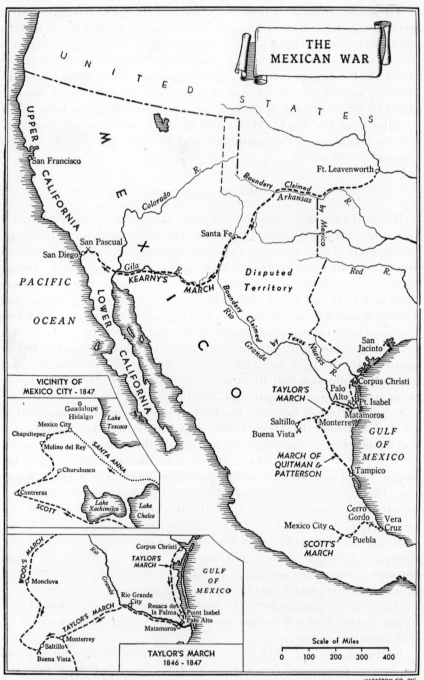

THE
MEXICAN WAR

UNITED STATES

M E X I C O

UPPER CALIFORNIA

San Francisco

Colorado R.

Ft. Leavenworth

Boundary Claimed
Arkansas
by Mexico R.

Santa Fe

San Pascual

San Diego

Gila R.

KEARNY'S MARCH

PACIFIC OCEAN

LOWER CALIFORNIA

Disputed
Territory

Red R.

Boundary Claimed by Texas

Rio Grande

Nueces R.

San Jacinto

Corpus Christi

**VICINITY OF
MEXICO CITY - 1847**

Guadalupe
Hidalgo

Mexico City

Chapultepec

Molino del Rey

Churubusco

Contreras

SANTA ANNA

Lake
Texcoco

Lake
Xachimilco

Lake
Chalco

SCOTT

TAYLOR'S
MARCH

Palo
Alto

Pt. Isabel

Matamoros

Saltillo

Buena Vista

Monterrey

GULF
OF
MEXICO

**MARCH OF
QUITMAN &
PATTERSON**

Tampico

Cerro
Gordo

Vera
Cruz

Mexico City

Puebla

**SCOTT'S
MARCH**

WOOL'S MARCH

Monclova

Rio Grande

Corpus Christi

**TAYLOR'S
MARCH**

GULF
OF
MEXICO

Rio Grande
City

Resaca de
la Palma

Point Isabel

Palo Alto

Matamoros

TAYLOR'S MARCH

Monterrey

Saltillo

Buena Vista

**TAYLOR'S MARCH
1846 - 1847**

Scale of Miles

0   100   200   300   400

HAGSTROM CO., INC.

some months was stationed near Corpus Christi, on the west bank of the Nueces River, about one hundred and fifty miles from the Rio Grande. When Polk saw that Slidell's mission would fail he ordered Taylor to move over to the Rio Grande. After this was done Taylor received a message from the Mexican commander demanding that he withdraw beyond the Nueces River. Up to this time the Mexican authorities had claimed all of Texas and had refused to recognize American ownership of any part of it; but this demand indicated that they might acquiesce in the annexation of Texas if the Nueces were accepted by the United States as the boundary.

As Taylor refused to comply with the demand of the Mexican general, the latter made an attack on the American forces and killed some of them. Polk had decided upon war before news of this skirmish reached Washington, but this attack gave him the opportunity to charge Mexico with having begun the conflict. Taking advantage of this turn in affairs, he now asked Congress for a declaration of war on the ground that the Mexican troops had invaded the United States. Congress thereupon fell in line with the suggestion and declared that we were at war by action of Mexico. *War declared*

The plan of campaign for the Americans included three lines of attack against Mexico. Colonel Stephen W. Kearny was directed to lead an expedition to the southwest and conquer New Mexico and California. As he approached Santa Fé the Mexican army, four thousand strong, withdrew without offering battle. Kearny remained in New Mexico long enough to organize a temporary government and then advanced to California with a small band of troops. On the way he fought a battle at San Pascual, after which he proceeded to San Diego. *Military events: Kearny's expedition*

He was too late, however, for the conquest of California. This had already been effected by the American naval and land forces under the command, first of Commodore John D. Sloat, and later of Commodore John F. Stockton. The coast towns had been captured and the interior posts taken. Among those who had figured actively in the land movements was Colonel John C. Frémont, who on account of his explorations in that region was known as the "Pathfinder of the West." In the spring of 1847 a provisional government was set up for California. *The conquest of California*

Before Congress had issued a declaration of war General Taylor had begun his attack on the Mexican forces near the mouth of the Rio Grande. On May 8 and 9, 1846, he defeated the Mexicans in two small engagements on the Texas side of the river and then crossed over and advanced into Mexican territory. In a three days' fight at Monterrey he defeated the Mexicans and captured the city. Three other towns were also occupied before the end of the year. *Taylor's campaign* *Battle of Monterrey*

In the meantime Mexico had undergone one of her periodic revolutions and had recalled Santa Anna, who had been living in exile at Havana since his expulsion from Mexico the previous year. Through secret agents Santa Anna promised Polk that if he were allowed to return to Mexico he would favor peace with the United States. On the basis of this understanding the American naval commander off the coast of Mexico, in obedience to orders from Washington, allowed Santa Anna to pass through the blockading squadron. But after he had been restored to power Santa Anna denied that he was bound by any pledge and went ahead with a vigorous prosecution of the war.

Being now at the head of the Mexican army, he infused new energy into the efforts to resist invasion. In February, 1847, the opportunity had come, as he thought, to take the offensive against the Americans. Taylor's army, stationed at Buena Vista, had been greatly reduced by the withdrawal of contingents of troops sent to reinforce General Scott. Upon learning this, Santa Anna with a force of twenty thousand men attacked the little American army, which was only about one fourth this size. Taylor had not used good judgment in placing his men, and in the first encounter they were forced to give ground. Later, inspired by his brave leadership, they stopped the advance of the Mexicans and forced them to retire. At the end of a day of furious struggle (February 23, 1847) each army held about the same position it had occupied the day before; but the morale of the Mexican army was broken, and in the night Santa Anna withdrew to San Luis Potosi. Taylor therefore reported the engagement as a great American victory.

A third expedition, under command of General Winfield Scott, was to advance from the coast town of Vera Cruz to the heart of Mexico. A landing near Vera Cruz was made without opposition and the city was captured after a four-day bombardment. Scott then advanced rapidly toward the interior to reach the upland region before yellow fever should set in in the lowlands. He met with no opposition

until he reached the pass of Cerro Gordo, where Santa Anna had stationed a strong force. Although Santa Anna's army was considerably larger than Scott's, he was badly defeated and lost his ammunition and supplies. This American victory was due in large measure to a bold undertaking suggested by Captain Robert E. Lee. Another young officer, Lieutenant Ulysses S. Grant, had a share in the honor of carrying out this plan.

Scott then advanced from Cerro Gordo to Pueblo, where he rested his army for three months. Resuming his march, he met with no resistance until he neared the approaches of Mexico City. After a hard-fought battle he captured the stronghold of Cherubusco and was then in possession of the outer defenses of the city. At this juncture Scott was duped by Santa Anna into signing a truce, which lasted two weeks. During this time Santa Anna consolidated his forces and made ready for a stronger defense. Realizing the purpose of his antagonist, Scott renewed the attack, and after fierce engagements at Molin del Rey and Chapultepec, drove into the city of Mexico. At Chapultepec American soldiers showed great bravery and the "terraces literally ran with blood."[1]

The Mexican Eagle before the War!   The Mexican Eagle after the War!

PLUCKED.

Yankee bumptiousness in the 'forties. From *Yankee Doodle,* 1847.

In the spring of 1847, Nicholas P. Trist, chief clerk in the State Department, was sent to join Scott's expedition as a commissioner to negotiate peace when the time for such a move should seem opportune. This policy of waving the olive branch with one hand and flourishing the sword with the other was Polk's idea of "conquering a peace." Since Trist was lacking in sound judgment and took himself too seriously, he was not the type of man needed for this responsible mission. His mismanagement of the negotiations brought him into disfavor with the Washington authorities and an order for his recall was issued. As the capture of the city of Mexico had opened up the opportunity for peace, he went ahead and signed a treaty with the

Nicholas P. Trist as peace commissioner

---

1 Nathaniel W. Stephenson, *Texas and the Mexican War* (Yale University Press), 249-250.

Mexican government although he had received the order cancelling his authority to conduct negotiations.

Treaty of Guadalupe Hidalgo

In a letter to Secretary Buchanan giving reasons for violating his instructions Trist made statements that were insolent and insulting to the President. The latter was highly indignant and pronounced the letter "a most extraordinary document." Besides, Trist's action in making the treaty was not official and the President was not bound in any way by it. But the treaty was a satisfactory one, although it granted only a minimum of the demands mentioned in Trist's instructions. Despite his indignation at Trist's insubordinate action Polk wisely disregarded the irregularity connected with the negotiation of the treaty and submitted it to the Senate. After making some modifications (which were accepted by Mexico) the Senate ratified the treaty by a large majority.

Terms of the treaty

By the Treaty of Guadalupe Hidalgo (signed February 2, 1848, at a town of that name near Mexico City), Mexico agreed to accept the Rio Grande as the Mexico-Texas boundary and to cede New Mexico and California to the United States. For this cession the United States agreed to assume all claims held by its citizens against Mexico and pay that country an additional sum of fifteen million dollars.

CHAPTER XXXI

Transportation and Trade (1783=1860)

STAGES IN THE DEVELOPMENT OF TRANSPORTATION

WITH independence and the subsequent expansion westward, there came a recognition of the need of better facilities for transportation and communication. This need has advanced with the growth of the country, and efforts to solve the problem have brought about several stages of development in the means of internal transportation. The periods have overlapped each other, but in each there was one type of transportation which was predominant. These stages have been, in the order of chronological succession, the first turnpike period, the river and canal period, the railroad period, and the second turnpike period.

During the first quarter of the nineteenth century the turnpike was the most popular and useful means of transportation. Private companies were carrying on a feverish activity in the construction of macadamized roads. This enthusiasm was stimulated in large measure by the success of the Philadelphia-Lancaster Turnpike, completed in 1794, which was the first hard-surfaced road of any considerable length in the United States. This road traversed a prosperous agricultural region and was the scene of a heavy line of traffic. The receipts of its nine tollgates were so large as to yield a fifteen per cent dividend to the stockholders of the company. The road had a graded width of thirty-seven feet, twenty-four feet of which were covered with stone and surfaced with gravel.

The first turnpike period

The Philadelphia-Lancaster Turnpike

A more noted turnpike of this period was the Cumberland Road, or National Turnpike, which ultimately extended from Cumberland, Maryland, to Vandalia, Illinois. The funds for the initial construction of this highway were derived from the sale of public lands in Ohio (see p. 322). An act of Congress in 1806 provided for surveys, but construction did not begin until 1811, and only twenty miles of the road had been finished by the end of the War of 1812. By 1818 it was completed to Wheeling, Virginia, on the border of Ohio. From time to time Congress voted funds for its extension until 1838, when Federal appropriations were stopped. With Federal and later state

The Cumberland Road

THE STAGECOACH.

Reprinted by permission of the publishers, The Arthur H. Clark Company, from Charles H. Ambler's "History of Transportation in the Ohio Valley."

From THE CHRONICLES OF AMERICA. *Copyright Yale University Press*

A CONESTOGA WAGON.

Photograph from the original in the National Museum, Washington.

and local aid the road was gradually pushed westward reaching Columbus, Ohio, in 1833, and Vandalia, Illinois, in 1852.

Other turnpikes built by Maryland connected the Cumberland Road with Baltimore, and the "National Pike" at once became an important highway to the West. Over this wide road the emigrant traveled to the new country with greater ease, and commodities were carried east and west with less cost and more speed than ever before. Both passenger and freight traffic soon became heavy.

Passengers were conveyed in large stagecoaches, which were *Stagecoaches* painted in bright colors and drawn by four or six horses. The speed *and freight* of these big coaches was almost incredible. One driver made the distance of twenty miles between Uniontown and Brownsville in forty-five minutes. Another, entrusted with the announcement of the declaration of war against Mexico, drove one hundred and thirty-one miles in twelve hours. Freight wagons were also numerous. The most noted of these was the Conestoga wagon. It had a capacious curved bed, the lower part of which was gaily painted in blue and the upper in red. Resting on heavy wheels bound by broad metal tires, and drawn by six strong horses, this vehicle had a large capacity for freight and was the best means for its overland conveyance.

For the accommodation of drivers and passengers there were lo- *Inns and* cated on the highways numerous inns and roadhouses. The former *roadhouses* were more expensive and better appointed than the latter, and were generally patronized by the passengers of the stagecoaches. At the less pretentious roadhouses stopped the teamsters and stockdrivers, who were regaled with an abundance of strong drink and plain but nutritious food.

During and long before the first turnpike period, western rivers *The river* were used extensively for transportation purposes. Even when the *and canal* chief reliance was on the flatboat and the barge, these rivers served *period* as the main outlet for western produce. Their importance in transportation was greatly enhanced by the introduction of the steamboat *Importance* on the Ohio River. Before this time river voyages were slow and *of the* the difficulty of conveying cargoes upstream were almost insuper- *steamboat* able. Trips could now be made more speedily and return cargoes could be carried without difficulty.

This improvement in navigation was made possible by Robert *Fulton's* Fulton's invention of the steamboat. Prior to Fulton's venture a *steamboat* number of more or less hopeful experiments in steamboating had been made, some of which had attained a measure of practical success. Using a superior engine built in England, Fulton was able to achieve a greater success than any of his predecessors. In August, 1807, the *Clermont* in the face of a gentle wind made the trip from

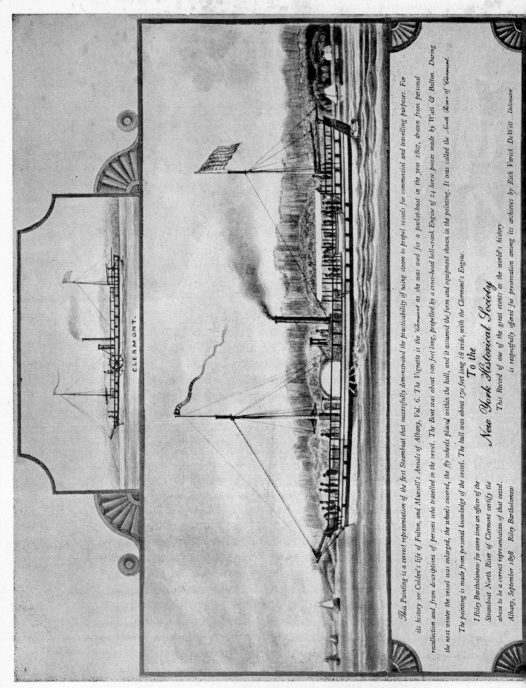

CLERMONT.

This Painting is a correct representation of the first Steamboat that successfully demonstrated the practicability of using steam to propel vessels for commercial and travelling purposes. For its history see Colden's life of Fulton, and Mansell's Annals of Albany, Vol. 6. The Vignette is the *Clermont* as she was used for a packet-boat in the year 1807, drawn from personal recollection and from descriptions of persons who travelled in the vessel. The Boat was about 100 feet long, propelled by a cross-head bell-crank Engine of 24 horse power made by Watt & Bolton. During the next winter the vessel was enlarged, the wheels covered, the fly wheels placed within the hull, and it assumed the form and equipment shown in the painting. It was called the North River of Clermont.

The painting is made from personal knowledge of the vessel. The hull was about 150 feet long 18 wide, with the Clermont's Engine.

To the

New York Historical Society

This Record of one of the great events in the world's history is respectfully offered for preservation among its archives by Rich Varick DeWitt. Delineator

I Riley Bartholomew for some time an officer of the Steamboat North River of Clermont certify the above to be a correct representation of that vessel.

Albany, September 1878   Riley Bartholomew

Courtesy of The New-York Historical Society, New York City

FULTON'S "CLERMONT."

New York to Albany, a distance of one hundred and fifty miles, in thirty-two hours. This was the longest and most promising voyage ever made up to that time by a steamboat and it proved that this type of craft was commercially practicable.

Four years later (1811) the first steamboat—the *New Orleans*— was launched on the Ohio River. The steamboat proved a great boon to the West and in time found its way on all the navigable streams in that section. Grain, merchandise, and other types of freight were taken down stream, and sugar, cotton, and rice brought back. There was also a rapid growth in the passenger service. As a result of improvements in design and construction, vessels plying the Mississippi were in later years large in size and luxurious in their appointments. *The first steamboat on the Ohio*

The period from 1840 to 1860 was the golden age of steam navigation in the West. The extension of the cotton kingdom to the Southwest had created in that section a market for the products of the middle and upper Mississippi Valley. Before 1850 the railroads did not parallel the rivers but served to connect them with each other and with eastern markets. They were therefore feeders to, rather than competitors of, the river trade. *The golden age of steam navigation in the West*

The use of the canal in this country as a means of transportation goes back as far as that of the hard-surfaced road. The Dismal Swamp Canal, the first constructed in this country, was opened in 1794, the year which also saw the completion of the Philadelphia-Lancaster Turnpike. A number of other canals were dug in the last decade of the eighteenth century and the first decade of the nineteenth, but construction did not start out on a grand scale until after the completion of the Erie Canal. Its success stirred up the country into a feverish activity in canal building, and the second quarter of the nineteenth century was the period in which this type of waterway played its most prominent role in transportation. *Early canals*

The Erie Canal was built by the state of New York and connected Lake Erie at Buffalo with the Hudson River at Albany. It was begun in 1817 and completed in 1825, at which time it was opened with dramatic ceremonies. A flotilla made the journey from Buffalo to New York. Two kegs of water taken from Lake Erie were emptied into New York harbor, symbolizing the marriage of the Great Lakes to the Atlantic Ocean. *The Erie Canal*

The project was a great financial success, as the toll receipts for the first ten years were sufficient to defray the cost of construction. It gave western New York an inlet and outlet for its trade and thus led to the rapid development of this part of the state. It also provided transportation facilities for all that region which was within

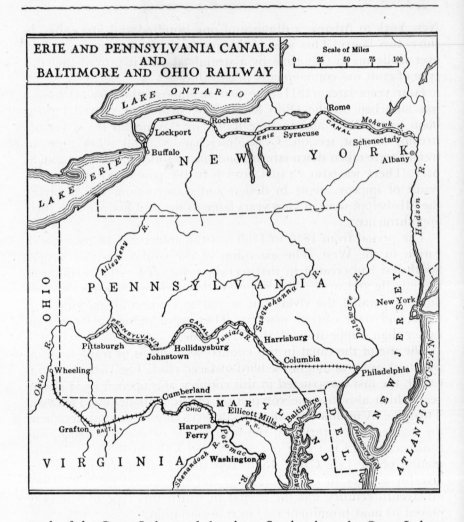

reach of the Great Lakes and the rivers flowing into the Great Lakes.
This area of accessibility was enlarged by the building of other

Its usefulness enlarged by other canals

canals in the Northwest connecting rivers with each other and with
the lakes. Some of these canals linked up the Illinois, Ohio, and
Mississippi Rivers with the Great Lakes, and in so doing diverted
considerable trade eastward which had hitherto been going down
the Mississippi to New Orleans and up the Ohio to Pittsburgh.

Effect on the West

The Erie Canal was an important factor in the development of
the West. The pioneers now had an easy way to reach the Northwest
and a good means of conveyance for the products which they wished
to sell to and buy from the East. Freight charges from Buffalo to
New York, which had been $100 a ton, were now cut down to $25

and less, and the time of conveyance was reduced from twenty to eight days. Thanks to this scaling down of freight rates, the Northwestern farmer could sell his grain and other produce at much better prices and at the same time purchase his tools and other commodities made in the East at much lower costs. In this way both East and Northwest were benefitted, and the canal served as a strong economic tie to bind the two sections together.

This waterway gave New York City the lion's share of the western *Effect on* trade and made it the most important seaport in the United States. *New York* All products shipped to the seaboard through the canal and all *City*

THE FLATBOAT.
Reprinted by permission of the publishers, the Arthur H. Clark Company, from Charles H. Ambler's "History of Transportation in the Ohio Valley."

foreign imports sent to the interior by the same route had to pass through New York. Such an advantage aroused the emulation of neighboring coast cities and caused them to bestir themselves in efforts to secure their share of the western trade.

Philadelphia's plan for making a connection with the Ohio River *The* was to build a combination canal and railroad from the Schuylkill *Pennsylvania* River to Pittsburgh. This ambitious project, known as the Pennsyl- *Canal* vania Canal, was prosecuted so energetically that the line was ready for traffic by 1834. The first part of the line was a horse railroad, which extended from Philadelphia to Columbia on the Susquehanna River. There was also a portage railroad over the mountains between Hollidaysburg and Johnstown. The rest of the distance was covered by canals.

The most picturesque part of the route was the thirty-three mile strip over the Allegheny Mountains. Between Hollidaysburg and

Johnstown there were five mountains to be crossed. This difficult break in the waterway was bridged over with inclined planes, on which first horse and later steam power was used. Charles Dickens, who traveled in the United States in 1842, gave the following account of his experiences in going over these mountains: "The canal extends to the foot of the mountain, and there, of course, it stops; the passengers being conveyed across it by land carriage, and taken on afterwards by another canal boat, the counterpart of the first, which awaits them on the other side . . . . There are ten inclined planes; five ascending and five descending; the carriages are dragged up the former, and let slowly down the latter, by means of stationary engines; the comparatively level spaces between being traversed, sometimes by horse, and sometimes by engine power, as the case demands . . . . It was very pretty, traveling thus at a rapid pace along the heights of the mountains in a keen wind, to look down into a valley, full of light and softness; catching glimpses, through the tree-tops, of scattered cabins; children running to the doors; dogs bursting out to bark, whom we could see without hearing; terrified pigs scampering homewards; families sitting out in their rude gardens cows gazing upward with a stupid indifference; . . . and we riding onward, high above them, like a whirlwind."[1]

The Chesapeake and Ohio Canal

When the completion of the Erie Canal gave New York the best route to the West, Baltimore also made a determined effort to secure her share of the western trade. At first she entered enthusiastically into a grandiose project to build a canal from Georgetown (now a part of Washington), at the head of navigation on the Potomac, across the Allegheny Mountains to an affluent of the Ohio River. One branch canal was to lead from the Ohio to the Great Lakes and another to connect Washington with Baltimore. But a preliminary survey of the route from Washington to Pittsburgh showed that the cost of carrying out the original plan would be prohibitive, and engineers reported that it would not be practicable to construct a canal from Baltimore to Washington. The plan was thus narrowed down to a canal from Washington to Cumberland. Such a waterway would divert the western trade away from Baltimore and channel it into Washington and other Potomac towns. Baltimore therefore lost interest in the canal and boldly decided to reach out to the Ohio by means of a railroad. However, the corporation which was sponsoring the project proceeded with its plans and was able to begin work in the summer of 1828. Finally, after many delays and discouragements

---

[1] Charles Dickens, *American Notes*, 218, 223-224.

the Chesapeake and Ohio Canal was completed to its western terminus at Cumberland (1850).[1]

Canals in the South

Canals were built in the South to a much less extent than in other parts of the country. There was, however, far less need for them in

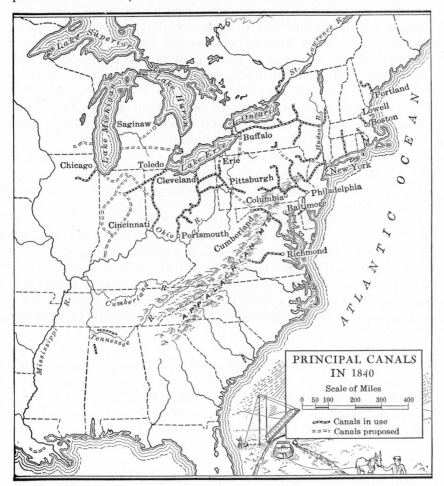

PRINCIPAL CANALS
IN 1840

Scale of Miles

0 50 100   200   300   400

Canals in use
Canals proposed

that section, for the navigable rivers of the Southern states were very numerous and flowed directly into the Gulf of Mexico or the Atlantic Ocean.

---

[1] The greater part of the money for financing the project was furnished by the state of Maryland, though liberal contributions were also made by the Federal government and by the terminal cities. The canal was handicapped in the contest with its northern rivals for the western trade partly by the competition of the Baltimore and Ohio Railroad and partly on account of its failure to cross the mountains and link up with a tributary of the Ohio. It therefore did not prove to be a successful undertaking.

*Canals
usually
built by
the states;
reasons*
The canal projects were generally financed by the state governments. There were several reasons for this. The financial outlook for such ventures did not always appeal favorably to corporations looking for gainful investments. At this time too there was a prejudice against corporations. The canals were to serve the interests of the public, and profits were to be a secondary consideration. Most of the money would have to be borrowed from abroad and could be obtained by public more easily than by private agencies. The United States government had paid off all its debt in 1835 and because of this was enjoying high credit in Europe. Undiscriminating foreign investors did not differentiate as closely as they should between the Federal and the state governments and therefore were willing to extend to the latter a very generous credit.

*Over-
optimism
in the con-
struction
of canals*
In the delirium of over-optimism that characterized the dozen years following the completion of the Erie Canal, more canals were constructed than the country needed and many of them were located at places where they could not be used to advantage. Besides, owing to extravagance and mismanagement, if not fraud, the cost of many of them was greater than it should have been. When the panic of 1837 came, some of these canals were abandoned when half completed and many of those that survived had a struggle for existence during the period of hard times. When the depression lifted they were confronted with the growing competition of the railroads. The railroads finally ran ahead in the race with the canal and by 1850 the former had become more important than the latter as a means of transportation.

*The railroad
period:
The Baltimore
and Ohio
Railroad*
When Baltimore, realizing her handicap in the race for water communication with the West, launched upon a bold experiment in transportation, the outcome of her venture was the building of the Baltimore and Ohio, the first important railroad in the United States.[1] The work of construction was begun in 1828 and in two years a stretch of thirteen miles was completed and open for traffic. The road was gradually extended westward until by 1853 it had reached Wheeling on the Ohio River. At first, horses were used for pulling the cars on the road and for a short time sails were experimented

---

[1] The Charleston and Hamburg Railroad in South Carolina was a close competitor of the Baltimore and Ohio for the distinction of being America's first railroad of importance. The former road was chartered in January, 1828, and was the first one in the country, and probably in the world, to be constructed for the use of steam. About six miles of the line were completed by January, 1830, and a year later, after some experimentation with sails and a horse treadmill, the steam locomotive was formally adopted. Before either of these roads was constructed, several tramways had been built in the United States. The first of these to use iron rails was a short line running from a stone quarry to Neponset in Massachusetts. Over it was transported granite for use in the construction of the Bunker Hill Monument.

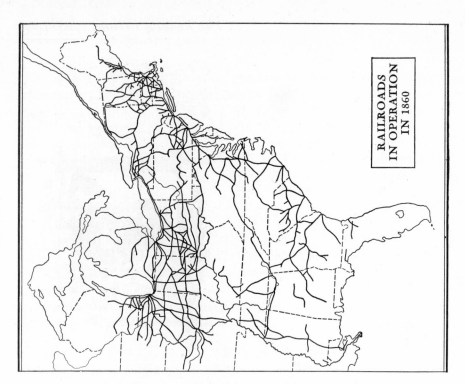

RAILROADS IN OPERATION IN 1860

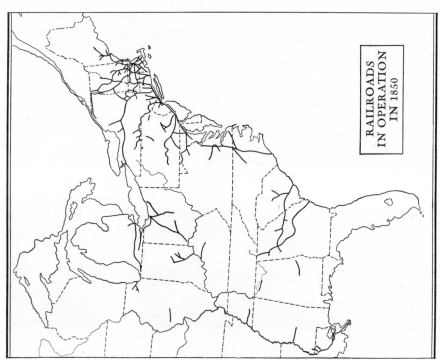

RAILROADS IN OPERATION IN 1850

with as motive power. It was not long, however, before the steam locomotive came into use.

Character of the railroads before 1840

In the meantime railroads were built in other regions and by 1860 there were more than thirty thousand miles of track in the country. In the early years the rails consisted of wooden beams whose upper edges were protected against wear by iron strips. Passenger coaches were modeled after the stagecoaches and were uncomfortable. They were heated by wood stoves, and wood was also used for firing the engines. Owing to the numerous sparks that poured out, a train was quite a fire hazard to the countryside through which it passed.

Courtesy of the Pullman Company

THE "FLYING DUTCHMAN."

Railroads after 1840

After 1840 certain mechanical improvements were introduced in the building of railroads, which greatly increased their efficiency as public carriers. One of the most

Courtesy of Railway Express Agency, Inc.

AN EXPRESS TRAIN IN THE 'FIFTIES.

important of these advances was the use of iron rails in place of wooden beams faced with iron strips. These stronger rails made possible larger cars with heavier loads, as well as greater speed.

In 1840 the roads were short and disconnected, and a lack of uniformity in gauge prevented the transfer of freight cars from one track to another. In the decade of the 'fifties, however, there was a strong tendency to consolidate these railroads into continuous lines, each owned by a single corporation. As a result of this trend, rail connection was established between the Atlantic seaboard and Chicago in 1853, and the Mississippi River in 1854. These through routes of transportation served as bonds to tie the West economically to the East; and this solidarity of economic interests was an important factor in deciding the central and northern West to unite with the North against the South in the great struggle of the 'sixties.

How railroad construction was financed

As has already been seen (p. 514), after the states had burnt their fingers in canal building, nearly all of them repudiated the policy of defraying the cost of internal improvements out of public funds. The Federal government had previously taken the same stand on the ground that it did not have the constitutional authority to participate in such activities. The building of railroads was therefore left mainly to private corporations. In the beginning, however, there were a few states which tried to finance the construction of their railroads. Other states gave aid to railroad corporations by buying stock, lending them money, or guaranteeing the sale of their securities. Subsidies were also voted by counties and cities. In the 'fifties the Federal government made lavish gifts of land to Western states for the benefit of their railroads.

COMMERCE AND SHIPPING

Effect of the Napoleonic wars on American commerce and shipping

During the first period of the Napoleonic wars (prior to 1807) American shipping and trade with foreign countries grew with great rapidity. Owing to her naval superiority England was able to drive French shipping off the high seas. British and neutral vessels therefore had a monopoly of the carrying trade. The United States, as the leading neutral power, profited greatly by this monopoly. The wars also created a strong demand for American food products and our exports were greatly increased.

American commerce from 1807 to 1861

During the Restrictive Period (1807-1815) American commerce and shipping declined as a result of the restraints imposed upon them just prior to and during the War of 1812. With the return of peace (1815), commerce with Europe again became active and for a while goods were imported from England in large quantities and at low prices. To protect the infant industries of this country against this competition, laws raising the tariff were enacted. These acts, together with the tariff measures of European countries, tended to discourage American foreign commerce during the decade of the 'twenties After 1830, however, commerce between the United States and Europe entered upon an era of expansion which was continuous until 1861 except for interruptions caused by the panics of 1837 and

Reproduced from THE PAGEANT OF AMERICA, *Copyright Yale University Press*

STEAMSHIP "SAVANNAH," 1819.

1857. This enlargement in foreign trade was brought about by the great increase in cotton exports due to the rapid extension of cotton culture to the Southwest.

American shipping from 1815 to 1840

After the War of 1812 was over, the European countries began again to transport their products in their own ships, and for a quarter of a century there was only a slight increase in American tonnage engaged in foreign trade. As there had been a decided gain in population, the per capita tonnage had declined from 13.43 to 4.25 from 1810 to 1839. One reason for this was that the high tariff of the period discouraged shipbuilding by increasing the costs of materials used for the construction of ships. In promoting manufactures in this country the tariff also discouraged the importation of foreign goods. After 1830 English shipping increased rapidly and entered into a vigorous competition with the American merchant marine.

By 1840, however, conditions had begun to change in favor of American shipping. There had been developed in the United States a fine type of sailing vessel, the American clipper, which could easily outdistance other sailing vessels and even steamboats when the winds were favorable. So far ahead of its competitors was it in speed that it could make three trips to England in the time taken for two by English vessels. Owing to the use of improved mechanical devices the clipper ship required a smaller crew for its management than did any other sailing craft. The superior skill of American seamen also gave them an advantage over their rivals. Moreover, the growth of

Circumstances favorable to the growth of the American merchant marine after 1840

CLIPPER SHIP "FLYING CLOUD."

the American merchant marine was promoted by a series of occurrences in world affairs. The British-China war of 1840 transferred a good part of the China trade from British to American vessels. A like diversion of foreign trade to American ships was caused by the revolutionary uprisings of 1848 in Europe, the Crimean War (1853-1856), and the famine in India in 1857. The lowering of the tariff by the act of 1846 also had the effect of lessening the cost of building ships in the United States. Numerous immigrants were coming into the country and fortune hunters were rushing to the gold fields of California and Australia. American ships were reaping a rich harvest in transporting these passengers. Owing to such favorable conditions, the American merchant marine, including vessels engaged in the fisheries and the domestic trade, was in 1861 about equal in tonnage to that of Great Britain.

*British
shipowners
more
progressive
than
American*

During this time, however, British shipowners were laying foundations for a future victory over their American competitors. In 1838 the *Great Western* and the *Sirius* crossed the ocean on their own steam, thus proving the practicability of the steamboat for ocean transportation. In this same year iron began to be used for the construction of the hulls of vessels. Great Britain put herself in line with these trends and by 1853 more than one fourth of her merchant fleet was of iron and nearly one fourth was propelled by steam. The United States was backward in taking advantage of these improvements. At that time only twenty-two per cent of American ships were propelled by steam and scarcely any were built of iron.

*Domestic
commerce*

More important than American foreign commerce was the interchange of goods between the different sections of the United States. Manufactures, fish, and other articles were shipped along the coast from the North to the South, and cotton, tobacco, and food supplies were brought back as return cargoes. By an act of Congress of 1793 this coastwise trade was reserved exclusively to American ships and this monopoly proved an important stimulus to the growth of the country's merchant marine.

*Advantage
of the rail-
road over
the canal*

The interior commerce was of greater value than either the foreign or the coastwise trade. The interchange of goods between the northern West and the southern West constituted an important part of our domestic commerce. Prior to the middle of the century most of this trade was carried by water, but after 1860 two thirds of it was diverted to the railroads. In the race for supremacy the railroad had some decided advantages over the canal. The latter had a more limited range of location, its cost of construction per mile was greater, and its speed of conveyance was less rapid than was the case with its rival. Besides, the railroad could be used throughout the entire year, whereas traffic on the canal was tied up by ice in the winter months.

COMMUNICATION WITH THE FAR WEST

*Trails to
the Far
West*

Long before the United States had come into undisputed possession of Oregon and had acquired New Mexico, routes to these far-off regions had been marked out. As the Missouri River was navigable to Independence, Missouri, this place was the starting point of the trails to the Far West. The most noted of these routes were the

Santa Fé Trail and the Oregon Trail. The American frontiersmen had begun a profitable trade with the Spanish settlers in New Mexico before the middle 'twenties. Every year a caravan of wagons, under the guidance of a capable leader, made a return trip from Independence to Santa Fé, carrying for sale hardware, cloth, needles and

GREAT TRAILS
TO THE
FAR WEST

thread, and other articles highly prized on the frontier, and bringing back mules, furs, and gold and silver. After the Lewis and Clark expedition (1804-06) traders began to make journeys to Oregon, using different routes to reach their destination. By the eighteen-thirties, however, it was found that the Oregon Trail was the best route to the Northwest.

In the decade of the 'fifties the Far West was brought in touch with the East by Federal mail routes. The first of these, established in the summer of 1850, extended from Independence to Santa Fé. The distance of eight hundred and fifty miles was usually covered in two weeks by coaches drawn by six mules and running day and night.

Postal routes

Each had room for eleven passengers besides the driver and eight heavily armed men who acted as guards. The coaches "were beauti-fully painted and made watertight that they might be used as boats in crossing streams." Provision was also made for carrying the mail from St. Joseph, Missouri, to Salt Lake City.

From 1858 on, the mail was sent regularly from two points on the Mississippi (Memphis and St. Louis) to Los Angeles and San Francisco. From St. Louis to Tip-ton the pouches were carried by train and from there to Fort Smith by stagecoach. To this point too the mail was brought overland from Memphis. Leaving Fort Smith, the stage ran by a southern route to Los Angeles and then on

Courtesy of Railway Express Agency, Inc.

THE PONY EXPRESS.

to San Francisco. By this line a regular mail service was established between the Mississippi River and the Pacific Ocean. Other routes were soon opened which linked the East with the Far West.

Courtesy of Pennsylvania Railroad

CROSSING THE ALLEGHENIES IN 1840.

Sectional canal boat being hauled over the inclined planes of the Portage Railroad.

*The
Pony
Express*

The overland mail to California went too slowly over these routes to meet the demands of this hurried age. Accordingly, the Pony Express was organized to provide a more rapid means of communication with the Far West. Beginning in 1860 letters and telegraphic messages were conveyed once a week each way by pony riders from St. Joseph to Sacramento, California. Along the line, ten or fifteen miles apart, there were stations at which the riders transferred themselves and their pouches to fresh ponies, which were awaiting them already bridled and saddled. The first trip from the Pacific Coast to St. Joseph was made in ten days and the last hundred miles in eight hours.

The means of communication were greatly improved by the invention of the magnetic telegraph. With the assistance of an appropriation by Congress, Samuel F. B. Morse constructed a telegraph line from Washington to Baltimore which was opened for use in June, 1844. Other lines were quickly put up and by 1860 there were 50,000 miles in operation. One was extended to San Francisco in 1861 and the Pony Express was discontinued.

The magnetic telegraph

CHAPTER XXXII

Industry, Agriculture, and Farm Tenure

INDUSTRY (1820-1860)

Condition of manufactures in 1815

WHILE the Industrial Revolution in the United States had its beginning in the Restrictive Period (1807-1815),[1] it did not get well under way until the third decade of the nineteenth century. Many infant industries, which had sprung up behind the shelter of the virtual protection afforded by the commercial restrictions and the war, were forced to shut down when foreign goods were dumped upon the American market. This bad situation was aggravated by the panic of 1819. With the return of prosperity in 1823, manufacturing took on a new lease of life and continued to advance (except for interruptions by the panics of 1837 and 1857) until the end of this period. In 1860 the number of persons engaged in manufacturing in the United States was four times as large as it was in 1820, and the value of manufactured goods was probably more than eight times as great.

Growth of manufactures after 1823; reasons

Of course, the use of machinery was the main factor in this rapid expansion. There were, however, other conditions that gave the American manufacturer an advantage over his European competitor. One of these was the originality and inventiveness of the American worker. To this intellectual quality we owe many new inventions and the successful improvement and adaptation of old ones. Besides, workmen with a flair for mechanics can make more effective use of machines than can those who are not so endowed. The expense of transoceanic shipment added considerably to the cost of European goods and gave the American producer an advantage in the competition for the home market. This advantage was accentuated by American protective tariffs, though the increase in price of raw materials because of the tax on them served in some instances to offset this aid.

The sewing machine

Invention in the United States was stimulated by the patent laws, which gave inventors a monopoly of their inventions for a number of years. Of the American inventions which greatly aided the development of manufactures, the sewing machine was one of the most

---

[1] For the stimulus given manufacturing in the Restrictive Period, see p. 381.

important of this period. It was invented by Elias Howe in 1846, and in a few years was improved by Singer and others. It was not only a great labor-saving device for the housewife, in that it relieved her of the tedium of hand-sewing, but it was also valuable in the manufacture of ready-made clothing. Owing to an improvement added by McKay, the sewing machine could be used for stitching leather, thereby leading to the machine production of boots and shoes.

Other reasons for the development of manufactures were: the rapid growth in population; the expansion in railroad construction; the abrogation of the British corn laws; and the discovery of gold in California. When the English corn laws were repealed (1846) an excellent market for American grain was opened up. This brought prosperity to the farmers and increased their purchasing power for manufactured goods. The discovery of gold in California made money more plentiful and caused a continuous rise in prices. The general prosperity of the country also stimulated manufacturing. Wealth was pretty equally distributed and the buying capacity of the masses gave a broad base to the home market.

Machinery was at first used mainly in the manufacture of textiles, but by 1840 the factory system had spread to a number of other industries. Of the pure manufactures (not counting the grinding of corn and wheat and the production of sawed lumber) that of cotton cloth soon took the lead and held it to the end of the period. Not until about 1830, however, did machine production exceed home production. In this period the woolen industry did not advance as rapidly as the cotton industry. Wool was not produced in great quantities in the United States and the tariff on it increased the difficulty of getting it from abroad.

The manufacture of textiles

Because the greater number of the cotton and woolen mills were run by water, most of them were located in New England where there was abundant water power. Other reasons for the primacy of New England in the manufacture of textiles were: an abundance of labor and capital; good means of inland transportation and easy access to the sea; and a comparatively large urban population, which furnished a local home market. In the manufacture of cotton goods the United States had the advantage of an ample supply of raw material furnished by the Southern plantation and a growing home market protected by a high tariff.

The Middle Atlantic states ranked next to New England in the manufacture of textiles. In the West and in the South spinning and weaving were also carried on in the home and in the mill. But in both these sections machinery was not employed as extensively as it was in the Northern and Middle states. In the South, cotton mills were located along the fall line of some of the rivers; but the slave labor of this section lent itself better to the growing of cotton than to its manufacture. Consequently, the number of spindles in this

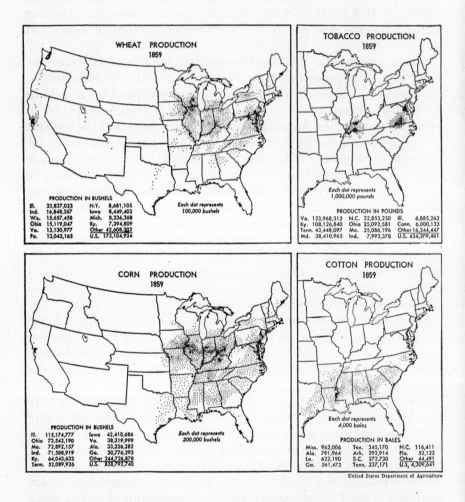

United States Department of Agriculture

region was comparatively small. However, the old-fashioned spinning wheel and loom were much in use, especially in the upland regions. On the big plantations in the Tidewater section the spinning and weaving were done by the slaves; in the homes of the yeomanry this work was done by the wives and daughters of the family.

The iron industry

As in the case of textiles, the manufacture of iron got a good start in the Restrictive Period. As long as charcoal was used in smelting, the abundance of wood in the United States gave our manufacturers of pig iron an advantage over their English competitors. But owing to later improvements by the British in machinery and in the methods of production, among them the use of bituminous coal instead of charcoal, the English took the lead over the American iron manufacturers. In 1840 anthracite coal was first used in this country in smelting. This advance and others led to a marked increase in the production of iron. In the last decade of this period coke and uncoked bituminous coal were used, but only to a slight extent until after 1860. Railroad expansion also stimulated manufacturing. The use of iron rails in the latter part of the period created a demand for iron that encouraged its production. The railroads also made it easier to transport the raw materials to the factories and the finished products to market.

The rich deposits of iron ore in various parts of the Appalachian region and other places gave a wide range to the manufacture of pig iron. All three sections—North, South, and West—thus had a share in this important industry. After 1810 Pennsylvania held the lead in the smelting of iron,[1] but larger iron deposits were discovered in the Lake Superior region after 1846.

COMMERCIAL FARMING AND ANIMAL HUSBANDRY (1783-1865)

The development of commercial farming and animal husbandry on an unprecedented scale was the outstanding characteristic of the history of American agriculture during the post-colonial period with which we are here concerned. There was no country in the world with so many types of crops which could be produced on such a scale and sold upon the market. In the colonial period there had been a few outstanding money crops, notably tobacco and rice and, to a lesser extent, wheat. The raising of livestock for export—horses, cows, sheep, and swine—was also a source of considerable gain in the South and the Middle states, and was always a basic element in subsistence farming. It was not, however, until the nineteenth century that these staples attained great importance. In this latter period other money crops, such as hay and sugar, took their place alongside the older staples, and one of them, cotton, outranked them all as a cash

Commercial farming in the colonial era

Development of commercial farming in the nineteenth century; reasons

---

[1] Iron and textiles did not by any means exhaust the list of important manufactures of the country. Other commodities produced in considerable quantities were machinery, farm tools, clothing, cordage, bagging, and distilled liquors. Milling, meat packing, and the sawing of lumber were also important industries. These various types of industry were carried on extensively in the Ohio River region as well as in other sections. The leading centers of western industry were Pittsburgh, Cincinnati, Louisville, and Chicago.

product. The extensive production of so many money crops may be attributed to several basic causes: the existence of what seemed to be an inexhaustible supply of cheap, or free, rich lands capable of producing some or all of these staples; the expansion of domestic markets through the growth of the cities, particularly in the East; the opening of foreign markets; the creation of cheap transportation, thus bringing the market closer to the producer; and the invention and manufacture of better farm implements and machinery.

An abundance of cheap, rich land

Some conception of the quantity of vacant land open to farming during the period under discussion may be gained when it is stated that, with the exception of a few scattered settlements in Tennessee and Kentucky and what is now West Virginia, all the land from the Appalachian Mountains to the Pacific Ocean was to be at the disposal of state or Federal government within the period of about a hundred years. In the five states of the cotton kingdom—Alabama, Mississippi, Louisiana, Arkansas, and Florida—the public lands in 1850 approximated 100,000,000 acres, which was far in excess of the lands owned by the people of those states. The amount of unappropriated land in Texas was even greater than this. The North Central states had, perhaps, an equally great supply of rich prairie land at this time. With so much land available, extensive production of those crops which offered cash returns was to be expected if the other conditions were favorable.

The development of cities and the opening of foreign markets

The towns and cities, which had sprung up or which had been greatly expanded by the rise of the factory system, furnished a larger home market for cereals, livestock, wool, vegetables, and dairy products. As for the foreign markets, American cotton had found few obstacles from the beginning, but the cereals, beef and pork, and other farm products came into the world market only after the removal of trade restrictions in Europe and the West Indies during the second quarter of the nineteenth century.[1]

Better transportation facilities

Agriculture was also greatly advanced by the building of hard-surfaced turnpikes, which connected cities, fanned out from the cities into the hinterland, and formed connecting links between navigable streams. The use of the steamboat on the rivers and the construction of canals and railroads did still more toward transforming subsistence farming and stockraising into commercial farming and commercial animal husbandry. (See pp. 505-517.)

The invention and manufacture of more efficient farm imple-

---

[1] The reopening of the British market to American grain was helped by the removal of restrictions on American trade with the British West Indies in 1830 as a result of a treaty negotiated between the United States and England; by the repeal of the British corn laws (1846); by the Irish famine in the late forties; and by the Crimean War (1853-1856).

ments and machinery were partly the cause and partly the result of *Improvement in farm implements* commercial farming. The fundamental tool in a more extensive agriculture—whether cotton, wheat, corn, or tobacco—was the improved type of plow. As has been noted, the plow used to break the land during colonial times was in no way superior to the one used in ancient times. Thomas Jefferson, a few years before the close *The new plows* of the eighteenth century, designed a plow on mathematical principles which had a moldboard or wing. From the time of Jefferson's contribution till 1830, more than one hundred and twenty patents were granted to inventors of plows; but the most important of them all was that of Jethro Wood of New York. Wood's plow was made of separate castings joined together by lugs, so that a share and moldboard or wing could be worn out or broken and a new part substituted. Samuel Withrow and David Pierce in 1839 contributed the final feature which gave the plow all its modern outlines: they added to the wing or moldboard the necessary twist for pulverizing the furrow slice. Although these inventions had been known for several years, the new type plows did not come into general use until between 1820 and 1830. In the western prairies it was not until the steel moldboard was introduced—which would acquire a high polish and prevent the dirt from clogging the plow—that the modern plow was widely adopted. Quickly following the development of the steel and cast iron plow was the invention of iron harrows and cultivators.

These were the tools which were fundamental to most crops. However, each staple called forth special implements. Of these staples cotton was probably the first which proved that necessity is the mother of invention. The Industrial Revolution in England had *The cotton gin* created such a demand for cotton that a cheaper and more efficient method of separating the lint from the seed was necessary. Several types of gins were produced in America, where cotton had long been raised for domestic use; but Eli Whitney's saw gin, invented in 1793, proved far superior to all others, and it soon enabled the Southern farmer to separate several hundred pounds of lint from the seed in the time heretofore taken in processing a few pounds. The result was that the Southern states dominated the world cotton *Special implements for the cultivation of cotton* market for over a hundred years. In addition to the harrows, cultivators, and double shovels, which could be used in the cultivation of most of the staple crops, special implements were invented for the planting and cultivation of cotton. A "planter," or cotton seed drill, considerably different from corn droppers or small grain drills, was developed, and sweeps, scrapes, and light draft bar plows and turn-plows were constructed for the special cultivation of cotton— though these might be used to some extent in the cultivation of corn and tobacco. In the cultivation of cotton and tobacco the horse and mule were found infinitely superior to the slow and awkward ox. However, the ox continued to be of paramount importance in breaking land, logging, and wagoning through rough and muddy places.

Implements used in the cultivation of sugar, grain, and hay

Sugar cane culture and the sugar industry, which developed almost simultaneously with cotton as a commercial enterprise, soon required better tools and machinery. Iron and steel rollers were substituted for the old-fashioned wooden rollers in grinding the cane stalk; steam engines took the place of draft animals in propelling the cane mills; and vacuum pans outmoded the old open evaporators in making syrup and sugar. In connection with the growing and harvesting of small grain and hay, a series of inventions and improvements —in addition to those general farm tools already mentioned—brought other agricultural implements into common use from 1840 to 1860 which made possible large scale production. These implements were the seed drill, gang plow, horse rake, and the mowing and reaping machines—first patented by Obed Hussey and Cyrus McCormick in 1833 and 1834, respectively—all mounted on wheels and ridden by the driver. Truly, the great wheat fields were filled with a mechanized army of farmers, and wheat, more than all other American crops, was placed upon a mass production basis.

AGRICULTURAL REFORM

Exploitative nature of commercial farming

The one feature common to all commercial farming except truck farming and animal husbandry (sheep raising, horse and mule breeding, the raising of beef cattle, and dairy farming) was its exploitative nature. The presence of so much cheap land created a wasteful attitude toward the land. The idea was to "wear it out and turn it out because there is plenty more just like it!" The American people acted too much as if they thought that everything would last forever or, if not, that when the natural fertility and resources began to give out, they would move on to another country.

The need of soil conservation realized

The consequences of exploitation were first seen in the coastal area of the older states, particularly in Virginia and Maryland, where commercial farming had been highly developed in colonial times. Land which had been dark brown from the presence of humus began to grow a sickly yellow or red from sheet erosion and overcropping; or great red gulleys and scrub pines appeared in the old fields that had been cultivated so long. The yield of tobacco and grain began to decrease alarmingly. The natural pasturage derived from worn-out fields became less and less sustaining to the livestock. Toward the end of the eighteenth century thoughtful men became seriously perturbed over the blight which was spreading over the countryside in the older states. A movement was started, which gained volume and momentum, to restore the worn-out soil, save the fresh lands, breed better livestock, and introduce better methods of husbandry.

Little was known at the end of the eighteenth century about the chemistry of soils and the essential elements of plant life; but great progress in soil conservation and renovation had been made in Europe by the process of trial and error. These practices were occasionally adopted in America in the latter half of the eighteenth century. In the Middle states and upper South, in particular, the use of clovers, animal manures, crushed limestone, lime sulphate, and marl, and the rotation of crops began before 1800 to receive attention from the more intelligent farmers under the leadership of several gentlemen farmers such as Richard Peters and Chancellor Robert Livingston of Pennsylvania, and Washington, Jefferson, and John Taylor, of Virginia. Agricultural societies sprang up everywhere, the chief function of which was to popularize the methods of the "New Farming," as already well established in Europe and just being tried out here and there in America. *Beginning of improved methods of agriculture*

While much knowledge of a practical nature was thus obtained, it was not until the basic principles of plant and soil chemistry were understood that agriculture could be put upon a scientific basis. Sir Humphry Davy's lectures on the chemistry of soils, begun in 1803 and published in book form in 1813 under the title of *Elements of Agricultural Chemistry*, was the first work to become available to the agricultural leaders. It was this book and its later editions which formed the basis of the career of Edmund Ruffin in Virginia, perhaps the most outstanding scientific agronomist of the entire country in the ante-bellum period. In 1804 Nicholas-Théodore De Saussure's work on plant chemistry—*Chemical Research on Plants*—was published in French, which perhaps limited its use. A much broader and more accurate knowledge of soil and plant chemistry was made possible after the publication in 1841 of the American edition of Liebig's *Chemistry in its Application to Agriculture and Physiology* (1840). *Knowledge of chemistry of plants and soils basis of scientific agriculture*

The interest in scientific agriculture, as a means of increasing production and saving the land, resulted in the establishment of farm journals in every part of the country and the spread of agricultural societies from the old into the new states. A few journals were established from 1819 to 1840; but the bulk came in the period of 1840-1860, when agricultural reform assumed widespread importance. There had been agricultural societies for a long time, but their spread into the remoter parts of the country took place during the *Farm journals and agricultural societies, 1840-1860* last two decades of the period. These journals and societies sponsored agricultural fairs where the best agricultural products, the finest livestock, and the best farm tools were displayed. Scientific farming was also promoted by the agricultural schools which began to appear in the latter part of the ante-bellum period.

"A Cotton Plantation on the Mississippi"
From a Currier and Ives print

Introduction of better breeds of livestock

Alongside the development of a better knowledge of field husbandry was the rapid introduction of purebred livestock from Europe. The finest breeds of saddle and carriage horses had been brought over in colonial times, and other imported breeds were now added. Robert Livingston and David Humphreys, the ministers to France and Spain respectively, brought over the first Merino sheep about 1802-1804. Washington had already introduced the Andalusian jack, which was soon to give rise to mule breeding, and between 1800 and 1840 most of the fine breeds of swine were imported from England—usually by gentleman farmers like Livingston and Jefferson. However, it was chiefly after 1840 that the average American farmer became interested in building up the native breeds by crossing them with the imported strains.

Some of the improved farm tools already discussed were also of decided value in soil conservation and in improving the yield. Deep plowing not only gave a better root bed for the growing plant, but it created a reservoir for the water so that erosion was checked. However, even deep plowing was not sufficient to check or prevent erosion in most of the South, which lay unprotected by snow and ice and exposed to the driving winter rains; so contour plowing was popularized by Edmund Ruffin and John Taylor of Virginia. Ruffin in particular was responsible for the widespread building of contour terraces and hillside ditches which, more than anything except sod, were calculated to prevent erosion and leaching. *Contour plowing and terracing*

Thus, by crop rotation, the use of animal manures, some commercial fertilizers, and clovers and grasses, deep plowing, and terracing and contour plowing, old land was improved, the destruction of new land retarded, and much of the bad effects of commercial farming eradicated, particularly in the older parts of the country where these effects were so much in evidence. But, as we shall see later, the great accomplishments of the agricultural reform were brought to naught in the South by the Civil War and Reconstruction, which impoverished the farm population and widely established the tenant system and a subsequent tendency toward the single crop system. On the other hand, scientific farming and scientific animal husbandry have gone forward in the North and Middle West with little interruption down to the present day.

LAND TENURE

During the period 1783-1860 the ownership of land in the North seems to have been fairly well distributed among the farm population, and the sizes of farms were usually medium or small. It has been estimated that farm ownership ranged from about 66 to 75 per cent of the total farm population in certain parts of the East. In other areas in the East, tenancy was very high; for example, the famous Wadsworth estate of New York comprising 25,600 acres was operated entirely by tenant farmers. Considerable tenancy existed in Ohio, Indiana, Illinois, and even Iowa, at the end of the ante-bellum period. But the great quantity of cheap or free lands in the West enabled the bulk of farmers in that section to become landowners. It seems from a cursory examination of the unpublished census reports of 1850 and 1860 that tenancy was decreasing in the Northwest and that by the latter date as high as 80 per cent of the farmers in the more settled areas were landowners. *Distribution of land ownership in the North*

In the middle decades of the nineteenth century the average size of farms in the Northern states was seldom excessively large. The number of acres in the average farm in certain Northern states, as determined by P. W. Bidwell and J. I. Falconer in their *History of* *Sizes of farms in North and West*

Agriculture in the Northern States, 1620-1860, is as follows:

	1850	1860
Massachusetts	98.5	93.8
Connecticut	106.2	99.5
Ohio	125.0	113.8
Illinois	158.0	145.9
Iowa	184.8	164.6

But 787 estates in the North, exclusive of the border states, were over a thousand acres in size; some of these were greater than any of the Southern plantations.

Land ownership in the South

In the South, as shown by the unpublished census reports and county tax lists, the bulk of the farm population consisted of small farmers, the greater proportion of whom owned their land. Eighty per cent of the farm population in the lower South and about 75 per cent in the upper South were landowners in 1860. About 80 per cent of the nonslaveholding landowners possessed up to 200 acres each, and 20 per cent from 200 to 1000 each. As to the slave-holders, about 60 per cent outside the Black Belt[1] and 35 per cent

Sizes of farms and plantations

in the Black Belt owned less than 300 acres of land. Only about 4 per cent of the slaveholders had over 2000 acres. The mass of South-ern farmers, slaveholders and nonslaveholders, were plain, hard-working people.

[1] The Black Belt consisted of those portions of the South where the slave population outnumbered the whites, and where, as a rule, the land was fertile.

FARMING TOOLS, 1790.

CHAPTER XXXIII

Labor, Immigration, and Reform

THE LABOR MOVEMENT

WHEREVER the Industrial Revolution has occurred labor problems have emerged. The United States was no exception to this rule. The labor movement in this country, however, owed its origin not so much to the rise of the factory system as to a change in market conditions. When labor began to agitate for its rights, machinery was not predominant in industry but was confined mainly to the production of textiles. Besides, a large majority of the workers in factories were women and children. *Conditions which gave rise to the labor movement*

Prior to 1820 most manufacturing was conducted on a small scale and under conditions similar to those of the colonial period. A master craftsman worked with a small group of apprentices and journeymen, sometimes in the home of the master. Under this system employer and employee were closely associated with each other, with no wide gulf, economic or social, separating them. There was little occasion for disputes over hours of labor or working conditions. The small output of goods was disposed of in the community on order.

In the 'twenties the market for manufactured goods began to expand, owing to the growth of population, the improvements in the means of transportation, and the development of the West. Production on a large scale now became possible. This created an opportunity for a middleman between manufacturer and consumer—the merchant capitalist. The latter bought the products and disposed of them at wholesale. By controlling the price paid he brought master craftsmen and their workers under his control. The economic independence formerly enjoyed by the master and shared by his assistants was now lost. To meet the keen competition growing out of the new conditions, the master felt compelled to press down upon his workers. It was as a protest against this new situation that the labor movement was started.

In the meantime the factory system was advancing and the number of laborers was increasing, but the Industrial Revolution in the United States did not effect such a violent shock to the social order as it did in England. The application of machinery to industry— *Effect of the Industrial Revolution* at first mainly to the production of textiles—was gradual and did not cause any serious dislocation of the old household industries. The American people had been accustomed to buy most of their manufactures from abroad, and therefore the number of workers which were supplanted by machines was not large.

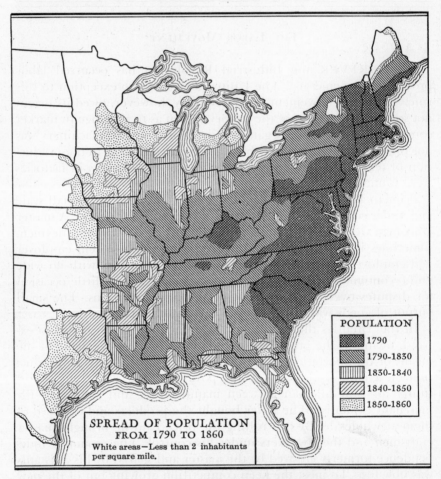

POPULATION

▨	1790
▧	1790-1830
▥	1830-1840
▨	1840-1850
░	1850-1860

SPREAD OF POPULATION
FROM 1790 TO 1860
White areas—Less than 2 inhabitants
per square mile.

Working conditions

There were, however, some evils connected with the introduction of machinery and the growth of towns around the mills. Laborers were crowded into cramped areas with poor housing conditions. Hours were long—from sunrise to sunset—and wages inadequate to maintain a high standard of living. A large majority of the workers were women and children. This work kept these children out of school and confined them in dark factories at an age when they needed sunshine and play. The women who were employed in the

New England factories seem to have been treated fairly well by their employers. Daughters of farmers from the neighboring countryside came to these mills to earn wages for a few years before marrying and settling down in their homes. An English traveller, who visited the mills at Lowell in 1854, reported that the young women employed there were admirably provided for. They had good food, well-furnished, airy bedrooms, and the use of a large living room in which they could entertain callers. While they spent the greater portion of their earnings for gay bonnets, parasols, and dresses, they devoted some of their time to reading books of a wholesome character which they borrowed from the town library.[1]

Despite this favorable view, the conditions under which these young women worked were far from ideal. The hours were long—thirteen hours in summer and from daylight to dark in winter. Their daily tasks were performed in rooms which were poorly ventilated and ill-regulated as to heat; their meals were eaten hurriedly on account of the short time allowed for them; and in the boardinghouses their quarters were too cramped to afford sufficient privacy.

In addition to the hardships resulting from the Industrial Revolution, workers had certain other grievances, some of which were a hangover from the colonial period. The children of poor laborers could attend the schools without paying tuition, but in most sections of the country only at the price of being branded as paupers. Employees were frequently paid in bank notes which were not worth face value. The laws did not give them a first lien on the products of their labor, and lawyers' fees were so high that the courts of justice were almost closed to the poorer class. The militia laws were enforced in such a way as to relieve wealthy men of militia duty by the payment of a fine, whereas the poor laborer had no such way of escape. *Older grievances of labor*

By the time Andrew Jackson came to the Presidency most of the states had broadened the suffrage so as to enfranchise the laboring class. Politicians now began to court the influence of this class and so the workers tried to gain their rights by political action. A "Workingmen's" Party was formed in Philadelphia in 1828, and in a little while similar parties sprang up in all the seaboard states north of Maryland. They nominated candidates for local offices and for Congress and conducted newspaper propaganda in favor of the rights of labor. The party, however, was never organized on a national basis, since the reforms demanded by it required state action. *The "Workingmen's" Party*

---

1 See E. L. Bogart and C. M. Thompson, *Readings in the Economic History of the United States*, 533-534. See also Charles R. Weld, *A Vacation Tour in the United States and Canada* (London, 1855), 50-53.

The Workingmen's Party did not last long and its membership was absorbed in the main by the Democratic Party. The reforms advocated by it were afterwards carried out by Federal or state legislation.

The demands of labor

One of the most persistent of the demands of labor was a ten-hour day. After a successful strike in Philadelphia in 1835, involving seventeen occupations, acceptance of this demand was won in that city. President Van Buren gave strong moral support to the reform by decreeing (1840) a ten-hour day for Federal workers. In 1847 New Hampshire enacted a ten-hour law for factory operatives and in five years five other states had adoped the same policy. Other reforms demanded by labor included the abolition of imprisonment for debt, universal education, abolition of chartered monopolies, equal taxation, revision or abolition of the militia system, a less expensive legal system, election of all officers directly by the people, a lien law for laborers, and freedom from legislation on religion.

Extent to which labor was organized prior to 1820

Prior to 1820 no serious efforts were made to unionize labor in the United States. Workmen's organizations had been formed in various trades, but they were mostly for benevolent purposes. There had even been occasional strikes, but no well organized movement in favor of labor had been attempted. While there was a considerable rise in wages immediately after the Revolutionary War, the workingman was still not getting his just deserts, considering the prosperous condition of the country. He was not in a good position to make a successful fight for his place in the sun. The workers did not constitute a large or influential class and were not class conscious. Few, if any, of them expected to remain laborers all their lives. Under such conditions a strong permanent labor organization could not be effected.

The labor movement in the 'twenties and 'thirties

In the 'twenties, however, conditions began to change, and in this and the succeeding decade labor awoke and made an effort to gain recognition of its rights. These efforts took the form of trades-unions and were confined mainly to skilled workmen. In 1827 a union was formed in Philadelphia made up of carpenters, glaziers, painters, bricklayers, and members of other crafts. A similar general union was formed in New York City in 1833, and by 1835 there were in most of the larger industrial centers general unions representing the various trades of the entire city. In 1834 these organizations sent delegates to a national convention, a body not unlike the later American Federation of Labor.

Attempts were also made to organize the individual trades on a national basis. A national cordwainers' union was established in 1836 and other crafts soon followed this example. This stage of labor organization came to an end with the depression that started in 1837. With mills closed and unemployment widespread, labor was in no position to continue its fight.

In the 'forties, interest in the labor movement was merged in the general feeling of humanitarianism which characterized that decade. The experiment of Robert Owen at New Harmony, and the phalanges advocated by Fourier, were attempts to better the condition of the laborers (see p. 546). A number of communistic settlements were begun, all of which proved unsuccessful. Since the idealists had failed to lead the laboring man to Utopia, he fell back upon a policy of realism. *Effect of communistic experiments on the labor movement*

After an abortive effort at co-operation, the laborer accepted as the plan for his protection the labor union of the modern type, with the use of the strike and the boycott as weapons. When the depression following the panic of 1837 was over, a period of prosperity set in, which lasted until 1857. During this time, especially the latter half, prices were soaring and so the cost of living was high, but the increase in wages was greater than the rise in prices. In addition to this improvement in his economic status, the workingman had secured most of the social reforms for which he had been agitating. Notwithstanding these gains, however, labor unions were formed and strikes were carried out. These were mostly of a local character, and only four trades had been organized on a national basis by 1860. *Organization of labor in the later period*

IRISH AND GERMAN IMMIGRATION

During the first four decades after the Revolution the number of foreigners who landed on American shores was comparatively small, and those who came were mostly from the British Isles. Beginning in 1820, the stream of immigration gradually increased during the next third of the century, though it slackened in the last half of the 'fifties, partly because of the hard times resulting from the panic of 1857. *Increase in migration to the United States after 1820; reasons*

Improvements in the means of ocean transportation facilitated the moving of the vast throng from the old world to the new. The marvelous prosperity in America (except during the panics of 1837 and 1857) made a strong appeal to Europeans who were dissatisfied with political, economic, and social conditions in the homeland. They were informed as to the opportunities in the United States by letters received from their friends and relatives there. These "America Letters" pictured in vivid colors a land of plenty where an honest laborer was respected, where he enjoyed full liberty, and where he had the opportunity by work and thrift to become prosperous. To a humble European peasant who had difficulty in eking out a scant livelihood for his family and who was accustomed to indignities from his social superiors and restraints on his freedom of action, such a country seemed a veritable Promised Land.

Irish immigration; reasons

Of the foreigners who migrated to the United States during this period (1820-1860), the Irish and the Germans were by all odds the most numerous. As has already been seen, there had been a large immigration of Scotch-Irish to the American colonies in the eighteenth century. There were also Celtic Irish here in colonial days, and they continued to come in after the Revolution. It was not until the decade of the 'twenties, however, that they began to arrive in considerable numbers. The inflow kept on increasing until it reached a volume of over nine hundred thousand in the decade of the 'fifties. There were a number of reasons to account for this persistent exodus from Ireland. The Irish were chafing under English domination and at times broke out in revolt against the restraints on their liberties. They also resented their exploitation by absentee landlords and the restrictions on their rights and privileges as loyal adherents of the Catholic Church. These grievances caused a rising tide of emigration, which reached its flood in the time of the famine of 1846-1847. The potato crop was a partial failure in 1845 and a complete failure the two succeeding years. As potatoes were the chief article of food for the masses, one quarter of the population was swept away by hunger and disease. The one way of escape from this awful plight was emigration to America.

The Irish become day laborers

The Irish peasant did not resume his occupation of tilling the soil in the new world. He did not have enough capital to become an independent farmer in the old settlements or to pay his way to the West. He therefore became a day laborer and found employment near the port of debarkation. Fortunately his services were much in demand for the construction of turnpikes, canals, and railroads, and he was the chief reliance for this heavy work. When the project on which he was working was completed he settled down in a near-by city, where he usually became a common laborer, or in a rural community, where he established himself as a farmer.

Opposition to the Irish; reasons

It was not long before the Irish immigrant began to meet with difficulties in his new home. While he was kind and agreeable when in a good humor, he became combative and self-assertive when he felt that his personal dignity had been infringed. Furthermore, this combativeness was too often stimulated by an intemperate use of alcoholic liquors. He was thus drawn into quarrels more frequently than was good for his reputation as a law-abiding citizen. The Irish generally congregated in certain localities in the cities and developed clannish customs. They usually voted as a unit and thus had a strong voice in politics. Some of them soon developed great ability for political leadership, and were able to exert a controlling influence over their fellow countrymen. In this way the Irish immigrant lent himself to machine politics. His religion also gave trouble since he was an ardent Catholic and the native stock had a strong prejudice against Catholics. But the greatest cause of opposition to the Irish was their willingness to work for low wages. They could live more parsimoniously than could the American workers and the latter could not successfully compete with them without lowering their standard of living.

The stream of German immigration, which was so strong in the eighteenth century, slackened after the Revolution. It began to flow again in 1820, and by 1830 had assumed large proportions. The number of immigrants each year grew constantly in size until it reached a total of a million and a quarter during the period between 1845 and 1860. *German immigration after 1820; reasons*

The causes of this great transfer of population were both economic and political. Many people found it hard to make a comfortable adjustment to the new economic order brought in by the Industrial Revolution. This difficulty was aggravated by the shortsighted policy of petty European rulers who were more inclined to exploit their people than to promote their prosperity. The passing of the regime of Napoleon had left in Germany as elsewhere a good deal of political dissatisfaction. There was a strong element which clamored for constitutional government and the unification of Germany. An uprising in favor of these objectives occurred in 1830 and a more important one in 1848. Both of these efforts were crushed by the conservatives and the old regime continued for a while undisturbed. Owing to these failures many liberals were unhappy and lost hope for the success of their cause in the homeland. Some of them, therefore, emigrated to the United States, where liberal views were accepted as commonplace opinion.

The German immigrants of this period usually had sufficient funds to begin farming on their arrival in the new country. Accordingly, they did not stop in the seaboard cities but moved on to the interior. The greater portion of them went to Ohio, Indiana, Illinois, Michigan, and Wisconsin. Some became artisans in the western cities, but most of them took to farming. By hard work and Spartan economy they were soon able to gain possession of valuable farms. On these were erected large barns for their stock, while during the early years their families were lodged in small log houses. It was not long, however, until log cabins were supplanted by comfort- *German settlers as farmers* able frame dwellings and the farm lands took on an air of prosperity.

The German immigrants brought with them the customs and cultural ideals of the homeland. Many of them had a higher appreciation of art and music than did their American neighbors. Thanks to this quality they were able to make a much-needed contribution to the spiritual ideals of the West, and in so doing aided in the process of toning down the rawness in frontier life. Their educational ideas were also often in advance of those of their neighbors. Unfortunately, however, some of their customs clashed with the practices and prejudices of the native American stock. The Westerners in general were still adhering to many of the Puritan principles which they had inherited from their New England and Southern ancestors. Serious-minded native Westerners, therefore, looked with marked disapproval upon the fondness of the Germans for beer and their laxity in observing the Sabbath.

The sentimental attachment of the German settlers for the institutions of the fatherland was not mixed with any disloyalty to their adopted country. They were not Fifth Columnists; on the contrary, they were in agreement with the political system of this country and were antagonistic to that of their native land. It was for this reason that many of them had left home. Some of them, notably Carl Schurz, became leaders in liberal movements in their adopted country. At first the Germans, owing to their strong individualism, were inclined to affiliate with the Democratic Party. But later, influenced by their opposition to slavery and their strong nationalism, the majority of them became Republicans.[1]

The coming of the foreigners in such large numbers was regarded by some of the American people as a menace to their ideals and institutions. It revived the old fear of the political power of Catholicism and aroused the latent hostility to foreigners. The antialien feeling was directed mainly against the Irish though it extended in some degree to all classes of immigrants. This antagonism sometimes found expression in mob violence. In 1834 an attack was made on a Catholic convent in Charlestown, near Boston. Later there were anti-Irish riots in Philadelphia and New York. In Philadelphia two Catholic churches and one schoolhouse were burned by mobs.

The opposition to aliens also gave rise to political agitation against

---

[1] This view is contested by Mr. Andreas Dorpalen in an article in the *Mississippi Valley Historical Review*, XXIX, 55-56. He contends that a large proportion of the Germans, a majority in some localities, voted the Democratic ticket in 1860 and that those of them who were Republicans were attracted more by the homestead than by the antislavery plank of the platform.

them. The old parties were not willing to incur the ill feeling of the Irish by declaring against them and so the antiforeign movement was carried on by independent political groups, which were active from time to time, beginning as early as the middle 'thirties. By 1852 this movement had become widespread, and for four years played an important role in national politics under the name of the American, or "Know-Nothing," Party. This third party had grown out of a secret society known as "The Supreme Order of the Star-Spangled Banner," which had a grip, pass words, and the other mysteries and ceremonies characteristic of fraternal orders. When a member was inquired of as to the principles of the society he would always answer, "I know nothing." Hence the name "Know-Nothing" Party. This secret organization advocated more rigid immigration and naturalization laws, the deportation of alien paupers, and the limitation of officeholding to native Americans of the Protestant faith. *The American, or "Know-Nothing," Party*

Partly as a result of the inflow of immigrants the population increased rapidly from 1820 to 1860. In 1820 it was 9,638,453; by 1830 it had increased 33.5 per cent; by 1840 it had gone beyond the seventeen million mark; and for each of the next two decades the rate of increase was more than 35.5 per cent. By 1860 the total population had reached 31,443,321. *Growth of population*

During these four decades the rate of increase of population had been about twice as high for the cities as for the rural areas. The South did not keep pace with the rest of the country in growth of population, because comparatively few of the immigrants settled in this region. There were not many manufacturing plants in the South to attract hired laborers, and would-be farmers from foreign countries disliked slavery and felt that the small farmer was put at a social and economic disadvantage in competing with the large planter using slave labor. Also, the North and West offered him the type of field crops which he was accustomed to cultivate.

HUMANITARIANISM AND REFORM

During the greater part of the period from the War of 1812 to the War for Southern Independence, the United States was blessed with peace and prosperity. The only break in peace was the Mexican War and the only interruptions in prosperity were those caused by periodic panics. Such conditions were most favorable for the rise and growth of humanitarianism. The tendency toward altruism was stimulated by the intellectual renaissance and by influences from abroad. Hence during the three decades preceding the Civil War *Circumstances favorable to reform* there was considerable agitation in favor of reform. Earnest and in some cases effective efforts were made to better the condition of the unfortunate and the underprivileged.

Changes in debtor laws and the criminal code

One such reform was an improvement in the laws against debtors. The old practice of imprisonment for debt was continued from colonial days, and at the time of Jackson's accession (1829) about seventy-five thousand persons each year were thrown into prison for debt. This practice worked a severe hardship on the members of the laboring class because many of them were imprisoned for small debts. The workingmen's parties, as well as the philanthropists, therefore strongly urged a repeal of these unjust debtor laws.

The new Western states took the lead in this reform, and their constitutions generally forbade imprisonment for debt except in cases of refusal of a debtor to surrender his property to his creditors. In the older states, too, debtor laws were gradually changed until imprisonment for debt was virtually abolished. Other desired changes

Prison reform

in the criminal code were also introduced. The severity of the penalties for crime was mitigated and the number of capital offenses was reduced. Improvement was also made in the treatment of prisoners. The idea that prisons should be used for reformation as well as punishment gradually gained in favor.

Dorothea L. Dix

Prominent among those who advocated prison reform was Dorothea L. Dix of Massachusetts. She also urged with great earnestness a better method of caring for paupers and the insane. With a New England conscience animated by the Quaker religion, she had a spiritual equipment which well fitted her for the role of reformer. She appeared before state legislatures and induced them to make appropriations in support of her cherished reforms. Effective appeals were also made to the philanthropic instincts of the wealthy. As a result of her endeavors, many old insane asylums were reorganized and many new ones were built. Furthermore, numerous jails and almshouses were constructed and run in accordance with the reform ideas.

The peace movement

World peace was one of the objectives of some of the reformers. A few peace societies were organized as early as 1815. In 1828 was formed the American Peace Society consisting of representatives from about fifty local societies. This national organization advocated the establishment of an international congress which, meeting periodically, would codify international law and create a world court for deciding controversies between nations.

In the meantime a similar movement had started in England. The merging of these two plans was signalized by the meeting in London in 1843 of a universal peace congress, at which thirty-seven

American delegates were present. Five years later an international peace congress was held at Brussels, at which the American plan was endorsed. International congresses were held frequently thereafter and the peace movement seemed to be advancing promisingly until it was seriously checked by the Crimean War and the War of Secession.

Another reform advocated in this period was that of temperance. *Temperance reform* At the end of the first third of the nineteenth century the American people were still freely indulging the appetite for strong drink which had come down to them from their ancestors of the colonial era. Drinking was common among both men and women, though intoxication among the latter was very unusual.

In 1826 societies whose members were pledged to abstain from the *Temperance societies* use of liquor began to appear in Boston. So rapidly did these organizations spread that in five years there were over a thousand of them. By 1833 the local groups were federated into a national organization. The movement made the greatest headway in the North and Northwest, sections in which the New England influence was strong. It did not, however, make much progress in the South.

The agitation was carried on by means of lectures, pictures, and *Methods of agitation* books and other printed materials. The main arguments advanced were the evil effects of alcohol on the health and efficiency of the drinker and the harm done to his immortal soul by a sinful practice. Most of the religious denominations supported the propaganda, and many of the speakers were ministers. After 1840 the principal lecturers were reformed drunkards. Many of these cheapened the cause by their tawdry efforts at self-advertisement; but some of them, notably John B. Gough, were sincere and eloquent speakers who could bring from the storehouse of their own experience unanswerable arguments against intemperance. Some of the outstanding writers of the day also helped in the literary campaign against liquor. The most famous of the books on temperance was *Ten Nights in a Barroom* (1854). When it was dramatized it vied in popularity with *Uncle Tom's Cabin*.

The advocates of temperance after a while decided to take their *Neal Dow and the Maine Law* fight into the realm of government. These reformers argued that the addicts of drink should be delivered from the liquor habit by legal action. The next step therefore was the restriction or prohibition by law of the manufacture and sale of intoxicating liquors. Neal Dow of Maine took the lead in this phase of the movement. Due to his influence Maine passed (1846) the first state prohibition law ever enacted in this country. In the next ten years a dozen other states in the North and West had followed Maine's example.

Results of the
temperance
movement

The results of the temperance movement were on the whole quite beneficial. By the end of the 'fifties drinking had virtually ceased among women except in the higher social circles and there it seldom went to excess. There was also considerably less drinking among men than there had ever been before in this country.

Communist
experiments

As was to be expected, the spirit of reform led to experiments in the social order. Of these one of the earliest and most noted was the one made (1825) at New Harmony, Indiana, by Robert Owen, a Scotch cotton manufacturer. Here a large tract of land was bought and a co-operative community was established. Although this experiment was not successful, its failure did not stop the search for panaceas. In the decade of the 'forties alone more than forty attempts were made to establish communistic settlements. The inspiration for these efforts was the Utopian philosophy of Charles Fourier, a French Socialist. The best advertised of these projects was Brook Farm, which was established near Boston (1841) by a group of intellectuals. Despite the support it received from a few of the noted writers of New England it proved a failure in a few years. All of these communistic colonies were short-lived except a few that were held together by the cement of religion. Of this latter group the one established by the Mormons in Utah was the most outstanding success.

The suffrage
revolt in
Rhode
Island

As has already been seen (p. 428), a movement in favor of political democracy was in progress throughout the country at the accession of Andrew Jackson (1829), and in time the trend became general in favor of virtual manhood suffrage for whites. One of the last of the states to accept a broadening of the suffrage was Rhode Island, which until 1841 was still using its colonial charter as a constitution. Under this conservative plan of government more than half of the adult males were deprived of the right to vote, and there was no provision in the charter for its revision. In response to the great demand for change, the people, under the leadership of Thomas W. Dorr, took the situation in hand and called a constitutional convention (1841). This convention framed a constitution which provided for manhood suffrage. The procedure was irregular and the old government did not recognize its legality. The new government was set up, however, with Dorr as governor. There was a clash between the two governments and the insurgents were defeated, but the victors had the good sense to make concessions to the malcontents by broadening the suffrage (1843).

Grievances
of women

The advance in democracy throughout the country did not alter the political status of women, and they were everywhere denied the right of suffrage. There were also certain legal discriminations against them. At marriage the husband acquired title to his wife's personal property and the right to manage her real estate. He also had the authority to punish her if he saw fit—and was able to do so. He was the guardian of the children and could by will make arrangements for their control after his death. From these laws it would seem that the father was a miniature despot in the home. This was far from the case, however. These powers were more theoretical than actual, and few heads of families could or would exercise them in a tyrannical way. Women occupied a high place in society and the respect usually accorded them by public sentiment almost always served as a shield against any real mistreatment. In no country in the world was the position of women more enviable. For these reasons (the law to the contrary notwithstanding) the actual government of the household was probably vested in the mother as often as in the father.

A number of the reformers were women. It was only natural that in their program for social betterment should be included the redress of their own grievances. The class consciousness of the feminist leaders was aroused by Frances Wright, a brilliant and attractive young Scotch woman who visited America in 1818. Besides supporting numerous other "isms," she was an ardent advocate of woman's rights. Soon leaders among American women arose to carry the torch which had been lighted by the beautiful Scotch visitor. Prominent among these were Lucretia Mott, Susan B. Anthony, and Elizabeth Cady Stanton. *Leading agitators for women's rights*

A new impetus was given to the woman's movement in 1840 when several woman delegates to an international antislavery convention in London were refused admission on account of their sex. Smarting under this indignity, the leaders of the movement in this country entered upon a vigorous crusade in favor of the rights of women. In furtherance of this cause they held a woman's rights convention at Seneca Falls, New York, in 1848. At this meeting they adopted a platform of principles, which declared "that all men and women are created equal," and demanded that men and women be made equal before the law and granted equal opportunities in education and business and the right of suffrage. *Platform of the women's organization*

The women's organization held meetings nearly every year and waged a persistent fight for these objectives. While in this period women did not win a complete victory they succeeded in gaining some of their demands. Prior to 1860 laws granting to married women the right to control their own property were enacted in a number of states. Schools for the higher education of women were established and girls were admitted to a few colleges and one state *Reforms secured prior to 1860* university before the Civil War. For the privilege of voting, however, they had to wait until a later day.

Of all the reforms proposed, the abolition of slavery was the most persistent and aroused the most intense opposition. This movement was of such importance that it deserves a fuller treatment than can be given in this chapter. (See Chapter XXXVIII.)

IRISH EMIGRANTS LEAVING THE HOMELAND.
Receiving the Priest's Blessing.

CHAPTER XXXIV

Schools and Colleges (1783=1860)

*T*HE immediate effects of the Revolution were detrimental to education. The schools suffered greatly from the destructive activities of the war. Some of the private and charity schools and most of the parochial schools were discontinued. Many of the academies and Latin grammar schools were forced to close because student attendance at them had been so reduced. Work in some of the colleges was suspended and the others were left with a scant remnant of students. So much of the energy of the people was taken up with the prosecution of the war that interest in public education declined. *Effects of the Revolution on schools and colleges*

The problem of education was left to the states by the Constitution of 1787. It was not long, however, before the Federal government by grants of land began a policy of aiding the new states in solving their educational difficulties. When Ohio was admitted into the Union (1803), the new state was given the sixteenth section in every township for the maintenance of schools in that township. This same policy was pursued in the admission of all the other new states until 1850. When California was admitted in that year she was granted two sections in each township. The other Western states which have been admitted into the Union since 1850 (not including Texas) have been given the same amount of land, except that Utah, Arizona, and New Mexico each received three sections in every township. *Education aided by Federal land grants*

Owing partly to the mismanagement of these lands and the limited demand for them, the revenue derived from them was not sufficient to sustain an adequate school system. The grants, however, created a sentiment in the West in favor of state schools and aided these new states in their efforts to establish a public educational system. They also influenced the older states to set aside funds or lands for the support of schools.

THE FIGHT FOR THE PUBLIC SCHOOL

By the end of the first quarter of the ninteenth century, public education on the primary level had made little advance beyond colonial conditions. In each of the New England states (except

Public edu-
cation at
the end of
the first
quarter
of the
nineteenth
century

Rhode Island) there were public schools which were free to pupils of all classes. In the other portions of the country the best schools were private and were supported by tuition fees. In addition to these there were, in all the states, schools for indigent pupils, supported by taxation or by donations of charitable and religious organizations. From these same sources funds were available for the payment of the tuition fees of poor children who attended the private schools. Schooling obtained through these aids was branded with the stigma of pauperism and many self-respecting parents would not allow their children to take advantage of these opportunities. The "pauper school" was, therefore, a very unsatisfactory means of primary education. During the second quarter of the nineteenth century a persistent fight was made for the establishment of a public free school system which in the primary grades would apply to rich and poor on equal terms.

Reasons
for the
advance in
public
education

By 1830 most of the states had virtually accepted the principle of white manhood suffrage, and public education was one of the demands of the common people. This demand could not be ignored by political leaders who were bidding competitively for the votes of the recently enfranchised citizens. The movement in favor of free schools also received the support of the political liberals and reformers who felt that an ignorant electorate would be a menace to good government, now that the masses were in control of the state and Federal governments. Jefferson said that if "a nation expects to be ignorant and free in a state of civilization it expects what never was and never will be." In colonial days education was encouraged as a means to the promotion of religion, and so the school was the ally of the church. Now one of the main objects of education was to promote good citizenship and therefore the logical policy was a union between school and state.

Public
education
in the
South

The alliance between the common people and the intellectuals proved to be a strong combination, and by 1860 had won a decisive victory for public elementary education throughout the North and Northwest. By this time too the principle of public education supported by taxation seems also to have been accepted by the South. In this section, however, the principle was not, to any great extent, put into practice until after the Civil War. State laws providing for a public school system were passed, but the acceptance of these laws was generally left optional with the counties, and many of the counties failed to make the appropriations necessary to execute the general plan. Therefore, in a good part of the South the number of public schools established in this period was small, and in such localities the main result of these laws was merely to give indigents a few months of schooling.[1]

The South, however, encouraged the establishment of academies, and ran ahead of the North in promoting seminaries for girls. In fact the progress made by the South in public education during this period has often been greatly underestimated. It is true that it did not keep pace with the North in the establishment of public schools, owing mainly to the fact that in the rural South there were few towns of importance and the people were too widely scattered for easy co-operation in school plans. But in time the renascence in education which started in New England found its way to Dixie. In the latter section the reform movement drew its inspiration largely from Thomas Jefferson, who had been the most ardent champion of public education in the South, and to his influence was added the impetus that came from later Southern leaders.[2] As a result of the activity of these leaders, by the middle of the century an interest in state-supported public schools had become widespread. Educational conventions were held, propaganda in favor of public education was carried on by contributed articles in newspapers, and measures looking toward the establishment of a free school system were urged by governors upon their too-often reluctant legislatures. In some of the Southern counties and cities there were good schools supported by taxation, and plans for a general system of public education had been formed in a number of the states by 1860. The outbreak of the war checked this forward movement.

The educational revival in the South

The fight for public education was a strenuous one, even in the sections which accepted the reform. Property owners often objected to being taxed to educate other people's children. Many of them felt that the school should be a private enterprise and considered its management and support by the state as rank socialism. A conservative of Rhode Island boasted that he would use his shotgun on Henry Barnard if this radical reformer should ever be caught on his farm advocating "such heresy as the partial confiscation of one man's property to educate another man's child." Individuals and religious foundations interested in private schools contended that their vested rights would be infringed if their schools were forced into competition with those which had been financed from public funds.

Opposition to public education

---

[1] For maps showing the advance in public free schools in the South and the country as a whole, see C. L. and E. H. Lord, *Historical Atlas of the United States*, 84-85.

[2] Prominent in the list of later Southern educational leaders were: Henry Ruffner, of Virginia; Archibald D. Murphey and Calvin Wiley, of North Carolina; and William F. Perry and J. L. M. Curry, of Alabama.

THE REFORM MOVEMENT IN EDUCATION

It was not enough to give a wider range to public education; it was just as necessary to make improvements in the school system which had come down from colonial days. Foitunately there arose in the 'thirties some capable leaders to direct this reform movement. This leadership came out of New England, a section in which public education had already gone farther than in any other part of the country. Here, however, as elsewhere, the schools were far below what one might expect in a vigorous and prosperous young republic.

Horace Mann

At the head of the list of reformers stood Horace Mann, who was able to diagnose the maladies which afflicted the New England school system and apply the heroic treatment needed for its relief. After graduating from Brown University he took up the study of the law and later went into politics. Although he was quite successful both as a lawyer and a politician, he sacrificed fine prospects in these fields to become secretary of the newly created Massachusetts State Board of Education (1837).

Courtesy of the Commonwealth of Massachusetts

HORACE MANN.

His work in Massachusetts

This proved a wise choice as he became one of the most outstanding leaders in public education that this country has ever produced. He did not make any discoveries or new contributions as to method, but was instrumental in putting into effect much-needed reforms. His connection with the state board enabled him to give valuable service by integrating the schools into a system and bringing them under state supervision and direction. In his reports on conditions in the schools of Massachusetts he showed the great need of change, and by lectures at school meetings he aroused public sentiment in favor of his proposals. New ideas gained from the study of European school conditions, especially those of Prussia, were urged upon the Massachusetts authorities.

Despite the opposition of obstinate conservatism, Mann was able at the end of a dozen years of service to point to a remarkable record of achievement. In Massachusetts, appropriations for public schools had been doubled, the school term had been lengthened, the pay of teachers had been increased by more than fifty per cent, and three normal schools for the training of teachers had been established. The first of these, which was also the first normal school in the United States, was opened at Lexington in 1839 with only three students.

Mann's influence was not confined to his own state, for his work in Massachusetts gave an impetus to educational progress throughout the country. The reforms carried out by him and other leaders not only led to the improvement of the schools but also gave inspiration and encouragement to those who were fighting for an extension of the public school system.[1] *His influence in other sections of the country*

After the Revolution native authors became active in the preparation of textbooks for American schools. One reason for this was the difficulty or impossibility of getting books from England during the war. Furthermore, along with the political separation from the mother country went the desire to become culturally independent. *Textbooks*

In 1783 Noah Webster published his *American Spelling Book.* This "Blue-backed Speller," as it was called, was used in the teaching of both spelling and reading, for it contained a number of "moral reading lessons" to be assigned to the pupils. It superseded the *New England Primer,* which had been widely used in the primary schools for nearly a century. The Speller quickly attained a remarkable popularity and sales were enormous. According to a reliable estimate, eighty million copies were sold by 1880. It "did more than any other single force to create a unified American language for the new nation."[2] *Webster's "Blue-backed Speller"*

Other readers and spellers came out from time to time. Of these the most popular during the first third of the century was Webster's *An American Selection,* or *Third Part.* This was the first reader of the modern type published in the United States. In 1836 there appeared the first two of the most noted series of readers ever produced in this country. These were William H. McGuffey's *First* and *Second Readers.* In a few years there had been added a *Third, Fourth,* and *Fifth Reader* and still later the *Sixth Reader* appeared, ending the series. For sixty years these readers were the ones most widely used throughout the country except in New England. The stories, fables, and literary excerpts were permeated with a sound moral tone, and *McGuffey's Readers*

---

1 Henry Barnard performed a service for education in Connecticut and Rhode Island comparable to that done by Mann in Massachusetts. As Secretary of the Connecticut State Board of Education he organized (1839) the first teachers' institute ever held in this country. It was, however, as editor for more than thirty years of the *American Journal of Education* that he made his finest contribution to education.

2 E. P. Cubberley, *Public Education in the United States* (Boston, 1934), 290-291.

all tended to make American ideals attractive to the young. In this way they exerted a profound influence in inspiring youth with high ethical and patriotic ideals.[1]

SECONDARY SCHOOLS

The academy

During the first half-century after the Declaration of Independence the chief interest in education was seen in the encouragement given to academies and colleges. The aristocratic notion of the colonial period that education should be for the training of the privileged few for leadership had not given way to the democratic idea of training the many for citizenship. Higher education was, however, changing its scope and purpose in order better to meet the new conditions. The old Latin grammar school of the colonial era, with its emphasis on the classics and its objective of preparing for college, was not adapted to the needs of the new country. It was therefore being supplanted by the academy, which was more practical in its aim and offered a curriculum of more useful subjects than those of the Latin grammar school. While Latin and Greek were continued as a part of the curriculum of the academies, special emphasis was placed on English grammar and to some extent also on oratory and declamation. It was probably due to this emphasis that the style of American writers and speakers was so good during this period. Other subjects were arithmetic, algebra, geometry, geography, and astronomy. In some academies surveying, rhetoric (including some literature), natural and moral philosophy, and Roman antiquities were also included in the list of studies.

Some of the academies were sponsored by religious denominations, but a good number of them were privately owned and run as business ventures. All of them had a religious tone, but they were usually careful to avoid the imparting of sectarian views. They were financed mainly by tuition fees, although many of them were subsidized by local or state funds or were aided by endowments. Most of the best-known ones were incorporated under charters granted by the states and were under the supervision of boards of trustees, while many others were managed by their owners. Some of the academies were

---

[1] In the class with Webster's "Blue-backed Speller" and McGuffey's *Readers* was Warren Colburn's *First Lessons in Arithmetic on the Plan of Pestalozzi,* which was published in 1821. This book contained a large number of problems which could be solved without difficulty by mental calculation. It simplified arithmetic and made it one of the most popular of the subjects taught in the common schools. Other outstanding textbooks for this period were: Lindley Murray's *English Grammar* (first published in 1795; an abridged edition later); Jedediah Morse's *American Universal Geography* (published first in 1784; republished in 1795 with the title of *Elements of Geography*); and Samuel Goodrich's *A History of the United States* (1822).

for girls only, and many of the others were coeducational. As a rule the academies had dormitories or boardinghouses.

From the Revolution to the War of Secession the academy was the chief agency in secondary education. In the South, where this type of school was widely prevalent, it held its primacy much longer, for in this section it was not outdistanced by its competitor, the public high school, until the last decade of the nineteenth century. The academy was a suitable intermediary between the primary school and the college, though its curriculum often overlapped that of the other two. Not only did it prepare students for college, but it also served as a "people's college," giving many young men their final training for life. Furthermore, most of the teachers in the primary schools were trained in the academies. Many men in all sections of the country who attained eminence in politics or the professions finished their formal education in the academies.

The academy was less aristocratic than was the old Latin grammar *The public high school* school, which served only the few privileged students who were able to go to college. The academy therefore suited the democratic trend of the time better than did its older rival. But it was far from being a democratic institution. Its portals were not wide open to the sons of the poorer classes. The progress of democracy therefore brought in a feeling of dissatisfaction with the academy. The rapid advances in industry and commerce were calling for a wider general education than that supplied by the state-supported primary schools.

Accordingly, there arose in the second quarter of the nineteenth century a demand from forward-looking leaders for the extension of the public school system so as to include secondary education. For some time many voters opposed this plan on the ground that the state had no right to tax the people for the support of higher education. But in the decade of the 'fifties economic prosperity, bringing increased earnings on the part of heads of families, postponed the age limit at which sons and daughters had to begin work. This change gave to youth a longer period for schooling than it had formerly enjoyed. It was to meet this new situation that the high school was brought in as a part of the state-supported school system.

The first public high school was the one established in 1821 in Boston. The high schools increased slowly in number until 1840, at which time there were only about fifty in the entire country, and half of these were in Massachusetts. The main reason for this slow development was probably the fact that urban life had not as yet attained any importance. At that time there were only forty-four cities in the United States with eight thousand or more inhabitants and more than ninety-one per cent of the population lived on farms or in villages.

By 1860 the number of high schools in the country had increased to three hundred and twenty-one. More than half of these (167) were in the states of Massachusetts, New York, and Ohio, and only about twelve per cent of them (38) were south of Mason and Dixon's Line and the Ohio River.

At first the main purpose of the high schools was to prepare boys for college, and they were therefore quite similar to the old Latin grammar schools. Later, however, they began to offer courses which would be useful for students who would not, as well as for those who would, be able to go to college. The high school thus became both a "people's college" and a college preparatory school.

HIGHER EDUCATION

Old and new colleges

The nine colonial colleges continued or resumed their work after the Revolution and twenty-nine new ones had been established by 1820. During this post-Revolutionary period, however, the standard of scholarship upheld by these colleges was not high and the intellectual atmosphere created by them was far from stimulating. The number of students and professors was still small. The older colleges had been reorganized and in them, as well as in those newly founded, an attempt had been made better to adjust the course of study to the demands of a new country, and there was less slavish imitation of the English universities. Less emphasis was put on theology, and other changes were made in the curriculum.

Denominational colleges

In the decade of the 'twenties higher education in this country entered upon an important stage of development both as to the number of institutions and the quality of the work done. During the four decades that preceded the War of Secession a large number of small denominational colleges came into being, some of which were shortlived while others later grew into importance. The denominational college had a student body ranging from one to three hundred, which was cared for by a faculty of from six to a dozen instructors. The equipment both as to library and laboratory facilities was usually ludicrously inadequate, and the professors were seldom noted for profound scholarship. Daily attendance at chapel was required and a religious observance of the Sabbath was expected.

Situated on a high elevation which commanded a fine view, with the buildings surrounded by shady lawns, these little colleges afforded their students a favorable milieu for study and were free from many of the temptations to idleness which beset present-day institutions of higher learning. Unfortunately, however, they were seldom able to offer the aids or create the atmosphere which were necessary for the promotion of sound and thorough scholarship. In the task of building character they probably scored a greater success than in that of diffusing knowledge. At these modest institutions a great many young men were indoctrinated with ideals which furnished the inspiration for fine achievement in later life.

In the later middle period (1820-1860) the older and stronger colleges made great improvement in the quality of their work. The impetus to this change was the influence exerted on our colleges by the German universities, which were at the height of their usefulness during this time. For this favorable influence—especially in its initial stage—the American college is largely indebted to four brilliant young men[1] who between 1815 and 1820 studied at two of the noted German universities. These students were deeply impressed with the high standard of scholarship of these universities and with the learning of the professors and the academic freedom enjoyed by them. On their return home they were given positions in Harvard and they used their utmost exertions to put this American college in the line of progress which had been marked out by the German universities. As a result of their efforts Harvard became the center of a productive scholarship and the leader in the fight for academic freedom—the fight to free scholarship from the restraints imposed by religious and political opinion and prejudice. Unitarianism was also a contributing factor in bringing Harvard to this liberal view. Other colleges caught this spirit of progress and higher education was benefited by it throughout the country. There was a small but constant stream of young men going abroad for advanced study and so the influence of the German universities was continuous. *Improvement in the older colleges; reasons*

With the progress of democracy there gradually developed a feeling of opposition to the aristocratic character of the old colleges. From this feeling there arose an agitation in favor of state control of higher education. The outcome of this attitude was the establishment of the state university, an institution which was free from sectarian influence. *State universities*

Early in this later period the state university began to assume an important place in higher education. By 1825 eight states had either founded state universities or had taken steps for their future establishment. The oldest of these, the universities of North Carolina and Georgia, were opened for students in 1795 and 1805, respectively.

[1] These young scholars were: Edward Everett, Joseph C. Cogswell, George Ticknor, and George Bancroft.

A new impetus was given to the movement in favor of state universities by the establishment of the University of Virginia in 1825.

*influence
of the Uni-
versity of
Virginia*

Thomas Jefferson was the founder and first rector of this institution, and the fathering of this his youngest brain child was an
achievement of which he was very proud. His aim was to create a
free and secular university of the highest type, supported and managed by the state. The instructors were to be free from all political
and religious restraints in the exercise of their duties. Emphasis was
to be put upon the teaching of science, and theology was not to be
included in the curriculum.

For the location of this new university a proper site was chosen
in the foothills of the Blue Ridge Mountains. Here under the eye of
the Sage of Monticello suitable buildings were erected for the accommodation of students and professors and for the housing of libraries
and laboratories. The landscape and architectural planning were
in that fine taste which could be expected of one of the most cultured
men of the time. The long colonnades which façaded the structures,
and the lawn enclosed by them, were worthy of the golden age of
ancient Athens. Up to this time the muses had never found such a
beautiful home on the American continent.

It was Jefferson's plan to select as professors the most renowned
teachers that could be found. If this idea had been realized a university of the type of Heidelberg or Göttingen would have sprung full-
armed from the Jovian brain of the great Virginian. A lack of funds
prevented the realization of this dream; but the young institution
started off with every prospect of success and almost at once took its
place as the leading American state university.

*State uni-
versities
numerous
in the
West*

From 1825 on the number of state universities continually
increased. By 1860 there were seventeen state institutions of higher
learning and two or three others that had some sort of a connection
with the state governments. State universities were more numerous
in the South and West than in the North and East. The founding
of these institutions in the West was greatly aided by land grants
made by the Federal government. Beginning with Ohio in 1803, each
new state that came into the Union (except Texas, which retained
its own public lands) was granted two townships as an endowment
for "a seminary of learning."

*Higher
education
for women*

At the opening of the nineteenth century there was not a college
in the United States to which women were admitted. It was not until
1865 that Vassar College was opened, which is generally considered
the first college for women in the country. This claim is contested,
however, by two institutions in the South. Elizabeth Academy, a
Methodist school at Old Washington, Mississippi, was chartered as

a college in 1820. In 1836 the Georgia Female College (now Wesleyan College at Macon) received a charter authorizing it to grant degrees. Neither of these institutions is willing to yield to Vassar the primacy usually conceded to it, and each claims for itself priority in the field of college education for women. But the claim that the instruction given in these institutions prior to 1865 was on the college level is challenged by many if not most educators of today.

Excepting these Southern schools the only colleges which admitted women students before 1860 were a few coeducational institutions in the West. The first of these was Oberlin College, which opened its doors in 1833 to twenty-nine men and fifteen women students. Oberlin was an institution of high standing, as its curriculum compared favorably with those of the old Eastern colleges. Prior to 1860 several other Western colleges and one state university (Iowa) had become coeducational. *Coeducational colleges*

It must not be inferred, however, that these coeducational colleges were the only institutions of higher learning to which women were admitted. As has already been seen, there were many "female seminaries" and academies for girls. It was in these schools that women students had their first opportunity for higher education. By 1860 there were sixty-one of these institutions in the entire country. *"Female seminaries" and academies*

Of the many girls' schools of this period the most noted was Mt. Holyoke Seminary at South Hadley, Massachusetts (established in 1837). Mary Lyon, the founder of this seminary, was a young woman of rare intellectual gifts and exceptional strength and fineness of character. She had overcome great obstacles in achieving a broad education and regarded teaching as a sacred profession. Probably no other woman in America at that time was better qualified to inspire girls with a high idealism, a love of learning, and a sane philosophy of life. *Mary Lyon*

College life in this period was similar to that of colonial days, except that the Puritan rigor which characterized discipline in the older time was gradually relaxing in favor of greater freedom. Students indulged in very much the same sort of pranks as did their ancestors of the colonial era and as do their descendants of the present day. Indeed, many of these antics probably came down in a direct line of descent from the early mediaeval universities. *College life*

Unlike his successor of a later era, the college student of the middle period took his classroom duties more seriously than his extracurricular activities. Nor were there many outside interests to divert students from their regular work. No time was devoted to intercollegiate athletics by the boys and none lost by the girls in priming themselves for beauty contests. The literary society was the noncurricular activity which commanded the greatest interest. In it young men received practice in debate, oratory, and essay writing. These exercises afforded useful training in public speaking, an art which was highly valued by the politician, lawyer, and clergyman of that day. In the third decade of the nineteenth century the social fraternity began to take its place in the American college and by the end of the period a considerable number of these organizations were firmly established. For some years the fraternity combined literary with social activities.

PROFESSIONAL AND TECHNICAL SCHOOLS

Theological schools

One of the main purposes of the colonial college was the training of young men for the ministry. By the end of the eighteenth century the religious tone of the colleges had declined, and ardent churchmen felt that new arrangements for theological training should be made. It was this feeling that led to the organization of separate theological schools. The first of these was founded by the Dutch Reformed Church in 1784, when Dr. John H. Livinston, pastor of the Collegiate Church of New York City, was made professor of divinity for the whole denomination. Candidates for the ministry were taught by him without charge. Ministers in other localities aided him in the teaching, but prospective preachers could not enter upon their profession until they had been examined by him and received a license to preach. In 1810 Dr. Livinston was made professor of theology in and president of Rutgers College. In this way his theological school was absorbed by this college and it has maintained this connection since that time.

The second theological school was St. Mary's Seminary in Baltimore, established by the Roman Catholics in 1791. Other such schools were founded from time to time and by the middle of the century each of the leading denominations had one or more institutions for the training of ministers.

Theology was one of the important subjects included in the curricula of some of the leading colonial colleges. There was, however, no well-organized plan in these colleges for preparing students for the ministry until 1819, when a school of divinity was established at Harvard. Three years later Yale established a theological department, and these examples were gradually followed by other colleges.

Rise of the law school

Prior to 1860 (and for years afterwards), it was the practice for many, if not most, lawyers to get their training by reading law under the direction of a successful practitioner. In keeping with this custom Judge Tapping Reeve, an eminent attorney at Litchfield, Connecticut, had a number of young men studying under his supervision. Out of this association there had developed by 1784 the first law school in the United States. For fourteen years Reeve was the sole instructor and thereafter he had only one assistant. The school had such a wide reputation that it attracted students from every state in the Union. In the list of 1024 students enrolled during the entire period of forty-nine years there were included a large proportion of men who afterward occupied high place in the official life of state and nation, one of whom was John C. Calhoun.

Two other attempts to establish law schools in the eighteenth century were unsuccessful. One of these was at the University of Pennsylvania in 1791; the other at Columbia College in 1797. The first permanent law school with degree-granting power was organized at Harvard in 1817. Law schools were soon established in other colleges, in Yale in 1824 and the University of Virginia in 1826. By 1840 there were only about a half-dozen law schools in the United States, and the total number of students in attendance at them was very small in comparison with the number of practitioners in the profession. This shows that the great majority of the lawyers were still being trained in the offices of older attorneys.

In colonial days the greater number of medical students received their training by being associated with practicing physicians. They served a sort of apprenticeship to their instructors while they were reading medicine (see p. 153). It is estimated that there were about three thousand practicing physicians in the country at the end of the Revolutionary War and only about four hundred of these were graduates of medical schools. The others had been trained under this quasi-apprentice system. The first regular medical school was the Medical College of Philadelphia (now a part of the University of Pennsylvania), which was founded in 1765. The second one was established two years later as the medical department of King's College (now Columbia University). By 1820 the number of medical schools had increased to nine. *Medical schools*

By 1860 there had grown up several dental schools and less than a half-dozen schools of pharmacy. The first dental college, the Baltimore College of Dental Surgery, was founded in 1839. The first school of pharmacy, the Philadelphia College of Pharmacy, began its career in 1822.

Washington recommended to Congress the establishment of a military academy, but it was not until July, 1802, while Jefferson was President, that the Military Academy at West Point was opened. Starting out with ten students, this school has been going continuously from the beginning except for one year at the time of the War of 1812. In addition to being the chief reliance in the training of officers in our armies, until 1825 it was the only engineering school in the country. A number of technologists and superintendents of public works have therefore been trained there. Just before the outbreak of the Mexican War (1845) the United States Naval Academy was established at Annapolis, Maryland.

Technical schools

Another technical school was the Rensselaer Polytechnic Institute, founded by Stephen Van Rensselaer at Troy, New York (1825). For the first ten years it offered courses in agriculture as well as engineering and therefore may be classed as the first agricultural college. From 1850 on it gave a regular four-year course in engineering. By 1860 a technical school, or school of applied science, had been established in affiliation with each of the older New England colleges—Harvard (1847), Yale (1847), and Dartmouth (1851).

Training for farmers

The need of scientific education for farmers was not generally felt until after the Civil War and therefore little was done toward the founding of agricultural colleges before 1860. For the first two and a half centuries of our history land was so abundant and cheap in this country that the people were slow in awakening to the importance of scientific farming. There was, however, at times some agitation in favor of providing better training for farmers, and at one time there seem to have been some small private agricultural schools in New York. It was near the end of the period (1857) when the first state agricultural college was established. This was the Michigan State Agricultural College at Lansing. Two years later Maryland established a state agricultural school near Washington.

ADULT EDUCATION

Public meetings

Schools and colleges were not the only agencies employed in education. Opportunities for intellectual development were open to adults as well as to those of school age. Men were brought into association with each other in town meetings, on court days, and at elections and political gatherings. In this way many persons who were denied the privilege of formal schooling received the kind of training which results from the contact of mind with mind.

In many towns there were public libraries affording useful reading material to the general public. In the cities and some of the larger towns there were mechanics' institutes which had night schools for vocational training. More widespread than either of these was the

Lyceums

lyceum, which was "an association for popular instruction by lectures, a library, debates, etc." This movement was inaugurated by Josiah Holbrook, when in 1826 he established the first of these local organizations at Milbury, Massachusetts. The idea became popular and lyceums were formed not only in the larger towns but also in many small villages, especially in New England. Public lectures and scientific demonstrations were promoted by these associations, and in this way the people were brought in touch with the leading intellectual lights of the country. The lecturers who appeared before the lyceums included such prominent men as Ralph Waldo Emerson, Henry Ward Beecher, and Oliver Wendell Holmes.

Probably the most important agency for adult education was the *News-* newspaper. The press had been free in this country since long before *papers*

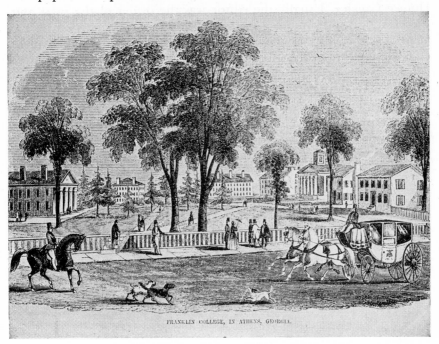

FRANKLIN COLLEGE, IN ATHENS, GEORGIA.

THE UNIVERSITY OF GEORGIA IN ANTE-BELLUM TIMES.

the Revolution and had played an important part in molding and expressing public opinion. It was not until the decade of the 'thirties, however, that the newspapers rose to their full measure of influence. Prior to that time they devoted too much space to political discussions and stale news from abroad and not enough to stories of human interest. The price to subscribers was high and so the circulation was limited.

The newspaper started on a new era when in 1833 the New York *Sun,* under the management of Benjamin H. Day, was offered to the public at one cent a copy. The owner properly anticipated that the financial gain from the advertisements attracted by wide circulation would more than compensate for the loss occasioned by lowering the price of subscription. This reduction in price was also encouraged by improvements in the mechanics of printing such as the application of steam to the Napier press (1835) and the use of the Hoe press (1846). The interest of the reader was aroused by sensational stories, some of which furnished thrill at the cost of truth.

Other papers soon followed the example set by the *Sun.* Outstanding among these were: the New York *Herald,* edited by James Gordon Bennett; and the New York *Tribune,* founded in 1841 by Horace Greeley. Usually the editor was the owner of the press and therefore was untrammeled in the expression of his views on public affairs. The result was that there came from the sanctums of these competent editors able discussions on the problems of the day. These editorials were usually warped by political prejudice and deeply colored with vituperation. The reader therefore was given an excellent opportunity to use his skill in discriminating between cold fact and heated opinion. Thanks to these improvements, newspapers had a wide circulation and exerted a marked influence during the quarter-century preceding the Civil War.

CHAPTER XXXV

Art, Science, and Literature (1783-1860)

ART AND MUSIC

SOON after the Revolution the young republic gave promise of *Post-Revo-* developing a native art. There were several portrait painters of merit, *lutionary* the most noted of whom was Gilbert Stuart (1755-1828). He made a *painters* number of portraits of Washington and of other American statesmen, including most of the early Presidents. Charles Wilson Peale (1741-1827) was a portrait painter who also made canvases of prominent Americans of the same period. He was able to inspire others with artistic appreciation and was influential in founding the Pennsylvania Academy of Fine Arts (1805). John Trumbull (1750-1843) not only made portraits, but also many paintings of dramatic events of the Revolution. All the American artists of this period received their training in Europe and some of them spent a good deal of their time abroad, where they could receive the inspiration and criticism of fellow craftsmen.

In the post-Revolutionary period, architecture was greatly influ- *Post-Revo-* enced by the classical tradition. The Roman dome and Greek *lutionary* portico were often used in the construction of public buildings, *architecture* and tall columns of the Greek type frequently constituted the façades even of private homes, especially in the South. Thomas Jefferson, in planning his own home, the Capitol at Richmond, and the buildings of the University of Virginia, followed closely the classical idea and exerted considerable influence in making it fashionable. The collection of buildings which originally housed this university is said to be "the finest example of classical architecture in America."

The promise as to art which was held out in the beginning was *Backward-* not fulfilled in later years. During the three decades which preceded *ness in art* the Civil War there was no advance either in painting or sculpture, *of the later* but rather a decline. At a time when literature was in full bloom the *period* buds of art showed no sign of swelling. In architecture the classical ideal dominated until about the middle of the century. Then a violent change occurred and there was a revival of the Gothic tradition with overdone ornamentation. Lack of taste and ugliness ran rampant in building construction. In painting, conditions were no better.

There were portrait and landscape painters, to be sure, but none of marked distinction. Nor was any advance made in sculpture. What little originality there was in this field was put in a strait jacket by a slavish adherence to Roman ideas.

Music   During this period, however, the American people were awakening to an appreciation of music. In the larger cities there were musical performances by artists from abroad who were touring the country. The most noted of the foreign singers were Adelina Patti (1843-1919) [1] and Jenny Lind (1820-1887). At a very early age Patti traveled for a year throughout the United States singing Italian productions. In 1850 Jenny Lind, the Swedish singer, made a tour of the country under the direction of P. T. Barnum. Her voice of unusual sweetness made a most favorable impression on the masses as well as the cultured classes.

In the long period between the Revolution and the Civil War there were few musical composers in the United States and none of outstanding reputation. There are, however, a number of hymns and popular songs which date from this era. In this field the Negroes made a real contribution. The songs used by them when at work and the hymns employed in public worship were largely the creations of the black race. While the originals of these hymns and songs may have been borrowed from the whites, they had been made over and appropriated by the Negroes, who had stamped their own sentiments and ideas upon them.

The type of song which idealized the plantation life of the old South was suggested but not created by the Negroes. Many of these songs—such as "The Old Folks at Home," "Old Black Joe," "My Old Kentucky Home," and "Massa's in the Cold, Cold Ground"—were composed by Stephen C. Foster (1826-1864), who was a native of Pennsylvania. He understood the spirit of the Negro remarkably well for one not to the manner born, and in interpreting it showed little sign of his Northern origin.

The   In the interval between the two wars for independence the
theater   theater in this country gradually became more American and less British in character than it had been in the colonial period. Prior to the Revolution nearly all the plays presented in English America were written by British authors and acted by British performers. This was also the case for some time after the Revolution. From the 'thirties on, there were usually stock companies in the larger towns and cities with which professional actors on tour co-operated in giving

---

[1] Adelina Patti was born in Madrid of Italian parents but was brought up in New York City.

their performances. The most popular of these itinerant stars were from England, but there were a few noted American actors, such as Edwin Forrest, Edwin Booth, and Charlotte Cushman. At the end of this period (the late 'fifties) Joseph Jefferson, after a long, hard apprenticeship, was coming into prominence. It was not until after the Civil War, however, that he entered upon his famous career in the role of Rip Van Winkle.

The tragedies and comedies of Shakespeare and other English classics were usually preferred by American audiences, and so not many of the dramas given in this period were written by American authors. There were, however, a few contemporary plays of both English and American authorship which had a very popular appeal.

SCIENCE AND INVENTION

In the field of science and invention a better showing was made than in that of the fine arts. For much of this advance we were indebted to two foreign-born scholars who had come to the United States to live. These were Louis J. R. Agassiz, an emigrant from French Switzerland, and J. J. Audubon, who was of French birth and education. Agassiz was well educated and was for a while a professor at Harvard. By organizing the data he had collected he made important contributions to the sciences of geology and botany. He was also able to inspire his students with an interest in scientific research. Audubon's work was in the study of birds. He spent his time wandering about in the forests and swamps observing and drawing pictures of them. The descriptions and drawings were remarkably accurate and thus constituted a valuable contribution to ornithology. Another noted American scientist was Asa Gray, who did much to promote the science of botany. *Advance in science*

The most important advance in science made during this period was the use of anesthetics in surgery. In 1842 a Georgia physician, Dr. Crawford W. Long, made the discovery that pain could be deadened during an operation by the use of ether. He did not publish his discovery until seven years later, and in the meantime Dr. Horace Welles, a dentist of Hartford, Connecticut, had discovered (1844) that nitrous oxide gas would serve as an anesthetic for the extraction of teeth. Two years later a Boston dentist, Dr. W. T. G. Morton, with the help of a noted chemist, C. T. Jackson, repeated Dr. Long's discovery and proved that ether could be successfully used as an anesthetic. This discovery was given wide publicity by a successful operation with ether in the Massachusetts General Hospital. *The discovery of anesthetics*

During this period there was a greater advance in the field of

Inventions

invention than in that of pure science. Some of the most useful inventions of the century were made by Americans. Prominent in this list are the magnetic telegraph, the reaper, and the sewing machine (see pp. 523, 525, 530). In 1847 the rotary printing press, invented by Richard M. Hoe, came into use. The revolver was invented by Samuel Colt of Connecticut, who first patented it in England and later (1836) in the United States. The process of vulcanizing rubber was discovered (1836) by another son of Connecticut, Charles Goodyear.

A number of other inventions introduced from Europe were improved and adapted to the needs of this country. The English locomotive, for example, was changed before it could be used effectively on American railroads. Much of the machinery employed in the factories there was also adjusted to the factories here. The daguerreotype was developed into the photograph. Matches were imported from Europe. Improvements were made in stoves both for cooking and heating, and by the middle of the century lamps using whale oil were superseding candles. At that time too in some of the cities gas was used for lighting, and houses were heated with furnaces and supplied with plumbing.

LITERATURE

Literature in the period of the Revolution and the Confederation

During the Revolutionary era and the period of the Confederation, there was very little American literature except orations and essays of a political character. According to tradition, James Otis and Patrick Henry attained great heights in their oratory, but the portions of their speeches which have come down to us are too fragmentary to confirm or deny the traditional view. Of the essays written at that time, which were printed as pamphlets or as newspaper articles, the most noted were Tom Paine's *Common Sense,* the *Declaration of Independence,* and the group of articles written by Hamilton, Madison, and Jay, and known as *The Federalist* (see p. 271). Other than political discussions, the one outstanding literary production of this period was Franklin's *Autobiography.* It was begun in 1771, but was not completed until 1789. In simplicity and clearness of style and directness of statement it is a classic in biographical narration. It is the most noted autobiography in American literature. With the exception of this book and political essays and orations, no works of marked literary excellence were produced in the United States from the beginning of the Revolution until near the end of the first decade of the nineteenth century, although efforts at writing poetry and prose fiction had been made with some degree of success.

In 1820 Sydney Smith stated that the United States had done *The Knick erbocker Group of writers* nothing in the fields of art and literature during the thirty or forty years of its separate existence. No one in any quarter of the globe, he said, read an American book or witnessed an American play or looked at an American statue or picture. This indictment was too severe, for at that time there had begun in the new republic a literary movement which was commanding the favorable notice of the English public. This movement was inaugurated by three young men who lived in New York and are therefore generally known as the Knickerbocker Group. These pioneers in American literature were Washington Irving, James Fenimore Cooper, and William Cullen Bryant.

Washington Irving (1783-1859), born and reared in New York City, was the writer who *Irving* first brought his country into literary prominence. For four years (1842-1846) he was United States minister to Spain, and he also traveled widely in other parts of Europe, especially England. Some of his works therefore have an English setting and some are based on observations and study in Spain. He began to write in his early twenties and by 1809 had published his *History of New York,* which is an amusing caricature of the leading actors and events in the Dutch period of

Courtesy of the New-York Historical Society, New York City

WASHINGTON IRVING.

From daguerreotype portrait about 1855.

New York history. The *Sketch Book* (1819) was the work which received the widest acclaim in Europe. Irving was especially happy in his short narratives and is properly recognized as one of the pioneers in the writing of the modern short story. Among his tales "Rip Van Winkle" and "The Legend of Sleepy Hollow" are outstanding. They portray in humorous vein the life of the Hudson Valley in the olden time. In his other writings are included some important historical and biographial works, such as the lives of Columbus, Mahomet, Goldsmith, and Washington. His five-volume life of Washington, written at the end of his career, was his most noted contribution to history and biography. Irving's style, which was modeled after that of Addison and Steele, was often spiced with a kindly humor. He pointed out to Americans the value of European culture and was the first to win for American literature recognition abroad.

Bryant

No outstanding poem had ever been published in English America until 1817, when *The North American Review* brought forward "Thanatopsis." This poem had been written by William Cullen Bryant (1794-1878) when he was only seventeen years of age. It has always been one of the most popular of American lyrics, and has won for Bryant the title of "Father of American Poetry." Next to "Thanatopsis" his most noted poem is "To a Waterfowl." Although he was lacking in warmth and fervor, Bryant was the greatest of the early American poets.[1]

He was also an able writer of prose and contributed articles to *The North American Review*. In 1825 he left Massachusetts, where he had been born and reared, and settled in New York. Soon thereafter he became the editor of the *Evening Post*, a position which he ably filled for more than fifty years. He continued to write poetry, however, and published late in life the *Flood of Years*.

Reproduced from THE PAGEANT OF AMERICA
Copyright Yale University Press

JAMES FENIMORE COOPER.

Cooper

James Fenimore Cooper (1789-1851) was the first of American novelists to gain distinction. Although born in New Jersey, he was reared in central New York, then a frontier region. He was thus able to observe at first hand the conditions of pioneer life described by him in some of his best novels. In 1821 he published the first of his successful works, *The Spy*, America's first historical novel. He also wrote a number of sea stories, of which *The Pilot* was the first and probably the most popular. Prominent in the list of his stories are the *Leather Stocking Tales*, which describe the relations between

---

[1] Among the minor American poets, each of whom was the author of at least one well-known poem, the following may be mentioned: Joseph Hopkinson, who wrote "Hail Columbia"; Francis Scott Key, "The Star-Spangled Banner"; Samuel Woodworth, "The Old Oaken Bucket"; and John Howard Payne, "Home, Sweet Home."

the whites and the Indians in pioneer days. One of the best of these is *The Last of the Mohicans*. In these novels thrilling incidents are detailed with great skill, and the grandeur and beauty of the natural setting of these dramatic events are described with rare vividness. In his characterization of women he is weak, but to the leading trappers and Indian chiefs who figure in these tales he gave a permanent place in the list of the well-known personalities of fiction. Despite a style which is occasionally prolix and sometimes even ungrammatical, Cooper deserves the high rank he holds as one of America's greatest novelists.

In New England during the quarter-century preceding the War of Secession there was an outburst of intellectual activity which is sometimes designated a renaissance. The movement was brought on by a galaxy of brilliant writers in both prose and poetry that gave to the United States its Golden Age of literature. The stern Calvinism of the seventeenth and eighteenth centuries had laid foundations of unhewn rock in the New England character on which was now being built a superstructure of polished marble. The flowering of Puritanism, which had been noted for its sternness in the olden time, was—to change the figure—like the unfolding of beautiful blossoms on prickly cactus stems. *New England in flower; explanation*

This unusual phenomenon was the result of forces both from without and within New England. During and immediately preceding this time, the European universities were exerting their greatest influence on American thinking, and this stimulus from the outside was doubtless a factor in bringing on a new intellectual movement. The rise and progress of liberalism in theology is also given as a cause. During the eighteenth century there had been a gradual breaking away in New England from some of the sterner aspects of Calvinism. Early in the nineteenth century many intellectual leaders in Boston and in Harvard College had revolted against the determinism of the old Puritan faith, which placed a low estimate on human nature. They maintained that there is a divine spark in man and that he has infinite possibilities for development. Out of these theological notions came Unitarianism. The new faith gradually spread among the educated classes throughout eastern Massachusetts and to some extent in other states.

That the acceptance of a liberal theology on the part of the religious leaders of New England was responsible for the literary outburst is a clever explanation, but one for which it is difficult to adduce proof. The idea is that just as a bare-footed boy when he casts aside his shoes in the spring celebrates his pedal freedom by a long and rapid run, so the New England mind when it first threw off its theological trammels signalized the event by speeding up its activity.

Associated with the literary movement was the rise of a philosophy known as Transcendentalism. This doctrine, like Unitarianism, placed emphasis on the perfectibility of man. Truth could not be found by observation and reasoning alone; it transcended the senses and the conclusions based on observation. Hence the term transcendentalism. Every person has a sort of divine intuition which is the true guide of life. A willingness to follow this divine instinct is the essence of wisdom and high character.

In 1836 a small number of New England intellectuals met in Boston and formed a club for the study of philosophy and religion. This was the origin of the Transcendental Club. Later its membership included several writers of note, the most eminent of whom were Emerson and Thoreau.

Emerson

Ralph Waldo Emerson (1803-1882) was born in Boston and educated at Harvard College. Descended from a long line of scholars and clergymen, he had inherited a flair for theological and metaphysical reasoning. For a while he was pastor of a Unitarian church, but later resigned from the ministry because he felt that he could follow his inner light better as a layman than as a minister.

He gave expression to his views through lectures and by the publication of his prose and poetry. The lyceums throughout the country afforded him a good opportunity for the dissemination of his beliefs. One of the most outstanding of his addresses was the Phi Beta Kappa oration, "The American Scholar," delivered at Harvard in 1837. In this address he proclaimed the doctrine of that higher self-reliance which causes one to follow his noblest impulses. In keeping with this doctrine he urged that American writers throw off the trammels that bound them to the old world culture. In so doing he was, as has been said, issuing a declaration of cultural independence.

His finest literary productions were the *Essays,* which contained the ideas previously presented in his lectures. In the list of his essays which have exerted the greatest influence, those on "Self-reliance," "Compensation," and the "Oversoul," hold a high place. In them he upholds with great force his doctrine of the oversoul. Within everyone, he maintained, is a holy impulse or instinct, corresponding to the Inner Light of the Quakers or the Holy Ghost of the early Christians. We are at our best when we are acquiescent to its demands and obedient to its orders. The surrender of our intellects to this deity leads to genius; of our wills, to virtue; and of our emotions, to love.

Thoreau

Closely associated with Emerson was his younger friend, Henry David Thoreau (1817-1862). He was born at Concord, Massachusetts, and after his graduation from Harvard lived for a while in Emerson's home. He was very fond of nature and spent a good deal of time rambling alone in the woods. Simplicity in living was one of his pet ideas. "A man is rich," he said, "in proportion to the number of things he can do without." By holding to a primitive standard of living he would not have to devote effort to procuring unnecessary luxuries and would have more time for reading, meditation, and the study of nature.

Thoreau took the principles of Transcendentalism quite seriously and made a lifelong effort to embody them in his character. He had eccentricities to begin with and the attempt to live up to this philosophy and to guard his intellectual honesty accentuated them. His marked individualism and meticulous conscientiousness caused a nonconformity as to social conventions which was at times almost laughable. His outstanding literary productions were: *A Week on the Concord and Merrimac Rivers* (1849), and *Walden; or Life in the Woods* (1854). In these works he showed himself to be one of the greatest of American prose writers.

High in the top rank of American novelists stands Nathaniel *Hawthorne* Hawthorne (1804-1864). Born at Salem, Massachusetts, he inherited from his Puritan ancestry certain traits that strongly colored his personality. He was graduated from Bowdoin College in 1825 in the class with Longfellow. He was a product, though not an admirer, of Puritanism. He hated Calvinism and repudiated other tenets of his ancestral faith. While the fire of the Puritan religion did not burn within him, the smoke of this fire hovered around his character. There was a strain of gloom in his personality which found expression in his writings. His first important book was a volume of stories published under the title of *Twice Told Tales* (1837).

From time to time he wrote other short stories, but it was as a novelist that he won his highest title to fame. His greatest novel, *The Scarlet Letter,* is probably the best romance that has ever been produced in the United States. In this remarkable work the author X-rays the human soul and shows what influences hinder and what help its proper functioning. The reaction of the two leading characters to a mutual sin is the theme of the book. The woman's offense is made public and she is subjected to disgrace; but in adjusting herself to this dire situation she develops a beauty of soul which would do honor to a saint. The man's guilt is not known and he retains the high esteem of the community; but there is a lifelong inner prodding which destroys his happiness but ultimately effects his spiritual redemption. In *The House of the Seven Gables,* which Hawthorne regarded as his best work, sin is discussed as a hereditary taint, transmitting moral obliquity and trouble from generation to generation.

Longfellow

Of the New England group of poets of this period Henry Wadsworth Longfellow (1807-1882) was easily the most popular. He was born in Portland, Maine, and educated at Bowdoin College. By extensive travel in Europe and wide reading he qualified himself for the continuance of the work which had been so ably begun by Irving, of interpreting the new world to the old. He spent a number of years in the teaching of modern languages, first at Bowdoin (1829-1834) and afterwards at Harvard (1836-1854).

Prominent in the list of his short poems which enjoyed a marked popularity were: "The Psalm of Life," "Hymn to the Night," "The Village Blacksmith," "Excelsior," "The Bridge," and "The Day is Done." Of the longer poems three have been especially well received: *Evangeline* (1847), *Hiawatha* (1855), and *The Courtship of Miles Standish* (1858). The popularity of Longfellow's poems has been greatly enhanced by the use made of them in the schools of the country. Parts or all of many of the short ones have found a place in the school readers and some of the longer ones have for a long time been taught in high schools and colleges.

Courtesy of Craigie House, Cambridge, Mass.

HENRY W. LONGFELLOW.

Age 33. Portrait by G. C. Thompson in 1840.

In his day Longfellow was ranked in America as her greatest poet and he also had a wide vogue in England. The favorable reception accorded his poems was due in part to the moral and religious idealism that breathed from them. That unsophisticated age placed a high estimate on religion and morality and did not taboo literature for preaching these virtues. It was even willing to overlook defects in craftsmanship if a poem was inspired with fine sentiment. The present generation does not place so high a value on the productions of the New England bard. It points out his lack of genius and originality and finds fault with the orthodoxy of his preachments. But even the severest of modern critics express admiration for his beautiful character and winsome personality.

Longfellow's friend and contemporary, John Greenleaf Whittier (1807-1892), also held an honored place in the list of New England poets. He was born at East Haverhill, Massachusetts, of Quaker parentage, and he adhered to the faith of his family during his entire lifetime. Whittier never received much formal schooling, and did not have the benefit of travel abroad, as did many of the other New England writers. He commenced to write verses in early youth and continued almost to his death at the ripe age of eighty-five. The emotional impetus for many of his poems was his crusading zeal in favor of abolition. The sentiment of these poems was so acceptable to his antislavery readers that they were inclined to shut their eyes to shortcomings as to content and mode of expression. Whittier never had the genius that inspires great poetry nor the technique that adorns inspiration with artistry. One of his most popular poems, "Snowbound," which is a beautiful portrayal of a rural scene in winter, did not appear until 1866, when he was mellowing with age and had laid down the weapons with which he had been fighting slavery. *Whittier*

An account of the flowering of New England, however brief, would be incomplete unless it included two other well-known authors, Oliver Wendell Holmes (1809-1894)[1] and James Russell Lowell (1819-1891).[2] Both of them were writers of prose and poetry and both enlivened their literary productions with wit and humor. With each, literature was an avocation rather than the main business of life. Both were born in Cambridge, were educated at Harvard, and were deeply imbued with the New England spirit. Having been reared in the atmosphere of eastern Massachusetts, they were firmly *Holmes and Lowell*

---

[1] Holmes was by profession a physician, and for thirty-five years was professor of anatomy and physiology at Harvard. He found time, however, for writing essays, three novels, and occasional poems. Of the poems the following should be mentioned: "The Last Leaf," "The One-Hoss Shay," and "The Chambered Nautilus." His best-known novel was *Elsie Venner* (1861), a weird tale of a young woman who was handicapped by a very unusual physical affliction. The best of his prose compositions is *The Autocrat of the Breakfast Table* (1858). This is a series of essays in humorous vein—a sort of running commentary on things in general.

[2] Lowell was a man of affairs as well as a writer. At one time or another he was editor of *The Atlantic Monthly,* assistant editor of *The North American Review,* and professor of modern languages at Harvard. He also served as United States minister to Spain for three years and to England for five years. Sandwiched in with his other work was a large amount of literary activity. By travel and residence abroad and by wide reading he acquired a breadth of view which served him in good stead in his literary pursuits. These included the writing of poems and essays and the delivery of brilliant lectures. The most noted of his long poems was the *Biglow Papers,* first published in 1848 as a satire on the Mexican War.

convinced that Boston was the intellectual capital of the Western Hemisphere. Holmes said facetiously, but probably with real belief, that Boston was the Hub of the Universe.[1]

Whitman   Standing in a class all to himself and having no connection with the New England group, was the unconventional poet, Walt Whitman (1819-1892). Born on Long Island, he spent the greater part of his active life in or near New York City. He received only a common school education, but this lack of formal training was compensated for in part by a deep interest in reading. By his practice of making contacts with all classes of people he learned to understand and sympathize with the masses.

In 1855 he published a small volume of poems under the title of *Leaves of Grass*. The collection was reissued and enlarged from time to time until by 1876 it comprised two volumes. More popular than this collection was a volume of war poems entitled *Drum Taps*, published in 1865. After the Civil War he produced some prose works of merit, among them *Democratic Vistas*. Owing to his great sympathy for the common man and his firm faith in the mission and destiny of his country, democracy and patriotism are the two sentiments which are featured in his poems. Although his poetry is not popular with the common people his main service was to interpret the masses to the reading public.

Whitman is still and has always been a center of literary discussion, with ardent admirers praising and harsh critics finding fault with his works. He did not conform to the accepted canons as to rhythm and he treated in an unabashed manner delicate questions which in the opinion of some of his critics are not proper subjects of discussion. His admirers, on the other hand, point out his originality of thought and feeling and acclaim his democracy and sound Americanism. For some time he has been highly rated in England and on the Continent, and in recent years has been accorded by critics in this country high rank among America's greatest poets.

Melville   Contemporary with Whitman was another New Yorker, Herman Melville (1819-1891), who won distinction as a writer of fiction. With a limited formal education, which was supplemented by extensive reading, he entered upon a business career at an early age. Later he spent a number of years at sea, visiting among other places picturesque islands in the South Seas and learning the customs of the natives. To the experiences of these voyages he was indebted for the materials used in his best literary productions. Of several novels dealing with the life of the South Sea islanders, the most popular is

---

[1]For an account of Harriet Beecher Stowe (1811-1896) see pp. 646-47.

Moby Dick, published in 1851. This is his masterpiece and is considered one of the most outstanding prose works of this entire period. It is noted for its clarity of expression, accuracy of description, and correctness in the portraiture of personality.

While New England can rightfully boast of having played the *Poe* leading part in the creation of the Golden Age of American literature, it did not have a complete monopoly of the great literary lights of that day. Certainly one outstanding figure cannot be appropriated by this section, although he was born in Boston and spent a few years

EDGAR ALLAN POE.

there in mature life. This writer was Edgar Allan Poe (1809-1849). He lived in a number of cities (Boston, Richmond, Baltimore, Philadelphia, and New York), but he always considered himself a Southerner. Before he was three years old he was left a waif in Richmond by the death of his parents, who were strolling players. He was adopted by John Allan, a Richmond tobacco merchant of means, whose name Poe added to his own. Except for a short and apparently unprofitable attendance at the military academy at West Point, his formal education ended with one term's residence at the University of Virginia. His health failed at the age of twenty-five and he had to contend with a neurasthenic temperament. His sensitive nature recoiled at the humiliations of poverty and the other blows dealt him by hostile circumstances. To his other misfortunes were added the invalidism and death of his wife, of whom he was devotedly fond. These troubles aggravated a habit of intemperance which had been fastened upon him early in life.

Poe's fame rests mainly on his poems and short stories, although his work as a critic was of a high order. In 1845 there appeared "The Raven," his most noted production. This poem of gloom and despair has a jingle and a rhythm probably not surpassed by any poem in the English language. Other noted poems were: "The Bells," "Israfel," "To Helen," and "Annabel Lee." Poe was a master of the short story. "The Gold Bug" and "The Purloined Letter" are among the best detective stories ever produced in this country, and "The Black Cat" has few, if any, equals as a gruesome tale.

Poe did not preach, as did the moralist-poets of the North. Poetry should give pleasure not impart truth, he contended. Artistry therefore is the one essential in verse. That he met this requirement with unusual success his bitterest critic must admit; but this quality did not win him proper appreciation in his lifetime. His failure to conform to the literary standards set by the New England bards, coupled with his intemperate habits, caused many of his contemporaries to put a low estimate on him and his work. Foreign critics, however, have always held him in high esteem and now regard him as America's greatest poet. In recent years opinion in this country has also grown more favorable to him, and today is strongly inclined toward the European view.

Courtesy of the New-York Historical Society, New York City

WILLIAM GILMORE SIMMS.

Simms

The claim of the South to a share in the literary renaissance does not rest on Poe's writings alone. There were other authors in both prose and poetry who played a part in this literary movement. At the top of this list stands William Gilmore Simms (1806-1870). Born and reared in South Carolina, he was a typical Southerner. He was a voluminous writer, having to his credit a large amount of both poetry and prose fiction. In childhood his imagination was fired by stories of the Revolution and of the Indians related by his grandmother and father. It is not strange therefore that many of his novels have a background in the Revolution and the relations between the Southerners and their Indian neighbors. Outstanding among his Indian stories is *The Yemassee,* considered by some critics as the best American historical novel. *The Partisan* is a story of the Revolution dealing with the guerrilla activity in the South. In his novels Simms takes a position in direct opposition to that of Harriet Beecher Stowe in that he represents slavery as a blessing.[1]

POLITICAL AND HISTORICAL WRITING

The South also made an important contribution to political thought during this period. John Taylor of Virginia (1753-1824) published several political treatises in which he argued ably in favor of agrarian liberalism and the Jeffersonian doctrine of states' rights. John C. Calhoun was one of the most original thinkers in the field of political science that this country has ever produced. (See pp. 438 ff.) The doctrine of slavery was ably upheld by William Harper of South Carolina (1790-1847) and Thomas R. Dew (1802-1846), professor in and president of William and Mary College. *Political writings in the South*

Conversation was a fine art in the Old South. The well-to-do planters had good private libraries and plenty of time for reading. Most representatives of the patrician families therefore were able to talk interestingly on literary, as well as political, questions. *Conversation*

During this period there were in the United States several magazines which promoted the literary movement. The oldest of these was *The North American Review* (established in 1815). Under the editorship of Jared Sparks it attained prominence in the 'twenties, and throughout this period it attracted contributions from the ablest historians and other literary men. *The Atlantic Monthly,* edited by James Russell Lowell, was started under favorable prospects (1857). In its columns appeared many articles written by the outstanding writers of New England. The most noted of the literary magazines of the South was *The Southern Literary Messenger.*[2] *Magazines*

In the writing of history New England easily took the lead over all other sections. There are a number of reasons for this. The libraries in Boston and Cambridge contained the finest collections of *Historians*

---

1 Other noted writers of the Old South that deserve mention were: the poets, Henry Timrod (1829-1867) and Paul Hamilton Hayne (1830-1886); and the novelists, Nathaniel Beverley Tucker (1784-1851) and John Pendleton Kennedy (1795-1870). Kennedy won distinction in both politics and literature. In *Swallow Barn* he idealized the life of the aristocracy of old Virginia as did Thomas Nelson Page at a later time. His best-known novel, however, was *Horse-Shoe Robinson,* a romance of the Revolution. Tucker's *George Balcombe* (1836) was regarded by Edgar Allan Poe as "the best American novel.'

2 Other magazines that deserve mention were: *Harper's New Monthly Magazine* (1850), *Harper's Weekly* (1857), and *Godey's Lady's Book* (1830). The last-named was primarily a fashion magazine, though it also contained stories and articles giving advice on manners and morals. Business magazines were: *De Bow's Review, Hunt's Magazine,* and the *Banker's Magazine. De Bow's Review* had a wider circulation than any other Southern magazine. *Niles' Weekly Register* (1811) was a most useful news publication. It discussed the important issues of the day and reprinted editorials and news stories taken from the daily press throughout the country. For this reason it was an excellent reflector of public opinion and is today a valuable storehouse of historical information. (The date following each title is for the first year of publication.)

the source materials of history that could be found in the United States. It happened too that in this region there were several scholars with a leaning toward historical research and with the means to prosecute that ambition.

Sparks The first in point of time of these historians was Jared Sparks (1789-1866). This many-sided and much-working man was a Unitarian minister, a professor in and president of Harvard, an editor of *The North American Review,* and an untiring searcher after historical documents. He wrote a number of biographies of leading American statesmen. He also published valuable collections of documents. These included the *Diplomatic Correspondence of the American Revolution* and the writings of Washington and Franklin. In preparing these papers for publication he made revisions of the original texts for which he has been criticized by later historians. His reason for taking these liberties was that he considered it disrespectful to the fathers of the country to advertise any slips in spelling or grammar which they may have made, believing, as has been said, that the founders of the republic should never appear in public except in full dress.

Courtesy of the New-York Historical
Society, New York City

GEORGE BANCROFT, Historian.
From portrait about 1868.

Bancroft A more successful historian than Sparks was George Bancroft (1800-1891). He was born and reared in Massachusetts and educated at Harvard. After his graduation he went to Germany and took an extensive course in the University of Göttingen. With this equipment of scholarship, an earnest patriotism, a strong belief in democracy, and an ornate style, he was just the man to write a history of the United States that would appeal to mid-century Americans. His interest in politics, however, led him into public activities which slowed up his historical writing. Among the governmental places held by him were those of Secretary of the Navy, minister to England, and minister to the German Empire.

His great literary production was the *History of the United States* in twelve volumes, the first of which appeared in 1834 and the last in 1882. Although this work is so voluminous it does not carry the narrative beyond 1789. In his last years Bancroft compressed the twelve volumes into six. The first volume was written in a rhetorical and philosophical style, which seems a little too florid to modern readers. The later volmes were, however, less rhetorical and more in keeping with present-day historical standards. Throughout the entire work the author has allowed his democratic beliefs and his ardent patriotism to impart more color to the narrative than is allowed by the canons of objective historical writing.

The greatest of all the historians of this period were a trio of writers—Prescott, Motley, and Parkman—whose names are familiar to students of history. All three of them lived in or near Boston and bore the stamp of Harvard. They came from families in easy financial circumstances and were never hampered by a lack of means in the prosecution of their studies. All were well-educated and traveled and were endowed with the spirit of sound scholarship. Their writings, especially those of Parkman, were based on careful research and were couched in good literary style. The subjects treated were interesting, the selection of facts wise, and the method of expression clear and often ornate. In short, never before or since has the writing of history in this country been more of a fine art than it was under these noted historians.

Courtesy of the New-York Historical Society, New York City

FRANCIS PARKMAN.
After engraving by J. J. Cade.

William Hickling Prescott (1796-1859) was born in Salem, Massachusetts, and came from a well-known *Prescott* family. In early manhood he was the victim of an accident which destroyed the sight of one eye and impaired that of the other. Despite this handicap he was determined to win a place in American historiography comparable to that which Gibbon had attained in England. He wrote unhurriedly in pursuit of this ambition and the result was the production of four great works. These were: the *History of the Reign of Ferdinand and Isabella* (1837); the *History of the Conquest of Mexico* (1843); the *History of the Conquest of Peru* (1847); and the *History of the Reign of Philip II* (only three volumes of which were finished at his death). These works were written in a dignified and interesting style, though later scholarship has questioned the accuracy of some of the statements. These mistakes arose from the use of sources which have since proved less trustworthy than Prescott considered them.

Motley

John Lothrop Motley (1814-1877) was born near Boston and belonged to the Massachusetts aristocracy. After graduating from Harvard he studied at the University of Göttingen. Here he formed a friendship with a young German nobleman who later became famous as Prince Bismarck. Like Bancroft, Motley tried his hand at diplomacy, though not very successfully. During and after the Civil War he was, in succession, American minister at Vienna and London, but was recalled from both places.

JOHN LOTHROP MOTLEY (1814-1877).

His outstanding historical works were *The Rise of the Dutch Republic* (1856) and *The History of the United Netherlands,* which came out between 1860 and 1868. In these works he displayed great skill in describing events and in depicting historical characters, along with a brilliance in style that is rare in historical writing. His hatred of Spanish tyranny gave a spice to his narrative which was very acceptable to the reader but detracted from the objectivity which is so much appreciated in modern writers.

Parkman

The youngest and greatest of this noted trio was another Bostonian, Francis Parkman (1823-1893). His first book, *The Oregon Trail,* was published in 1847 and was the result of travels in the western wilderness. The exposure incident to this journey and the overtaxing of his physical strength caused a loss of health from which he never recovered. His affliction led to a serious impairment of his eyesight, and for fourteen years he was unable to do any writing. After that he could use his eyes for only half an hour without stopping to give them a rest. At times he could write only about six lines a day. He had planned to write a full history of the conflict between France and England for the control of the greater part of North America. Before the break in his health came he had completed only one of this series of works—*The Conspiracy of Pontiac* (1851). The other volumes (there were eleven volumes in the whole series) did not appear until after 1860, and do not belong to this period.

Parkman was highly skilled in both the science and art of historical writing. In his search for documents and the appraisal and use of them he met the high standards of accurate scholarship; and in the arrangement and expression of facts he used a style which was clear, interesting, and colorful.

Courtesy of the New-York Historical Society, New York City

JENNY LIND (1820-1887).
By an unidentified artist.

CHAPTER XXXVI

The Decline and Revival of Religion
(1783=1860)

$\mathcal{D}$URING the years immediately following the Revolution some of the leading religious denominations, like the states and the Federal Union, began to form constitutions which would give them more effective organization. In the seventeen-eighties the Methodists, Catholics, Presbyterians, and Episcopalians were all organized on a national basis. In New England, strange to say, the trend toward nationalism in church government did not appear, although political nationalism was making greater headway there than in many other parts of the country. The old congregational idea of democracy and decentralization in church government was being revived and the Congregationalists refused to effect a national organization. By this refusal they put themselves at a disadvantage in the contest with the denominations which were more efficiently organized.

The Baptists were likewise committed in theory to the doctrine of democracy and decentralization, as their form of church government was also congregational, but a spirit of nationalism soon grew up among them. The necessity of uniting their membership in all sections in the fight for religious freedom (in which they took a leading part) caused the churches of this denomination to develop a machinery of co-operation. Accordingly, associations grew in number and importance, and in 1814 a national convention was organized to direct foreign missions.

THE WESTWARD MOVEMENT IN THE CHURCHES

With the westward movement which followed the Revolution there came to the various denominations a great opportunity for expansion. Of the several religious groups the Presbyterians especially were in a strategic position to take possession of this Promised Land. The Scotch-Irish, who were the backbone of the denomination,

584

were nearest to the new land, since they were located on the frontier all the way from New England to South Carolina. The Presbyterians had shown a zealous loyalty in the Revolution and consequently enjoyed a reputation for true-blue Americanism. Their leaders were capable ministers, most of whom were well educated.

The Presbyterians and Congregationalists outdistanced the other *Baptists* denominations in establishing schools and spreading culture in the West, but they were not so successful in gathering in members as were the Baptists and the Methodists. The numerical strength of the Baptists in the West was due partly to the number of emigrants of this faith from the older states, and partly to their success in winning converts in the new land. In the early part of this period many of the Baptists belonged to the humbler classes, who welcomed an opportunity to better their economic condition by acquiring cheap lands in the West. With such a good reason for going west, they made excellent pioneers. Their system of church government, by which all the members had an equal voice in the administration of church affairs, was in accord with the democratic ideals of the frontier. There was also a strain of mysticism in their religion which made a strong appeal to the emotions.

The Baptist ministers were usually farmers who supported themselves by their own labor, with the aid of small contributions from their members. Religious meetings were held in private homes at first and later in rough log meetinghouses. As a rule the farmer-minister had had little formal education, but, thanks to his manner of living (which forced him to meet the problems of his parishioners), he had firsthand information as to the spiritual needs of his flock. In his preaching there was a frequent repetition of Scripture texts, a practice which enabled his illiterate hearers to gain a knowledge of the Bible. By drawing from his own religious experience he was able to impart to his impromptu talks a freshness of inspiration which was too often lacking in learned discourses.

Each congregation held a business meeting once a month. An important part of this business was the enforcement of a strict discipline upon the membership. Delinquents were admonished and rebuked and if they proved recalcitrant were excluded from the church. The other denominations also held their members up to a rigid standard of conduct. The enforcement of this discipline proved a valuable aid to the authorities in their effort to preserve law and order on the restless frontier.

The Methodists likewise were able to secure a strong foothold in *Methodists* the West. Their system of circuit riders, which had been devised by Wesley for England, was well adapted to a new and sparsely settled country. Under this plan the minister would travel over a large district, visiting the churches as often as possible and preaching daily at such places as would furnish him an audience. The Methodist doctrine, like the Baptist, had a warm emotional content which found a ready response in the hearts of backwoodsmen. With a zeal and energy worthy of a great cause, the circuit riders went along the highways and byways organizing new churches and strengthening those which had already been established. As they moved on from place to place, class leaders and local preachers were left behind to keep the fires burning. These efforts were attended with great success and the church grew rapidly in numbers and influence throughout the western country.

Courtesy of the New-York Historical Society, New York City

St. Joseph's Church and Convent.
Oldest Catholic Church in Ohio.
From Howe's "Historical Collections of Ohio, 1847."

Catholics   In the early years the Catholic Church did not play as prominent a part in the indoctrination of the West as did the Protestant denominations. The few Catholic immigrants from the East were served by itinerant priests, and missionary priests were sent out to the French settlements at Detroit and in the Illinois region. By 1808 there were enough Catholics in the trans-Allegheny region to warrant the establishment of a diocese. Bishop Joseph Flaget was put in control of this diocese, which included Tennessee, Kentucky, and all the Northwest Territory. The Catholic cause in both the West and the East was greatly strengthened by the coming of the Irish and German immigrants, for virtually all the former and a large portion of the latter were Catholics.

THE SECOND AWAKENING

The general deterioration in religion and morality which resulted *Religious* *and moral* *conditions* from the Revolution (see pp. 232 f.) lasted until near the end of the eighteenth century. During this period the American church is *immediately* thought to have reached the lowest point in spirituality and moral *after the* *Revolution* efficacy ever plumbed in its entire history. Far worse than the material losses of the churches occasioned by the war were the deep inroads which unbelief was making on the faith of the people. Contact with the English and French soldiers had brought in skepticism, deism, and downright infidelity. The attitude of "half-belief or unbelief" was becoming fashionable and many people took pride in ridiculing religion. Tom Paine was the apostle and his *Age of Reason* was the *Koran* of the unbelievers—especially those among them who posed as intellectuals.

In the official pronouncement of the Presbyterian General Assembly made in 1798 there appeared the following severe indictment of the moral and religious conditions of that time: "We perceive with pain and fearful apprehension a general dereliction of religious principles and practice among our fellow-citizens, a visible and prevailing impiety and contempt for the laws and institutions of religion, and an abounding infidelity, which in many instances tends to atheism itself. The profligacy and corruption of the public morals have advanced with a progress proportionate to our declension in religion. Profaneness, pride, luxury, injustice, intemperance, lewdness, and every species of debauchery and loose indulgence greatly abound."[1]

Nor were conditions in the West any better than those in the East. *Religious* *and moral* *conditions* The raw frontiersmen were even able to shock the Easterners with *in the West* their profanity, disregard of the Sabbath, brutality in fighting, and general lack of respect for law. Peter Cartwright, the noted Methodist evangelist of the West, spoke in the most disparaging terms of Logan County, Kentucky, which soon afterwards became the center of a great revival. It was, he said, known as "Rogue's Harbor," and was a haven for counterfeiters, horse thieves, highway robbers, and escaped murderers.

Moral integrity and religious earnestness were, however, too deeply imbedded in the American character to be uprooted by adverse circumstances and a dangerous exotic philosophy. So in the last years of the century the American people began to slough off immorality and infidelity and yearn for the garments of salvation. The time was

---

[1] Quoted by W. W. Sweet in *The Story of Religions in America*, 324. Used by permission of Harper and Brothers.

thus ripe for a religious revival, which made a good start about the turn of the century.

To differentiate this revival from that of the first half of the eighteenth century, we speak of it as the Second Awakening. It started in the East, in all probability partly as a result of the evangelical activity of the Methodists in Boston. Strange to say, the Eastern colleges, which had recently been the strongholds of skepticism and deism, now became important centers of the revival. Timothy Dwight, the president of Yale, was able to exert a strong influence on his students in favor of religion, and a revival began there in 1802 which led to the professed conversion of one third of the student body. This fine beginning was followed by other revivals occurring at frequent intervals. Amherst, Williams, and Dartmouth had like experiences.

The revival, however, was not confined to New England and the colleges, but spread throughout the entire country and affected all classes. In the West it took a very serious and colorful form. Here the emotions of the people were stirred to the depths and feeling was expressed in dramatic fashion. At the meetings some of the people would engage in such physical performances as spasmodic jerking, running, dancing, rolling, and barking. That outward exercises of an unusual nature should accompany a deep inner spiritual upheaval is not surprising. Conversion was regarded as the most outstanding experience in the personal history of any individual. It brought to the sinner a sense of pardon for all his sins and qualified him for a life of joy and peace throughout eternity. It was thought that persons who had not been converted, despite the possession of high moral character, were after death dragged by their sins into a state of eternal punishment. When under conviction the sinner was brought down to the hell of despair; with conversion came a sense of relief which exalted him to the heaven of religious ecstasy.

The revival in the West started in Logan County, Kentucky, in 1796, under the preaching of James McGready, an earnest Presbyterian minister. From this center the movement spread under the leadership of Presbyterian, Methodist, and Baptist ministers until the whole Western country had experienced a religious awakening. Meetings were held which lasted day and night for days at a time. These were attended by hundreds and sometimes thousands of earnest listeners. At one gathering the number present was estimated at from 10,000 to 25,000. Families came to these meetings bringing their provisions with them and prepared to stay several days in their tents. Out of this practice developed the camp meeting, the weird picturesqueness of which is described by a competent observer as follows:

"The glare of the blazing camp-fires falling on a dense assemblage ... and reflected back from long ranges of tents upon every side; hundreds of candles and lamps suspended among the trees, together with numerous torches flashing to and fro, throwing an uncertain light upon the tremulous foliage, and giving an appearance of dim and indefinite extent to the depth of the forest; the solemn chanting of hymns swelling and falling on the night wind; the impassioned exhortations; the earnest prayers; the sobs, shrieks, or shouts, bursting from persons under intense agitation of mind; the sudden spasms which seize upon scores, and unexpectedly dashed them to the ground; all conspired to invest the scene with terrific interest, and to work up the feelings to the highest pitch of excitement."[1]

Camp meetings

The Second Awakening was followed by small local revivals which occurred periodically throughout the country. Each year virtually every community had an evangelistic campaign which resulted in winning new recruits for the church and in increasing the spiritual fervor of those who had previously been converted. The camp meeting played an important part both in the Second Awakening and in these follow-up revivals. Bibles, tracts, and other literature distributed by colporteurs also helped to stimulate the spirit of religious fervor.

Local revivals

The spark of evangelism which was kept alive by these means again burst into flame in the "Great Revival of 1858."[2] The panic of 1857 was an important factor in this revival. The suffering incident to hard times was interpreted by many as a sign of God's displeasure with the sin and worldliness of the prosperous years. The panic also caused many people to appreciate the deceitfulness of material wealth and to look to spiritual sources for consolation. Thus as doors to earthly opportunity were closing, windows looking toward heaven were opening. This later religious movement was largely interdenominational in character, and except in rural sections was not characterized by emotional excesses.

The "Great Revival of 1858"

In this era of religious fervor there were a number of preachers who attained eminence as spiritual leaders. Among the Western revivalists Peter Cartwright (1785-1872) was one of the most outstanding. He was an ideal circuit rider and a past master of camp-meeting technique. For a while he was active in Kentucky and

Peter Cartwright

---

1 Sweet, *op. cit.*, 331.
2 In the eighteen-twenties also the country had been swept by a great revival.

Tennessee, but the greater part of his career was spent in Illinois. In his picturesque personality were embodied most of the higher ideals of the frontier, and his role in Western religion was comparable to that of Andrew Jackson's in Western politics. As he was blessed with an iron constitution, he was able to endure the exposure and hardships of circuit riding on the frontier without any impairment of his health. He believed in and practiced "muscular Christianity," and unlucky were the ruffians who by trying to interfere with his meetings invited physical encounters with this pugilistic minister. His courage, self-reliance, sense of humor, and "his readiness with tongue and fist" rendered him the model preacher to the frontiersmen.

Courtesy of the New-York Historical Society, New York City

PETER CARTWRIGHT.
After engraving by A. H. Ritchie.

Effects of the waves of evangelism

The imprint made on the American character by the successive waves of evangelism was both good and bad, but, according to the best-informed opinion, the good far outweighed the evil. One practical result was a decided increase in church membership. A more intangible, but none the less important, result of the revivals was the deepening of the spiritual life of professed Christians. They imparted to religion a warmth and zeal in which it had stood greatly in need. New churches were erected, and the pulpit attracted the energies of able and consecrated men who served the cause of religion with a zeal, courage, and self-devotion in keeping with their high calling.

The series of evangelistic movements brought on a revival of orthodoxy as well as religion, and a belief at variance with the fundamentals of Christianity was no longer popular. Reverence for the Bible went almost to the verge of bibliolatry. The Scriptures were regarded as having been verbally inspired and quotations from them were cited as unanswerable arguments in all sorts of controversies. In the sermons, prayers, and hymns of church worship, strong emphasis was placed on otherworldliness. According to the church leaders, the great aim of religion was not to improve social conditions on earth but to prepare the individual for a career of happiness and usefulness in the world to come.

Another effect of the revivals was an improvement in the morals of the people. One observer, who seemed inclined to give a judicial appraisal of the movement, spoke of it (1803) as follows: " . . . some neighborhoods, noted for their vicious and profligate manners are now as much noted for their piety and good order. Drunkards, profane swearers, liars, quarrelsome persons, etc., are remarkably reformed."[1]

One cost of the revival was the restraint which a renewed interest in religion imposed upon certain types of intellectual freedom. With the triumphant return of orthodoxy, church leaders became hostile to any views which were in conflict with their conception of religion. Scientific theory and liberal philosophy, therefore, did not now enjoy such freedom of expression as they had in the post-Revolutionary decade.

THE RISE OF NEW DENOMINATIONS

Another result of the Second Awakening was the emergence of church schisms in the West. When people take their religion seriously (as they did during and after the revival) they attach significance to theological divergences which to the indifferent seem unimportant. Among the Western Presbyterians there arose disagreements which quickly widened into two permanent breaches. Both of these schisms started in Kentucky, each in a section where the revival had been especially successful. In the Cumberland region a number of Presbyterians, who were warmly evangelistic and only slightly Calvinistic, withdrew from the regular organization and formed the Cumberland Presbyterian Church. *Cumberland Presbyterians*

About the same time Barton W. Stone, a prominent leader in the revival, caused another breach in the Presbyterian Church. He and his followers rejected all forms of church polity which they did not believe to be authorized by the Scriptures, and invited all Christians to unite on a nondenominational basis under the name of "The Christian Church." This "New Light" movement, as it was called, spread rapidly in Kentucky and Ohio. Immersion was accepted as the only form of baptism, and this made the New Lights acceptable to the Baptists, many of whom left their own denomination to join in the new movement. *The Christian Church*

Parallelling the effort of Stone and his associates for church unity

---

[1] Sweet, *op. cit.*, 333.

was a similar movement which was started in western Pennsylvania and western Virginia. It was led by two Presbyterian ministers, Thomas Campbell and his son, Alexander. The Campbells were not in accord with their fellow Presbyterians in that they were opposed to all church practices not accepted by them as upheld by the Bible, and were in favor of the union of all Christians on this basis. These ideas led to a permanent breach with the Presbyterians, and the Campbells organized a church of their own (1811). Alexander Campbell was an able speaker and under his leadership the new movement made rapid progress in the West. For a while the reformers were affiliated with the Baptists, but by 1826 they had begun to separate from the Baptist churches and form independent congregations. The members of these new congregations called themselves "Disciples of Christ."

It was soon observed that the "Christians," followers of Stone, had aims similar to those of the "Disciples," and the two groups were able to coalesce and form a new denomination. The congregational form of church government was adopted and for some time there was no central authority for the whole denomination. The members in some places were called "Disciples" and in others, "Christians." The latter term predominated and has become the permanent name of the denomination. In this way a movement which had originated as a protest against sectarianism and in favor of Christian unity had led to schism in two old denominations and the formation of a new one.

The Methodists also had to contend with schism. The alleged autocracy of Bishop Asbury in the government of the denomination aroused dissatisfaction and led to a long period of agitation in favor of a larger participation of laymen in church affairs. The "Reformers," as the dissatisfied members termed themselves, asked that presiding elders be elected and that laymen be admitted as delegates to conferences. Baltimore was the center of the agitation. The refusal of these demands by the General Conference in 1828 caused the malcontents to withdraw and organize themselves into the Methodist Protestant Church (1830).

While the West proved a more important recruiting ground for new sects than the East, the latter section was not entirely free from church schism. A serious breach in the Congregational Church grew out of a controversy over a belief in the Trinity. Ever since the Great Awakening of the first half of the eighteenth century there had been a group of ministers and laymen in New England who did not accept the Calvinistic doctrines of Congregationalism. They were generally opposed to the revival and advocated a liberal theology.

They taught that the individual enjoyed freedom of will and could and must perform a part in his own salvation. Emphasis was placed on the fatherhood of God, the brotherhood of man, and man's capability for development into grandeur of character. These liberals finally repudiated the doctrine of the Trinity and the deity of Christ and became Unitarians.

The first Unitarian church in America was formed (in 1786) from the Episcopal church of King's Chapel in Boston. There was also a strong trend away from Trinitarianism in the Congregational churches in Boston and a large majority of them had become Unitarian in belief before the end of the first decade of the nineteenth century. The liberals, however, still wore the Congregational label and they and the conservatives did not come to the parting of the ways until 1819. In that year William Ellery Channing in a famous sermon made a severe attack on orthodoxy and precipitated a permanent break between the Unitarians and the Trinitarians in the Congregational fold. The former now separated from the latter and in 1825 organized the American Unitarian Association.

The Unitarian denomination developed considerable strength in Boston and eastern Massachusetts and won a small following among the educated classes in other parts of New England, but it never made a strong appeal to the masses, and it never gained a firm foothold in other sections of the country.

When religion is charged with a high emotional voltage the increase in fervor is in some instances purchased at the cost of intellectual poise. As the evangelistic movement swept in successive waves over the country it left a doctrinal sediment in which religious irregularities might easily sprout. Accordingly, there arose a number of religious movements which were considered vagaries by the orthodox. Prominent in the list of unconventional denominations which grew out of evangelical soil was Mormonism. The founder of this new church was Joseph Smith, a young man of western New York, who had imbibed from superstitious parents a firm belief in visions. In a trance at the age of eighteen, so he maintained, he was directed by an angel to locate a buried book made up of golden plates or pages. By the aid of two miraculous lenses found with the plates he was able to read them. The book purports to be an account of America going back as far as the Tower of Babel, with emphasis on the ups and downs of God's chosen people in this hemisphere. This golden book after having been translated by Smith with the aid of four helpers was published as the Book of Mormon and became the sacred book of the Mormons.

Smith was soon able to win adherents to the new faith, and a

Mormonism

Joseph Smith and the Book of Mormon

Organization
and early
history of
the church
church was organized in Seneca County, New York (1830). In the same year began the missionary activity which has done so much to promote the Mormon cause. But Smith fell into disfavor with his neighbors, and troubles arose which led to a move to Kirtland, Ohio, and then to Far West, Missouri. At the latter place the strife between the Mormons and the older inhabitants became serious and the former then withdrew from Missouri and settled at Nauvoo, Illinois.

The new community at Nauvoo started off promisingly and in a few years was in a flourishing condition. Trouble soon came, however, for in 1843 Smith professed to have received a new revelation authorizing polygamy. Opposition to the Mormons now became intense and civil strife again arose between them and the anti-Mormons. Smith and his brother were put in jail at Carthage on the charge of treason. With the connivance of the authorities a mob attacked the jail and shot the Smith brothers (1844).

Brigham
Young as
leader of the
Mormons
Two years later, under the able leadership of Brigham Young, the Mormons left Nauvoo and started on their long trek to a new and permanent home. Before the end of 1848 there were five thousand of the faithful in Utah ready to change the arid valley of the Great Salt Lake into a land of milk and honey. Irrigation projects were planned and carried out and soon the desert flowered into beauty and ripened into fruitfulness. Missionaries were sent out to gather in recruits, many of whom came from foreign lands. An emigration fund was established to aid new converts in their long journey to the Promised Land.

THE MISSIONARY MOVEMENT

Home
missions
The religious fervor generated by the great revival and sustained by subsequent evangelistic efforts aroused a feeling of humanitarianism which found expression in missionary activity at home and abroad and in other efforts at human betterment. In the period that overlapped the eighteenth and nineteenth centuries a number of societies for promoting home missions were formed by several denominations in the Middle and New England states. These organizations were generally local and interdenominational in character. Later, societies for home missions were organized on a denominational basis in all the leading denominations.

Some of these missionaries worked faithfully in sparsely settled communities preaching to the frontiersmen, while others were putting forth their best efforts to convert the Indians. In the 'thirties the Methodists were represented by Jason Lee in far-away Oregon, where he and his associates were earnestly trying to bring the Indians to a knowledge of Christ. The Presbyterians also were active in the same region in that decade. Marcus Whitman, whom they had sent as a medical missionary to work with the Indians (1836), is noted not only for his sacrificial work among the natives but also for an heroic journey on horseback from Oregon to Boston and Washington (1842).[1] The Catholics from Canada were also active as missionaries in Oregon, and this rivalry whetted the desire of the American Protestant missionaries for the acquisition of the region by their own country.

Foreign missions

Early in the nineteenth century there began to grow up among American Protestants the feeling that the gospel should be taken to the heathen of foreign lands. This conviction caused them to organize societies for the promotion of foreign missions. The movement had a dramatic beginning when five consecrated and zealous young men were ordained at Salem, Massachusetts, in 1812, and sent out to preach to the people of India. The organization which sponsored this first mission was under the auspices of the Congregational and Presbyterian churches. Other denominations followed suit and in time all the larger ones had national missionary societies. Foreign missions were established in China, Japan, and other distant regions. In Hawaii the missionaries had marked success in Christianizing and civilizing the natives.

The Sunday School

The Sunday School was another agency for imparting religious instruction during this period. The first Sunday School in this country was organized by the Methodist bishop, Francis Asbury, in Hanover County, Virginia, in 1786. The example set by the Methodists was followed by other denominations and the movement soon became widespread.

The Young Men's Christian Association

Later in this period (1851) the Young Men's Christian Association was brought to the United States. By 1865 it had made considerable headway in the larger cities.

THE CHURCH AND SLAVERY

During the first half-century after the Declaration of Independence official pronouncements against slavery were made by religious groups in the South, as well as in the North, especially among the

---

1 While the long trip was probably made primarily in the interest of his mission, Whitman is thought to have interviewed President Tyler and Secretary Webster, who received him cordially and respectfully. Tradition relates that this rugged pioneer, dressed in leather breeches and worn and torn furs, and whose hands had been frozen on his three-thousand-mile ride, made a deep impression on the President and his Secretary of State when he pointed out to them the great value of this far-off region. On his return to his mission he accompanied a large group of emigrants to Oregon. See O. P. Chitwood, *John Tyler,* 335.

*Earlier and
later atti-
tude of
Southern
churches
toward
slavery*
Methodists, Baptists, and Presbyterians. This agreement on the slavery question between the Northern and Southern branches of these churches was not seriously disturbed until about 1830, when the second and more violent period of slavery agitation began. The advocacy of emancipation was now frowned upon by public senti- ment in Dixie, and the attacks on slavery gradually grew fiercer in the North. Under such conditions it was only natural that the slavery dispute should invade the churches.

The denominations which had the largest membership were the Methodists and the Baptists. As the controversy over slavery grew in intensity and bitterness the Southern Baptists and Southern Methodists took an increasingly firm stand in favor of slavery while their brethren in the North became more and more outspoken in favor of abolition. Schism was the inevitable outcome of this feeling.

*Division
of the
Baptist
denomi-
nation*
The breach in both denominations came in the middle 'forties. In October, 1844, the board that had charge of Baptist home missions refused to appoint James E. Reeves as a missionary in the home field because he was a slaveowner. Later in the same year the board for foreign missions declared that it would not send out any slaveholder as a foreign missionary unless he liberated his slaves. Thereupon the Southern Baptists severed their relation with their Northern asso- ciates and organized (1845) the Southern Baptist Convention. The division proved to be permanent, though now it is along geographi- cal lines and the maintenance of separate organizations is for admin- istrative convenience and does not indicate a disagreement on theo- logical and moral questions.

*The
Methodist
Church
divides*
In the meantime the Methodist General Conference in a meeting in New York in 1844 had considered the case of Bishop James O. Andrew of Georgia, who had by marriage become the owner of a few slaves. This was the first time that a Methodist bishop had been handicapped by such an encumbrance. After a debate of eleven days a resolution was passed asking Bishop Andrew to abstain from his episcopal activities until he had disposed of his slaves. The Southern annual conferences now seceded from the national organization and next year (1845) organized at Louisville, Kentucky, the Methodist Episcopal Church South, creating a breach which remained open for nearly a century (until 1939).

*Effect of
slavery on
the unity
of the Pres-
byterian
Church*
In 1837-38 the regular Presbyterians divided into two groups, the New School and Old School Presbyterians. The New School group was strongly antislavery in sentiment and its General Assembly finally (1857) adopted a resolution vigorously condemning slavery. This resulted in the withdrawal of a number of Southern members who organized the United Synod of the South. The Old School

Presbyterians refused to take any official stand against slavery and thus escaped division until after the outbreak of the War.

After their division both the Methodists and the Baptists increased in membership and in missionary activity, but the numerical gain was purchased at the cost of weakening the cause of political union. Hitherto the national unity of these large denominations had been an important tie in binding North and South together. The snapping of this tie subjected the political bond to additional strain and thereby aggravated the trend toward disunion.

Effect of the division of the churches

CAMP MEETING IN A WESTERN FOREST.

From Woestemeyer & Gambrill's "The Western Movement."
D. Appleton-Century Company, Inc.

CHAPTER XXXVII

American Life at Mid=Century (1840=1860)

COUNTRY LIFE

Small farmers

DURING the decades of the 'forties and 'fifties a large majority of the American people followed agriculture as an occupation and therefore lived on isolated farms or in small villages. The greater portion of the land in all sections was held by small landowners, who cultivated it with the aid of their sons and often one or more hired men. The wives and daughters also sometimes lent a helping hand with the outdoor work. Usually, however, the latter were kept busy with their own allotted tasks. These included not only cooking and housekeeping, but also such miscellaneous duties as milking and churning, drying fruit, poultry raising, sewing, and spinning and weaving. Neighborhood co-operation was still practiced in the performance of such tasks as house-raising, grain threshing, logrolling, and other similar kinds of work which called for the joint labor of a number of men. These co-operative activities gave opportunity for neighborhood gatherings at which work and social intercourse were pleasantly combined. On these occasions there was an abundance of food which had been carefully prepared by the solicitous housewives and their assistants and which was consumed with keen relish by the hungry workers. These working parties tended to promote a wholesome community spirit and good feeling among neighbors.

The yeoman farmers were the backbone of American society. They had much in common whether they lived in the North or the South. Their manners and customs and ethical and religious ideals were quite similar in all sections. They prized highly the homely virtues of courage, honesty, industry, and frugality, and had a great respect for religion.

The yeomanry in the North

Owing to diversities as to soil, labor systems, and social conditions, the economic outlook was different in different sections of the country. In New England the hillsides had worn thin and the farmers were making a losing fight in competition with the grain growers of the West. In more favored regions of the North and in the Northwest the small farmer enjoyed the great advantage of a fertile soil; consequently, he generally lived in a comfortable house, had good barns

598

for his stock, and was well supplied with necessary food and clothing. Except for a few owners of large landed estates, there were no great inequalities of wealth among the farmers in these sections.

Less fortunate than the yeoman of the Northwest was the small farmer of the South. There were, however, some points in favor of the latter. The long summers were an advantage in crop production, and land was so cheap that any industrious worker could hope to become a landowner. But the lands which the yeomen held were frequently not of the best grade and the crop yield on them was not large. Furthermore, in disposing of their small surpluses they had to accept prices which were fixed by large-scale production with slave labor. Then, too, many of them could not give their children the opportunities for elementary education which were enjoyed by the masses in the North and Northwest, for the South had lagged behind these sections in public education. *The yeomanry in the South*

Despite these drawbacks the yeomanry owned the greater portion of the farms in the South. A small proportion of the families in this group had a few slaves, but most of them were nonslaveholders. Many young men of this class had to begin as tenants. Those who were energetic and thrifty were able to purchase land in a few years, but some remained tenants all their lives, sometimes paying a money rent for their land and sometimes giving a part of the crop. However, the proportion of sharecroppers to the whole number of farmers was small.

The small farmer of the South was, generally speaking, not in as good financial circumstances as his brother of the North. Furthermore, his long lanky appearance, his carelessness as to dress, and his untidiness in the use of tobacco caused him to appear at a disadvantage when in the presence of strangers. In descriptions of the South written by hurried and sometimes biased travelers he therefore plays an unattractive role. These observers were quick to note his somewhat ungainly exterior but were not able to appreciate his good qualities—his industry, honesty, love of freedom, courage, reverence for religion, respect for womanhood, and loyalty to friends. It was these deeper inner traits which later enabled him to make a successful adjustment to a new social order brought in by war and reconstruction.

In all countries and in every age there is a stratum of people who owing to physical or mental handicaps and a lack of economic opportunity fall into poverty or petty criminality or both. There was such a class in every region of the United States. In the Northwest, because of the abundance of fertile land, it was small, although it was recruited to some extent by pauper immigrants from abroad. In the *The "poor whites"*

South it was larger than in other sections, partly on account of the excess of poor land and partly on account of the prevalence of hookworm and malaria in certain localities. With their physical and mental vigor sapped by disease and malnutrition, the poor whites could not put forth the exertion needed to earn a comfortable living. These unfortunates were termed by the Negroes "poor white trash," and many of them merited the designation.

The mountain whites

Another group of small farmers in the South consisted of the mountain whites, who occupied the Appalachian region from Maryland to northern Alabama. Since they were not in easy reach of transportation routes, they were shut off from the main stream of progress. As a result of this isolation, living conditions among them were very much as they had been in pioneer days, the manners and customs of the colonial age having been preserved with slight change. Dwelling in a log cabin, the hardy mountaineer cultivated a small acreage in the elevated valleys, or "coves," as they were called, and managed to grow enough grain to supply his family and the few razor-back hogs and other livestock that he kept. Seldom did he have the assistance of a slave, for there were very few Negroes in the entire region. The furnishings of his house were scant and most of the utensils were of wood. An attractive feature of the humble dwelling was a large fireplace over which were suspended pothooks and a crane used in the family cooking.

Large landholders of the South

The group in the South which has attracted the most attention of the writers of both fiction and history is that of the wealthy landed proprietors. Everywhere in the Southland there were big estates manned with numerous slaves. In each case the owner lived in a mansion, supplied with costly furnishings and surrounded by beautiful lawns and gardens. The house was usually located in a grove on a lofty eminence and was approached through an avenue lined with trees. Sometimes it overlooked a broad and lazy river which coursed along at the foot of the hill. Some of these mansions were ancestral homes which had been built in the early eighteenth century; most of them, however, were of later construction. In some cases broad columned porticos, wide halls, and beautiful wainscoting were characteristic architectural features.

The mansion house was usually the center of a group of buildings which gave the plantation the appearance of a village.[1] The surrounding buildings consisted of a kitchen, smokehouse, laundry, storerooms, office, granaries, barns, poultry houses, schoolhouse, blacksmith shop, weaving room, and, at some distance away hidden behind a

---

[1]In the lower South the mansion house was often located, not on the plantation, but in a near-by town or village.

clump of trees, a group of Negro cabins, each with its small yard and larger vegetable garden.

The owners of these big estates, although constituting a very small minority of the people, dominated to a great extent the economic, political, and social life of the South. Seldom, if ever, in a political democracy had a social aristocracy enjoyed such an unchallenged ascendency. This privileged class used its opportunity in developing a style of living which in some of its aspects was objectionable and in others picturesque and beautiful. The traditions which grew out of it discredited manual labor in the eyes of the aristocracy; condoned dueling; and showed too great a tolerance of excessive social drinking. On the other hand, they tended to inspire the men with courage, self-reliance, and a chivalric attitude toward womanhood.

The mansions were the scene of a most delightful social life. Long and numerous visits were interchanged between the patrician families on holidays and at other times. The social intercourse of these occasions was informal and natural and generally most enjoyable. Feasting, drinking (on the part of the men), cardplaying, dancing, and the fine art of conversation were indulged in. Every planter prided himself on his well-stocked wine cellar, which was generally supplied with hard liquor as well as champagne and madeira. The choicest foods were well prepared and served in lavish abundance. *Life on the big plantation*

The following account of a supper dance given (in 1855) at the home of a planter in Tidewater Virginia is typical of the period: ". . . Wednesday night we all attended the party at Dr. Wilcox's. . . . We had a most merry time of it. . . . We danced incessantly till one o'clock, when the first supper was announced. . . . The table was beautiful. . . . There were three large pyramids of iced cake surmounted by three corresponding designs. . . . The mottoes and confectionery were of the most expensive kind—candied fruits, and liqueur drops of every description, with the fruits, ices, etc. etc. in abundance. This over we danced again until three, when the second supper was announced. . . . Here was profusion indeed. Such turkeys and such saddles of mutton! the fat on the former *three inches* thick—then there were venison, wild ducks, etc. etc. Champagne flowed unceasingly—of the nicest kind. . . . With all the jollification not a gentleman showed evidence of having drunk too much except one . . ., who perhaps looked a little funny. The windows of the dancing rooms (four in number) shewed piles upon piles of negro heads. . . ."[1]

Life on the big plantation was conducive to the rearing of a high

---

[1] See O. P. Chitwood, *John Tyler,* 422.

type of womanhood. The patrician women of the Old South, both maids and matrons, were noted for their charm. Young girls were shielded from temptation and kept in ignorance, as far as possible, of the sordid and seamy side of life. Their relationships with young men were regulated by the strictest Victorian conventions. Despite these restrictions, however, the young women managed to exhibit marked individuality, a winsome vivacity, and at times an imperiousness which were very attractive to admiring beaux.

After marriage the aristocratic dame withdrew from society and assumed the responsibilities of mistress of the plantation. She had to supervise not only the housekeeping and cooking, but the making of clothes for the slaves, the nursing of the sick, and the caring for the needs of all the inmates of the mansion house and the dwellers on the plantation. Every large estate was at that time not only a farming community but to some extent an industrial plant as well. The lady in the "big house" could make ends meet in the farm economy only when she was an efficient entrepreneur. The activities of the matron on a large plantation afforded her a dignified employment that lifted her above the frivolities which are so often the curse of the idle rich. The interchange of hospitalities and the practice of the amenities occasioned by it gave her a charm of manner which would be an ornament to the social life of any age.

CITY LIFE

At mid-century there were throughout the North landed estates comparable in size to those of the South; but in the former section the wealthy class owed its affluence to manufacturing, banking, and commerce rather than to agriculture. This favored group therefore lived mostly in the cities and large towns. The patricians in the North and South had much in common as to manners and customs, styles of dress, and social ideals. The luxury of the rich Southern planter was more than matched by that of the Northern merchant prince. The main difference between the Northern and the Southern aristocracy was that the former rested largely on an urban and the latter on a rural economy.

The development of American industry and the marked improvement in transportation facilities were attended by the rapid growth of the older cities and the rise of new ones. In 1790 the census reports listed only two cities (Philadelphia and New York) as having a population of twenty thousand and more. By 1800 the number had increased to five. They were, in order of size, Philadelphia, New York, Baltimore, Boston, and Charleston. It was twenty years before another, New Orleans, was added to the list. The number increased rapidly during the next three decades, having climbed up to eight by 1830, to sixteen by 1840, to thirty by 1850, and to forty-three by 1860. If five thousand be taken as the minimum of population which

The game between the Squire and the Postmaster. Taken from A. B. Frost's A BOOK OF DRAWINGS, (P. F. Collier and Son Co., 1904). Reproduced in THE PAGEANT OF AMERICA, vol III, p. 133, with permission of Dodge Publishing Co.

entitles a town to rank as a city, the number of cities in the entire country had by 1860 reached the approximate total of three hundred. There had also been a considerable growth in the size as well as in the number of cities, and the largest ones—those of one hundred thousand or more—had by this time increased to nine in number. These larger cities (arranged in the order of size) were: New York, Philadelphia, Brooklyn, Baltimore, St. Louis, Boston, New Orleans, Cincinnati, and Chicago. The states having the largest number of cities were New York and Massachusetts, with seventy-one and forty-eight, respectively. In Arkansas, Florida, and Oregon there were no cities that could claim a population of five thousand. There were only twenty-eight cities within the area which was soon to be organized into the Southern Confederacy.

At the opening of the century Philadelphia, with a population of more than sixty-nine thousand, was the largest city, but by the *New York* end of the first decade New York had won first place, a rank which it has held ever since.[1] With a population (1840) of more than three hundred thousand, New York had become the great commercial and financial center of the country. Some of its citizens lived in small gaily-painted cottages while others dwelt in five-story brick edifices. Broadway was the great avenue of traffic and the promenade of fashion. Along this poorly-paved street, dimly lighted by gas, there passed a continuous stream of vehicular traffic. The endless procession was made up of omnibuses, hackney coaches, handcarts, phaetons, and every other sort of conveyance. Conspicuous in the line of pedestrians along the sidewalks were the women dressed in costly furs or in bright-colored silks and satins. Until 1842, when the Croton Water began to be piped into the city, much of the water supply was obtained by use of hand pumps scattered throughout the city.

Philadelphia   Next to New York in size and importance came Philadelphia, a city still noted for its Quakerlike calm and quiet. According to the census of 1840 its population was around 220,000 and by 1850 about 340,000. Its clean and well-paved streets were straight and monotonously regular. Along them behind beautiful rows of trees could be seen pretentious mansions, with white doors and marble steps. With its fine public squares and well-stocked shops the city presented an attractive appearance.

Baltimore   Baltimore and Boston, third and fourth respectively in size, were
and Boston   also growing rapidly in importance and were attracting favorable comment from foreign observers.

New Orleans was the largest city in the South and the most pic-

---

[1] The following is a list of the cities having a population of twenty thousand and above with the population of each as given by the census of 1850:

City	Population	City	Population
New York	515,547	Rochester	36,503
Philadelphia	340,045	Lowell	33,383
Baltimore	169,054	San Francisco	34,776
Boston	136,881	(according to state census of 1852)	
New Orleans	116,375	Chicago	29,963
Cincinnati	115,436	Troy	28,785
Brooklyn	96,838	Richmond	27,570
St. Louis	77,860	Syracuse	22,271
Albany	50,763	Allegheny City	21,261
Pittsburgh	46,601	Detroit	21,019
Louisville	43,194	Portland, Me.	20,815
Charleston	42,985	Mobile	20,515
Buffalo	42,261	New Haven	20,345
Providence	41,513	Salem, Mass.	20,264
Washington	40,001	Milwaukee	20,061
Newark	38,894		

Of these thirty cities, only four (New Orleans, Charleston, Richmond, and Mobile) were in the states which afterwards formed the Southern Confederacy. The aggregate population of these four cities was 307,445; the total population of the thirty was 2,271,774.

turesque one in the country. As a protection against the river there *New Orleans* had been constructed a broad levee which rose eight feet above the level of the city and which was approached by a gradual inclined plane. Four miles of this levee were used as a wharf. On it were piled products which had been floated down from the upcountry. Some of these products were to be distributed among the planters of the neighboring regions and some were to be sent abroad on the numerous ships which stood ready in the deep river channel. New Orleans was the most cosmopolitan of all our cities. A part of it was like any other large American city. In one quarter visitors were reminded of Paris by the language, mode of life, amusements, shops, and restaurants of the French and Creole population. There was a third portion which was reminiscent of Cadiz. Here dirty and grass-grown streets and dilapidated wharves and houses proclaimed poverty and distress.

Charleston was the second city in the region south of the Potomac *Charleston* River, but it was lagging behind its rivals in growth. It was still, however, the center of a charming social life and the guardian of patrician traditions.

Cincinnati was the metropolis of the West and the leading pork- *Cincinnati* packing center in the United States. Its pork industry and other businesses afforded employment for ten thousand workers. Foreign observers were impressed with the attractiveness of the city and commented favorably on its broad, well-paved streets, beautifully adorned with shade trees, and its private residences remarkable for their elegance and neatness. It was a center of culture as well as prosperity. It could boast of two fine public libraries, six daily newspapers, and several colleges, including a medical college, a law school, and a theological seminary.

Chicago was exhibiting youthful vigor but was not giving promise *Chicago* of its future greatness. It had been organized into a city in 1839 and by 1840 had a population of more than five thousand. There were board sidewalks, but the streets were unpaved. Therefore, the mud in the streets in rainy weather was so deep that the young men had to wear high boots when making calls. In the summer many of the streets were green with a luxuriant growth of prairie grass. After 1842 the city had a water system, by which water was conveyed to the more thickly settled portions of the town through hollow logs. By 1850 the population had increased to nearly thirty thousand.

The most phenomenal growth of all the cities was that made by *San Francisco* San Francisco. The waving of the magic wand of gold had suddenly transformed it from a little town of slightly over eight hundred inhabitants (in 1848) to a city of more than thirty-four thousand (34,776) by 1852.

Hotel accommodations

In the 'forties and 'fifties hotel accommodations were as a rule not so good in any of the cities as would be expected from the general appearance of these cities. Guests were called out of bed at seven-thirty in the morning and summoned to breakfast by a gong at eight. At the long breakfast table were seated a score of persons who ate hurriedly and ravenously.

Living conditions

The cities were not properly drained, and in none of them was there a proper disposal of refuse. Rubbish was thrown into the gutters, and garbage was allowed to accumulate in alleys and back yards. In some places the air was polluted by vile odors emanating from slaughterhouses and malodorous manufacturing plants. Dogs were allowed the freedom of the streets, and under the wooden sidewalks lived innumerable rats. The hogs that roamed at will in virtually all the cities served as scavengers, but often were a nuisance in that they impeded traffic and dug unsightly holes in the streets for wallowing places. As late as 1853 there were said to be more hogs than people in the town of Urbana, Illinois, now the seat of a great state university.

In the cities housing conditions were generally bad, almost beyond belief. Many of the poor "lived in damp, dark, ill-ventilated, vermin-infested, underground rooms." By 1850 a number of cities had been furnished with community water systems, but there was no guaranty that the water supplied by them would be pure. For example, the water which was piped into Chicago from Lake Michigan was frequently contaminated by the drainage from the manure piles on the lake shore. Nowhere was the public protected against the sale of milk from diseased cows, and it was charged that in New York eight thousand children annually lost their lives as a result of infection from milk.

Conveniences in the home

In the mid-century decades families of means were beginning to enjoy many of the conveniences of the machine age. In some homes there were hot and cold running water, bathrooms, cookstoves, and occasionally a hot-air furnace. German and Irish immigration had brought in a good supply of servants, who were relieving the women-folk of drudgery in prosperous families in the North, while slaves were performing the same service for the wealthy in the South.

Epidemics and plagues

Since the rules of sanitation were largely ignored, it is no wonder that the cities were often scourged with epidemics. In winter small-pox was widely prevalent. Vaccination was practiced to some extent but was not an adequate curb on the disease since it was not compulsory. The South was time and again the victim of yellow fever, and whenever midsummer approached, the people in this section stood in dread of its recurrence. There was a violent outbreak of this plague in the summer of 1853. It was at its worst in New Orleans.

Starting in May, it attained the greatest virulence in August. On the 21st of that month the number of deaths in the city for one day was nearly three hundred. The mortality was as high as that in London from the great plague. The only bright spot in the awful situation was the heroism and wisdom displayed by the physicians, nurses, and others who cared for the victims of the disease. Two years later the South was again attacked by this fearful scourge. This time it was particularly severe in Louisiana, Mississippi, and in the coast towns of Portsmouth and Norfolk, Virginia. In those portions of Virginia where it was epidemic one fifth of the population died. So heavy was the death toll that the dead were often buried in trenches without coffins.

Worse even than the yellow fever were the epidemics of cholera. The greatest scourge from this disease began in the spring of 1849. Starting in the South it gradually spread throughout the country. It reached the Pacific coast by 1851, and three years later returned to New York and Chicago, this time in a most virulent form. When a city was in the throes of the plague no one could be seen on the streets except doctors, undertakers, and coffinmakers. "Thousands fled panic-stricken before the scourge, while days of fasting, humiliation and prayer were appointed in view of its probable advent."

One would expect that there would be little ill-health due to improper diet in the prosperous America of this period. Yet, according to contemporary accounts, the people of that day had more than their share of stomach trouble. This was due, it was thought, to the rapid eating of rich foods which had been improperly cooked. The editor of *Harper's Monthly* saw in the youth of the middle 'fifties "a pale pasty-faced, narrow chested, spindled-shanked, dwarfed race." While this appraisal is doubtless an exaggeration, it is quite likely that the health of the people suffered considerably from the "invalid habits" of the country. *Improper eating*

One hindrance to good health was the use of patent medicines and fake remedies. Besides, the regular physicians were so little versed in their craft that they often aggravated rather than alleviated disease. So backward was medical science that Dr. Oliver Wendell Holmes felt justified in making this severe indictment (1860) against his fellow practitioners: ". . . if the whole materia medica, *as now used,* could be sunk to the bottom of the sea, it would be all the better for mankind,—and all the worse for the fishes." *The backwardness of medical science*

AMUSEMENTS

The evil effects of improper eating were counteracted in many cases by the wholesome outdoor amusements participated in by the

THE DRUNKARDS PROGRESS.

STEP 1. A glass with a Friend.

STEP 2. A glass to keep the cold out.

STEP 3. A glass too much.

STEP 4. Drunk and riotous.

STEP 5. The summit attained. Jolly companions. A confirmed drunkard.

STEP 6. Poverty and Disease.

STEP 7. Forsaken by Friends.

STEP 8. Desperation and crime.

STEP 9. Death by suicide.

people. These included skating, boating, horseback riding, yacht *Outdoor* *amuse-* *ments* sailing, hunting and fishing, and the playing of such games as football and baseball. Baseball, which had developed from "Old Town Ball," was played in the early 'fifties very much as it is today, except that the number of players on each side ranged from eleven to thirteen. By 1858 a National Association of Baseball Players had been organized, and the game had been standardized under a regular code of rules. Every community of any importance had its local team, and colleges and high schools had taken up the popular sport.

The circus was a great attraction to all classes. It had developed *The* *circus* into greater importance in the 'fifties by the consolidation of small troupes into large organizations and by the use of the railroad for the transportation of circus equipment. P. T. Barnum was the dean of circus managers.

In the cities the theater offered a type of recreation which was very *Indoor* *amuse-* *ments* popular (see pp. 566 f.). The small towns located on the navigable rivers were also favored with occasional theatricals given on showboats. In these towns the people gladly welcomed the periodic visits of the showboats and were thrilled with the loud and stirring music of the steam pianos and brass bands.

The indoor amusements were also similar to those of the present time. Cards, chess, checkers, billiards, and other games were popular. The spelling match was in high favor with the youth as it was both an intellectual contest and a social diversion. Dancing also had a wide vogue, and masquerade balls were quite common. While the quadrille was still the most usual form of dancing, the polka and the waltz were often indulged in in fashionable circles. To stern moralists with conservative leanings the waltz was an improper type of amusement. When Senator John Tyler (afterwards President) first witnessed the waltz (1827) he was shocked by the performance. In writing to his daughter about it he described it as "a dance which you have never seen, and which I do not desire to see you dance. It is rather vulgar I think." In the cities there were public dance halls which were regarded as "sinks of iniquity."

Every family of the opulent class tried to make at least one tour of *Summer* *resorts* Europe—the "Grand Tour," as it was called. For the wealthy the summer resort also served as an important center of recreation, amusement, and social intercourse. In the 'fifties Newport, Rhode Island, took the lead as a seaside resort. Every summer the cottages and hotels of this watering place were crowded with well-dressed women, accompanied by their prosperous husbands and fathers. They whiled away the time in dancing, horseback riding, bowling, bathing, and flirting. Of these amusements bathing was the most popular. The awkward costumes worn by the women gave them a picturesque appearance but greatly hampered their movements in the water. Their swimming suits were a combination of long-sleeved red frocks and white pantalets coming down to their ankles.

Mineral springs in the interior also attracted large numbers of summer visitors. Of these Saratoga Springs of New York and White Sulphur Springs in Virginia were especially noted. These fashionable spas were patronized by the wealthy from all parts of the country. Some of the patrons were lured by the hoped-for benefit of the medicinal waters, but the majority were attracted by the opportunities for amusement and social intercourse.

Courtesy of the New-York Historical Society, New York City

CADET HOP AT WEST POINT.

From woodcut in Harper's Weekly, Sept. 3, 1859. From drawing by Winslow Homer.

For a long time Southern planters and Northern manufacturers and merchants met each other on most friendly terms at these summer colonies. This mingling of the social leaders of the two sections had a wholesome effect in that it tended to counteract the trend toward sectionalism. But in the late 'fifties the ill feeling between North and South found its way to the summer resorts, and the Southern guests began to complain of a lack of cordiality toward them by their Northern associates. Accordingly, a movement was started in favor of boycotting Northern resorts and developing those of the South.

Unfortunately, most of the amusements listed above were open only to the prosperous classes. In the cities little or nothing had been done to provide recreation for the poor. This lack was in large measure supplied by the barroom and public dance hall. It was therefore under these unwholesome surroundings that many of the youth, especially in the poorer quarters, found their diversion. That immorality and crime would be encouraged under such conditions should have occasioned no surprise. *Lack of proper amusements for the lower and middle classes*

Nor did the yeomanry in the country have sufficient opportunities for amusement. There was, however, a variety of inexpensive diversions which were open to them. These included (in addition to the semisocial working parties) outdoor games, hunting and fishing, dancing and indoor games, visiting, churchgoing, and attendance at public meetings. One useful form of recreation indulged in by the rural classes was conversation. Farmers meeting each other at the inn, country store, church, or the county seat on court days, elections, and other public occasions, exchanged views on politics, condition of crops, and the questions of the day. Often this conversation took the form of anecdote and sometimes of coarse jokes. These meetings served as a clearinghouse of views, afforded amusement, and kept alive a sense of humor in a rather drab countryside.

One form of diversion which appealed to all classes, especially the rural portion of the population, was the political rally. The main objection to it was that it came too infrequently. In Presidential campaigns, however, political meetings furnished the people with numerous occasions for enjoying this kind of recreation. Politics is a great leveler of social barriers, and at political gatherings patrician candidates and their henchmen meet plebeian voters as social equals. On such occasions the latter are not made uncomfortable by the condescension or patronage of their rich or prominent neighbors. These meetings also furnish exceptional opportunities for recreation. If the assemblage is a large one it attracts patent-medicine quacks, who intersperse their sales talk with jokes and clever repartee; and cheap-John peddlers, who in recommending their wares display a fluency of speech and a cleverness at sleight of hand that are wonderfully interesting. Then, too, there is the ubiquitous lemonade vender, who offers at a low price to the thirsty and perspiring youth a marvelous drink with a nectarine flavor and sweetness. *Political rallies*

These attractions, however, furnish only the minor and preliminary thrills while the crowd is awaiting the more exciting events of the day. In the Presidential campaigns of this period the procession *Presidential campaigns* was usually the outstanding feature. Callous-handed farmers, with their tired wives and timid children, while looking at or taking part in these processions, threw off their embarrassment and self-consciousness, despite the stiffness and discomfort imparted by their "Sunday clothes," and joined in the enthusiasm aroused by the stirring band music and the loud hurrahs of the crowd. They observed with keen enjoyment local leaders prancing back and forth on white horses, and visiting statesmen seated in moving carriages, constantly raising their silk hats in response to cheers.

The political speeches also afforded great amusement. They were usually enlivened with a homely imagery and numerous jokes, some of which, though old, had not yet circulated throughout the countryside. But the crowning event of the day was the barbecue. Long tables loaded down with barbecued meat and other kinds of food invited the hungry crowd to appease an appetite that had been sharpened by long waiting and ardent expectation.

DRESS

*Extrava-
gance in
dress
among
women*

The two decades immediately preceding the War of Secession were an era of extravagance, especially as to the wearing apparel of women. The hundred-dollar gowns, costly shawls, and beautiful ribbons with which well-to-do matrons and maids adorned themselves offended the sense of thrift of old-fashioned Americans. The strict moralists also objected to the low-necked dresses worn in fashionable circles. Criticism was leveled against the length of the skirts, which were termed "street-sweepers." So far had this silly fashion gone that it aroused a protest from Mrs. Amelia Bloomer, a prominent advocate of woman's rights. She set the example of wearing a costume which was a combination of a short skirt and a pair of full "trousers." For a few years this new garb, known as "bloomers," gave promise of being popular and was adopted by so well-known a personage as Mrs. Elizabeth Cady Stanton. But masculine ridicule was too much for feminine persistence, and after 1853 the costume was seldom worn except by suffragettes and other zealous advocates of the independence of women.

The hoop skirt which followed had better luck than the "bloomer." This new fashion was set by the Empress Eugenie, who introduced it at the French court in 1853. With such high sponsorship it is no wonder that this fad was popular and held its own for some years beyond the end of this era.

The men at this period were less pretentious in their mode of dress than were their fair wives and daughters. The frock coat and the stovepipe hat were still much in use among the well to do. For a *Mode of.* while the severity of this style of dress was relieved by colored vests *dress* of velvet or satin. Men, both young and old, frequently wore beards *among* and mustaches, and the mustache cup was in great demand. *men*

"GROWING PAINS"

American life in the 'forties and 'fifties presented both attractive and unattractive features. The latter are regarded by a present-day historian[1] as the "growing pains" of an otherwise healthy young society. It could hardly be expected that a generation which was tingling with youthful enthusiasm would be entirely free from the frailties which beset human nature. Some of these shortcomings could be traced to bad economic conditions. Unemployment, which in times of panic became widespread, was a prolific source of poverty and crime. In the year of the panic of 1857 thousands of workers in the large cities faced starvation, although there was an abundance of food in the country. The sufferers assembled in groups and threatened to raid the shops and banks to get food for their families. Their threats as a rule were not carried out, and very little violence occurred despite the fact that little was done to meet the needs of the sufferers. Naturally crime had a hothouse growth under such conditions.

In the cities theft, robbery, and murder grew more and more com- *Crime in* mon, and prostitution plied its trade with unabashed boldness. Often *the cities* young boys were caught pilfering and picking pockets. More serious *and min-* were the gangster.organizations which infested all the larger cities. *ing camps* Another evil which had recently grown into great proportions was that of professional beggary introduced by German and Irish immigrants. The restraints on crime were weakened by the inefficiency and laxity of the police and the misplaced clemency of pardon officials. It was in the gold diggings of California that crime flaunted itself with the most brazen impudence. San Francisco for a time was terrorized by thugs and other criminals. Conditions became so intolerable that the law-abiding element was forced to organize itself into vigilance committees which restored law and order.

All the crime, however, could not be charged to the economic sit- *Drunk-* uation. Drunkenness, for example, was a vice of the prosperous as *enness* well as of the poverty-stricken. The consumption of hard liquor was lessened as a result of the fight against it by the temperance agitators. But by 1856 this reform movement was on the decline, and the trend

---

[1] See A. C. Cole, *The Irrepressible Conflict* (1850-1865) , ch. VII.

Gambling

toward abstinence was checked by the drinking of beer. This practice, begun about 1850 by the native Americans in imitation of the German immigrants, had become widely prevalent in a decade.

Gambling was also a very common vice. In the big cities, in the mining camps, and on the steamboats which went up and down the Mississippi River this evil practice was engaged in to the greatest extent. Dueling was still practiced among the upper classes in the South, but by this time an affair of honor was very unusual in the North.

Courtesy of the New-York Historical Society, New York City

COSTUMES OF 1842.

From Graham's Magazine, March 1842.

American life still sound at the core

In thus considering the evils of this period we are to guard against exaggerating its shortcomings and overlooking its many good points. It must not be forgotten that the two decades which overlapped the mid-century, despite much that is to be deprecated, were in some respects a golden age. In a large portion of the country the great natural resources were being appropriated for the uses of man, and the people were enjoying material comforts and leisure for the cultivation of the finer things of life. There was still left enough of the sturdy virtues of pioneering days to furnish society with a sound moral basis. Maturity had not brought on cynicism and undue sophistication, but was coupled with a breezy optimism which proclaimed the hopeful youthfulness of the age. Lingering traces of an earlier liberalism and a lively faith in religion gave a wholesome spiritual content to American social philosophy. This philosophy was finding expression in philanthropic and reform movements. Although society was a long way from the millennium of which cheerful optimists dreamed, progress toward a better day was gradually going forward, when war came to end many cherished hopes.

CHAPTER XXXVIII

The Antislavery Movement (1783=1860)

OPPOSITION TO SLAVERY BEFORE 1830

*Effect of the
Revolution
on the
slave trade*

AT the end of the colonial period there were slaves in all the Original Thirteen Colonies. But the liberal philosophy behind the Revolution, which is embodied in the Declaration of Independence and the bills of rights of the states, was in conflict with the practice of slavery. This sentiment was reflected in state legislation limiting or forbidding the importation of slaves, and in the Association, or non-intercourse agreement, voted by the First Continental Congress, containing a provision which prohibited the bringing in of any more slaves. Owing to these restrictions the importation of blacks from Africa was brought almost to an end during the Revolutionary period. It was due largely to this liberal philosophy that slavery was excluded from the Northwest Territory and the slave trade was prohibited by an act of Congress (effective 1808).

*Emancipation
in the North
and reason
for its failure
in the South*

The liberal philosophy of the Revolution, combined with the unprofitableness of slavery, resulted in a policy of gradual or immediate abolition in all the Northern states. The same philosophical and economic motives operated strongly in the South at this time and many slaves were granted their freedom. In Virginia alone the number of slaves emancipated in eight years was equal to the whole slave population of Rhode Island and Connecticut in 1775. The proportion of slaves to freemen in the South was so great, however, that the emancipation of all the blacks would have imposed upon the whites an economic burden which they did not feel able to bear. The race problem resulting from freeing slaves seemed even more serious than the economic burden. For this reason the most liberal advocates, like Jefferson, favored emancipation only upon the condition that the freemen be colonized outside the country—preferably in Africa. They feared that a large proportion of the Negroes, when released from the restraints and supervision of slavery, would lapse into crime or pauperism and thus become a burden on, or a menace to, society, since they had not had the opportunity to develop the initiative and self-discipline needed for the responsibilities of freedom. But if the blacks could be taken away from the South when freed, one serious

616

objection to emancipation would be met. It was with the hope of removing this barrier that the American Colonization Society was founded.

This society was organized in Washington in 1816. Its membership included many of the leading Southerners of the day, such as Henry Clay, William H. Crawford, John Randolph, and Chief Justice Marshall. The object of the society was to promote the colonization of free Negroes in Africa. In 1820, eighty-six Negroes were sent to Africa, and two years later Liberia was founded on the west coast. The American Colonization Society started out under very favorable auspices. The national organization was supported by many state societies, two of which, those of Maryland and Virginia, were aided by state appropriations. Other state legislatures, both in the North and the South, expressed approval of the plan, and the Federal government maintained a friendly attitude toward it. Despite these favoring influences, however, the movement was doomed to failure from the beginning unless a more accessible territory could be acquired. The distance to Liberia was so great as to make virtually prohibitive the cost of colonization on any considerable scale. Besides, most of the settlers after their arrival were unable to cope with the torrid climate and the diseases bred by it. Only 1162 Negroes were landed in Africa during the first decade (1820-1830), and the greater portion of these died within a few years.

The American Colonization Society

Other developments soon undermined the Southern emancipation sentiment. The invention of the cotton gin and the opening of the rich lands of the Southwest, as well as the spread of cotton culture into the Piedmont section of the seaboard states of the Southeast, had greatly increased the demand for more slaves after the War of 1812. The increased value of slaves resulting from this greater demand quite naturally caused slavery to be looked upon with more favor than when it was less profitable. However, there was very little defense or justification of slavery until the commencement of a vigorous abolitionist assault from the North. As this attack increased in violence, the Southern grip on slavery was tightened, and since the wind of abolitionism continued to blow more and more fiercely from the North, the South wrapped the mantle of slavery more and more closely around itself (see pp. 624 ff.). In time, therefore, slavery became so firmly intrenched that in the deep South assaults were seldom made upon it except by suicide squads. The few free lances who had the boldness to attack the peculiar institution were confined mostly to the upper South, where the number of slaves was not so large as in the Cotton Kingdom and the problem of the free Negro was not so difficult. Here, too, successful experiments with free labor

Effect of the invention of the cotton gin and the abolition crusade

had been carried out, and the culture of the people—older than that of the Southwesterners—still held lingering traces of Jeffersonian liberalism and Quaker idealism.

THE ANTISLAVERY CRUSADE

Types of antislavery movements

The new antislavery movement in the North was quite aptly termed a crusade by the leaders of the movement itself. Those who participated in the agitation were not all of one mind or of one purpose; on the contrary, they had different and not infrequently conflicting motives. On only one thing were they agreed: the ending of the influence or, as they put it, "the domination," of the "slave power." The "emancipationists"—weak in influence and rarely heard after 1830—would end it by gradual emancipation with compensation to owners and the colonization of the freemen. The "free-soilers" would lessen or destroy the power of the slaveholding section by closing all Federal territories to slavery so that no more slave states would be created. The abolitionists would effect the same result by the immediate and uncompensated emancipation by the national government of all slaves, without any regard to costs or consequences.

The "free-soilers"

The "free-soilers" appear to have made up the bulk of Northern people as early as the Missouri Compromise debates of 1819-1821. The sectional nature of the vote on the compromise measures seems to indicate this.[1] Such a sectional solidarity was possible at this early date because of the breakdown of political parties due to the absorption of most Federalist leaders into the Jeffersonian Party. The restoration of the two-party system under the names of Whig and Democrat during the Jacksonian era had a tendency to counteract the growing sectionalism with reference to the political aspects of slavery, so that it is probable that not again until the Mexican War was a majority of the Northern people found in opposition to the creation of more slave states. After that time political parties again broke down rapidly and sectional lines were more and more tightly drawn. One might, as a matter of convenience, if not of absolute fact, speak of the *abolition movement* as the moral phase of the antislavery movement, and the *free-soil movement* as the political phase, though in truth it seems that fundamentally the abolitionists were greatly influenced by political considerations and, as time passed, the free-soilers were influenced likewise by moral considerations.

The earliest phase of the political antislavery movement related

---

[1] In the settlement of the Missouri dispute 20 Southern Senators and 4 Northern Senators voted for the main compromise and 18 Northern Senators voted against it.

to the Federal ratio of representation in the lower house of Congress *The three-*
and in the Electoral College. It will be recalled that in the Constitu- *fifths rule*
tional Convention a compromise between the North and the South *the North* *opposed by*
was reached whereby three fifths of the slave population were to be
counted in apportioning both direct taxation and representation.
It seems definitely to have been understood to be a sectional bargain
by which the free states and the slave states would establish an approximate balance or equality of power in the national government.[1]
The three-fifths rule proved very objectionable to the North in
general and to New England in particular. The loss of political
supremacy of the latter section which came with the election of
Jefferson was attributed to slave representation. The Boston *Columbian Sentinel,* December 24, 1800, expressed the opinion that "those
500,000 slaves (at least their masters for them) chose 15 Electors of
President" and thereby elevated Jefferson to office. The *Mercury
and New England Palladium,* January 20, 1801, declared that Jefferson and Burr "ride into the Temple of Liberty upon the shoulders
of slaves." The constant repetition of such sentiment by the New
England press and leaders could not fail to create hostility to slavery
and to the South. It can hardly be questioned, if one follows the ever-
growing resentment of New England and finally of the North as a
whole against "slave representation," that the identification of the
three-fifths ratio and Southern political power formed one of the
strongest roots of the antislavery and the abolition movements.

The results of this agitation against the three-fifths ratio can be *This rule*
seen clearly in the Missouri Compromise debates. For the first time *played an*
the free states and the slave states stood almost solidly against one *part in the* *important*
another on the question of admitting more slave states. Northern *Missouri*
leaders in Congress were perfectly frank in contending that this was *Compromise*
primarily a struggle between the slave and the free states for control *debates*
of the Federal government. They would, because of the three-fifths
ratio, oppose the admission of more slave states. In the Missouri
debates the Northern leaders attacked the society and morals of the
South, and they demanded that the balance of power be overthrown
in the political interest of the North.

The emotional intensity of this movement to prevent the spread
of slavery into the territories became greater and greater, and the
language and tone of its leaders became much like that of the aboli-

---

[1] See Albert F. Simpson, "The Political Significance of Slave Representation, 1787-
1821," in *The Journal of Southern History,* VII (August, 1941), 315-342. For a discussion
of this point in the Constitutional Convention see Max Farrand (ed.), *The Records of
the Federal Convention of 1787* (1911-1937), I, 575, 579, 580, 581-83, 585, 586, 587, 591-93.
594-97; II, 219, 221-23, 364; Jonathan Elliot (ed.), *Debates on the Federal Constitution,*
V, 377, 391-93, 457-461.

tionists. However, the great majority of Northern political leaders, like their constituents—though influenced by the abolition movement into a more unfriendly emotional attitude toward the South—never lost sight of the political ends in view, namely, the overthrow of the sectional balance of power in favor of the Northern sections.

Two principal classes of abolitionists

More aggressive in the antislavery cause than the free-soilers were the abolitionists. These arch-opponents of slavery were divided into several categories, though as time passed they all tended to fuse into one body. In general, one may consider them as falling into two classes, those who were radical in their views and activities and those who were mild and philosophic. The latter argued against slavery upon the basis of abstract moral and political principles and made little use at first of sectional advantages or prejudices. Their appeal was directed *to* rather than *against* the Southern slaveholder. Their condemnation of slavery was in nowise different from that of the older generation of Southerners of whom Thomas Jefferson was the outstanding representative. Closely connected, personally and in attitude, with this mild class was the Eastern—largely New England—group of writers, among whom were Ralph Waldo Emerson, John G. Whittier, and James Russell Lowell. But as time passed the philosophical and literary abolitionists more and more adjourned their philosophy and their literature and entered the field of agitation and propaganda writing, and so the philosophical and literary abolitionists tended to coalesce into one great volcanic body with the radical abolitionists.

Benjamin Lundy

One of the most active of the philosophical abolitionists was Benjamin Lundy, whose opposition to slavery was inspired by his Quaker religion. He was born in New Jersey but resided at different times in several slave states. In 1815 he began to organize antislavery societies and six years later established *The Genius of Universal Emancipation,* the first of the abolitionist journals. His plan was to persuade masters to liberate their slaves, and in pursuit of this aim he traveled a great deal and held many antislavery meetings.

Two groups of radical abolitionists

The radical abolitionists accepted the philosophical and moral principles of the mild abolitionists, but dramatized them and clothed them in forms that would appeal to the emotions, the prejudices, and the sectional advantage of the Northern people. They did not appeal *to* the Southern people, but *against* them, directing their appeal to persons in the North and wherever possible to the Negro slaves themselves. For convenience the radical abolitionists may be divided into two groups: the Eastern, which was dominated by William Lloyd Garrison and other New England leaders; and the Western, under the leadership of Theodore Weld, Charles G. Finney, and

James G. Birney. The former constituted the left wing and the latter the right wing of the body. The Western, or Weld, group favored political action as a means toward accomplishing its aims and took an active part in elections, frequently tipping the scales in favor of certain candidates. The Eastern group advocated a policy of non-participation in any kind of political activity, but at the same time demanded that the Federal government abolish slavery without compensation. It gave its approval to the exclusion of slavery from the territories by Federal action and advocated the secession of the non-slaveholding states should they fail to obtain the abolition of slavery.

Courtesy of The New-York Historical Society, New York City

WILLIAM LLOYD GARRISON.

The most radical of all the abolitionists was William Lloyd Garrison. For a while he was associated with Lundy in the publication of *The Genius of Universal Emancipation.* His hatred of slavery, however, soon outran the mild philosophy of this Quaker journalist and led him into a more violent type of agitation. To propagate his ideas he decided to establish a newspaper of his own. Accordingly, he founded *The Liberator,* which for a third of a century (1831-1865)

William Lloyd Garrison

was the most violent of all the antislavery journals. In the first number he said: "I shall strenuously contend for the immediate enfranchisement of our slave population—I will be as harsh as truth and as uncompromising as justice on this subject—I do not wish to think, or speak, or write with moderation—I am in earnest—I will not equivocate—I will not retreat a single inch, and I *will be heard!"* Garrison spoke as well as wrote against slavery, and in 1832 he organized the New England Antislavery Society. In December of the following year the American Antislavery Society was organized at Philadelphia with Beriah Green as president. Local societies were now quickly formed and by 1840 they numbered about two thousand. So bitter was Garrison's opposition to slavery that in later years he became hostile to the Constitution and government of the United States because both recognized and permitted slavery. At the head of *The Liberator* was placed the statement that "the compact which exists between the North and the South is a covenant with death and an agreement with hell." In 1854 he went so far as to burn publicly a copy of the Constitution, uttering loudly this imprecation: "So perish all compromisers with tyranny!" These extreme views were not shared by a majority of the abolitionists. Many of their prominent leaders did not accept the theory that the Constitution was proslavery and therefore made no attack on it.

The post office and abolitionist pamphlets

One means of reaching the slaves was the distribution of pamphlets throughout the South. By the use of these tracts the abolitionists could hurl incendiary bombs into the camp of the enemy without being subject to a return fire. In these circulars slaveholders were held up as brutal tyrants and the slaves as innocent victims of the most cruel barbarities. This agitation was calculated to create dissatisfaction among the slaves and arouse in their masters the fear of insurrection. It goes without saying that such a course stirred up in the South great excitement and a violent feeling against abolitionism. The Southern people strenuously objected to the use of the postal system as an agency for this dangerous propaganda. Amos Kendall, Postmaster General under Jackson, sympathized with the Southern position on this question and ruled that postmasters would have to receive the abolitionist pamphlets but would not have to deliver them. For, so ran his instructions, "we owe an obligation to the laws, but a higher one to the communities in which we live." Acting on this broad hint, the postmaster at Charleston refused to deliver the objectionable pamphlets.

Antislavery petitions in Congress

The abolitionists tried to enlist the support of Congress in their agitation against slavery. Petitions were sent, asking that body to put an end to the domestic slave trade and to abolish slavery in the District of Columbia. The South objected to these petitions, since they were usually so phrased as to contain arguments against slavery and, if they were printed at public expense, the government would be financing antislavery propaganda. The Southern members finally (1836) succeeded in getting a resolution passed by the House of Representatives which provided that all petitions relating to slavery should be laid on the table without being printed or referred to a committee. This "Gag Resolution," as it was called by its opponents, was renewed in substance at each session until 1844, when it was finally dropped. The adoption of this resolution was not good tactics on the part of the South, for it not only aroused the bitter opposition of the North but it laid the South liable to the charge of upholding the cause of slavery at the cost of sacrificing the right of petition.

Regardless of whether the abolitionists were Westerners or Easterners their attack upon slavery and the South was stereotyped both in ideas and in language; and it is of great significance that this abolitionist assault, launched by Garrison and Weld in 1831, was essentially the same as the attack of the political leaders of the East during the Missouri Compromise debates. The onslaught, ever increasing in volume and, if possible, in violence, created in the South fear and profound resentment, and the Southerner's conception of the North was that of a section of self-righteous and meddling fanatics. The Southern defense of slavery resulting from this opposition (though generally more restrained than that of the abolitionist denunciation) was nevertheless bitter, and it in turn aroused further bitterness in both the Northern and Southern mind. According to the opinion of the late Albert J. Beveridge (expressed in his *Abraham Lincoln*), "had it not been for what they [the abolitionists] said and did and the fear and anger they aroused, it is not altogether impossible that there would have been no war." *The abolitionist attack creates fear and resentment in the South*

In their attack upon slavery and the South, the abolitionists pursued the following line of argument: First, it was the major premise that all men were brothers in the sight of God and therefore equal. Granting this to be true, it logically followed that it was a violation of the ordinances of God for man to prevent by law or by any other method the exercise of this brotherhood and equality. Hence, any man-made law which violated the laws of God was null and void. This meant specifically that all laws and constitutions, Federal or state, which in any way recognized man's ownership of man, were null and void. This view was not essentially different from the doctrine of natural rights so profoundly impressed upon the minds of all who lived during the time of the American Revolution. It had, indeed, no greater champions than Southerners of the Jeffersonian school who applied it very specifically to the institution of slavery. This doctrine of the supremacy of natural over legal rights became known as the "higher law" doctrine during the antislavery crusade. The adherents of this doctrine rejected the laws and constitutions of state and Federal government wherever such laws conflicted with what they believed to be God's will, and therefore they refused to recognize all laws upholding slavery. Standing upon what they chose to consider divine authority, they thundered down upon the South in language never surpassed in violence. They made specific applications that quickly lost sight of any philosophical principle. The slaveholder held property that was not his. He was therefore "a thief," "a robber," "a manstealer," "a kidnaper." *The abolitionist argument against slavery*

The slaveholders thus classed as robbers were accused of the most heinous crimes against the slaves. The slaves were regularly worked to death in seven years; they were beaten with hundreds of lashes;

they had their teeth knocked out with clubs and their ears cropped for purposes of identification; they were thrown to the bloodhounds and chewed; they had turpentine, red pepper, and vinegar rubbed into their wounds; they were not given enough clothes to protect them from the weather; and were systematically starved and forbidden religious instruction. The slaveholders and their poorer neighbors were pictured as arrogant, boastful, murderous, and universally immoral. In the charge of immorality, Southern women and the ministers of the churches were singled out as special objects of attack. It was charged that Southern pulpits were often filled by "manstealing, girl-selling, and slave-manufacturing preachers." "The abolition assault on Southern clergymen," says Beveridge, "was more virulent than the attack on any other body of men in the South."[1] The climax of this argument was that the nation was ruled by this brutal, immoral Southern people, in reality the political argument that even the most unpolitical abolitionists seldom failed to use. Finally, the most fearful of all to Southerners, was the propaganda which might lead to slave revolt carried on by William Lloyd Garrison and other prominent abolitionists. It was from men like these that John Brown received aid and encouragement in his raid.

*The aboli-
tionist assault
causes a
change in the
Southern
position on
slavery*
The attack upon slavery and the South resulted in the development of a philosophical defense of slavery and angry attacks upon Northern society. The bitterness of feeling expressed by the North toward the South during the Missouri debates and afterward, gave great alarm to Southern leaders. It (together with the increase in the value of slaves as a result of the rapid expansion in cotton growing) caused them to weaken their efforts at emancipation and in some cases to reconsider their former position upon the slavery question—namely, that it was a necessary evil—and to come to the conclusion that slavery was a positive good. Several Southern writers during the ten years following the Missouri Compromise completely reversed the position of former Southern spokesmen and justified slavery upon moral, religious, and social principles. Nevertheless, this philosophical defense of slavery gained little popular notice and probably would have been relegated to oblivion had not the radical abolitionists, under the leadership of Weld and Garrison, begun in 1831 the abolition crusade which demanded immediate and uncompensated emancipation of the slaves by act of the national government. So violent and dangerous did this new crusade appear to Southerners that a revolution in Southern thought immediately took place. Chancellor William Harper, Thomas Cooper, Edmund Ruffin,

---

[1] A. J. Beveridge, *Abraham Lincoln*, II, 25-26. For the best short discussion of the slavery controversy, see Beveridge, *op. cit.*, II, ch. I.

Thomas R. Dew, John C. Calhoun, and James H. Hammond, to mention only a few of the Southern leaders, formulated a new doctrine, which has usually been termed the "philosophy of slavery." Within a few years the South, under the teachings of these new proslavery champions, became firmly convinced that far from being an evil slavery was a positive good. This justification of Negro slavery was carefully thought out by men of keen and logical minds. With the abolition invective for its background, the new philosophy carried conviction to the majority of Southerners. Those who did not agree with it as a whole usually accepted it in part; and under abolition pressure most were agreed as to the practical necessity of maintaining slavery under the circumstances.

Courtesy of Heustis Cook

THOMAS R. DEW.

The proslavery argument can be *The proslavery argument* stated briefly. To those who accepted the literal meaning of the Scriptures, and most Americans did at that time, the Bible supplied scores of passages which seemed unequivocally to sanction slavery. Then it was pointed out that all past civilizations had developed apparently upon the very backs of slaves, that, in other words, the sanction of history rested upon the institution. Turning from the Biblical and historical justification, the proslavery champions pointed out the practical, materialistic advantages of Negro slavery and the losses entailed by its abolition. Billions of dollars were directly and indirectly invested in slaves, land, and the staples such as tobacco, cotton, rice, and sugar cane. This, of course, was not a new idea. Since the invention of the cotton gin and the expansion of slavery into the Southwest, there had been a strong but quiet support of slavery in the lower South as a practical institution but, as previously stated, prior to 1830 there was little or no justification expressed by Southern leaders, while there was wide Southern condemnation. Next, there was the social justification which appealed more or less to every Southerner. This was the race problem, namely, that two racial groups so different from one another as the whites and the Negroes could not live in the same community or country upon terms of equality. One must dominate or destroy the other or be destroyed. The whites declared it their right to dominate, first upon the *assumption,* and later upon the alleged *scientific proof,* that the blacks were inferior to the whites. Finally, without reference either to the assumption of white superiority or to scientific proof, the Southerners were thoroughly agreed that the Caucasians should dominate the Africans in order to maintain the integrity and civilization of the former. With the so-called scientific proof omitted, this social justification will be recognized as that of the old emancipationists like Jefferson, who advocated freeing the slave only upon condition of colonization outside the country.

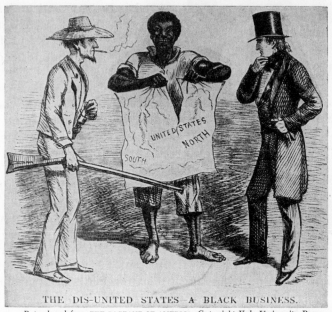

THE DIS-UNITED STATES A BLACK BUSINESS.

Reproduced from THE PAGEANT OF AMERICA, *Copyright Yale University Press*

The comity of sections destroyed by agitation of the slavery question

In proclaiming this philosophy, the Southern leaders replied to the abolitionist vituperation in language which, though neither violent nor unrestrained, was caustic and severe toward the entire North. Moreover, the terrible picture of the South presented by the abolitionists colored the thinking to some extent of most of the Northern people and aroused the bitterest resentment in the South. The Southern proslavery arguments and accompanying counter accusations against the North had a further effect in creating mutually hostile feelings in both the North and the South. The comity of sections disappeared with the abolition crusade and a national state such as the United States, composed of sections resembling—as Frederick Jackson Turner has so often pointed out—nations themselves, could

THE HERMITAGE

PART OF THE HERMITAGE SLAVE QUARTER, 1889

ANOTHER PART OF THE HERMITAGE QUARTER, 1928

Mansion and Cabins on the Savannah

PLANTATION LIFE IN THE SOUTH.

hardly avoid disruption and war where intersectional goodwill had disappeared. The psychosis of war developed out of the abolition attack upon the South and the counterattack of the South. In an atmosphere so taut with emotion a reasonable and peaceable solution of the slavery problem could hardly be expected. To remove slavery from the social order at this time, while public sentiment was so inflamed, was to perform a major operation after infection had set in.

CHAPTER XXXIX

Controversy and Compromise

THE SLAVERY CONTROVERSY GIVEN A NEW IMPETUS

*T*HE accessions of territory resulting from the Mexican War added *The Wilmot Proviso* new fuel to the fires of controversy over the slavery issue. Indeed, before these accessions were made, the blaze began to flare up in anticipation of an extension of the national domain. In August, 1846, a bill was offered in the House of Representatives providing for an appropriation of $2,000,000 to be used by the President in the prospective negotiations with Mexico. To this measure was attached a rider proposed by David Wilmot of Pennsylvania. The Wilmot Proviso, as it was called, stipulated that the appropriation be made on the condition that slavery be excluded from all the territory which should be acquired from Mexico. The proviso stirred up a great deal of excitement and, although it was stricken out by the Senate, it gave a new impetus to the controversy over slavery. It solidified and strengthened the antislavery sentiment in the North and the pro-slavery sentiment in the South. The opponents of slavery now had a definite platform to which all of them could rally. The principle underlying the proviso was a disturbing factor in the political situation, and both of the old parties tried to eliminate it as an issue. But, like Banquo's ghost, it would not down.

In general the Northern people, especially the antislavery element, *Causes of dispute between the North and the South* accepted the principle of the Wilmot Proviso and thus opposed the extension of slavery into any of the new acquisitions. The Southerners were just as strong in their demand that the recent accessions should be open to slavery. They contended that they had done their full share in winning the new territory and should not be prohibited from emigrating to it with their labor system. Furthermore, if slavery were excluded from the Mexican cession, the political balance between the North and the South would be upset to the disadvantage of the South. Arkansas and Michigan had been admitted as states in 1836 and 1837, respectively; Florida and Texas in 1845; and Iowa and Wisconsin in 1846 and 1848. As a result of this policy of balance in admitting new states, there was in 1848 an equal number of slave and free states. The South felt, however, that this equilibrium could

629

not be maintained in the future if slave states could not be carved out of the Mexican cession; for Minnesota would soon be ready to come into the Union as a free state, and in time free states would be created in the Oregon country. These apprehensions were accentu- ated when, in 1848, despite the persistent opposition of Southern Congressmen, Oregon was organized as a territory without any stipulations as to slavery, which meant that the government of the territory would be on an antislavery basis.

The North and the South were also not in agreement as to the western boundary of Texas. The Texans and Southerners generally held out for the Rio Grande to its source. If this claim were allowed, Texas, a slave state, would have a large part of the New Mexico area, all of which would be slave territory. The North, therefore, was un- willing to concede such a boundary.

Nevertheless, not all the bitterness of feeling between the North and the South, which had now reached a new height, was rooted in the problems connected with American expansion. Some of this ill will arose from old and chronic causes of dispute. The Southerners were enraged at the abolitionist propaganda and frightened by its possible effect on the Negroes. They also felt that the Northern- ers were depriving them of their property rights by refusing to return fugitive slaves to their owners, in plain violation of the Constitution and a Federal statute. The status of slavery and the slave trade in the District of Columbia was still a subject of violent discussion.

These old causes of trouble were assuming new importance be- cause fresh heat had been imparted to them by the friction between the sections which had arisen over the new territorial acquisitions. The antislavery element in the North was clamoring for the abolition of the slave trade and slavery in the District of Columbia. As Congress was the legislature for the District it was contended that it had the constitutional authority to decide as to slavery. Some of the moderates of the South were willing to grant the abolition of the slave trade in the District, but the conservatives and the radicals of this section were a unit in contending that Congress, regardless of its constitu- tional powers, had no moral right to abolish slavery in the District. To do so would be, they maintained, to break faith with Maryland, since that state had ceded the land of the District to the Federal government with the implied understanding that the laws of the District would not be so changed as to menace the security of her own institutions. The creation of a center of freedom in an area of slavery would constitute such a hazard.

THE CAMPAIGN OF 1848

There was a slight lull in the slavery agitation at the time of the Presidential election of 1848, for during the campaign sectionalism was to some extent tempered by partisanship. The Democrats held their national convention in Baltimore in May. The first and most difficult problem which this body had to face was a decision as to the claims of two rival delegations from New York. At that time the Democrats in that state were divided into two factions, known as "Barnburners" and "Hunkers." The disagreement had arisen over state issues, the former advocating a policy of liberalism in state management and the latter one of conservatism. The Barnburners were so called because their opponents regarded them as extreme radicals, being, as they charged, like the Dutchman who burned down his barn to get rid of the rats.[1] The Barnburners and Hunkers each sent a delegation to the national convention in 1848. Both delegations were offered seats in the convention with the understanding that the vote of the state would be divided equally between them. Neither faction was willing to accept this decision and the Barnburners would not promise to support the party nominee. Withdrawing from the Democratic convention, they later (June 22) met at Utica and nominated Van Buren for the Presidency.

"Barnburners" and "Hunkers"

The Barnburners nominate Van Buren for President

In the platform of 1844 the Democrats had declared in favor of the one-term principle, and Polk, therefore, was not a candidate for the succession. The convention chose General Lewis Cass of Michigan as its candidate for the Presidency. The platform contained a strong endorsement of Polk's administration, a justification of the war, and a condemnation of the opposition which had been arrayed against it. An effort to commit the party in favor of the Wilmot Proviso was voted down.

Action of the Democratic Convention

The Whigs held their convention at Philadelphia in June, 1848. Again passing over Clay, they chose a war hero, Zachary Taylor of Louisiana. He was a slaveowner, a point in his favor with the Southern but against him with the Northern wing of the party. A resolution endorsing the Wilmot Proviso was tabled and no platform was adopted. For Vice-President the Whigs nominated Millard Fillmore of New York.

The Whig Convention

The Liberty Party had held its convention as early as November, 1847, at which time it had nominated John P. Hale of New Hamp-

---

[1] Just why the Hunkers received this designation we do not know. It is quite likely, however, that the term was used because it is an ill-sounding one and aided the Barnburners in their effort to stamp their rivals as a bad lot.

The conven-
tion of the
Free-Soil
Party
shire for the Presidency. As the Barnburners were in favor of the Wilmot Proviso, it was felt that a union between them and the Liberty Party should be effected. This was done by issuing a call for a national convention representing all the antislavery elements. The convention was held in August, 1848, and by it was launched the National Free-Soil Party. The new party declared in favor of free homesteads for actual settlers on the public lands and against the extension of slavery into any of the territories. Its slogan was, "Free Soil, Free Speech, Free Labor, and Free Men." Van Buren was named for President and Charles Francis Adams for Vice-President. Hale withdrew in favor of Van Buren, who in the main received the support of the antislavery groups.

Result of
the election
As in the election of 1844, the vote of New York was the deciding factor. The division in the Democratic ranks enabled the Whigs to carry that state and thereby to elect Taylor and Fillmore.

ZACHARY TAYLOR AS PRESIDENT

President
Taylor;
personal traits
General Taylor was a man of limited education and strong prejudices. He was honest, had sound judgment, and was possessed of unusual moral and physical courage. In acting upon his firm convictions he displayed a fixed determination which was reminiscent of Andrew Jackson. His previous career afforded no experience which would qualify him for high office. He had never held a civil office and, prior to his nomination, had never voted in a Presidential election. As he owned a large sugar plantation manned with several hundred slaves, Taylor was naturally inclined to view the slavery question with Southern eyes. But it was not long before he fell under His attitude
toward
compromise the influence of Seward and then he inclined toward the Northern view of the slavery question. He therefore was not in favor of yielding to the South on that issue and was opposed to Clay's compromise measures. Any hint of secession aroused in him violent antagonism, and he let it be known that an effort in that direction would be met by a boldness like that shown by Jackson in the Nullification crisis.

The Clayton-
Bulwer
Treaty
For Secretary of State Taylor selected John M. Clayton of Delaware, who was able to score a noted diplomatic success, the negotiation of the Clayton-Bulwer Treaty. The settlement of the Oregon dispute and the acquisition of California had given the United States a new interest in the construction of a canal which would connect the Atlantic with the Pacific Ocean. In pursuit of this interest the United States secured from New Grenada (now Colombia), by a treaty signed in 1846, the right of transit across the Isthmus of Panama. Taking advantage of the opportunity offered by this

agreement, American capitalists built the **Panama Railroad** in the half decade of 1850-1855.

One of the three possible routes for a canal was through Nicaragua, in a location on which Great Britain had designs. She had already obtained the eastern and was trying to get the western terminus. The rival plans of England and the United States made it necessary for the two powers to come to an agreement, which was embodied in the treaty negotiated (1850) by Secretary Clayton and Sir Henry Bulwer, British minister at Washington. Under the terms of the agreement any canal constructed in Nicaragua would be protected and its neutrality guaranteed by both countries. Both powers were pledged never to obtain exclusive control over the canal or to erect fortifications commanding it or to exercise any dominion over any part of Central America. They also agreed to extend their protection to any other canal or any railroad that might be constructed across the isthmus, and especially to any waterway that might be constructed either at Panama or Tehuantepec. The canals and railroads were to be open to the use of the citizens of other nations on the same terms as those granted to the citizens of England and the United States.

THE COMPROMISE OF 1850

When the new Congress met in December, 1849, the witches' cauldron was boiling furiously. Resolutions adopted by state legislatures and other bodies showed that there was intense feeling on the slavery question throughout the country. Henry Clay described the situation as follows: "At this moment we have in the legislative bodies of this Capitol and in the States twenty-odd furnaces in full blast, emitting heat and passion and intemperance, and diffusing them throughout the whole extent of this broad land."[1] From these expressions of opinion it was evident that there was an overwhelming sentiment in the North against the extension of slavery to California and New Mexico, whereas feeling in the South was equally strong in favor of keeping the new territories open to it. As the views of the country were reflected in Congress an amicable agreement on the questions at issue could be reached only as a result of compromise.

Intense feeling between the North and the South

In the efforts at compromise no co-operation could be expected from the radicals of either side. The Northern and Southern extremists in Congress were unyielding in their insistence, the former on the exclusion of slavery from the Mexican cession and the latter on the protection of slavery in the new territory. There were, however, moderates from both sections who, in a spirit of compromise,

Possible solutions of the questions at issue

---

[1] Quoted by J. F. Rhodes, in his *History of the United States*, I, 124.

were willing to meet their opponents on middle ground. One group of these advocated the division of the territory between the North and the South by extending the line of 36° 30′ to the Pacific. South of this line slavery would be permitted and north of it it would be prohibited. Another group suggested that the question of slavery in the territories be determined by the people who had settled in them. A third plan was for Congress to take no action as to slavery in the territories and allow the territorial and Federal courts to settle all controversial questions which might arise on this score.

Urgency of the problem

In the meantime events in the Far West were moving rapidly and changing some of these bitter academic disputes into practical quarrels. In New Mexico, Utah, and California, affairs had taken such a turn as to demand immediate action by Congress. New Mexico was in need of a territorial government and Utah was asking for statehood. The Mormons there had organized a government for the new state of Deseret (1849), elected Brigham Young as governor, and applied for admission into the Union. In the new commonwealth, church and state were to be united, slavery prohibited, and polygamy allowed.

California under Spanish rule

The problem of greatest urgency had arisen in connection with California. To understand the situation there it is necessary to take a hurried glance at the history of this part of the new acquisition. It had been in the nominal possession of Spain since before the middle of the sixteenth century, but no serious effort had been made to occupy the country until the last third of the eighteenth century. At that time fear of British aggression caused the Spanish authorities to strengthen their claim by settlement. Missionaries, soldiers, and settlers were sent from Mexico (beginning in 1769), and soon a series of missions was established, extending from San Diego to Sonoma. The early missionaries were zealous and self-sacrificing Franciscan monks, who had considerable success in converting the Indians and teaching them agriculture and the handicrafts. For the first half-century, however, the development of the colony was slow. The settlers were few in number and not very energetic or capable. The soldiers stationed at the posts were inefficient and the governing officials were often corrupt.

Americans in California

As Spain's main purpose was to pre-empt the ground against rival powers, and as she was not interested in developing a strong agricultural colony, immigration to California from non-Spanish countries was discouraged. Despite this attitude, however, Americans and other foreigners gradually drifted into the province. By 1845 the total white population of California was approximately seven thousand persons, about one tenth of whom were Anglo-Americans. Of the non-Spanish immigrants who came to California before the Mexican War, the most noted was Captain John A. Sutter, a native of Germany, who arrived at San Francisco in 1839. He settled at the confluence of the American and Sacramento Rivers on an area which covered nearly a hundred square miles. Here he built a large fort, which was well equipped with cannon and manned with soldiers in uniform.[1] *John A. Sutter*

It was not until near the middle of the century that California entered upon her phenomenal growth. Nine days before the Treaty of Guadalupe Hidalgo was signed, gold was discovered in California (January 24, 1848), but neither the Mexican nor the American authorities were aware of it at the time the negotiations were pending. A workman digging a millrace at Sutter's Fort observed in the dirt shining particles which proved to be gold. At first Sutter and his associates tried to prevent this valuable knowledge from spreading, but such a secret could not be kept. It was publicly divulged when a Mormon rode from Sutter's Fort to San Francisco to announce the discovery. Holding up a bottle of gold dust in one hand, he walked along the street crying out "Gold! Gold! Gold from the American River." The news was soon broadcast everywhere, and thousands of people rushed to the new El Dorado. "Blacksmiths, carpenters, masons, farmers, bakers, tapsters, boarding-house keepers, soldiers, and domestics all left their occupations. . . . Privates from the army and sailors from the naval ships deserted and repaired to the gold diggings."[2] In this heterogeneous group there were many good citizens but also a considerable number of criminals and outlaws. In 1849, eighty-one thousand emigrants went to California. *The gold rush*

The military government of California had not been devised for such a situation and was not able to cope with the new conditions. Strife over mining titles led to fights, and there were numerous brawls of other kinds. A sort of lynch law, regulated by the better element, was nearly all that stood between the people and anarchy. The need of law and order was strongly felt by all well-meaning citizens, and a constitutional convention was called to organize a government. Meeting in September, 1849, before the gold rush was well under way, it framed a state constitution which prohibited slavery. In taking steps toward the formation of a new government, the people were assisted by the confidential agent of the President, for Taylor stated *A free state constitution ratified by the people*

---

1 Inside the large enclosure of the fort there were a cannery, a gristmill, a distillery, and a blacksmith shop. Grain, fruits, and vegetables were cultivated, and on his extensive lands there roamed thousands of cattle, horses, and sheep. By good treatment he was able to secure efficient service from his Indian trappers and thus reap rich gains from the fur trade.

2 Rhodes, *op. cit.*, I, 111. (Quoted by permission of The Macmillan Company.)

that he "desired to substitute the rule of law and order there for the bowie-knife and revolver." The constitution was ratified by the people and application was made to Congress for admission into the Union.

Clay offers a group of compromise resolutions

In the Congress that met in December, 1849, Henry Clay was one of the most prominent leaders. At this trying time he came forward to perform his last public service. Owing to frail health and his advanced age, he had given up all hope of the Presidency, and so his judgment was free from the bias of personal ambition. He now assumed the role of peacemaker and offered eight resolutions which provided for a compromise settlement of the questions at issue. These resolutions led to one of the most remarkable debates ever staged in Congress. Prominent among the noted speakers who took part in it, besides Clay himself, were Calhoun, Webster, Stephen A. Douglas, William H. Seward, and Jefferson Davis. A few days after offering his resolutions (February 5, 1850), Clay appeared on the floor of the Senate to uphold them. When he arose to speak he faced an appreciative audience that overflowed the galleries. With deep earnestness he urged each section of the country to make concessions to the other for the sake of the Union. The North, he contended, should accept a law that would provide for the return of fugitive slaves to Southern owners. Nor should the North insist upon applying the Wilmot Proviso to the new territory, for the restriction was entirely unnecessary. If admitted at all, California would come into the Union with her antislavery constitution, and slavery could not exist in New Mexico because physical conditions there were unfavorable to it.

A notable debate

Attitude of Calhoun toward the Compromise

About a month later (March 4), Calhoun was slated to appear before the Senate. He was nearing death's door and was not strong enough physically to deliver his speech. Swathed in bandages, he tottered into the Senate chamber, where he sat quietly while his speech was being read by Senator James M. Mason of Virginia. In this serious address he expressed opposition to the compromise resolutions on the ground that they did not go far enough in recognizing the rights of the South. He pointed out how the South with its system of slave labor had lagged behind the North with its system of free labor in the apportionment of the territorial additions to the Union. The tariff and the policy of internal improvements had favored the North at the expense of the South. Furthermore, the centralization of political authority had deprived the states of their legitimate powers. All of these practices had tended to retard the South and weaken the bonds that held it to the Union. Some of the strong spiritual, ecclesiastical, political, and social ties which had bound the North and South together were now broken, and soon there would be nothing but force left to hold the two sections together. The only remedy for this situation was for the North to show a willingness to return to the South her runaway slaves; stop the slavery agitation; allow the South an equal share in the public domain; and consent to an amendment to the Constitution which would restore the political equilibrium between the sections.

A few days after Calhoun's speech was presented, Webster took *Webster's* the floor in favor of compromise. His speech made on March 7 was *Seventh-* a great forensic achievement and deserves to rank with his reply to *of-March* Hayne. In it he advocated compromise for the sake of the Union and *speech* pointed out grievances of which the South had a right to complain. Like Clay, he urged the adoption of a stricter fugitive slave law and contended that slave restrictions by Congress on California and New Mexico were unnecessary. Even if there were no such restrictions slavery could not exist in those regions, and therefore to apply the Wilmot Proviso to them would only serve to antagonize the South. Since California and New Mexico were destined to be free, "I would not," he said, "take pains uselessly to reaffirm an ordinance of nature, nor to re-enact the will of God. I would put in no Wilmot Proviso for the mere purpose of a taunt or reproach."

By taking such a stand, and especially by supporting the new fugitive slave act, he aroused the bitter antagonism of the abolitionists in the North. So unpopular with them was this Seventh-of-March speech that for a while he was the butt of violent abuse. Horace Mann said of him: "Webster is a fallen star! Lucifer descending from Heaven!" In a meeting at Faneuil Hall, Theodore Parker said: "I know no deed in American history done by a son of New England to which I can compare this but the act of Benedict Arnold."[1] Later, however, with the coming of sober second thought, fair-minded people in the North took a more just attitude toward Webster and came to realize that his action on this occasion was prompted by the patriotic desire to save the Union. He was opposed to slavery, to be sure, but his hatred of slavery was not as strong as his love of the Union. In the Southland the speech was well received and the editorial comment of most of the newspapers was very favorable.

This was the last joint appearance on the public stage of that triumvirate of elder statesmen which had figured so prominently for a generation. Calhoun died in less than a month after the delivery of his address, and both Clay and Webster passed away before the end of 1852.

Clay's resolutions were opposed by extremists in both the North

---

[1] *Ibid.*, 147, 154.

*Attitude of
Northern and
Southern
extremists
toward the
Compromise*

and the South. With the Northern radicals the hatred of slavery was greater than their fear of disunion, while with the Southern ultras the love of the Union was less strong than their dread of abolition and the dominance of the North. The former therefore opposed the proposed compromise on the ground that it did not sufficiently loosen the shackles of slavery, whereas the latter opposed it because it did not give adequate recognition to the rights of the slaveowner. Prominent in the list of the younger statesmen who for these reasons opposed the measure were William H. Seward of New York, on the one

side, and Jefferson Davis of Mississippi, on the other. Seward said that there was a "higher law than the Constitution, which regulates our authority over the domain." Although Davis maintained that all the territories should be open to slavery, he was willing to make this concession: ". . . the drawing of the line of 36° 30′ through the territories acquired from Mexico, with the condition that in the same degree as slavery is prohibited north of that line, it shall be permitted to enter south of the line, and that the States which may be admitted into the Union shall come in under such constitutions as they think proper to form."[1]

Clay seemed to think that his compromise could be floated through Congress "upon a sea of stately speeches"[2] and he appeared on the floor of the Senate seventy times in support of his proposals. It was, however, the political strategy of Douglas, rather than the eloquence of Clay, that secured the enactment of the measures, and for their successful outcome Douglas probably deserves more credit than anyone else. They were carried through the Senate under his leadership and through the House by his friends.[3] The debates in Congress showed that Clay's resolutions could not pass if tied together in one bill, for few of the members were willing to support all of them. They were therefore broken down into separate measures, each of which was passed by Congress and signed by the President.

This group of acts, which embodied in substance the original proposals of Clay, is known as the Compromise of 1850. It contained some provisions favorable to the North and some favorable to the South. California was to be admitted as a free state. The South was compensated for this concession to the North by a new fugitive slave law, providing for a more effective return of slaves escaping to free states. A neutral measure was the one that provided for the organiza-

---

[1] Rhodes, *op. cit.*, 168-169.

[2] G. F. Milton, *The Eve of Conflict*, 74.

[3] For an excellent account of the part played by Douglas in the fight for the Compromise, see an article by F. H. Hodder in the *Mississippi Valley Historical Review*, XXII, 525-536.

tion of the Territories of Utah and New Mexico with no provision for slavery during the territorial period. When these territories, or any portions of them, were ready for statehood they were to be admitted into the Union with or without slavery as their constitutions should prescribe at the time of admission. Texas was to receive $10,000,000 from the Federal government if she would cede to the United States the large area of land in dispute on her western and northern borders. This agreement was favorable to the North, as it took territory from the slave state of Texas and added it to the Territory of New Mexico from which could be carved free states. Concessions were made to both sides in the slave law for the District of Columbia. By it slavery was continued, but the slave trade was prohibited in the Federal district.

The Compromise was a truce in the slavery conflict which post- *Significance* poned secession for ten years. During this decade the economic bonds *of the* between the northern West and the northern East were strengthened *Compromise* by the numerous railroads which linked the two sections together. It was in large measure due to this solidarity that the northern West supported the North in the War of Secession and thus assured the success of the Union cause.

While the debates on the Compromise were in progress a conven- *The Nashville* tion met at Nashville (June 3) to consider plans for concerted action *Convention* on the part of the South. Nine slave states were represented. Although the delegates from Mississippi and South Carolina advocated radical measures, no aggressive action was taken. The resolutions adopted declared that the territories were the joint property of all the states and any act of Congress prohibiting slavery in them was unconstitutional. If, however, the majority in Congress would not recognize this principle, it was demanded that the public domain be divided between the North and the South by the extension of the line of 36° 30′ to the Pacific.

The Compromise was anathema to the extremists in both the *The* North and the South, but the country as a whole welcomed a cessa- *Compromise* tion of the strife over slavery. Despite its strong objection to the *accepted by* admission of California as a free state, the South, except South *the country* Carolina and Mississippi, accepted the Compromise as a satisfactory settlement. It was also favorably received in the North, although the Fugitive Slave Law was a bitter pill to the people of that section. At well-attended meetings held in Boston, New York, Philadelphia, and other Northern cities, resolutions were voted expressing satisfaction with the new laws and a willingness to carry them out.

THE PRESIDENCY OF MILLARD FILLMORE

A new Cabinet

On July 9, 1850, after a short illness, occurred the death of President Taylor. Millard Fillmore, who at once took up the reins of government, was more fortunate than have been most of our Vice-Presidents who have succeeded to the Presidency, in that he was able to choose his own Cabinet. On the death of Taylor the Cabinet resigned and Fillmore selected a new one. Webster was made Secretary of State and became the dominant personality in the group.

Personal traits of Fillmore

He favors the Compromise

Millard Fillmore (1800-1874) was a self-educated man of ability who had had considerable experience in governmental affairs. For eight years he had been a member of the House of Representatives and had presided over the Senate as Vice-President with dignity and impartiality. He had a pleasing personality and a suavity of manner that disarmed political opponents. Prior to his election to the Vice-Presidency he had been an opponent of slavery, but he had now come to fear that a further advance of the crusade against slavery would jeopardize the Union. Consequently, he was in favor of the Compromise. Webster also exerted his great influence in its favor, and so the passage of the compromise measures was furthered by the coming in of the new Administration.

The campaign of 1852

The breach in the Democratic Party had been healed when it held its national convention at Baltimore early in June, 1852. The outstanding candidates for the nomination were Cass, Buchanan, Douglas, and Marcy. For a number of ballots the convention was deadlocked and it became evident that none of these leaders would be selected. Then on the forty-ninth ballot there was a stampede to Franklin Pierce of New Hampshire, and he was nominated almost unanimously. William R. King of Alabama was named for the Vice-Presidency. The platform gave an unqualified endorsement of the Compromise of 1850.

The Whigs held their convention in Baltimore later in this same month of June. Before it were presented the names of Fillmore, Webster, and General Scott. Fillmore started out with a plurality (not a majority) of the votes, but later he fell behind Scott, who was nominated on the fifty-third ballot. Scott owed his victory to the fact that the pro-Administration forces were divided between Fillmore and Webster. The platform, like that of the Democrats, endorsed the Compromise, including the Fugitive Slave Act.

There was little excitement in this campaign. The Whigs tried without success to stir up enthusiasm for their military hero and thus repeat the performance of 1840. So far as their platforms went, there was no real issue between the parties. Nevertheless Scott, although reared and educated in Virginia, was thought to lean toward the antislavery cause. This opinion arose from his close association with Seward, who had effectively supported his nomination. Pierce, on the other hand, was supposed to be wholeheartedly in favor of the Compromise, and his election therefore offered the better guarantee that the slavery controversy would not be reopened.

Scott did not receive the cordial support of the whole Whig Party. *Result and* The antislavery element liked the candidate but objected to the *significance* platform. Quite a number of the Southern and conservative Whigs, *of the election* on the other hand, endorsed the platform but were dissatisfied with the candidate. Pierce had behind him a united party and was able to make a strong appeal to the independent voters. The people were tired of slavery agitation and wanted a vacation from controversy. Times were good and the business interests feared that this prosperity would be frightened away if the slavery dispute were reopened. For these reasons Pierce was elected by an unusually large popular and electoral majority, carrying every state but four. The Free-Soil Party did not make nearly so good a showing as it had in the previous campaign. This was another indication that the country was weary of the strife over slavery and was longing for rest.

CHAPTER XL.

A Relapse into Sectional Strife

FOREIGN POLICY OF PRESIDENT PIERCE

*F*RANKLIN PIERCE (1804-1869) was in his forty-eighth year and was thus the youngest man elected President up to that time. He had an attractive personality, was an eloquent speaker, and enjoyed a reputation for strict honesty and earnest religious convictions. He was a successful lawyer and had been in public life for a number of years, having served in the New Hampshire legislature and in both houses of Congress. In the Mexican War he had displayed courage and ability, serving under General Scott as a brigadier general.

The inauguration of the good-looking new President was witnessed by the largest crowd that had ever assembled on such an occasion. His inaugural address, which was a well-phrased literary production, was effectively delivered, not read. It advocated a strict enforcement of the Compromise measures and such territorial expansion as would be necessary for

*Courtesy of the New-York Historical Society,
New York City*

FRANKLIN PIERCE.

home defense. "The policy of my administration," he said, "will not be controlled by any timid forebodings of evil from expansion."

If the snow falling on his bare head as he took the oath of office was an unfavorable omen, the other auspices pointed to a successful administration. It was a time of great prosperity. Immigrants were pouring into the country, and railroad construction was booming. The acceptance of the Compromise by both of the great political parties gave the impression that the evil spirit of slavery agitation

642

had finally been exorcised. The business interests were anxious to maintain the *status quo* as to slavery, fearing that a renewal of the dispute would frighten away the good times.

Pierce's outstanding weakness as President was his indecision of *The Cabinet* character, a fault which was aggravated by his intense desire to please everybody. The wisdom or unwisdom of his policy would therefore be determined largely by the influences that would be brought to bear upon him. For this reason the selection of his official advisers was an important step. In his Cabinet there were three men who had attained eminence in public life. These were: William L. Marcy of New York, Secretary of State; Jefferson Davis of Mississippi, Secretary of War; and Caleb Cushing of Massachusetts, Attorney General. Davis was rapidly becoming the leading champion of the Southern cause and the other two took a moderate attitude toward slavery. Under such guidance the President was more cordial toward Southern interests than ordinarily would be expected of a Northern President.

At his accession Pierce probably looked forward to the annexation *Pierce's plans* of Cuba as the principal objective of his administration. By this *for expansion* time, however, the question of expansion was so interlaced with that of slavery that there was no way of separating them. The South favored and the North opposed the acquisition of Cuba because expansion southward would seemingly enlarge the area of slavery and thereby give the South a stronger position in the Union. With sentiment thus divided at home, the President was not able to carry out his desire for expansion. Furthermore, no outward event occurred which opened the way for an agreement with Spain looking to the purchase of Cuba.

In 1854 the *Black Warrior,* an American merchant vessel, was seized by the Cuban authorities, and the United States had a grievance which might develop into an opportunity to seize the coveted island. But the Cuban authorities made a satisfactory adjustment with the owners of the *Black Warrior,* and no excuse for further action was left.

In this same year, however, a suggestion was made which, if it had *The Ostend* been carried out, might have led to the acquisition of the Pearl *Manifesto* of the Antilles. The American ministers to England, France, and Spain—James Buchanan, John Y. Mason, and Pierre Soulé, respectively—met at Ostend, Belgium, and drew up a memorandum suggesting that Spain be offered one hundred million dollars for Cuba and that if this offer were refused the United States would be justified in seizing the island. This memorandum was known as the Ostend Manifesto. There was a loud outcry against this proposal—both at home and abroad—and Secretary Marcy repudiated the Manifesto.

The Gadsden Purchase

The only new territory gained was a small area south of the Gila River, which was bought from Mexico (1853) for ten million dollars. This acquisition is known as the "Gadsden Purchase" because the purchase was negotiated by James Gadsden, American minister to Mexico. This land was coveted because the surveyors thought it would be needed for the proper location of a southern railroad to the Pacific. A boundary dispute and other causes of friction had

Courtesy of the New-York Historical Society, New York City

PERRY IN JAPAN.

been disturbing relations between the United States and Mexico and each country had grievances against the other. Gadsden was instructed to negotiate a treaty by which all points of difference would be settled, and Lower California and a large area south of the Rio Grande would be granted to the United States. The Mexican government, however, was unwilling to alienate so large a portion of its domain and refused to consider the cession of territory beyond the minimum necessary for the adjustment of the boundary and the location of the prospective railroad.

The treaty with Japan

The Administration scored a diplomatic success in the Far East which led to results important not only for the United States but for the world at large. Soon after a commercial treaty with China was signed (1844) [1] an unsuccessful attempt was made to open commercial relations with Japan. At that time the Japanese were strongly prejudiced against foreigners; no trade was allowed with the outside world except with the Dutch, and that only to a limited extent. Foreign sailors shipwrecked on her coast were harshly dealt with. In 1852, Commodore Matthew C. Perry was sent by President Fillmore to Japan with instructions to negotiate a treaty of commerce with that eastern power. Not succeeding, he returned with a large squadron (1854) and overawed the authorities into the acceptance of a treaty. By the terms of this agreement two ports were opened to American trade, and shipwrecked American sailors were to be cared for. This was the entering wedge of Occidental influence in Japan. It led to a breakdown in the isolation of the island kingdom and ultimately to the acceptance of western civilization.

THE FUGITIVE SLAVE ACT; UNCLE TOM'S CABIN

The letup in the slavery dispute resulting from the Compromise of 1850 proved to be only a short-lived truce, during which hostilities did not entirely cease. The spirit of bitter controversy had for the time being left the halls of Congress but was still exciting the minds of the people throughout the country. During this interval the centers of disturbance were the Fugitive Slave Law and *Uncle Tom's Cabin*.

The Fugitive Slave Act

The Fugitive Slave Act of 1850 was more stringent than the one of 1793, which had become a dead letter. The newer law imposed upon Federal marshals and their deputies the obligation to take every step necessary for the recapture of runaway slaves and made it an offense punishable by fine or imprisonment for anyone to aid in their escape. Negroes accused of being fugitives were brought before Federal courts or commissioners appointed by them and were denied the right of trial by jury. They were not allowed to testify in their own behalf, whereas the evidence of the claimants or their agents was accepted. The enforcement of the law tended to aggravate rather than alleviate the strife over slavery. The South contended that the opposition to the law on the part of abolitionists in the North was causing many fugitives to escape and was thereby inflicting heavy financial losses on slaveowners. The opposition became stronger after public sentiment had been inflamed by the Kansas-Nebraska Act. The abolitionists sometimes went to the extent of releasing fugitives by mob violence. The North, on the other hand, was dissatisfied with the workings of the act, alleging that free Negroes were being enslaved under its enforcement.

---

[1] In 1844 a treaty negotiated by Caleb Cushing was signed with China, by which American citizens were allowed full trading privileges in certain Chinese ports.

The "Underground Railroad"

That the people in the North who opposed slavery on moral grounds did not co-operate in the enforcement of the Fugitive Slave Act is beyond question. Some of these refused to assist in carrying out the law, while others were active in opposing enforcement. For aiding slaves to escape to free states and Canada the latter group had an effective organization called the "Underground Railroad." Along routes of escape there were designated places at which runaways were received and given assistance. These were the stations. The persons who led the fugitives from one station to another were called conductors. By this secret system a considerable number of Negroes were assisted in their flight from slavery to freedom. To the owners of the escaped slaves this meant the loss of valuable property.

Uncle Tom's Cabin

An important use was also made of literature in the fight for abolition. The most effective indictment ever made against slavery was the novel, *Uncle Tom's Cabin*. Its author, Harriet Beecher Stowe, was born and reared in New England, but it was while she was living at Walnut Hills, near Cincinnati, that she gained what firsthand knowledge she had of slavery. Her father, husband, and seven brothers (one of whom was Henry Ward Beecher) [1] were all ministers. With such a background it was only natural that her opposition to slavery would be based on deep religious conviction. *Uncle Tom's Cabin* appeared first as a serial in an antislavery newspaper. It did not create much excitement, however, until it came out in book form in 1852. At once it attained great popularity, and the number of sales was almost incredible. Its fame extended to other lands, and it was translated into twenty foreign languages. The number of copies sold in the British empire is said to have reached a million and a half. It was soon dramatized, and large numbers of people who were unable to read the book witnessed the play. It exerted a great influence on young people and children, and many boys reading it in their teens are said to have imbibed a deep hatred of slavery which caused them to vote the Republican ticket on reaching their majority.

As a literary production the work was far from being a masterpiece. The style was commonplace, the language in places inelegant, and the portrayal of plantation life far from accurate; but, measured by the influence wielded, "it stands at the very top of American fiction." It was received in the North with great acclaim and it intensified there the opposition to slavery and also the hostility to the South. The people of the South, on the other hand, felt that the

---

[1] Henry Ward Beecher (1813-1887) was the most eloquent preacher of his day. For a number of years he was the minister at the large Plymouth Church (Congregational) in Brooklyn. He too was an ardent champion of the antislavery cause.

book held up their section in a false light before the world. A Southern minister spoke of it as "that book of genius, true in all its facts, false in all its impressions." This alleged slander increased the Southerner's hatred of Northern abolitionists. This difference in reaction revealed the gulf that separated the two sections and widened and deepened it.

THE KANSAS-NEBRASKA ACT

The good auspices under which Pierce entered office soon gave way to portents of trouble. After less than a year of smooth sailing, *Stephen A. Douglas*

Courtesy of the New-York Historical Society, New York City

STEPHEN A. DOUGLAS.

the Administration ship hit upon a rock—the Kansas-Nebraska controversy. The leading part in this dispute was assumed by Stephen Arnold Douglas (1813-1861), a statesman who was born in Vermont but had moved to Illinois in young manhood. Although he came from an old New England family his character was molded more by Western ideals than by Eastern traditions. He easily imbibed the breezy optimism of the broad prairies and had the bustling energy which was characteristic of the West at that time. He was short of stature, but his large head and broad shoulders gave the appearance of physical strength, while his brilliant mind raised him far above the ordinary intellectual level. On account of these mental and physical traits he was called the "Little Giant." He was a master politician and "his party was his religion." He was loyal to his friends and was usually able to win the devotion of young men.

As an aid to a correct understanding of the controversy of which Douglas was the center, a glance should be taken at the map of the trans-Mississippi region. West of Missouri, Iowa, and Minnesota Territory, and north of the present Oklahoma, there was a vast area of unoccupied land which extended to the Rockies on the west and to Canada on the north. In this extensive region there were wide prairies well suited to farming, and the Westerners were eager for the opportunity to settle in this favored land. But before it could

Reasons for organizing a territorial government for Nebraska

be occupied the land would have to be surveyed and provision made for a territorial government. Furthermore, for some time there had been considerable talk of a railroad to the Pacific. The North and the South each wanted this railroad to be linked up with its own section, and three possible routes were under consideration—a northern, a central, and a southern. The organization of a territorial government for the region described above would be favorable to a northern or a central location for the road.

Provisions of the Kansas-Nebraska Act

A bill was offered (December, 1853) by Senator Augustus C. Dodge of Iowa providing for the organization of the Territory of Nebraska. The proposal was referred to the Committee on Territories, of which Douglas was chairman. A bill in line with Dodge's suggestion was promptly reported by Douglas (January 4, 1854). It carried, however, the important additional provision that the people living in the territory were to decide through their legislature whether they would or would not have slavery. Douglas termed this principle of government popular sovereignty. But as there were very few settlers in this territory, the question would have to be determined by the newcomers, or "squatters," who would rush into this new country. The opponents of the bill therefore called the policy "squatter sovereignty."

Repeal of the Missouri Compromise

The slavery clause was contrary to the Missouri Compromise and if passed would supersede that measure. But as there was enough vagueness in the provision to give rise to different interpretations, Senator Archibald Dixon of Kentucky announced his intention to move an amendment definitely repealing the Missouri Compromise. The Southern ultras supported Dixon in this stand and, to win their support to his measure, Douglas accepted in principle the Dixon amendment. As a result of this and other changes, the bill in its final form provided for the repeal of the Missouri Compromise and the organization of two territories—Kansas and Nebraska—in each of which the slavery question was to be decided by popular sovereignty.

The bill supported by the Administration

In the meantime Pierce had been induced to give to the measure the entire support of the Administration. In coming to this decision he was doubtless greatly aided by Jefferson Davis, his Secretary of War, who exercised a strong influence on his chief. With this backing, the bill was passed (1854) by safe majorities in both houses of Congress.

Opposition in the North to the measure

The enactment of this law proved the opening of Pandora's Box, and the evils of slavery agitation began to swarm out with unabated fury. The controversy, now renewed, continued with accelerated momentum until slavery met its death in a terrible fratricidal war. Public sentiment in a large part of the North was lashed into fury over the repeal of the Missouri Compromise. It is true that this compromise was only an act of Congress and legally could be repealed as could any other act of Congress. But the North chose to consider it a sort of compact between the two sections and contended that it was more binding morally than an ordinary law. As the Kansas-Nebraska Act made it possible for the people of one or both of these territories to vote in slavery, it was jeopardizing an area which the North had already staked off for itself. A great deal of excitement was thus aroused, both inside and outside of Congress.

Douglas had not advised with the Southern Congressmen before *Attitude of* presenting his bill, and at first they were a little suspicious of his *the South* intentions. But after he had added the amendment repealing the Missouri Compromise they came out strongly and almost unanimously for it.[1] Many of them gave the measure their endorsement more on account of the abstract principle it contained than because of any practical advantage which might accrue to their section. Their support was won by its recognition of the equal rights of the sections in the territories rather than by the possibility of slavery extension which it offered; for many of the Southern leaders seem not to have expected that either of the proposed territories would accept slavery. This attitude was also reflected by the newspaper press. The bitter opposition to the measure in the North did not, therefore, find a counterpart in exuberant enthusiasm in the South. On the other hand, the latter section accepted the act with a composure which almost verged on indifference.

Douglas contended that his doctrine of popular sovereignty was virtually the same as that embodied in the Compromise of 1850, for the provision as to slavery in the Kansas-Nebraska Bill was like that in the measure for the organization of Utah and New Mexico. It was therefore not a repeal but an extension of this compromise. Besides, the slavery issue, he contended, would now be taken out of Congress and placed before the people of the territories, where it rightfully belonged. It is needless to say that the antislavery Congressmen did not accept this view.

It was through the skillful management of Douglas that the bill *Douglas* was pushed through Congress, and he therefore became the butt of *attacked for* severe criticism in the North. The motive for his action, it was *his sponsor-* charged, was the selfish desire to strengthen himself in the South and *ship of the bill* thus enhance his chances for the Presidency. So unpopular was he in the North that, as he afterwards said, he could travel "from Boston to Chicago by the light of his own effigies." This bitterness of feeling

---

[1] In the passage of the bill the number of negative votes in the Senate from the South was only two and in the House of Representatives only nine.

was largely due to the propaganda carried on by the abolitionists and their political allies. Not only was Douglas grossly slandered by his political opponents, but he has also received unfair treatment at the hands of historians. The older historians—those of a generation ago—inclined too far toward the abolitionist estimate of him and therefore did not present him in a true light. Later writers are more charitable toward him and less disposed to question the purity of his motives. In the light of recent research we may safely assume that one strong motive (and probably the main one) of Douglas' action was his desire that the Pacific Railroad should take the central route and make Chicago its eastern terminus. The organization of territorial governments for Kansas and Nebraska would aid in the furtherance of this plan. The provision as to slavery would win the support of Southern Congressmen and thus ensure the passage of the bill. Furthermore, popular sovereignty was in keeping with the democratic principles to which he adhered. The hope of aiding a political friend, Senator David R. Atchison of Missouri, may also have had some influence.[1]

"BLEEDING KANSAS"

Nebraska organized as a free territory

After the Kansas-Nebraska Act had been passed, settlers moved into Nebraska from Iowa and took steps toward organizing a government. The Southerners made no attempt to win this region for slavery, and so Nebraska at once became a free territory. The citizens of Iowa had taken a prominent part in the election of members of the Nebraska legislature, and some of them had resorted to the practice of stuffing the ballot boxes. However, these irregularities did not attract the attention of other parts of the country, since the slavery question did not figure in the election.

The political situation in Kansas

Very different was the reaction from the outside to the efforts to organize a government for Kansas, as both the proslavery and antislavery forces made a vigorous fight for supremacy. Whether the territory would be free-soil or slaveholding would depend upon the proportion of the settlers from the North to those from the South. Antislavery leaders in the North formed the New England Emigrant Aid Company and other similar organizations to encourage by financial support active emigration from the Northern states to Kansas, hoping that these settlers would be numerous enough to

---

[1] Atchison was in an awkward position because his constituents favored the opening of the Nebraska lands to settlement. But his proslavery sentiments and commitments prevented his advocacy of the organization of another free territory. By tacking on the repeal amendment to his bill Douglas relieved Atchison of all embarrassment on this score with his constituents.

outvote the proslavery men and thus organize the territorial government on a free-soil basis. This method of stimulating settlement gave the antislavery party quite an advantage over its opponents in the race for the control of Kansas. Later on, the South tried the same plan and emigrant aid societies were formed in nearly all the Southern states. These efforts, however, met with little success, for comparatively few planters were willing to assume the risks involved in taking their slaves to a territory from which slavery might be excluded.

An election was held in Kansas in the spring of 1855 to choose members of the territorial legislature. Slaveholders from Missouri came over in large numbers and took part in the election. In the contest the proslavery party was successful. The free-soilers contended that this victory was due to the illegal participation in the election by the voters from the Missouri border, to whom Horace Greeley applied the term of "Border Ruffians." This outside interference was a serious blunder; but whether the proslavery party needed this assistance to win the election is difficult to determine.[1]

Despite the irregularity of the election in which the Missourians had heavily stuffed the ballot boxes, the territorial legislature so chosen was recognized by President Pierce. This legislature created the machinery for a territorial government and adopted a civil and criminal code which included laws favorable to slavery. The antislavery party denied the legality of the acts of this legislature. Moreover, it held a convention at Topeka, which framed an antislavery constitution. Although the call for this convention did not rest on a legal basis, the free-soilers contended that it represented a majority of the settlers and asked that Kansas be admitted as a state with this antislavery constitution. This request for the admission of Kansas to the Union was voted on favorably by the House of Representatives but was rejected by the Senate.

A proslavery government organized in Kansas

With two governments thus facing each other in Kansas, each with a group of adherents enraged against the other side, serious friction was the inevitable outcome. Accordingly, the territory soon fell into a condition of strife which gave rise to the term "Bleeding Kansas." It was a case of Greek meeting Greek, and both sides were at fault. The Missourians who crossed the border were not loath to use the arms with which they were equipped. In the North money was raised not only to send emigrants to Kansas but also to supply them

Civil strife

---

[1] According to a census taken late in the preceding winter the number of *bona fide* settlers from the South was greater than that from the North. But not all of the Southerners in Kansas were in favor of slavery and not all of the Northerners were against it. See George F. Milton, *The Eve of Conflict*, 192; and Avery Craven, *The Coming of the Civil War*, 362.

with rifles. Henry Ward Beecher warmly advocated the furnishing of arms to the free-state men and declared in public addresses that rifles might prove "a greater moral agency" than the Bible. For this reason the Sharps rifles supplied to the antislavery immigrants were usually called "Beecher's Bibles." The slavery controversy was the main but not the only cause of this strife. Some of it grew out of frontier conditions and some of it was caused by personal differences and disagreements over land titles. Furthermore, the seriousness of the situation was exaggerated by distorted newspaper reports.

The Lawrence incident

At first the free-state colonists were located in one part of Kansas and the proslavery settlers in another. Being thus separated, they did not come immediately into conflict with each other. It was not long, however, before there arose a bitter feud between them. One of the deplorable incidents of this struggle was the sack of the antislavery town of Lawrence by the proslavery party. The United States marshal and a county sheriff led a posse of seven hundred and fifty men to Lawrence to make some arrests (1856). The men indulged freely in the whiskey

Courtesy of the Boston Athenaeum

JOHN BROWN.

found there and the posse was converted into a mob. After the arrests had been made some newspaper offices were destroyed, a hotel was burned, and the town was sacked.

John Brown at Pottawatomie Creek

A crime of still greater enormity was committed at Pottawatomie Creek (May, 1856) by a small group of antislavery men led by John Brown. Brown was a narrow-minded fanatic in whose religion there was a fierce strain of belated and decayed Puritanism. The milk of human kindness in his philosophy had soured, and earnestness had hardened into intolerance. The abolition of slavery was the one reform toward which he devoted his energies with unabated effort. He regarded the institution of slavery as a cancer on the social order which could be removed only by painful surgery. "Without the shedding of blood there is no remission of sins," was one of his favorite sayings. That this dangerous man should have gravitated toward strife-ridden Kansas was as natural as the pointing of the needle of the compass toward the magnetic pole. According to his estimate, five antislavery men had lost their lives in Kansas at the hands of the proslavery party. To avenge their death he and six associates (four of whom were his sons) captured five men on Pottawatomie Creek, killed them, and mutilated their bodies.

SECTIONAL FEELING REFLECTED IN CONGRESS

Contest over the election of the Speaker of the House

If Douglas thought that his bill would relieve Congress of slavery agitation he had less foresight than should be expected of a brilliant politician. When the Thirty-fourth Congress met early in December, 1855, the membership of the House of Representatives was divided into so many factions that no group was able to secure a majority vote for its candidate for Speaker. The Kansas question had been the main issue in the Congressional elections, and on it the Republicans had won more than one hundred seats in the lower house and (after many elected on other tickets had shifted their allegiance) were the most numerous group in that body. Under such conditions it could easily have been foreseen that the fighting in Kansas would have its counterpart in bitter, forensic battles in Congress. The first contest came with the effort to elect the Speaker of the House. For nearly two months the members engaged in balloting, with accompanying discussion, without making a choice. The deadlock was finally broken by an agreement to accept as Speaker the candidate who should win the largest number of votes, if this was a majority of the quorum. On the one hundred and thirty-third ballot Nathaniel P. Banks of Massachusetts[1] received the necessary plurality and was therefore declared Speaker of the House (February 2, 1856).

The assault on Senator Sumner

The fight over the Speakership had been characterizd by dignity and decorum and there had been no untoward incidents in connection with it. Unfortunately this was not always the case in the subsequent debates on slavery; too often Congressmen slipped from argument into personal abuse. Of the attacks on the Kansas policy the most malicious was the one made by Senator Charles Sumner of Massachusetts. In his speech on "The Crime against Kansas" he indulged in the most abusive expressions and inexcusable personal allusions without taking the trouble to veil his insults in diplomatic language. In this speech Sumner made a violent onslaught on the character of Senator Andrew P. Butler of South Carolina. Two days later Senator Butler's nephew, Preston S. Brooks, a member of the House of

---

[1] Banks was elected to this Congress on the "Know-Nothing" ticket, but his position on the slavery issue was satisfactory to the Republicans and soon afterward (1857) he received and accepted the nomination by them for the governorship of Massachusetts.

Representatives from South Carolina, avenged the insult to his relative by attacking Sumner while he was seated behind his desk in the Senate chamber, beating him over the head with a gutta-percha cane until he became unconscious. So severe was Sumner's injury that it was not until December, 1859, that he returned to full-time attendance in the Senate, although in 1857 he made a trip overseas to visit the spas of Europe. His political enemies accused him of exaggerating his injury to be able to pose as a martyr and charged that his sightseeing tour demanded the strenuous exertions of a well man.

An effort to expel Brooks from the House of Representatives failed because it was not sustained by the necessary two-thirds vote. He was saved from this disgrace by the support given him by his Southern colleagues.[1] A majority of the Representatives, however, voted in favor of expulsion, and Brooks resigned his seat. He was re-elected almost unanimously, as only six votes were cast against him. The people of South Carolina in general approved of Brooks' action and there was considerable sentiment in his favor in other localities in the South. This sympathy was expressed in gifts of canes and in newspaper statements and editorials. However, the predominant feeling of the South (outside South Carolina) was that the assault was rash, unwise, and indefensible, and would injure the South and the cause of slavery. It is said that Brooks himself during the last months of his life (he died in 1857) was troubled with the fear that he had harmed rather than helped his section.[2]

The cooler headed leaders in the South were correct in their view that this unfortunate affair would strengthen the antislavery and weaken the proslavery cause. The Northerners regarded the attack on Sumner as a cowardly and brutal act inspired by the slave power. The event therefore intensified their hatred of slavery. The action of Brooks' constituents and his Southern colleagues in the House of Representatives, together with the efforts of Southern apologists to excuse him and blame Sumner, enabled the abolitionists with some show of reason to contend that the South as a whole acclaimed or at least condoned what they termed a dastardly act. They were now able to tip with fresh venom the weapons which they were using against the South. It also furnished ammunition for the use of the Republican Party in its first national campaign. "Bleeding Sumner" was added to "Bleeding Kansas" to make a campaign slogan.

---

[1] The Southern Representatives held that the House had no authority to punish its members for acts committed outside the Hall of the House of Representatives. G. F. Milton, *op. cit.*, 236, note.

[2] For an excellent appraisal of the attitude of the South toward Brooks, see Avery Craven, *op. cit.*, 374-377.

THE ELECTION OF 1856

One important result of the Kansas-Nebraska Act was the formation of a new political party. Prior to 1854 the two great national parties—the Whigs and Democrats—had been able to maintain their national character despite the inroads of sectionalism. The Kansas-Nebraska Act led to a division of the Democratic Party and to the destruction of the Whig Party. The Northern Whigs were almost unanimous in their opposition to the act, while a majority of the Southern wing were in favor of it. The Democrats were also divided into pro-Nebraska and anti-Nebraska factions.

Origin of the Republican Party

While the Kansas-Nebraska Act was under discussion a number of meetings were held in various parts of the country to protest against the proposed measure. At one of these meetings, held at Ripon, Wisconsin (March, 1854), it was suggested that a new party, assuming the name Republican, be organized to oppose the extension of slavery. In July of this same year a convention was held at Jackson, Michigan, by the antislavery party and a state ticket was nominated. A few other states followed this example and put out state tickets. The Republican Party had thus been successfully launched before the end of 1855.

The "Know-Nothing" Party

The American, or "Know-Nothing," Party had come into prominence by 1854 (see p. 543). In this year it carried Massachusetts and received a strong vote in New York and Pennsylvania. Next year it carried three New England states. While this party made its chief appeal by its opposition to Catholics and foreigners,[1] it could not ignore the slavery issue. In 1855 the General Council of the party declared that Congress should not prohibit slavery in any of the territories or the District of Columbia. It also refused to demand the restoration of the Missouri Compromise. This pro-Southern stand alienated the antislavery wing of the party in the North. The "Know Nothings" entered the race in 1856 with Millard Fillmore as their candidate for the Presidency.

The Whig Party divided

The Whig Party was unable to stand up against the onslaughts of sectionalism. Since the Compromise of 1850 it had been badly split, and after the Kansas-Nebraska Act is was hopelessly divided. The Southern adherents of the party felt disgruntled at the attitude of their Northern associates toward the Kansas-Nebraska Act. Some of them joined with the "Know Nothings" and others with the Demo-

---

[1] The "Know Nothings" did not advocate the closing of the doors of the country against all immigrants. They were, however, strongly against the admission of alien felons and paupers and demanded that officeholding be confined to native-born Americans who did not recognize allegiance to any foreign prince or power. This meant the exclusion from office of Catholics who acknowledged the authority of the pope.

crats. In the North the antislavery Whigs united with the Republicans. The remnant of the old Whig Party endorsed the nomination of Fillmore.

*Frémont
nominated
for President
by the
Republicans*

The Republican Party was now forging rapidly to the front. The main element in this new coalition was the group of former antislavery Whigs. The party also included Free-Soilers, anti-Nebraska Democrats, and "Know Nothings" who had seceded from their party because of its recent proslavery stand. In February, 1856, the Republican Party was organized on a national basis in a convention meeting at Pittsburgh. Another national convention was held at Philadelphia (in June of the same year), at which John C. Frémont was nominated for the Presidency. He was also endorsed by the antislavery

*Position
of the
Republicans
on the
slavery issue*

wing of the "Know-Nothing" Party. The platform, which was unanimously adopted, declared that Congress should "prohibit in the Territories those twin relics of barbarism, polygamy and slavery." It also demanded the immediate admission of Kansas to the Union with her free-state constitution. William H. Seward of New York was the most prominent member of the party, but he was passed by because he had made enemies, especially among the "Know Nothings," and his availability was questioned. Frémont had had little experience in governmental affairs but had won the title of "Pathfinder of the West" from his explorations in that region. Because of his somewhat overrated adventurous career in California, he was crowned with a halo of romance which made a strong appeal to voters and stamped him as a suitable leader for an enthusiastic young party.

*Buchanan
the nominee
of the
Democrats*

The Democratic Convention met in Cincinnati in June (1856). The platform declared in favor of the Kansas-Nebraska measure and commended the Kansas policy of the Administration. As Douglas and Pierce had been the chief sponsors of this policy, one or the other of them was the logical candidate. But the Kansas-Nebraska Act and its aftermath had aroused so much hostility in the North that anyone prominently identified with it would be seriously handicapped. Because of this lack of availability neither of these leaders was named and, after considerable balloting, James Buchanan was chosen. He had been minister to England and therefore had not been associated with the Kansas-Nebraska Act. His record in Congress had been quite satisfactory to the South, and as he was from Pennsylvania it was hoped that he would carry this close but important state. John C. Breckinridge of Kentucky was nominated for the Vice-Presidency.

*Result of
the election*

It soon developed that the "Know-Nothing" Party would be out of the running and the real contest would be between the Democrats and the Republicans. The Republicans tried to make "Bleeding Kansas" the main issue by harping on the unsettled conditions in that territory. The Democrats contended that only by their continuance in power could the Union be saved—that the South would secede if the sectional Republican Party should come into power. Fillmore carried only one state, Maryland. The rest of the South went solidly for Buchanan. While Fillmore received a fair popular vote in this section, Frémont's popular vote south of the Mason and Dixon Line, the Ohio River, and the Missouri Compromise line was negligible. In the North many conservatives supported Buchanan, who represented the only national party. Pennsylvania was carried by the Democrats and Buchanan was elected. Frémont carried eleven states and received one hundred and fourteen electoral votes.

CHAPTER XLI

Storm Clouds

*Buchanan;
personal
traits and
previous
career*

FEW, if any, of our Presidents have had better training through experience than James Buchanan (1791-1868). He was a good lawyer and in the beginning of his practice earned an unusually large income. The greater part of his life, however, was spent in the public service. He was in Congress for more than a score of years, having been in the House of Representatives for nearly half of this time and in the Senate for the remainder. He was minister to Russia for two years, Secretary of State during Polk's entire term, and minister to England from 1853 to 1856. In all these important positions he had worthily discharged his duties, though he had at no time in his career exhibited any marked brilliance or originality. In his relations with others he showed courtesy, tact, discretion, and moderation. Presenting a rather cold exterior and maintaining due reticence, he gave an impression of sagacity. He was of a conservative turn of mind, and to this temperament he doubtless owed his attitude toward slavery. While he was opposed to slavery in the abstract he recognized that the slaveowner had certain legal rights which ought to be respected. Furthermore, he was always opposed to any measures which might cause trouble between the slaves and their masters. He was therefore more considerate of the rights of the Southern slaveholder than were most of his antislavery associates in the North. Abhorring sectionalism and strife, he deprecated the formation of political parties along geographical lines. For these pro-Southern leanings he was dubbed by his opponents a "doughface," a Northern man with Southern principles. Any President with such a political philosophy would have had great difficulty in pleasing a constituency among whom the feeling against slavery had been raised to white heat.

His Cabinet

In line with his policy of peace and moderation, Buchanan, in choosing his Cabinet and in making appointments to office in general, tried to maintain "the sacred balance" between the sections. Four members of his Cabinet were from slave states and three from free states. His Cabinet was not an outstanding one—it was not equal in ability to that of his predecessor. Prominent members of it were: Lewis Cass of Michigan, Secretary of State; Howell Cobb of Georgia, Secretary of the Treasury; and Judge Jeremiah S. Black of Pennsylvania, Attorney General.

James Buchanan is the only one of the American Presidents who was never married. The young lady to whom he had been engaged died when he was a young man, and never thereafter did he have enough interest in women to assume the responsibilities of matrimony. The social life at the White House did not, however, suffer in the slightest because of his bachelorhood. His niece, Harriet Lane, did the honors of First Lady, and so great was her charm that his administration was able to score a fine social success. *Social life at the White House*

One of the most urgent problems that confronted Buchanan on his accession was the Kansas situation. The murders committed by John Brown on Pottawatomie Creek led to a sort of guerrilla warfare between the rival groups which resulted in the death of two hundred people. The original territorial government was in the hands of the proslavery party but it was not accepted by the free-state men. Robert J. Walker of Mississippi, who had been in the United States Senate for a number of years and had served as Secretary of the Treasury under Polk, was now appointed Governor of Kansas. He made an honest effort to put down the strife and give the territory a government which would represent a majority of the people. *Persistence of the Kansas trouble*

With the view to carrying out this purpose, the governor issued a call for a convention to meet at Lecompton to frame a constitution. By that time the free-soilers were decidedly in the majority and could have controlled the convention if they had participated in the election of delegates. Unfortunately they acted under the guidance of an unwise leadership and refused to take part in the election. The Lecompton Convention was therefore completely in the hands of the proslavery party. A constitution favoring slavery was adopted (1857), and its slavery provisions were to be referred to the people for their approval or disapproval. But the terms under which the referendum was to be carried out were such that the voters could not reject the constitution but could only pass upon the further introduction of slavery. The free-state men refused to vote under these conditions, and the constitution with strong proslavery clauses was overwhelmingly accepted. *The Lecompton Constitution*

In the fall election the free-state men voted and gained control of the legislature, which submitted the Lecompton Constitution to the voters for the second time. The proslavery men refused to vote in this referendum and the constitution was rejected. The Lecompton Constitution had now been accepted by one referendum and rejected by another, and in both cases the majorities were overwhelming.

The second vote, against this constitution, was much larger than the first, in its favor, and showed that the free-state men were greatly in the majority. Popular sovereignty therefore would have meant the organization of the territory on an antislavery basis.

The Lecompton government recognized by President Buchanan

Buchanan, however, continued to recognize the proslavery government and asked Congress to admit Kansas as a state with the Lecompton Constitution. Douglas now came out strongly against the acceptance of this constitution until there should be a real, not a partial, ratification of it by the people. He contended that to recognize a government upheld by a minority and opposed by a majority of the voters was to violate the principle of popular sovereignty. In taking this stand he sacrificed much of his popularity in the South and aroused the bitter enmity of the President, who after this used the powerful influence of the Administration against him.

Final settlement of the Kansas dispute

The proposal to admit Kansas as a state with its proslavery constitution was passed by the Senate but rejected by the House. The deadlock in Congress was broken by the adoption by both houses of a proposal made by Senator William H. English of Indiana. This measure provided for submitting the Lecompton Constitution again to the people of Kansas. If ratified by them Kansas would at once be admitted as a state, with a gift of public land approximately the same in amount as that usually granted to new states. If the constitution were rejected Kansas would remain a territory until it had a population as great as that of a regular Congressional district. The constitution was rejected by the voters, and therefore Kansas did not come into the Union until January, 1861, when after some Southern members had withdrawn from Congress she was admitted as a free state.

THE DRED SCOTT CASE

In his inaugural address President Buchanan referred to the dispute over slavery in the territories as "a judicial question which legitimately belongs to the Supreme Court of the United States before whom it is now pending, and will, it is understood, be speedily and finally settled." This reference was to the Dred Scott case, which was decided two days later. The facts in this noted case are as follows:

Facts of the case

Dred Scott was a Negro slave who had been taken by his owner, Dr. John Emerson, an army surgeon, first into Illinois (1834) and then (1836) to Fort Snelling in the northern part of the Louisiana Purchase (now Minnesota). Two years later Scott returned to Missouri with his master and was held as a slave until after Emerson's death. In 1846 Scott brought suit in a Missouri court against Emerson's widow, demanding his freedom on the ground that his sojourn in a free state and free territory had removed the shackles of bondage from him and his family. Slavery had been legally prohibited in Illinois first by the Ordinance of 1787 and later by the state constitution. It was also forbidden in the Louisiana Purchase north of 36° 30′ by the Missouri Compromise. The case was taken by appeal to the supreme court of Missouri (1852), where it was decided that the condition of slavery reattached to Scott on his return to Missouri regardless of his status while he was away.

Courtesy of the New-York Historical Society, New York City

ROGER B. TANEY.

In the meantime Mrs. Emerson had married again and her second husband was an ardent advocate of the antislavery cause. She was willing to co-operate in the effort to win a court decision in favor of Scott, and in order to get his case before a Federal court she transferred him by a fictitious sale to the ownership of her brother, J. F. A. Sanford of New York. The Constitution states that the judicial power of the United States shall extend to controversies between citizens of different states. On the basis of this provision Scott's antislavery lawyers, contending that he as a citizen of Missouri had a right to sue a citizen of New York in a Federal court, brought the case before the Federal Circuit Court in Missouri and then to the Supreme Court of the United States.

At this time the United States Supreme Court was made up of five justices from the slave states (including Chief Justice Roger B. Taney) and four from the free states. Since the death of John Marshall it had been the practice of the Court to concern itself with the strictly legal aspects of cases and as far as possible to steer clear of political questions. For this reason it held a high place in the estimation of conservatives and moderates, and its decisions carried great weight. Not all of its opinions, however, had been acceptable to the abolitionists, and they had already started an effective propaganda to undermine its influence. *High standing of the Supreme Court*

At a meeting in February, 1857, it was agreed by a majority of the justices to hand down a decision to the effect that Dred Scott was still a slave and to give no opinion as to the political questions involved. The precedent followed in this opinion was a unanimous decision given by the United States Supreme Court in a similar case in 1850. If this had been the final act of the Court—as was expected at the time it was taken—the decision would have been generally accepted and would have caused little or no excitement.

Unfortunately the Court soon afterward decided to widen the scope of its opinion and make it cover the political as well as the legal questions involved. This reversal of the original agreement resulted from the decision of the two minority justices (McLean and Curtis) to argue in their dissenting opinions in favor of the constitutionality of the Missouri Compromise. Inasmuch as the minority would present their views on the important political questions, the majority felt that they also should uphold their side of the case. Accordingly, it was decided that the opinion should cover all the points at issue and should be written by Chief Justice Taney. In coming to this conclusion the majority were influenced by the arguments of Justice Wayne, who felt that a decision by the highest tribunal in the land would allay the strife over the troublesome slavery question. The final decision as reported by Taney and upheld by a majority of the Court was as follows:

1. Dred Scott was not a citizen of Missouri in the constitutional sense and had no right to sue or be sued in a Federal court. According to Taney's argument no Negroes were citizens. The rights and privileges guaranteed in the Constitution applied exclusively to the white race. Negroes, whether free or slave, did not come under the shelter of its protection. At the time the Constitution was framed it was not considered that the Negro had any rights which a white man was bound to respect.

2. Congress did not have any right to prohibit slavery in any of the territories carved out of the Louisiana Purchase. The Missouri Compromise (1820), which prohibited slavery in this area north of the parallel of 36° 30′, was therefore unconstitutional and null and void.

3. Dred Scott was still a slave since his status was determined by the law of Missouri which, as interpreted by its highest court, did not recognize any change of his status by virtue of his temporary residence outside the commonwealth.

The decision at once became a political issue. By declaring that Congress had no authority to prohibit slavery in the territories it struck at the cardinal principle of Republican doctrine. If the view of the Court should prevail this new party would lose its reason for being. Self-preservation therefore demanded that it strike back, which it did not hesitate to do. The adherents of this party declared that the decision, in so far as it referred to slavery in the territories and the Missouri Compromise, had no relation to the case before it and was therefore *obiter dictum*. To them it was not a decision but only an opinion—one which they expected to be reversed when the personnel of the Court had been made over to their liking. The decision proved a great boon to the Republicans since it furnished them a fresh issue. The people were getting bored with "Bleeding Kansas," and the party needed a new object of attack.

The Northern Democrats accepted the decision but were somewhat embarrassed by it, inasmuch as it struck at the doctrine of popular sovereignty (see p. 648). The Southern Democrats, however, enthusiastically acclaimed the decision, for it was an endorsement of a principle which Calhoun and other Southern leaders had been proclaiming for years.

Those well-meaning justices who thought that the decision would *Effect of* quiet the slavery controversy were sadly disappointed, for it had just *the decision* the opposite effect. The antislavery leaders and newspapers in the North raised a storm of opposition greater than ever encountered, before or since, by a decision of the United States Supreme Court. An editorial in Horace Greeley's influential *New York Tribune* said that the decision "is entitled to just so much moral weight as would be the judgment of a majority of those congregated in any Washington barroom." The *New York Independent,* which had a wide circulation among Congregationalists, said: "If the people obey this decision, they disobey God."

The refusal of an influential element in the North to accept the opinion intensified the feeling of bitterness in the South against that section. Another unfortunate result of the decision was that it caused the Supreme Court to lose prestige and influence. This loss of prestige was due partly to the decision itself and also largely to the campaign of misrepresentation which was carried on against it. Even before the decision was rendered the abolitionists had started propaganda against the Court, which received added momentum from the unpopularity of the decision in the North.

THE PANIC OF 1857

Buchanan had been in office less than six months when the panic *Causes* of 1857 started. It was caused by overactive speculation, especially in real estate, and overexpansion in railroad building, manufacturing, and agriculture during the preceding years. Prior to this time, except for a brief interruption in 1854, the 'fifties had been a period of exceptional prosperity. The great output of gold in California was increasing the supply of money and causing a constant rise in prices. Inflation was encouraged by this abundance of gold and by the banking practice of the day. Since Jackson's administration there had been no national bank in the country and the numerous state banks had been issuing notes more freely than they had before that time. The notes, which circulated as currency, were better supported by specie reserves in some cases than in others, and so there was considerable difference in the value of the paper put out by the various banks. Such a condition meant confusion and overexpansion in the money supply. Easy credit and rising prices were stimulating activity in all lines of business. American shipping was at the greatest height in its history. The steamboat on the Mississippi was enjoying its golden age. Railroads had been constructed in sparsely settled regions where they were not called for by traffic needs. Manufacturing had gone beyond the available demand of the country and had piled up goods for which there was no sale. The Crimean War had raised among farmers expectations of high prices for grain, and they had greatly increased their indebtedness to extend the acreage of production.

The financial crash

In the winter of 1856-57 business leaders began to show nervousness over financial conditions, and by August optimism had given way to distrust. Banks were calling in their loans and this greatly increased the feeling of uneasiness. The crash was precipitated by the suspension of the Ohio Life Insurance and Trust Company (August 24), which was engaged in a large banking business. Soon there appeared all the symptoms of a full-fledged panic. Manufacturing plants closed, throwing laborers out of employment; mercantile establishments failed; stocks declined, and a number of railroads went into bankruptcy; and for a short time all but a few of the banks in the country suspended specie payment.

Hard times

The financial panic was followed by a period of hard times which lasted until the end of the decade. Farmers in the North felt the pinch, as well as manufacturers, speculators, and business men. In the breathing space between European wars the demand for grain declined and prices fell, leaving many farmers with an indebtedness which they could not meet. The cotton planter of the South, however, was more fortunate than the grain grower. Cotton still commanded a high price, as the foreign demand for it did not fall off. The continuance of prosperity in this section at a time when the rest of the country was suffering from depression gave the South greater confidence than ever in the soundness of its economic system. It encouraged *De Bow's Review,* the leading economic journal of the South, to make this boast: "The wealth of the South is permanent and real, that of the North fugitive and fictitious." Hammond of South Carolina delared in the Senate that "cotton is king."

One effect of the panic was the demand by Northern manufacturers *The tariff* for an increase in the tariff. The tariff had been lowered by the act of *issue renewed* 1846 and still further reduced by that of 1857. Urged on by the industrial interests of his own state, Buchanan recommended the raising of the import rates. In May, 1860, the Morrill Bill, which provided for an increase in the tariff, was passed by the House but defeated in the Senate. Later (March, 1861), after the Senators and Representatives from seven Southern States had left Congress, the Morrill Tariff Act was passed.

THE LINCOLN-DOUGLAS DEBATES (1858)

Douglas' opposition to the Kansas policy of the President had *The Illinois* made him popular in the North. By contending that Kansas should *Senatorial* be turned over to the free-state majority he won the favor of *election* Republicans, as well as Northern Democrats. His term as Senator would soon expire (1859), and Eastern Republican leaders advised the Illinois Republicans not to oppose his re-election. The latter did not take this advice and put up Abraham Lincoln against him.

In accepting the nomination Lincoln made the famous speech *Lincoln's* in which he said: " 'A house divided against itself cannot stand.' I *speech of* believe this government cannot endure permanently half slave and *acceptance* half free. I do not expect the Union to be dissolved—I do not expect the house to fall—but I do expect it will cease to be divided. It will become all one thing or all the other. Either the opponents of slavery will arrest the further spread of it, and place it where the public mind shall rest in the belief that it is in the course of ultimate extinction; or its advocates will push it forward till it shall become alike lawful in all the states, old as well as new—North as well as South." This was a very radical stand for an aspiring politician to take, and some of Lincoln's friends had advised against his making so strong an utterance, while the Democrats were jubilant over what they considered an unwise move on the part of the Republican nominee. It gave Douglas the opportunity to accuse him of favoring a settlement of the slavery issue by agitation and warfare between the sections. Lincoln denied the charge, affirming that he had repeatedly declared against the interference with slavery in the states. As the Senator would be chosen by the legislature, Lincoln was trying to secure the election of a Republican legislature and. Douglas a Democratic one.[1]

Joint debates

Douglas and Lincoln each carried on a very active campaign throughout the state. Of the numerous speeches made by them, those that attracted most outside attention were a series of seven joint debates. These meetings were held in the open in groves or on the prairie because no halls could be found which would accommodate the crowds. Speaking from the same platform, they addressed audiences numbering from five to ten thousand, and on one occasion it was estimated that twenty thousand people heard the discussion. Douglas was an able debater and the best-known statesman in America, while Lincoln was just entering upon a national career. The Little Giant appeared more at ease and was quicker and more skillful at retort than his antagonist, though the latter had a good style and was very clever in the use of homely illustrations and humorous anecdotes.

The Freeport Doctrine

The most historic of these joint debates was the one held at Freeport. It was here that Lincoln asked his opponent a question the answer to which is known as the Freeport Doctrine. Lincoln had declared against the Dred Scott decision and Douglas had expressed his acceptance of it. The question put to Douglas was: "Can the people of a United States territory, in any lawful way, against the wish of any citizen of the United States, exclude slavery from its limits prior to the formation of a state constitution?" To appreciate the dilemma in which Douglas was now placed it must be remembered that according to his doctrine of popular sovereignty the people of a territory acting through the territorial legislature could accept or reject slavery. But in the Dred Scott decision the Supreme Court had declared that Congress had no power to exclude slavery from the territories. As the authority of a territorial legislature was derived from that of Congress, it followed by implication that a territorial legislature also had no power to interfere with slavery.

When Lincoln directed his embarrassing query to his rival he knew what the answer would be, for the Little Giant had already stated his position on this question in a number of speeches. As early as June 12, 1857, he had declared in an address at Springfield, Illinois, that although Congress could not divest a slaveowner of his right to take his slave to any territory, this right could be rendered barren by nonaction on the part of a territorial legislature. If the people of a territory were opposed to slavery the legislature, reflecting this feel-

---

[1] Douglas was opposed by the Administration Democrats who put up legislative candidates to divide the vote between him and Lincoln; but this group was not strong enough seriously to weaken Douglas.

ing, could refuse to give it the necessary police support and provide adequate penalties for the protection of the rights of the slaveowner. Without such local legislation slavery could not exist.[1] At Freeport, Douglas gave Lincoln a forthright answer and reaffirmed this position declaring that no matter what the decision of the Supreme Court might be on the abstract question of slavery in the territories, "the people have the lawful means to introduce it or exclude it as they please." This clever explanation, which is known as the Freeport Doctrine, relieved Douglas, for the time being, from an embarrassing situation, but it was a virtual denial of the efficacy of the Dred Scott decision.

Long excerpts from the speeches made in these joint debates were published in the metropolitan press and other leading newspapers, and so the country was able to follow the discussions. Douglas won in the Senatorial contest, but he owed his victory to his personal popularity and his skill in debating, for the Republican state ticket was elected. Few campaigns in the history of the country have had a wider significance than did this off-year contest. The Little Giant's views were acceptable to some Southern statesmen, but the Freeport Doctrine and his later utterances—notably an article which he contributed to *Harper's Magazine*—alienated many of the political leaders of the South. By thus weakening his hold on the Southern wing of his party, the Senatorial campaign, although it gave him the unchallenged leadership of the Northern Democrats, destroyed his availability for the Presidential nomination by a united Democracy. On the other hand, it greatly increased the prestige of Lincoln and enhanced his availability for the Republican nomination in 1860. *Significance of the campaign*

JOHN BROWN'S RAID

In the following year the slavery controversy was brought to a crisis by an untoward abolitionist stroke, John Brown's raid. Brown's hatred of slavery had by the fall of 1859 developed into a dangerous obsession. He had conceived the idea of seizing and fortifying a position in the mountains of Virginia and using it as a center from which forays into the surrounding country would be made for the liberation of the slaves. When the movement was well under way slaves from the South and free Negroes from the North would join his standard, and slave property would become so insecure that masters would rapidly emancipate or otherwise dispose of their slaves. The movement would gradually eat its way farther and farther into the South *Brown's plans*

---

[1] See G. F. Milton, *The Eve of Conflict*, 260, 344.

and would ultimately lead to the abolition of slavery throughout the entire region. This solution of the slavery problem might occasion the shedding of some blood but not as much as a civil war, which would result if slavery were not abolished. He made known his plans to some idealistic but impractical philanthropists of the North who furnished the money for the project.

Using as the base of operations a farm on the Maryland side of the Potomac four miles from Harper's Ferry, Brown with eighteen armed followers, five of whom were Negroes, marched into this little Virginia town on a dark, cold Sunday night in mid-October (1859). Arms had been provided not only for the attacking force but also for expected recruits. In this equipment were included fifty pikes for use of the slaves who were expected to enlist under his banner. Other arms would be taken from the United States armory at Harper's Ferry as soon as the village should be captured. These were the plans and preparations for capturing a town of fourteen hundred people and defying the commonwealth of Virginia and the government of the United States. The foolhardiness of such a venture was ruled out by Brown, who declared that "if God be for us, who can be against us?"

He captures Harper's Ferry

Taken unawares, Harper's Ferry, including the United States armory, was by midnight completely in the hands of the invaders (October 16). A party was sent out which brought in as prisoners two neighboring planters, one of whom was Colonel Lewis Washington, a great-grandson of George Washington's brother. Some slaves were also brought in on this roundup. When pikes were put in the hands of the Negroes and they were ordered to strike for freedom they stood dumb with amazement. They showed a disposition to make no use of them or rather to use them in aid of their captive masters.

The insurrection put down and Brown captured

Brown and his men fortified themselves in the armory enginehouse, which was taken by assault by a company of United States marines sent down from Washington under the command of Colonel Robert E. Lee. Brown and four of his followers were captured, but not until after he had received several saber cuts and bayonet thrusts. The casualties of this unfortunate affair included fifteen killed and nine wounded. Ten of those killed were Brown's followers, and five killed and nine wounded were citizens or members of the attacking force. The first fatality was that of a free Negro, who was shot while peaceably attending to his duties as baggagemaster.

The leader and his captured associates were put in jail at Charles Town, there to await a speedy trial. The prisoners were represented by able counsel and the hearing was an impartial one.[1] On the last day of October the jury brought in a verdict against Brown, declaring him guilty of treason, conspiracy, and first degree murder. This sen-

A PREMATURE MOVEMENT.
JOHN BROWN. "Here! Take this, and follow me. My name's Brown."
CUFFEE. "Please God! Mr. Brown, dat is onpossible. We ain't done seedin' yit at our house."

Reproduced from THE PAGEANT OF AMERICA, *Copyright Yale University Press*

tence was carried out without delay, and the stoic prisoner was publicly hanged at Charles Town (December 2).

During his trial and the period of his imprisonment, Brown in

---

[1] Brown stated that he felt entirely satisfied with the treatment accorded him on his trial. "Considering all the circumstances, it has been," he said, "more generous than I expected; but I feel no consciousness of guilt." It may be, however, that perfect fairness would have demanded a consideration of the plea of insanity. Seventeen of his friends and neighbors had signed affidavits declaring their belief that he was mentally deranged, but these statements were not admitted as evidence. At one stage in the trial a plea of insanity was made by his counsel. On hearing this, Brown, who was lying on a pallet in the courtroom because of his wounds, arose and objected declaring that he was not demented. It is doubtful, however, as to whether this disclaimer on the part of the prisoner should have been considered. After the deplorable affair at Pottawatomie Creek his hostility to slavery seemed to develop into a monomania. There was a deep strain of mental disease in his family, as his mother, grandmother, five first cousins, and two of his sons were of unsound mind. It is not improbable that a constant brooding over the slavery question had caused his mind to give way to this family weakness.

letters to his family and in interviews with visitors exhibited a composure, courage, and depth of religious conviction which elicited the highest admiration in many quarters in the North. His Spartan fortitude and religious earnestness even won the respect of some proslavery advocates who were brought in touch with him.

Significance of the raid

Some of the Northern idealists regarded him as a God-inspired prophet who had put himself in the class of the early Christian martyrs. Others considered him a misguided but honest enthusiast and, while they deprecated the sin, they admired the sinner. Some of the former class allowed their zeal to run away with their discretion. Emerson, in an address which was loudly cheered, spoke of John Brown as "that new saint, than whom none purer or more brave was ever led by love of men into conflict and death—the new saint awaiting his martyrdom, and who, if he shall suffer, will make the gallows glorious like the cross."

To the South, on the other hand, the raid was an act of the deepest criminality—one that was fraught with grave danger to the peace and security of its people. Fear of a slave insurrection had from ancient times been a nightmare to trouble the sleep of slaveowners. Southerners saw in Brown's thwarted plan the stark attempt at slave insurrection peeping through the mist of Northern glorification. They felt that the lives of their wives and children were menaced. It is difficult for the present generation to appreciate the fear occasioned by this raid.

The fact that the raid was hailed as a worthy deed by some prominent leaders in the North and condoned by others led many Southerners to feel that the two sections could no longer pull together. In this way the ill will which was widening the breach into an "irrepressible conflict" was greatly intensified. It also pushed forward the doctrine of secession as a practical policy for the South. Long before this time radical proslavery advocates had predicted that the abolitionists of the North would come into Dixie to stir up slave insurrections. The moderates had laughed off these fears as bugaboos. The radicals were now in a position to claim fulfillment for their gloomy prophecies. The effect of the raid on the South was, therefore, to weaken the feeling of loyalty to the Union and to strengthen the belief in the necessity of secession.

THE CONTEST OVER THE SPEAKERSHIP

Why the yeomanry of the South acquiesced in slavery

Since a majority of the families in the South had no slaves and since slavery was against their economic interests, one wonders why the yeomanry did not use their power of the ballot to put an end to the institution. Instead of welcoming the antislavery agitation, the plebeian nonslaveholder opposed the abolitionists as violently as did his patrician neighbor. He resented outside interference, and his conservatism revolted against what he deemed the fanatical radicalism of the Northern abolitionists. Furthermore, he, as well as his wealthy slaveholding neighbor, felt that free blacks and whites could not live together in peace and security. But probably the main reason for this acceptance of slavery was that the yeomanry were not class conscious. The line that separated the common people from the aristocracy was not an insuperable barrier. This barrier could be and sometimes was scaled by energetic and ambitious plebeians, who thus joined the ranks of the looked-up-to patricians. A successful nonslaveholding farmer hoped some day to be a slaveowning planter. This expectation was often realized, for many of the outstanding political leaders of the planter class were sons of middle-class farmers. Nonslaveholders who were capable of leadership, on acquiring sufficient wealth to become slaveholding planters, usually graduated from their own class and joined that of the privileged order, leaving the former group without adequate leadership.

A serious effort to create among nonslaveholders a feeling of class consciousness was made by Hinton Rowan Helper of North Carolina, who in 1857 published his book, *The Impending Crisis of the South.* He belonged to the yeoman class, being a son of a small farmer who owned only one family of slaves. This work is a severe indictment of slavery on economic grounds. Basing much of his discussion on the data furnished by the census of 1850, he declared that the South had lagged behind the North in education, economic prosperity, and general civilization. This backwardness he attributed to slavery. A strong point in his argument was the economic dependence of the South on the North. "In infancy," he said, "we are swaddled in Northern muslin; in childhood we are humored with Northern gewgaws; in youth we are instructed out of Northern books; at the age of maturity we sow our 'wild oats' on Northern soil; . . . in the decline of life we remedy our eye-sight with Northern spectacles, and support our infirmities with Northern canes; in old age we are drugged with Northern physic; and, finally, when we die, our inanimate bodies, shrouded in Northern cambric, are stretched upon the bier, borne to the grave in a Northern carriage, entombed with a Northern spade, and memorized with a Northern slab!"

Hinton Helper and his book against slavery

The abolition of slavery, without compensation to owners, was advocated, not on moral grounds but in justice to the nonslaveholding whites. The author had no love for the Negro but regarded slavery as the curse of the poor and middle-class whites. He made a violent attack on the intelligence and morality of the advocates of slavery.

The yeomanry were urged to organize against the "lords of the lash" and the suggestion was thrown out that slave uprisings might be used in furtherance of the movement toward abolition. If he had succeeded in indoctrinating the yeomanry with his beliefs the institution of slavery might have been overthrown by the masses in the South without any outside assistance. The great planters, therefore, were following a true instinct when they saw in this vituperative work an assault on the foundations of their peculiar institution.

The book condemned in the South

At first the book did not arouse much excitement. In 1858 Horace Greeley published it as a campaign document to aid the Republican Party. To give it a proper introduction he secured the endorsements of fifty leading Republicans, prominent among whom was John Sherman of Ohio. By this time the South had become aware of the danger in the book and violently resented the action of these politicians in giving it this publicity. Southern leaders bitterly denounced Helper and those who had aided in spreading what they considered a malicious slander against their section. The newspapers echoed the cry, and to such a pitch was public sentiment aroused that it became a crime to circulate this objectionable book in some of the states in the Southland.

New states admitted to the Union

Three days after John Brown was hanged, the Thirty-sixth Congress assembled (December 5, 1859). Two new states, Minnesota (1858) and Oregon (1859), had been admitted into the Union by the previous Congress, and there were now fifteen slave and eighteen free states. The Southern Congressmen had not opposed the admission of Minnesota despite the fact that it had come in with a free-soil constitution. A majority of the Republicans, however, were not in favor of admitting Oregon, although it would be a free state, partly because it did not have the population of a regular Congressional district (as had been required in the terms for the admission of Kansas), and partly because its constitution prohibited free Negroes and mulattoes from entering the state. Another reason for Republican opposition was that Oregon was expected to line up with the Democratic Party. As a matter of fact, both Minnesota and Oregon gave their vote to Lincoln in 1860.

The Speakership contest

In this Congress the Democrats still had a majority in the Senate but had lost control of the House of Representatives. Of the four groups represented in the House[1] the Republicans had the largest number but not a majority of the membership. No one could be elected Speaker, therefore, without winning votes from more than one faction. The attempt to organize the House would of necessity

---

[1] The membership of the House consisted of 119 Republicans, 88 Administration Democrats, 13 Anti-Lecompton Democrats, and 27 Americans ("Know Nothings").

involve a long if not bitter fight. After the first ballot the Republicans centered on John Sherman of Ohio for Speaker, and he received a large vote on the numerous successive ballots. But his chances for election were destroyed when Clark of Missouri offered a resolution declaring that any Representative who had endorsed and recommended Helper's *The Impending Crisis of the South* was unworthy of the Speakership. Since Sherman along with other prominent Republicans had approved the publication of this book, the resolution was aimed at him.

Not only did Clark's motion cause the defeat of Sherman, but it also unleashed an ill-natured debate which degenerated into a chronic quarrel of unrestrained bitterness. The clerk who was acting as chairman could not control the unruly members, and at times the sessions were characterized by unparliamentary language and physical disorder. According to a letter written at the time by Senator James W. Grimes of Iowa, the Representatives on both sides were "mostly armed with deadly weapons, and it is said that the friends of each are [were] armed in the galleries." Finally, after the deadlock had lasted nearly two months, Sherman withdrew from the race, and William S. Pennington of New Jersey was elected Speaker (February 1, 1860).

THE CAMPAIGN OF 1860

The violent disagreement between North and South over the slavery question, which had figured so dramatically in the Speakership contest, was destined to work havoc in the ranks of the Democratic Party. At the Cincinnati Convention (1856) the Democrats had selected Charleston, South Carolina, as the place for their next national convention (in 1860). Owing to the growth of sectional strife in recent years, Charleston—a city in which the Southern feeling was especially strong—was not considered by some leading Democrats as a suitable place for a national convention. The atmosphere there was not conducive to the spirit of unity which the convention so much needed if it were to weather the approaching storm. Furthermore, Douglas' chances for the nomination would not be so good in a city whose people were in opposition to his views. For these reasons an effort was made to change the place of meeting, but without success. *The Democratic Convention in Charleston*

When the Democrats assembled in national conclave at Charleston (April 23), they were divided into two opposing camps. The issue between them was Douglas and his doctrine of popular sovereignty. The Little Giant was the outstanding leader of the North- *Division of the Democratic Party*

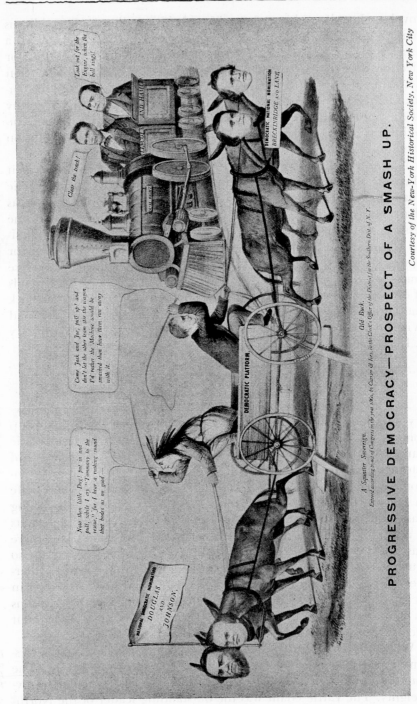

PROGRESSIVE DEMOCRACY—PROSPECT OF A SMASH UP.

THE CAMPAIGN OF 1860.

Courtesy of the New-York Historical Society, New York City

ern Democracy, and his policies were acceptable to that wing of the party. He also had a considerable following among the rank and file of the Southern Democrats, but the radical proslavery advocates, "Fire-eaters," as they were called by their opponents, were strongly opposed to him. The ultras insisted upon a straightforward

Courtesy of the New-York Historical Society, New York City

WILLIAM LOWNDES YANCEY.

statement of the principle that slavery should be protected by the Federal government in the territories. They were ably led by William L. Yancey of Alabama. This eloquent orator, with his soft, musical voice and picturesque personality, was the dean of the "Fire-eaters." In a brilliant speech before the convention he boldly stated the demands of his section and earnestly urged the adoption of a platform which would meet them.

William L. Yancey

The Douglas men were in the majority and were able to dictate the platform and name the candidate. If either the platform or the candidate had been satisfactory to the South a breach might have been averted; but the Northern delegates would not yield on either of these

Northern delegates in control

points. They felt that a clear-cut statement in favor of the Southern position and the selection of any candidate other than Douglas would be unacceptable to their section and would invite defeat at the polls. A platform was thus adopted which did not meet the wishes of the ardent advocates of Southern rights, though it went farther in that direction than any party had ever gone before.

Upon the adoption of the platform the delegations from Alabama, Mississippi, Texas, and Florida, and a majority of those from several other Southern states withdrew from the convention. Under the rule then adopted, no nomination could be made with less than two thirds of the original number of delegates. For two days they balloted on a candidate for President. On several ballots Douglas received a majority of the votes of the original convention, but could never obtain a two-thirds majority. The body was hopelessly deadlocked and, after fifty-seven ballots had been taken, adjourned to meet again in Baltimore on June 18.

Southern delegates withdraw from the convention

After leaving the Charleston Convention the bolting delegates

THE YEAR 1860: A COMPARISON

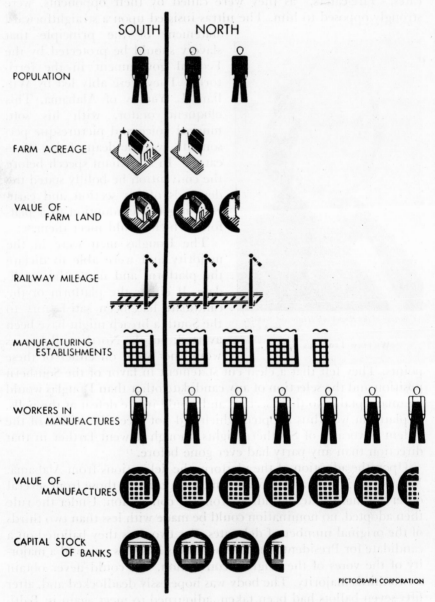

SOUTH   NORTH

POPULATION

FARM ACREAGE

VALUE OF
FARM LAND

RAILWAY MILEAGE

MANUFACTURING
ESTABLISHMENTS

WORKERS IN
MANUFACTURES

VALUE OF
MANUFACTURES

CAPITAL STOCK
OF BANKS

PICTOGRAPH CORPORATION

The chart is from Louis M. Hacker, *The United States: A Graphic History,* p. 61.
Modern Age Book, Inc., N. Y., 1937.

met in that city and adopted a platform in line with Southern rights. They called another convention to meet at Richmond on June 11 and invited that portion of the Democratic Party which was in sympathy with them to send delegates to this convention. The Richmond meeting, which was held at the appointed time, after a two days' session, adjourned until June 25 to await the action of the Baltimore Convention.

When the adjourned convention assembled in Baltimore some of the Charleston seceders and other Southern delegates appeared to take part in the proceedings. Dissension arose over the seating of some of the delegates who had bolted at Charleston and, after several days of bitter wrangling, the delegates from Virginia, Tennessee, North Carolina, Kentucky, and Maryland, and some from other states, withdrew from the meeting. Douglas was then nominated for President and Senator Benjamin Fitzpatrick of Alabama for Vice-President. The latter afterwards declined and Herschel V. Johnson of Georgia was named for the place by the national committee. *Nominees and platform of the Northern Democrats*

The platform expressed strong disapproval of legislative enactments which violated the Fugitive Slave Law; advocated the annexation of Cuba "on such terms as shall be honorable to ourselves and just to Spain"; and declared that the decisions of the Supreme Court of the United States as to the power of a territorial legislature regarding slavery should be enforced by every branch of the general government.

The delegates who had withdrawn from the regular Baltimore Convention and those who had been denied seats in it promptly assembled in the same city and adopted the platform which the Southern leaders had presented at Charleston. The main plank in this platform was the declaration that it was the duty of the Federal government, in all its departments, to protect slavery in the territories. John C. Breckinridge of Kentucky was nominated for President and Joseph Lane of Oregon for Vice-President. The adjourned convention at Richmond reassembled and accepted this platform and these nominees. The Democratic Party, which had for so long been a unifying influence in the country, was now broken in twain. This division of the only remaining national political party meant the breaking of one more important tie that had bound the North and South together. It boded ill for the continuance of the Union. *Nominees and platform of the Southern Democrats*

In the interval between the adjournment of the Charleston Convention and the assembling of the Democrats in Baltimore, a convention was held in Baltimore (May 9) by the "Constitutional Union" Party. This new party was made up of remnants of the Whig and Native American Parties and other conservatives who wished to save *The "Constitutional Union" Party* the Union by calling a halt on slavery agitation. It nominated John Bell of Tennessee for President and Edward Everett of Massachusetts for Vice-President. The only principles advocated in the platform were "the Constitution of the country, the union of the states, and the enforcement of the laws."

Platform of the Republican Party

One week after the assembling of the "Constitutional Union" Party in Baltimore, the Republicans held their convention in Chicago. Opening on May 16, it adopted with great enthusiasm a platform which denied "the authority of Congress, of a territorial legislature, or any individual, to give legal existence to slavery in any territory of the United States." It also declared in favor of a homestead law; pronounced John Brown's raid "as among the gravest of crimes"; recognized "the right of each state to order and control its own domestic institutions"; and advocated such an adjustment of the tariff rates as would "encourage the development of the industrial interests of the whole country."

Lincoln nominated

Several names were before the convention, but it soon developed that the real race was between Seward and Lincoln. Seward's long public career had made him better known than his rival, and he had a strong following among both the leaders and the rank and file of the party. Unfortunately for him, however, his availability was questioned. His reference in one of his speeches to the slavery controversy as an "irrepressible conflict" and his enunciation of the "higher-law" doctrine stamped him as an extreme radical,[1] and this arrayed many conservative leaders against him. Lincoln's House-Divided-against-Itself speech was just as radical, but Lincoln's statement was susceptible of two interpretations. The prophecy that the country would become all slave or all free could be held out to the abolitionists as a promise of the destruction of slavery in the states, while to the conservatives it could be explained as referring to a gradual process to take place in the distant future. It was feared that Seward could not carry the doubtful states of Pennsylvania, New Jersey, Indiana, and Illinois. Promises as to Cabinet positions made by Lincoln's manager to prominent delegates also helped the cause of the Illinoian. Lincoln did not authorize these pledges, but he carried them out after he became President.

Although the slavery question was the outstanding issue of the campaign, the tariff also played an important part in Pennsylvania and New Jersey. While the tariff plank in the Republican platform was vague, it was accepted in these two states as a pledge in favor of protection. Such an interpretation was favorable to Lincoln,

---

[1] As a matter of fact, Seward was not so radical as these utterances (as interpreted by his conservative opponents) indicated.

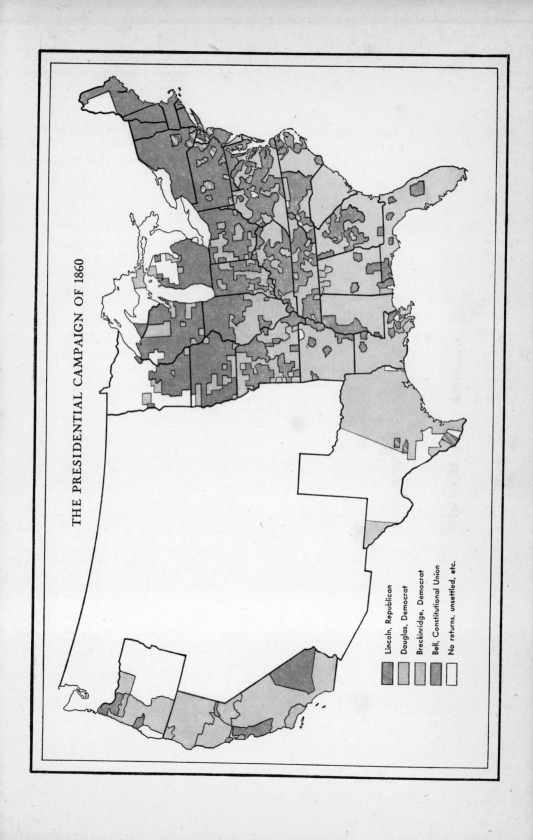

THE PRESIDENTIAL CAMPAIGN OF 1860

Lincoln, Republican

Douglas, Democrat

Breckinridge, Democrat

Bell, Constitutional Union

No returns, unsettled, etc.

as the sentiment in both states was strong for a higher tariff. The provision advocating free homesteads was also a winning card with prospective emigrants to the West.

Lincoln was elected by a good-sized majority of the electoral vote, although he received only forty per cent of the total popular vote.[1] The Republicans, however, failed to gain control of either house of Congress.

Result of the election

Lincoln's support came almost entirely from the states north of the Potomac and Ohio Rivers. The Republican platform, it was said, could not cross these streams. Although the South was opposed to the economic policies of the Republicans, its main attack was directed against the antislavery plank in the platform. Its objection to this plank seems to have been more a matter of principle than of policy. For there were in 1860 only forty-six slaves in all the territories, and soil and climate had decreed that none of these territories could ever become slave states. Furthermore, there was a fear on the part of some of the Southern leaders that the Republican Party if successful would not stop at the exclusion of slavery from the territories but would demand its abolition in the states.[2]

---

[1] The electoral vote was as follows: Lincoln, 180; Douglas, 12; Breckinridge, 72; and Bell, 39. The popular vote was: Lincoln, 1,857,610; Douglas, 1,365,967; Breckinridge, 847,953; Bell, 590,631.

[2] See H. H. Simms, *A Decade of Sectional Controversy*, 211.

PART IV

The War for Southern Independence
1860=1865

CHAPTER XLII

Secession

FUTILE EFFORTS AT COMPROMISE

*T*HE election of a President by one section of the United States *Election of Lincoln by the North* was a new experience in American history, and this alone would have created apprehension in the remainder of the country had there been no other factors of discontent. But the platform of the Republican Party that elevated Lincoln to the Presidency and the declarations of its prominent leaders, so it appeared in the South, seemed to be fashioned in the exclusive interest of the Northern states and against the welfare and perhaps the existence of the South. The newly elected Governor of South Carolina, Francis W. Pickens, gave voice to this widely held opinion in his inaugural address of December 17, when he expressed the conviction that Lincoln had been elected "upon issues of malignant hostility and uncompromising war to be waged upon the rights, the interests, and the peace of half the states of the Union."

While the people of South Carolina and the majority in the lower *Secession of South Carolina* South were in agreement as to the meaning of Lincoln's election, they differed as to what should be done about it. South Carolina would withdraw from the Union at once; but the other Southern states would attempt to reach a compromise settlement with the North. On November 8, two days after the election, the South Carolina legislature passed an act for the election of a state convention to meet on December 17 to consider the future relations between the state of South Carolina and the Union. On the appointed date the convention met at Columbia and listened to the governor's address in which he urged secession. The next day it adjourned to Charleston because of the smallpox epidemic then raging in Columbia. On December 20 the convention by a unanimous vote passed the ordinance of secession.

Despite widespread resentment and fear in the other states of the *The Crittenden Compromise* South, the local and national leaders of this section were not without hope that a compromise between the sections might be reached, and the Union preserved. The first and most important compromise

683

measure presented to Congress was that offered on December 18, 1860, by John J. Crittenden of Kentucky, who had succeeded Henry Clay in the Senate. This measure was offered as a series of constitutional amendments. Its basic feature was the proposal to ban slavery in the territory north of latitude 36° 30′ and permit it south of this line. Other items of the compromise provided that Congress should have no power to abolish slavery in places under its exclusive jurisdiction and situated within slaveholding states — such as army camps and forts — or in the District of Columbia without compensation and the consent of its inhabitants, and those of Maryland, and of Virginia; that Congress should have no power to interfere with the transportation of slaves between the territories and slave-holding states; and that the United States should grant compensation for fugitive slaves not recovered. Finally, these proposed amendments were not to be amended or repealed.

Courtesy of New-York Historical Society
ABRAHAM LINCOLN.

The Committee of Thirteen

This measure—and several others of less importance—was submitted to a senatorial committee of thirteen of which Crittenden was chairman. In the House, also, a committee of thirty-three was appointed to consider proposals for compromise. The committee of thirteen was composed of five Republicans, W. H. Seward, B. F. Wade, Jacob Collamer, J. W. Grimes, and J. R. Doolittle; two representatives from the lower South, Robert Toombs and Jefferson Davis; three Democrats from the North, H. M. Rice, Wm. Bigler, and Stephen A. Douglas; and three representatives, John J. Crittenden, L. W. Powell, and R. M. T. Hunter, from the upper South. It was agreed in advance between Toombs and Davis that if the Republican members would support the compromise, they too would support it. Had the compromise been thus adopted in committee it seems probable that the lower South would have accepted it. Hence the outcome of the compromise depended upon

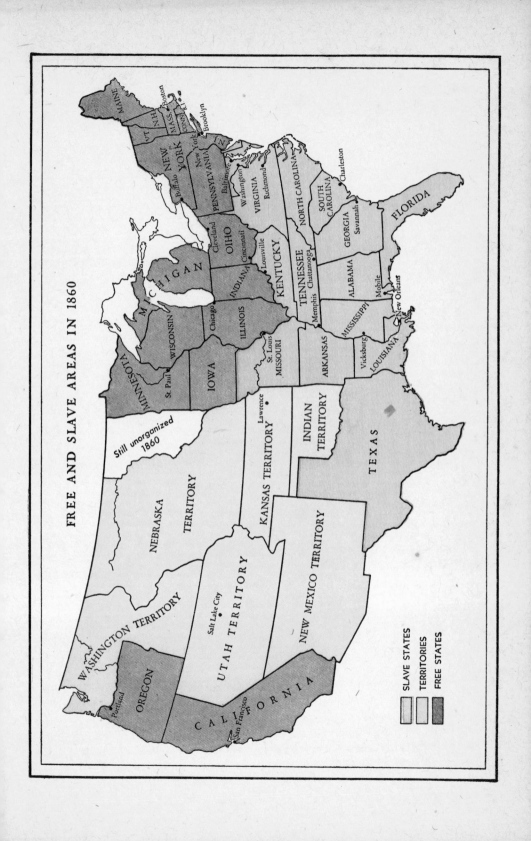

FREE AND SLAVE AREAS IN 1860

MAINE
VT.
N.H.
Boston
MASS.
CONN. R.I.
Brooklyn
New York
NEW YORK
PENNSYLVANIA
Baltimore
Buffalo
Washington
VIRGINIA
Richmond
Charleston
OHIO
Cleveland
Cincinnati
Louisville
NORTH CAROLINA
SOUTH CAROLINA
FLORIDA
MICHIGAN
INDIANA
KENTUCKY
TENNESSEE
Chattanooga
GEORGIA
Savannah
ALABAMA
Mobile
Chicago
ILLINOIS
WISCONSIN
Memphis
MISSISSIPPI
New Orleans
IOWA
St. Paul
St. Louis
MISSOURI
ARKANSAS
Vicksburg
LOUISIANA
MINNESOTA
Still unorganized 1860
Lawrence
KANSAS TERRITORY
INDIAN TERRITORY
TEXAS
NEBRASKA TERRITORY
NEW MEXICO TERRITORY
WASHINGTON TERRITORY
Salt Lake City
UTAH TERRITORY
Portland
OREGON
San Francisco
CALIFORNIA

SLAVE STATES
TERRITORIES
FREE STATES

the action of the Republican members of the committee. But the attitude of the Republican committeemen, with the exception of "Bluff Ben Wade" who had made it clear that he would not budge an inch toward conciliation of the South, was dependent upon that of Seward and President-elect Lincoln.

Seward favored the compromise; but Lincoln, who had offered *Lincoln's* to make Seward Secretary of State in his prospective Cabinet, was *attitude* known to be strongly opposed to any compromise sanctioning the extension of slavery into the territories. He had, for example, a few days before the formation of the Crittenden committee, written Congressman William Kellogg of Illinois to "entertain no proposition for a compromise in regard to the extension of slavery"; and he had urged Congressman E. B. Washburne of Illinois to "hold firm as a chain of steel" against such concessions.

In the hope of winning Lincoln's support of the compromise, *Republican* Seward had his old friend, Thurlow Weed, go to Springfield for a *rejection* consultation with the President-elect. Weed, who was editor of the *of all* *Albany Journal* and one of the most influential leaders of the *compromises* moderate element of the Republican Party, was a strong advocate of a compromise embodying the essential features of the Crittenden proposal. But Weed was unable to move Lincoln from his stand on the territorial questions; and as a result Seward displayed no further interest in the Crittenden Compromise. The Republican members of the committee of thirteen voted against the measure; and Davis and Toombs in accordance with their agreement cast their votes with the Republicans. Thus ended in committee the first and greatest effort at compromise. Later this measure and similar measures were brought up on the Senate and House floors; but the attitude of the Republican members, who were pledged to oppose them, resulted in the failure of all such efforts. Crittenden proposed to submit his plan to a popular referendum, but the Republicans prevented Congress from taking action on his proposal.

Another important attempt to avoid a conflict was made when *The Peace* at the call of the Virginia legislature a peace convention met in *Convention* Washington in February, 1861. It was attended by delegates from twenty-one states and was presided over by ex-President John Tyler. The convention was able, finally, to agree upon a compromise (one that was less favorable to the South than the Crittenden Compromise) , the essential feature of which was the extension of the Missouri compromise line to the Pacific. But the proposed settlement received very little support in Congress; it was rejected by the Senate and did not come up for consideration in the House.

The refusal of Lincoln and of the Republican members of Con-

*Secession of
the Cotton
States*

gress to accept the Crittenden Compromise convinced most of those in the lower South, who had counselled delay in the hope of compromise, that there could be no settlement in the Union; whereupon five of the states of this section—Georgia, Alabama, Florida, Mississippi, and Louisiana—seceded during the first part of January. In February the seceded states met in convention at Montgomery, Alabama, and established the Confederacy. Even then many hoped that by secession a state, or the Southern states together, could reach a more equitable agreement with the North than they could by remaining in the Union. Until the firing on Fort Sumter many Southerners, including Jefferson Davis, hoped for a reconstruction of the Union on terms which would protect the minority section.

Courtesy of New-York Historical Society

Jefferson Davis.

ESTABLISHING THE CONFEDERATE GOVERNMENT

*The
provisional
government*

On February 4, 1861, six of the seven states of the lower South — Texas had not completed all the formalities of secession — met in convention, drew up a provisional constitution, and set up a provisional government which remained in operation until February, 1862. The convention by unanimous vote elected Jefferson Davis provisional President and Alexander H. Stephens provisional Vice-President. Jefferson Davis, who had had a distinguished career under the old government as soldier, Senator, and Secretary of War, accepted the office with reluctance because of his desire to serve the South in a military capacity. Stephens, the Vice-President, was as great a constitutionalist as Davis, and more of a strict constructionist; and he finally came to believe that Davis was attempting to set up a despotism at Richmond and waged an unrelenting war upon the Confederate President.

Davis' first Cabinet was not, with the exception of Judah P. Benjamin, former Whig Senator from Louisiana, and Robert Toombs, *Davis'* one time Whig Senator from Georgia, composed of outstanding men; *Cabinet* and even these two exceptions were placed where they were least fitted to serve. Benjamin was made Attorney General, then acting-Secretary of War, and finally Secretary of State. Toombs was made Secretary of State, a job for which he was peculiarly unfitted and which he looked upon scornfully. From among the Democrats Davis selected Christopher Memminger of South Carolina as Secretary of the Treasury; J. H. Reagan of Texas, Postmaster General; Stephen Mallory of Florida, Secretary of the Navy; and L. P. Walker of Alabama, Secretary of War. Davis left out such powerful secession leaders as William Lowndes Yancey and Robert Barnwell Rhett.

The permanent constitution adopted by the convention at Mont- *The* gomery on March 11, 1861, deserves some notice. Fundamentally, *Confederate* as would be expected, the Confederate constitution was the Federal *constitution* constitution. Some changes were made, however, in the details. For example, the President could serve only one term of six years; and he could veto items in a bill without invalidating the rest of the measure. Cabinet members, though they could not vote, could sit in Congress and explain their reports or answer questions. The Confederate judiciary was to consist of the district courts and a Supreme Court. While the Confederate district courts functioned regularly during the existence of the Confederacy, the Supreme Court waited on the coming of peace to be organized. In addition to certain minor changes such as those mentioned, the Confederate constitution cleared up other questions which had been subject to dispute under the Federal constitution: a protective tariff could not be levied; the Confederate government could not appropriate money for internal improvements; Negro slavery was to be protected in the territories by Confederate law; and the foreign slave trade was prohibited. Additional provisions settled other controversial matters: no state could be admitted without the consent of two thirds of both houses of Congress, and an executive budget system was provided for.

Under this constitution, despite the state sovereignty theory, retained both in the letter and the spirit, a real national government was established which, under the stress of war, set up a system of economic control with a strangely modern aspect.

BUCHANAN'S UNWILLINGNESS TO COERCE THE SOUTH

President Buchanan met secession with no positive action, but *Buchanan's* on the contrary temporized during the period from the election of *inaction* Lincoln to the latter's inauguration; and such lack of direction *due to:*

*(a) His
conception
of the
Union*

seemed to the Radicals near akin to treason. Actually, the President's hands were stayed by his conception of the Federal Union and the constitution. He thought of the United States as being held together by mutual desire and not by force. "Our Union," he said, "rests upon public opinion and can never be cemented by the blood of its citizens shed in civil war. If it cannot live in the affections of the people, it must one day perish." His theory of the Federal constitution was fundamentalist: he believed in the strictest division of powers between state and Federal government, and considered that the incursion of either government into the jurisdiction of the other was an unconstitutional act. While a strong believer in the indestructible rights of a state, he looked upon secession as unconstitutional; but at the same time, harking back to the Federal Constitutional Convention, where the coercion of a refractory state had been proposed and rejected, he believed that the Federal government had no legal power to force a state to remain in the Union.

*(b) His
constitu-
tional
theory*

*(c) Public
opinion*

Furthermore, Buchanan was restrained from coercive action against the seceded states by practical considerations. He realized that any attempt to retake the Southern forts, or to strengthen Sumter and Pickens, would put an end to all attempts at the restoration of the Union by a compromise settlement, and would precipitate sectional war and the secession of most, if not all, of the upper slave states. Nor did he find any decided trend in Northern opinion during his last few months in office which could be considered a mandate to force the seceding states back into the Union. Perhaps a majority of Northern Democrats held views not far dissimilar to those of Buchanan; and at this time the extreme Garrisonian abolitionists were loud in their expressions that the withdrawal of the slave states should be welcomed as a cause of great rejoicing in the North. Then the conservatives of the Bell-Everett Party, and the general business class who had joined the Republican Party to obtain a high tariff and other governmental favors, were strongly in favor of compromise and looked with disfavor upon any proposal to use force. Only a minority, though a large one, of the Republican Party, calling themselves "stiff-backed Republicans," were demanding of Buchanan an uncompromising use of force; and these were the men and principles which Buchanan blamed for bringing on the great crisis.

*The Star
of the West*

However, Buchanan was not entirely inactive, for he made one futile effort at provisioning Fort Sumter, which Major Robert Anderson had seized under the impression that his orders so permitted. On January 9, 1861, the *Star of the West* attempted to enter the harbor with provisions for Sumter, when it was fired upon by South

Carolina artillery and forced back. This attempt to maintain the Federal garrison at Sumter fell within Buchanan's conception of the constitution; but the resistance of South Carolina warned him that such efforts would bring war, and war was coercion which would end all efforts at settlement. The firing on the *Star of the West* could have been as easily regarded as an act of war as the firing on Sumter on April 12 had Buchanan desired to make an issue of it. As it was, Northern opinion remained relatively quiet.

LINCOLN IN COMMAND

When Lincoln assumed office, he appointed a cabinet composed of practically all of the men who had been his rivals for the presidential nomination, as well as representatives of some other political elements. Seward was made Secretary of State; Salmon P. Chase, Secretary of the Treasury; Simon Cameron, Secretary of War; Gideon Welles, Secretary of the Navy; Edward Bates, Attorney General; Caleb Smith, Secretary of the Interior; and Montgomery Blair, Postmaster General. Only a man of Lincoln's tactfulness, patience, and lack of sensitiveness could hope to manage such a dissident group. Yet, if he could manage them, he would go far toward uniting the many conflicting elements of the Republican Party. *Lincoln's Cabinet*

The policy of the new administration for over a month appeared on the surface to be one of inaction like that of Buchanan. But Lincoln's inaugural address had in skillful and subtle language promised quite a different policy from that of his predecessor. Like Buchanan, he took the position that secession was illegal; but unlike the former he asserted that he would enforce the "laws of the Union" in "all the states." In enforcing the law, said the President, there would be no bloodshed unless the law were resisted, or, as he put it, "unless it be forced upon the national authority." He also asserted that he would use the powers of government "to hold, occupy, and possess the property and places belonging to the government, and to collect the duties and imposts" and to maintain the mail service. In short the President proposed to carry on the chief functions of the Federal government in the seceded states, and would use no more force than was necessary to accomplish this aim. Moreover, long before his inaugural address Lincoln had indicated privately that he would maintain Federal authority in the South. On December 22, 1860, he had written Major David Hunter that "if the forts fall, my judgment is that they are to be retaken" after the inauguration; and two days later he had informed Senator Lyman Trumbull that he was considering announcing "publicly at once *Lincoln's intentions to use force on the South* that they [the forts] are to be retaken after the inauguration." One may be assured, therefore, that the new President during the first month in office was not passively watching the Union disintegrate, but that he was grappling with the problems of its preservation.

The problem of the border slave states

But Lincoln could hardly begin any attempt to retake the Southern forts and enforce the Federal laws before he had been assured that he would not lose the bulk of the upper slave states. He was aware, as Buchanan had been, that any attempt to retake the Southern forts or to reinforce Pickens and Sumter, still under Federal control, might precipitate the secession of North Carolina, Virginia, Maryland, Tennessee, Kentucky, Arkansas, and Missouri. This, of course, would doom to failure any attempt to restore the Union. Accordingly, the first month of Lincoln's administration was considerably preoccupied with organizing and, wherever possible, arming the Union elements in the border slave states for the day when the move against the Southern forts would be made and the issue of secession be presented to these states. Nor was the President neglecting the old Whig and conservative Democratic leaders in the upper South, who, though pro-Southern in their feelings, were reluctant to see the Union dissolved.

The difficulty of relieving Fort Sumter

At the same time that Lincoln was thus strengthening the hand of the Union, especially in Missouri, Kentucky, and Maryland, he was struggling to formulate a policy for dealing with Fort Sumter. Here in Charleston harbor the fort with a small garrison under Major Robert Anderson was the one remaining symbol of the Federal Union, and its position placed it at the mercy of Confederate batteries. Both Major Anderson and General Scott had warned Lincoln, when he assumed office, that it would require a powerful fleet and an army of no inconsiderable size to relieve Fort Sumter.

Plans to send supplies to Sumter

The President, however, had no such army and navy at his disposal. As an alternative he proposed at a Cabinet meeting on March 15 that small, swift vessels be sent to reprovision and reinforce Sumter; but the Cabinet, with the exception of Blair and Chase, opposed this plan as calculated to draw the fire of the Confederate batteries and thus precipitate war. Unless Anderson could be relieved, Sumter must fall within a few weeks. On March 29 Lincoln held another Cabinet meeting at which the pressing question of Fort Sumter was discussed; and this time only Smith and Seward opposed all efforts at sending relief to Sumter. These two urged the alternative of reinforcing Fort Pickens at Pensacola, which, because of its distance from the shore, could be approached from the sea without being fired upon. But the President, determined to do something about Sumter, presently ordered a naval expedition to be made ready to proceed to that place. At the same time an expedition was prepared to reinforce Pickens. Lincoln could, with little reason, suppose that such an expedition could reach Sumter without drawing the fire of the Confederate batteries. Indeed, Gustavus Fox and Ward H. Lamon, whom he had recently sent to Charleston, had explained to him that any attempt to reinforce Sumter or send in fresh provisions would precipitate civil war; but on April 4 Lincoln gave formal orders for the expedition to proceed. On April 6 he sent by the hand of R. S. Chew of the State Department a message to Governor Pickens that Fort Sumter would be reprovisioned, "and that, if such an attempt be not resisted, no effort to throw in men, arms, or ammunition will be made without further notice, or in case of an attack upon the fort."

Reaction of the South

The reaction in the South to the knowledge that the Federal government was at last dispatching an expedition to Sumter was very strong. Furthermore, it was the general opinion that Lincoln had practiced deception in dealing with the South; for it was common knowledge that Seward, the supposed spokesman for the President, had time and again assured the Confederate commissioners in Washington, through Judge John A. Campbell of the Supreme Court, that Fort Sumter would be evacuated. That Seward had probably assumed such authority without the consent or even knowledge of the President could not be known in the South.

Confederate and Federal conflict over Sumter inevitable

Here, then, was an issue that would have to be met. Under the Southern belief that secession was legal, Fort Sumter belonged to the Confederacy and must be taken. But, regardless of theory, the fort lying in one of the South's best ports could hardly be left in the hands of a foreign power. On the other hand, under the theory that a state could not withdraw from the Union except by successful revolution, Sumter belonged to the United States, and must be held if possible or surrendered only after a struggle. Lincoln must try to hold, and the Confederacy try to take, the fort under such conflicting beliefs. It would seem inevitable, under the circumstances, that war must begin here.

The attack upon Fort Sumter

When Davis received word that an expedition was on its way to Sumter, he and his Cabinet decided to compel Anderson peaceably or by force to evacuate the fort. After some negotiations the Federal commander promised to withdraw his garrison by noon of April 12, unless reinforced or ordered to stay. But the imminent approach of the Federal expedition made such a delay seem dangerous to the Confederate authorities; and Davis ordered P. G. T. Beauregard, who was in command of the Charleston area, to ask the immediate evacuation of Sumter and to reduce the fort should Anderson not comply with the request. Anderson, with the knowledge that the relief expedition might soon arrive, would not agree to surrender earlier than April 15; and at 4:30 A. M. of April 12 the Confederate batteries opened upon the fort and the United States flag. The next afternoon Anderson surrendered, and he and his men marched out with honors of war.

Each side considered the other the aggressor

The war had begun, and in the North the South was considered the aggressor because it had fired upon the flag, troops, and a fort of the United States. Feeling in the North was deeply stirred. In the South, Lincoln and his party were deemed the aggressor for the refusal to surrender Sumter and the attempt to reinforce it. Southern feeling, too, was aroused and bitter.

IMMEDIATE REACTION TO FORT SUMTER

The call to arms in the North

The surge of indignation in the North at the firing on the United States flag and troops enabled Lincoln to implement his declared purpose of repossessing Federal property and maintaining the authority of the United States government in the Confederate States. On April 15 he issued a proclamation calling for 75,000 volunteer militiamen to serve for three months. The avowed purpose was to send these troops into the Southern states to put down combinations "too powerful to be suppressed by the ordinary course of judicial proceedings" and "to cause the law to be duly executed." Volunteers soon exceeded the quota of April 15; and the President, on May 3, authorized the enlistment of 42,000 volunteers for three years, and directed that the regular army and navy be strengthened by the addition of 22,700 and 18,000 men respectively. The three months' volunteers were called under the provisions of the Militia Act of 1795; but the President had no legal authority for enlisting the three-year volunteers and increasing the size of the army and the navy. Nor did Lincoln consider the situation grave enough to convene Congress before July 4.

Secession of the Southern border states

Lincoln's call for volunteers to be used against the seceded states was considered in the South to be a declaration of war by the President of the United States, and it imposed upon the upper Southern states the necessity of choosing sides. Virginia, North Carolina, Tennessee, and Arkansas quickly chose the side of the Confederacy, nor is it entirely doubtful that Maryland and Kentucky would have taken similar steps had not the secession movement been disorganized by the arrest by the Federal government of prominent leaders and the attempt of Kentucky and Maryland to remain neutral.

The decision of the upper Southern states that seceded is typified

in the personal decision of Robert E. Lee. Lee was resentful toward *The*
the lower South for seeming precipitate and toward the Northern *decision of*
states for the vicious attack upon the Southern people by the Re- *Robert E. Lee*
publicans and abolitionists; he devoutly desired a quieting of the
waters and a cessation of mutual crimination. Nor was there a man
anywhere who loved the Union more than Lee; but his conception
of the Union was a spiritual union, not a mere physical body held
together by a governmental mechanism. Hence, when he came east
from Texas, where he was stationed, and viewed the sectional
quarrel at close range, he realized that real union no longer existed
and that secession, like a final divorce decree, merely recorded outwardly what had already occurred. To Lee, the dissolution of the
Union was a profoundly tragic thing, for the Lee family had done as
much as any family in American history to make the United States
great. Since to him the Union did not longer exist, it was a matter
now of taking sides with the North or the South, and most particularly it was a matter of taking sides for or against Virginia. To Lee
there was only one choice. He could not raise his hands against
his mother state nor against the Southern people. The more one
studies the secession movement in the South the more is one overwhelmed by the impression that Lee's attitude was typical not only
of the people of the border states but of many of those of the lower
South. Actually there was no great difference, for example, between
the attitudes of Robert E. Lee and Jefferson Davis. To the latter,
and to hundreds of thousands of his fellow citizens of the lower
South, the moment for decision had come earlier.

The reaction of the whole South to Lincoln's call for volunteers *Raising the*
and his declaration of a blockade of the Southern waters on April 19 *Confederate*
—later to be extended to Virginia and North Carolina—was, if any- *armies*
thing, more vigorous than that of the North against the firing upon
the flag and troops at Fort Sumter. The Confederate Congress on
March 6 had provided for the raising of 100,000 one-year volunteers;
but apparently recruiting was slow under the terms of this act until
after the fall of Sumter. Before that date few Southerners had expected war and, like their Northern brethren, they preferred to remain in the ranks of the state militia which, with honorable exceptions, was martial only in dress. But with the outbreak of hostilities
volunteers came forward in large numbers to enlist in the Confederate army for one year. Davis convened Congress in special
session on April 29; and the Confederate Congress immediately
passed an act recognizing that a state of war existed between the
Confederate States and the United States. A few days after Lincoln's
Proclamation increasing the armed forces of the United States, the

Confederate Congress enacted a law authorizing Davis to accept as many volunteers as he deemed necessary "for and during the existing war, unless sooner discharged." In August another act provided for the recruiting of an army of 400,000 men to serve for not less than one year nor more than three. In addition individual states called out their militia, which in most cases was mustered into Confederate service. By August, 1861, there were at least 200,000 Southern men in the military service of the Confederacy, and many thousands more in the service of the states. Before the end of the first year of war, according to the reports of the Confederate War Department, 600,000 men offered their services to the Confederacy, though scarcely more than half of this number were accepted because of lack of equipment.

FUNDAMENTAL CAUSES OF THE WAR FOR SOUTHERN INDEPENDENCE

Sectional structure of the Union

Before proceeding with the story of the military struggle between the Northern and Southern states, a brief recapitulation of causes leading to this conflict will be helpful. A glance back over the history of the United States from its founding till the outbreak of this fratricidal war will disclose one constant source of conflict, namely, the sectional structure of the American Union. The sections, as Frederick Jackson Turner has frequently pointed out, were no artificial creation, but were the inevitable products of certain physical and social forces. Nature had marked off the United States into geographic provinces where soil, climate, rivers, and harbors predisposed those regions for certain economic activities. Adding powerfully to this physical demarcation of the country into natural provinces was the human factor: these geographical areas were inhabited severally by provincial, self-conscious, aggressive, and ambitious populations of various origins. The geographic and human factors combined to create in them diverse social and economic systems, and the passage of time and the cumulative effects of history sharpened the sectional pattern.

Loss of intersectional good will

Each section strove to exercise the greater influence in the Federal government partly out of sectional self-consciousness and pride, but chiefly out of the natural desire to protect and further through the instrumentality of the Federal government the interests, both social and economic, of that section. The East would control the Federal government in the interest of a high tariff, a central banking system, internal improvements, and the restriction if not the abolition of slavery. On the contrary, the South would control the central government in the interest of low tariff, the protection of slavery, and a general policy of governmental noninterference in local affairs. If the West should dominate the Federal government it would have free homesteads, internal improvements at national expense, and cheap money. This sectional rivalry was inevitable. It was dangerous, but perhaps not dangerous enough either to divide the nation spiritually or disrupt it physically as long as such rivalry was conducted with the proper regard for the comity of sections. But, as observed in a previous chapter, intersectional good will and mutual courtesy disappeared under the impact of the slavery controversy, and, in the sectional quarreling during the forty years preceding the election of Lincoln, the essence of national unity was destroyed.

Embittered by this quarreling, a majority, perhaps, in the Northern and Southern sections had come by 1860 to distrust and even hate *The development of two nations* one another; and after the election of Lincoln and his refusal to compromise, the South had come to the point where it regarded a continuation under the same government with the North as undesirable and dangerous. Feeling thus, the South withdrew from the Union, basing its action upon the principle of state sovereignty which would enable a state legally to withdraw from the Union and upon the basic American doctrine of the right of a people to choose their own government. For, by 1861, Southern sectionalism had developed into Southern nationalism, laying claim to the right of self-government. Lincoln on the other hand appealed to the principle that the majority had the right and obligation to govern, and the minority, even though the latter had developed into a separate nationality, was under obligation to acquiesce. The Southerners in 1861 did not reject the principle of majority rule, and propose to substitute the rule of the minority—the Confederate constitution and the history of the Confederacy demonstrate the attachment of the South to democratic ideology. What the South rejected in 1861 was the government of one nation by another and hostile nation—for now, too, the North was a nation.

CHAPTER XLIII

Military Operations from Sumter to Fredericksburg

COMPARATIVE STRENGTH OF THE WARRING SECTIONS

Population and man power

*I*N considering the military phase of the Civil War[1] a comparison of man power and material and technological resources would seem to place the South at a great disadvantage. The population of the Northern and upper Southern states that remained in the Union was about 22,700,000, half a million of which were slaves; and that of the Confederacy was approximately 9,000,000, three and a half million of which were Negro slaves and 140,000 free Negroes. During the war, however, the North obtained thousands of soldiers from the Southern mountain regions and recruited the bulk of its 183,000 Negro troops from the slave population of those portions of the Confederacy overrun by Federal armies. On the other hand, the Confederacy drew tens of thousands of troops from the slave states which had not become part of the Confederacy. Although it is obvious then that the potential man power of both North and South cannot be exactly estimated, it is probable that the Confederacy could count upon not less than a 6,000,000 white population as a recruiting ground, whereas the North could draw from about 21,500,000 whites and free Negroes within the Union and about 1,000,000 Southern Negroes.

Industrial superiority of the North

While there had been a rapid industrialization of the South during the ten years preceding the War, nevertheless, the Confederate states were seriously lacking in the industrial and technological equipment so necessary in the waging of war. The North, of course, had far better industrial equipment than the South, but it was not self-sufficient for war in 1861. Until 1864 great quantities of military supplies had to be purchased from Europe.

The North had other distinct advantages over the South. It had

---

[1]The term "Civil War" will be used for convenience rather than the longer phrase "The War for Southern Independence."

696

an established government of three quarters of a century's standing, *Other* with all its functions well organized and its departments well staffed. *advantages of the* Internationally, it was not only recognized as the legitimate govern- *North* ment of the North but of the seceded states also. Its financial and monetary system was in good standing at home and abroad. It had the regularly organized army of about 20,000 and, above all, the Federal navy. Finally, the North had the advantage of interior lines in the West. The Cumberland, Tennessee, and Mississippi Rivers spread like the spokes of a wheel into the heart of the Confederacy, from the Cairo-Paducah area which may be thought of as a hub. The railroads from Paducah and Bowling Green were auxiliary spokes. The Federals could concentrate along any one of these spokes while the Confederates must scatter their forces along the outer rim which they must defend. In the East, the situation was not so favorable to the North; but even there, the James, York, and Potomac Rivers, dominated by the United States naval forces, gave entrance to interior Virginia.

There was a lack of comprehension on the part of each section as *Magnitude of* to the duration and magnitude of the oncoming conflict. Lincoln *the war not* and Seward, whose views were those of the greater part of the North- *foreseen* ern public, insisted that the mass of Southern people were loyal at heart to the old Union and only deluded and coerced by the slav-ocracy; and they believed for months that one crushing victory over the Southern armies would disperse the soldiers homeward. The Southern opinion of the North was that the abolitionists and their sympathizers were agitators but not fighters, and that the commercial and industrial magnates of the North were so devoted to making money that they would not want to make war on their best customer. The mass of Northern people were considered unfriendly, but it was not believed that they would support a war against the South. Even should the North undertake a real war, political leaders at first hoped, and many believed, that England and France would inter-vene in the struggle and thus make an early termination of the con-flict in order to obtain the Southern cotton on which their textile industries were based. Unlike the majority of Southerners, however, Davis feared a long war, and he urged vainly, until after Lincoln's call for volunteers, that a strong force be raised to meet any invasion.

The aged, irritable, and vain Winfield Scott, general-in-chief of the *Scott's grand* United States forces, clearly saw the military problem of the conquest *strategy* of the South in its broad outlines. His policy was to strangle the South by blockade, seize its rivers—particularly the Mississippi and its tributaries—and railroads, and thus cut it into isolated segments. Even before the upper Southern states seceded, Scott had urged upon

Lincoln the necessity of raising and thoroughly training at least 300,000 three-year troops, who would require fully three years to finish the task of conquest. But the Northern press and public scoffed at any idea of a real war; and until after the humiliation of Bull Run in July, 1861, Lincoln did not fully believe in the necessity of such a long-range military policy.

Military problem of the South

The military problem of the South was to prevent the success of the Northern grand strategy. Southern military strategy was of necessity to be a defensive type, preferably an offensive-defensive, that is, an offensive against the enemy within Southern territory.

WAR IN THE EAST, 1861

Battle of Bull Run

In early July President Lincoln, harassed by the popular clamor for an immediate march upon Richmond, ordered General Irvin McDowell with his army of 30,000 near Alexandria to advance against the Confederate force of 23,000 under General P. G. T. Beauregard near Bull Run. At the same time General Robert Patterson, with a force of about 19,000 men occupying the lower end of the Valley of Virginia, was ordered to prevent Confederate General Joseph E. Johnston's detachment of 9,000 men from joining Beauregard. McDowell on July 21 executed the first of those brilliant flanking movements that were so characteristic of the Civil War strategy. While a portion of his army remained on the north bank of Bull Run opposite Beauregard's forces on the south bank, he marched the remainder of his army to the west, crossed the Run several miles above the Confederate left, and came down upon that flank in a surprise attack. McDowell's forces swept all before them down Matthew Hill, across the Warrenton turnpike and up Henry Hill; and the Confederate left was thrown into confusion and panic. But unfortunately for McDowell, Johnston had eluded Patterson in the Valley, and the best of his troops under General Thomas J. Jackson came up from behind the crest of Henry Hill, met the charging Federals with point blank rifle and cannon fire, and countercharged with bayonets. Seeing Jackson halt the Federal charge in his determined stand on the crest of Henry Hill, General Barnard E. Bee is reported to have exclaimed to his disorganized and retreating brigade: "See Jackson standing like a Stonewall! Rally behind the Virginians." Thus Jackson won his sobriquet "Stonewall." E. Kirby Smith's men—the last of Johnston's Valley troops—arrived upon the Confederate left at this juncture and attacked the Federal right flank; and Johnston ordered heavy reinforcements to the Confederate left, which enveloped the Federal right so that the flankers were outflanked. The battle suddenly turned against McDowell, and his troops, abandoning their arms and equipment, broke and fled in panic. The Confederate army was almost as badly disorganized by this surprise victory as were the Federals, and no effort at pursuit was made.

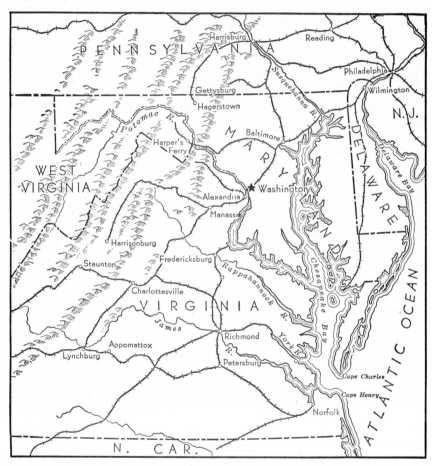

EASTERN WAR AREA.

The effects of Bull Run were beneficial to the North and harmful *Effects of* to the South. In the North popular pride was stung almost beyond *the battle* endurance, and both the public and the President began to comprehend the magnitude of the struggle that the South would make for a separate existence. The military forces of the United States were soon raised to more than half a million men, well-equipped and enlisted for three years or the duration of the war. These armies were given intensive training under the supervision of such able young generals as Ulysses S. Grant, W. T. Sherman, and George B. McClellan; and the latter on July 24, just after Bull Run, was given the command of all the Federal forces in the department of Virginia. In the South, there was much rejoicing and some gloating over the rout of the "Yankees." The Confederate military leaders, on the contrary, were apprehensive at the inevitable effect of over-confidence in the South. Events were soon to confirm their fears, for thousands of soldiers, homesick and believing that the war was about over, took this occasion to visit home—frequently without leave. During the same time volunteering slackened considerably.

Conscription adopted in the South

This popular letdown, accompanied by the shortsighted policy of state governors in building up state military organizations for local defense, and the Confederate defeats in the West in the early part of 1862, had one good effect: the passage in April by the Confederate Congress of the Conscription Act, which required, with certain exceptions, the military service of all men between 18 and 35 years of age—soon to be extended by further legislation to 45. The chief service of these acts was to retain the large army existing in April, 1862, and to bring many thousands as "volunteers" who did not like to be conscripted.

McClellan Lincoln's ablest general in 1861

General McClellan, who had the task of training the Army of the Potomac, was without doubt the best selection that Lincoln could have made at this time. Though a graduate of West Point, he had been a railroad executive for some time, and his large business experience was of service now. He was a great organizer, drillmaster, and a popular commander. But as a combat general he had several shortcomings: he was a stickler for detail, too often when detail was not vital; he overestimated the size but not the striking power of the opposing armies; he was cautious and deliberate to an excessive degree; and he was opinionated, outspoken, and not always courteous in dealing with the President and other civilian officers of the government. But he never made any major error in the conduct of a battle; and in a war of attrition he inflicted more relative damage upon the Confederate army in 1862 than Grant did in 1864.

McClellan's refusal to be hurried

For months after Bull Run, McClellan showed no intention of doing battle with the Confederates. President Lincoln wheedled him, pricked him with good-natured sarcasm, ordered him to attack, and offered to borrow the army if he did not want to use it, while the congressional committee on the conduct of the war accused him of treason and demanded his removal. On November 1, 1861, the President, in the face of radical criticism, made him general-in-chief of all the armies of the United States. McClellan, however, would not budge before he was convinced that his army was strong and seasoned enough to stand up against the Army of Northern Virginia. Indeed, it was not until in March, 1862, that he was ready to move against the Confederate army; and when he did move it was by way of the peninsula formed by the York and James Rivers. In the meanwhile the opposing forces in the West had been engaged in decisive battles.

MILITARY OPERATIONS IN THE WEST, 1861-62

Missouri had perhaps been prevented from joining the Confederacy by the quick action of Francis P. Blair, Jr., and Captain Nathaniel Lyon in organizing Union guards. The governor and legislature were favorable to the Confederacy until deposed by a Unionist convention, and they authorized General Sterling Price to raise a Confederate army in Missouri, which soon reached a total of 20,000 men. Lyon, now brigadier general, marched against a Confederate force of 7,000 at Wilson's Creek, near Springfield, on August 10, three weeks after Bull Run, and in a desperate battle his army was defeated and he was killed. Price now marched back through Missouri, and on September 20 he captured Lexington after defeating the Illinois "Irish Brigade" of Colonel John A. Mulligan. General John C. Frémont in command of the Northern army of the Missouri area took over active command after Lyon's death, and with a force of about 40,000 attempted to drive Price from the state. He marched on Springfield, Missouri, near the end of September and Price fell back. Then followed over a month of virtual inactivity. *In Missouri*

In the meantime, Frémont issued a proclamation freeing the slaves of all "rebels and rebel sympathizers," and to cap the climax threw in jail Frank Blair, his patron, the person who had been most responsible for his appointment to the Missouri post. Lincoln was forced by these ill-advised and arrogant measures, as well as by Frémont's military incompetence, to remove the general; and he placed General Henry W. Halleck in command of the Department of the West, which eventually included all armies west of the Alleghenies. But to placate the Radicals, Frémont was given a berth in a very vital spot: he was made commander of an army of about 18,000 men to operate in and near the Shenandoah Valley and toward southwest Virginia. *Frémont's highhanded conduct*

The majority of the people in the section of Virginia west of the mountains seem to have been Unionist in sentiment, and certainly they held long standing grievances against eastern Virginia. Consequently, when McClellan and his successor, W. S. Rosecrans, defeated and drove out the Confederate forces under Robert E. Lee, the *Western Virginia* thirty-nine transmontane counties formed themselves into the state of West Virginia which was admitted into the Union on December 31, 1862.[1] The creation of West Virginia out of a Confederate state was soon to have great influence upon the attitudes of people in the mountainous portions of the neighboring states of Kentucky, Tennessee, and North Carolina.

Position of the opposing armies

In the winter and spring of 1862 the Army of the Ohio, under Don Carlos Buell, and General Halleck's forces were scattered along a line from southern Missouri through southern Kentucky to the mountains. Facing this sprawling Union line was a weak and poorly equipped Confederate army under the command of General Albert Sidney Johnston, who had been a colonel and the highest ranking officer in the old regular Federal army to take an active part in the war.

Grant's plan to gain control of the lower Mississippi Valley

General Grant, in command of a force at Cairo in Halleck's department, had been quick to grasp one portion of Scott's grand strategy and to elaborate it, and to seize upon a much easier method of execution than had been contemplated by Scott. Instead of attempting to conquer the mighty Mississippi by direct assault of gunboat and army, Grant proposed to pierce the Confederate center by moving with a combined army and gunboat fleet up the Cumberland and Tennessee Rivers. This would probably force the Confederate left to withdraw far down the Mississippi. Indeed, such a move would carry the Federal transports to Pittsburg Landing within twenty-three miles of the Memphis-Charleston Railroad, where it formed a junction with the Mobile and Ohio at Corinth. Control of these main lines might enable the Federals to flank the entire Mississippi and take it from the rear, as it were.

Capture of Forts Henry and Donelson

In January, 1862, Grant obtained Halleck's approval of his plan, and was assigned the ironclad gunboat fleet under Commodore Andrew H. Foote. On February 6, Foote attacked Fort Henry on the Tennessee. The fort, lying on a low bank, was easily reduced; but the gunboats found Fort Donelson quite a different problem from that of Fort Henry. Situated upon the high bluffs of the Cumberland, its batteries aimed a plunging fire at the gunboats, which were beaten back and several of them disabled. Grant then placed 28,000 men about the fort and prepared either for siege or assault. The Confederates drove back the Union center and right, which had closed the river road to Nashville below the fort. But, instead of continuing the attack upon the Federal right and thus keeping the escape route open, General John B. Floyd, the senior Confederate

[1] The formation of West Virginia will be discussed in more detail in connection with Lincoln's policy of reconstruction, Vol. II.

officer, shifted a portion of his army up the river to meet an assault at that point, and permitted the Federal right to reform its ranks and close the road to Nashville again. Then during the night the generals decided to surrender the garrison of about 15,000 men. General Simon B. Buckner was given the distasteful duty of surrendering the fort, while Floyd and Gideon J. Pillow escaped across the river; and the cavalry leader, Nathan Bedford Forrest, who had angrily protested that he could take the entire Confederate garrison to safety, led his own men through the backwater.

This surrender in the eyes of the Southern soldiers and people *Immediate* ranked in its cowardice with that of General William Hull's sur- *consequences* render of Detroit. It was a staggering blow in itself, but its strategic consequences were to be appalling to the South. A. S. Johnston, who might have relieved Fort Donelson before its capture, was now forced to abandon middle Tennessee and fall back to Corinth in northeast Mississippi, where he could assemble the other portions of his scattered army and await reinforcements. The morale of the South, both on the home front and in the armies, was severely shaken, and that of the North greatly strengthened.

Soon after the fall of Fort Donelson, Grant proceeded to Nash- *Federals* ville and, for some reason, lost touch with Halleck, who immediately *occupy west* concluded that he had reverted to his old habit of strong drink. After *Tennessee and* temporarily suspending Grant and diverting much of his army to *assemble* west Tennessee, which was quickly occupied, Halleck again per- *armies at* mitted him to resume his operations against Johnston's army at *Pittsburg* Corinth. The plan was that Buell with an army of 35,000 operating *Landing* from Nashville should join Grant's army of 45,000 at Pittsburg Landing, twenty-three miles northeast of Corinth.

At this point Grant must have become overconfident, for he placed *Exposed posi-* his main forces centered at Pittsburg Landing in a very dangerous *tion of* position. Their backs were to the Tennessee River, their flanks were *Federals* cut by several creeks swollen by spring floods, which emptied into the Tennessee, and their front was not entrenched or fortified, nor were adequate outposts thrown out. In this exposed situation the Federal army settled down to wait for the coming of Buell's army. Grant had reached Pittsburg Landing on March 17, and it was not until April 5 that Buell arrived with a portion of his army at Grant's headquarters at Savannah—eight miles down the river—where he halted to rest for the night.

This period of nearly three weeks permitted Johnston to assemble, *The battle* reorganize, and equip his main army of 40,000. Then on April 6, *of Shiloh* before Buell had left Savannah, Johnston's army attacked Grant's force encamped in the neighborhood of Shiloh Church. It was a

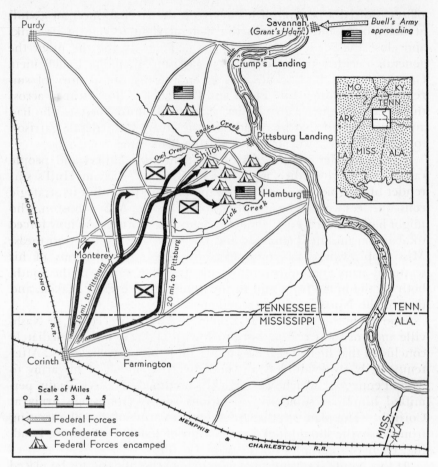

A. S. Johnston's Attack on Grant's Army at Shiloh.

complete surprise, and the Union army, though making a desperate fight, was thrown back in great disorder. By late afternoon when Grant arrived, thousands of demoralized Federal soldiers had sought protection under the river bluff. Before the day was done, however, Johnston was mortally wounded and died on the battle field. His place was taken by Beauregard, who did not continue the fighting after nightfall, and thus ended whatever possibilities there had been for a victory. The next morning Buell and General Lew Wallace, who had been cut off from Grant's main force by the flooded Snake Creek, had arrived with 20,000 fresh soldiers, and Grant had somewhat reformed his disorganized troops. He launched a counterattack which threw the Confederates back and forced them that night to withdraw toward Corinth.

The battle was one of the bloodiest in history. The Federals lost 13,000 killed, wounded, and captured, out of 63,000 engaged; and the Confederates, 11,000 out of 40,000. There was a popular clamor for Grant's removal, but Lincoln dryly remarked, "I can't spare this man; he fights." Nevertheless, Halleck superseded Grant by taking personal command of the army. However, the former was extremely timid in engaging the Confederates and it took him seven weeks to advance his strong force to the Confederate position at Corinth. *The results*

While Halleck was slowly moving his army upon Corinth and Buell was attempting to gain possession of the railroad from Corinth to Chattanooga, General Braxton Bragg, who had succeeded Beauregard in command of the Army of Tennessee, began a spectacular flanking movement. He shipped most of his army by rail from Corinth to Mobile, from Mobile to Montgomery, from Montgomery to Atlanta, and from Atlanta to Chattanooga. From Chattanooga his forces moved northwestward toward Nashville in the general direction of Louisville, Kentucky, while a force under Kirby Smith moved toward Cincinnati. *Bragg's wide flanking maneuver*

The immediate effect of this counteroffensive was to compel Buell to fall back all the way from north Alabama to Louisville, Kentucky, and thus to clear the greater part of Tennessee and over half of Kentucky of most Federal forces—all without a battle. However, Bragg's strategy came to little; for lacking energy and daring, he made no serious effort at cutting Buell off from Louisville, but marched slowly through the blue grass region collecting rich supplies and enlisting a small brigade of soldiers. While he was doing this Kirby Smith's army stopped at Frankfort and installed a secessionist governor. With his army thus divided, Bragg permitted Buell to reach Louisville, obtain fresh recruits and supplies, and turn upon him at Perryville. The night after the battle, in which each side lost about 4,000 men, Bragg withdrew from the field and began a retreat. He was not strong enough to continue the campaign so far from his base and against an enemy now greatly reinforced, and he withdrew from Kentucky. *Federal withdrawal and counter-offensive*

The withdrawal of the forces under Smith and Bragg was well executed: enormous wagon trains, droves of fresh horses, and herds of beef cattle were brought back into Confederate territory without loss. The Federal army was not able to regain middle Tennessee in 1862, for Bragg brought his army to Murfreesboro and blocked its advance. The end of 1862, then, found the Confederate position in the West much better than it had been immediately after the battle of Shiloh. *Confederate position improved by Bragg's Kentucky campaign*

WAR IN THE EAST IN 1862: THE PENINSULA THROUGH FREDERICKSBURG

McClellan's new plan; its defects

In the East the armies had by the end of 1862 waged five campaigns, all save one of which, the invasion of Maryland, had ended favorably for the Confederates. McClellan's new plan of an assault upon Richmond by way of the peninsula formed by the York and James Rivers had the great advantage of an all-water communication. But the one defect of the plan was that it would either uncover Washington or compel the government to retain a force between that city and Richmond to protect the capital from quick attack by Confederate armies operating in the Valley under Stonewall Jackson.

Lincoln's interference hampers McClellan

When McClellan informed Lincoln that he had decided to move against Richmond by way of the Peninsula, the President gave his consent with great reluctance. He soon revealed his waning confidence in the general by several acts that went far toward destroying the effectiveness of the Peninsular strategy. First he deprived McClellan of his position as general-in-chief of all the armies. This removed from his control the forces of 18,000 men under Frémont in the mountains on the west side of the Valley of Virginia, and that of 26,000 under General Nathaniel P. Banks at Strasburg and Harper's Ferry. Next, McDowell's corps of 40,000 men was detached from McClellan's army to protect Washington. To cap the climax, Lincoln placed Secretary of War Stanton in charge of all military operations and allowed him to stop recruiting.

McClellan's cautious advance up the Peninsula

McClellan had his main army at Fortress Monroe by early April; but when he moved up the Peninsula he found Joseph E. Johnston's army lying across his path at Yorktown. McClellan deployed his army and brought up his siege guns. Johnston retreated to Williamsburg on May 3, where his rear guard fought a delaying action until he could withdraw his main force to the outworks at Richmond. McClellan then moved up the York River and established his base at White House Landing on the Pamunkey River, within twenty miles of Richmond. At about the same time the Confederates abandoned Norfolk and blew up the Confederate ram, the *Merrimack* (*Virginia*), to prevent its falling into Federal hands. This cleared the river to Drury's Bluff, six miles from Richmond, so that Federal gunboats and transports moved without interruption up the James almost to the Confederate capital.

McDowell recalled again to defend Washington

McClellan kept the greater part of his army north of the Chickahominy River, in the hope of having McDowell's army join him. Finally, on May 18, Lincoln yielded to McClellan's importunities and ordered McDowell to place himself on McClellan's right near Fredericksburg; but six days later, in great haste and anxiety, the

President ordered him to march back to defend Washington against the Confederate forces operating under Jackson in the Valley.

The withdrawal of McDowell was the one object of Jackson's Valley Campaign; and when McDowell moved to place himself on McClellan's right wing, Jackson went into action. He first fell upon Robert H. Milroy, who commanded an advanced portion of Frémont's army on the western edge of the Valley of Virginia, and drove him back into the mountains. Quickly turning upon Banks at Strasburg in the Valley, Jackson forced him north to Winchester, and there, May 25, overtook and defeated him and drove him back across the Potomac. Jackson next occupied Harper's Ferry for a brief space, and then it was that Lincoln ordered McDowell to move back from Fredericksburg so as to cover Washington. General James Shields, who had been attached to McDowell's command, was now to move to the rear of Jackson, up the east side of the Valley, Frémont was to close in from the west and rear to join Shields, and Banks was to come in from the direction of Harper's Ferry. Thus would Stonewall be trapped. With incredible swiftness Jackson struck and threw off balance the forces under Shields and Frémont before they could join and before Banks could come up. Then he slipped from the Valley and marched rapidly to join the Confederate forces to the northeast of Richmond now under Lee. *The Valley Campaign of Stonewall Jackson*

McClellan's force, despite the withdrawal of McDowell's corps, numbered by this time 105,000 men, who were in fine spirits, well-equipped, well-trained, and confident. He retained three corps north of the Chickahominy in order to co-operate with McDowell, should that general be permitted to join him; and two were placed south of the river. On May 31, 1862, Joseph E. Johnston, who had under his command at Richmond about 75,000 troops, attacked the weak left wing of the Federals south of the river at Fair Oaks; but before the day was over Sumner's corps crossed to the south bank of the Chickahominy and helped check the Confederate assault. On the succeeding day the Confederates were driven back to their original position near the city. The severe wounding of Johnston, and rains that made the ground impassable, put a halt to the fighting. *The battle of Fair Oaks*

Robert E. Lee, who had had little experience as a commander in battle, now took over the Confederate army. Lee, however, while making many errors in his first independent command, nevertheless gave evidence at once of military talent of a high order. He rapidly erected stronger earthworks, so that McClellan's long range siege guns would do less harm, reorganized and re-equipped much of the army, and studied the disposition of McClellan's army. On June 12 he sent J. E. B. Stuart, his young cavalry chief, to reconnoiter the *Lee's plan to attack McClellan's right flank* country to the north and east of McClellan's right wing. The daring and imaginative Stuart, however, rode completely around the Federal army and reported back to Lee on June 15 with accurate information concerning the disposition of McClellan's entire army. Their position was soon exactly reversed from what it had been when Johnston had attacked at Fair Oaks. The Federal right wing, under Fitz-John Porter, lay north of the Chickahominy and numbered only about 25,000, while the bulk of the Federal army lay south of the river. Lee held a conference with Jackson, and it was agreed that the latter should bring his forces from the Valley and join with A. P. Hill, D. H. Hill, and James Longstreet in an attack upon McClellan's right wing north of the Chickahominy. If this combined movement were successful, Porter's corps might be destroyed and the Confederates placed in the rear of the main Federal army.

The Seven Days' Battle McClellan's skillful retreat

On June 26, Lee, retaining only about 30,000 men to defend Richmond, sent the remainder of his army across the Chickahominy to join Jackson in the surprise attack. But Jackson was a day late, and the assault of A. P. Hill's single division upon Porter at Mechanicsville robbed the movement of the element of surprise. McClellan ordered Porter back to Gaines' Mill (Cold Harbor) where he reinforced him. On June 27, Jackson's men were on the field and the Confederates now had 55,000 men against Porter's 34,000; but instead of a flanking movement they were forced at great cost to storm by frontal assault the well-chosen position of the Federals. McClellan skillfully withdrew Porter from the north bank of the river. Lee had cut McClellan's line of communication with his base at White House and expected him to withdraw down the Peninsula, or attempt to drive the Confederate army back. He did neither, but shifted his base to Harrison's Landing on the James River twenty miles below Richmond, to which he began withdrawing on June 28. It was not until the next day that Lee discovered McClellan's purpose. By that time the Federal general had his army well in hand and, when Lee attacked at Savage Station and Frayser's Farm, McClellan was able by strong rear-guard action to prevent serious interference with the withdrawal of his army. Finally, July 1, McClellan's army, now in easy reach of its base and the protection of the big guns of the James River fleet, waited upon Malvern Hill to receive Lee's attack. Lee, believing that the Federal army was demoralized, ordered an attack across open fields that were swept with artillery and musket fire. The attack was a failure. It was poorly co-ordinated and was one of Lee's great mistakes.

The relative success of each command

The Confederates in the Valley and on the Peninsula had won this campaign in three major respects: they had prevented the forces under McDowell and McClellan from uniting in an assault upon Richmond which must have proven successful; they had compelled McClellan to withdraw from before the Confederate capital; and they had increased McClellan's cautiousness, for he was convinced now that Lee had 200,000 men. But in one decisive phase the Federal general had gained a great victory: in the war of attrition he had inflicted relatively more damage upon Lee's army than Lee had upon his. Lee's forces, which at the beginning of the Seven Days' Battle numbered about 86,000, suffered over 20,000 casualties in killed, wounded, and captured, while McClellan's army of 117,000 lost only 16,000. A continuation of such relative losses soon would have destroyed the Confederate armies.

While Lee as a rule expended his men less extravagantly after this, it was Lincoln who unintentionally did the most at this juncture to conserve the man power of the Confederacy by withdrawing his full support from McClellan. Influenced by Stanton and Halleck, now the chief military adviser of the President, Lincoln refused to send further reinforcements to McClellan, which would enable the general to attempt an advance upon Richmond by way of Petersburg—the route to be used successfully by Grant in 1864; and finally on August 3 he permitted Halleck to order McClellan's army back to Aquia Creek near Fredericksburg.

Lincoln's failure to give McClellan his support

No sooner had McClellan withdrawn to Harrison's Landing than the divisions of McDowell, Banks, and Frémont were assembled in northern Virginia under command of General John Pope, who boastfully proclaimed to his men that in the West where he came from he had only "seen the backs of our enemies." At about the same time General Ambrose E. Burnside arrived at Fortress Monroe off the Peninsula with a considerable force aboard transports. It seemed to Lee that the Confederates were in a situation similar to the one in which they had been at the commencement of the Peninsular Campaign. Pope's army would attack from the north while McClellan resumed the offensive from the south.

Advantageous position of the Federal armies

Naturally, Lee could not know that McClellan would not move without reinforcements, and that such reinforcements would be refused and the army itself withdrawn. Jackson, however, insisted that McClellan would withdraw or remain inactive for a long time, and he proposed that Lee retain only a small force to watch McClellan and throw the bulk of his army upon Pope before the latter could assemble his forces. Lee, however, would take no such risks. McClellan was too close for comfort, and he only sent Jackson and a few thousand men north to Gordonsville, the junction of the Virginia Central and the Orange and Alexandria railroads.

Jackson sent against Pope's vanguard

Lee decides to attack Pope before McClellan and Burnside join him

On August 9, Jackson had a brush with Pope's advance guard at Cedar Run, which seemed to indicate that the Federal general was already moving on Richmond from the north. A few days later Lee received reliable information that Burnside's forces had already reached Fredericksburg on the way to join Pope, and that Mc-Clellan's army was being sent to Aquia Creek for the same purpose. Without waiting for McClellan to evacuate more than a fraction of his army, Lee detached a small garrison to remain near Richmond and sent the rest of his forces to join with Stonewall Jackson in an effort to defeat Pope, or drive him out of northern Virginia before McClellan could join him.

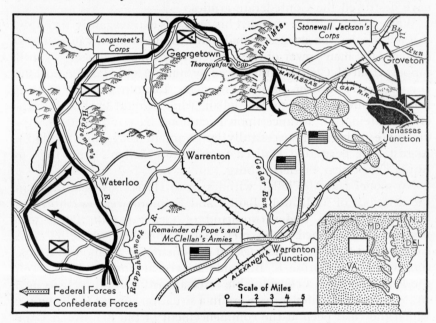

SECOND BATTLE OF BULL RUN.

Lee maneuvers Pope away from McClellan

Soon after Lee reached the Rappahannock River, the north bank of which was strongly held by the enemy, he learned from captured Federal dispatches that Burnside had already joined Pope, and that reinforcements from McClellan's army at Aquia Creek were approaching. In order to prevent Pope and McClellan from uniting and to find a good opportunity to attack, Lee shifted his army up the south bank of the river to the west. This movement drew Pope away from McClellan, but developed no favorable openings for Lee to attack. As for Pope, he would not take the offensive until large reinforcements from McClellan had reached him.

On August 25, after five days of such maneuvering, the two armies had come in sight of the Bull Run Mountains, lying in a northeasterly direction and perilously near to Pope's line of communication. Here was the great opportunity to attack Pope and force him from northern Virginia and beyond aid from McClellan. Accordingly, on August 25, Lee sent Jackson with a detachment of 23,000 men on a forced march behind the Bull Run Mountains; and within two days Stonewall had cut Pope's line of communication with Washington and had destroyed his base at Manassas Junction. When Pope became aware of Jackson's movements he began withdrawing his army toward Manassas to deal with this apparently reckless commander. As soon as Lee discovered that Pope was withdrawing, he sent Longstreet along the same route followed by Jackson, so that on August 29 he came upon the field (near Manassas Junction) where Jackson was already engaged.   The next day, just as the bulk of Pope's tired and hungry army threw itself upon Jackson's men, who were almost out of ammunition and badly battered, Longstreet opened a devastating artillery fire on the left flank of the Federals and launched an assault upon this flank that forced the Federal army back across Bull Run. Here at Centerville, Pope met large reinforcements from McClellan's army. He made no serious effort to organize them and launch a counterattack, but retreated to Washington.

The Second Battle of Bull Run

When the despondent Federal armies were brought back to the Washington defenses, McClellan was immediately restored to active command of all the troops in the East. Under his genius for organization and his gift for inspiring confidence, the army was back in good spirits in a few days.

McClellan restored to command

Lee, with the consent of Davis, decided after the victory of Second Bull Run to carry the Confederate army across the Potomac into Maryland and Pennsylvania. His reasons were good. He would by maneuvering draw the Federal army away from Virginia and permit the war-ridden population a respite and an opportunity to harvest their crops; he would permit the Confederate army to subsist itself in fresh territory, though there was to be no looting or seizure of private property; he believed that Maryland might join the Confederacy if given a fair chance; and, finally, and of great importance, Lee hoped that an invasion of Maryland and Pennsylvania, accompanied by a successful battle, might well result in foreign intervention of some kind. Nor was his calculation ill-founded in this last respect.

The decision to invade Maryland

After crossing the Potomac east of the Blue Ridge Mountains, Lee was compelled to send the entire left wing of his army under Jackson to seize Harper's Ferry, where a Federal garrison of 11,000 obstructed his proposed line of communication in the Valley of

Jackson captures Harper's Ferry

Virginia. The remainder of his army under Longstreet and D. H. Hill was to remain at Boonsboro and Hagerstown to the west of South Mountain. Jackson captured Harper's Ferry and Martinsburg without much difficulty.

McClellan disrupts Lee's plans

But Lee's order which thus divided his force and scattered it fell into the hands of McClellan. McClellan now moved with the rapidity of Lee himself. He overwhelmed the Confederate force defending Turner's Gap in South Mountain and broke through Crampton's Gap in the rear of the Confederates who were attacking Harper's Ferry, and thus wrecked Lee's plans for maneuvering over Maryland and Pennsylvania; Lee, however, refused to retreat from the state without a real fight.

The battle of Antietam

On August 15 he withdrew to Sharpsburg near Antietam Creek a few miles northeast of the Potomac where Jackson joined him on September 16. At the same time McClellan moved with complete assurance toward the same place. In the early dawn of September 17 the battle commenced. General Joseph Hooker's corps of the Federal army struck Jackson's divisions on the Confederate left and cut a gap in the lines. With A. P. Hill's division still at Harper's Ferry, Lee had few reserves with which to meet this attack, and he threw in reinforcements from the right of his line, not yet heavily engaged. Thus reinforced, Jackson was able finally to check Hooker's charge, and that of the corps of J. K. F. Mansfield and Edwin V. Sumner, which followed in quick succession upon the Confederate left. After McClellan's attack against the Confederate left wing had been at great cost partially stemmed, the Federal commander sent W. B. Franklin's corps in a similar fashion against the Confederate center, driving it back and opening it up; but by reinforcing the center from that part of the line relatively quiet, Lee again checked the assault. At length, near the close of the day, Burnside's corps on the Federal left attacked across the Antietam. But A. P. Hill arriving from Harper's Ferry at this time attacked Burnside's left and forced him back across the Antietam.

So ended the bloodiest single day of the war. Lee with about 40,000[1] men had casualties of 10,000 killed, wounded, and captured; while McClellan with about 87,000 on the field had casualties of 12,400. McClellan's relative loss was smaller than Lee's but, in the entire Maryland campaign including Harper's Ferry, this was not true. Lee had 13,600 casualties and McClellan, 27,760. But Lee's army was greatly weakened and he was forced to withdraw across the Potomac.

---

[1] Lee's army had been greatly weakened by straggling, much of which was due to lack of shoes, but some of which was due to the unwillingness of the Confederate soldier to invade enemy territory.

Lincoln was impatient with McClellan for his failure to pursue *McClellan* Lee to Winchester, and he had Halleck order McClellan to "cross the *replaced by* Potomac and give battle to the enemy or drive him South." On *Burnside* October 6, 1862, McClellan detached a large force to hold the lower end of the Valley and, on October 26, he proceeded with the main army to Warrenton, Virginia, east of the Blue Ridge Mountains.

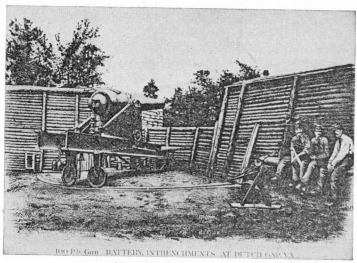

100 Pd. Gun BATTERY, INTRENCHMENTS AT DUTCH GAP, VA.

Atlas of Official Records of the Union and Confederate Armies

100 Pdr. Gun Battery.

As McClellan was approaching Warrenton on November 7, 1862, with the reluctant purpose of attacking Lee's army, strategically placed near the mountain gaps, Lincoln dismissed the general from command and placed in his stead the Radicals' favorite, General Ambrose E. Burnside.

Burnside understood quite well that he was expected to defeat *Fredericks-* Lee's army and to capture Richmond, and he moved his army to *burg* Stafford Heights opposite Fredericksburg. Lee anticipated Burnside's movements and placed his army upon the heights overlooking Fredericksburg from the southwest. Longstreet's corps was placed along the steep ridge just above the town to the westward, with his right flank resting on Marye's Heights. Jackson's corps was stretched out on the high ground to the south of Longstreet. On December 13 Burnside began throwing pontoons across the river and, after many futile efforts and considerable loss, finally succeeded. He ordered Franklin's and Sumner's "Grand Divisions" into a frontal assault. Sumner sent wave after wave against the Confederate position on Marye's Heights; but Longstreet's infantry, at the foot of

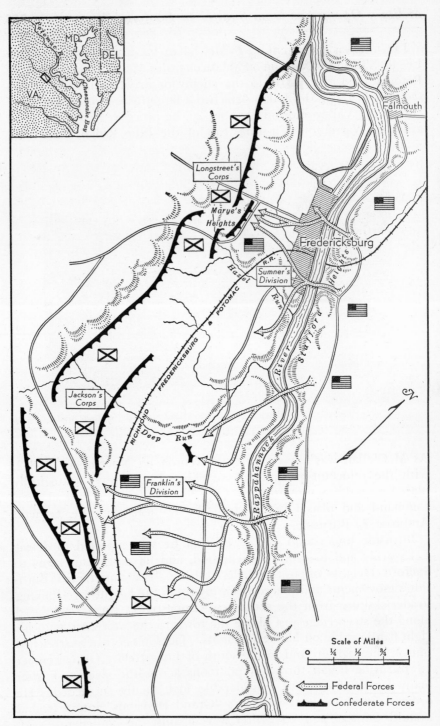

BATTLE OF FREDERICKSBURG.

the Heights in a sunken road lined by a stone wall and supported by artillery atop the ridge, threw back every desperate charge. Franklin in his attack upon Jackson's corps was more successful, and he penetrated the Confederate lines to a considerable depth before he was repulsed.

The battle was a dangerous blunder, but Burnside, who was almost demented from the carnage and defeat, wished to renew the assault. His generals, however, were unwilling to order the soldiers to another such slaughter. The Federal army of 120,000 suffered 12,650 casualties and the Confederate army of 78,000 had 5,300. Lincoln now intervened and ordered Burnside not to make another attack without consulting him.

A dangerous blunder

CHAPTER XLIV

Military Operations from Stone's River to Appomattox

THE WEST IN 1863: STONE'S RIVER TO CHATTANOOGA

Rosecrans harassed by Wheeler's cavalry

ABOUT December 25, 1862, after two months spent in reor-ganizing and outfitting his army, W. S. Rosecrans, who had succeeded Buell, began to move out of Nashville upon Bragg at Murfreesboro; but Bragg's cavalry under the command of General Joseph Wheeler obstructed and harassed his march so effectively that it required four days for the Federal army to cover the thirty miles between Murfreesboro and Nashville. On the night of December 29-30, Wheeler rode completely around Rosecrans' army, destroyed about 500 wagons filled with supplies valued at over $1,000,000, and captured many ambulances and prisoners.

Battle of Murfreesboro, or Stone's River

Bragg, having his army in position before Rosecrans had made all his dispositions, took the initiative. On December 31, General William J. Hardee's corps on Bragg's left wing and General Leonidas Polk's corps in the center attacked Rosecrans' right and center, and by the close of the day had forced them back several miles along the Nashville turnpike. Thinking that the Federals were defeated, Bragg refrained from attack on January 1. The next day he found Rosecrans still in front of him, and he decided to complete the execution of his plan by having Breckinridge attack the Federal left. This was Bragg's fatal error, for Federal General Thomas L. Crittenden had concentrated his artillery on high ground from which he swept the entire advancing Confederate lines with an oblique fire. This reckless charge cost Bragg 2,000 men and con-vinced him that he could not dislodge the Federals from their strong positions. He was so shocked by his failure to defeat Rose-crans that he withdrew to Tullahoma. The losses on both sides had been so disastrous that neither army was in any condition to renew the struggle. The Federals lost in killed, wounded, and captured

12,906 out of an army of 47,000; and the Confederates suffered a casualty of 11,739 out of 38,000.

After six months of recuperation, Rosecrans on June 24, 1863, recommenced his maneuvers against Bragg. These were skillfully carried out and, without more than cavalry skirmishes, the Federal general by flanking movements was able to force Bragg all the way to Chattanooga by September 9, 1863.

Bragg forced back to Chattanooga

In the meantime Grant had carried on a series of operations against Vicksburg, which was the chief obstacle to Federal control of the Mississippi. In the fall of 1862 he tried to approach the town from Holly Springs by way of Jackson, Mississippi, only to have General Earl Van Dorn's cavalry capture his base and destroy his supplies, and Forrest's cavalry demolish the railroad almost to Paducah, Kentucky. Then Grant sent Sherman down the Mississippi against Vicksburg, but the Confederates from their heights easily defeated this attempt. He next cut a canal across a bend in the Mississippi in the hope of getting his troops and supplies below Vicksburg without having to run the Confederate batteries at that place, but the spring floods destroyed the canal.

The Vicksburg campaign: failure of Grant's early attempts to recapture the town

At last, without advice from government or fellow officers, Grant struck upon a plan which proved successful. With remarkable swiftness he transferred his army through the swampy country west of the river, crossed over and occupied Bruinsburg on May 1, captured Port Gibson nearby, and from there marched his army between the town of Jackson and Vicksburg along the railroad connecting these two points. In this position his army lived off the country, which, however, was not a difficult task, since this was one of the richest farming areas of the South. Grant now had his army of 43,000 lying between General John C. Pemberton's army of 40,000 based on Vicksburg and a Confederate force of 12,000 at Jackson, soon to be commanded by Joseph E. Johnston. At Raymond on May 12, and at Jackson, May 14, he defeated the smaller Confederate force and drove it back to the northeast.

Grant's plan to attack from below

Johnston, who had been put in command of the Department of the West, ordered Pemberton to maneuver north and eastward so as to unite the two Confederate forces and avoid being trapped in Vicksburg; but Pemberton, in ignorance of Johnston's orders, marched southward instead of north and east, in the expectation of forcing the Federal general to retire by threatening his line of communication and his supposed base at Grand Gulf. Grant, however, had cut loose from his base and, far from retreating, attacked Pemberton and defeated him at Champion Hill, May 16, and near Black River, May 17. Then Johnston ordered Pemberton not to

Pemberton and Johnston unable to coordinate their efforts

fall back to Vicksburg; yet that is just what he did on May 17, and this sealed his doom. He was never able to break out again nor was Johnston able to assemble an army strong enough to raise the siege. He seemed to have received Johnston's instructions in each case after he had begun or completed the move which Johnston had ordered him not to make.

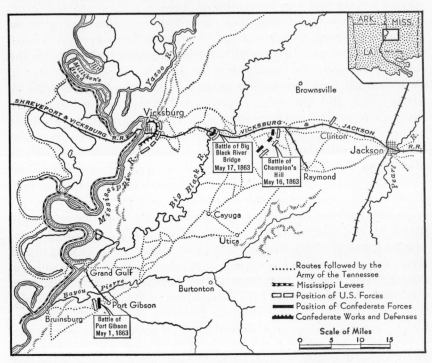

VICKSBURG CAMPAIGN.

The order to hold Vicksburg at any cost, a fatal blunder

It is possible, however, that Pemberton could have withdrawn from Vicksburg before Grant placed it under siege, but the Confederate President had ordered him to hold Vicksburg at all cost. Davis knew that the loss of Vicksburg and the consequent severance of the trans-Mississippi territory from the rest of the Confederacy would be a serious if not fatal blow to the South; for the trans-Mississippi Department had come to be the principal source from which horses, cattle, and swine were obtained for the Southern armies. Johnston agreed with Davis in the importance of keeping open the route to the trans-Mississippi Department. He believed, however, that to stand siege would be fatal, and that only by maneuver could the Confederates hope to defeat Grant and hold Vicksburg. The capture of the town and Pemberton's army, after a few weeks of siege, seems to bear out the strength of Johnston's arguments and to mark Davis' order to hold Vicksburg at any cost as a fatal blunder.

The siege of Vicksburg lasted until July 4, 1863, when Pember- *Fall of* ton surrendered his army of 31,000 men, 50,000 modern rifles, 175 *Vicksburg* pieces of artillery, and large military stores. Four days later Port Hudson with 5,000 men surrendered to General N. P. Banks. Grant had in this campaign effectively wrecked the Confederate army in Mississippi—originally part of the Army of Tennessee. Of more importance, he had gained for the Federals the control of the Mississippi River.

As already observed, Rosecrans had pushed Bragg to the vicinity *Chickamauga* of Chattanooga, one of the vital railway junctions of the South. On September 9, 1863, the Federals entered Chattanooga and shortly began a move toward Chickamauga Creek where Bragg had taken position. On September 18 Rosecrans ran afoul of the Confederate army. Bragg's force, now reinforced by Longstreet's corps and Buckner's division, numbered on paper around 60,000, while Rosecrans had about 58,000. The ensuing battle, which lasted two days, September 19-20, was another of those desperate and sanguinary conflicts so characteristic of American soldiery. The lines were sometimes only a few paces apart where the men fired point blank at one another from behind brush heaps and felled trees. On the second day the Confederates discovered a wide gap in the Federal lines and charged through it in great force. The Union right and center were thrown into confusion and then into panic. The rout of this portion of the army of veterans was a near disaster to Rosecrans. However, the Confederate army was unable to follow up their success, for the Federal left wing under the command of General George H. Thomas held firm, and this enabled Rosecrans to assemble his disorganized units within the works at Chattanooga.

The losses of both armies were nearly a third of their total *Heavy losses* strength. Bragg lost 18,000 killed, wounded, and captured, while Rosecrans lost about 17,000. Quite naturally neither Federal nor Confederate army was in condition to resume active campaigning for some time to come.

Chattanooga, however, was no place for an army to reorganize *Bragg lays* and re-equip. It lies in a valley nearly surrounded by mountainous *siege to* ridges. Southward lie Lookout Mountain and Missionary Ridge, *Chattanooga* which come close to the Tennessee River; and upon these ridges commanding the river, and all of the approaches to the town except one mountain road, Bragg placed his army. The Confederate commander, now quarreling with most of his leading subordinates, refused to accept the advice of his generals to attack the disorganized Federals. On the contrary he proposed to win by laying siege to Chattanooga. Overlooking the possibilities of the enemy's being reinforced, he presently weakened his own army by detaching Longstreet's command, and most of his own cavalry under Wheeler, to operate against Burnside's army at Knoxville.

Grant saves the besieged army

This procedure was hardly rational in view of what was taking place in the Federal armies in the West. General Grant had, on October 18, been placed in command of the Military Division of the Mississippi, and he promptly dismissed Rosecrans from command of the Army of the Cumberland and appointed General George H. Thomas in his place. Thomas and W. F. Smith quickly seized a strong position down the Tennessee River that enabled the Federals to open a line from Bridgeport to Chattanooga and relieve the starving army. Hooker, who had been dispatched from the East and had been waiting at Bridgeport with an army corps, was able within a few weeks to enter Chattanooga. Sherman, now in command of the Army of the Tennessee (Grant's old command), was at Bridgeport by November 13 with part of his force.

The battle of Chattanooga

Grant had come to Chattanooga on October 23, and within a month he had his forces well organized, plentifully supplied, and their morale restored. On November 23 he set his army in motion to attack Bragg upon the near-by ridges. Hooker was on the right with his corps, Thomas in the center with the Army of the Cumberland, and Sherman on the left with the Army of the Tennessee. Since Bragg's army was now temporarily relieved, by his own request, of some of its ablest officers—Polk, Buckner, and Longstreet—Wheeler's cavalry absent, and the men in the ranks lacking both confidence in, and respect for, their commander, the powerful Union force had no great difficulty in practically routing the Confederates from their high perch. Hooker's spectacular assault up Lookout Mountain did something to erase his recent humiliation of Chancellorsville (see pp. 722-23); but the real defeat was inflicted by Thomas' army, which charged up the slopes of Missionary Ridge and broke the Confederate center. The Confederate army withdrew to Dalton, Georgia, where it remained until the Spring of 1864.

Bragg replaced by Joseph E. Johnston

President Davis, despite his affection for Bragg, was now forced to remove his favorite from command, and he was induced by popular clamor and the demands of the men and officers of the Army of Tennessee to appoint the sensitive, stubborn, prideful but able Joseph E. Johnston to command the beaten army. But, instead

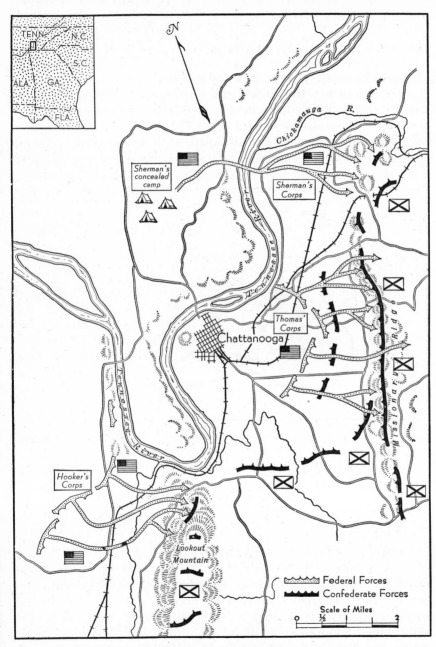

BATTLE OF CHATTANOOGA.

of dismissing Bragg from the army, he promoted him by making him his military adviser.

CAMPAIGNS IN THE EAST, 1863: CHANCELLORSVILLE TO GETTYSBURG

Hooker in command of the Army of the Potomac

After the battle of Fredericksburg, Lincoln wisely gave Burnside a leave of absence from the army and placed in his stead another favorite of the Radicals, General Joseph Hooker. Hooker had been a good corps commander and, like McClellan, an excellent organizer and drillmaster. By the end of April, with the unstinted support of the President and Congress, he had the largest and best equipped

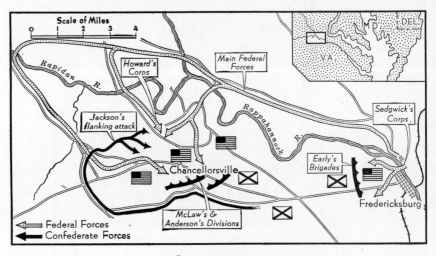

CHANCELLORSVILLE.

army ever assembled on the North American continent up to that time. Directly under his command near Fredericksburg were 138,000 men of all arms, while near-by in Washington was a large garrison and across the Blue Ridge were other forces, all of which he could call upon.

Chancellorsville; Hooker's excellent strategy

Hooker, aware of the weakened condition of Lee's army, which numbered about 63,000 with most of Longstreet's corps in North Carolina, was ready for battle when the roads became passable the last of April. He had conceived an excellent plan. He began, in modern military terminology, a pincer movement. To encircle Lee's right wing he moved General John Sedgwick's corps of 20,000 men across the Rappahannock River at Fredericksburg in the early morning of April 29, 1863. In the meanwhile he rapidly marched the main body of his troops up the Rappahannock and across into the vee formed by this river and the Rapidan. On April 29, when Sedgwick's troops were crossing at Fredericksburg, he began moving his forces over the Rapidan near Chancellorsville and against the left wing of the Confederate army.

Lee improvised plans to meet Hooker's strategy. He detached 10,000 men under General Jubal A. Early to remain at Fredericksburg to engage Sedgwick's force. He then placed Lafayette McLaws' and R. H. Anderson's two divisions of about 20,000 across Hooker's front at Chancellorsville. When this was done Jackson and Lee agreed that Stonewall should attempt a flanking attack against Hooker's right wing; and before nightfall of May 2 Jackson had repeated the strategy of the Second Battle of Bull Run on territory of far less dimensions. He had marched completely behind the right flank of Hooker's army with 28,000 men. Hooker and General O. O. Howard, who commanded the right wing, had refused to believe that the Confederates were flanking the Federal army, but insisted that Jackson was retreating to Richmond. The Federal army was therefore unprepared for the attack, and the right wing was badly disorganized. In the twilight, however, Jackson ventured out to reconnoiter and was mortally wounded by his own men. J. E. B. Stuart took over Jackson's command and continued the fight through the next day. Hooker now showed no signs of taking the offensive, and Lee detached a portion of his army to help Early drive Sedgwick back across the Rappahannock. This accomplished, Lee again prepared to attack Hooker, but the Federal general had withdrawn his men north of the Rappahannock.

Stonewall Jackson's last flanking attack

The casualties at Chancellorsville were very heavy. The Confederates lost in killed, wounded, and captured about 12,500, while the Federals lost slightly over 17,000. Though the Confederates had won the battle their casualties were again relatively higher than those of the Federals. The loss of Jackson was irreparable. Lee's army never again would be able to strike so swiftly and with such force as it had when Stonewall commanded the left wing.

Heavy casualties

Shortly after Chancellorsville Lee determined to invade the North for the second time and, for reasons similar to those that prompted his first invasion, namely: to draw the enemy away from Virginia; supply his army at Northern expense; encourage the peace movement; and gain foreign recognition by a victory on Northern soil. Lee planned the invasion in order to gain the enemy's country before Hooker should discover what he was about. He would invade by way of the Valley of Virginia. With great skill he began withdrawing from the Rappahannock on June 3, and by June 26 his entire army, with the exception of Stuart's cavalry, was across the Potomac. Gen-

Lee's second invasion of the North

724 The War for Southern Independence, 1860–1865

eral Richard Ewell, whose corps had gone ahead to gather supplies, reached Carlisle, Pennsylvania, June 27. On the same day Longstreet and A. P. Hill were at Chambersburg, where Lee established headquarters. But Lee was in hostile territory without knowledge of the movements of the Federal army on which to base his plans, because Stuart was absent with the cavalry on a wild ride around Hooker's army.

Meade succeeds Hooker in command

When Hooker learned that the Confederate army was entering the Valley, he concluded that Lee was going to attempt an invasion of the North. He broke camp on the Rappahannock and, keeping east of the Blue Ridge Mountains so as to cover Washington, marched his army to Frederick, Maryland. On June 27, quarreling with Halleck and distrusted by his subordinates, he offered his resignation as commander of the Army of the Potomac, and, probably to his surprise, he received Lincoln's order accepting it and appointing George Gordon Meade as his successor. Meade, in contrast to Hooker, was popular with his colleagues and highly respected by his opponent, General Lee.

Gettysburg: The Federals driven back to Cemetery Ridge

The day on which Meade took over command of the Army of the Potomac, Lee learned somewhat to his chagrin that the Federal army was at Frederick headed north. In view of this fact he began on June 29 to concentrate his army at Cashtown, near Gettysburg. Here he proposed to await the enemy's attack. Meade, on the other hand, selected Pipe's Creek below the Maryland border as a good defensive position where he planned to await Lee's expected attack. A rather trivial, almost casual, incident changed the scene of battle to Gettysburg and caused Lee with a force of about 73,000 to assume the offensive against Meade's army of 93,000. A. P. Hill's barefooted soldiers entered Gettysburg in search of shoes on July 1 and encountered the Union cavalry and John F. Reynolds' force, which had been sent to Gettysburg to delay Lee's expected move. Soon Ewell's corps arrived to join with that of Hill. The Confederates now had the advantage of numbers, and they quickly transformed a skirmish into a major battle. With the weird rebel yell they charged the Federals and, after inflicting severe casualties, drove them badly disorganized up Cemetery Ridge, south of the town. But the day now was drawing to a close, and Ewell failed to press the attack.

Federal position ideal for defense

General Winfield Scott Hancock, who had been sent up to take the place of the mortally wounded Reynolds, saw at a glance that Cemetery Ridge was an excellent defensive position. He quickly reorganized his troops and sent a message urging Meade to bring up the remainder of the army. Meade, who soon arrived, confirmed Hancock's opinion and, on the following day (July 2), the greater

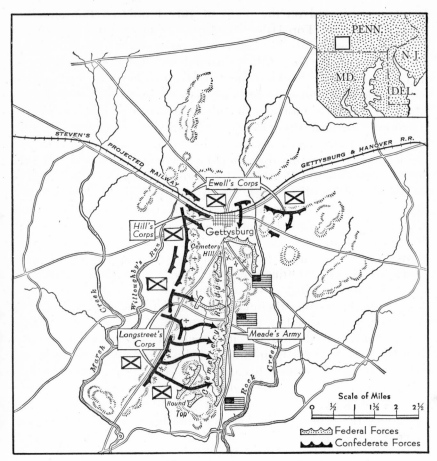

BATTLE OF GETTYSBURG.

part of his army was on or near Cemetery Ridge. This ridge lay roughly parallel with Seminary Ridge, a mile or so to the west, on which Lee placed two of his three corps. At each end of Cemetery Ridge were two hills: Little Round Top and Big Round Top on the south; and Cemetery Hill and Culp's Hill on the north. Federal artillery placed on these hills would protect both flanks and sweep the front with a cross fire; but if the Confederates gained these elevations they would deliver an enfilading fire against both ends of the Federal line with crushing effect.

The real strategic contest of Gettysburg was for possession of these hills. Meade would not be able to get his batteries and the supporting infantry placed on the Round Tops and Culp's Hill in sufficient strength to hold them before well into the day of July 2. *The struggle for the hills dominating Cemetery Ridge*

Lee knew this and on the night of July 1 ordered Longstreet to storm the Round Top Hills, and Ewell to seize Culp's Hill in the early morning of July 2. However, Longstreet, who had opposed any attempt to take these hills by frontal assault, but who had argued in favor of a wide flanking movement around Meade's left, made only feeble efforts to execute Lee's plans. Instead of beginning the attack in the early morning of July 2, he did not move until late afternoon. By that time Meade had strongly fortified the Round Tops, and Longstreet's assault failed to dispossess the Federals. While undertaking this operation he encountered General Daniel Sickles' corps in the Peach Orchard just to the north and after a prolonged and costly struggle he drove the Federals back up the ridge. Farther north, Ewell, who had likewise delayed his assault upon Culp's Hill until late afternoon, was halted by darkness just short of his goal.

Meade prepares for an attack on his center

By the night of July 2 Meade had his troops well placed and his position fortified. While Longstreet and Ewell had pushed back the right and left wings of his army and had wrought great destruction, at the same time their failure to win the heights dominating Cemetery Ridge was fair assurance of the impregnability of his flanks. With sound military judgment he anticipated that Lee would deliver his next main attack against the center, and he made every preparation to meet this attack.

Pickett's charge

Meade was right. On the night of July 2 Lee ordered Longstreet to move out in the early morning of July 3 with about 15,000 men and attack the center of the Federal lines held by Hancock. Longstreet remained inactive till nearly three in the afternoon when he reluctantly set his troops in motion against the Federal center. This attack is known as "Pickett's Charge." The Confederates, like the Union troops at Fredericksburg, marched to the attack as if on dress parade, while the artillery from the Round Tops tore their flanks into shreds, and the guns on the ridge in front cut gaps from one end of the line to the other like a giant mowing machine. When the Confederates were within a distance of about two hundred yards, the Federal riflemen from behind stone walls and entrenchments opened point blank fire. Yet the decimated Confederate divisions swept on over the stone wall, past the Federal artillery, and well to the rear of the ridge. But they were spent. The men were captured or driven back, and the battle of Gettysburg came to an end with the close of the day (July 3, 1863).

Lee expected a counterattack from Meade and waited all day July 4 for him to make it. Meade's army, however, was badly shattered. During the three days' fighting he had lost in killed, wounded, and captured 23,000 men and great quantities of equipment, and he contented himself with having repulsed Lee. As for Lee, he had lost 20,000 men, and his supplies and ammunition were not sufficient for another battle. On the night of July 4-5 he withdrew his army southward. After waiting a few days for the swollen river to subside, he withdrew to Northern Virginia without interference from Meade. Lincoln was sorely disappointed at his new general's failure to follow up the advantage he had gained over the Confederates.

Both armies too badly crippled to resume the battle

THE EAST IN 1864: THE WILDERNESS TO THE CRATER

The President's disappointment was not lessened when Meade eventually moved across the Potomac into Northern Virginia; for the Federal commander consumed the remainder of the summer and fall in petty maneuvers in a cautious attempt to get between Lee and Richmond. As an offensive leader, Meade was surely reminiscent of McClellan in the fall and winter after First Bull Run. Lincoln cast about him to find a leader who was both able and aggressive in the presence of Lee. He would have to draw from the West again for, despite his mistake in the case of Pope, Lincoln was by this time well aware that his western generals were his best. The campaigns of Donelson, Vicksburg, and Chattanooga marked Grant (the ranking general in the West) as a military leader of a high order, and Lincoln called him to Washington in the spring of 1864 and placed him in command of all the armies of the United States, with the rank of Lieutenant General. Grant would take personal command in the East or designate one of his ablest subordinates to do so.

Grant given supreme military command

This rather small man, with slightly stooped shoulders, untrimmed beard, wrinkled uniform, and a cigar or pipe clinched between his teeth, did not look the part of a hero any more than had the seedy and unobtrusive Stonewall Jackson. But Grant, despite the unhappy experiences of his early years[1] that had given him a feeling of inferiority, was not meek. He was the best general in the United States army and no one knew it any better than he did. He was not arrogant or conceited, but rather self-assured; and before assuming the responsibilities of general-in-chief he exacted terms from Lincoln that no one else had obtained: there was to be no meddling by the Administration with his conduct of military affairs, and he was to be given everything in men and equipment that he asked.

Grant, the ablest Federal general

Grant had devised a strategic plan for the defeat of the Southern

[1]After graduation at West Point, Grant served in the regular army until he resigned his commission as captain in 1854. From that time until he was commissioned colonel of volunteers in Illinois he engaged in various business enterprises and failed in each.

armies. Sherman was to take over command in the West and, with the combined armies of the Ohio, the Cumberland, and the Tennessee, drive the Confederate Army of Tennessee back into the lower South until it was destroyed. By such a movement he was to sever the lower South from the eastern theater of war, devastate it and break the morale of the people, and dry up the sources of supply in men, food, and equipment. Grant would himself direct military operations in Virginia. In this department, Franz Sigel and David Hunter were to drive the Confederates from the Valley and thus cut Virginia off from the Southwest; Benjamin F. Butler was to operate up the south bank of the James, seize Petersburg and the railways connecting Virginia with the lower South; and the Army of the Potomac, over which Grant would exercise active command—though Meade was to remain as nominal head—was to move out from its position north of the Rappahannock against Richmond and compel Lee to waste his army in a fight against overwhelming numbers.

On May 4, 1864, Grant launched the campaign intended to bring the war to a close within a few months. He crossed the Rappahannock and the Rapidan and entered the Wilderness about Chancellorsville, where Stonewall Jackson had inflicted such a stunning blow against Hooker on May 2, 1863. This time as his army of over 100,000 entered the dense thickets there were no shots from Confederate sharpshooters to greet it. Grant was striking out southward to seize the two railways that intersected at Hanover Junction. This move would cut the Confederate supply line to Northern Virginia. He did not expect Lee to offer battle until the latter had withdrawn much nearer to the Confederate capital, because he knew that the Army of Northern Virginia had in it less than 65,000 men. Grant, however, underestimated Lee's aggressiveness and his swiftness in maneuver, for the Confederate general had hoped and doubtless prayed for this opportunity to strike the Federals on the march here, where the thick undergrowth would render their superior artillery useless; and on May 5-6 he ambushed Grant in the middle of the Wilderness. He almost repeated the battle of Chancellorsville by sending Longstreet around Grant's left flank just as he had sent Jackson around Hooker's right, and he inflicted a much greater relative loss upon Grant than he had upon Hooker. Grant's casualties were 17,700, and Lee's were about 7,600.

Grant, unlike his predecessors, had no intention of withdrawing across the Rappahannock. On the night of May 6 he attempted to outflank Lee and get in between him and Richmond, skillfully and rapidly marching by the left flank southeast to Spotsylvania Court House. Lee anticipated Grant's move and had his army awaiting the

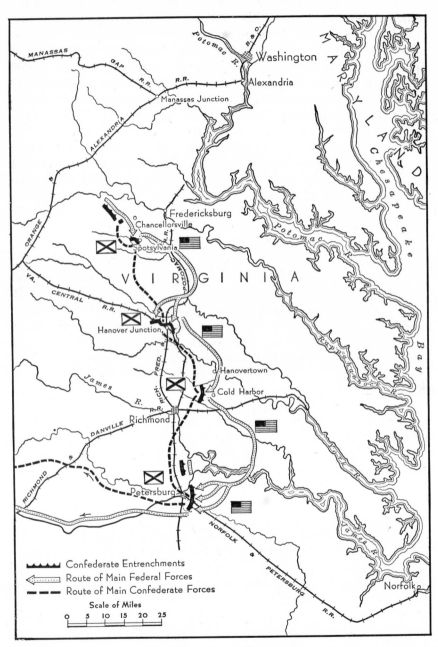

THE WILDERNESS TO PETERSBURG.

Federals when the Army of the Potomac arrived. Both armies entrenched, but Grant threw his men against Lee's works in desperate assault in an almost continuous battle from May 8 to 12. Heavy rains after that put an end to the battle. Grant lost 13,500 men at Spotsylvania. He was undismayed by the staggering loss of 31,000 men since May 4. "I propose," he wrote Halleck at this time, "to fight it out along this line, if it takes all the summer." It would, however, take him more than a summer, and he would be unable to fight it out along this line.   Grant had, however, inflicted upon Lee grievous losses in men and officers; but the greatest had been in the death of "Jeb" Stuart, who had fallen mortally wounded on May 11 in a battle between his cavalry and that of Philip Sheridan near Richmond.   Despite his boyish pranks, Stuart was one of the greatest cavalry leaders of all time.   "He never brought me a piece of false information," said Lee, when he learned of Stuart's death.

Grant on his marches keeps a river between himself and Lee

Unable to drive Lee from his entrenchments by frontal attack, Grant on May 21 moved again by the left flank for the purpose of threatening the Confederate line of communication with Richmond and thereby compelling the Southern army to come out into the open to fight. But Grant would never put himself in the position to be ambushed again: the lesson of the Wilderness was sufficient. From now on he conducted his army on its marches with alertness and skill. He moved upon the Confederate capital, after Spotsylvania, always well screened by the system of rivers flowing into the York not far from the capital. He first moved along the north bank of the tributaries of the Mattapony River, then along the north bank of the Mattapony itself, which flows into the York dangerously near to Richmond.   On coming to the railroad running south to Richmond he crossed the river and marched to the North Anna, a tributary of the Pamunkey, which joins the Mattapony to form the York. He followed the North Anna and then the Pamunkey until he reached Hanovertown, only fifteen miles northeast of Richmond. During most of this maneuver Lee had been unable to attack except at great disadvantage across a river. Only once did Grant really expose himself. At Ox Ford on the North Anna he threw both wings of his army across the river to attack Lee, but found the Confederates in such a strong position that he wisely refused to commit his army to a large scale battle.

Cold Harbor

On reaching Hanovertown, Grant forsook the rivers, turned south until he reached Cold Harbor, ten miles from Richmond, where McClellan had engaged Lee two years before. He was practically in sight of the Confederate capital, but Lee, who had moved on shorter, interior lines, was waiting for him behind entrenchments.

Grant, not yet convinced by his great losses at Spotsylvania, of the hazards of a frontal assault upon entrenched positions, flung his army against the fortified Confederate line in complete disregard of the cost in human life. In the chilly dawn of June 3 wave after wave of Federal soldiers charged across the rain soaked fields only to be cut down by Lee's veteran riflemen and by artillery fired at point blank range. Grant wasted over 7,000 men, most of whom were killed or died in the blazing woods where they lay wounded. Lee suffered less than 1,500 casualties. Up to this point the war of attrition was working against the Federals.

Atlas of Official Records of the Union and Confederate Armies

PONTOON BRIDGE ON THE JAMES RIVER.

While Lee was waiting for Grant to make the next move after Cold Harbor, he detached most of his cavalry to operate against General Philip Sheridan, who was devastating the country to the west of Richmond, and sent a corps under Jubal Early to attempt to drive the Federals from the Valley, which they were putting to the torch. On June 13 Grant began a brilliant maneuver. He disappeared from the Confederate front, and Lee, stripped of his cavalry and with J. E. B. Stuart dead, was unable to locate any part of Grant's army for twenty-four hours. Nor could he fully determine the Federal general's purpose until the maneuver was completed five days later. What Grant had done was to undertake the maneuver that McClellan had wished to try in 1862: cross to the south side of the James and take Petersburg and Burkeville, which would

Grant crosses the James to attack Petersburg

virtually cut Richmond off from the South and force the Confederates to abandon it. When Grant brought his army across the river, he was able to extricate Butler, whom Beauregard had hemmed in against the river, and thus add about 30,000 men to his army.

The failure to take Petersburg by assault

On June 18, when Lee was at last convinced that Grant had committed his main forces to an assault upon Petersburg, he transferred the bulk of his own army to that point to join with Beauregard's garrison. It was just in the nick of time, for Grant now began a series of frontal assaults which would have driven out a weaker force. But the massive breastworks that the Confederates had constructed enabled Lee to inflict further serious loss upon the Federals. By July 30 Grant had lost about 10,000 men in his attempts to carry the breastworks by storm, and on this day he lost another 4,000 when he mined and blew a big hole in the Confederate works. In their attempt to charge through the opening in the line, the Federal troops were thrust into the "crater" where a great number lost their lives before they could effect a surrender. At last, Grant and the President were convinced that the type of combat used up to this point was too costly and would probably fail to bring the war to a close. Siege, blockade, slow starvation, the demoralization of Lee's army—and other Confederate armies—by bringing down want and fear upon their families at home would have to replace the type of war which Grant preferred.

Lee forced to stand siege by Davis' determination to hold Richmond

Lee's army was not surrounded and forced to stand siege. At any time prior to the winter of 1865 it could have abandoned the defense of the Confederate capital, retired to the Valley, and continued the war of movement which Grant had found too costly. Davis, however, was fixed in his determination to hold Richmond at all costs, just as he had determined to hold Vicksburg. He was afraid of the political effects of giving up his capital and was unwilling to lose the Tredegar Iron Works which manufactured a great deal of heavy equipment for the armies. Lee on the contrary held, as Joseph E. Johnston had in the case of Vicksburg, that for the weaker Confederate army to stand siege would mean the loss of both the army and the capital. Obliquely and tactfully he presented this view to Davis, but the Confederate President could never bring himself to abandon the capital until it was too late to extricate Lee's army. The remainder of the summer and fall of 1864, from June 18 to the winter rains, were thus committed to a war of attrition in which the weaker side stands always to lose.

Early's incursions into Maryland and Pennsylvania

Grant's plan to drive the Confederates from the Valley had not gone well up to this point. On the contrary ⌐arly had driven both Hunter and Sigel out and, on July 11, had pursued the latter to the outskirts of the national capital. Here reinforcements from Grant's army halted Early and drove him back across the Potomac. Four days later he was back across the river, and he burned Chambersburg, Pennsylvania, partly because of the refusal of that town to pay the money that he had demanded of it, but chiefly in retaliation for the destruction wrought in the Valley by Hunter and Sigel. Aside from its barbarity such retaliation was extremely unwise, since it served to give further excuse for the policy of devastation which the Federal government was now adopting as its basic strategy.

Determined now to bring a final end to the Confederate use of the Valley, Grant sent the young, brilliant General Philip Sheridan with a force larger than the Army of Northern Virginia to cope with Early. The Confederate general, considerably reinforced, stood his ground for a short while, but Sheridan's army soon inflicted three severe defeats upon him in the battles of Winchester, Fisher's Hill, and Cedar Creek, which occurred on September 19 and 22, and October 19, respectively. Sheridan under Grant's orders then completed the devastation of the Valley and many residences were burned; livestock, wagons, farm implements, grain, hay, and other food for man and animal were carried off or put to the torch. When Sheridan completed this assignment, he sent Grant a message which quoted Grant's instructions to him: he had wrought such destruction that "a crow flying over the country would need to carry his rations." The Valley was now finally cleared of the Confederates.

Sheridan defeats Early and devastates the Valley

THE WEST IN 1864: CHATTANOOGA TO ATLANTA

On May 5, 1864, while Grant was moving into the Wilderness, Sherman led his army of 100,000 Western troops out from Chattanooga against Johnston's army of 63,000 entrenched along the ridges near Dalton, Georgia. The Federal general did not throw his army in frontal assault upon the Confederate works as Grant was soon to do at Spotsylvania, but carried out a maneuver strongly reminiscent of McDowell's flanking movement at First Bull Run (where Sherman had commanded the force near Stone Bridge), or Lee's flanking operations at Second Bull Run and Chancellorsville. He used a strong force to engage Johnston's front while he sent General J. B. McPherson's corps down a valley to attack the Confederates on their left flank and in the rear. Johnston, however, was screened by a very alert cavalry, under the command of Joseph Wheeler, so that he soon discovered Sherman's maneuver to his left flank. He withdrew to the south toward Atlanta, along the Western and Atlantic Railroad, and entrenched at Resaca.

Sherman flanks Johnston out of his position at Dalton

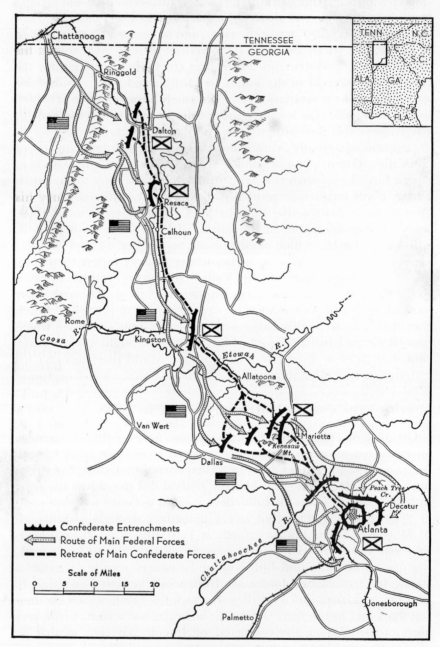

CHATTANOOGA TO ATLANTA.

Here Sherman threatened to outflank him, and once more John- *From Resaca*
ston withdrew his army along the railroad. From Resaca to Kenesaw *to Peach Tree*
Mountain the Federal commander maneuvered against the Army *Creek*
of Tennessee in this manner. Each time Johnston withdrew his
army, intact, nearer to the strongly fortified base at Atlanta. At
length, on June 27 Sherman, in the belief that he had found a
weak place in the Confederate center on Kenesaw Mountain, made
a frontal attack which cost the Federal army 3,000 men and the
Confederates only about 800. Sherman quickly resumed his flanking
maneuvers and Johnston fell back before Atlanta, south of Peach
Tree Creek.

Here in a well entrenched position, with the powerful Atlanta *Johnston in a*
fortifications just to his rear, and his army supplied by railroads from *strong defen-*
Montgomery, Macon, and Savannah, Johnston considered himself in *sive position*
as a result of
an ideal position to defeat Sherman. The Federal general was 120 *his masterful*
miles from his Chattanooga base, and Chattanooga in turn was even *retreat*
farther from Nashville, his next base. These places were connected
by one railroad which ran through hostile territory. At any time
John H. Morgan or Bedford Forrest could operate against this
precarious line of communication with devastating effects. Indeed,
Johnston had urged Davis to send Forrest against Sherman's rear,
but Davis had insisted that Forrest was more profitably occupied elsewhere.

Obviously the President and the General did not hold to the same *Davis replaces*
strategic principle. Johnston's chief concern was the enemy's army *Johnston*
and he cared little, perhaps too little, for any particular bit of *with Hood*
territory, while Davis from political pressure if not from conviction
was as greatly concerned with holding on to certain positions as he
was with destroying the forces of the enemy. Now, because of
Johnston's failure to halt Sherman, Davis removed him from command before Atlanta, and placed in his stead John B. Hood, one of
the best subordinate, fighting generals Lee ever had.

Hood's appointment meant that the Confederates would no *Hood stands*
longer pursue Johnston's strategy of retreat—so successfully used by *and fights*
the Russians in Napoleon's invasion of Russia in 1812 and, after
Johnston's time, in the Second World War. Hood was expected to
come into the open and fight an army twice the size of his. This he
did bravely and skillfully in the battles of Peach Tree Creek, July
20, Atlanta, July 22, and Ezra Church, July 28. In this series of
engagements he shuttled army corps from left to right, turned the
enemy's left flank at Decatur, and used his cavalry with such skill that
Wheeler was able to capture a portion of Sherman's cavalry and de-

feat the rest. But this open warfare was ruinous, for in this series of battles Hood lost about 11,000 men, and Sherman with an army nearly twice the size of his lost only about 10,000. Sherman was delighted at the new turn of affairs.

Atlas of Official Records of the Union and Confederate Armies

CONFEDERATE FORT ON CHATTANOOGA RAILROAD, ATLANTA, GA.

Fall of Atlanta   Hood's lack of experience as an independent commander now began to count against the Confederates in the several ill-judged measures which he adopted after his bloody encounters with Sherman. First, he sent Wheeler's cavalry to cut Sherman's railway communications with Chattanooga and thus deprived himself of the only means of keeping informed of the enemy's movements. Wheeler did very little damage to the railroad, but, in his absence, Sherman proceeded methodically to envelop Atlanta and, on September 2 Hood, faced with siege and capture, evacuated the town.

ATLANTA TO NASHVILLE

The futile attempt to cut Sherman off from his base   Hood's next undertaking was more reckless than stripping himself of his cavalry: he marched his army northward toward Chattanooga with the intention of cutting Sherman off from his base. But his army was not strong enough for such an undertaking nor could

it be adequately supplied. Sherman with only part of his army reinforced the garrisons at Altoona and other stations on the railroad and
soon compelled Hood to give up any plans of further attacks on this
line of supply. Hood now determined to march his army by way of
Decatur, Alabama, back to Nashville and, perhaps, to Louisville,
Kentucky. By thus operating at a distance upon Sherman's line of
communication, he hoped to force the enemy to fall back northward.

Sherman, however, sent Thomas and General J. M. Schofield *The battle*
back toward Nashville with a portion of the army to deal with Hood, *of Franklin*
while he remained in Atlanta and prepared for his march through
Georgia, South Carolina, and North Carolina. On November 30,
Hood came up with Schofield's army of about 29,000 at Franklin,
Tennessee, twenty miles south of Nashville. Schofield's force was
marching to join Thomas' command, and it was placed in Hood's
path to delay the Confederate army until Thomas could prepare
the Nashville defenses. Having failed to bag Schofield at Springhill
where the Confederates had gotten between the Union army and
the town of Franklin, Hood now made a suicidal frontal assault,
which finally drove Schofield's force back north of the town to the
Harpeth River, where it found the bridge badly wrecked. Here by
hasty entrenchment the Federals were able to hold back the Confederate army until darkness enabled them to withdraw in good
order to Nashville. Hood's force was badly shattered. He lost 6,000
men and many of his best officers. Schofield lost hardly more than a
third of this number. The Army of Tennessee had already been
reduced to scarcely 30,000 by sickness, lack of food, clothing, and
shoes, and by desertion and straggling. But with this battle-weary
skeleton of an army Hood moved on to the hills south of Nashville
to attack the powerful army of an unbeaten general. Like Burnside
after his failure at Fredericksburg, Hood seemed bereft of all sane
judgment.

But Thomas needed to reorganize Schofield's corps—the old Army *The battle*
of Ohio—for it had been severely shaken by Hood's ferocious assaults. *of Nashville*
Strangely enough, Grant, whose army at this time was lying relatively
idle before Lee's works at Petersburg, insisted on instant battle
and, when Thomas failed to attack immediately, he instructed General John A. Logan to take over the command. Logan, with the
orders in his pocket to supersede Thomas, forebore taking the final
step to carry out these orders because, being on the ground, he
realized Thomas' difficulties, one of which was the coating of ice over

the surface of the earth. At last, on December 15, the careful and deliberate Thomas moved out against Hood's army, and in two days reduced it to 15,000 infantrymen and a few hundred cavalrymen.

This was the virtual death of the Army of Tennessee. Gallant and futile had been its career since July 17 when Hood succeeded Johnston in command.

SHERMAN AND TOTAL WAR

Sherman, the prophet of modern war

Sherman had over 60,000 veterans about Atlanta in November, 1864, and there were only a few thousand Confederate cavalrymen to offer any military opposition. How then was he to use this army in the midst of an unarmed population? Within the framework of the accepted principles of civilized warfare he could use it to destroy railroads, bridges, and all public property having military value. By marching through Georgia and the Carolinas he could in this way cut off all supplies to Lee's army from outside southern Virginia and western North Carolina and bring about the inevitable defeat of the Army of Northern Virginia. Sherman did this. But he did far more; like Sheridan in the Valley and as he himself had done in Mississippi in 1862-63, he undertook a policy of almost total devastation of private as well as public property. Sherman was, indeed, as Lloyd Lewis has contended (with ample evidence), a prophet of modern total war. He conceived of war as a conflict with the civil population as well as with the armed forces of the enemy. He stated this view—one frequently expressed on other occasions—in a letter to Halleck on December 4, 1864. "I attach more importance to these deep incisions into the enemy's country, because this war differs from European wars in this particular: we are not only fighting armies, but a hostile people, and must make old and young, rich and poor, feel the hard hand of war, as well as their organized armies."

Sherman's march through Georgia

On November 20, 1864, Sherman began his famous march to the sea. He carried with him sufficient rations to feed his army for three weeks, but his jocular order to "forage liberally" made such careful preparation unnecessary. His army lived upon the fat of the land, and what they could not eat or carry off they destroyed. For many weeks the country through which he passed reeked with the stench of dead cattle, horses, and fowls which Sherman's army had wantonly slaughtered; and the air was filled with smoke from the gins, barns, mills, court houses, and even residences which had been burned. Like a colossus swinging his scythe, Sherman cut a swath sixty miles wide through Georgia from Atlanta to the sea. He estimated that he had destroyed $100,000,000 worth of property, four fifths of which were "simple waste and destruction." He arrived at Savannah on December 10 and, after a ten day siege, he forced Hardee's garrison of 15,000 men to give up the town and withdraw northward.

In January, 1865, Sherman moved into South Carolina. Before setting out upon his march he had received a letter from Halleck urging him to burn Charleston and, like the Romans had done after they had burned Carthage, sprinkle salt on the spot where the city had stood. Sherman's reply to Halleck gives an insight into the motives and character of his devastations. "I will bear in mind your hint as to Charleston," he wrote, "and do not think that 'salt' will be necessary. When I move into S. C. the Fifteenth Corps will be on the right of the right wing, and their position will naturally bring them into Charleston first; and if you have watched the history of this corps, you will have remarked that they generally do their work pretty well. The truth is the whole army is burning with an insatiable desire to wreak vengeance upon South Carolina. I almost tremble at her fate, but feel that she deserves all that seems in store for her. . . . I look upon Columbia as quite as bad as Charleston and I doubt if we shall spare her public buildings as we did at Millidgeville." Sherman's destruction of South Carolina was far more widespread than it had been in Georgia and as complete as it had been in Mississippi. From the lower Ashley and Cooper Rivers at Charleston, to Columbia, the land was devastated. The people were to a great extent, deprived of clothing, shelter, and the means of subsistence.

The devastation of South Carolina

Disease and death, especially among old people and children, from exposure and want of food, and the physical and mental anguish of an uprooted and scattered population, crushed the spirit of those who had thus felt "the hard hand of war." Nor were the people in those areas yet untouched by Sherman—and Sheridan, Hunter, and Sigel—much less discouraged; for they felt that a detachment from Sherman's army would burst upon them—a fear well founded, as was shown in the Wilson raid through central and southern Alabama.

The suffering of the people breaks their spirit

The knowledge of this suffering at home, reaching the soldiers in the Army of Tennessee and the Army of Northern Virginia in letters from their families and neighbors, undermined the morale of the fighting men. But those thousands who could get no word either

The desperate plight of their families undermines the morale of the fighting men

from their families or from their neighbors were the most affected. Desertions and absences-without-leave, resulting partly from this situation at home, cut Hood's army by half before it reached Franklin, Tennessee, in November, 1864, and so reduced Lee's army that as spring approached it found itself almost enveloped at Petersburg by Grant's forces.

THE CURTAIN FALLS

Sherman's North Carolina campaign

Sherman began meeting some opposition from Confederate forces in North Carolina. Johnston, now restored by Lee's orders —Lee so belatedly made general-in-chief of all the Confederate armies—headed a small Confederate army made up of the remnants of Hood's command and such troops as Hardee and Beauregard had been able to collect. It was poorly equipped and had a large element of state militia, always nearly worthless in a sustained campaign. But Johnston placed it across Sherman's path, thirty miles north of Fayetteville at Averesborough. Stemming the overwhelming tide at this point only for a short time, the skillful retreater drew his ragged host back to Bentonville where another brief stand was made. But the great power of Sherman's army, now having 20,000 more men under Schofield within easy reach, threatened to overwhelm him. Once again Johnston fell back, first to Goldsboro, only about one hundred and fifty miles from Richmond, then to Raleigh, and finally upon Greensboro.

Grant denounced as a "butcher"

Turning now to Grant and Lee on the Petersburg-Richmond line, it will be recalled that the battle of the "crater" ended Grant's aggressive strategy. From May 5 to July 30, 1864, he had lost at least 65,000 men, mostly veterans, while Lee had lost fewer than half that number. "Grant the butcher" was on many Northern lips and pressure for his removal increased during the summer after Cold Harbor. Lincoln, however, would not this time yield to such pressure, but he did caution Grant against any further attempts to destroy Lee's army by assault and Grant began the slow, distasteful work of siege.

Failure to win a decisive victory in summer of 1864 creates spirit of defeatism

The failure of Sherman and Grant to win a decisive victory over Johnston and Lee in the summer of 1864 brought Northern morale to its lowest point in the war. Had Sherman not been successful in his campaign to take Atlanta—and the probabilities are that he would not have been if Johnston had been retained in command—the war would perhaps have reached a stalemate in the fall of 1864 with the possibilities of a Democratic victory in the elections and a negotiated peace. But Sherman's capture of Atlanta and his march through Georgia immediately raised Northern morale and, as already pointed out (pp. 739-40), lowered that of the Southern people.

In the early spring of 1865, Grant began extending his left flank until it had reached almost to the one remaining railroad which supplied Lee's army from southwest Virginia and western North Carolina. Because of the critical military situation Lee abandoned Petersburg and Richmond April 3 with the purpose of striking out down the Richmond and Danville Railroad to join with Johnston. But successful withdrawal of the weakened army of Northern Virginia was now doubtful. The Confederate officials abandoned Richmond, and Lee started his army to Amelia Court House on the Danville Railroad. His men and horses were nearly starved, and the spirits of many were hopelessly crushed to find, on reaching that point on April 4, that no food was there. When they retreated down the Danville Railroad to meet Johnston, who was falling back on Greensboro fifty miles below Danville, they were confronted on April 5 by Sheridan with a strong force. Lee turned off in the direction of Lynchburg, but Sheridan's cavalry soon threw themselves across Lee's path at Appomattox Court House. Pursued from the rear and blocked in front, Lee decided that further resistance would be a useless shedding of blood and he asked Grant for terms of surrender. *Lee's futile attempt to join Johnston*

Generals Lee and Grant with their staffs met under a flag of truce at the McLean House in Appomattox on April 9 and, after some discussion of details, Lee surrendered his army to Grant. It must be understood, of course, that Grant had no authority to prescribe conditions or make concessions of a political character; his authority was of a strictly military nature. However, he showed rare graciousness in arranging details of the surrender: he permitted all officers to retain their side arms and personal belongings; allowed the men to take their horses home—looking the other way when they took those belonging to the Confederate government; and finally he paroled the men and officers and permitted them to go home on condition that they would not take up arms again until exchanged. This condition was a mere formality since both armies regarded Lee's surrender as the end of the war. So it was. *Lee and Grant at Appomattox*

Though Davis had joined Johnston in North Carolina, he was unable to induce that general to retire to the mountains or to the West and carry on the struggle. Lee's example was too powerful. The average soldier under Johnston, now that the great

Johnston and his army not willing to continue the struggle

leader had laid down arms, was unwilling to continue the unequal struggle, particularly in view of the general understanding that Lincoln's peace terms involved no humiliating and grinding conditions.

Sherman and Johnston prepare an armistice

Johnston met Sherman near Durham, North Carolina, April 17 and 18, and the two drew up armistice terms. Johnston on his part not only proposed to surrender his own army but to arrange for the surrender and parole of all other Confederate armies. Sherman in return offered the same kind of parole and military honors as Grant had given Lee's army. In addition he was to propose that the President recognize the present state governments of the South and re-establish the Federal courts. Doubtless Sherman considered this a good bargain on his part, for he was of the opinion that Johnston's army and other Confederate armies might continue the fight.

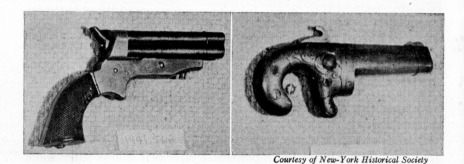

Courtesy of New-York Historical Society

TWO FIREARMS.

The assassination of Lincoln

Lincoln, though, was dead. On the night of April 14, he had attended the Ford Theater; and during the performance John Wilkes Booth, under the delusion that he was aiding the South, entered the President's box and shot him. Booth, who managed to elude capture for the moment, was soon caught in a burning barn in Maryland where he was killed. Four other conspirators, along with an innocent woman, Mrs. Surratt, were soon hanged, and others were imprisoned.

Surrender of the remaining Confederate armies.

Vice-President Johnson now became President, and he and Stanton, greatly embittered over the belief that the Southern leaders had prompted Booth in the assassination, swept aside Sherman's political concessions. Finally, on April 26, Johnston accepted purely military terms identical with those Grant had given Lee. On May

4, Taylor surrendered his forces in Mississippi and Alabama; and *The capture of Davis* May 26, Kirby Smith surrendered the troops in the trans-Mississippi Department on similar terms.   On May 10, Jefferson Davis was taken prisoner near Irwinville in Southern Georgia and thus suddenly collapsed the entire military and civil structure of the Confederacy.

CHAPTER XLV

The Federal and Confederate Navies

THE WORK OF THE FEDERAL NAVY

U. S. Civil War navy devised almost solely to defeat the South

*I*N 1861 the Federal navy of about fifty sail ships and forty wooden steamers, though obsolete in comparison with the ironclad fleets of France and Britain, was all-powerful in relation to that of the Confederacy, and it retained this position of inferiority and superiority with reference to the respective European and Southern navies until the end of the Civil War. Secretary of the Navy Welles devised a navy for the special and almost sole purpose of aiding in the defeat of the South and with little thought of competing for sea power with France and Britain. He had no vessel constructed that was comparable with the class of ironclads represented by the French and British warships, the *Gloire* and the *Warrior*. The most powerful naval vessels that Welles had built were those of the experimental *Monitor* type, that were slow, frequently unseaworthy but effective against the "homemade" Confederate ironclads and land fortifications. The chief functions of the United States navy during the Civil War were threefold: to blockade the Confederacy; to co-operate with the army in amphibious warfare; and to capture or destroy the Confederate raiders such as the *Alabama* and the *Florida*.

THE BLOCKADE

The United States establishes the British type of blockade

Lincoln proclaimed a blockade of the coast of the Confederate States on April 19, 1861, which he extended to include that of North Carolina and Virginia when they seceded. But an ordinary blockade of the South was impossible. The Confederate shore line was over 3,500 miles in extent, and great stretches of this were composed of long, narrow islands screening almost continuous bodies of water —such as Biscayne Bay and Indian River in Florida, Albemarle and Pamlico Sounds in North Carolina—through which flat-bottomed steamers and sail vessels could pass without being observed from the sea. There were not enough warships in the world to surround and guard effectively such a long and complex shore line, which, according to American doctrine and that of continental Europe, was the only legal method of blockade. What the President did was to lay down the British type of blockade, which, it will be recalled, had a great deal to do with the War of 1812. As soon as the navy had sufficient strength, an arc of naval vessels was placed around each of the principal Confederate ports, and other ships patrolled at intervals the long intervening stretches of coast. The swifter ships were sent to cruise off the West Indies and in the Gulf Stream to capture suspected blockade runners, and almost habitually such squadrons effectively blockaded the neutral ports on these islands or used them as bases of operation.

Blockade running

The very announcement by Lincoln of the blockade served in the beginning to frighten foreign ships away, but as the price of naval stores, tobacco, and cotton rose, so did the courage of the merchantmen. In a few months they began coming back into the Southern trade despite the risks of capture. As the Federal navy strengthened its squadrons and made it more hazardous for ordinary steamers and sail vessels to attempt to run the blockade, vessels were specially constructed for this business. These were long, slim craft, driven by screw propellers instead of side or stern wheels, and they were capable of such speed that few naval vessels could overtake them in a chase. They ran from the Bermudas, Nassau, Cuba, and St. Thomas into Charleston, Wilmington, Mobile, and Galveston, passing usually along the coast out of range of the Federal naval guns. Not infrequently they ran through the cordon of blockading ships. One daring blockade runner came into Wilmington with the Federal fleet when that port was captured and, on discovering the error the next morning, successfully ran out again. Blockade running was exciting, spectacular, and very profitable. Young men of daring and skill from the South and from Great Britain manned the blockade runners, the stories of whose adventures rival any of our tallest tales.

Noted seamen and famous ships

There were many noted seamen among those who manned these boats, but none who gained such renown as the two Englishmen, Captains Augustus C. Roberts and William Watson, and the Confederate, Captain John Wilkinson. Perhaps the blockade runners themselves gained as much fame as their masters, for these craft had their own personality and their special "fans," who laid bets on their goings and comings. None were more famous than the *Pet*, the *Kate*, and the *Little Hattie*, which ran the blockade, chiefly at Wilmington and Charleston, forty, forty-four, and sixty times, respectively, before capture or destruction, and the *Robert E. Lee*, that Captain

Wilkinson conducted through the Federal squadrons twenty-one times in ten months.

Blockade not effective according to previous American doctrine

Although the Federal navy was able to destroy the normal export and import trade of the South and thus contribute greatly to the defeat of the Confederacy, it was never able to establish a blockade which would have been considered effective according to previous American definitions when dealing with Great Britain. The blockade runners made thousands of successful trips through the blockade. About 1,000,000 bales of cotton were shipped out, and 600,000 to 1,000,000 stand of small arms, a good portion of the artillery, and much food and clothing were brought in.

COMBINED SEA AND LAND OPERATIONS

The South Atlantic and Gulf coasts

One of the chief objectives of the co-operative expeditions of the navy and land forces along the coast and up the tidal rivers was to strengthen the blockade. In August, 1861, the navy seized the inlets to Pamlico and Albemarle Sounds. In January, 1862, a land force under Burnside captured Roanoke Island, flanked by these two sounds, and presently occupied New Bern and Plymouth on the mainland. This cut off a considerable strip of coast and supplied bases of operation for the blockading fleet. In the fall of 1861 the South Atlantic squadron captured Port Royal, South Carolina, and in April, 1862, took Fort Pulaski at the mouth of the Savannah River. On April 25 Admiral David Glasgow Farragut, after running past the Confederate forts with part of his fleet and a land force under General Benjamin Butler, captured New Orleans and thus blockaded more effectively the Gulf coast.

The Virginia coast: the Monitor and the Merrimack

The fight for control of the Virginia coast and tidal rivers was carried out successfully in 1862 by McClellan and the James River Fleet, commanded a portion of the time by the obstreperous Charles Wilkes. On March 8, 1862, the Confederate ironclad ram, the *Virginia,* better known as the *Merrimack,* steamed out of Norfolk and attacked the wooden fleet on blockade duty near Hampton Roads. It destroyed the *Cumberland,* the *Congress,* and three smaller vessels and captured two steamers. It was a monstrous looking affair. The Confederates had constructed this ironclad ram by cutting the hull of the old United States frigate *Merrimack* down to the water's edge and building over it a low roof of heavy timbers, covered by four inches of iron plate. On the next day it returned to its business of destruction only to meet an even stranger looking craft than itself, one which had its deck almost even with the water and on top of which was a revolving gun turret. This queer naval craft, "a cheese box on a raft," was the *Monitor,* designed by the naval architect, John Ericsson, for the express purpose of meeting the *Merrimack,* whose construction had caused wild rumors to spread throughout the Northeast. The fight between the *Monitor* and the *Merrimack* did little damage to either vessel, but because of its defective engines the *Merrimack* did not return to the fray. The work of the *Merrimack* in destroying the wooden ships rendered obsolete all the United States deep sea naval vessels except the *Monitor.* These were not the first ironclads, although this was the first time two ironclads had fought. Federal ironclads had already attacked Forts Henry and Donelson and were sinking wooden steamers on the western rivers (see p. 702).

The Merrimack sunk by its own crew

The Confederate vessel would have steamed up the James River toward Richmond and thus contributed much to the frustration of McClellan's march up the Peninsula, but the draft was too great. For that reason, when Norfolk fell into the hands of the Federals as a result of McClellan's outflanking it with his army, the *Merrimack,* now left without a base, was blown up by its own crew. After this, the coast of Virginia and the James and York Rivers fell permanently into the hands of the Federals.

Captured ports useful as Federal bases

As time passed, other points along the Confederate coast were taken, and the blockade was thus reinforced by the occupation of places by the land forces. These harbors thus taken were vital in the work of the blockading squadrons, but their importance in directly cutting off trade can be easily overemphasized. As bases of operation for land forces they were of equally great importance.

THE CONFEDERATE DEEP SEA NAVY

Building the Confederate navy

The Confederacy had no seagoing navy to begin with, but Secretary Stephen Mallory and his able subordinates constructed several powerful ironclad rams at home, among which was the *Merrimack.* Furthermore, the Confederate naval agents in Europe, James D. Bulloch and James North, performed miracles. First, in 1861-62 Bulloch planned and had constructed in England the two famous raiders, the *Florida* and the *Alabama.* Then in 1862-63 he had the Lairds build two ironclad rams, the size of modern destroyers. North had the Thompsons of Glasgow, Scotland, build at the same time an ironclad ram as large as a modern light cruiser. In France, 1863-64, Bulloch had two powerful ironclads and four corvettes or cruisers similar to the *Alabama* constructed with the connivance of Emperor Napoleon III. John Bigelow said of the two ironclads built in France that, had they escaped to sea, "they would not only have opened every Confederate port to the commerce of the world, but they might have laid every important city on our seaboard under contribution." The same could have been said of the ironclads built in England. With the exception of the *Alabama* and *Florida,* however, none of these war vessels was permitted to leave either the French or British ports for Confederate service, though by a ruse, the Confederacy got possession of the *Stonewall* just before the war ended.

Work of the Confederate commerce raiders

The Confederate cruisers, headed by the *Alabama* under the command of Raphael Semmes, directly and indirectly inflicted staggering damage upon the American merchant fleet. These and other Confederate cruisers and privateers captured or sank over two hundred ships, but their greatest destruction was by indirection. Their presence upon the high seas was such a menace to the commerce of the United States that by the end of the war the better part of the merchant fleet had been sold to the British or transferred to British registry.

The difficult task of capturing or destroying the raiders

The task of running down and destroying these swift cruisers was a difficult one indeed for the American navy. It is improbable for example that the *Alabama* could ever have been bagged, had not Raphael Semmes in order to maintain the prestige of the Confederate service—and perhaps his own pride played a part—gone out to fight the powerfully armed and stronger built *Kearsarge.* Off Cherbourg, France, on June 19, 1864, he steamed out to meet his fate and the famous raider was sunk. Nor were the Federals able to catch the *Florida* upon the high seas; not until they violated Brazil's neutrality and sent their warships into the port of Bahia (São Salvador) after her were they able to catch this famous raider.

THE FRESH WATER NAVIES

Creating the Federal river fleet

Both Federal and Confederate governments had their "fresh water" navies operating on the inland waterways of the South. Indeed, as has already been intimated, the river fleet of the United States played a decisive roll in the western campaigns of Halleck, Grant, and Pope. In the spring of 1861, the United States War Department undertook the odd task of purchasing and building a navy for the Mississippi and its tributaries, and by early December it had ten or more partially ironclad river gunboats. In July, 1862, Admiral Farragut, who had brought his deep sea squadron up the river, was given command of the Mississippi flotilla, with Commodore David D. Porter in immediate command.

The work of the Federal river fleet was twofold: clearing the rivers of Confederate gunboats—which proved no easy undertaking *Its principal* despite the defective machinery and poor equipment of these boats— *functions* and co-operation with the armies as transports, convoys, and fighting units.   It was the river gunboats under Flag Officer Foote that reduced Fort Henry, though they were not successful against Donelson; and the river fleet was primarily responsible for the fall of Columbus (Kentucky), Island Number 10, and Memphis.

While the Federal river fleet was being constructed the Con- *The Confed-* federate government was building and reconstructing old river *erate river* vessels.   At New Orleans a few armored but inadequately powered *fleet* rams were completed, or were in the process of completion, when Farragut started up the river for the purpose of taking New Orleans. One of these rams was the ironclad *Manassas,* which in October, 1861, had attacked and defeated some of the advanced units of the Federal flotilla anchored in the lower reaches of the Mississippi. Another Confederate ironclad river gunboat of note was the *Arkansas.* This vessel had poor engines and bad steering gear, but a good crew and an excellent commander, Captain Isaac Brown.   Brown is reported to have remarked whimsically that the steering gear of the *Arkansas* was so unmanageable that the ram could not always be brought around the numerous bends in the Mississippi, and that it frequently cut across through the woods.   On one occasion the *Arkansas,* which had been lurking in the Yazoo swamps, chased the Federal gunboats down the Yazoo, out into the Mississippi where, without stopping, it plowed through the combined fleets of Admiral Farragut and Flag Officer Davis and managed to reach Vicksburg.

The Mississippi flotilla of the United States before the end of *The Federals* 1862 controlled all the Mississippi River except that stretch of water *drive all Con-* between Vicksburg and Port Hudson. In the winter of 1863 the *federate* Federals made a serious effort to sweep this part of the river clear of *the Mississippi* Confederate craft, but running the gauntlet at Vicksburg caused considerable damage to begin with and the gunboats met disaster farther down stream.   The ram, *Queen of the West,* was disabled by the Confederates and immediately taken over by them and repaired. Whereupon the Federal ironclad, *Indianola,* was sunk by this same captured *Queen of the West* with the aid of other Confederate rams and gunboats.   The Confederacy thus secured the Mississippi from Vicksburg to Port Hudson until the late spring of 1863. When Vicksburg and Port Hudson were taken in the summer of 1863 the Confederate ironclads retreated up the Red River and other Mississippi tributaries and continued traffic across the Mississippi—though at considerable hazard and in greatly reduced volume—until the end of the war.

CHAPTER XLVI

Foreign and Domestic Affairs

THE DIPLOMATIC FRONT: MOTIVES FOR EUROPEAN INTERVENTION

ALTHOUGH the people of the North and South were opposed to permanent European entanglements, they were not unaware of the potentialities of diplomacy as a weapon of warfare. French intervention in the Revolution had been decisive in establishing American independence, and, in 1861, the South hoped and the North feared that the Confederacy might receive similar aid in its war for independence. The motives for such action seemed obvious: England and France must have Southern cotton; the British disliked the Americans and would like to see their power reduced; and Napoleon III shared this desire because a United States weakened by division could not frustrate his ambition to annex Mexico.

British and French dependence on Southern cotton

The dependence of England and France upon Southern cotton was very great. About eighty-five per cent of the raw staple used in those two countries came from the Confederate States. In England half the foreign trade, a fifth of the population, and a tenth of the wealth were committed to the cotton industry; and in France the manufacture of cotton textiles was the most important business.

Confederates ask that blockade be repudiated

Southern belief in the power of cotton to force intervention was widespread during the first year of the war. "If England and France were willing to engage in a war with China to secure commerce in opium with the Chinese people against their will and the decree of their government," asked one of the King Cotton champions, why would those countries "not raise a blockade for commerce in cotton?" It was on the basis of such assumption that the Confederate commissioners, chief among whom were W. L. Yancey, James M. Mason, and John Slidell, urged Great Britain and France to break or repudiate the blockade in order to obtain cotton. Their argument, of course, was that the blockade was ineffective and, therefore, illegal.

Napoleon III was easily convinced that the United States was imposing a "paper blockade," and his opinion was in keeping with the traditional French view of an effective blockade and the recent

Declaration of Paris. Actually, of course, he had little respect for legality. The distress in the textile industry and his ambition to establish Mexico as a French vassal state determined his attitude toward the blockade. He accordingly assured Slidell that he would send his fleet, if Great Britain would contribute a portion of hers, and raise the blockade.

The British government would not listen to such proposals. On the contrary, in the spring of 1862, it openly pronounced itself satisfied with the effectiveness of the blockade. Britain's general policy of nonintervention in the domestic struggles of first class powers was an important factor in that country's acceptance of the effectiveness of the blockade. The fact, however, that the United States, the long-standing opponent of "paper blockades," had set up one of her own was more important, for henceforth the United States would be unable to offer effective argument against similar action on the part of Great Britain. *British accept blockade as effective*

Had the British not accepted the legality of the blockade, the adequate supply of cotton during the first year of the war would have been a deterrent to any drastic action against it. The British textile industry had accumulated an enormous surplus of raw cotton and manufactured goods, and, in the spring of 1861, the manufacturers and buyers had on hand about 700,000 bales of American cotton and 300,000,000 pounds of manufactured goods in excess of the normal supply. Cotton goods were selling at less than cost, the mills were faced with a shutdown, and the operatives were confronted with a long period of unemployment. Indeed, it was believed in financial circles that England was on the brink of a serious panic. But the blockade cut off the source of cheap and plentiful cotton, and within two years the surplus had been disposed of at a profit of over $200,000,000. The cotton famine came in the fall of 1862, and 500,000 operatives were thrown out of work, and many of the small mills went into bankruptcy. But the larger, well financed mills "rode their oars" for a few months, and then began to readjust their operation upon the basis of Egyptian, Indian, Brazilian, and Chinese cotton. With this and the Southern cotton received through the blockade they were able to go on during the remainder of the war piling up excellent profits. The operatives were reabsorbed in part by the larger mills and in part by the greatly expanded linen and woolen industries, so that before the end of the war there was very little unemployment in the textile centers. *Blockade enabled British to make great profits from surplus stocks*

The French millowners and operatives were not so fortunate as the British. They had very little surplus cotton, the factories were

*Napoleon still
unable to per-
suade the
British to join
him in inter-
vention*
smaller and not well financed, and within a few months there was great destitution in the cotton textile centers followed by a strong demand that the government help put an end to the American war. But Napoleon could no more persuade Britain to join him in outright intervention than he had been able to get her to send her fleet along with his to break the blockade. It is true that for a short time during Lee's invasion of Maryland in September, 1862, the British Cabinet was seriously considering intervention because of the rapidly developing cotton famine; but the battle of Antietam arrested this move for the time being, and the rapid recovery from the cotton shortage together with the general prosperity of the country after 1862 laid it permanently on the table.

*British atti-
tude toward
the Americans
not friendly*
At the time of the Civil War the British had long been in the habit, like the ancient Greeks, of regarding other peoples more or less as barbarians, and, if their newspapers, journals, reviews, and travel literature are any gauge of public opinion, they considered the American as semibarbarian. The London *Economist* on September 28, 1861, spoke of them as "so rough, so encroaching, so overbearing, that all other governments felt as if some new associate, untrained in the amenities of civilized life and insensible alike to the demands of justice and courtesy, had forced its way into the areopagus of nations." But the Americans were not merely a terribly rough folk, they had become in just a few years one of the great powers of the earth, spoiling for a fight, so it appeared—especially with the mother country. The London *Times* expressed a common attitude when on August 15, 1862, it spoke of the United States as the "American Colossus" between whose legs—should the giant continue to increase in size—"the tallest empire of the old world will easily walk." The downfall of the Colossus, by the secession of the Southern states, was in the opinion of the *Times* "the riddance of a nightmare."

*Sympathy for
the South
developed
after 1860*
While the British held opinions not flattering to the American people in either the North or the South before the outbreak of the war, after that event Confederate propaganda, British jealousy of the "American Colossus," and the brilliant military achievements of the Confederacy caused a shift of opinion very flattering to the South. It was no longer a dreary wasteland of slavery and half-savage poor whites, but a highly cultured country controlled by gentlemen like the English aristocracy—and descended from them—and inhabited by independent small farmers. Henceforth the ill-bred, swaggering American bully lived north of the Confederate boundary.

Nevertheless, it was an ill-founded hope in the South and fear in the North that the British would interfere in the Civil War because of likes and dislikes of Americans in one or the other section, or of dread of the Western Colossus. Their sympathies were, with the exception of certain individuals, entirely passive, whereas the fear and jealousy of a powerful United States were not as great or as immediate as the fear of Russia, Prussia, and France. *British dislike and fear of the Western Colossus insufficient grounds for intervention*

Napoleon's scheme to annex Mexico was of long standing; but it was not until the United States was involved in a civil war that he undertook to carry it out. Jointly with England and Spain he sent troops into Mexico in 1861, ostensibly to collect the debts which that strife-torn country had not been able to pay. When the other intervening powers withdrew from the venture he revealed his ulterior purpose by reinforcing his army and proceeding to subjugate the republic. Seward had attempted to prevent European intervention by an offer to pay the interest on the Mexican debts, but the offer was not accepted. He and the United States minister at Paris, William Dayton, in carefully guarded words constantly warned Napoleon that the United States, while it recognized the right of France to make war on Mexico, could never accept French interference with the Mexican government or annexation of Mexican territory. This, of course, was the essence of the Monroe Doctrine. Napoleon gave fair words of assurance that he had no ultimate designs upon Mexico, although while he was saying these things he was overthrowing the republic of Mexico and setting up a puppet empire under Maximilian, the Austrian Archduke. But the United States government had to bide its time and Seward had to pretend that he accepted Napoleon's promises. *Napoleon's intervention in Mexico and the attitude of the United States*

The French Emperor should have understood quite well the chances of the game he was playing: that if the United States were not reduced in strength by the Confederacy's establishing its independence, his Mexican venture was doomed to failure. Maximilian recognized this and attempted to commit Napoleon to aiding the South before he went to Mexico in 1864, but the Emperor tricked him. The Confederate diplomatic agents saw even more clearly than the puppet emperor that the independence of the Confederacy was an essential condition to French success in Mexico. They pressed this idea home upon Napoleon for two years, and they always received the same answer given them when they urged that France intervene for the purpose of obtaining cotton: the Emperor would not act without the co-operation of Great Britain. In thus holding aloof from the American war, Napoleon offers the perfect example of the man who would keep the cake and eat it too. Until 1865 he was convinced that the Confederacy would win without foreign aid, *Confederate independence, Napoleon's only chance of success in Mexico* and that the United States, rendered powerless to interfere effectively with his Mexican plans, would make the best of a bad situation and remain at peace.

Confederate friendship essential, and must be paid for by French intervention

In the spring of 1864 Slidell suddenly and bluntly warned the French Emperor that he was deceiving himself in supposing that he could thus get what he wanted for nothing. The safety of his Mexican empire depended not only upon the establishment of the *independence* of the Confederacy but upon its *friendship* as well, and this friendship came at a high price, namely, French intervention on the side of the South. If such aid were not forthcoming, the South would, as soon as it gained its independence, form with the North "an offensive and defensive alliance, for the establishment of an American policy [the Monroe Doctrine] on our continent, which will result in the suppression of monarchical institutions in Mexico." This was no idle threat, for French intervention in Mexico was as unpopular in the South as it was in the North, and Confederate acceptance of it would be the price to be paid for Napoleon's aid.

Napoleon afraid to pay the price

The Emperor's unpopularity at home, his fear of war with Russia and Prussia, his distrust of Great Britain, and his fear of war with the United States rendered him too timid to pay this price. Consequently the Mexican situation, like the other reasons for European intervention, did not work out as hoped in the South and feared in the North.

THE IRRITATIONS OF WAR

Seward's truculent attitude toward the British

These were the chief factors at the beginning of the war that seemed to point to foreign intervention, yet none of them operated as anticipated. In the course of the war, however, others developed which might have resulted in intervention had England desired to join the ever-willing Napoleon. In the face of a situation dangerous to the United States, Seward, while very cautious in dealing with the French, assumed a truculent attitude toward the British. Before going into office he had told the Duke of Newcastle that when he became Secretary of State it would be his business to insult England and that he intended to do it. The Duke passed this remark on, and soon it was in circulation throughout England. On the heels of this came the rumor, essentially correct, that Seward had proposed to Lincoln on April 1, 1861, that the United States declare war on Great Britain and France as a means of bringing the Southern states back into the Union. In May, Seward and Adams had angrily protested against the British proclamation of neutrality which recognized Confederate belligerency, and seldom after that did either of these men send a communication to the British government in which some sharp reference to this proclamation was not made. At about the same time Seward sent a warning to the British against receiving the Confederate commissioners, which was in essence an ultimatum. The effect of this bellicose attitude was to create the impression among the British people as well as in the government that Seward, as spokesman of the United States, was spoiling for a fight.

With the British thus convinced that the United States was seeking an opportunity to start a war with them, it is easy to understand the violent reaction of the people and the government to the *Trent* affair. On November 8, 1861, Captain Charles Wilkes of the U.S.S. *San Jacinto* stopped the British steamer *Trent* while en route to England and seized the two Confederate commissioners, James M. Mason and John Slidell, together with their secretaries. Though this was a violation of the principles of the freedom of the seas, as heretofore proclaimed by the United States, Wilkes' act was greeted with applause throughout the North, and the stamp of official approval was put on it by the House of Representatives and the Secretary of the Navy offering the Captain their congratulations. When the news of the *Trent* affair reached England about November 27, the British naturally accepted it as a challenge, and the popular demand for war compelled the government to send an ultimatum to the United States demanding the surrender of the prisoners and an apology. At the same time 8,000 troops were dispatched to Canada. Lincoln and Seward agreed that the United States could not fight two wars at once and released the prisoners. But Seward offered no apology. While the *Trent* affair did not make the British love Seward or the Americans, it did convince them that the Secretary of State was not seeking war between the United States and Great Britain. It likewise showed Seward that Great Britain was not seeking an excuse to declare war on the United States.

The Trent Affair

The construction of the Confederate ironclads and cruisers in England and France aroused deep and prolonged resentment in the North and brought the United States close to breaking off diplomatic relations with both countries, and even to talk of war. Adams, through his secret service agents, had learned that the several cruisers and ironclads being constructed in British ports were intended for the Confederacy. The British government, too, had evidence pointing to the same conclusion, yet neither the evidence furnished by Adams nor that obtained by the British agents afforded the legal proof necessary for the condemnation of the

Britain and United States clash over legal right of neutrals to build warships for belligerents

ships under British law (the Enlistment Act of 1819) or international law as interpreted by British and American courts. As a test case the British government had seized the Confederate ship, the *Alexandra*, and had lost the suit. The Enlistment Act did not prohibit the building of such vessels so long as they were not armed and equipped in British ports; and the government took the position, quite sincerely, that the two Confederate cruisers, the *Alabama* and the *Florida*, that left British ports in 1862, were not armed in British ports. However, the British contended that under international law warships could be built, armed, and equipped in neutral ports, and sold to belligerents as merchandise, provided such ships were delivered at a port of the belligerent before they were permitted to begin operations. The British Foreign Office supported its position in part by former American practices sanctioned by the United States courts in the cases of the ships, *Santissima Trinidad*, the *President*, and the *Independence*. These had been built as warships in American ports, had been armed there, and two of them sold to belligerents as merchandise.

British seize ships as a matter "of policy and not of strict law"

But Adams would not for one moment listen to Russell's citation of opinions of the United States Courts in such cases. The Confederate ships must be seized. When the *Alabama* escaped, he began a ceaseless demand for indemnity to cover the damage done by that cruiser. In July, 1863, when the ironclads seemed almost ready to depart, he began submitting stacks of proof of Confederate ownership, and in a succession of notes ever increasing in grimness he demanded that the British government seize these vessels. Finally, on September 5, he sent Russell a note observing that if the ironclads were permitted to leave port, "It would be superfluous in me to point out to your Lordship that this is war." Three days previously, however, Russell had ordered the seizure of the Confederate ships as a matter "of policy though not of strict law." Seward and his minister had left no doubt in the minds of the British Cabinet that war with the United States would be the consequence of the failure to stop the departure of the ironclads.

Napoleon's policy relating to the building of Confederate warships, a matter of expediency

Napoleon, as would be expected, did not take a stand upon either national or international law but upon expediency in permitting the building of the Confederate cruisers and ironclads in French ports. As soon, therefore, as Dayton and John Bigelow, American Consul General in Paris, discovered that these vessels were being built for the Confederacy, the Emperor pretended to be very indignant at what the Confederate agents were doing and promised to seize the ships at once. But he delayed the seizure from the fall of 1863 till the late spring of 1864, when Seward had Dayton warn the Emperor that, if the vessels were permitted to leave, there would be war. Just how little in earnest Seward was in this ultimatum may be judged by the later statement of Bigelow that one of these ironclads could have broken the blockade.

Even after the *Trent* affair the British had many serious grievances against the United States, which could have caused war had either desired it. These grew primarily out of the methods of enforcing the blockade. While the British accepted the revival of the practice of the seizure of ships on the grounds of ultimate destination, at the same time there was much friction over the facts in the case. The blockade of neutral, especially British, ports, or the use of these ports as bases of operation against blockade runners and the Confederate raiders, almost precipitated a naval battle between the British and the American fleets on more than one occasion. The imprisonment by the United States of the British crews of blockade runners was the source of strong resentment in England during the last two years of the war. Though this practice was banned by international law, Adams stoutly defended it when the British government protested. All British subjects engaged in blockade running, Adams contended, "must incur a suspicion [that they are in the services of the Confederacy] strong enough to make them liable to be treated as enemies, and if taken, to be reckoned as prisoners of war." But Great Britain met all such infringements of her neutrality with angry protests only. Why?

British grievances against the United States

It has already been pointed out why the British government did not intervene to obtain cotton or to weaken the "American Colossus." But why permit the capture of her merchant vessels sailing from one British port to another, when suspected of the ultimate intention of violating the blockade or of delivering contraband by way of Mexico? In this and other ways, not less than 1,000 British vessels with their rich cargoes were captured. Why permit the imprisonment of civilian crews of blockade runners? Why submit to the many other grievances? The answer is too complex for more than a few brief suggestions here. As pointed out in the case of the disposal of the surplus cotton and cotton goods, the war brought great profits to the British. It has been estimated that the woolen and linen industries made an excess profit of over $250,-000,000; the wool and flax growers reaped proportionate gains; tens of thousands of cotton textile workers were absorbed in the expanded woolen and linen industries; the shipyards did a land-office business in constructing blockade runners, and the blockade runners sometimes ran up a profit of 1,000 per cent on one voyage. Perhaps the greatest profit was the transfer of the best portion of the American

War profits and general British prosperity

merchant marine to the British because of the depredations of the Confederate cruisers. Finally, employment outside of the cotton textile districts was so much higher than it had been before, that it brought the national average above normal. There was then no economic motive for intervention. On the contrary a war with the United States would have been ruinous to British commerce and would have turned these profits into losses. Then there was the need for American wheat caused by a partial failure of the wheat crop in Britain and western Europe. While grain could have been obtained from central and eastern Europe, it would have been at much greater cost and would have added to the suffering attendant upon a war with the United States. It must be observed, however, that, had the United States been unable to sell its wheat abroad at this time, it would have been deprived of its only medium of international exchange now that cotton was no longer available. War with England would thus have been ruinous to the United States too.

The slavery question

The slavery question would have acted as a moral restraint upon the British had there been grounds for intervention. However, the attitude of the United States government, as expressed by Lincoln in his first inaugural and in his Emancipation Proclamation, that the freeing of the slaves was incidental to and not the purpose of the war doubtless neutralized to a great extent British sentiment on the slavery issue.

THE HOME FRONTS: LIFE IN THE NORTH

Economic depression

In the beginning the North experienced a severe economic depression as a result of secession and war. Banks suspended specie payments and many closed their doors forever. Thousands of business houses failed. Cotton factories were soon deprived of their normal supply of raw material and were compelled to close down or run only part time.

Industrial recovery and prosperity

But the North soon began to recover, then to prosper as never before. Army contracts were let on such terms that contractors netted incredible profits. Dividends of forty per cent in the textile mills were common. The heavy industries, the munitions factories, and the private arsenals reaped larger profits out of a government desperately arming under war conditions. Salvage companies raised old, rotten ships from watery graves and sold them to the Federal government for troop transports. Millions were made in the lumber business and the production of coal. At the same time rich, newly-discovered gold and silver mines were being worked in

Nevada, Arizona, and Colorado, and the petroleum industry developed during the war into one of major importance.

Northern agriculture profited temporarily from the war. The succession of bad grain crops in western Europe and the needs of the armies stimulated the production of grain and wool in the North far beyond anything of prewar days. Millions of acres of fresh land were brought into cultivation and sowed in small grain or planted in Indian corn. The grain farmers supplied Great Britain forty per cent of her flour and wheat and quantities of Indian corn, rye, barley, and peas. To enable the farmers, whose sons were frequently away on the battle front, to cultivate and harvest so much grain, the use of farm machinery—the riding cultivator, reapers, threshers, and gang plows—was expanded upon a scale never dreamed of. It is estimated, for example, that there were not less than 250,000 reapers in use in the North in 1865. The production of wool almost quadrupled under war demands, while hogs and beef cattle were marketed in greater numbers than ever before.

The prosperity of the farmer

The transportation of troops and military supplies, and the increased production of every commodity, except cotton textiles, greatly stimulated railroad building, so that railroads which had been practically bankrupt before 1860 found themselves paying excellent dividends even on watered stock.

The railroads

The high prices of wartime were not all the result of extraordinary demand and of profiteering, but were in part due to inflation of the currency. This inflation, high prices, and lack of organization excluded the laboring classes and those on fixed salaries from the prosperity of the banker, the industrialist, the merchant, and the farmer. Indeed the lot of the laborers was hard: their real wages were much lower than in prewar times, and as a result of their poverty they were unable to buy exemption from military service or hire substitutes as could others who so desired. For this reason they came to have a feeling that it was "a rich man's war and a poor man's fight." This attitude was made stronger when, by looking around, one saw neighbors hiring substitutes or buying exemptions for a mere bagatelle compared with the enormous profits they were wringing from the United States government from which they had bought this exemption.

The hard lot of the laboring classes

The third inalienable right of man was in great evidence during the war: all except the soldiers and the laboring classes seemed strenuously engaged in the "pursuit of happiness." Theaters were crowded from gallery to orchestra, where bedizened dames from gambling halls and cheap cabarets occupied conspicuous boxes cheek by jowl with the old elite and the "shoddy aristocracy"—those who

"The pursuit of happiness"

had made their fortunes by selling "shoddy" uniforms to the Federal government. The race course, the barroom, and more questionable resorts did a land-office business. "Who at the North would ever think of war, if he had not a friend in the army, or did not read the newspapers?" asked the New York *Independent* in the fourth year of the conflict.

LIFE IN THE SOUTH

Factors undermining Southern economy

The South suffered a greater shock than the North as a result of the severance of the national political structure and the outbreak of war. Unlike the North, it never recovered from the first shock. The reasons for this are that the South was blockaded by the Federal navy and invaded and occupied, piece by piece, by the Federal armies. The blockade, while never effective according to the early American definition, destroyed the normal export of cotton, tobacco, and rice from the South, upon which the economic life of that section had so greatly depended (see p. 746). The extra-legal cotton embargo, which lasted until the spring of 1862, aided the blockade in preventing export trade.

Return to domestic manufacture

Since the markets for their staple crops were partially cut off, and because they hoped by withholding cotton to induce Britain to break the blockade, Southern farmers and planters turned more and more to subsistence farming. At the same time they were forced to fall back upon household manufacture, and the rural population except in the path of the invader was not long in becoming self-sufficient in a crude but not uncomfortable fashion.

The cities of the Confederacy suffer want

The cities, however, suffered want, for they must buy everything with depreciated currency from farmers and merchants who were more and more reluctant to part with their produce in exchange for such money. Then, too, the railway systems of the South were unable to carry the extra load of war and at the same time transport ordinary articles of trade to the cities and seaports. This failure of the Southern railroads was due in part to the inadequate facilities for repairing rails and rolling stock and in part to the destruction or capture, by the invading armies, of many of the most important roads, which resulted in overburdening those remaining in Confederate hands. The Confederate armies, so dependent upon imports of guns, munitions, uniforms, blankets, and eventually certain foods, were weakened by poor transportation. But more than anything else the breakdown of the railroads undermined the finances and credit of the Confederate government by severely limiting the export of cotton and other supplies.

There was much gaiety in Richmond and a few other urban communities where soldiers on furlough and their families met, war profiteers assembled, and gambling resorts and other such places of doubtful fame sprang up; but in the South generally life was somber and tragic. Since the Confederacy had at most a white population of only 6,000,000 to draw from, and 700,000 or more saw active military service first and last, it becomes quite clear that nearly every family had sons or a father at the front. At least one third of all the men whom the South sent to the front never returned, while perhaps an equal proportion were crippled. *Life in the South somber and tragic*

CREATING THE NORTHERN ARMIES

For the first two years of the war the North relied upon volunteer enlistments and state drafts to fill the armies, but long before this period expired, volunteering had almost ceased. It became necessary in the spring of 1863 to resort to the draft, and on March 3 an act was passed making all men between the ages of 20 and 45 subject to military service. The law, however, permitted a man to gain exemption by paying $300, or by employing a substitute, even though the substitute died or deserted the day after he entered the service. Sole supporters of aged parents and fathers of young children were exempt. Each state was assigned its quota at first on the basis of population and then on the basis of the total number of those registered. States and registration districts were given credit for all the soldiers that they had previously furnished. *Methods of raising troops volunteer enlistments and the draft*

The result of this was interesting. The West had already furnished most of its quota for the first draft, while the East was far behind. Great numbers in the East in comfortable circumstances paid their $300 or hired substitutes. The draft, then, came to bear heavily upon the poor in that section. Finally, in some large cities the Democrats, many of whom were Irish, were probably drafted out of proportion to their numbers. The Irish-Americans, and the Eastern Democrats generally, already angry because of Lincoln's Emancipation Proclamation, deeply resented what they believed to be the unfair operation of the draft law. In New York City on July 13, the second day of the draft, a mob drove the provost marshal from his office and destroyed the registration lists. Then for about four days the city was in turmoil. A vast mob stormed the city, burning, stealing, and killing Negroes, policemen, and even soldiers. Trouble occurred in other Eastern cities. General Meade, who was reorganizing his army after Gettysburg in preparation for another invasion of Virginia, was compelled to detach 15,000 troops to quell the *Draft riots* riot in New York, where a large number of persons had been killed or injured, and to put down threats of resistance in other Eastern cities.

The bounty system

The draft brought a relatively small return directly; indirectly it brought in hundreds of thousands. In order to raise their quotas, cities, counties, and states offered large bounties for "volunteers" and substitutes. Even the Federal government resorted to bounties to obtain "volunteers." In New York the combined local, state, and Federal bounties aggregated nearly $700 for each three-year enlistment. Bounty brokers and Federal agents swarmed over Ireland, Great Britain, Germany, and the Low Countries recruiting soldiers in the guise of laborers.

The recruiting of mercenary troops

This policy of recruiting foreign mercenaries was instituted by the United States Secretary of State. In a document—Circular 19— distributed widely throughout Europe, Seward promised free land and good jobs to all able-bodied men who would immigrate to the United States, and made veiled references to military bounties for those who would enlist. Under this policy of disguised recruiting in foreign countries many thousands of mercenary soldiers were enlisted. John Bigelow, who had charge of the recruiting, was convinced that the foreign mercenary was the decisive military factor in the Civil War. He was of the opinion that the State Department Circular 19, on which the recruiting of mercenaries was based, explains "the mysterious repletion of our army during the four years of war, while it was notoriously being so fearfully depleted by firearms, disease and desertion."

RAISING THE ARMIES IN THE SOUTH

Volunteering and conscription

The Confederacy had far more volunteers than it could arm during the first year of the war. Before the first year ended, however, the great enthusiasm for enlistment had cooled, or young men had satisfied their sense of duty by joining one of the local defense organizations. The bulk of those in Confederate service had enlisted for one year, and their terms would begin to expire in the spring of 1862. In order to save its veteran armies, as well as to get new recruits, the Confederate government April 16, 1862, passed a conscription act. Under this act men between 18 and 35 were liable to military duty. A few months afterward by a supplementary act the age limit was extended to 45. In 1864 the military age was extended to include all men from 17 to 50. Under the laws many were exempt: state officials, ministers, school teachers, newspaper editors, apothecaries, conscientious objectors, railway employees, millers, blacksmiths, and one white man of military age on any plantation where there were twenty or more slaves—sixteen by a subsequent act. Then, too, for the first two years of the war a man could hire a substitute; but as the price rose with the depreciation of Confederate currency, only the affluent could afford substitutes. This partiality for those who had money gave rise just as in the North to the devastating slogan, "a rich man's war and a poor man's fight." It was, however, not usually the planters but the business men, especially the war profiteers, who hired substitutes. The planters as a class contributed both their wealth and their share of man power to the Confederate military service.

The several Confederate conscription acts, like the Federal draft acts, did not directly bring many into the army. What it did was to cause that class of young men to volunteer who had offered their services in 1861, but who had "cooled off."

Conscription was the most drastic and centralizing piece of legislation ever enacted in America up to that time. It violated the theory of state rights and state sovereignty, which formed the legal basis of secession and which was stressed in the Confederate constitution. Lee and Davis, however, threw the weight of their prestige in the balance, and most of the governors of the states of the Confederacy accepted it as constitutional. But the state rights leaders, especially Governors Joseph E. Brown of Georgia and Zebulon Vance of North Carolina, waged a war of sabotage against the law and did much to cripple its operation by the wholesale creation of minor state offices and by granting state military commissions. This state exemption probably served to keep out of the Confederate army, not the worthless conscript, but the young man who, had he not had his conscience salved by service to his state as a civil or military officer, would have volunteered for the Confederate forces and made a good soldier. Despite the opposition to conscription offered by the extreme state rights governors and leaders like Rhett and Stephens, the state courts—even of Georgia—upheld conscription as constitutional. *Opposition of the state rights leaders*

FEDERAL FINANCE

When the Federal Congress met in extra session on July 4, 1861, it had already become apparent that the war was going to be an expensive undertaking. But Congress, being unwilling to ask the people to pay for the war and fight it at the same time, quickly decided to depend chiefly upon borrowing. In the two acts of July 17 and August 5, 1861, Congress authorized the Treasury to borrow *War financed largely on credit: sale of bonds and notes*

$250,000,000 by the sale of treasury notes and bonds; but this was inadequate to meet current needs, and in February, 1862, a bond issue of $500,000,000 was provided for. Soon the growing magnitude of the war, rising prices, and the depreciation of the currency made other and greater loans necessary. The act of March, 1863, provided for an issue of $900,000,000, the two of March and June, 1864, together, for $400,000,000 and that of March, 1865, for $600,-000,000. Thus a grand total of $2,650,000,000 was raised by the sale of treasury notes and bonds. The interest on these ranged from five to seven and three tenths per cent.

Legal tender paper money or greenbacks

Another form of borrowing was the issuing of legal tender paper currency. Under the loan acts of 1861 about $60,000,000 in such paper had been issued, but the notes were promptly retired on reaching the Treasury. By the loan act of February 25, 1862, Congress authorized an issue of $150,000,000 of such notes, now called "greenbacks," and made them legal tender in all transactions except the payment of import duties and the interest on the public debt. By successive acts to March 3, 1863, the volume of greenbacks authorized was increased to $450,000,000, all but $17,000,000 of which were issued.

The national banking system

Beginning with the act of February 25, 1863, Congress passed a series of laws creating the national banking system, the purpose of which was to establish a uniform currency to supplant the 12,000 kinds of state bank notes, create a market for Federal bonds, and provide an agency for their disposal. Each bank on becoming a member of the system was permitted, on depositing bonds with the United States Treasury, to issue national bank notes up to 90 per cent of the market value of such bonds, provided the value was not above par. These notes were not legal tender except between banks, but were receivable for all government dues except imports. The amount of notes that could be issued by these banks was at first $300,000,000 to be apportioned among the states—including the Confederate states when brought back into the Union—according to population and the banking needs of the states. Despite the advantages of a uniform currency the state banks and other financial associations were slow in organizing under the national banking laws, and only a few hundred had become national banks by the end of the war. On March 3, 1865, an act was passed imposing a 10 per cent annual tax on all state bank notes. This forced the retirement of such bank notes, and these local institutions hastened to reorganize under the national banking laws. The national banking system was thus of no great value in Civil War finance; its greatest usefulness was in the period of Reconstruction.

Although both Congress and the Administration were apprehensive about the popular reaction to any serious attempt to pay the cost of war by current taxation, nevertheless excise duties, income taxes, and tariffs on imports were levied at increasing rates as the war progressed, and the public became accustomed to being taxed. In 1861 Congress levied direct taxes averaging 22 cents per capita, and a tax of three per cent on all incomes above $800 a year; and in 1862 it enacted a far more comprehensive revenue law. Moderate duties were placed upon tobacco, beer, spirituous liquors, carriages, yachts, billiard tables, plate, railroads, banking houses, insurance companies, slaughtered cattle, sheep, hogs, etc., and a license tax was imposed upon numerous occupations and professions. In 1864 the rates were raised and additional articles were included. At the same time Congress elevated the income tax rates and lowered the exemptions so that all who earned from $600 to $5,000 paid five per cent and those whose incomes were higher paid ten per cent. To protect the manufacturers from cheaper priced foreign goods as well as to raise revenue, the protective tariff, inaugurated by the Morrill Tariff of March, 1861, was raised correspondingly with the elevation of the excise and income tax rates. *War taxes and tariffs*

The net receipts of the Federal government during the Civil War period amounted to $3,389,000,000. Four fifths of this were obtained by loans and the remainder by the tariff, excise, direct tax, and income taxes. *Net receipts during Civil War period*

CONFEDERATE FINANCE

In the matter of finance the Confederacy held itself up by its boot straps for the duration of the war. It used the printing press more freely than did the Federal government; nor were the state and municipal governments and private corporations timid in their resort to paper. However, neither bonds nor paper currency ever reached such astronomical proportions as they did in central Europe in the 1920's. The Confederacy issued about two billion dollars in bonds and over a billion in paper money, and for the first year of the war both bonds and paper currency maintained a level comparable with that of the Federal government. *Bonds and paper money*

However, the armies could not have been supported in the field by government paper alone; the Confederacy supplemented this paper by having its armies "live off the country" to a remarkable extent. It commandeered or "impressed" food, mules, and horses, railroad iron, rolling stock, and Negro slaves to work on fortifications. All these things were paid for at market price until 1863. *Impressment of supplies*

On March 26, 1863, a law was passed which legalized and limited the impressment of goods and slaves. Unfortunately, those parts of the country near railroads and in the vicinity of the armies were compelled to bear most of the burden of impressment.

Tithe tax

Closely related to impressment was the tithe tax on agricultural products and livestock. This was an income tax on the farmers and planters which was paid in produce and live or slaughtered animals. It was of very doubtful constitutionality since it taxed only certain occupations, and it aroused great opposition. It was by this tax that the Confederate armies were to a large extent fed during the last year or more of the war.

The Confederacy in the blockade-running business

The financing of the purchases of ships, munitions, clothing, and food in Europe was even more striking than the domestic methods. In the summer of 1861 the Confederate government floated a produce loan, by which it paid bonds for 400,000 bales of cotton and quantities of turpentine and tobacco. In the spring of 1862 the Confederacy began to dispose of the cotton to blockade runners who were bringing in government supplies. Such low prices were paid for the staple, and such exorbitant prices were charged for goods brought in, that in 1863 the Ordnance Bureau bought four blockade runners—and the government soon purchased additional ones—and began doing business on its own account. This enterprise was so successful that the Confederate government in 1863 compelled all private blockade runners to devote one third of their cargo space to exporting and importing on government account. In 1864 one half of the cargo was to be on Confederate account.

Confederate credit in Europe

The government cotton thus carried through the blockade during the remainder of the war greatly strengthened Confederate credit in Europe. In the spring of 1863, Slidell was able to float a loan of $15,000,000 in cotton bonds, through Émile Erlanger, the French banker. And in the winter of 1865, Duncan Kenner, special Confederate agent, was able to obtain favorable consideration in British financial circles of a loan of $45,000,000.

Centralization of purchasing and shipping under three agencies

The Confederacy's belated success in its financial operations in Europe was the direct result of the centralization in 1864 of all purchasing and shipping under one agency abroad and two agencies at home. In Europe all purchasing agents and financial transactions were placed under the control of C. J. McRae. In the Confederacy east of the Mississippi the purchase and shipment of cotton, tobacco, and naval stores were handled by the Bureau of Foreign Supplies, and west of the Mississippi such matters were managed by the Cotton Bureau.

LINCOLN AND EMANCIPATION

Before 1860 Lincoln had said that if he were a Southerner he would not know what to do with slavery, but that whatever was done would have to be done gradually. With the outbreak of war, however, his attitude began to change. On August 6, 1861, he approved a confiscation act containing a provision that allowed the emancipation of slaves employed in digging trenches, building fortifications or constructing any other Confederate military project. While the confiscatory feature dealt with property in the North that might be used to aid the South, it was in part a retaliatory measure against the Confederate Sequestration Act of May 21, 1861. But the section dealing with slavery was the real point of the measure for it was the entering wedge of emancipation, meant to appease the Radicals. *The emancipation provision of the Confiscation Act of 1861*

The Confiscation Act was as far as Lincoln could go and retain popular support at the time; consequently, when John C. Frémont on August 30, 1861, issued an order freeing slaves of Confederates in his department, Lincoln removed him. This satisfied the moderate element and the border slave states, but aroused the Radicals whose blistering anger made Lincoln very uneasy. He therefore returned to the problem of emancipation in March, 1862, when he suggested that Congress enact a law offering an average of $400 each for the slaves in the border states of Maryland, Delaware, Kentucky, and Missouri, and the District of Columbia. Both Congress and the border states turned a deaf ear to the proposal, but in April slavery was abolished with compensation in the District of Columbia. *Lincoln's removal of Frémont and his advocacy of compensated emancipation*

The Radicals were pushing Lincoln very hard during the summer of 1862 and he stood to lose their support in the Congressional elections. General David Hunter, advised by Radicals and now in command of the Federal forces at Beaufort, South Carolina, published on May 9, 1862, an order emancipating the slaves in South Carolina, Georgia, and Florida. The President revoked the order, but attempted to placate the Radicals by again urging the border slave states to accept compensated emancipation. Representatives of the border states suggested that Congress should take the initiative; again that body refused to act. *Lincoln again advocates compensated emancipation*

Instead of adopting a plan for compensated emancipation, Congress passed the Second Confiscation Act, which Lincoln, with some doubt as to its constitutionality, signed July 17, 1862. This act which provided for more drastic confiscation of Confederate property declared free all the slaves of Confederates and those who supported the Confederate cause. As far as slavery was concerned, it *The provision in the Confiscation Act of 1862 to abolish slavery in the Confederate States* in no fashion differed in principle from Lincoln's Proclamation of Emancipation soon to be issued in a preliminary form.

Lincoln's decision to emancipate slaves by executive decree

On July 22, 1862, the President announced to the Cabinet his intention to declare free on the following New Year's Day all slaves held in Confederate territory. Montgomery Blair objected to the proposal because of the political effects it would have in the border states. The other members of the Cabinet, however, approved of the idea, but induced Lincoln to postpone action until after some important Federal victory, lest it be regarded as a confession of impotence.

The public made ready to accept the abolition of slavery in the Confederacy as a means of saving the Union

While the plan for emancipation by Presidential order was to be kept secret, nevertheless the public must be prepared for such a move. Lincoln was doubtless casting about for some effective means of winning popular approval of his prospective Emancipation Proclamation when Horace Greeley, editor of the New York *Tribune,* gave him his opportunity. On August 20 in an editorial entitled "The Prayer of Twenty Millions" Greeley upbraided the President for revoking Frémont's and David Hunter's emancipation orders, for his failure to execute the provision of the Second Confiscation Act freeing the slaves, and for his tender regard for the border states and their "fossil politicians." Lincoln published in the *Tribune* on August 22 a reply to Greeley's editorial, which had a profound effect. It prepared people of the border states and the Northerners of moderate views to accept or acquiesce in the forthcoming Proclamation of Emancipation, as an instrument for the preservation of the Union. This reply was one of the most adroit moves Lincoln ever made in giving direction to public opinion. "As to the policy I 'seem to be pursuing,' as you say [wrote the President], I have not meant to leave anyone in doubt. I would save the Union. I would save it the shortest way under the Constitution. The sooner the national authority can be restored, the nearer the Union will be the 'Union as it was.' If there be those who would not save the Union unless they could at the same time save slavery, I do not agree with them. If there be those who would not save the Union unless they could at the same time destroy slavery, I do not agree with them. My paramount object in this struggle is to save the Union, and is not either to save or destroy slavery. If I could save the Union without freeing any slave, I would do it; and if I could save it by freeing all the slaves, I would do it; and if I could save it by freeing some and leaving others alone, I would also do that. What I do about slavery and the colored race, I do because I believe it helps to save the Union."

After the battle of Antietam on September 17, 1862, followed by Lee's retreat two days later, Lincoln issued (September 23) the preliminary Proclamation of Emancipation. It warned that the slaves in all the states in arms against the Federal government on January 1, 1863, should be free. On January 1 the final Proclamation was published which declared all the slaves free in the Confederate States, except those of Tennessee and portions of Louisiana and Virginia, where reconstructed governments had been set up. *The Preliminary Proclamation of Emancipation*

The Emancipation Proclamation as previously suggested differed in no fundamental respect from that part of the Second Confiscation Act freeing the slaves. But Lincoln, doubting the constitutional authority of Congress to enact such a law, was convinced that the war powers of the President did give him the right to free the slaves as a war measure. The Proclamation was issued on the grounds of military necessity. But it seems that the reasons were largely political and personal: first, to hold the support of the Radicals; second, to stimulate greater sympathy for the North in western Europe, particularly in England and France; and finally, to give slavery a severe blow, something that he doubtless had wished to do for a long time.

POLITICS NORTH AND SOUTH DURING THE WAR

The regular Republicans, who were not abolitionists but were opposed to slavery, accepted the Emancipation Proclamation as a war measure and nothing more—just as they had other arbitrary acts of the executive. The Radical Republicans were inclined to regard it as a timid effort at abolition for its own sake and were, consequently, impatient to get along much faster with the business. The "war Democrats," who composed a small minority of their party, continued to co-operate with the Administration; but in private many prominent leaders of this group, like Governor Horatio Seymour of New York, were gravely concerned over the social and political implications of the emancipation decree. *Varying degree of approval of the Proclamation*

The regular Democrats regarded it, together with the Second Confiscation Act freeing the slaves, as further evidence that the Republican Party was waging war not to preserve the Union but to free the Negro slaves, and that to accomplish this purpose it was subverting the constitution and destroying the liberty of the white man. They now reviewed the succession of arbitrary acts of the Administration. The President had after the fall of Fort Sumter during the period of over two months raised an army, carried on war, and financed it without convening Congress. He had suspended the writ of *habeas corpus* without Congressional consent, and under *The Democratic opposition* his authority the mayor of Baltimore, members of the Maryland legislature, and many other prominent men had been arrested and held without trial on hearsay and suspicion of having Southern leanings. The Democrats, now convinced that the war was not being waged primarily for the preservation of the Union, began demanding that a truce be called between the warring sections and that a convention of all the states North and South be held for the purpose of compromising the sectional differences and restoring the Union.

Disapproval shown in state and Congressional elections

As a result of this feeling, the Democrats in the fall of 1862 carried the state elections in Pennsylvania, New Jersey, New York, Ohio, Indiana, Illinois, and Wisconsin, and gained thirty-three additional members in the House of Representatives. The Administration carried the border states in the face of the Emancipation Proclamation and arbitrary arrests. Troops had been stationed at the polls in many places, however, and the Democrats accused the President of military coercion.

The Copperheads

The most violent opponents of the war and of the Republican Administration were the extreme state rights element of the Democratic Party, which soon won for itself the name of "Copperheads." Though they must have known that the Republicans had in mind the poisonous reptile of that name, these Democrats chose to ignore the opprobious implications of the title and turned it into a compliment to themselves and a reproof to their enemies. They wore badges, made of the copper cent bearing the head of the Goddess of Liberty, and assumed the role of champions of freedom. There were doubtless traitors among the Copperheads, men and women who were pro-Southern to the extent of working for the independence of the Confederacy. Most of them, however, were desirous of seeing the Union restored, but like Buchanan they did not believe that real union could be built upon force and conquest. They wished to end the war for this reason and because they were convinced that the war was devouring the freedom of the Northern people. There was probably little difference in their convictions and those of the Democratic Party as a whole, yet they were more violent —indeed seditious—in their denunciation of Lincoln and the Republican Party.

Vallandigham

One of the most prominent leaders of the Copperhead movement was Clement L. Vallandigham, former member of Congress from Ohio, who in 1863 became a candidate for governor of that state. Vallandigham, a powerful speaker, constantly denounced the Republican Administration for its disregard of the Bill of Rights and the principles of free government. General Burnside, now in command of the area, had Vallandigham arrested on charges of disloyalty and tried by a military commission—though the civil courts were open in Ohio—which condemned him to prison for the duration of the war. President Lincoln, with his usual adroitness, commuted Vallandigham's sentence to that of banishment to the Confederacy, which avoided making him a martyr in the eyes of all save the Copperheads, but instead made Vallandigham seem ridiculous in the eyes of many otherwise potential sympathizers. Going from Richmond to Canada, Vallandigham waged from a distance a campaign for governor of his state. The Federal victories at Gettysburg and Lincoln's discrediting of Vallandigham ended, however, in the election of the rival candidate. At the same time, the elections in several other Northern states went favorably for the Administration.

THE PRESIDENTIAL ELECTION OF 1864

Lincoln's political strategy had such finesse that his Radical colleagues utterly failed to comprehend it, and they misjudged him a weak and timid man. In 1864 the elect of the Radicals groomed Chase for the Republican nomination, and Lincoln with good-natured tolerance for Chase's naïve political maneuvering permitted his ambitious Secretary of the Treasury to run his course. Chase, when his own state of Ohio nominated Lincoln, relinquished temporarily his chronic ambition and settled down to administering the business of the Treasury. The Radicals then turned to Frémont to displace Lincoln, but Lincoln had the party convention so thoroughly in hand that, when it met on July 7, he not only obtained a unanimous nomination for himself but was able to have his friend Andrew Johnson, a Union Democrat, nominated for Vice-President. *Lincoln renominated*

There was no such unanimity in the North at large as there was in the nominating convention of 1864. Grant's staggering and seemingly futile losses in the Wilderness-to-Petersburg Campaign, and Sherman's inability to bag Johnston's army, all brought a wave of defeatism throughout the North during the months of May, June, July, and August. There was such a feeling of despair of bringing the struggle to a successful close that the President expressed the widespread belief that he would not be re-elected. *The spirit of defeatism*

The Democratic Party seems to have reached the position held by the Copperheads, and the military disasters of the summer of 1864 added a sense of defeat to its disapproval of the conflict. The Democrats now adopted a Copperhead platform demanding a cessation of the war and the calling of a national convention to work out a *The Democrats adopt the Copperhead platform, but nominate McClellan* sectional agreement for the purpose of restoring the Union and constitutional government. General George B. McClellan, despite his rejection of the peace plank, was nominated.

Defeatism ended by military success

Military successes, however, brought a turn in the tide of Northern defeatism. Farragut captured Fort Morgan and Mobile Bay in August; Sherman captured Atlanta, September 3, and the march through Georgia was being prepared by the middle of October. Sherman probably saved Lincoln from defeat. As it was, he received 212 electoral votes to McClellan's 21. Lincoln's popular majority, however, was very small. It showed public opinion closely and deeply divided even after it began to appear certain that the North would win the war. Unquestionably, much of the Democratic strength was based on the fear that four more years of Republican rule would destroy many of the great principles of civil liberty and democratic government.

Opposition to Davis: the Whigs and state rights Democrats

In the Confederacy, a political situation strikingly similar to that in the North developed. The fall elections of 1861 under the permanent constitution retained Davis and Stephens in office and returned a Congress friendly to the Administration. But after 1862 both state and Confederate elections revealed a widespread and rapidly mounting opposition to the Davis regime. The most important opposition at first was that of the old national Whigs, so many of whom were great planters, merchants, and industrialists. Such persons had always deprecated sectional agitation, and they had accepted secession and war with grave doubts of success and sure knowledge of what they might lose. They entered the Civil War resentful toward the Democratic Party, which had taken the lead in the secession movement, and critical of every act of the Confederate government dominated by that party. The state rights Whigs, like Robert Toombs and Zebulon Vance, secessionists though they were, were just as critical and suspicious of the Democratic administration as were the national Whigs. The extreme state rights Democrats, among whom were the most prominent leaders of the secession movement like Robert Barnwell Rhett, W. L. Yancey, and Joseph E. Brown, governor of Georgia, soon joined with the state rights Whigs in opposition to most of the war measures adopted by the Confederate government.

Opposition to war measures as violation of the constitution

These groups opposed as a violation of state rights and the Confederate constitution such measures as the conscription acts, the tithe tax, impressment of supplies, Confederate control of blockade running, the suspension of the privilege of the writ of *habeas corpus* and many other features of Administrative policy. Their opposition did much to cripple the effectiveness of military operations.

When the conscription acts were passed, the state rights governors relieved thousands of able-bodied young men from active military service—who would have volunteered to avoid conscription—by enrolling them in the state militia or by appointing them to minor state offices. By their insistence upon the right and the duty of each state to supply its troops in the Confederate service, this state rights group did great but unintentional injury to the military arm of the Confederacy. Governor Vance of North Carolina, for example, supplied the Confederate troops from his state with adequate clothing, tents, and blankets, and had 93,000 surplus uniforms and other vital supplies stored in Richmond during the Petersburg Campaign when the soldiers from other states were ragged and without shoes.

The state rights groups were not aiming at the defeat of the Confederacy. One cause of their intransigent position was that neither they nor their supporters had an adequate conception of how to conduct a war. But to a great extent their opposition was due to the fear that Davis and the old army clique, the "jannissaries" as Toombs called them, aimed at the overthrow of constitutional government and the establishment of Davis as a dictator. It is obvious that the Northern Copperheads and the Southern state rights faction were identical twins. *Fear of overthrow of constitutional government*

Another form of opposition to Davis and to the Confederacy was that of the peace societies, known variously as the Red Strings, the Order of the Heroes of America, the Peace Society, etc. These were composed in part of deserters, draft dodgers, and Unionists, although largely of persons of Confederate sympathies, who had come to look upon the continuation of the war as a hopeless slaughter of their loved ones. They were the destitute victims of the ravages of war. They were the defeatists and, like the state rights element, they too had their counterpart in the North. *The peace societies*

In 1864 the peace element in the South was rapidly gaining the ascendency, just as it was in the North before Sherman captured Atlanta. The peace societies and the state rights factions in the South were advocating the same approach to peace as that of the Copperheads and the regular Democrats in the North, a convention of all the states, North and South, to discuss peace terms. The Southerners would insist on separation as the basis of peace, and the Northerners would insist upon union as the basis. In the meanwhile, both were willing to declare a truce. In the summer of 1864 both the Northern and the Southern peacemakers would have settled for less than they were demanding; and, if the war had continued stalemated, peace by negotiation would probably have been attained and the Union reconstructed by mutual concessions. *Peace elements in both North and South almost in ascendency in 1864*

Bibliographical Notes

THE UNITED STATES TO 1865

GENERAL HISTORIES

These bibliographical notes do not purport to be a full bibliography of American history. They are presented, however, with the hope that they will aid students in gaining an acquaintance with the best-known general histories and such special works as will enable them to find their way to adequate secondary authorities and primary sources on any topic which may enlist their serious interest.

Single works

One of the outstanding general histories of the United States is Edward Channing's *A History of the United States*, 6 volumes, covering the period 1492-1865 (1905-1925). While the main emphasis of these volumes is on narrative history, considerable attention is given to social and economic life. The clear and interesting style of this scholarly work appeals to the general reader, and the references to primary sources, together with the interesting discussions of bibliographical materials, serve as a useful guide to the special student. Another well-known general history is E. M. Avery, *A History of the United States and Its People*, 7 vols. (1904-1910). There are a large number of good pictures, maps, and plans in this work which add greatly to its value. It does not, however, cover the whole period of American history. Woodrow Wilson's *A History of the American People*, Documentary edition (1917, 1918), is very useful. Each of the ten volumes contains important documents and numerous illustrations. The style of the text is clear and interesting. A recent history of wide popularity is *The Rise of American Civilization*, 4 vols. (1927-1942), by Charles A. and Mary R. Beard. Emphasis is placed on interpretive rather than factual narration. Another useful interpretation of the history of the country is J. T. Adams' *The March of Democracy*, 2 vols. (illustrations; 1933). An old work, brief in scope but useful because of its numerous pictures, is Benson J. Lossing, *New History of the United States* (1875, 1881).

Co-operative works

A very readable series of books, covering the entire period of American history (to 1921), is *The Chronicles of America*, 50 vols. (1918-1921), edited by Allen Johnson. These volumes are all interesting and most of them are products of ripe scholarship. There are no footnote references to primary sources, but the bibliographical notes given at the end of each volume are in some instances quite useful. Of more value to the special student, but probably of less interest to the general reader, is another co-operative work, *The American Nation: A History from Original Sources*, 28 vols. (1904-1918). The series was edited by Albert B. Hart, and each volume was prepared by a competent authority. The numerous citations to primary sources in the footnotes are helpful to the serious student. The most valuable of the pictorial histories of the country is *The Pageant of America*, 15 vols. (1925-1929), edited by Ralph H. Gabriel and others. In each volume the rather brief narrative is profusely illustrated with pictures, some of which are imaginary, but many are reproductions of old portraits or prints.

An extensive history of the South is a co-operative work, *The South in the Building of the Nation*, 13 vols. (1909-1913). This work, to which many writers have contributed, deals with economic and social, as well as political, history. A convenient and useful single-volume history of the South is William B. Hasseltine's *A History of the South* (1936).

Source books   Important documents bearing on the general history of the United States are easily accessible in the following works: H. S. Commager, *Documents of American History*, 2 vols. in one (1934, 1943); H. S. Commager and Allan Nevins, *The Heritage of America* (good illustrations; 1939); T. C. Pease and A. S. Roberts, *Selected Readings in American History* (1928); William MacDonald, *Documentary Source Book of American History, 1606-1926* (1926); Ina F. Woestermeyer and J. M. Gambrill, editors, *The Westward Movement* (1939); A. B. Hart, ed., *American History Told by Contemporaries*, 5 vols. (1897-1929); and Willard Thorp, Merle Curti, and Carlos Baker, *American Issues*, 2 vols. (an anthology of intellectual history; 1941).

SPECIAL WORKS

International relations   There are several brief works each of which covers the field of American diplomatic relations. Of these, mention should be made of the following one-volume treatises: S. F. Bemis, *A Diplomatic History of the United States* (1942); R. G. Adams, *A History of the Foreign Policy of the United States* (1926); Thomas A. Bailey, *A Diplomatic History of the American People* (1940); J. H. Latané, *A History of American Foreign Policy* (revised ed., 1934); Louis M. Sears, *A History of American Foreign Relations* (revised ed., 1935); Robert L. Jones, *History of the Foreign Policy of the United States* (1933); and J. W. Foster, *A Century of American Diplomacy* (1901). See also Willis F. Johnston, *America's Foreign Relations*, 2 vols. (1921).

The texts of the various treaties between the United States and other nations are given in *Treaties, Conventions, International Acts, Protocols and Agreements between the United States of America and Other Powers, 1776-1937*, 4 vols., compiled by William M. Malloy (1910-1937). David H. Miller is collecting and editing a series of documents of like character, entitled *Treaties and Other International Acts of the United States of America*. Volume VI, published in 1942, goes as far as 1855.

Constitutional history   There are only a few general works on American constitutional history. Those best suited to the general reader and college student are: H. C. Hockett, *Constitutional History of the United States, 1776-1876*, 2 vols. (1939; a third volume to appear later); A. C. McLaughlin, *A Constitutional History of the United States* (1935); and Carl B. Swisher, *American Constitutional Development* (1943). A volume of well-selected documents is Allen Johnson's *Readings in American Constitutional History, 1776-1876* (1912).

Historical geography   Useful map books are: D. R. Fox, ed., *Harper's Atlas of American History;* C. O. Paullin, *Atlas of Historical Geography of the United States* (1932); J. T. Adams, *Atlas of American History* (1943); and C. L. and B. H. Lord, *Historical Atlas of the United States* (1944). The following works show the influence of geography on American History: A. P. Brigham, *Geographic Influences in American History* (1903); H. H. McCarty, *The Geographic Basis of American Economic Life* (1940); and E. C. Semple, *American History and Its Geographic Conditions* (revised ed., 1933). Good descriptive geographies are Isaiah Bowman's *Forest Physiography* (1911); and N. M. Fenneman, *Physiography of Eastern United States* (1938), *Physiography of Western United States* (1931), and "Physiographic Divisions of the United States" (Association of American Geographers' *Annals*, XVIII).

Economic and social histories   In recent years there have been published a number of single-volume economic histories which serve as useful supplements to the general treatises on American history. In this list should be included the following works: A. C. Bining, *The Rise of American Economic Life* (1943); E. L. Bogart, *Economic History of the United States* (latest edition, 1942); H. J. Carman, *Social and Economic History of the United States*, 2 vols. (1930-1934); H. U. Faulkner, *American Economic History* (1943); E. Q. Hawk, *Economic History of the South* (1934); E. F. Humphrey, *An Economic History of the United States* (1937); W. W.

Jennings, *A History of Economic Progress of the United States* (1926); E. C. Kirkland, *A History of American Economic Life* (1934); Isaac Lippincott, *Economic Development of the United States* (1921); R. C. McGrane, *The Economic Development of the American Nation* (1942); Fred A. Shannon, *Economic History of the People of the United States* (1934); C. M. Thompson and F. M. Jones, *Economic Development of the United States* (1939); T. W. VanMetre, *Economic History of the United States* (1921); and Chester W. Wright, *Economic History of the United States* (1941).

Of the works which deal with certain phases of economic life the following are useful for the special student: Emory R. Johnson and others, *History of the Domestic and Foreign Commerce of the United States* (1915); Victor S. Clark, *History of Manufactures in the United States*, 3 vols. (1939); R. M. Tryon, *Household Manufactures in the United States, 1640-1860* (1917); B. H. Meyer and others, editors, *History of Transportation in the United States before 1860* (1917); J. R. Commons and others, *History of Labor in the United States*, 4 vols. (1918-1935); L. C. Gray, *History of Agriculture in the Southern States to 1860*, 2 vols. (1933); P. W. Bidwell and J. I. Falconer, *History of Agriculture in the Northern United States, 1620-1860* (1925); and Seymour Dunbar, *A History of Travel in America*, 4 vols. (1915). For an excellent collection of pictures illustrative of economic development, see three volumes of *The Pageant of America*, namely: R. H. Gabriel, *Toilers of Land and Sea* (III, 1926); and Malcolm Keir, *The Epic of Industry* (V, 1926), and *The March of Commerce* (IV, 1927). *Special phases of economic history*

For governmental policy with reference to economic development see: Amelia C. Ford, *Colonial Precedents of Our National Land System as it Existed in 1800* (1910); B. H. Hibbard, *A History of the Public Land Policies* (1924); Roy M. Robbins, *Our Landed Heritage: The Public Domain, 1776-1936* (1942); D. R. Dewey, *The Financial History of the United States* (rev. ed., 1931); W. R. Shultz and M. R. Caine, *Financial Development of the United States* (1937); W. G. Sumner, *History of Banking in the United States* (1896); Horace White, *Money and Banking* (1935); David K. Watson, *History of American Coinage* (1897); F. W. Taussig, *The Tariff History of the United States* (revised 1931); and Edward Stanwood, *American Tariff Controversies in the Nineteenth Century*, 2 vols. (1903).

A dip into the primary sources of economic history is afforded by A. L. Bogart and C. M. Thompson, *Readings in the Economic History of the United States* (1916); H. U. Faulkner and F. Flügel, *Readings in American Economic History* (1929); and L. B. Schmidt and E. D. Ross, *Readings in the Economic History of American Agriculture* (1925). *Source readings in economic history*

There is no complete work which deals satisfactorily with the whole field of American social life. The nearest approach to an adequate treatment of this subject is *A History of American Life*, edited by A. M. Schlesinger and D. R. Fox (1929-1944), a useful series consisting of twelve volumes. There are, however, a number of discussions of certain phases of economic and social life. For living conditions on the frontier and among foreign immigrants the following are useful: F. J. Turner, *The Frontier in American History* (a series of essays published in 1920); L. R. Hafen and C. C. Rister, *Western America* (1941); F. L. Paxson, *History of the American Frontier, 1763-1893* (1924); Dan E. Clark, *The West in American History* (a textbook covering the whole period; 1937); E. Douglas Branch, *Westward: The Romance of the American Frontier* (1930); M. L. Hansen, *The Atlantic Migration, 1607-1860* (1940); A. B. Faust, *The German Element in the United States*, 2 vols. (latest ed., 1927); C. K. Bolton, *Scotch-Irish Pioneers in Ulster and America* (1910); L. J. Fosdick, *The French Blood in America* (1906); and George Cohen, *The Jews in the Making of America* (1924). *Social life*

For the everyday life of the people see: W. C. Langdon, *Everyday Things in American Life, 1607-1776*, 2 vols. (many valuable pictures; 1937-1941); E. R. Dulles, *America Learns to Play: A History of Popular Recreation, 1607-1940*

(1940); O. S. Coad and Edwin Mims, Jr., *The American Stage* [*The Pageant of America,* XIV; 1929; pictures]; Arthur Hornblow, *A History of the Theatre in America,* 2 vols. (numerous quotations from the sources; pictures; 1919); Dixon Wechter, *The Saga of American Society* (1937); A. W. Calhoun, *Social History of the American Family,* 3 vols. (1917-1919); Allan Nevins, ed., *American Social History as Recorded by British Travellers* (1923); and Elizabeth McClellan, *History of American Costume, 1607-1870* (excellent pictures; an invaluable work; 1904, 1937). W. E. Woodward, in *The Way Our People Lived* (1944), gives a popular, semi-fictional treatment of certain aspects of social life; pictures.

Education

A very readable brief history of education in the United States is E. E. Slosson, *The American Spirit in Education* [*The Chronicles of America,* XXXIII; 1921]. A fuller account is S. G. Noble's *A History of American Education* (1938). Other useful general works are: E. G. Dexter, *A History of Education in the United States* (1904); E. P. Cubberley, *Public Education in the United States* (1919); Edgar W. Knight, *Education in the United States* (1929, 1941); T. A. Woody, *A History of Women's Education in the United States,* 2 vols. (1929); and C. F. Thwing, *A History of Higher Education in America* (1906). A valuable work on intellectual history is Merle Curti's *The Growth of American Thought* (1943).

Religion

The whole field of religion in the United States is covered by W. W. Sweet in *The Story of Religions in America* (1930); and in *The American Church History,* 13 vols. (a co-operative work, 1893-1897; the 13th volume, *A History of American Christianity,* by L. W. Bacon, gives a summary of the whole subject). Other works that might prove useful are: J. G. Shea, *History of the Catholic Church in the United States,* 4 vols. (1886-1892); Theodore Maynard, *The Story of American Catholicism* (1943); Peter G. Mode, *Source Book and Bibliographical Guide for American Church History* (1920); S. H. Cobb, *The Rise of Religious Liberty in America* (1902); T. C. Hall, *Religious Background of American Culture* (interpretive; 1930); H. G. Townsend, *Philosophical Ideas in the United States* (1934); Woodbridge Riley, *American Thought from Puritanism to Pragmatism* (1923); Henry K. Rowe, *The History of Religion in the United States* (1924); and Luther A. Weigle, *American Idealism* [*The Pageant of America,* X; 1928]. In the last-named volume the brief narrative is supplemented with valuable pictures.

Art

There are a number of books on American art. Of these the following might be mentioned: Thomas E. Tallmadge, *The Story of Architecture in America* (1927); Lewis Mumford, *Sticks and Stones* (an interpretive account of American architecture; 1924); T. F. Hamlin, *The American Spirit in Architecture* [*The Pageant of America,* XIII; numerous pictures; 1926]; H. H. Shurtleff, *The Log Cabin Myth* (1939); F. J. Mather, Jr., C. R. Morey, and W. J. Henderson, *The American Spirit in Art* [*The Pageant of America,* XII; 1927; pictures]; Samuel Isham and Royal Cortissoz, *The History of American Painting* (numerous pictures; 1936); C. S. Coffin, *The Story of American Painting* (many good illustrations; 1907); E. Neuhaus, *History and Ideals of American Art* (numerous illustrations; 1931); Alan Burroughs, *Limners and Likenesses: Three Centuries of American Painting* (excellent illustrations; 1936); Homer Saint-Gaudens, *The American Artist and His Times* (illustrations; 1941); and Lorado Taft, *The History of American Sculpture* (fine illustrations; 1925).

Music

The general history of American music is given by L. C. Elson in *The History of American Music* (1925); and J. T. Howard in *Our American Music. Three Hundred Years of It* (1929, 1931).

Science

For the history of science and invention, see: E. S. Dana and others, *A Century of Science in America* (1918); George Iles, *Leading American Inventors* (1912); F. R. Packard, *History of Medicine in the United States,* 2 vols. (1931); R. H. Shryock, *The Development of Modern Medicine* ("an interpretation of the social and scientific factors involved"; 1936).

So much has been written on the history of American literature that it is not *Literature*
easy to make a selection of titles. Readable brief accounts are: P. H. Boynton,
Literature and American Life (1936) ; Bliss Perry, *American Spirit in Literature*
[*The Chronicles of America*, XXXIV; 1918]; and S. T. Williams, *The American
Spirit in Letters* [*The Pageant of America*, XI; 1926]. The latter volume is valuable chiefly for the numerous pictures given. Of the fuller works, two especially
deserve mention: *The Cambridge History of American Literature*, 4 vols., edited
by W. P. Trent and others (1917-1921) ; and *Main Currents in American
Thought: An Interpretation of American Literature from the Beginning to
1920*, 3 vols., by Vernon L. Parrington (a literary masterpiece; 1927).

Of the works concerned with historical literature and journalism, the following *History and*
should be listed: Michael Kraus, *A History of American History* (1937) ; J. F. *journalism*
Jameson, *History of Historical Writing in America* (1891) ; F. L. Mott, *American
Journalism, 1690-1940* (1941) ; W. G. Blyer, *Main Currents in the History of
American Journalism* (illustrations; 1927) ; J. M. Lee, *History of American
Journalism* (1917) ; F. L. Mott, *A History of American Magazines, 1741-
1885*, 3 vols. (good pictures; 1930-1938).

The history of the army and navy is covered by the following works: Colonel *Military*
O. L. Spaulding, *The United States Army in War and Peace* (many good maps; *and naval*
1937) ; Captain D. W. Knox, *A History of the United States Navy* (illustrations; *history*
1936) ; Edgar S. Maclay, *A History of the United States Navy from 1775 to
1901*, 3 vols. (1902) ; and J. R. Spears, *The History of Our Navy*, 4 vols. (1897).

The census reports published by the Federal government are an inexhaustible *Reference*
mine of statistical information. Much of this data can be found in more usable *works and*
form in the current *Statistical Abstract of the United States*. Of the numerous *bibliographies*
other books of reference, the following are not only useful but quite accessible:
Allen Johnson and Dumas Malone, editors, *The Dictionary of American Biography*, 21 vols. (1928-1944) ; J. T. Adams, editor, *The Dictionary of American
History*, 6 vols. (1940) ; and E. R. A. Seligman and others, editors, *Encyclopedia
of Social Sciences*, 15 vols. (1930-1935). For pictorial statistics see *The United
States; A Graphic History* (1937), a useful and attractive volume by Louis M.
Hacker, Rudolf Modley, and George R. Taylor.

Most of the works already listed contain extensive bibliographies which will
prove helpful to serious students. As supplements to these, the following works
should be listed: S. F. Bemis and Grace G. Griffin, *Guide to the Diplomatic History of the United States* (1935) ; F. J. Turner and Frederick Merk, *List of
References on the History of the West* (rev. ed., 1922) ; and Grace G. Griffin,
Writings on American History, a series of volumes, one each year, which have
been published since 1906 as a part of the *Annual Report of the American Historical Association*. In the last-named volumes are listed the books and articles
on United States and Canadian history published each year. The most complete
guide to the source materials of American history is Henry P. Beers, *Bibliographies in American History* (late edition, 1942). This is a bibliography of bibliographies, and is so organized that one can by its aid easily locate the literature on
any subject in the field of United States history.

PART I: THE COLONIAL ERA, TO 1763

GENERAL HISTORIES AND BIBLIOGRAPHIES

Many of the general works listed in the preceding section bear on the colonial *Secondary*
era. In addition to these the following works, which are devoted exclusively or *authorities*
mainly to this period, should be mentioned: C. M. Andrews, *The Colonial Period
of American History*, 4 vols. (1934-1938), is probably the best general history of
the American colonies, but there is less emphasis on social and institutional history than in some of the other works. Another scholarly work, though old and in

some respects out-of-date, is *The Narrative and Critical History of America,* 8 vols., edited by Justin Winsor (1884-1889). It is still valuable for its appraisal of primary and secondary authorities and its reproduction of old maps and contemporary pictures. A well-known English work is John A. Doyle's *English Colonies in America,* 5 vols. (1880-1907). For colonial institutions the best authority is H. L. Osgood, *The American Colonies in the Seventeenth Century,* 3 vols. (1904-1907), and *The American Colonies in the Eighteenth Century,* 4 vols. (1924-1925). The greater part of George Bancroft's *History of the United States of America,* 6 vols. (latest edition, 1891-1892) is concerned with the colonial and Revolutionary periods.

Useful one-volume works are: H. S. Bolton and T. M. Marshall, *The Colonization of North America* (considerable space given to Spanish and French colonies; 1920); O. P. Chitwood, *A History of Colonial America* (1931); E. B. Greene, *Foundations of American Nationality* (1922, 1935); M. W. Jernegan, *The American Colonies* (1929); C. P. Nettels, *The Roots of American Civilization* (emphasizes British background; 1938); Max Savelle, *The Foundations of American Civilization* (1942); and J. B. Sanders, *Early American History, 1492-1789* (1938).

The best cross-sectional view of the British colonies, both insular and continental, at the end of the colonial period is given by L. H. Gipson in his definitive work, *The British Empire before the American Revolution,* 5 vols. (1936-1942). Some space is also devoted to the British West Indian plantations by Savelle in *The Foundations of American Civilization,* and by C. M. Andrews in *The Colonial Period of American History.* See also F. W. Pitman, *The Development of the British West Indies, 1700-1763* (1917).

Source books   Of the source books which are concerned entirely or mainly with the colonial period, the following are useful and easily accessible: *Original Narratives of Early American History,* 19 vols., edited by J. F. Jameson (1906-1917); *Select Charters and Other Documents Illustrative of American History, 1606-1775,* compiled by William MacDonald (1899); and *A Source Book in American History,* edited by W. M. West (1913). For an excellent collection of pictures, illustrative of the life of the people, see J. T. Adams and others, *Album of American History; Colonial Period* (1944).

Bibliographies   All of the one-volume general histories mentioned above contain useful bibliographical material. A fuller bibliography than any of these is E. B. Greene and R. B. Morris, *A Guide to the Principal Sources for Early American History (1600-1800) in the City of New York* (1929). If more references are needed the student can always fall back on the exhaustive work of H. P. Beers, *Bibliographies in American History,* listed above.

SPECIAL WORKS

CHAPTER I—THE LAND AND ITS ORIGINAL INHABITANTS

European background   For the physical basis of colonial development, see the geographical works listed on p. 776. The European background of colonial history is discussed at great length by E. P. Cheyney in his *European Background of American History* [*The American Nation,* I; 1904]. A good brief account can be found in the first four chapters of *The Roots of American Civilization,* by C. P. Nettels.

Indians   The economic, social, and cultural life of the Indians is discussed at length in Clark Wissler's valuable work, *The American Indian* (1922). Other accounts of the aborigines that might prove useful are: P. Radin, *The Story of the American Indian* (1927, 1934); F. W. Hodge, ed., *Handbook of American Indians North of Mexico,* in two parts (an encyclopedia with numerous illustrations; 1907-1910); Livingston Farrand, *Basis of American History* [*The American Nation,* II; 1904]; and E. R. Embree, *Indians of the Americas* (1939).

CHAPTER II—THE DISCOVERY OF AMERICA

Of the general works listed on p. 775, Channing is particularly good on the *The Norse* period of discovery and exploration. Most readers and students will find his *discoveries* treatment of the Norse discoveries adequate. For a fuller discussion see the well-known work of Geoffrey M. Gathorne-Hardy, *The Norse Discoveries of America* (1921). It evaluates the sources of information for the Norse discoveries and contains English translations of the sagas and other documents. More recent volumes on this subject are: Hjalmar R. Holand, *Westward from Vinland* (contains a lengthy discussion as to the genuineness of the Kensington Stone; 1940); A. D. Fraser, *Norse Discoveries* (1943); and Einar Haugen, *Voyages to Vinland* (a new translation of the old manuscripts with arguments in favor of the historicity of the Norse traditions; 1942). For English translations of the sagas and other documents, see J. E. Olson and E. G. Bourne, eds., *The Northmen, Columbus, and Cabot* (1906).

Most of the information regarding Columbus which the general reader and *Columbus* average student will be interested in can be found in the general histories already listed (pp. 775, 779f.) and in the works given in the next two paragraphs. A valuable supplement to these is S. E. Morison, *Admiral of the Ocean Sea: A Life of Christopher Columbus,* 2 vols. (scholarly and readable; 1942).

For more than half a century Columbus has been the subject of a warm dispute among scholars, and a voluminous literature has grown out of this long debate. A good deal of this discussion is so meticulous that it has little or no value except as exhibitions of skill in mental gymnastics. Anyone interested in these labored and over-refined arguments should consult Henry Harrisse, *Christoph Colomb* (he takes issue with the traditional favorable view of the Great Navigator; 1884); and a later work, also in French, Henry Vignaud, *Histoire Critique de la Grande Enterprise de Christoph Colomb* (concerned largely with Columbus' motive in making the historic voyage). Other references, to both primary and secondary sources, can be found on pp. 714-716 of O. P. Chitwood's, *A History of Colonial America.*

There are many readable and useful works on the early explorations in *Early* America. Of these the following might be mentioned: John B. Brebner, *The* *explorations* *Explorers of North America, 1492-1806* (1933); E. G. Bourne, *Spain in America* [*The American Nation,* III; 1904]; Herbert I. Priestley, *The Coming of the White Man, 1492-1848* [*A History of American Life,* I; 1929]; I. B. Richman, *The Spanish Conquerors* (1919); William Wood, *Elizabethan Sea-Dogs* (1918); W. B. Munro, *Crusaders of New France* (1918); and H. E. Bolton, *The Spanish Borderlands* (1921). The four titles last named are in the *Chronicles of America* series.

The best collection of easily accessible primary sources on the early discoveries *Primary* and explorations is that found in five of the volumes of *The Original Narratives* *sources* *of Early American History.* These volumes are: J. E. Olson and E. G. Bourne, eds., *The Northmen, Columbus, and Cabot;* F. W. Hodge and T. H. Lewis, eds., *Spanish Explorers in the Southern United States, 1528-1543* (1907); H. E. Bolton, ed., *Spanish Explorations in the Southwest, 1542-1706* (1925); H. S. Burrage, ed., *Early English and French Voyages, 1543-1608* (1906); and W. L. Grant, ed., *Voyages of Samuel de Champlain, 1604-1618* (1907).

CHAPTER III—THE BIRTH OF A NATION

The early history of Virginia is given with considerable fullness in the *General* general works listed on pp. 779f., especially in those of Andrews, Doyle, and *accounts* Osgood. A few other titles should be added: John Fiske, *Old Virginia and Her Neighbors,* 2 vols. (brilliantly written and very readable; 1897); Alexander Brown, *The First Republic in America* (1898); Lyon G. Tyler, *England in*

America, 1580-1652 [*The American Nation*, IV; 1904]; Matthew P. Andrews, *Virginia, the Old Dominion* (1937); P. A. Bruce, *History of Colonial Virginia, 1606-1764* (the first volume of a three-volume co-operative history of the Old Dominion; 1923); and Mary N. Stanard, *The Story of Virginia's First Century* (1928). An excellent account of Bacon's Rebellion is T. J. Wertenbaker's *Torchbearer of the Revolution* (1940). See also *Virginia under the Stuarts* (1914) by the same author.

Economic and social life

The economic and social life of the Old Dominion for certain periods has been carefully treated in the scholarly works of P. A. Bruce. Of these the following especially deserve mention: *Economic History of Virginia in the Seventeenth Century*, 2 vols. (1896); *Institutional History of Virginia in the Seventeenth Century*, 2 vols. (1910); and *Social Life in Virginia in the Seventeenth Century* (1907). L. G. Tyler's *Narratives of Early Virginia, 1606-1625* [*Original Narratives of Early American History*, V; 1907] is a good collection of source materials.

CHAPTERS IV AND V—EARLY NEW ENGLAND

General accounts

The literature of New England history is so voluminous that it is difficult to choose among many useful works. Most of the general histories listed on pp. 775, 779f. devote a good deal of space to the New England colonies. This is especially true of Andrews, Avery, Bancroft, Channing, Doyle, and Osgood. There are also a number of excellent works which are concerned exclusively with New England. High on this list stands J. G. Palfrey's *The History of New England*, 5 vols. (1858-1890). This history, though old and with a strong leaning toward Puritanism, is valuable for both the general reader and the special student. As a counterpoise to its pro-Puritan orthodoxy, should be placed J. T. Adams' heterodox, anti-Puritan volumes: *The Founding of New England* (1921), and *Revolutionary New England, 1691-1776* (1923). Adams in his excoriations of the Puritan clergy more than redresses the balance which had been tipped by Palfrey in favor of the early Puritans. A good brief account of the early history of this section is C. M. Andrews, *The Fathers of New England* [*The Chronicles of America*, VI; 1921].

Special works

Of the more specialized discussions, the following are of value: R. G. Usher, *The Pilgrims and Their History* (sympathetic, but inclined toward the modern view; 1918); D. W. Howe, *The Puritan Republic* (lengthy discussion of social life; 1899); Thomas Hutchinson, *History of Massachusetts Bay*, 3 vols. (1936); S. E. Morison, *Builders of the Bay Colony* (interesting biographical sketches of the early leaders in Massachusetts; 1930); G. L. Clark, *A History of Connecticut* (1914); C. M. Andrews, *Connecticut's Place in Colonial History* (1924); Isabel M. Calder, *The New Haven Colony* (1934); I. B. Richman, *Rhode Island: Its Making and Its Meaning*, 2 vols. (a full, scholarly account; 1902); S. H. Brockunier, *The Irrepressible Democrat: Roger Williams* (1940); W. H. Fry, *New Hampshire as a Royal Province* (1908); H. S. Burrage, *The Beginnings of Colonial Maine, 1602-1658* (1914); and L. C. Hatch, ed., *Maine, a History*, 5 vols. (1919). W. B. Weeden's *Economic and Social History of New England*, 2 vols. (1890), is valuable for the study of economic and social life. For lists and appraisals of other authorities, both primary and secondary, see pp. 779f.

Primary sources

The sources for New England history are also full and accessible. In the *Original Narratives of Early American History* there are four entire volumes devoted to this period. These are: *Bradford's History of Plymouth Plantation, 1606-1646*, ed. by W. T. Davis (1908); *Winthrop's Journal:* "History of New England," 1630-1649, 2 vols., ed. by J. K. Hosmer (1908); and *Johnson's Wonder-Working Providence, 1628-1651*, ed. by J. F. Jameson (1910).

CHAPTER VI—THE MIDDLE AND SOUTHERN COLONIES

The titles listed on pp. 779-80 will doubtless furnish the average reader with all the guidance he needs in his search for information on the Middle and Southern colonies. It might be well, however, to add a few special works which treat more intensively the history of each colony. *Secondary authorities*

A good brief account of colonial New York is Maud W. Goodwin's *Dutch and English on the Hudson* [*The Chronicles of America*, VII; 1921]. Of the numerous other works concerned with the Middle and Southern colonies, the following, might be mentioned: W. E. Griffis, *The Story of New Netherland* (readable; 1909); D. R. Fox, *Yankees and Yorkers* (1940); John Fiske, *The Dutch and Quaker Colonies in America*, 2 vols. (interesting; 1899); S. G. Fisher, *The Quaker Colonies* [*The Chronicles of America*, VIII; 1921]; W. R. Shepherd, *History of Proprietary Government in Pennsylvania* (1896); Edward C. O. Beatty, *William Penn as Social Philosopher* (1939); Christopher Ward, *New Sweden on the Delaware* (1938); Amandus Johnson, *The Swedish Settlements on the Delaware, 1638-1664*, 2 vols. (illustrations; numerous references to the sources; voluminous and thorough; 1911); E. P. Tanner, *The Province of New Jersey, 1664-1738* (1908); and E. J. Fisher, *New Jersey as a Royal Province, 1738-1776* (1911). The two last-named volumes are voluminous and scholarly and are concerned mostly with government. A work similar in character to these is *Maryland as a Proprietary Province* (1901) by N. D. Mereness. A later and more readable account of early Maryland is *The Founding of Maryland* (1933) by M. P. Andrews.

Of the special works on the Carolinas attention should be called to *The History of North Carolina*, 3 vols., a co-operative work by three well-known scholars. The first volume, which covers the colonial and Revolutionary periods, was written by R. D. W. Conner (1923). Other histories deserving mention are: C. L. Raper, *North Carolina, A Study in English Colonial Government* (1904); Archibald Henderson, *North Carolina: The Old North State and the New*, 2 vols. (1941); Edward McCrady, *History of South Carolina under the Proprietary Government, 1670-1719* (1897); and Verner W. Crane, *The Southern Frontier, 1670-1732* (1928).

The most accessible contemporary accounts of events in the Middle and Southern colonies are those given in the *Original Narratives of Early American History*. Five volumes of this series are devoted to this group of colonies. They are: J. F. Jameson, ed., *Narratives of New Netherland, 1609-1664* (1909); B. B. James and J. F. Jameson, editors, *The Journal of Jasper Danckaerts, 1679-1680* (1913); A. C. Myers, ed., *Narratives of Early Pennsylvania, West New Jersey, and Delaware, 1630-1707* (1912); C. C. Hall, ed., *Narratives of Early Maryland, 1633-1684* (1910); and A. S. Salley, ed., *Narratives of Early Carolina, 1650-1708* (1911). *Primary sources*

CHAPTER VII—AMERICA BETWEEN TWO REVOLUTIONS

The period covered by Chapter VII is discussed more or less fully by some of the special works listed in Chapter VI and by most of the General Works listed on pp. 775, 779f. A good short account of the "Glorious Revolution" in England is given in W. E. Lunt, *History of England* (1928), pp. 500-509. Good brief accounts of Stuart rule in the colonies and the revolts against it can be found in the works of Osgood, Andrews, and Channing, already cited. The best single volume on the Revolution of 1689 in New England and the events that preceded and led to it is *The Dominion of New England* (1923), by Viola Barnes. *Stuart rule and the "Glorious Revolution"*

Other topics of this period are discussed by one or more of the following: E. B. Greene, *Provincial America* [*The American Nation*, VI; 1905], and *The Provincial Governor in the English Colonies of North America* (1898); Lois K. Mathews, *The Expansion of New England* (1909); George L. Kittredge, *New England, the Carolinas, and Georgia*

Witchcraft in Old and New England (1929); C. L. Raper, *North Carolina: A Study in English Colonial Government* (1904); Archibald Henderson, *The Old North State and the New,* 2 vols. (1941); Edward McCrady, *The History of South Carolina under Royal Government, 1719-1776* (1899); W. R. Smith, *South Carolina as a Royal Province* (1903); A. H. Hirsch, *The Hugenots of Colonial South Carolina* (1928); E. M. Coulter, *A Short History of Georgia* (1933); J. R. McCain, *Georgia as a Proprietary Province* (1917); P. S. Flippin, *The Royal Government in Georgia* (1923); Harriett C. Cooper, *James Oglethorpe, the Founder of Georgia* (1904); and A. A. Ettinger, *James Edward Oglethorpe: Imperial Idealist* (1936).

The Old West   The pioneer in the writing of Western history was Frederick Jackson Turner. For the study of the Old West the best of his works is *The Frontier in American History* (1921). This is a collection of essays on frontier life, including his epoch-making article, "The Significance of the Frontier," which was first published in 1893. Numerous other books on the West are listed in F. J. Turner and Frederick Merk's *List of References on the History of the West* (1922). For special topics see the following: M. L. Hansen, *The Immigrant in American History* (1940); Carl Wittke, *We Who Built America: The Saga of the Immigrant* (1939); C. K. Bolton, *Scotch-Irish Pioneers in Ulster and America* (lengthy quotations from the primary sources; 1910); H. J. Ford, *The Scotch-Irish in America* (diffuse; lengthy quotations from the sources; 1915); A. B. Faust, *The German Element in the United States,* 2 vols. (scholarly; references to primary sources; probably the best work on German settlements in America; 1909); and Lucy F. Bittinger, *The Germans in Colonial Times* (readable; 1901).

Source   Most of the works already listed for this chapter give citations in the footnotes
materials   to primary sources. In the *Original Narratives of Early American History* there are three volumes which bear on this period. These are: C. M. Andrews, *Narratives of the Insurrections, 1675-1690* (1915); G. L. Burr, *Narratives of the Witchcraft Cases, 1648-1706* (1914); and C. H. Lincoln, *Narratives of the Indian Wars, 1675-1699* (1913).

CHAPTER VIII—BRITISH AND FRENCH RIVALRY IN AMERICA

General   Most of the general histories listed on pp. 775, 779f. devote a good deal of
accounts   space to British and French rivalry in America. There are also a number of special works concerned with this period. Of these the following volumes of *The Chronicles of America* are readable and useful: W. B. Munro, *Crusaders of New France* (1918), and George M. Wrong, *Conquest of New France* (1918). With these are to be classed: G. M. Wrong, *The Rise and Fall of New France* (1928); R. G. Thwaites, *France in America* [*American Nation,* VII; 1905]; W. Wood, *The Fight for Canada* (a valuable work; full bibliography; 1906); Theodore Roosevelt, *The Winning of the West,* 4 vols. (1894-1896); G. L. Beer, *British Colonial Policy, 1754-1765* (valuable; 1907); six volumes of the *Chronicles of Canada* (of a popular nature; 1922); Carl Wittke, *History of Canada* (1933); and A. G. Bradley, *The Fight with France for North America* (1900). But the best discussion of this period is to be found in the scholarly and interesting volumes of Francis Parkman. The works of this noted historian (20 volumes in all) are historical classics. Of these, the following are especially valuable for this chapter: *Pioneers of France in the New World* (1865, 1895); *Frontenac and New France under Louis XIV* (1894); *Half-Century of Conflict,* 2 vols. (discusses Queen Anne's War and King George's War; 1894); *Montcalm and Wolfe,* 2 vols. (1884, 1896); and *Conspiracy of Pontiac and the Indian War after the Conquest of Canada* (1895).

Special works   Of the numerous discussions of certain phases of the subject the following will prove helpful to the special student: V. W. Crane, *The Southern Frontier, 1670-1732* (1929); K. P. Bailey, *The Ohio Company of Virginia and the*

Westward Movement, 1748-1792 (1939); L. K. Koontz, *The Virginia Frontier, 1754-1763* (1925), and *Robert Dinwiddie* (1941); Hayes Baker-Crothers, *Virginia and the French and Indian War* (1928); C. H. Ambler, *George Washington and the West* (1936); Rupert Hughes, *George Washington, The Human Being and the Hero, 1732-1762* (1926); Frederick J. Turner, *The Frontier in American History;* T. W. Clarke, *The Bloody Mohawk* (1940); and A. T. Volwiler, *George Croghan and the Western Movement* (1924). For new light on Braddock's defeat, see an article by Stanley Pargellis in the *American Historical Review* for January, 1936.

The occupation of Tennessee and Kentucky is discussed in: Archibald *The Old* Henderson, *The Conquest of the Old Southwest* (1920); Constance L. Skinner, *Southwest* *Pioneers of the Old Southwest* [*The Chronicles of America*, XVIII; 1919]; Carl S. Driver, *John Sevier, Pioneer of the Old Southwest* (1932); Thomas Abernethy, *From Frontier to Plantation in Tennessee* (1932); W. S. Lester, *The Transylvania Colony* (1935); John Bakeless, *Daniel Boone, Master of the Wilderness* (1939); H. A. Bruce, *Daniel Boone and the Wilderness Road* (1929); and Temple Bodley, *Our First Great West* (1938).

CHAPTER IX—ECONOMIC DEVELOPMENT IN THE COLONIES

The economic development of the colonies is discussed with considerable *General works* fullness by the economic histories listed on pp. 776f. The bibliographies of these volumes also list fuller works for intensive study.

For the growth and distribution of population see: Evarts B. Greene and *Special works* Virginia D. Harrington, *American Population before the Census of 1790* (1932); Stella H. Sutherland, *Population Distribution in Colonial America* (1936); and *A Century of Population Growth, 1790-1900* (1909; published as a part of the report of the Twelfth Census). Other special works are: T. P. Kettel, ed., *Eighty Years' Progress* (1861); P. A. Bruce, *Economic History of Virginia in the Seventeenth Century*, 2 vols.; W. B. Weeden, *Economic and Social History of New England, 1620-1689*, 2 vols.; L. C. Gray, *History of Agriculture in the Southern United States to 1860*, 2 vols.; P. W. Bidwell and John I. Falconer, *History of Agriculture in the Northern United States, 1620-1860; American Husbandry* (originally published in 1775 but recently [1939] reprinted under the editorship of H. J. Carman; a valuable original account); A. S. Salley, *The Introduction of Rice Culture into South Carolina* (1919); Melville Eggleston, *The Land System of the New England Colonies* (1883); Arthur C. Bining, *British Regulation of the Colonial Iron Industry* (1933); William Smith, *The History of the Post Office in British North America, 1639-1870* (1920); U. B. Phillips, *American Negro Slavery* (1918); and C. G. Woodson, *The Negro in Our History* (1924). For works on immigrants to America, see p. 784.

CHAPTER X—SOCIAL LIFE IN THE COLONIES

For an excellent brief account of local government in England at the *Government* beginning of the seventeenth century, see E. P. Cheney, *A History of England from the Defeat of the Armada to the Death of Elizabeth*, 2 vols. (1914-1926), Vol. II, chs. 37-41. Governmental institutions in the various colonies are discussed at considerable length in the works of Osgood cited above. Of the numerous works dealing with certain phases of colonial government, the following are useful: C. F. Bishop, *History of Elections in the American Colonies* (1893); A. E. McKinley, *Suffrage Franchise in the Thirteen English Colonies in America* (1905); L. W. Labaree, *Royal Government in America* (1930); E. B. Greene, *The Provincial Governor in the English Colonies of North America* (1898); J. F. Sly, *Town Government in Massachusetts, 1620-1930* (1930); E. E. Proper, *Colonial Emigration Laws* (1900); Anne B. MacLear,

Early New England Towns (1908); Alice M. Earle, *Curious Punishments of Bygone Days* (1896); G. Myers, *Ye Olden Blue Laws* (1921); P. S. Reinsch, *English Common Law in the Early American Colonies* (1898); and Ernest L. Griffith, *History of American City Government: The Colonial Period* (1938). There are also a number of valuable monographs on colonial government in the Johns Hopkins University *Studies in Historical and Political Science.*

Social life   Some of the general histories listed on pp. 775, 776ff., 779, notably those of Osgood, Bruce, and Weeden, devote considerable space to social life in the colonies. C. M. Andrews, in his *Colonial Folkways* [*The Chronicles of America,* IX; 1921] gives an interesting brief account of colonial life in the eighteenth century. Two of the volumes of *A History of American Life* are also concerned with the colonial era. These are: *The First Americans, 1607-1690* (1927), by T. J. Wertenbaker, and *Provincial Society, 1690-1763* (1928), by J. T. Adams.

There are a number of special works dealing with the life of the people. Mrs. Alice M. Earle has been especially productive in this type of historical writing. Of her works the following should be mentioned: *Costume of Colonial Times* (1894); *Child Life in Colonial Days* (1899); *Colonial Dames and Good Wives* (1895); *Home Life in Colonial Days* (1898); and *Stage Coach and Tavern Days* (1900). Other accounts of a similar character are: H. D. Eberlein, *The Architecture of Colonial America* (1924); T. J. Wertenbaker, *The Golden Age of Colonial Culture* (1942), and *The Old South: The Founding of American Civilization* (1942); Elsie Lothrop, *Early American Inns and Taverns* (1926); S. G. Fisher, *Men, Women, and Manners in Colonial Times,* 2 vols. (1898); Elizabeth A. Dexter, *Colonial Women of Affairs* (1931); Carl Holliday, *Woman's Life in Colonial Days* (1921); Elizabeth McClellan, *Historic Dress in America, 1607-1800* (1904, 1910); Anne H. Wharton, *Colonial Days and Dames* (1895); Julia C. Spruill, *Women's Life and Work in the Southern Colonies* (1938); and Mary S. Benson, *Women in Eighteenth-Century America* (1935).

Religion   The best single volume on the colonial church is William W. Sweet's *Religion in Colonial America* (1942). In the Johns Hopkins University *Studies in Historical and Political Science* there are several scholarly monographs which discuss certain phases of colonial religion. Of the special works that might be added are: S. H. Cobb, *The Rise of Religious Liberty in America* (a valuable work; 1902); R. M. Jones, *The Quakers in the American Colonies* (1911); Lars P. Qualben, *The Lutheran Church in Colonial America* (1940); J. G. Shea, *The Catholic Church in Colonial Days* (1886-1892); and Carter G. Woodson, *The History of the Negro Church* (1921).

Good brief accounts of the Great Awakening can be found in Adams, *Provincial Society* (pp. 279-286), and Osgood. *The American Colonies in the Eighteenth Century* (III, pp. 407-451). The best contemporary account is *The Christian History,* edited by Thomas, Prince, 1744-1745 (a weekly publication detailing the events of the revival).

Education and literature   There is an abundance of material on colonial education and literature to be found in the general works listed on pp. 778f. Of the additional titles which might be added, the following deserve mention: Elsie W. Clews, *Educational Legislation and Administration of the Colonial Governments* (valuable for the special student; 1899); Colyer Meriwether, *Colonial Curriculum* (1907); Samuel E. Morison, *The Founding of Harvard College* (1938); M. C. Tyler, *A History of American Literature, 1607-1765,* 2 vols. (1878-1879); H. W. Schneider, *The Puritan Mind* (1930); Perry Miller, *The New England Mind: The Seventeenth Century* (1939); Ola E. Winslow, *Jonathan Edwards, 1703-1758* (1940); Carl Van Doren, *Benjamin Franklin* (1938); Elizabeth C. Cook, *Literary Influences in Colonial Newspapers, 1704-1730* (1912); and L. R. Schulyer, *The Liberty of the Press in the American Colonies before the Revolutionary War* (1905).

PART II: THE AMERICAN REVOLUTION, 1763-1783

GENERAL WORKS

Most of the general histories (see p. 775) devote considerable space to the Revolutionary era. This is especially the case with Bancroft, by whom the facts are stated with substantial correctness, but they are deeply colored with patriotic fervor and are thus given a strong bias in interpretation. Of the same character is John Fiske's brilliant and interesting narrative, *The American Revolution*, 2 vols. (1891). Among the later and more scientific historians of the Revolution the late C. H. Van Tyne holds a high place. His works are the product of years of careful study and are not marred by prejudice against Great Britain. One of his volumes, *The American Revolution, 1776-1783 [The American Nation, IX; 1905]* gives a general account of the Revolution; the others are concerned with certain phases of it (see below). Other general accounts are: S. G. Fisher, *The Struggle for American Independence,* 2 vols. (1908); and E. W. Whitton, *The American War of Independence* (1931). There is a good collection of source readings in S. E. Morison's *Sources and Documents Illustrating the American Revolution and the Formation of the Federal Constitution, 1764-1788* (1923).

There are two fine, impartial histories of the Revolution by English writers. These are: G. O. Trevelyan, *The American Revolution*, 3 vols. ("on the whole the work on the Revolution best worth reading"; 1905); and W. E. H. Lecky, *The American Revolution, 1763-1783* (taken from his *History of England in the Eighteenth Century*, 8 vols., and edited by J. A. Woodburn; one of the best single volumes; 1898). For a good pictorial history of the war see W. Wood and R. H. Gabriel, *The Winning of Freedom [The Pageant of America*, VI; 1927]. There are also many valuable pictures in the older work of Benson J. Lossing, *The Pictorial Field-Book of the Revolution*, 2 vols. (1850, 1860). The ideology of the movement is ably set forth by M. C. Tyler in *The Literary History of the American Revolution, 1763-1783*, 2 vols. (1897). See also V. L. Parrington, *The Colonial Mind, 1620-1800* (1927).

SPECIAL WORKS

CHAPTER XI—FROM CONTROVERSY TO CONFLICT

Very readable discussions of the policy of the British government in dealing with the colonial possessions are given by G. L. Beer in his scholarly works. Of these the following are especially useful for this period: *The Old Colonial System, 1660-1754,* 2 vols. (1912); *British Colonial Policy, 1754-1765* (1907); and *Commercial Policy of England toward the American Colonies* (1893). For discussions of special topics, see the following: L. W. Labaree, *Royal Government in America;* O. M. Dickerson, *American Colonial Government, 1696-1765* (a study of the British Board of Trade in its relation to the American colonies; 1912); A. H. Basye, *The Board of Trade, 1748-1782* (1925); and E. R. Turner, *The Privy Council of England in the Seventeenth and Eighteenth Centuries*, 2 vols. (1927-28). *[British colonial policy]*

The literature on the causes of the Revolution is abundant. The following are a few of the many works which discuss this topic: Carl Becker, *The Eve of the Revolution [The Chronicles of America*, XI; brief and readable; 1921]; G. E. Howard, *Preliminaries of the Revolution [The American Nation*, VIII; references to primary sources; 1905]; C. M. Andrews, *The Colonial Background of the American Revolution* (good discussion of the indirect causes of the Revolution; 1924); C. H. Van Tyne, *Causes of the War of Independence* (1922); and A. M. Schlesinger, *The Colonial Merchants and the American Revolution, 1763-1776* (1917), and *New Viewpoints in American History* (1922), Ch. VII. For a *[Causes of the Revolution]* disagreement with the views of Andrews and Van Tyne, see an article "The First American Revolution," by Louis M. Hacker in *Columbia University Quarterly*, XXVII, No. 3. See also John C. Miller, *Origins of the American Revolution* (pictures; 1943.)

For the political theory behind the Revolution, see C. H. McIlwain, *The American Revolution: A Constitutional Interpretation* (1923). C. S. Callender, *Selections from the Economic History of the United States, 1765-1860* (1909), is a good short collection of source materials. Useful biographies are: M. C. Tyler, *Patrick Henry* (1887); John C. Miller, *Sam Adams, Pioneer in Propaganda* (1936); and Ralph V. Harlow, *Samuel Adams, Promoter of the American Revolution* (1923). Julian P. Boyd, *Anglo-American Union: Joseph Galloway's Plans to Preserve the British Empire, 1774-1788* (1941) should also be listed.

The Declaration of Independence

A valuable work on the Declaration of Independence is C. L. Becker, *The Declaration of Independence* (numerous extracts from the sources; 1922). Other full accounts of the Declaration are: H. Friedenwald, *The Declaration of Independence, an Interpretation and an Analysis* (1904); and J. H. Hazelton, *The Declaration of Independence; its History* (1906).

CHAPTERS XII AND XIII—THE WAR FOR INDEPENDENCE

Military history

The military history of the Revolution can be found in considerable fullness in the general works listed on p. 787. Other good general accounts are: George M. Wrong, *Washington and His Comrades in Arms* [*The Chronicles of America*, XII; 1921]; F. V. Greene, *The Revolutionary War and the Military Policy of the United States* (many excellent maps; 1911); and C. H. Van Tyne, *The War of Independence* (1929). Detailed accounts of military events can also be found in any one of a number of biographies of Revolutionary generals. Of these, one of the most popular is Rupert Hughes, *George Washington,* 3 vols., 1926-1930 (volumes II and III are concerned with the Revolution). Other readable and easily accessible lives of Washington are L. M. Sears, *George Washington* (1932); Nathaniel Stephenson and W. H. Dunn, *George Washington,* 2 vols. (1940); Norwood Young, *George Washington, Soul of the Revolution* (1932); and Bernard Knollenberg, *Washington and the Revolution* (1940). For the conquest of the Northwest, see J. A. James, *The Life of George Rogers Clark* (1928); and Temple Bodley, *George Rogers Clark: His Life and Public Services* (1926). New light on Arnold's treason has been shed by the recent work of Carl Van Doren, *Secret History of the American Revolution* (1941). An authoritative work on the Whigs and Tories is C. H. Van Tyne's *The Loyalists of the American Revolution* (1902).

Naval history

For naval history see A. T. Mahan, *Major Operations of the Navies in the War of American Independence* (1913); C. O. Paullin, *The Navy of the American Revolution* (1906); and G. W. Allen, *A Naval History of the American Revolution,* 2 vols. (1913).

Army administration

Conditions in the army are discussed by C. K. Bolton, *The Private Soldier under Washington* (1902); and L. C. Hatch, *The Administration of the American Revolutionary Army* (1904). See also V. L. Johnson, *The Administration of the American Commissariat during the Revolutionary War* (1941).

Diplomatic history

For diplomatic relations see: S. F. Bemis, *The Diplomacy of the American Revolution* (1935); E. S. Corwin, *French Policy and the American Alliance of 1778* (1916); J. B. Perkins, *France in the American Revolution* (1911); Carl Van Doren, *Benjamin Franklin* (1938); and Bernard Faÿ, *Franklin, the Apostle of Modern Times* (1928). Good collections of documents are: Francis Wharton, ed., *Revolutionary Diplomatic Correspondence of the United States,* 6 vols. (1889); and Jared Sparks, ed., *Diplomatic Correspondence of the American Revolution,* 12 vols. (1892).

CHAPTER XIV—POLITICAL AND SOCIAL ASPECTS OF THE REVOLUTION

Government

Many of the authorities already given for Part II contain material on the political and social aspects of the Revolution. Only a few additional titles need be listed. Allan Nevins in *The American States during and after the Revolution, 1775-1789* (1924), treats authoritatively the subject indicated by this title. The definitive work on the Continental Congress is E. C. Burnett's *The Continental Congress* (1941). For source materials on the Continental Congress, see *Letters of Members of the Continental Congress,* 8 vols., compiled by the same author (1921-1936); and *Journals of the Continental Congress, 1774-1789,* 34 vols., compiled by W. C. Ford and others (1904-1937). See also Merrill Jensen, *The Articles of Confederation* (1941).

Miscellaneous

A brief but valuable work on the social aspects of the Revolution is J. F. Jameson's *The American Revolution Considered as a Social Movement* (readable and scholarly; 1926). See also Dixon R. Fox, *Ideas in Motion* (1935); and E. B. Greene, *The Revolutionary Generation, 1763-1790* [A History of American Life, IV; 1943]. For the study of financial history see C. J. Bullock, *Finances of the United States from 1778 to 1789* (1895). There are a number of valuable documents dealing with the economic aspects of the Revolution in G. S. Callender, *Selections from the Economic History of the United States.* See also R. A. East, *Business Enterprise in the American Revolutionary Era* (1938).

PART III: THE FEDERAL PERIOD, 1783-1860

GENERAL WORKS

General accounts

This period is discussed at considerable length by each of the general histories listed on p. 775. Of the well-known works that are devoted mostly or entirely to the eight decades which separate the two American revolutions, the following deserve special mention: John B. McMaster, *A History of the People of the United States from the Revolution to the Civil War,* 8 vols. (readable and scholarly; social life emphasized; 1883-1913); James Schouler, *History of the United States of America, under the Constitution,* 7 vols. (style ornate and stately; 1895-1913); and Hermann Edward von Holst, *The Constitutional and Political History of the United States,* 8 vols. (strongly biased in favor of nationalism; 1876-1904). The latter part of this period is covered by James Ford Rhodes in his masterly work, *A History of the United States from the Compromise of 1850 to the End of the Roosevelt Administration,* 9 vols. (latest edition, 1892-1929). The social life of about half of the period is treated in a scholarly way by J. A. Krout and D. R. Fox in *Completion of Independence, 1792-1830* [A History of American Life, V; 1944]; pictures.

Diplomatic history

The diplomatic, economic, and social histories given on pp. 776ff. are especially useful for this period. To these should be added: Charles E. Hill, *Leading American Treaties* (1922); R. B. Mowat, *The Diplomatic Relations of Great Britain and the United States* (1925); and John W. Foster, *A Century of American Diplomacy* (1900).

SPECIAL WORKS

Observations of foreigners

A large number of books have been written on certain phases of the history of this period. Of these the following titles will prove adequate for supplying the special student with information and for directing him to the other authorities: *A Century of Population Growth, 1790-1900,* published by the Bureau of the Census (1909); Ralph Gabriel, *The Course of American Democratic Thought; An Intellectual History since 1815* (1940); Allan Nevins, ed., *American Social History as Recorded by British Travellers;* Max Berger, *The British Traveller in America, 1836-1860* (1943); and Jane L. Mesick, *The English Traveller in*

America, 1785-1835 (1922) . One of the most noted accounts of travels in America is Harriet Martineau's *Society in America,* 3 vols. (interesting observations by a clever English woman of American life in the eighteen-thirties; London, 1837) .

Pictures
An insight into the manner of living of the people is afforded by the pictures of such publications as *Harper's Weekly, Godey's Lady's Book,* and *Gleason's Pictorial Drawing Room Companion* (succeeded in 1859 by *Ballou's Pictorial Drawing Room Companion*) . Other views of American life are afforded by the noted drawings of Currier and Ives. A number of these drawings have been collected and published by Harry T. Peters under the title of *Currier and Ives, Printers to the American People,* 2 vols. (1929-1931). A one-volume edition under the same title has recently (1942) been published by the same collector. For interesting cartoons, see Allan Nevins and Frank Weitenkampf, *A Century of Political Cartoons* (1944) .

Governmental agencies
In this supplemental list should be included a number of works which show how the agencies of government have functioned. Of this group the following deserve mention: K. H. Porter, *A History of Suffrage in the United States* (1918) ; William E. Binkley, *American Political Parties: Their Natural History* (1943) ; William O. Lynch, *Fifty Years of Party Warfare, 1789-1837* (1931) ; Burton J. Hendrick, *Bulwark of the Republic: A Biography of the Constitution* (1938) ; Edward Stanwood, *A History of the Presidency* (1898) ; Harold J. Laski, *The American Presidency, an Interpretation* (1940) ; E. S. Corwin, *The President, Office and Powers* (1940) ; Charles Hurd, *The White House, a Biography* (the story of the Executive Mansion, its occupants, and its place in history; 1940) ; H. B. Learned, *The President's Cabinet* (1912) ; Mary L. Hinsdale, *A History of the President's Cabinet* (1911) ; Gaillard Hunt, *The Department of State of the United States. Its History and Functions* (1914) ; S. F. Bemis, ed., *The American Secretaries of State and their Diplomacy,* 10 vols. (a co-operative work of value; 1927-1929) ; R. V. Harlow, *A History of Legislative Methods before 1825* (1917) ; George H. Haynes, *The Senate of the United States. Its History and Practice,* 2 vols. (1938) ; Lindsay Rogers, *The American Senate* (1926) ; Charles Warren, *The Supreme Court in United States History* (1932) ; and C. A. M. Ewing, *Judges of the Supreme Court, 1789-1937* (1938).

History of the sections
Of the various works dealing with the history of the sections the following might be listed: F. J. Turner, *The Significance of Sections in American History* (1932) ; R. L. Cotterill, *The Old South* (1936) ; William G. Brown, *The Lower South in American History* (1930) ; W. E. Dodd, *Statesmen of the Old South, or From Radicalism to Conservative Revolt* (1921) ; Cardinal Goodwin, *The Trans-Mississippi West, 1803-1853* (1922) ; Amelia C. Ford, *Colonial Precedents of Our National Land System as It Existed in 1800* (1910) ; and B. H. Hibbard, *A History of the Public Land Policies* (1924) .

CHAPTER XV—THE PERIOD OF THE CONFEDERATION

General accounts
A good general account of the period of the Confederation is given by Andrew C. McLaughlin in *The Confederation and the Constitution* [*The American Nation,* X, 1905]. A very interesting and brilliantly written discussion is John Fiske's *The Critical Period of American History* (1888) . Both of these works, especially the latter, lean too far toward the old tendency to exaggerate the shortcomings of the Confederation government. For foreign relations and conditions in the states, see, respectively, A. B. Darling, *Our Rising Empire, 1763-1803* (1940), and Allan Nevins, *The American States During and After the Revolution, 1775-1789* (1924). A contemporary account of the rebellion in western Massachusetts is given in George R. Minot's *History of the Insurrection in Massachusetts* (1810) .

Western problems
Western problems are discussed by a number of books, of which the following might be of interest to the special student: Thomas P. Abernethy, *Western Lands and the American Revolution* (1937) ; Payson J. Treat, *The National*

Land System, 1785-1820 (1910); Justin Winsor, *The Westward Movement* (1897); F. A. Ogg, *The Old Northwest* [*The Chronicles of America,* XIX; 1919]; B. A. Hinsdale, *The Old Northwest; the Beginnings of Our Colonial System* (1899); Beverley W. Bond, *The Civilization of the Old Northwest* (1934); Jay A. Barrett, *Evolution of the Ordinance of 1787* (1891); and A. P. Whittaker, *The Spanish American Frontier, 1783-1795* (1927).

CHAPTER XVI—THE CREATION OF A NEW GOVERNMENT

Good brief accounts of the formation and ratification of the Constitution are given in McLaughlin, *Confederation and the Constitution,* and Max Farrand, *The Fathers of the Constitution* [*The Chronicles of America,* XIII; 1921]. Of the fuller discussions, the following are useful: A. T. Prescott, *Drafting the Federal Constitution* (documents; rearrangement of *Madison's Notes;* 1941); Charles Warren, *The Making of the Constitution* (documentary; 1928); Robert L. Schuyler, *The Constitution of the United States; an Historical Survey of Its Formation* (1923, 1928); H. L. McBain, *The Living Constitution* (1927); and Max Farrand, *The Framing of the Constitution of the United States* (1913). For certain aspects of the Constitution and the motives behind its creation and acceptance, see Charles A. Beard, *An Economic Interpretation of the Constitution of the United States* (1913); *The Supreme Court and the Constitution,* by the same author (1912); and O. G. Libby, *The Geographical Distribution of the Vote of the Thirteen States on the Federal Constitution, 1787-88* (detailed; large map; 1894). See also: F. J. Klingberg, *The Morning of America* (1941); Abbott E. Smith, *James Madison: Builder* (1937); and E. M. Burns, *James Madison, Philosopher of the Constitution* (1938). *Secondary authorities*

The best collections of primary sources on the work of the Constitutional Convention are: Max Farrand, ed., *Records of the Federal Convention of 1787,* 3 vols. (1911); and Charles C. Tansill, *Documents Illustrative of the Formation of the Union of the American States* (1927). The debates on the Constitution that were carried on in the state conventions are given in Jonathan Elliott's *Debates on the Federal Constitution,* 5 vols. (1827-1845). *The Federalist* has been published a number of times. Good editions are the ones edited by Paul Leicester Ford (1898) and by E. H. Scott, 2 vols. (1898). *Primary sources*

For the history of the Constitution, see Burton J. Hendrick, *The Bulwark of the Republic: A Biography of the Constitution* (1937). *History of the Constitution*

CHAPTER XVII—WASHINGTON AT THE HELM

The first dozen years under the Constitution was one of the most important periods in the history of the country. This fact has been so well recognized that the general histories and special works already listed (see pp. 789f.) have, almost without exception, given the events of the era a full-length treatment. For this reason few titles need be added. Two good general accounts are: J. S. Bassett, *The Federalist System* [*The American Nation,* XI; 1906]; and Henry J. Ford, *Washington and His Colleagues* [*The Chronicles of America,* XIV; 1918]. Of the numerous lives of Washington, see those listed on p. 788. An interesting contemporary account of the events connected with the organization of the government is given in E. S. Maclay's *Journal of William Maclay* (1890). *General accounts*

For Hamilton's financial policy see Bassett, *op. cit.* (a good brief account), or a biography of Hamilton. H. C. Lodge's *Alexander Hamilton* (1882) is still useful, though it leans strongly toward the Hamiltonian view of government. A later biography is F. S. Oliver, *Alexander Hamilton* (1921). The bank question is adequately covered by John T. Holdworth in a joint work by him and D. R. Dewey, *The First and Second Banks of the United States.* The political issue between Jefferson and Hamilton is discussed at length by C. A. Beard in *Economic Origins of Jeffersonian Democracy* (1915, 1936), and by Claude *Hamilton's financial policy*

Bowers in *Jefferson and Hamilton, the Struggle for Democracy in America* (favorable to the Jeffersonian view; 1925).

CHAPTER XVIII—DOMESTIC AND FOREIGN PROBLEMS

Only a few additional titles need be given for this chapter since it is so well covered by the general histories already mentioned and the special works listed in the previous chapter. In F. J. Turner's *The Significance of Sections in American History* (1932) there are two good chapters on Franco-American relations during the administrations of Washington and Adams. Other useful works on this period are: Leland D. Baldwin, *Whiskey Rebels: The Story of a Frontier Uprising* (1939); William Findley, *History of the Insurrection in the Four Western Counties of Pennsylvania* (a contemporary account; 1796); S. F. Bemis, *Jay's Treaty* (1923), and *Pinckney's Treaty* (1926); V. H. Palsits, *Washington's Farewell Address* (1935); A. B. Darling, *Our Rising Empire, 1763-1803;* and B. W. Bond, *The Monroe Mission to France, 1794-1796* (1907).

CHAPTER XIX—THE ADMINISTRATION OF JOHN ADAMS

A brief account of the administration of John Adams is given by Ford and a full one by Bassett. For biographies of the second President, see J. T. Adams, *The Adams Family* (1930), and Gilbert Chinard, *Honest John Adams* (1933). The following special works might also be listed: E. W. Warfield, *The Kentucky Resolutions of 1798* (1894); and G. W. Allen, *Our Naval War with France* (1909).

CHAPTERS XX AND XXI—JEFFERSON IN POWER

Jefferson's first term

Good general discussions of the events of Chapters XX and XXI can be found in E. Channing's *The Jeffersonian System* [*The American Nation*, XII; 1906]; and Allen Johnson's *Jefferson and His Colleagues* [*The Chronicles of America*, XV; 1921]. A part of the next volume in this series, *John Marshall and the Constitution* (1920) also bears on this chapter. But the great authority on the administrations of Jefferson and Madison is Henry Adams' *History of the United States, 1801-1817,* 9 vols. (1889-1891). This interesting and scholarly work is an exhaustive treatise on the events of the decade and a half covered by it. Good, readable biographies of Jefferson are Saul K. Padover, *Jefferson* (1942); Gilbert Chinard, *Thomas Jefferson, the Apostle of Americanism* (1929); and James T. Adams, *The Living Jefferson* (1936). See also Claude G. Bowers, *Jefferson in Power, the Death Struggle of the Federalists* (biased in favor of Jefferson; 1936). For special topics see: Avery O. Craven, *Democracy in American Life* (1941); James K. Hosmer, *The History of the Louisiana Purchase* (1902); E. W. Lyon, *Louisiana in French Diplomacy, 1759-1804* (1934); Arthur P. Whittaker, *The Mississippi Question, 1795-1803* (1934); H. C. Hockett, *Western Influence on Political Parties to 1825* (1917); and O. D. Wheeler, *The Trail of Lewis and Clark, 1804-1904,* 2 vols. (numerous illustrations; 1926).

Jefferson's second term

Many of the works listed for the preceding chapter, as well as the general works on p. 789, are concerned with Chapter XXI. To supplement these the following titles might be added: W. F. McCaleb, *The Aaron Burr Conspiracy* (1930); Holmes Alexander, *Aaron Burr, The Proud Pretender* (1937); Henry Adams, *Life of Albert Gallatin* (1879); John A. Stevens, *Albert Gallatin* (1896); I. J. Cox, *The West Florida Controversy, 1798-1813* (1918); L. M. Sears, *Jefferson and the Embargo* (1927); and W. W. Jennings, *The American Embargo, 1807-1809* (1921).

CHAPTER XXII—JAMES MADISON AND THE WAR OF 1812

General accounts

The best account of Madison's administration and the War of 1812 is the one given by Henry Adams in his history cited above. Another good general account, though much briefer, is K. C. Babcock, *The Rise of American* Nationality [*The American Nation*, XIII; 1906].

In the following volumes can be found biographical material regarding *Biographies* President and Mrs. Madison: Irving Brent, *James Madison; the Virginia Revolutionist* (in progress; and interesting, though discursive, account of his early life to 1780; 1941); A. E. Smith, *James Madison: Builder* (1937); Gaillard Hunt, *The Life of James Madison* (1902); and Lucia B. Cutts, ed., *Memoirs and Letters of Dolly Madison* (1886).

Adequate details of the War of 1812 and the war with the Barbary States, *The War* including diplomatic, military, and naval events, can be found in the following *of 1812* works: Frank A. Updyke, *The Diplomacy of the War of 1812* (1915); R. B. Mowat, *The Diplomatic Relations of Great Britain and the United States* (1925); Ralph Paine, *The Fight for a Free Sea* [*The Chronicles of America*, XVII; 1920]; William Wood, *The War with the United States* [*The Chronicles of Canada*, XIV; 1915; presents the Canadian side]; C. P. Lucas, *The Canadian War of 1812* (1906); Theodore Roosevelt, *The Naval War of 1812* (1882, 1910); Captain A. T. Mahan, *Sea Power in Its Relation to the War of 1812*, 2 vols. (1905); Edgar S. Maclay, *A History of the United States Navy from 1775 to 1901*, 3 vols. (1901, 1902); Gardner W. Allen, *Our Navy and the Barbary Corsairs* (1905); and Harold and Margaret Sprout, *The Rise of American Naval Power, 1776-1918* (1939). An old work on the War of 1812, still valuable because of the numerous pictures, is *The Pictorial Field-Book of the War of 1812*, by Benson J. Lossing (1868). For sidelights on the peace negotiations, see C. F. Adams, ed., *Memoirs of John Quincy Adams*, 12 vols. (1874-1877; Vols. II and III); and *The Diary of James Gallatin, 1813-1827*, edited by **Count** Gallatin (1916).

The special student might also wish to consult the following biographies of *Military and* military and naval leaders: Dorothy B. Goebel, *William Henry Harrison, A* *naval leaders* *Political Biography* (1926); Freeman Cleaves, *Old Tippecanoe* (full on military events; 1939); Marquis James, *Andrew Jackson: The Border Captain* (1933); Rodney Macdonough, *Life of Thomas Macdonough* (1909); and Charles J. Dutton, *Oliver Hazard Perry* (1935).

Theodore Dwight's *History of the Hartford Convention* is a contemporary *The Hartford* account written by the secretary of the Hartford Convention though it was *Convention* not published until 1933.

CHAPTER XXIII—THE REVIVAL OF NATIONALISM

In each of the economic histories listed on p. 776f. can be found a discussion *General* of the influence on American industry of the restraints on commerce imposed *accounts* during the period 1807-1815 (the Restrictive Period). For the nationalist measures adopted by Congress soon after the War of 1812 and the discussions centering about them, see the general histories already given (pp. 775, 789). These political topics, as well as a number of important judicial decisions, are also well treated, though briefly, by Babcock in the latter part of the work cited in the previous chapter. The judicial decisions are also covered by Edwin S. Corwin in *John Marshall and the Constitution*. Fuller discussions of the nationalistic decisions of the United States Supreme Court can be found in Charles Warren, *The Supreme Court in United States History*, 2 vols. (1932); and Albert J. Beveridge, *The Life of John Marshall*, 4 vols. (1916-1919).

For the establishment of a national bank and the inauguration of a pro- *Special topics* tective tariff policy, see R. C. H. Catterall, *The Second Bank of the United States* (1903); F. W. Taussig, *Tariff History of the United States;* and Edward Stanwood, *American Tariff Controversies in the Nineteenth Century*, 2 vols. (1903-1904).

CHAPTER XXIV—THE ERA OF GOOD FEELING

General works   Most of the general histories are quite full on the administrations of James
Monroe and John Quincy Adams. Aside from these, the best general account is
F. J. Turner, *Rise of the New West, 1819-1829* [*The American Nation,* XIV;
1906]. Of the small number of biographies of Monroe that have so far appeared
the old one by D. C. Gilman, *James Monroe* (1883), is probably as good as any.
A later biography is George Morgan's *Life of James Monroe* (1921).

The acquisi-   There are a number of scholarly works which deal with the outstanding
tion of Florida   events of Monroe's administration. The acquisition of East Florida is discussed
authoritatively by Herbert B. Fuller in *The Purchase of Florida: Its History and
Diplomacy* (1906); and by P. C. Brooks, *Diplomacy and the Borderlands: The
Adams-Onis Treaty of 1819* (1939). Shorter accounts of the same topic are
given in Babcock (Ch. 17) and in J. W. Burgess, *The Middle Period, 1817-
1858,* Ch. 2 (1897). See also Marquis James, *Andrew Jackson: The Border
Captain.*

The Monroe   Useful treatises on the Monroe Doctrine are: Dexter Perkins, *The Monroe
Doctrine*   *Doctrine, 1823-1826* (1927), and *Hands Off: A History of the Monroe Doctrine*
(1941); William F. Reddaway, *The Monroe Doctrine* (1905); and J. R. Clark,
Memorandum on the Monroe Doctrine (Government Printing Office, 1930).
For the background of the Monroe Doctrine see: Frederic L. Paxson, *The
Independence of the South American Republics* (1903); Charles C. Griffin,
The United States and the Disruption of the Spanish Empire, 1810-1822 (1937);
and Arthur P. Whittaker, *The United States and the Independence of Latin
America, 1800-1830* (1941).

The Missouri   Excellent short discussions of the Missouri Compromise are given by Turner
Compromise   (Ch. 10) and by Burgess (Ch. 4). There is also a good account of it in John P.
Gordy's *Political History of the United States,* Vol. II (1902). For constitutional
arguments advanced on both sides of the dispute, see Homer C. Hockett, *Constitutional History of the United States, 1776-1876,* Vol. II, 148-168 (1939). See
also W. O. Lynch, *Fifty Years of Party Warfare;* and F. C. Shoemaker, *Missouri's
Struggle for Statehood, 1804-1821* (1916).

The campaign   The campaign of 1824 is discussed with fullness by the general histories
of 1824   referred to above. Other works that might be included are: W. O. Lynch, *op.
cit.;* Edward Stanwood, *The History of the Presidency,* 2 vols. (1916); and
M. Ostrogorski, *Democracy and the Organization of Political Parties,* 2 vols.
(1908).

CHAPTER XXV—SECTIONALISM IN POLITICS

Biographies   So many of the authorities listed for the previous chapter overlap the
administration of John Quincy Adams that few titles need be added for this
chapter except on the westward movement. Adequate biographical data as to
the sixth President can be found in the following works: J. T. Morse, *John
Quincy Adams* (1882); B. C. Clark, *John Quincy Adams,* "Old Man Eloquent"
(good pictures; 1932); and James T. Adams, *The Adams Family* (1930). For
interesting source material regarding the second Adams see C. F. Adams, ed.,
Memoirs of John Quincy Adams, 12 vols. (1874-1877). Useful information on
this period can also be found in Glendon G. Van Deusen, *The Life of Henry
Clay* (1937); and Carl Schurz, *Henry Clay,* 2 vols. (1899, 1909). For other
biographies of Clay see p. 797.

The westward   The following are a few of the many works which are concerned with the
movement   westward movement: F. L. Paxson, *A History of the American Frontier, 1763-
1893;* F. J. Turner, *The Frontier in American History,* and *The Significance
of Sections in American History;* E. Douglas Branch, *Westward, The Romance
of the American Frontier* (1930); Dan E. Clark, *The West in American History*
(1937); Henry C. Hubbart, *The Older Middle West, 1840-1888* (1936); William

W. Sweet, *Religion on the American Frontier, 1783-1850* (1939) ; R. H. Gabriel, *The Lure of the Frontier* [*The Pageant of America,* II; pictures; 1929]; and T. D. Clark, *The Rampaging Frontier: Manners and Humors of Pioneer Days in the South and Middle West* (1939).

For contemporary accounts and other source materials on the West, see Timothy Flint, *Recollections of the Last Ten Years* (1826) ; J. M. Peck, *Guide for Emigrants to the West* (1837) ; R. G. Thwaites, *Early Western Travels, 1748-1846,* 32 vols. (1904-1907) ; Ina F. Woestemeyer and J. M. Gambrill, *Westward Movement* (source readings; 1939) ; and Henry Howe, *Historical Collections of the Great West,* 2 vols. (pictures; 1857).

Other works can be found in F. J. Turner and Frederick Merk's *List of References on the History of the West* (1922). See also references listed elsewhere in these Bibliographical Notes, especially p. 790.

For the campaign of 1828 see Claude G. Bowers, *Party Battles of the Jackson Period;* Marquis James, *Andrew Jackson: Portrait of a President;* and the references given under the campaign of 1824, p. 794. *The campaign of 1828*

CHAPTERS XXVI AND XXVII—THE ADMINISTRATION OF ANDREW JACKSON

There are a large number of books that deal with the administration of Andrew Jackson. Not only do the general histories (pp. 775, 789) devote a good deal of space to this period, but there are a number of works of briefer scope which discuss it at considerable length. Some of the latter group cover a period which extends beyond the end of Jackson's second term, and are useful for subsequent chapters. Four of the latter especially deserve mention: J. W. Burgess, *The Middle Period* (1905) ; F. J. Turner, *The United States, 1830-1850* (1935) ; Thomas H. Benton, *Thirty Years View; or, A History of the Working of the American Government, 1820-1860,* 2 vols. (a contemporary account; strong pro-Jacksonian leanings; 1854-1856) ; and G. W. Johnson, *America's Silver Age* (1939). *General accounts*

Valuable documentary material for this longer period can be found in *Selected Readings in American History,* by T. C. Pease and A. S. Roberts; and in *Documents of American History,* by H. S. Commager. Good general accounts confined to Jackson's administration are: William MacDonald, *Jacksonian Democracy* [*The American Nation,* XV; 1906]; F. A. Ogg, *The Reign of Andrew Jackson* [*The Chronicles of America,* XX; 1919]; and Claude G. Bowers, *The Party Battles of the Jackson Period* (readable; 1928). *The Autobiography of Martin Van Buren,* edited by J. C. Fitzpatrick (*Annual Report* of the American Historical Association for 1918, vol. II) gives a great deal of first-hand information regarding Jackson's administration.

The best-known of the biographies of Jackson are: James Parton, *Life of Andrew Jackson,* 3 vols. (very interesting, but in some respects out of date; contains many important excerpts from the documents and is thus a source book; 1860-1864) ; J. S. Bassett, *The Life of Andrew Jackson,* 2 vols. (scholarly and interesting; 1911) ; and Marquis James, *Andrew Jackson: Portrait of a President* (scholarly and brilliant; the most popular of all: 1937). Of the numerous biographies of other statesmen of that period, the following might prove useful: Gaillard Hunt, *John C. Calhoun* (1908) ; W. M. Meigs, *Life of John Caldwell Calhoun,* 2 vols. (1917) ; Arthur Stryon, *The Cast-Iron Man: John C. Calhoun and American Democracy* (1935) ; Claude M. Fuess, *Daniel Webster,* 2 vols. (a definitive work; 1930) ; G. Van Deusen, *The Life of Henry Clay* (1937) ; and Theodore Jervey, *Robert Y. Hayne and His Time* (1909). *Biographies*

For the campaign of 1832, see S. R. Gammon, Jr., *The Presidential Campaign of 1832* (1922) ; and Charles McCarthy, *The Antimasonic Party: A Study of Political Antimasonry in the United States, 1827-1840* (1903). *The campaign of 1832*

A good deal has been written about the nullification controversy. Of the *Nullification* works on this subject the special student might wish to refer to the following: C. E. Merriam, *A History of American Political Theories* (1915); J. G. Van Deusen, *Economic Basis of Disunion in South Carolina* (1928); D. F. Houston, *A Critical Study of Nullification in South Carolina* (1896); Chauncey S. Boucher, *The Nullification Controversy in South Carolina* (1916); and E. P. Powell, *Nullification and Secession in the United States* (contains documents; 1898). Light is also shed on the nullification crisis by the biographies listed above.

Jackson and the Bank

Jackson's bank policy is given with sufficient fullness by R. C. H. Catterall in *The Second Bank of the United States*. D. R. Dewey also discusses the same subject in *The First and Second Banks of the United States* by J. T. Holdsworth and D. R. Dewey. For useful accessible source material on the bank question see R. G. McGrane, *The Correspondence of Nicholas Biddle Dealing with National Affairs, 1807-1844* (1917).

Jackson's foreign policy

Useful information as to certain aspects of Jackson's foreign policy is given in G. A. King's *The French Spoliation Claims* (1912); R. A. McLemore, *Franco-American Diplomatic Relations, 1816-1836* (1941); and F. L. Benns, *The American Struggle for the British West India Carrying-Trade, 1815-1830* (1923).

The campaign of 1836

For the campaign of 1836 see A. C. Cole, *The Whig Party in the South* (1913); and E. M. Carroll, *Origins of the Whig Party* (1925).

Miscellaneous topics

Special works which touch on phases of Jackson's policy are: C. R. Fish, *Civil Service and the Patronage* (1906); E. Stanwood, *History of the Presidency,* 2 vols. (1916); K. H. Porter, *A History of Suffrage in the United States* (1918); W. E. Binkley, *American Political Parties;* Grant Foreman, *Indian Removal: The Emigration of the Five Civilized Tribes* (1932); Annie H. Abel, *The History of Events Resulting in Indian Consolidation West of the Mississippi* (1908); R. G. Wellington, *The Political and Sectional Influence of the Public Lands, 1828-1842* (1914); Benjamin F. Hibbard, *A History of the Public Land Policies* (1924); Roy M. Robbins, *Our Landed Heritage: The Public Domain, 1776-1936* (1942); and Ulrich B. Phillips, *Georgia and State Rights* (1902).

CHAPTER XXVIII—VAN BUREN AND THE PANIC OF 1837

Van Buren's administration

A good brief account of Van Buren's administration is given in F. J. Turner's *The United States, 1830-1850*. There are also several biographies of Van Buren which discuss the events of his presidency. Of these the following might be of interest to the special student or general reader: Holmes Alexander, *The American Talleyrand: The Career and Contemporaries of Martin Van Buren, Eighth President* (readable; good pictures and cartoons; 1935); D. T. Lynch, *An Epoch and a Man: Martin Van Buren and His Times* (good portraits; 1929); and E. M. Shepard, *Martin Van Buren* (1888, 1899). The Autobiography of Van Buren ends just before the time of his accession, but is useful as giving his earlier career.

The financial history of the administration is discussed in the following works: A. B. Hart, *Slavery and Abolition* [*The American Nation,* XVI; 1906], Ch. 20; R. C. McGrane, *The Panic of 1837* (1924); J. J. Knox, *A History of Banking in the United States* (1900); Horace White, *Money and Banking, Illustrated by American History* (1895, 1935); and David Kinley, *The Independent Treasury of the United States* (1893).

The campaign of 1840

Accounts of the campaign of 1840 can be found in: G. P. Garrison, *Westward Extension* [*The American Nation,* XVII; 1906], Ch. 3; O. P. Chitwood, *John Tyler: Champion of the Old South* (1939), Ch. 13; A. B. Norton, *Reminiscences of the Log Cabin and Hard Cider Campaign* (1888); and G. R. Poage, *Henry Clay and the Whig Party* (1936).

CHAPTER XXIX—A PRESIDENT WITHOUT A PARTY

A good brief account of the events of this chapter, as well as the one which *Harrison's* follows, can be found in G. P. Garrison's *Westward Extension* [*The American* *short term* *Nation*, XVII; 1906]. Harrison's incumbency of one month is briefly treated by Dorothy B. Goebel, *William Henry Harrison* (1926); Freeman Cleaves, *Old Tippecanoe: William Henry Harrison and His Time* (1939); and J. A. Green, *William Henry Harrison* (1941).

The older general histories (see pp. 775, 789) contain lengthy but unfair *General ac-* appraisals of Tyler's presidency. In a carefully prepared monograph, *Presi-* *counts of* *dential Politics in the United States, 1841-1844* (1936), O. D. Lambert discusses *Tyler's ad-* the politics of Tyler's administration, taking an unfavorable view of his policy. *ministration* Accounts favorable to Tyler are given in the following works: F. J. Turner, *The* *United States, 1830-1850;* G. R. Poage, *Henry Clay and the Whig Party* (1936); O. P. Chitwood, *John Tyler: Champion of the Old South* (1939); and Lyon G. Tyler, *Letters and Times of the Tylers*, 3 vols. (1884, 1896). The editor of the last-named work was the son of President Tyler, and his interpretations were colored by filial piety; this is, however, a most valuable collection of documents.

Many interesting details of the history of this period can be gleaned from *Biographies* C. M. Fuess, *Daniel Webster*, and the biographies of Henry Clay. Of the latter the following are recommended: Glyndon G. Van Deusen, *The Life of Henry* *Clay* (1937); and Carl Schurz, *Henry Clay*, 2 vols. (1899, 1909). Bernard Mayo's projected three-volume work, one volume of which (*Henry Clay: Spokesman of* *the New West;* 1937) has already appeared, gives promise of being a brilliant and scholarly achievement. See also C. M. Fuess, *The Life of Caleb Cushing,* 2 vols. (1923).

American relations with England are adequately covered by J. M. Callahan, *Relations with* *American Foreign Policy in Canadian Relations* (1937); J. F. Sprague, *The* *England* *Northeastern Boundary Controversy and the Aroostook War* (1910); and L. B. Shippee, *Canadian-American Relations, 1849-1874* (1939).

For the events that preceded and led to the annexation of Texas, see E. C. *Texas* Barker, *The Life of Stephen F. Austin, Founder of Texas* (1925), and *Mexico* *and Texas, 1821-1835* (1928); Marquis James, *The Raven: A Biography of* *Sam Houston* (1929); and Justin H. Smith, *The Annexation of Texas* (1911).

CHAPTER XXX—EXPANSION AND CONFLICT

There is an excellent brief discussion of Polk's administration in G. P. *General ac-* Garrison's *Westward Extension*. The best full account of Polk's presidency *counts of* and his previous career is E. I. McCormac's *James K. Polk* (1922). A good source *Polk's ad-* book for the inside history of the administration is *The Diary of James K. Polk,* *ministration* *during His Presidency, 1845-1849*, 4 vols., edited by M. M. Quaife (1910). There is a useful abbreviated edition of the Diary by Allan Nevins (1929).

The diplomatic relations of Mexico and the United States for this period *Diplomatic re-* are covered by each of the following scholarly works: Jesse S. Reeves, *American* *lations with* *Diplomacy under Tyler and Polk* (1907); J. M. Callahan, *American Policy in* *Mexico* *Mexican Relations* (1932); J. Fred Rippy, *The United States and Mexico* (1931); and George L. Rives, *The United States and Mexico, 1821-1848*, 2 vols. (1913).

An interesting brief account of the topics indicated in the title is given by *The Mexican* N. W. Stephenson in *Texas and the Mexican War* [*The Chronicles of America,* *War* XXIV; 1921]. For detailed accounts of the Mexican War see Justin H. Smith, *The War with Mexico*, 2 vols. (1919); H. Hamilton, *Zachary Taylor: Soldier* *of the Republic* (1941); Arthur D. H. Smith, *Old Fuss and Feathers; the Life* *and Exploits of Lt.-General Winfield Scott* (1937); and Charles W. Elliott, *Winfield Scott: The Soldier and the Man* (1937).

The treatment of the Oregon question by Garrison in *Westward Extension*

The Oregon dispute and by Constance L. Skinner in *Adventures of Oregon* [*The Chronicles of America*, XXII; 1920] is satisfactory except for special students. To these the following works might prove useful: H. M. Crittenden, *The American Fur Trade of the Far West*, 3 vols. (1902); Albert K. Weinberg, *Manifest Destiny: A Study of National Expansion in American History* (1935); Melvin C. Jacobs, *Winning Oregon: A Study of an Expansionist Movement* (1938); Clifford M. Drury, *Marcus Whitman, M.D., Pioneer and Martyr* (1937); and Cardinal L. Goodwin, *The Trans-Mississippi West, 1803-1853* (1922).

CHAPTER XXXI—TRANSPORTATION AND TRADE (1783-1860)

Considerable space is given to the economic and social life of the Federal Period (covered by Chapters XXXI-XXXVIII) in some of the general histories listed on pp. 775, 789, notably those of Channing and McMaster, and in the economic histories and special treatises listed on pp. 776f. Other general accounts can be found in three volumes of the *American Life* series: Carl R. Fish, *Rise of the Common Man, 1830-1850* (1937); Arthur C. Cole, *The Irrepressible Conflict, 1850-1865* (1934); and J. A. Krout and D. R. Fox, *The Completion of Independence, 1790-1830* (1944). These works will doubtless provide sufficient material for the general reader and the average student.

Transportation and travel For the benefit of special students the following titles might be added: A. B. Hulbert, *The Paths of Inland Commerce* [*The Chronicles of America*, XXI; an interesting general account; 1921]; Seymour Dunbar, *A History of Travel in America*, 4 vols. (1915); B. H. Meyer, Caroline E. McGill, and others, *History of Transportation in the United States before 1860* (1917); T. B. Searight, *The Old Pike: A History of the National Road* (contains numerous excerpts from the documents; 1894); Robert Bruce, *The Old National Road* (good maps; 1916); U. B. Phillips, *A History of Transportation in the Eastern Cotton Belt to 1860* (1908); C. H. Ambler, *A History of Transportation in the Ohio Valley* (1932); and Herbert and Edward Quick, *Mississippi Steamboatin'* (1926).

Railroads For railroads see: C. F. Carter, *When Railroads Were New* (1909); Slason Thompson, *A Short History of American Railways* (numerous illustrations; 1925); John W. Starr, *One Hundred Years of American Railroading* (1929; good pictures); William H. Brown, *The History of the First Locomotive in America* (1871); Lewis H. Haney, *A Congressional History of Railways in the United States to 1850* (1908), and *A Congressional History of Railways in the United States, 1850-1877* (1910); and Edward Hungerford, *The Story of the Baltimore and Ohio Railroad, 1827-1927*, 2 vols. (valuable pictures; 1928).

Commerce An important history of commerce is a co-operative work by Emory R. Johnson and others, *History of the Domestic and Foreign Commerce of the United States*, 2 vols. (1915). For other discussions of commerce and related subjects see: J. R. Spears, *The Story of the American Merchant Marine* (1910); R. D. Paine, *The Old Merchant Marine* [*The Chronicles of America*, XXXVI; 1920]; Malcolm Keir, *The March of Commerce* [*The Pageant of America*, IV; numerous pictures; 1927]; A. H. Clark, *The Clipper Ship Era, 1843-1869* (good pictures; 1910); and Carl C. Cutler, *Greyhounds of the Sea* (good pictures; 1930).

Communication with the Far West Communication with the Far West is, in some of its phases, treated in the following works: W. J. Ghent, *The Road to Oregon* (illustrations; 1929); R. L. Duffus, *The Santa Fé Trail* (1930, 1934); Josiah Gregg, *Commerce of the Prairies: or the Journal of a Santa Fé Trader*, 2 vols. (1844; reprinted in 1905 in R. G. Thwaites' *Early Western Travels*); James J. Webb, *Adventures in the Sante Fé Trade, 1844-1847*, ed. by Ralph P. Bieber (a contemporary account); L. R. Hafen, *The Overland Mail, 1849-1869* (1926); G. D. Bradley, *The Story of the Pony Express* (1913); and Arthur Chapman, *The Pony Express* (1936).

CHAPTER XXXII—INDUSTRY, AGRICULTURE, AND FARM TENURE

Some of the topics of this chapter are discussed in a general way in the *Industry* histories referred to in previous chapters, especially those of Channing and McMaster. The progress of invention and the advance of industry are described in the economic histories listed on pp. 776f. and in a number of special works, such as: B. T. Holland, *The Age of Invention* [*The Chronicles of America,* XXXVII; 1921]; Edward W. Byrn, *The Progress of Invention in the Nineteenth Century* (1900); George Iles, *Leading American Inventors* (1912); Robert Hoe, *A Short History of the Printing Press* (1902); Malcolm Keir, *The Epic of Industry* [*The Pageant of America,* V; good pictures; 1926]; V. S. Clark, *History of Manufactures in the United States,* 3 vols. (1916-1929); John G. Glover and W. B. Cornell, *The Development of American Industries* (1932); and A. H. Cole, *American Wool Manufacture,* 2 vols. (1926).

The most authoritative histories of agriculture for the period under discussion *Agriculture:* are: Lewis Cecil Gray, *History of Agriculture in the Southern United States to* *General works* *1860,* Vol. II (1933); and Percy Wells Bidwell and John I. Falconer, *History of Agriculture in the Northern United States, 1620-1860* (1925). Very useful shorter studies emphasizing the economic and social aspects of agriculture are: E. L. Bogart, *Economic History of American Agriculture* (1923); Joseph Schaefer, *The Social History of American Agriculture* (1936); and L. B. Schmitt and E. D. Ross, *Readings in the Economic History of American Agriculture* (1925).

For plantation agriculture in the South see U. B. Phillips, *American Negro* *Special works* *Slavery* (1918), and *Life and Labor in the Old South* (1929); Charles Sydnor, *Slavery in Mississippi* (1933); and Ralph Flanders, *Plantation Slavery in Georgia* (1933). Blanche Henry Clark, *Tennessee Yeomen* (1942), gives an excellent picture of agricultural practices and land tenure of the average Southern farmer. See also F. L. and Harriet C. Owsley, "The Economic Basis of Society in the Late Ante-Bellum South," *Journal of Southern History,* Vol. VI, no. 1, pp. 24-45 (1940), and same authors, "Economic Structure of Rural Tennessee, 1850-60," *Journal of Southern History,* Vol. VIII, no. 2, pp. 161-182 (1942). For the development of the reaper and mowing machine see William T. Hutchinson, *Cyrus Hall McCormick,* 2 vols. (1930).

For further bibliographical aids consult Everett Eugene Edwards, *A Bibli-* *Bibliography* *ography of the History of Agriculture in the United States* (1930), and *References on Agriculture in the Life of the Nation* (1939).

CHAPTER XXXIII—LABOR, IMMIGRATION, AND REFORM

For the labor and immigration questions see the following: Ralph H. Gabriel, *Labor and* *Toilers of Land and Sea* [*The Pageant of America,* III; good pictures; 1926]; *immigration* John R. Commons and others, *History of Labor in the United States,* 4 vols. (1918, 1935-36); Mary R. Beard, *The American Labor Movement, A Short History* (based largely on the work of Commons and others just cited; 1935); Anthony Bimba, *The History of the American Working Class* (1927); Norman Ware, *The Industrial Worker, 1840-1860* (1924); S. P. Orth, *Our Foreigners* [*The Chronicles of America,* XXXV; 1920]; Carl Wittke, *We Who Built America: The Saga of the Immigrant* (1939); G. M. Stephenson, *A History of American Immigration, 1820-1924* (1926); Albert S. Faust, *The German Element in the United States,* 2 vols. (1909, 1927); and W. F. Adams, *Ireland and Irish Emigration to the New World from 1815 to the Famine* (1932).

Among the discussions of humanitarianism and reform the following works *Humanita-* deserve mention: Henry N. Hurd and others, *The Institutional Care of the* *rianism and* *Insane in the United States and Canada,* 4 vols. (1916-1917); Frederick H. Wines, *reform* *Punishment and Reformation* (1919); Blake McKelvey, *American Prisons: A Study in American Social History prior to 1915* (1936); Francis Tiffany, *Life of*

Dorothea Lynde Dix (1892) ; Merle E. Curti, *The American Peace Crusade, 1815-1860* (1929) ; W. F. Galpin, *Pioneering for Peace: A Study of American Peace Efforts to 1846* (1933) ; John A. Krout, *The Origins of Prohibition* (1925) ; Johnson Wolley, *Temperance Progress of the Century* (1903) ; August F. Fehlandt, *A Century of Drink Reform in the United States* (1904) ; W. A. Hinds, *American Communities and Cooperative Colonies* (1902) ; and George B. Lockwood, *The New Harmony Movement* (1905).

Women's rights

There is a voluminous collection of documents on woman's suffrage in the *History of Women's Suffrage,* 6 vols. (1889-1922), compiled by Elizabeth Cady Stanton, Susan B. Anthony, and others. For other accounts of the woman's movement, see: Belle Squire, *The Woman Movement in America* (1911) ; Abbie Graham, *Ladies in Revolt* (1934) ; and E. A. Hecker, *Short History of Women's Rights* (1914).

CHAPTER XXXIV—SCHOOLS AND COLLEGES

Elementary and secondary education

The subjects covered by Chapters XXXIV-XXXVII are so fully treated in the volumes of Fish and Cole cited in the previous chapter and in the general treatises listed on pp. 778f., that not many titles need be added. To supplement these general accounts the following works might be listed for Schools and Colleges: *A Cyclopedia of Education,* 5 vols. (brief bibliographies; 1911-1913) ; E. G. Dexter, *A History of Education in the United States* (1904) ; E. E. Slosson, *The American Spirit in Education* [*The Chronicles of America,* XXXIII; 1921]; Merle Curti, *Social Ideas of American Educators* (1935) ; Frank T. Carlton, *Economic Influences upon Educational Progress in the United States, 1820-1850* (1908) ; E. P. Cubberley, *Public Education in the United States* (1919) ; E. A. Winship, *Great American Educators* (1899, 1927) ; B. A. Hinsdale, *Horace Mann and the Common School Revival in the United States* (1898) ; H. R. Warfel, *Noah Webster: Schoolmaster to America* (1936) ; E. E. Brown, *The Making of Our Middle Schools* (1914) ; S. C. Parker, *History of Modern Elementary Education* (1912) ; Rev. James A. Burns, *The Growth and Development of the Catholic School System in the United States* (1912) ; Carter G. Woodson, *The Education of the Negro prior to 1861* (1919) ; D. G. Tewksbury, *The Founding of American Colleges and Universities before the Civil War* (1932) ; C. F. Thwing, *A History of Higher Education in America* (1906) ; and E. M. Coulter, *College Life in the Old South* (1928).

Higher education

CHAPTER XXXV—ART, SCIENCE, AND LITERATURE

Art

Only a few special works dealing with this chapter need be added to the list given on pp. 778f. In this supplemental list might be included the following: Sadochi Hartman, *A History of American Art,* 2 vols. (1902) ; T. E. Tallmadge, *The Story of Architecture in America* (1936) ; Howard Major, *The Domestic Architecture of the Early American Republic: The Greek Period* (1926) ; and Samuel Isham, *The History of American Painting* (numerous illustrations; a valuable work; 1905).

Science

To the list of scientific works given on p. 778 might be added: H. B. Shafer, *The American Medical Profession, 1783-1850* (1936) ; and J. S. Chambers, *The Conquest of Cholera: America's Greatest Scourge* (1938).

Music and the stage

Additional works on music and the stage: F. J. Metcalf, *American Writers and Compilers of Sacred Music* (short sketches of writers, a sort of biographical dictionary; 1925) ; O. G. Sonneck, *Early Opera in America* (1915) ; and Mary C. Crawford. *The Romance of the American Stage* (good illustrations; 1913).

Literature

The special student of literature might wish to refer to the following works: Fred L. Pattee, *The First Century of American Literature, 1770-1870* (1935) ; Van Wyck Brooks, *The Flowering of New England* (a brilliant discussion; 1936) ; V. L. Parrington, *The Romantic Movement in America* (also brilliant; 1927) ; M. J. Moses, *The Literature of the South* (1910) ; Carl Holliday, *A History of*

Southern Literature (1906); W. M. Baskerville, *Southern Writers, 1798-1803,*
2 vols. (1897-1903); and Clement Eaton, *Freedom of Thought in the Old South*
(1940). There are one or more biographies of each of the well-known poets,
novelists, and essayists of this period, but they are too numerous to be listed here.

An additional title or so might be added to the list already given (p. 779) *Journalism*
for journalism and history: Algernon de Vivier Tassin, *The Magazine in America* *and history*
(1916); G. H. Payne, *History of Journalism in the United States* (1926); and
John S. Bassett, *The Middle Group of American Historians* (1917).

CHAPTER XXXVI—THE DECLINE AND REVIVAL OF RELIGION

For references for this chapter see p. 778. In the bibliography of C. R. Fish's *Religion on*
The Rise of the Common Man are given numerous references to contemporary *the frontier*
accounts of religious conditions in the United States in the 'thirties, 'forties, and
'fifties, see pp. 358-359. W. W. Sweet's *Religion on the American Frontier, 1783-*
1830, and other related works by him include a volume each on the Baptists,
Presbyterians, and Congregationalists, and two on the Methodists. Other works
that might be of use to special students are: Catharine C. Cleveland, *The Great*
Revival in the West, 1797-1805 (1916); Vardis Fisher, *Children of God: An*
American Epic (an interesting fictionized account of the Mormons; 1939); Nels
Anderson, *Desert Saints; The Mormon Frontier in Utah* (1942); N. R. Werner,
Brigham Young (1925); J. N. Norwood, *The Schism in the Methodist Church,*
1844 (documents in appendices; 1923); and W. P. Strickland, ed., *Autobiography*
of Peter Cartwright, Backwoods Preacher (1856).

CHAPTER XXXVII—AMERICAN LIFE AT MID-CENTURY

For a cross-sectional view of American life in the 'forties and 'fifties, see:
E. Douglas Branch, *The Sentimental Years, 1836-1860* (1934); Meade Minne-
gerode, *The Fabulous Forties, 1840-1850* (1924); John A. Krout, *Annals of*
American Sport [*The Pageant of America,* XV; pictures; 1929]; Foster R. Dulles,
America Learns to Play (a history of popular recreation from 1607 to 1940;
numerous illustrations; 1940); C. W. Brewster, *National Standard of Costume*
(1837); W. E. Dodd, *The Cotton Kingdom* [*The Chronicles of America,* XXVII;
interesting; 1920]; and R. Q. Mallard, *Plantation Life before Emancipation*
(1892). Good pictures of plantation life, more or less idealized, are also given in
the works of fiction by some Southern writers, such as the stories of Thomas
Nelson Page, *In Ole Virginia* (1887); Stark Young, *So Red the Rose* (1934);
and Margaret Mitchell, *Gone with the Wind* (1936).

CHAPTER XXXVIII—THE ANTISLAVERY MOVEMENT (1783-1860)

The following books and pamphlets are excellent examples of abolitionist *Primary*
and pro-slavery writings: Wilson Armistead, comp., *Five Hundred Thousand* *sources*
Strokes for Freedom, or Leeds Anti-Slavery Tracts (1853), Vol. II, Chapter I,
"The Seeds of War"; Albert Taylor Bledsoe, *An Essay on Liberty and Slavery*
(1856); Gilbert H. Barnes and Dwight L. Dumond (editors), *Letters of Theo-*
dore Dwight Weld, Angelina Grimke Weld and Sarah Grimke, 1822-44, 2 vols.
(1934); Dwight L. Dumond, ed., *Letters of James Gillespie Birney, 1831-*
1857 (1938); George Bourne, *Slavery Illustrated in its Effects upon Woman and*
Domestic Society (1837); William Ellery Channing, *The Duty of the Free States*
(1842); George B. Cheever, *God Against Slavery! And the Freedom and Duty of*
the Pulpit to Rebuke it, as a Sin against God (1857); Thomas R. Dew, *Review*
of the Debate on the Abolition of Slavery in the Virginia Legislature of 1831
and 1832 (1832); E. N. Elliott, ed., *Cotton is King and Pro-Slavery Arguments:*
Comprising the Writings of Hammond, Harper, Christy, Stringfellow, Hodge,
Bledsoe and Cartwright, on This Important Subject, with an Essay on Slavery
in the Light of International Law by the Editor (1860); S. S. Foster, *The*

Brotherhood of Thieves; or A True Picture of the American Church and Clergy (1844) ; and William Harper, *Memoir on Slavery* (1838) .

Secondary authorities

For recent evaluations of the slavery issue see: William S. Jenkins, *Pro-Slavery Thought in the Old South* (1935) ; Arthur Young Lloyd, *The Slavery Controversy* (1939) ; U. B. Phillips, "The Central Theme of Southern History," *American Historical Review*, XXXIV, pp. 30-43 (1929) ; Henry H. Simms, *A Decade of Sectional Controversy* (1942) ; Avery O. Craven, *The Coming of the Civil War* (1942) ; Frank L. Owsley, "Origins of the American Civil War," *Southern Review*, V, pp. 609-629 (1940) ; and Albert J. Beveridge, *Abraham Lincoln, 1809-1858,* 2 vols. (1928) .

CHAPTER XXXIX—CONTROVERSY AND COMPROMISE

Sectional controversy in the 'fifties: General accounts

The political history of the 'fifties is given at considerable length in the general histories of Schouler, Channing, and McMaster and in the constitutional history of Von Holst. The last-named work is strongly biased in favor of the Northern point of view. A fuller account can be found in J. F. Rhodes, *History of the United States*, 7 vols. (1893-1906; a later edition in 9 vols.; 1929) . The period originally covered by this work is from 1850 to 1877. The events of this tragic era are given in a clear and interesting style, but recent research has shown that some of the statements need modification. Other works that are concerned with the entire period (1850-1860) or the greater part of it are: A. C. Cole, *The Irrepressible Conflict, 1850-1865* [*A History of American Life*, VII; 1934]; H. H. Simms, *A Decade of Sectional Controversy, 1851-61* (1942) ; George M. Stephenson, *The Political History of the Public Lands from 1840-1862* (1917) ; Katharine Coman, *Economic Beginnings of the Far West* (1912) ; Avery Craven, *The Repressible Conflict, 1830-1861* (brief interpretive essays; 1939) , and *The Coming of the Civil War* (1942) ; and Dwight L. Dumond, *Antislavery Origins of the Civil War in the United States* (interpretive essays; 1939) .

Biographies

A good deal of information can also be found in the biographies of the statesmen who figured in the disputes of this decade. Of these the following are useful: Allen Johnson, *Stephen A. Douglas: A Study in American Politics* (1908) ; George F. Milton, *The Eve of Conflict: Stephen A. Douglas and the Needless War* (1934) ; T. K. Lothrop, *William Henry Seward* [*American Statesmen;* 1896]; A. B. Hart, *Salmon Portland Chase* [*American Statesmen;* 1899]; William E. Dodd, *Life of Jefferson Davis* (1907) , and *Statesmen of the Old South* (1911) ; Robert McElroy, *Jefferson Davis*, 2 vols. (1937) ; and G. H. Haynes, *Charles Sumner* [*American Crisis Biographies;* 1909].

The Taylor-Fillmore administration

For accounts of the Taylor-Fillmore administration, emphasizing the Compromise of 1850 and the events that preceded and led to it, see G. P. Garrison, *Westward Extension* [*The American Nation*, XVII; 1906]; and the general works listed above. The following special works might also prove helpful: I. D. Travis, *History of the Clayton-Bulwer Treaty* (1900) ; Robert C. Cleland, *A History of California: The American Period* (1922) ; Allan Nevins, *Frémont, Pathmarker of the West* (illustrations; 1939) ; S. E. White, *The Forty-Niners* [*The Chronicles of America*, XXV; 1920]; A. B. Hulbert, *Forty-Niners, The Chronicle of the California Trail* (1931) ; Carl Schurz, *Henry Clay*, Vol. II.; C. M. Fuess, *Daniel Webster*, Vol. II.; M. J. White, *The Secession Movement in the United States, 1847-1852* (1910) ; R. H. Shryock, *Georgia and the Union in 1850* (1926) ; U. B. Phillips, *The Course of the South to Secession* (1939) ; Roy F. Nichols, *The Democratic Machine, 1850-1854* (1923) ; and A. C. Cole, *The Whig Party in the South* (1913) . As a supplement to and a corrective of the older accounts of the Compromise of 1850, the special student should read an article by F. H. Hodder, "The Authorship of the Compromise of 1850," in the *Mississippi Valley Historical Review*, XXII, pp. 525-536. It gives more credit to Douglas than to Clay for the success of the Compromise.

CHAPTER XL—A RELAPSE INTO SECTIONAL STRIFE

Pierce's administration is discussed at considerable length by T. C. Smith, *Parties and Slavery* [*The American Nation*, XVIII; 1906], and the general histories given for the preceding chapter. See also the following special works: D. L. Dumond, *Anti-Slavery Origins of the Civil War* (1939) ; J. G. Randall, *The Civil War and Reconstruction* (1937) ; Roy F. Nichols, *Franklin Pierce* (1931) ; Paul N. Garber, *The Gadsden Treaty* (1923) ; P. J. Treat, *Diplomatic Relations between the United States and Japan, 1853-1895,* 2 vols. (1932) ; and Edwin A. Falk, *From Perry to Pearl Harbor: The Struggle for Supremacy in the Pacific,* Ch. I (1943) . *Pierce's administration*

For certain aspects of the slavery question, see Hinton R. Helper, *The Impending Crisis of the South,* first edition, 1857 (a violent attack on slavery by a Southern yeoman) ; A. Y. Lloyd, *The Slavery Controversy, 1831-1860* (1939) ; W. H. Siebert, *The Underground Railroad from Slavery to Freedom* (illustrations and maps; 1899) ; Forrest Wilson, *Crusader in Crinoline: The Life of Harriet Beecher Stowe* (good pictures; 1941) ; and Catherine Gilbertson, *Harriet Beecher Stowe* (1937) . *The slavery question*

For the Kansas-Nebraska Act and its aftermath, see H. H. Simms, *A Decade of Sectional Controversy, 1851-61;* Avery Craven, *The Coming of the Civil War;* George F. Milton, *The Eve of Conflict: Stephen A. Douglas and the Needless War;* P. C. Ray, *The Repeal of the Missouri Compromise, Its Origin and Authorship* (1909) ; and F. H. Hodder, "Genesis of the Kansas-Nebraska Act" [*Wisconsin State Historical Society Proceedings* for 1912], and "The Railroad Background of the Kansas-Nebraska Act" [*Mississippi Valley Historical Review*, XII]. For an excellent appraisal of the character and personality of John Brown and his record in Kansas, see James C. Malin, *John Brown and the Legend of Fifty-Six* (1942) . *The Kansas-Nebraska Act*

For details as to the campaign of 1856 see the following special works: R. J. Bartlett, *John C. Frémont and the Republican Party* (1930) ; A. W. Crandall, *The Early History of the Republican Party, 1854-1856* (1930) ; R. A. Bellington, *The Protestant Crusade, 1880-1860* (discusses the anti-Catholic prejudice and the rise of "Know-Nothingism"; 1938) ; and George M. Stephenson, *A History of American Immigration, 1840-1924* (Chapter X discusses "Know-Nothingism"; 1926) . *The campaign of 1856*

CHAPTER XLI—STORM CLOUDS

Many, if not most, of the references given for the two preceding chapters apply also to Buchanan's administration. Few titles, therefore, need be added. Of these the following might be included: G. T. Curtis, *Life of James Buchanan,* 2 vols. (1883) ; P. G. Auchampaugh, *James Buchanan and His Cabinet on the Eve of Secession* (liberal extracts from the primary sources; 1926) ; D. L. Dumond, *The Secession Movement, 1860-1861* (1931) , and *Antislavery Origins of the Civil War in the United States;* R. G. Randall, *op. cit.;* George W. Van Vleck, *The panic of 1857* (1943) ; and C. F. Dunbar, *Economic Essays* (contains an account of the Panic of 1857; 1904) . *Buchanan's administration*

The views of the older writers on the Dred Scott Case can be found in the works of Schouler, McMaster, and Von Holst. See also J. W. Burgess, *The Middle Period,* Chapter 21, and T. C. Smith, *Parties and Slavery,* Chapter 14. For newer and fairer appraisals, consult: C. B. Swisher, *Roger B. Taney* (1935) ; C. W. Smith, *Roger B. Taney: Jacksonian Jurist* (1936) ; Charles Warren, *The Supreme Court in United States History* (1932) , 2nd volume; E. S. Corwin, "The Dred Scott Decision, in the Light of Contemporary Legal Doctrines" (*American Historical Review*, October, 1911) ; and articles by F. H. Hodder in the *Mississippi Valley Historical Review* (see especially Vol. XVI, pp. 3-22) . *The Dred Scott case*

For the Lincoln-Douglas debates, see *Collections* of the Illinois State Historical Society, Vol III (a report of these speeches) ; Albert J. Beveridge, *Abraham* *Other special topics*

Lincoln, 1809-1858, 2 vols. (1928) ; and Carl Sandburg, *Abraham Lincoln: The Prairie Years,* 2 vols. (1926).

The following works give full accounts of John Brown's Raid: O. G. Villard, *John Brown, 1800-1859* (fine pictures; 1910) ; and John D. Lawson, ed., *American State Trials,* Vol. VI, pp. 700-864 (record of the trial of John Brown and his accomplices).

Accounts of the campaign of 1860 can be found in the general histories so often referred to, in E. D. Fite's *The Presidential Campaign of 1860* (1911), and in R. H. Luthin's *The First Lincoln Campaign* (1944).

PART IV: THE WAR FOR SOUTHERN INDEPENDENCE, 1860-1865

GENERAL ACCOUNTS

General Accounts of the Civil War period: J. F. Rhodes, *History of the United States,* Vols. III-V; J. B. McMaster, *A History of the People of the United States during Lincoln's Administration* (1927) ; Edward Channing, *A History of the United States: The War for Southern Independence,* Vol. VI (1925) ; J. K. Hosmer, *The American Civil War,* 2 vols. (1913) ; James Truslow Adams, *America's Tragedy* (1935) ; Walter G. Shotwell, *The Civil War in America,* 2 vols. (1923) ; N. W. Stephenson, *Abraham Lincoln and the Union; A Chronicle of the Embattled North* (1918) and *The Day of the Confederacy; A Chronicle of the Embattled South* (1919) ; Carl Russell Fish, *The American Civil War; An Interpretation,* edited by William E. Smith (1937) ; and J. G. Randall, *The Civil War and Reconstruction* (1937).

SPECIAL WORKS

CHAPTER XLII—SECESSION

Efforts at
compromise

Buchanan,
Lincoln,
and other
leaders

In Volume III of J. F. Rhodes' *History of the United States,* there is an excellent account of the several attempts at compromise, and a very sound analysis of public opinion. J. B. McMaster, *A History of the People of the United States during Lincoln's Administration* is good for the entire secession and Civil War period. P. G. Auchampaugh, *James Buchanan and his Cabinet on the Eve of Secession,* and Frank W. Klingberg, "James Buchanan and the Crisis of Union", *Journal of Southern History,* IX (1943), 455-474, present a more reasonable estimate of Buchanan's attitude toward secession and the sectional controversy. Buchanan's writings and speeches for this period are to be found in J. B. Moore, ed., *The Works of James Buchanan, Comprising His Speeches, State Papers and Private Correspondence,* 12 vols., (1908-1911). See also O. P. Chitwood, *John Tyler, Champion of the Old South* (1939), and Mary Scrugham, *The Peaceable Americans of 1860-1861; A Study in Public Opinion* (1921). Lincoln's attitude toward secession and compromise are found in Vols. III and IV of John G. Nicolay and John Hay, *Abraham Lincoln; A History,* 10 vols. (1917) ; David M. Potter, *Lincoln and His Party in the Secession Crisis* (1942) ; N. W. Stephenson, *Abraham Lincoln and the Union; A Chronicle of the Embattled North;* Ida M. Tarbell, *The Life of Abraham Lincoln,* 2 vols. (1919), Vol. II; John Shipley Tilley, *Lincoln Takes Command* (1941) ; and Thomas H. Williams, *Lincoln and the Radicals* (1941). Frederick Bancroft, *The Life of William H. Seward,* 2 vols. (1900) ; Mrs. Mary Chapman Coleman, *The Life of John J. Crittenden,* 2 vols. (1873) ; P. S. Flippin, *Hershel V. Johnson of Georgia; State Rights Unionist* (1931) ; Robert McElroy, *Jefferson Davis; The Unreal and the Real,* 2 vols. (1937) ; Louis Pendleton, *Alexander H. Stephens* (1908) ; U. B. Phillips, *The Life of Robert Toombs* (1913) ; Dunbar Rowland, ed., *Jefferson Davis, Constitutionalist; His Letters, Papers and Speeches,* 10 vols. (1923) ; Harriet A. Weed (ed. of Vol. I) and Thurlow Weed Barnes (ed. of Vol. II), *Life of Thurlow Weed, Including His Autobiography and a Memoir* (1884) ; *Diary of Gideon Welles,* 3 vols. (1911) ; and the biographies of Douglas, Sumner, and Chase previously cited should be consulted for the attitudes of the more prominent leaders toward compromise and secession.

Most of the books cited above contain sections on Fort Sumter, and this is *Fort Sumter* true of the books in the following section on secession. Especial attention is called to John Shipley Tilley, *Lincoln Takes Command;* Thomas H. Williams, *Lincoln and the Radicals;* P. G. Auchampaugh, *James Buchanan and His Cabinet on the Eve of Secession;* Frank W. Klingberg, "James Buchanan and the Crisis of Union", *Journal of Southern History,* (loc. cit.) ; and Mary Scrugham, *The Peaceable Americans.* In addition see Charles W. Ramsdell, "Lincoln and Fort Sumter" in the *Journal of Southern History,* III (1937), 259-288; S. W. Crawford, *The Genesis of the Civil War; The Story of Sumter, 1860-1861* (1887).

Dwight L. Dumond, *The Secession Movement, 1860-1861* contains excellent *The secession* accounts of the party conventions and state secession conventions. This *movement* should be used in connection with the same author's *Southern Editorials on Secession* (1931). J. G. Randall, *The Civil War and Reconstruction* and Carl Russell Fish, *The American Civil War: An Interpretation* are the two best short accounts of this entire period. Good background studies are: J. T. Carpenter, *The South as a Conscious Minority, 1789-1861* (1930) ; R. R. Russell, *Economic Aspects of Southern Sectionalism, 1840-1861* (The University of Illinois *Studies in Social Sciences,* XI, Nos. 1-2; 1924) ; John G. Van Deusen, *Economic Bases of Disunion in South Carolina* (1928) ; A. O. Craven, *Edmund Ruffin, Southerner; A Study in Secession* (1932) ; A. C. Cole, *The Irrepressible Conflict* (1934) ; and Laura A. White, *Robert Barnwell Rhett* (1931). Clarence P. Denman, *The Secession Movement in Alabama* (1933) ; Percy L. Rainwater, *Mississippi, Storm Center of Secession, 1856-1861* (1938) ; and Henry T. Shanks, *The Secession Movement in Virginia, 1847-1861* (1934) are excellent accounts of the movement in these states. For the border slave states see E. Merton Coulter, *The Civil War and Readjustment in Kentucky* (1926), Chapters I-VI; Matthew Page Andrews, *History of Maryland, Province and State* (1929), Chapter II; W. E. Smith, *The Francis Preston Blair Family in Politics,* 2 vols. (1933).

An excellent understanding of the Confederate government may be gained *The Con-* from: J. L. M. Curry, *Civil History of the Government of the Confederate* *federate* *States with Some Personal Reminiscences* (1901) ; William M. Robinson, Jr., *government* *Justice in Gray; A History of the Judicial System of the Confederate States of America,* 2 vols. (1941) ; and Jefferson Davis, *The Rise and Fall of the Confederate Government* (1881).

CHAPTERS XLIII AND XLIV---MILITARY AFFAIRS

Military The following military histories should be listed: G. C. Eggleston, *The* *histories* *History of the Confederate War; Its Causes and Its Conduct,* 2 vols. (1910) ; John Fiske, *The Mississippi Valley in the Civil War* (1900) ; J. K. Hosmer, *The appeal to Arms 1861-1863* (1907) ; R. S. Henry, *The Story of the Confederacy* (1931) ; Stanley Horn, *The Army of Tennessee; A Military History* (1941) ; R. U. Johnson and C. C. Buel, eds., *Battles and Leaders of the Civil War,* 4 vols. (1884-1888) ; J. C. Ropes, *The Story of the Civil War,* 2 vols. (1894-1898) ; J. F. Rhodes, *History of the Civil War, 1861-1865* (1917) ; and Matthew F. Steele, *American Campaigns* (1943).

A voluminous collection of documents is *The War of the Rebellion: A* *Official* *Compilation of the Official Records of the Union and Confederate Armies,* *records, maps,* 70 vols. (1880-1901). There is also a two-volume *Atlas* to accompany these Rec- *and photo-* ords (1891-1895). For other maps and for photographic material see *Harper's* *graphic* *Atlas of American History,* with maps by Dixon R. Fox (1920) ; Francis T. Miller, *histories* *The Photographic History of the Civil War,* 10 vols. (1911) ; Harper's *Pictorial*

History of the Rebellion, 2 vols. (1866-1868) ; and B. J. Lossing, *The Pictorial Fieldbook of the Civil War in the United States of America*, 3 vols. (1874).

*Autobiog-
raphies*

Autobiographies, memoirs, and personal narratives of military leaders: E. P. Alexander, *Military Memoirs of a Confederate* (1907) ; Heros von Borcke, *Memoirs of the Confederate War for Independence*, 2 vols. (1866) ; J. D. Cox, *Military Reminiscences*, 2 vols. (1909) ; B. F. Butler, *Autobiography and Personal Reminiscences of Major-General Benj. F. Butler; Butler's Book* (1892) ; C. A. Evans, ed., *Confederate Military History*, 12 vols. (1899) ; U. S. Grant, *Personal Memoirs of U. S. Grant*, 2 vols. (1885-1886) ; John B. Gordon, *Reminiscences of the Civil War* (1903) ; J. B. Hood, *Advance and Retreat* (1880) ; R. U. Johnson and C. C. Buel, *Battles and Leaders of the Civil War;* Alfred Roman, *The Military Operations of General Beauregard in the War Between the States, 1861-1865*, 2 vols. (1884) ; Joseph E. Johnston, *Narrative of Military Operations during the Late War Between the States* (1874) ; J. W. Jones, *Personal Reminiscences, Anecdotes, and Letters of General Robert E. Lee* (1876) ; Mrs. Thomas J. Jackson, *Memoirs of Stonewall Jackson* (1895) ; James Longstreet, *From Manassas to Appomattox; Memoirs of the Civil War in America* (1896) ; Armistead L. Long, *Memoirs of Robert E. Lee* (1886) ; George B. McClellan, *McClellan's Own Story* (1887) ; Robert E. Lee, Jr., *Recollections and Letters of General Robert E. Lee* (1904) ; Horace Porter, *Campaigning with Grant* (1897) ; W. T. Sherman, *Memoirs of General William T. Sherman*, 2 vols. (1886) ; Philip H. Sheridan, *Personal Memoirs of P. H. Sheridan, General, United States Army*, 2 vols. (1888) ; John McAllister Schofield, *Forty Six Years in the Army* (1897) ; Charles Dana, *Recollections of the Civil War* (1898) ; Richard Taylor, *Destruction and Reconstruction* (1879) ; Lewis Wallace, *Lew Wallace; An Autobiography*, 2 vols. (1906) ; John Allen Wyeth, *Life of General Nathan Bedford Forrest* (1899).

Biographies

Biographies: Alfred H. Burne, *Lee, Grant and Sherman; A Study in Leadership in the 1864-65 Campaign* (1939) ; L. A. Coolidge, *Ulysses S. Grant* (1917) ; Henry Coppée, *General Thomas* (1898) ; J. P. Dyer, *"Fightin' Joe" Wheeler* (1941) ; H. J. Eckenrode and Bryan Conrad, *James Longstreet; Lee's War Horse* (1936) ; Douglas Southall Freeman, *R. E. Lee; A Biography*, 4 vols. (1934-1935), and his *Lee's Lieutenants*, 3 vols. (1942-1944) ; J. F. C. Fuller, *Grant and Lee* (1929), and his *The Generalship of Ulysses S. Grant* (1929) ; G. F. R. Henderson, *Stonewall Jackson and the American Civil War*, 2 vols. (1926) ; B. H. Liddell Hart, *Sherman; Soldier, Realist, American* (1929) ; Lloyd Lewis, *Sherman, Fighting Prophet* (1932) ; Andrew Lytle, *Bedford Forrest and His Critter Company* (1931) ; Frederick Maurice, *Robert E. Lee, the Soldier* (1925) ; H. B. McClellan, *The Life and Campaigns of ... J. E. B. Stuart* (1885) ; William M. Polk, *Leonidas Polk, Bishop and General* (1915) ; W. S. Myers, *A Study in Personality, General George Brinton McClellan* (1934) ; J. H. Eckenrode, *George B. McClellan, the Man Who Saved the Union* (1941) ; John W. Thomason, *Jeb Stuart* (1930) ; Benj. P. Poore, *The Life and Public Services of Ambrose E. Burnside, Soldier—Citizen—Statesman* (1882) ; Francis Amasa Walker, *Winfield Scott Hancock* (1894) ; and James Grant Wilson, *General Grant* (1904).

CHAPTER XLV—THE FEDERAL AND CONFEDERATE NAVIES

*Official
records*

The basic source for the study of the work of the navies during the Civil War is *Official Records of the Union and Confederate Navies in the War of the Rebellion*, 30 vols. (1894-1922). The most outstanding memoirs and narratives by participants and observers of naval operations and blockade running

*Memoirs
and personal
narratives*

are in: D. D. Porter, *The Naval History of the Civil War* (1886) ; John T. Scharf, *History of the Confederate States Navy* (1887) ; Raphael Semmes, *Service Afloat* (1903) ; J. D. Bulloch, *The Secret Service of the Confederate States in Europe*, 2 vols. (1883) ; J. M. Morgan, *Recollections of a Rebel Reefer* (1917) ; *Diary of Gideon Welles;* John Wilkinson, *The Narrative of a Blockade*

Runner (1877) ; R. M. Thompson and Richard Wainwright, eds., *Confidential Correspondence of Gustavus Vasa Fox, Assistant Secretary of the Navy, 1861-1865,* 2 vols. (1918-1919) ; William Watson, *Adventures of a Blockade Runner* (1892) ; Thomas E. Taylor, *Running the Blockade* (1897) ; and John Bigelow, *France and the Confederate Navy* (1888) . W. C. Church, *The Life of John Ericsson,* 2 vols. (1890) ; Richard S. West, Jr., *The Second Admiral; A Life of David Dixon Porter, 1813-1891* (1937), and his *Gideon Welles, Lincoln's Navy Department* (1943) ; Charles Lee Lewis, *Admiral Franklin Buchanan: Fearless Man of Action* (1929) ; A. T. Mahan, *Admiral Farragut* (1892) ; W. A. Roberts, *Semmes of the Alabama* (1938) ; Colyer C. Meriwether, *Raphael Semmes* (1913) are indispensable biographies of Union and Confederate naval leaders. *Biographies*

For the development of the ironclad navy see J. P. Baxter, 3rd., *The Introduction of the Ironclad Warship* (1933) ; H. W. Wilson, *Ironclads in Action,* 2 vols. (1896) ; Robert S. McCordock, *The Yankee Cheese Box* (1938) ; Dudley W. Knox, *A History of the United States Navy* (1936) ; Fletcher Pratt, *The Navy, A History* (1941) . For further study of the blockade and blockade running see James R. Soley, *The Blockade and the Cruisers* (1883) ; F. B. C. Bradlee, *Blockade Running during the Civil War and the Effect of Land and Water Transportation on the Confederacy* (1925) ; and Frank L. Owsley, "America and the Freedom of the Seas" in Avery Craven, ed., *Essays in Honor of William E. Dodd* (1935) . W. M. Robinson, Jr., *The Confederate Privateers* (1928) is the principal account of this phase of naval warfare. George W. Dalzell, *The Flight from the Flag* (1940) , is an account of the destructive effects upon the American merchant marine of the operations of the Confederate raiders. *Development of the ironclad navies* *The blockade*

CHAPTER XLVI—FOREIGN AND DOMESTIC AFFAIRS

There is no comprehensive diplomatic history of the United States during the Civil War; but numerous phases of diplomacy have been dealt with in various volumes. Vol. V of G. E. Baker, *The Works of William H. Seward,* 5 vols. (1853-1884) is a basic document. E. D. Adams, *Great Britain and the American Civil War,* 2 vols. (1925), concerns itself with the relations of Great Britain with the United States and the Confederacy. It is written from the point of view of the British Foreign Office. Charles Francis Adams, Jr., *Charles Francis Adams* (1900) , and W. C. Ford, ed., *A Cycle of Adams Letters,* 2 vols. (1920) , are useful in studying Civil War diplomacy from the vantage point of the United States embassy in London. J. M. Callahan, *The Diplomatic History of the Southern Confederacy* (1901) , and Frank L. Owsley, *King Cotton Diplomacy; Foreign Relations of the Confederate States of America* (1931) , cover the chief diplomatic phases of Confederate history. W. Reed West, *Contemporary French Opinion on the American Civil War* in Johns Hopkins University *Studies in Historical and Political Science,* Series 42, No. I (1924), is an excellent study of the French metropolitan press; but L. M. Case, *French Opinion on the United States and Mexico 1860-67* (1936), in utilizing the secret reports to the minister of Justice from officials in the cotton textile regions, reaches different conclusions. D. Jordan and E. J. Pratt, *Europe and the American Civil War* (1931) , is a study primarily of public opinion in Western Europe. For French intervention in Mexico see Count E. C. Corti, *Maximilian and Charlotte of Mexico,* 2 vols. (translated into English in 1929 by C. A. Phillips) ; J. M. Callahan, *American Foreign Policy in Mexico* (1932) ; Dexter Perkins, *The Monroe Doctrine, 1826-1867* (1933), 318-548; Owsley, *King Cotton Diplomacy,* Chapters IV, XVII; J. Fred Rippy, *The United States and Mexico* (1931) ; and Case, *French Opinion on the United States and Mexico, 1860-67.* *United States diplomacy* *Confederate diplomacy* *Public opinion in Europe* *French intervention in Mexico*

Life in the North: E. D. Fite, *Social and Industrial Conditions in the North during the Civil War* (1910) , deals entirely with this subject. A. C. Cole, *The Irrepressible Conflict, 1850-1865* (1934) ; the same author, *The Era of the* *Life in the North*

Civil War, 1848-1870 (1919) ; Fred A. Shannon, *Economic History of the People of the United States* (1934) ; W. H. Russell, *My Diary, North and South* (1863) ; W. E. Smith, *The Francis Preston Blair Family in Politics,* Rhodes, McMaster, Channing, and the biographies of the leading political and intellectual leaders all contain sections on the life in the North. For special phases see: L. G. Vander Velde, *The Presbyterian Churches and the Federal Union, 1861-1869* (1932) ; C. W. Heathcote, *The Lutheran Church and the Civil War* (1919) ; W. W. Sweet, *The Methodist Episcopal Church and the Civil War* (1912) .

Life in the South

Life in the South: Matthew Page Andrews, *The Women of the South in War Times* (1920) , entire; N. W. Stephenson, *Day of the Confederacy.* Rhodes, McMaster, and Channing all contain some discussion of life in the South. But the best pictures are from such contemporary writings as: Mary Boykin Chesnut, *A Diary from Dixie* (1905) ; Sarah Morgan Dawson, *A Confederate Girl's Diary* (1913) ; Mrs. Burton Harrison, *Recollections Grave and Gay* (1912) ; Judith P. McGuire, *Diary of a Southern Refugee* (1867) ; J. B. Jones, *A Rebel War Clerk's Diary at the Confederate States Capital* (1935) ; and Sarah A. Pryor, *Reminiscences of Peace and War* (1904) .

The Northern armies

The Northern armies: In addition to the general accounts of the Civil War previously cited, see F. A. Shannon, *The Organization and Administration of the Union Army, 1861-1865,* 2 vols. (1928) ; F. L. Huidekoper, *The Military Unpreparedness of the United States; A History of American Land Forces from Colonial Times until June 1, 1915* (1915) ; Ella Lonn, *Desertion during the Civil War* (1928) ; and W. B. Hesseltine, *Civil War Prisons; A Study in War Psychology* (1930) .

The Southern armies

The armies of the South: A. B. Moore, *Conscription and Conflict in the Confederacy* (1924) , deals primarily with creating and maintaining the Confederate armies. Rhodes, Channing, McMaster, and other authors covering the Civil War period cited previously, deal more or less with this problem.

Wartime finance in the North

Federal finance: D. R. Dewey, *Financial History of the United States* (8th edition 1922) contains a general treatment of the subject. For special phases see section dealing with this period in R. A. Bayley, *History of the National Loans of the United States from July 4, 1796, to June 30, 1880,* in Vol. VII, United States 10th Census; W. C. Mitchell, *History of Greenbacks* (1903) ; F. W. Taussig, *Tariff History of the United States* (rev. ed. 1923) , 155-177; D. C. Barrett, *The Greenbacks, and Resumption of Specie Payments, 1862-1879* (1931) ; A. M. Davis, *The Origin of the National Banking System* (1910) ; E. P Oberholtzer, *Jay Cooke, Financier of the Civil War,* 2 vols. (1907) ; and James L. Sellars, "An Interpretation of Civil War Finance" in the *American Historical Review,* XXX, 282-297.

Finances of the Confederacy

Confederate finance: E. A. Smith, *History of the Confederate Treasury* (1901) ; J. C. Schwab, *The Confederate States of America, 1861-1865; A Financial and Industrial History of the South during the Civil War* (1901) ; H. D. Capers, *The Life and Times of C. G. Memminger* (1893) ; S. B. Thompson, *Confederate Purchasing Operations Abroad* (1935) ; and E. Q. Hawk, *Economic History of the South* (1934) .

Emancipation

Lincoln and emancipation: Rhodes, Vols. III-IV, Channing, Vol. VI, and McMaster, *History of the People of the United States during Lincoln's Administration;* N. W. Stephenson, *Abraham Lincoln and the Union;* the biography of Lincoln by Nicolay and Hay; and the several other general histories of the Civil War period contain chapters and sections on the progress of emancipation. See J. G. Randall, *Constitutional Problems Under Lincoln* (1927) ; W. E. Smith, *The Francis Preston Blair Family in Politics;* Allen Nevins, *Frémont, The West's Greatest Adventurer,* 2 vols. (1928) .

Politics in the North

Politics in North and South: W. E. Smith, *The Francis Preston Blair Family in Politics;* Wood Gray, *The Hidden Civil War; The Story of the Copperheads* (1942) ; H. G. Pearson, *Life of John A. Andrew, Governor of Massachusetts, 1861-1865,* 2 vols. (1904) ; E. C. Kirkland, *The Peacemakers of 1864* (1927) ; W. W. Pierson, "The Committee on the Conduct of the War" in the *American*

Historical Review, XXIII, 550-577; Robert S. Mitchell, *Horatio Seymour of New York* (1938); and E. M. Coulter, *The Civil War and Readjustment in Kentucky,* together with the general histories cited above, may be used for political life in the North. For the Confederate side see J. L. M. Curry, *Civil History of the Government of the Confederate States,* Davis, *Rise and Fall of the Confederate Government,* and the lives of Davis cited above; A. B. Moore, *Conscription and Conflict in the Confederacy;* F. L. Owsley, *State Rights in the Confederacy* (1925); P. A. Stovall, *Robert Toombs, Statesman, Speaker, Soldier, Sage* (1892); Henry Cleveland, *Alexander H. Stephens in Public and Private* (1866); L. B. Pendleton, *Alexander H. Stephens;* Louise B. Hill, *Joseph E. Brown and the Confederacy* (1939); and Georgia Lee Tatum, *Disloyalty in the Confederacy* (1934).

Political life in the South

Index

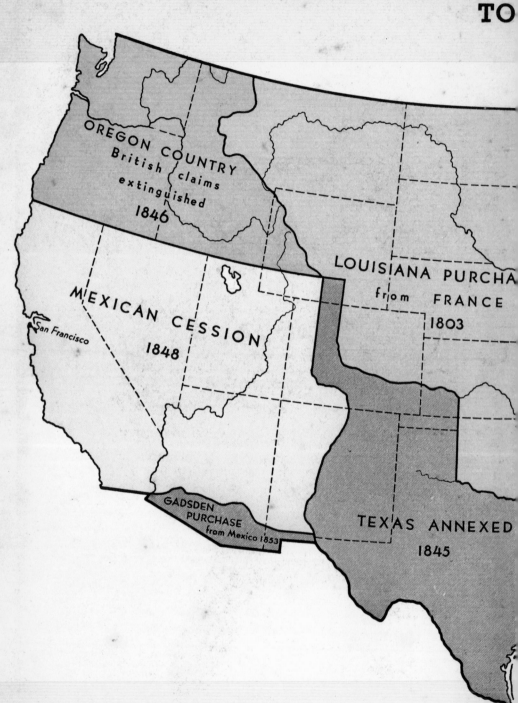

TERRITORIAL GROWTH
TO

OREGON COUNTRY
British claims
extinguished
1846

LOUISIANA PURCHA
from FRANCE
1803

MEXICAN CESSION
1848

San Francisco

GADSDEN
PURCHASE
from Mexico 1853

TEXAS ANNEXED
1845